HANDBOOK ON THE HISTORY OF ECONOMIC ANALYSIS VOLUME II

Handbook on the History of Economic Analysis
Volume II

Schools of Thought in Economics

Edited by

Gilbert Faccarello

Professor of Economics, Panthéon-Assas University, Paris, France

Heinz D. Kurz

Emeritus Professor of Economics, University of Graz and Graz Schumpeter Centre, Austria

 Edward Elgar
PUBLISHING

Cheltenham, UK • Northampton, MA, USA

Published by
Edward Elgar Publishing Limited
The Lypiatts
15 Lansdown Road
Cheltenham
Glos GL50 2JA
UK

Edward Elgar Publishing, Inc.
William Pratt House
9 Dewey Court
Northampton
Massachusetts 01060
USA

Paperback edition 2018

A catalogue record for this book
is available from the British Library

Library of Congress Control Number: 2016931730

This book is available electronically in the **Elgar**online
Economics subject collection
DOI 10.4337/9781785367366

ISBN 978 1 84980 111 9 (cased)
ISBN 978 1 78536 131 9 (cased 3-volume set)
ISBN 978 1 78536 736 6 (eBook)
ISBN 978 1 78897 238 3 (paperback)
ISBN 978 1 78897 240 6 (paperback 3-volume set)

Typeset by Servis Filmsetting Ltd, Stockport, Cheshire
Printed on FSC approved paper
Printed and bound in Great Britain by Marston Book Services Ltd, Oxfordshire

Contents

Figures and tables

Figures

Tables

Contributors

François Allisson, University of Lausanne, Switzerland

Roberto Baranzini, University of Lausanne, Switzerland

Michel Bellet, University of Saint-Étienne, France

Andrei A. Belykh, Bank Saint Petersburg, Russia

Corrado Benassi, University of Bologna, Italy

Alain Béraud, University of Cergy-Pontoise, France

Charles B. Blankart, Humboldt University, Berlin, Germany

Jérôme de Boyer des Roches, University of Paris Dauphine, France

Anthony Brewer, University of Bristol, Great Britain

Günther Chaloupek, Former director of the economic policy section of the Austrian Chamber of Labour, Vienna, Austria

Irina Chaplygina, Lomonosov Moscow State University, Moscow, Russia

Simon Cook, Independent scholar, Israel

John Creedy, Victoria University of Wellington, New Zealand

Thierry Demals, University of Lille, France

Ross B. Emmett, Michigan State University, USA

Gilbert Faccarello, Panthéon-Assas University, Paris, France

Christian Gehrke, University of Graz, Austria

G.C. Harcourt, University of Cambridge, Great Britain and University of New South Wales, Australia

John E. King, La Trobe University, Australia and Federation University Australia

Heinz D. Kurz, University of Graz, Austria

André Lapidus, University of Paris I Panthéon-Sorbonne, France

Marc Lavoie, University of Ottawa, Canada

Maria Cristina Marcuzzo, University of Roma La Sapienza, Italy

Arash Molavi Vasséi, University of Hohenheim, Germany

Pier Luigi Porta, University of Milano Bicocca, Italy

Annalisa Rosselli, University of Roma Tor Vergata, Italy

Malcolm Rutherford, University of Victoria, Canada

Neri Salvadori, University of Pisa, Italy

Bertram Schefold, Johann Wolfgang Goethe-University, Frankfurt am Main, Germany

Neil T. Skaggs, Illinois State University, USA

Ricardo Solis Rosales, Metropolitan University of Mexico City, Mexico

Peter Spahn, University of Hohenheim, Germany

Noel Thompson, Swansea University, Great Britain

Hans-Michael Trautwein, University of Oldenburg, Germany

Keith Tribe, Independent scholar, Great Britain

General introduction

The past is never dead. It's not even past. (William Faulkner)

The aim of this *Handbook on the History of Economic Analysis* is to provide a succinct overview of the development of economics since its systematic inception up until today. The *Handbook* has three volumes. Volume I deals with *Great Economists since Petty and Boisguilbert*. It provides short essays in biography of some of the most important economists in what is known as the "Western World". Volume II deals with *Schools of Thought in Economics*. A school is defined in terms of the analytical method(s) used, the approach chosen in tackling the problem(s) at hand, the results derived and the policy conclusions inferred. Volume III contains summary accounts of *Developments in Major Fields of Economics* reflecting the division of labour within the discipline.

There are different ways of approaching the history of economic thought. The focus of these volumes is on economic theories: their formation, including their philosophical and historical underpinnings, their conclusiveness and place within the field, and their possible use in formulating economic policies. We draw attention to those economists and their doctrines that we regard as especially significant. It hardly needs to be said that our choice unavoidably reflects a subjective element. We would have liked to include the portraits of several more important thinkers, but space constraints prevented us from doing so. The same applies *cum grano salis* to the schools of thought and developments in major fields covered.

Let us however acknowledge, at the outset, some of the important gaps in coverage. The focus is on European intellectual traditions and their continuation in the so-called Western World, but of course it is a fact that all advanced civilizations can point to notable achievements in the exploration of economic life – think of countries such as China or Japan, for example, or civilizations following philosophical or religious traditions such as Buddhism or Islam. In addition to geographic gaps, there are also some gaps in subjects covered, such as the omission of business administration and management theories.

Arthur Cecil Pigou once remarked that the history of economic thought is a history of the "wrong ideas of dead men". Certainly, it is partly also that, but not only, and moreover there is always much to learn from the alleged "errors". While there is progress in economics, there is also occasional regress. This should not come as a surprise: in a discipline dealing with as complex a subject matter as economics, it would be naive not to expect some intellectual "bubbles" that sooner or later burst, necessitating a fundamental re-orientation in the area of investigation under consideration. In the parlance of economists: the market for economic ideas is not a perfectly functioning selection mechanism that preserves all that is correct and valuable and discards whatever is wrong and useless.

This may also contribute to explaining the remarkable fact that certain ideas and concepts in economics, cherished at one time, get submerged and are forgotten afterwards, only to re-emerge in a new garb and liberated of their teething troubles at a later time. As Dennis Robertson once remarked with regard to the history of economics: "If you stand in the same place long enough, the hunted hare comes round again." Or, as Alfred Marshall put it: "We continually meet with old friends in new dresses." One of the most knowledgeable historians of economic thought ever, Joseph Alois Schumpeter, expressed the same view as follows: "Old friends come disguised to the party."

Modern economists frequently seem to believe that it not only suffices to know just the most recent economic doctrines and theories; they even seem to think, echoing Pigou's statement above, that it is detrimental to their intellectual development to expose themselves to the ideas and thoughts of earlier generations of economists. Since by assumption these must be partly or wholly wrong, or at least imperfect, it is not only a waste of time to study the "old masters", it may even be harmful to do so, because it may confuse readers and prompt them to deviate from the correct path to truth and wisdom. This position is a version of what the literary critic Norman Foerster called "provincialism of time", that is, "the measure of past literature by the ideas and moods of a narrow present". It is, among other things, based on the false presumption that it is the privilege of living economists to articulate only correct views.

Even a casual look at the history of economics, its various schools of thought and doctrines, shows that economics always lacked and still lacks a *unité de doctrine*, and that there is no reason to presume that this state of affairs will end any time soon. If economics were characterized by a relentless march towards ever-higher levels of knowledge and truthfulness, this fact would be difficult to explain.

There can be little doubt that the ideas of economists are important. John Maynard Keynes even insisted: "The ideas of economists and political philosophers, both when they are right and when they are wrong, are more powerful than is commonly understood. Indeed the world is ruled by little else." If this happens to be so, it is important to know the ideas of economists, especially when they are wrong. The history of economic analysis is not only a treasure trove of such ideas, it also informs about when and why certain ideas were challenged and some of them eventually rejected, at least in the form in which they were available at the time. Knowing the history of the discipline should help you to resist superstition, hysteria and exuberance in economic and social questions. And it should immunize you against falling victim to the ideas of some "defunct economist" (Keynes) all too easily.

The gestation period of the *Handbook on the History of Economic Analysis* was long – a great deal longer than originally planned. There are many factors that contribute to explaining the delays to the project. With some 140 authors, the probability was high that some of them could not deliver, for various respectable reasons, and had to be replaced. In some cases we had to act as writers of last resort. We also insisted that the three volumes should come out together, which necessitated the completion of them at roughly the same time. Bad health at different periods of time for each of the editors did not exactly help in propelling the project forward. Confronted with these and other difficulties, we are all the more pleased to be able to present the *Handbook on the History of Economic Analysis* to the scientific community. We take this opportunity to thank all of the contributors for their fine work. We are particularly grateful to those who delivered their entries in good time and for their patience thereafter. We also thank the referees we involved in assessing the different versions of the entries and for their useful comments, which helped to improve them.

May this *Handbook on the History of Economic Analysis* contribute to a better under-standing of the path economics took over time up until today and substantiate William Faulkner's claim that "History is not was, it is".

GILBERT FACCARELLO AND HEINZ D. KURZ

A note on the cross-references sections: the volume in which the cross-references appear is listed as follows:

(I)   *Handbook on the History of Economic Analysis Volume I: Great Economists since Petty and Boisguilbert;*
(II)   *Handbook on the History of Economic Analysis Volume II: Schools of Thought in Economics;*
(III) *Handbook on the History of Economic Analysis Volume III: Developments in Major Fields of Economics.*

Antiquity

Ancient and Modern Conceptions of the Economy

We attribute to the ancient Greeks the origin of the major disciplines in the natural sciences, such as physics or biology, of medicine, and also of disciplines in the humanities such as philosophy, rhetoric, and grammar. Among the social sciences, politics could be mentioned but not economics, although many single ideas of modern economics can be traced back to first formulations in the writings of ancient authors. However, this is little known because the mercantilists, such as Petty (Schefold 2011a: 13–40) and even Adam Smith (on Smith and antiquity, see the important study by Vivenza 2001), admitted only sparingly their debt to humanist and scholastic writers and to their invariably extensive readings of the ancients (Roover 1955: 161–90). When Antonio Serra discovered economics, he did not name it, but he was fully aware that its origin, as a discipline, was not in antiquity, in the sense of Aristotle neither part of politics nor of ethics (Schefold 1994: 5–27). Economic insights were thus found in ancient writings as part of historiography (Tukydides, Polybios, and Livius) and ethnology (Herodotos), as generalisations in writings about special economic activities, such as agriculture (Varro, Columella), as views on economic policy expressed by the orators, as regulations in Greek and especially Roman law, and as ethical judgements and rules in philosophy (Plato, Aristotle).

The historical school would read all these sources and occasionally use them to illustrate specific economic problems (for example, Roscher 1861: 353, on the role of credit during economic crises), but more often and systematically would use them to illustrate the historicity of economics, contrasting stages of ancient and modern economics (Hildebrand 1864: 1–24, 1869: 1–25, 130–55) and discussing changing ethical norms as a contribution to the emergence of sociology. A leading member of the youngest historical school, Karl Bücher (Schefold 1988: 239–67), launched a debate which is still topical among ancient historians and in historical sociology, by comparing a "primitivist" interpretation of antiquity with a "modernist" interpretation. The former emphasises the specificity of ancient institutions, patriarchal households, the striving for autarchy, gift giving in exchange and other remnants of the pre-monetary economy which were thought to be still relevant to the classical Athenian economy, while the modernists regarded the integration of the Mediterranean world through trade with the emergence of the Hellenistic and, later, the Roman empires, as evidence of economic growth and capitalist forces which suggested analogies between the economy of imperial Rome and the economic development reached in the early mercantilist period (Finley 1979). To reach a balanced view of the history of economic thought in antiquity, taking account of the real economic life behind it, remains a difficult task, but it is comparatively easy to follow the main texts, where economic considerations come up as simple illustrations of a more sophisticated ethical discourse. The gap between the modern and ancient conceptions can be bridged by recognising that both are concerned with action. Modern economists ask which actions produce efficient outcomes; the ancient philosopher asked which action was good. The Stoic philosophers prepared for the link: the creator has made the world harmonious so that the good is achieved by pursuing one's true self-interest (Kraus 2000).

We need to understand the economic insights of antiquity in their context, but this does not mean that there are no common regularities in economic rationality, behaviour, and causality. Xenophon is recognised to have been the first who observed and expressed the link between the degree of the division of labour and the extent of the market, and he seems to have seen that the causality runs both ways, as Adam Smith would later emphasise. He explicitly said that crafts can be more specialised (one example is the preparation of food) if the market (the city) is larger (Xenophon, *Cyroupaideia* VIII, 2, 5: ἐν δὲ ταῖς μεγάλαις πόλεσι διὰ τὸ πολλοὺς ἑκάστου δεῖσθαι ἀρκεῖ καὶ μία ἑκάστῳ τέχνη εἰς τὸ τρέφεσθαι). Elsewhere he expressed the idea of increasing returns (*Poroi*). However, he does not combine both to formulate, or at least to visualise, the principle of cumulative causation. In these separate observations, the economy does not feature as an independent subsystem of societal intercourse; on the contrary, economic insights are invariably part of reflections of larger societal interconnectedness, reflecting the embedding of the economy in society. Even to the extent that similar economic mechanisms and institutions were visible then which we have now – there was money, exchange, taxation, there was production and distribution – their combination was different and varied a great deal within the world of antiquity both in space and time (we mainly focus on Athens and Rome because of the sources available). Differences in rationality and economic functioning therefore become most visible where the situation is more complex. If we look at an isolated procedure such as the haggling in a market for a particular commodity, different mores may become apparent, but the economist may be pardoned if he abstracts from historical specificities such as different formulas of politeness in this context and speaks simply of supply and demand. But all aspects of culture inevitably come in, if it is a matter of financing the activities of the state. The Athenians expected donations from rich citizens to pay for choruses in the theatre or for the equipment of a military ship. These contributions were voluntary, but also prestigious. The social mechanism of this so-called liturgy system made it a matter of honour to pay, and a variety of subsidiary legal and moral institutions helped to keep it going. The proof of liberty was said to be in giving and spontaneous action (for the unfree, the slaves, are ordered around), the hierarchy of virtues reflected this conception of the dignity of free citizen and what we call economic concepts were structured accordingly (Schefold 1998: 235–56). We encounter a distinction between "visible" and "invisible" wealth made in the Athenian orators (we found this opposition, for example, in *Lysias* XX, 23, XX, 33). The visible part of the riches of a citizen consisted of the house, land, olive trees. Invisible, by contrast, were the credits outstanding. If the community wanted to challenge someone to provide for the state, they had to rely on what they saw. Hence the temptation to hide riches by lending and the consequent popular distrust of moneyed men (Salin 1963: 153–81). Such institutions served to avoid the build-up of a state bureaucracy, but they presupposed social cohesion. Contrasting roles had to be fulfilled: the citizen had to look after the family and his house, to engage in politics, to serve in war. To order one's priorities would not have been easy. The role conflicts help to explain the general and intense interest in philosophy as the basis of ethics and of all learning from the later classical period onwards (Schefold 2011c: 131–63).

Cultural and economic life and the forms of government varied in antiquity, but there were important continuities. There is the general view from Homer on the downfall of

Rome that the good life was to be led in the well-ordered house in which production and consumption were a whole (Finley 1973 [1975]). The *agora*, the place for the market and reunions, represented the economic and political centre. Household and firm would separate only much later in early modern times; hence the inevitable tension between the acquisitive principle which the household must respect to the extent that it is a producer and the satisfaction of needs as the principle of consumption. In the past there had been the royal and aristocratic households and the smallholdings of independent peasants. Later, the large latifundia of Roman times were the economic centres of the households of the ruling elite. Oikonomos (οἰκονόμος), householder, was the title of a royal manager of agricultural estates in Ptolemaic Egypt, and the economy of the country as a whole was planned and regarded as a royal household (Rostovtzeff 1941 [1972]). There were not only the households of the citizens in classical Athens, but also those of the metoikoi (μέτοικοι, immigrants), and there were considerable differences of wealth, with poor wage earners being at the bottom of the ladder, as far as the free were concerned, while the lot of the slaves varied enormously, depending on whether they were employed in a household and belonged to the family or whether they were estate managers or had to work in the fields or the mines. There was a contradictory tension in the crafts. The free would rather be farmers, if they had to work with their hands at all, but good handicraft was much admired and its historically exceptional quality during the classical period is obvious from archaeological remains. City life did not disappear but ceased to dominate the political process at large when the Hellenistic kingdoms formed and cosmopolitan intellectual currents took over, as seen in Hellenistic philosophy and in Stoicism in particular.

State and Justice in Plato

Plato's philosophy of the just life in the just state is concerned with economic problems, in so far as economic inequality is a threat for the cohesion of the city (Schefold 1989: 19–55). The ideal state, which he analyses in the *Republic*, was not meant as a model for the foundation of an actual state – many such models were conceived and realised through the foundation of the colonies in the Greek world – but it helped to establish the fundamental principles which would have to be modified in a second best or third best state which might be put into practice. As a matter of logic, the best state had to be governed by the best. The art of state craft was analogous to the rule in the household; both are concerned not with their own advantage but with that of the people or the family to be guided; hence the comparison with the good shepherd who is concerned with the well-being of his sheep and does not look forward to eating or selling them. The warriors defending the state have their property in common so that they do not set their individual interests above those of the community. For the producers, the state presupposes the division of labour which Plato motivated not so much by considerations of the quantity to be produced, but by the quality; people divide tasks because they have different talents (*Republic* 370 A–B). Markets and coins as signs are needed (ibid. 371 B–C). Nothing points here towards a theory of value, but there is a notion of a just price in so far as no one shall charge two different prices for the same commodity – Plato was concerned with the honesty of the trader (*Laws* 917 B). More specifically, economic considerations come up in Plato's late dialogue *The Laws*, where communism in production is rejected as something which is beyond the possibilities of human beings as we know them (*Laws* 740 A).

The communism of the ideal state (which did not mean communist production) should be interpreted as a philosophical expression of the ideal of the complete dedication of full citizens to the tasks of guiding and protecting the city together. However, as mentioned, the real Athenian citizen was the head of a household, a warrior, and a politician all in one. He had to reconcile the aims associated with the different forms of life. Plato regarded a person without moral principles in such a situation like a mass of people who are lumped together but do not form a state because they have no constitution (*Republic* 432 B–444 A). The task of philosophy is to provide an orientation that grows with the complexity of the life forms, but the basic requirement remains to be just. This includes the principle of fulfilling one's own tasks. Large differences of status and riches must be avoided. Wealth generates inertia and discontent, poverty, base thinking and bad work (*Laws* 919 C). Plato's descriptions, based on experiences of the possible degenerations of the state, frighten the modern reader by their analogies with fascist take-overs, hence the primary necessity of lawful and constitutional government. Plato mentions in the *Statesman* that there is a degenerate form to each of the lawful forms of government: monarchy, aristocracy, and democracy. Among the ideal states, the monarchic is the best and aristocracy comes second, but among the degenerate states – and the real state tends to be degenerate – the order of preference is reversed (*Statesman* 302 E–303 B). Then it is best to live in a democracy, even if it is imperfect, while an oligarchy is worse, and the most unpleasant form of life is in the wilfulness of lawless tyranny.

Thus an attempt is made to design more practical rules in the *Laws*, where the principle of avoiding large social discrepancies is to be realised by prescribing redistribution as soon as someone possesses more than four times what another possesses, and the emphasis is on agricultural production; the citizens and their slaves shall abstain from trade and the crafts and leave them to the metoikoi and their slaves (*Laws* 846 D, 919 D). Plato says, in a typical formulation which anticipates the Aristotelian insistence on the true goal:

> Therefore we say that gold and silver ought not to be allowed in the city, nor much of the vulgar sort of trade which is carried on by lending money, or rearing the meaner kinds of live stock; but only the produce of agriculture, and only so much of this as will not compel us, in pursuing it, to neglect that for the sake of which riches exist. (*Laws* 743 D)

What are the riches for, you may ask, reading this sentence. The natural riches are there to lead a good life, Aristotle will respond. The Socratic philosophers are suspicious of the traders and money lenders, for fear that their professions will prevent them from keeping the main aims of life in view. Plato's dialogues impress not only through their didactic elegance, but also through irony and wit and, in key passages, through their invocation of deeper truths which transcend the rational argument and are clad in mythology. The ultimate good is not revealed.

Aristotle: Production and Acquisition, Justice in Distribution and Exchange

The Aristotelian conception of man as a political animal is connected with his economic idea of the household as the fundamental unit of the city, following the venerable tradition of Hesiod (*Works and Days* 342–413). Economics, the art of house-holding, comprehends everything which holds house, estate, and family together. It is first concerned with the life of the family, including the slaves, whom Aristotle regards as indispensable (*Politics* 1253b8). Only if we had automatic weaving and music making, could we do without slaves. Aristotle as a rational thinker clearly feels that he is on uncertain ground with his defence of slavery. Perhaps some are, by their nature, born to be slaves? However, he admits that many are slaves, although they are neither of inferior talent nor barbarians (ibid. 1254a–1255b). It is observed in the pseudo-Aristotelian writing *Oeconomica* that slaves obtain a wage, in the form of nourishment. It is emphasised that slaves can reach high ranks in positions which require trust (for example, as supervisors). Aristotle recommends to treat them well and to free them after a predetermined time, and he ordered some of his slaves to be freed in his testament. However, uneasiness remained.

The problem, which is here dealt with by Aristotle in philosophical terms, had been treated poetically by Homer, where slavery is described as a tragic fate by the very heroes who will enslave others by conquest, if they can. Also, the god Hephaistos in Homer has made automata, maids made of bronze, who serve him like slaves; the god does not need to enslave living beings (Schefold 1997: 99–145). However, slavery is a tragic fate for humans, and this is reflected by the honest Aristotle in his avowed inability to provide a satisfactory philosophical justification.

The aim of house-holding is to provide the material basis of the good life of the Greek citizen and the family. This requires a level of material well-being which is neither so high that it distracts from the main aim nor so low that there is no room for philosophical reflection and political activity. Private property and material incentives are accepted, with a criticism of Plato as if the latter had ever made communism a general principle (*Politics* 1261a6). Aristotle differentiates between the art of house-holding and the art of acquisition (ibid. 1256a12). House-holding uses the means of the household, acquisition provides them. Acquisition is natural, if there is an analogy with the acquisition in nature, by animals. Hunting, fishing, farming, shepherding and robbing are thought to be natural in this sense – the last suggestion is a little shocking, but, as analogues of the lions, remember the conquerors of Homeric times. It also corresponds to nature, if surplus products of the house are exchanged for others which cannot be made yourself. It is an exchange of values in use, for which the need is limited; Aristotle explicitly rejects the saying by Solon, according to which it is a deplorable fate of man not to know the limits of riches (ibid. 1256b34). To have a measure, to correspond to a middle between extremes is the nature of the good. To increase the household indefinitely is an error which Aristotle ascribes to a kind of vitalism, to the desire to live instead of living well (εὖ ζῆν). The means of the good life must be defined and limited like the good life itself.

The other form of acquisition, the unnatural one, is an art to enrich oneself; we here call it by one of the expressions used by Aristotle, chrematistics. It is an acquisition which disregards the boundaries and has no limits (*Politics* 1256b40–1257a1, 1258a7).

The borderline between the two kinds of acquisition is drawn as follows: a shoe is really used if it is worn, but it can also be used as mean of exchange (*Politics* 1257a10). It is natural, and not a matter of chrematistics, if households complement each other, one providing shoes and the other providing corn. However, the shoe has not come into being for the sake of exchange (οὐ γὰρ ἀλλαγῆς ἕνεκεν γέγονεν, ibid. 1257a13). Hence there is an abuse if it is produced for exchange. We have to conclude that the cobbler must have the use of the shoe in mind, when he makes it, and not the selling price. The cobbler therefore is like the Platonic good shepherd, who is concerned with the welfare of his sheep and not with eating or selling them. It is not easy for us to think in this way, except if we have an artist or a scholar in mind who are completely dedicated to their tasks, without thinking of future success or an addition to the salary. The scholar offers his insights to the public and he gets some support, but he does not bargain. The opposite position would be a worker who works for piece wages. As we shall see, Aristotle ranks wage labour among the chrematistic pursuits.

Aristotle develops chrematistics historically. The exchange of values in use between households generated trade, a trade which transcended the limits of the city. Since many goods were difficult to transport, people consented to use and take in exchange things which were useful in themselves and easy to handle, such as iron and silver (*Politics* 1257a35). This is how money arose. It was a mean to facilitate exchange, but it became an end in itself for many people. They interpreted wealth as a mass of money and tried to obtain as much of it as possible, hence the definition "all men engaged in wealth-getting try to increase their money to an unlimited amount" (ibid. 1257b34).

> So when currency had now been invented as an outcome of the necessary interchange of goods, there came into existence the other form of wealth-getting (chrematistics), trade, which at first no doubt went on in a simple form, but later became more highly organised as experience discovered the sources and methods of exchange that would cause most profit. (Ibid. 1257b1–5)

Aristotle rejects this form of acquisition. Bravery shall not make money, but engender courage, and also the art of strategy and medicine shall not do that, but procure victory and health (ibid. 1258a11).

Exchange as such does not necessarily become chrematistic, as long as it takes place within the confines of house-holding, for which there are limits, and, to this extent, the art of exchange is natural (*Politics* 1257a29), but otherwise blameworthy (ibid. 1258b1). The art of acquisition of the household is necessary but not so chrematistics (ibid. 1258a15). King Midas had wished that everything that he touched would turn into gold. He died of hunger, when his wish was fulfilled. This example shows how meaningless it is to regard a mass of money as wealth. Natural wealth and chrematistics are different. Chrematistics is associated in the beginning with petty trade. Later it becomes a matter for powerful merchants and seafaring in long distance trade. Chrematistics will then begin to assimilate even other arts, for example, if medicine is used not to heal but to make money.

The difference between natural acquisition and chrematistics, therefore, is not only that the former has limits, while the latter is limitless, but in the attitude to production; it is not only a matter of ethics, but also of aesthetics. Aristotle sees profit only as arising from trade, not in production. Interest can therefore not be derived from production. Hence the famous denunciation: usury is an unnatural form of acquisition which is justifiably hated, since money begets money (*Politics* 1258b3). The argument would later be developed by the scholastic authors who, like Aristotle, defined money as a means of circulation (ibid. 1257a3) so that its use as an instrument of credit seemed illicit. Aristotle's reference to nature (*physis*) represented an important innovation. Without invoking divine law, order is created by the visible necessities of natural life; there are natural laws.

Aristotle proceeds from theoretical to practical considerations and enumerates the different forms of acquisition in the house; there then follow the chrematistic techniques of trade, money lending and wage labour, with transitional forms. It does not occur to him that they should be prohibited. He realises that they can be useful for the state. There is the pseudo-Aristotelian book (the second book of *Oeconomica*) which deals with the techniques of increasing the revenues of the state; it illustrates that the Aristotelian school analysed the monetary techniques at least empirically. We must conclude that Aristotle's teaching in the end amounts to advice for his students – young citizens – not to take up the chrematistic pursuits because they might miss the good life. His problem is not the alienation of work. It remains an ideal for the philosopher and free citizen not to have to worry about material sustenance. Chrematistic acquisition means to forget about the true aims and to make wealth-getting an end in itself instead of treating it as a mean for higher ends.

Aristotle's theory of just exchange is not directly linked with his theory of natural acquisition, in that it is part of his ethical theory (book V of *Nicomachean Ethics*), but we shall discover organic links between both approaches to what the moderns regard as an economic problem.

Aristotle develops his consideration of exchange in the context of a discussion of justice which is the most perfect virtue (*Eth. Nic.* 1129b26); virtuous life leads to human happiness which culminates in the vision of truth. We are here concerned only with justice which determines a share. It is divided into distributive and commutative justice. The former concerns the distribution of honour, money and other objects, which can be shared among the members of the community (ibid. 1130b32). Distributive justice takes proportionality into account, hence the situation in society of the person who shall receive. The principle of proportionality is general, but it must be based on a certain conception of dignity and merit, and these conceptions are different according to the form of governance. Democrats value freedom, oligarchs wealth, aristocrats virtue (ibid. 1131a25). If persons A and B stand in relation $A : B$, so must the objects a, b, which they are to receive, so that we have $A : B = a : b$. It is a symbolic proof that proportionality is preserved if the persons are augmented by what they receive (ibid. 1131b4); in fact we have, by the law of proportions:

$$A : B = a : b = (A + a) : (B + b).$$

"Mathematicians" call this proportionality "geometric", says Aristotle (*Eth. Nic.* 1131b13). Each receives according to desert, respecting the inequality of the members of the community. However, it may be difficult to decide in what desert consists. We only have to remember the Homeric poems in order to realise that this problem is central to Greek culture from the beginning; the Iliad turns around the question of who shall keep the main booty, the maiden Briseis: Agamemnon as the leader of the army or Achilles as the most eminent hero (*Ilias* I 182–351).

Another form of justice determining shares is commutative justice, which is needed in many matters of daily life such as commerce, credit, but also theft or other objects of litigation. Status plays no role here. If A has received a (which is too much) and B has received b (which is too little), hence, if $a > b$, both shall receive according to arithmetical proportionality. By this Aristotle (*Eth. Nic.* 1132a2) means what we call arithmetical mean; he intends a redistribution according to:

$$a - \frac{a - b}{2} = \frac{a + b}{2} = b + \frac{a - b}{2}.$$

Justice in exchange is based on reciprocity (*Eth. Nic.* 1132b20). This does not coincide with either justice in distribution or commutative justice, for reciprocity can be unjust. If an officer hits a soldier as punishment, reciprocity would mean to strike back, but this would not be just, for it would be against the law (ibid. 1132b30). Acting in appropriate reciprocity and donating keep the city together, otherwise it would be a city of slaves. Anthropologists ponder why one feels the obligation to reciprocate, but Aristotle emphasises that it does not suffice always to wait for gifts in order to respond with counter-gifts, but that one should precede the others in donating (ibid. 1133a6). The true wonder of the functioning of the community consists in the spontaneity of giving, and the dry philosopher recalls the beautiful custom to erect public altars for the Charites, the goddesses of grace and thankfulness. The central role of the liturgies in Athenian life was here alluded to in a philosophical doctrine in the evening glow of the independent city state, as also in his *Politics* (1261a31): τὸ ἀντιπεπονϑὸς σῴζει τὰς πόλεις (reciprocity saves the cities) (1261a31).

The discussion of reciprocity now moves from spontaneous donation (μετάδοσις, *Eth. Nic.* 1133a2) to immediate exchange against a counter-gift (ἀντίδοσις, ibid. 1133a6). It is not necessary to recall the Charites anymore, since gift and counter-gift follow each other immediately. The spheres of culture and politics and the economic sphere are not separated but touch each other. What is a proportionate counter-gift? Aristotle begins with objects and persons standing in a relation of proportionality as in distributive justice. In our notation $A : B = a : b$ as above (Aristotle's notation is a little different and refers also to geometrical illustrations). Exchange implies a "diagonal conjunction" (an Aristotelian technical term also to be found in *Eud. Eth.* 1242b12 and elsewhere): prior to exchange, A is equipped with a and B is equipped with b. A and B are on the top angles, a and b on the bottom angles of a quadrangle, hence after the exchange "along the diagonals", A has b and B has a. The diagram symbolises the exchange of property (Polanyi 1968: 107, is mistaken in his belief that the price is given by the point at which the two diagonals cross). Each person has given to the other some of his "work", an architect, and a cobbler exchange a house and shoes in Aristotle's example. Now the persons are unequal (*Eth. Nic.* 1133a18), as the text emphasises, but the objects are made equal (ibid. 1133a14). How can this be, as they are qualitatively different? It has been proposed – but the textual evidence for this is meagre – that this form of just exchange should be symbolised by a proportion of proportions, in which each person remains in relation to the object in the same proportion after the exchange as this person had held before:

$$A : a = B : b = (A : b) : (B : a).$$

This proportion of proportions (Soudek 1952, following Euclid) holds, as one verifies easily, if and only if $a = b$; the objects are equalised, while the persons are not. Aristotle continues, however, saying that, through exchange, the persons as well are "to be made equal" (ἰσασϑῆναι – *Eth. Nic.* 1133a19); the geometric proportion is used and total identity results: the initial $A : B = a : b$ becomes after the exchange $A : B = b : a$, hence $a = b$ and $A = B$ (ibid. 1133a34); the persons are equal as traders. Finally, the arithmetical mean is resorted to according to commutative justice to restore equality, if the exchange happened to be unequal, and the "too much" of the one has to be divided and to be given to the other (*Eth. Nic.* 1133b3).

Aristotle now has moved from gift exchange to commodity exchange without saying so. Gift exchange does not necessarily imply an exchange of equivalents, as Aristotle makes clear elsewhere when he discusses friendship, for the gift of the higher-ranking person may be of higher value than the counter-gift of the lower-ranking person if the former is friendly with the latter, but the converse may also happen, if the lower-ranking person wishes to obtain a favour from the higher-ranking person (*Eud. Eth.* 1242b17). Here, however, Aristotle is concerned with commodity exchange, for he asks why gifts and counter-gifts can be set as equal, although they are qualitatively different. He answers that it is need (*chreia, Eth. Nic.* 1133a28) which holds the exchange together. He also says that the relationship is not natural; money has been invented to measure things according to *nomos* which means law (ibid. 1133a31), but *nomos* is here meant as convention: people adopt money (and fix prices) by convention. Prices can also be prescribed; the estimation can be that of an overseer of a market – at any rate, everything has to be "estimated" (ibid. 1133b15). Money is a warranty for the future (ibid. 1133b13) and acts as an intermediate, being a "measure" to "set equal" (ibid. 1133b18). Aristotle uses an example (a house or a bed) in order to show that having an exchange ratio between different commodities is essentially the same thing as having one between commodities and money (ibid. 1133b24).

Many interpreters have tried to discover a theory of prices in Aristotle. The two great strands of price theory, labour theory or cost theory of value and the subjective theory of value both seem to originate here. Aristotle says that each of the exchanging persons gives of his work (*ergon*). In this view, both sides exchange equal increases of value, owing to equal effort, and "proportionality" would refer to equal arithmetical differences of value added (*Eth. Nic.* 1133a10–17). On the other hand, he says that it is need (*chreia*) which holds the exchange together. However, he also says that everything in the transaction has to be measured by some unit (ἑνί τινι πάντα μετρεῖσθαι, ibid. 1133a26), without saying to which specific quality the measure is to be applied. Aristotle may have had some intuition that prices were related to cost and demand, but the wording and the context do not yield much for the development of the corresponding theories. The term *ergon* refers to the object produced by work, not to labour time, and to measure labour time was not as much a concern for slave owners as it became when wages were to be paid in the early modern period. The term *chreia* emphasises objective need rather than desire.

How far removed this conception can be from subjectively determined demand becomes clear if we relate the Aristotelian exposition of the problem of just exchange to his theory of households. There, households were thought to exchange their surpluses in order to assemble the necessary means for the good life. This is reminiscent of Sraffa's idea of a production of commodities without a surplus (Sraffa 1960: 3). Let a_{ij} denote the amount of commodity j needed by household i and assume that each household has a surplus of only one commodity (the cobbler is dedicated to the production of shoes and he also owns a plot on which he produces vegetables, but he consumes the latter himself and brings only the shoes not needed by his family to the market). We assume that households of the same kind are aggregated. Together they form a city which is autarkic. If total output of each commodity j is normalised to 1, we must then have $a_{1j} + \ldots + a_{nj} = 1$, with n commodities being produced by the corresponding number of types of households; $i = 1, \ldots, n$; and it follows, if the resulting non-negative matrix $\mathbf{A}$ is indecomposable, as is natural to assume in this context, that a positive vector of prices $\mathbf{p}$ exists, such that:

$$\mathbf{Ap} = \mathbf{p};$$

prices are determined by the needs (*chreia*) of the households to reproduce themselves and by the product (*ergon*) they can bring to the market.

We might therefore say that Aristotle's philosophy of just exchange points not only towards subjectivism and the labour theory of value, but also towards the modernised classical theory of prices. The multiplicity of meanings is not evidence of inconsistency in Aristotle, but the result of his looking at exchange from different perspectives, using different mathematical analogues. His theorising is conceptual and not the construction of a formal model, but it has inspired model-building. If we add chrematistics, a pursuit of wealth beyond needs, the framework of static reproduction is broken and we can, looking back, again see two lines of thought develop towards the present. On the one hand is the idea of accumulation of capital without limits to growth and, on the other, that of equilibrium: profit-making firms must sell to households in order to obtain factors. In the latter case, households will provide labour only up to the point where the wage ceases to compensate for the disutility of work and they will provide capital only as long as the sacrifice for future consumption is compensated by the satisfaction from present consumption. We know that both Marx and Böhm-Bawerk felt indebted to Aristotle, both directly and via the medieval and early modern interpretations and developments of Aristotelian economics.

Economic Realities in Xenophon and among the Romans

Xenophon was probably, of all known authors of antiquity, the author whose economic ideas are closest to modernity. They appear mostly as challenges to the Socratic tradition which he at the same time represents. The latter predominates in his *Memorabilia*, where we encounter handicraft production. There appears a head of a household whom Socrates advises to overcome a difficult financial situation by requiring his relatives and slaves to take up weaving (*Memorabilia* II, 7). The emphasis in the *Memorabilia* is not just on the survival of the household, however, but on good work. The armour produced by a smith must be made to fit the body of a customer (ibid. III, 10, 9–15) and the sculptor endeavours to show the movements of the soul in the face and the body of the statue (ibid. III, 10, 8). A different approach is visible in Xenophon's *Poroi* where it turns out that he had some idea of a normal price in the long period, which covers cost of production, and the mechanism by which it is established. He wrote: "for if the number of copper smiths becomes too big, they abandon their craft, because their copper products become too cheap, and the iron smiths do the same" (*Poroi* IV, 6). This is the Marshallian idea: there is a certain demand for the product of each industry at the normal price, which covers costs. If there are too many suppliers, short run prices will fall below costs and some producers must leave the business. Xenophon contrasts this with the demand for silver. "But nobody ever required so much silver, that he could not make use of more. If, however, one had a big amount of it, one is no less pleased to bury what is superfluous than to use it" (ibid. IV, 7). Silver is the monetary commodity, hence there is no limit to the accumulation of silver, as Aristotle also observes – but in a more critical vein – in his theory of chrematistics. Xenophon even expresses the idea that there are diminishing returns in agriculture, for he states that it is no use to multiply the agricultural workers on a given amount of land indefinitely (ibid. IV, 5). His observation of the division of labour can, in this perspective, be interpreted as the identification of the external effects of agglomeration. Xenophon, who was very often translated by humanists, may have influenced Serra, who probably was the first to formulate laws on increasing and diminishing returns at the beginning of the seventeenth century (Serra 1613 [2011]).

What Aristotle attacks as chrematistics must have been defended by others. The *Oikonomikos* of Xenophon, also in the Socratic tradition, gives a more realistic picture. The core of the dialogue consists of a discussion between Socrates and Ischomachos, the latter being a rich landowner; it takes some time to discover whether he pursues his agricultural interests for the enjoyment of gardening or as a business. We first hear much about the pleasures of farming, and its natural character is proved by pointing out that nature itself teaches how to plant and to harvest – the arts of gardening and farming are visual: we learn from observation with a little instruction by experienced persons.

However, Ischomachos often has to be absent in the city. He seems to be engaged in considerable liturgies, of which he is proud, but he has to fight off exorbitant claims to pay even more. At any rate, he needs a supervisor for his estate, and he admits paying a large salary (πολὺν μισθόν) for a supervisor (*Oikonomikos* I, 4) who is able to enlarge the estate (αὔξειν τὸν οἶκον). It seems not to be a matter of living the good life on an estate, with modest and definite needs, but the question is how to improve it and to get more out of it. Management requires keeping order and discipline among the slaves – rewards, not only punishment, are needed, and so the dialogue offers us also some insight into the life of the family. Ischomachos seems to be a man in the middle of his life and he has married a very young wife. We imagine a sweet young person who is overwhelmed by the prospect of having to look after such a large estate with many dependents. We hear her asking, shyly, but determined to fulfil her duty: ῍Ο τι ἂν ἐγὼ ποιοῦσα συναύξοιμι τὸν οἶκον?" ("By doing what might I help to enlarge the household?") (ibid. VII, 16). To improve the estate thus appears at first as an extension of the natural activities. One should do well what one does. The wife should therefore help to keep good order among the male slaves and the maids, and among the instruments – is the good life not one in which one feels the pleasure of improvement?

This is what Ischomachos suggests (though he does not use the term "good life"), but Socrates then asks from whom Ischomachos got the estate and what he wants to do with it in the long run. Gradually, as Socrates presses him, it turns out that Ischomachos has bought it, that he is going to sell it at a large profit, because of the improvements, and that he has learnt the art of buying estates, improving them and selling them again with a profit, from his father and that he has exerted it many times. He is unmasked: he strives for money and operates farms not for the love of farming. As Socrates puts it, he loves his estate like a corn merchant loves his wheat (*Memorabilia* XX, 27): this is Xenophon's critique of chrematistics.

Max Weber's theory, according to which the household and the firm had to be separated for modern rational capitalism to develop, is illustrated by this episode (Schefold 2011b: 179–97). The tension between the rationality of house-holding, represented by the wife, who wants to keep the house in good order, and of profit-making, represented by Ischomachos, who wants to sell the estate, is obvious. However, households and firms could not be separated, since the firm was not a legal entity, and this institutional obstacle also came up in banking. The trapecites, who were money changers serving also as bankers, giving credit and receiving deposits, operated in a risky business, which Demosthenes defined as follows: "ἡ δ᾽ἐργασία προσόδους ἔχουσα ἐπικινδύνους ἀπὸ χρηρημάτων ἀλλοτρίων" (*Dem.* 36. 11). The banker works with the money of others and gets incomes beset with dangers. The dealings of the trapecite are made in person, but the banking business extends over years. Can an old and frail banker be trusted if he accepts a deposit for an indefinite number of years? Cohen (1992: 101–10) has drawn attention to the fact that the lack of the legal institution "firm" leads to tensions within the banks as households. The solution: the banker, in order to remain trustworthy, accepted his main slave, who was responsible for much of the business, as his heir. The slave was liberated in the banker's testament and the testament also arranged for this former slave to marry the banker's widow. The banker-heir thus was integrated into the Athenian society and could continue the business. If the continuity of the business was ensured through its continued personal representation, banks could accept long-run financial dealings.

The example demonstrates how the economic institutions were not modern, but historically specific. We turn briefly from economic specificities of the house as unity of household and firm to the state as economic organiser. Ancient reflections on political life and political constitutions were in part motivated by economic considerations and led to original economic experiments. Xenophon suggested, in the *Poroi*, using the proceeds from silver mining in Athens, carried out by means of state slaves, to provide for the basic needs of the poor citizens. He did not propose the modern solution: redistribution of the proceeds from taxation. Politicians gained influence in the *Polis* by means of suggestions of public services which often addressed economic issues. This remained true also among the Romans.

Cicero, in his *De officiis*, where he, on the whole, follows Panaitios (Schefold 2001), thought that it was wise to spend for public purposes, but not to the extent of damaging the family fortune. In his comparison of benficentia and liberalitas, he gave advice rather to render services (opera were regarded as praiseworthy) than spending money (pecunia). There was the danger of spending too much and of getting involved in corruption ("Tota . . . ratio talium largitionum genere vitiosa est" (*De officiis* II 52, 60). Services, performed as a lawyer, were applauded: ". . . opera . . . tum in universam rem publicam, tum in singulos cives conferuntur. Nam in iure cavere, consilio iuvare . . . et ad opes augendas pertinet et ad gratiam" (ibid. II 65).

The Roman economy was larger and had more developed means of communication, including credit, than most countries of the early modern period; yet Rome did not develop a theory of political economy. The best we have are conceptualisations of economic transactions in Roman law and the texts of the Agrarian writers. For example, Roman law stated that a transaction could be invalidated in court, if it could be shown that the price paid was less than half the just price (the market price according to experts, on *Laesio enormis*, see Gordon 1975: 130). The insights of the agrarian writers concerned management techniques. It was advised to have the dangerous work done by wage labourers and not by the more precious slaves. Further, it was recommended that the activities of the labourers should be evenly spread throughout the year, so that slaves would have to do the steady basic work and wage labourers had to be hired at harvest time. A principle of the division of labour was formulated: labour should be so divided as to avoid revolts. Plato had related the division of labour to the quality of work and Xenophon to productivity; here it was related to domination and control. The advice given by the agrarian writers continued to be studied by agriculturalists down to the eighteenth century, and calculation of an investment process, involving the use of the rate of interest as a measuring for profitability, can be found in *Columella* (III. 3.8–10), but compound interest is not mentioned.

The old discussions about the economic underpinnings of the good life reappeared in later Roman philosophy. Philodem, an Epicurean writer at the time of Cicero, wrote about the household principles which would be fit for an Epicurean philosopher: it is better for the Epicurean if he does not have to work and owns a fortune. If this is the case, he should not be distracted by attempts to enlarge it but try to develop an income from it by honest employments of the capital, for example, in house-letting or, preferably, in agriculture, but the best life is that of the philosopher who earns money from his pupils by means of his lectures, which should neither be demagogic nor hair-splitting (*Peri oikonomias* 21).

Much more important was Stoic philosophy. Cicero's discussion of asymmetric information in markets has remained famous (*De officiis* III, 12–13). Should a merchant who arrives with a ship full of corn at an island, where people are hungry because of a bad harvest, reveal that other ships with corn follow him and will arrive a day later? Or is he allowed to sell at a price reflecting his temporary monopoly? Cicero insisted that the apparent contradiction between the "useful" and the "honest" could be overcome by observing that it is not useful to be called a deceiver; the problem of the asymmetry of information therefore is solved by taking the value of a good reputation into account. The case was discussed by Scholastic authors and humanists alike. Other examples of the use of Stoic philosophy are Seneca's considerations (*Ad Lucilium* 90) of whether innovations are primarily due to the ingenious minds of the few or to the experience of the many – a discussion later reflected in Adam Smith who sided with practice. The most important heritage of the Stoics consisted in the idea that the creator of the world had made it such that anyone who recognises his true personal interest can benefit even from evil, much as the wrestler learns from his adversary: the wrestler gets training from a strong adversary, the philosophically minded person learns to bear if evil befalls him (Epictet, *Diatribes* III, 20; I, 19). This Stoic idea was taken up by the German author Fronsperger at the time of the Reformation who tried to prove that harmony resulted if each followed his own interest, as beautiful melodies emanate from an organ, not although but because the pipes are of different length (Fronsperger 1564). Later, the working of self-interest was described by Mandeville and Adam Smith, who also were indebted to the Stoic tradition (Vivenza 2001).

The famous *edictum* on prices and wages by Emperor Diocletian is more important for economic history than for the history of economic thought (Lauffer 1971), but it results from this text in which the emperor ascribed inflation to imperfect competition among merchants, not to his own debasement of the currency. This and other monetary reforms prove that there was some understanding of the working of metallic currencies; however, we do not possess much direct textual evidence of it. The *edictum* on prices and wages demonstrates that Emperor Diocletian related prices to remuneration and costs.

The latest additions to the economic thought of antiquity came from the Fathers of the Church (Seipel 1907 [1972]; Troeltsch 1912 [1994]). The New Testament gave dignity to work. Some Fathers radicalised the classical idea of gift-giving by postulating that charity be extended even at the risk of spending the fortune of the family – God would look after the children. Sophisticated theories of the prohibition of interest would arise only in the high Middle Ages, when charging interest was regarded as unnatural, following Aristotle, while the early Fathers of the Church thought that interest-taking simply resulted from avarice.

BERTRAM SCHEFOLD

See also:

Karl Heinrich Marx (I); Methods in the history of economic thought (III); Karl Polanyi (I); Political philosophy and economics: freedom and labour (III); Joseph Alois Schumpeter (I); Adam Smith (I).

References and further reading

Cohen, E.E. (1992), *Athenian Economy and Society. A Banking Perspective*, Princeton, NJ: University Press.
Finley, M.I. (1973), *The Ancient Economy*, reprinted 1975, London: Chatto & Windus.
Finley, M.I. (ed.) (1979), *The Bücher–Meyer Controversy*, New York: Arno Press.
Fronsperger, L. (1564), *Von dem Lob deß Eigen Nutzen. Mit vil schönen exempeln und Historien auß heyliger Göttlicher Schrifft zusammen gezogen*, Frankfurt am Main: Feyerabend, Hüter & Lechler.
Gordon, B. (1975), *Economic Analysis before Adam Smith*, London: Macmillan.
Hildebrand, B. (1864), 'Natural-, Geld- und Credit-Wirthschaft', *Jahrbücher für Nationalökonomie und Statistik*, **2**, 1–24.
Hildebrand, B. (1869), 'Die soziale Frage der Verteilung des Grundeigentums im klassischen Altertum', *Jahrbücher für Nationalökonomie und Statistik*, **12**, 1–25, 139–55.
Kraus, J.X. (2000), *Die Stoa und ihr Einfluß auf die Nationalökonomie*, Marburg: Metropolis.
Lauffer, S. (1971), *Diokletians Preisedikt*, Berlin: de Gruyter.
Polanyi, Karl (1968), *Primitive, Archaic and Modern Economics. Essays of Karl Polanyi*, ed. G. Dalton, New York: Anchor.
Roover, R. de (1955), 'Scholastic economics: survival and lasting influence from the sixteenth century to Adam Smith', *Quarterly Journal of Economics*, **69** (2), 161–90.
Roscher, W. (1861), *Ansichten der Volkswirthschaft aus dem geschichtlichen Standpunkte*, Leipzig: C. F. Winter, reprinted 1994 (Klassiker der Nationalökonomie), B. Schefold (ed.) with commentary volume *Vademecum zu einem Klassiker der historischen Schule*, Düsseldorf: Verlag Wirtschaft und Finanzen.
Rostovtzeff, M. (1941), *The Social and Economic History of the Hellenistic World*, vol. 1, reprinted 1972, Oxford: Clarendon.
Salin, E. (1963), 'Kapitalbegriff und Kapitallehre von der Antike bis zu den Physiokraten', in E. Salin, *Lynkeus. Gestalten und Probleme aus Wirtschaft und Politik*, Tübingen: J.C.B. Mohr (Paul Siebeck), pp. 153–81.
Schefold, B. (1988), 'Karl Bücher und der Historismus in der Deutschen Nationalökonomie', in N. Hammerstein (ed.), *Deutsche Geschichtswissenschaft um 1900*, Stuttgart: Steiner, pp. 239–67.
Schefold, B. (1989), 'Platon und Aristoteles', in J. Starbatty (ed.), *Klassiker des ökonomischen Denkens*, Munich: Beck, pp. 19–55.
Schefold, B. (1994), 'Antonio Serra: der Stifter der Wirtschaftslehre?', in *Vademecum zu einem unbekannten Klassiker*, commentary to the facsimile reprint of the 1st edn from 1613 of A. Serra, *Breve Trattato delle cause, che possono far abbondare li regni d'oro, & argento*, Klassiker der Nationalökonomie, ed. B. Schefold, Düsseldorf: Verlag Wirtschaft und Finanzen, pp. 5–27.
Schefold, B. (1997), 'Reflections of ancient economic thought in Greek poetry. Greek economic thought as a problem of historical dogma', trans. C. Shiley and B.B. Price of the German article 'Spiegelungen des

antiken Wirtschaftsdenkens in der griechischen Dichtung', in B.B. Price (ed.), *Ancient Economic Thought*, vol. 1, London and New York: Routledge, pp. 99–145.

Schefold, B. (1998), 'Spontaneous conformity in history', in H. Hagemann and H.D. Kurz (eds), *Political Economics in Retrospect. Essays in Memory of Adolph Lowe*, Cheltenham, UK and Northampton, MA, USA: Edward Elgar, pp. 235–56.

Schefold, B. (2001), 'Von den Pflichten', in *Vademecum zu einem Klassiker des römischen Denkens über Staat und Wirtschaft*, commentary volume to the facsimile reprint of the 1st edn from 1465, printed in Mainz, of M.T. Cicero, *De officiis*, Klassiker der Nationalökonomie, ed. B. Schefold, Düsseldorf: Verlag Wirtschaft und Finanzen, pp. 5–32.

Schefold, B. (2011a), 'Cameralism as an intermediary between Mediterranean Scholastic economic thought and classical economics', in H.D. Kurz, T. Nishizawa and K. Tribe (eds), *The Dissemination of Economic Ideas*, Cheltenham UK and Northampton, MA, USA: Edward Elgar, pp. 13–40.

Schefold, B. (2011b), 'A contribution to Weber's theory of modern capitalism: amortisation according to Sraffa as a rational substitution of missing markets', in C. Gehrke and N. Salvadori (ed.), *Keynes, Sraffa, and the Criticism of Neoclassical Theory. Essays in Honour of Heinz Kurz*, London: Routledge, pp. 179–97.

Schefold, B. (2011c), 'The applicability of modern economics to forms of capitalism in antiquity. Some theoretical considerations and textual evidence', *Journal of Economic Asymmetries*, **8** (1), 131–63.

Seipel, I. (1907), *Die wirtschaftsethischen Lehren der Kirchenväter*, Vienna: Mayer, 2nd edn, 1972, Graz: Akademische Druck- und Verlagsanstalt.

Serra, A. (1613), *A 'Brief Treatise' on the Wealth and Poverty of Nations*, reprinted 2011 with an introduction by S.A. Reinert (ed.), London: Anthem.

Soudek, J. (1952), 'Aristotle's theory of exchange. An inquiry into the origin of economic analysis', *Proceedings of the American Philosophical Society*, **96** (1), 45–75.

Sraffa, P. (1960), *Production of Commodities by Means of Commodities*, Cambridge: Cambridge University Press.

Troeltsch, E. ([1912], *Die Soziallehren der christlichen Kirchen und Gruppen*, 2 vols, reprinted 1994, Tübingen: J.C.B. Mohr (Paul Siebeck).

Vivenza, G. (2001), *Adam Smith and the Classics. The Classical Heritage in Adam Smith's Thought*, Oxford: Oxford University Press.

Economic thought in scholasticism

Medieval economic views can be reconstructed only indirectly, through the works of theologians, moralists, lawyers, and philosophers for whom such issues did not constitute a field that deserved to be considered separately. Even texts that are directly related to specific economic problems, such as money lending, only make sense as part of a more general perspective. In general, economic views are restricted to certain paragraphs in the *Summa*, the commentaries on Aristotle's works on ethics or politics, or comments on contracts in canon or civil law. These economic ideas therefore appear as a kind of projection from theological, philosophical, moral, political or legal concepts to the economic aspects of social life, especially as they concern human behaviour.

In this respect, the economic reasoning of the Middle Ages could not be considered an economic theory in the modern sense. Characterized by a comparative approach, it consists of two procedures. First, within the framework of general conceptions of society, a norm for economic activity is formed. Secondly, economic behaviour and, further, economic intentions, are analysed and assessed for whether they conform to that norm. Understanding this duality is particularly important since it permits an explanation of certain apparent contradictions between the various judgements of the schoolmen. Moreover, it helps prevent the erroneous though widespread tendency to read medieval economic analysis through exclusively normative glasses: whatever the norm is (a just price, for instance), the existence of a possible gap between this norm and actual transactions requires an explanation to support the judgement of the moralist, whether priest or judge. The elements of medieval economic analysis lie in this explanation.

This does not mean that apparently familiar economic categories (price, interest, exchange, money, and competition) can be understood as they would be today. What makes them unfamiliar is their dependence both on specific conceptions of society, and on the specific goals of the age.

Three main sources formed the intellectual basis of the economic thought of the Middle Ages. The first comprises the traditional teaching of the church, drawing on the Gospels and on the wide corpus of patristic literature. The second source is provided by the Latin translations of Aristotle, mainly his *Nicomachean Ethics* and his *Politics*, which spread across the western world during the thirteenth century. Usually these translations were indirect, since Aristotle's moral and philosophical works were known from previous translations by Muslim and Jewish commentators. The third source is Roman law, rediscovered through the works of glossators during the second half of the eleventh century. These three sources sustained an ambitious project, initiated by Albert the Great and his follower Thomas Aquinas, as a reaction against the spread of the doctrine of the double truth – truth of reason and truth of faith – attributed to Averroes, and taught in Paris by Siger of Brabant. The purpose of this project was the conciliation of reason and faith by showing that faith is founded on reason. Aristotle's philosophy here played a crucial role, in that it allowed the rationalization of theological doctrines.

On first sight, this seems far from economic matters. Nonetheless, philosophical positions such as Albert's and Thomas's brought with them a conception of society which is worth mentioning from the viewpoint of such matters. From Aristotle they borrowed a teleological and organicist conception of society. The first feature gives rise to a hierarchy of natures, which goes from inanimate things up to vegetables, animals, men, and, at the top of the pyramid, God. Since the end of each level in this hierarchy is to be found in the higher level, men appear on this earth not only as God's creatures, but as agents of the Creation, endowed with reason. The second feature draws on Aristotle's political philosophy, for instance, on *Politics*, book 1, where he argued that man is a "political animal", since his ends and capacities can be satisfied only through his function within the political organization of the City, just like any particular organ within the organism of which it is a part. This does not only mean that, as Thomas argued, again following "the Philosopher" (Aristotle), "the whole must of necessity be prior to the part" (Thomas Aquinas, *Summa Theologiae*, II^a–II^{ae}, q.58, a.5, resp.), but that our place in society as a part of it conforms to an external hierarchy of ends which, as beings endowed with reason, it is our task to discover.

However, society was far from being considered only from the point of view of Thomism. In 1277 – that is, three years after Thomas Aquinas's death – Averroist theses were condemned by the Bishop of Paris. It was clear to everyone that, behind Averroës, this condemnation was aimed at the teachings of Aquinas, whose eminent position was not all that firmly established outside the Dominican order. As early as the beginning of the fourteenth century, there was a gradually increasing influence of alternative trends of thought coming mainly from the Franciscan order, through figures such as John Duns Scotus and William of Ockham who set out what is now known respectively as "Scotism" and "nominalism". From a philosophical point of view, both might be seen as ways of importing other influences (Plato and, concerning Islamic philosophy, Avicenna), of reframing the influence of Aristotle, or even of moving away from it. However, it was also a way to provide more individualistic foundations to the conception of society, either through a contractualist approach (Scotism), or through an approach which dismissed the possibility that a category like "men" in general, independently from the particularities of each single individual, might constitute the basis of society (nominalism).

These considerations are far from strictly academic, since they explain some of the variants of the analysis of economic categories among the schoolmen.

Price and Just Price

Just price is the most typical example of an economic category which has different interpretations in medieval literature. Baldwin (1959: 8) found the first occurrence of the phrase in Babylon, at the time of the fourth successor of Hammurabi. However, the medieval theologians and jurists encountered it via Roman law, in the *Corpus Juris Civilis*, notably in passages related to contracts such as those concerning the problem of the *laesio enormis*. Further, the just price occurs in the theological literature of the end of the twelfth century, as in Peter Cantor, or at the beginning of the thirteenth century, as in Robert of Courçon or Alexander Hales.

Nevertheless, although the rough intuition of a price which might be considered as just from a moral or legal viewpoint does have an ancient origin, the first systematic presentation of the concept, accessible to contemporary economists, appears no earlier than in the writings of Albert the Great and his pupil Thomas Aquinas. As such, it expresses the basic requirements of any moralist broadly speaking (for instance, a priest or a judge): knowing whether such-and-such a price for such-and-such a transaction is morally acceptable or not requires (1) that a norm of acceptability is made explicit – the just price, and (2) that any difference from this norm is explained in moral terms. This basic requirement was evidently not restricted to Thomism, since it was shared by its opponents, and still appears as a major theme in the sixteenth century – within the revival of Thomism which since Marjorie Grice-Hutchinson's works has been known as the "School of Salamanca" (Grice-Hutchinson 1952, 1978; Tortajada 1992); in the works of the founders of natural law philosophy during the seventeenth century such as Hugo Grotius and Samuel von Pufendorf; and even in the eighteenth century, in Turgot's works. However, during this long process of evolution, its initial content vanished.

This should be taken seriously: not only had the meaning of the "just price" been transformed since its analytical origin in the thirteenth century, but it is too dependent on concerns different from ours to be easily approached through our current economic categories. However, there remains a persistent tendency to view the just price – that is, the norm of morality within a transaction – as something of a trailblazer for market price theory (see, for instance, De Roover 1958, 1971; Baldwin 1959; Barath 1960).

Intuitively, this point of view is far from unreasonable: the persistent struggle of schoolmen against corporations of merchants, trade associations and many other kinds of collusion, or the development of fairs all over Europe, suggest that the intuition of a market mechanism already existed. In the same way, reference in the works of several schoolmen, including Thomas Aquinas, to such notions as "demand" or "utility" contributes to this impression.

However, a more nuanced investigation shows that such an interpretation makes poor sense. For instance, the schoolmen's opposition to various kinds of monopoly does not lead to an understanding, similar to ours, of the competitive mechanism which leads to market price. Rather, it is linked to moral judgements, which condemn such contracts where justice is violated because of the asymmetric position of the parties. The existence of fairs, which we rightly consider today as "markets", only means that markets as institutions already existed; not that, for all those who were involved in that institution, the market was also a theory. Moreover, even though Latin expressions such as *indigentia* or *utilitas* were often translated respectively as "demand" or "utility", this does not imply that both of them had the subjective meaning to which we are today accustomed: *indigentia* denotes a social need, and *utilitas* refers to an admitted social use which has nothing to do with individual fancy.

Thomas Aquinas on the analysis of price
Thomas Aquinas's writings on price are not numerous. To his commentaries on Aristotle's *Ethics* and *Politics* should be added the questions on justice from the *Summa Theologica* (II^a–II^{ae}, especially question 77), as well as passages from more specific works, such as that on forward transactions, *De Emptione et Venditione ad Tempus*. These passages elaborate on the comments on Aristotle provided by Thomas Aquinas's master, Albert the Great, showing once again the influence of the philosopher, which brings with it both the Church Fathers' traditional teaching and the legacy of Roman law. The representation of price therefore appears as an outcome of a more general understanding of social interactions, within which the question of ownership plays a crucial part.

Private property and natural law   Although scholastic views on property had moved away from those of the Church Fathers, such as Ambrose or John Chrysostom, who argued in favour of collective property, private property never obtained the status of a full natural right. Thomas Aquinas's views typify this persistent gap between private property (to which he devoted the whole article 2 of question 66 from II^a–II^{ae} of the *Summa*) and natural law. He justified the principle of ownership (whatever its type) of external things as a consequence of the place of men in the plan of the Creation (*Summa Theologica*, II^a–II^{ae}, q.66, a.1, ad 1): as reasonable beings, men are not only created by God, they are also agents of the Creation, contributing to its accomplishment. The "power to manage and to distribute" (*potestas procurandi et dispensandi*) should therefore be understood not as the expression of an exclusive and transferable property right, but as a faculty required in order to fulfil the divine plan. Such a position legitimates human property as a way to reach the goals of human community as a whole, according to its place in the hierarchy of natures.

As a result, the introduction of private property should not be understood as a way to take into account a hitherto neglected individual and subjective dimension: it is only a way to reach the common goal more efficiently: Thomas reminds us of the greater "care" (*cura*) that we give to what we possess privately (*Summa Theologica*, II^a–II^{ae}, q.66, a.2, resp). Thus, the individual dimension appears only as a moral and religious one, through the responsibility of each human being to share or to reject this common goal. Similarly, although private property evidently has something to do with natural law, this is not immediate, as an unquestionable part of it, but only indirect. As for Augustine, and according to a distinction already present in Roman law, private property rights are considered something added by human reason as a more convenient way of contributing to the common good, pertaining to what will be known as the "human right" – *jus gentium*.

The theory of the just price   Thomas's conception of the just price is the core of question 77 from the *Summa Theologica* (II^a–II^{ae}). As such, it is a part of a reflection on the injustice committed in a context of voluntary exchange. This emphasis on justice or injustice in exchange shows that the just price is assumed to be "just" according to what Aristotle named "particular justice", which could be either commutative or distributive (*Summa Theologica*, II^a–II^{ae}, q.61, a.3, resp.). Rigorously speaking, Aristotle distinguished three (and not two) kinds of particular justice: distributive, reciprocal, and corrective. The confusion between the two last kinds of justice in the category of "commutative" justice seems to have been an effect of the Latin translations which were used throughout the Middle Ages, particularly in the works of Albert and Thomas (see, for instance, *Summa Theologica*, II^a–II^{ae}, q.61, a.1, sed contra).

In commutative justice, whose primary concern is "selling and buying", Thomas Aquinas said that "it is necessary to equalize thing with thing", whereas distributive justice deals with the distribution of "common goods" among individuals "according to proportion between things and persons", that is, according to the respective "position[s] in the community" in that it reflects individual contributions to the realization of the goals of the society (*Summa Theologica*, II^a–II^{ae}, q.61, a.2, resp). Again following Aristotle, he argued that commutative and distributive justice can be distinguished in that the first specie of justice achieves an arithmetic proportion, and the second one a geometric proportion (*Summa Theologica*, II^a–II^{ae}, q.61, a.2, ad 2).

The part played by commutative justice is obvious, since it explicitly deals with *commutatio*, that is, with exchange. The equality of thing to thing which characterizes it draws its importance from what it excludes: in one way, this equality depends on conditions of place, time and risk; but in another way, it depends neither on the social hierarchy between the persons involved in the transaction nor on any natural hierarchy between the things exchanged. This gives a determining part to what Thomas called *indigentia*, often translated as "need" or "utility", and explains why, in contrast with the hierarchy of natures and according to a well-known example from Augustine (*Of the City of God*, XI), a horse might be more expensive than a slave (see Aquinas's *Summa Theologica*, IIa–IIae, q.77, a.2, ad 3 and *Ethicorum ad Nichomachum* – hereafter *Ethicorum* – V, 9).

Among some commentators (see, for instance, De Roover 1971: 49–50), such reference to "need" constituted an argument in support of the idea that the scholastic theory of the just price constituted the first stone of a theory of price based on subjective utility. However, although it is obvious that exchange was viewed as a mutual advantage (*Ethicorum*, V, 9; *Summa Theologica*, IIa–IIae, q. 77, a.1, resp.), it is difficult to allow that phrases such as *indigentia* anticipate the subjective content of individual preferences in the modern sense (see Lapidus 1986: 20–21, 1992: 34, and the lexical discussion in Langholm 1987: 122–5). On the contrary, *indigentia* seems to refer to a socially acknowledged norm which associates things and human needs in the same way as a tool is associated to its use. Such universality shows that these needs accord not with individual fancy, but with the requirements of society as a whole – with public felicity.

This is why commutative justice is tightly connected with distributive justice. Now, distributive justice primarily deals with the distribution, among individuals, of a common good, ruled by their respective positions within the society. As Thomas Aquinas explains, "in distributive justice a person receives all the more of the common goods, according as he holds a more prominent position in the community" (*Summa Theologica*, IIa–IIae, q. 61, a. 2, resp.). The "common good" dimension of distributive justice should not mislead us. In the same question of the *Summa*, after having explained the differences between commutative and distributive justice, Thomas Aquinas stresses their similarity, using a most interesting analytical argument which states that externalities might be internalised in the same way as internalities might be externalised: "things can be taken out of the community in order to be distributed among individuals as much as exchanged between them" (*Summa Theologica*, IIa–IIae, q. 61, a. 3, resp.). This should be taken seriously. It means that selling private goods can be viewed as an equivalent to distributing a public good, through the income distribution to which it gives rise – what was to be called the "labour and expenses" of the merchants. It is obvious that this might give birth to two kinds of retrospective biases.

The first retrospective bias comes from the way we interpret the social hierarchy which is reflected by the hierarchy of incomes generated by the price of a good. Since this social hierarchy constitutes an expression of the relative merits of the members of a society, it seems rather easy to consider such merit as an expression of individual contributions, which would foreshadow marginal productivity (for a criticism of the marginal productivity interpretation of the incomes generated by distributive justice, see Wilson 1975: 63 ff.). Nonetheless, it should be stressed that although individual merit matters, it is not according to the production of material wealth, but to its contribution to a common end which gives rise to public felicity – in contrast to private well-being.

This should be kept in mind in order to avoid the second retrospective bias, which would lead us to question the consistency of the just price with both needs (according to commutative justice) and income distribution (according to distributive justice). When taken into account, such possible inconsistency has led commentators to support the idea of a coexistence of two alternative theories of the just price in Thomas's works (see Hollander 1965), or of a quasi-Smithian gravitation theory involving two prices (De Roover 1958: 421 ff.), or, finally, of a kind of prefiguration of the distinction between short-term and long-term market price (Barath 1960). However, the prerequisite for such interpretations – that is, the mere possibility that a price might be just in two different ways, generating two different magnitudes – would be meaningless at least within Albert's and Thomas's legacy, where a teleological and organicist conception of society results in the consistency between common end and social hierarchy (see Lapidus 1986, 1992).

Price and moral behaviour: the determination of actual prices   The just price constitutes a norm of acceptability of price, which is rooted in a moral point of view of what is "just". As such, it is a part of a broader device which takes into account the exchangers' morality in order to explain why such an actual price would depart from or, to the contrary, match the norm of the just price. Three types of situation give rise to a possible deviation from the just price: (1) lack of information; (2) manipulation of information; and (3) exchange by accident.

In the two first types of situation, the part played by the morality of the seller and of the buyer is linked to the role of information not about the just price itself (which is assumed to be known, or easily knowable, by everyone), but about the goods and on the conditions of the transaction. The examples which Thomas Aquinas introduced in question 77 of the *secunda secundae* all suggest the same kind of process (see Lapidus 1994): whereas in (1) a lack of information might make the actual price depart from the just price to the detriment of any of the parties without any sinful intention, the same lack of information by one party in (2) can also be manipulated purposefully to his detriment by the other party, so that the gap between the actual price and the just price now constitutes the fraud denounced in question 77. On the contrary, a potential transaction between a virtuous seller and a virtuous buyer, both accurately informed about the good and the transaction, represents a kind of reference to which the actual transaction is compared. In such virtuous and informed situations, the behaviour of each agent is described as a consequence of a switch between each one's point of view, drawing on Matthew 7.12: "All things whatsoever ye would that men should do to you, do ye even so to them" (*Summa Theologica*, II^a–II^ae, q. 77, a. 1, sed contra). When the buyer and the seller are both informed about the just price, this means that the first aims at paying at least the just price and that the second aims at paying at most the just price, so that this last becomes the only actual price acceptable by the two sides of the transaction. In the last type of situation, (3), exchange is viewed as an accidental operation (exchange *per accidens*, which relates to the Aristotelian theory of categories; see *Summa Theologica*, II^a–II^ae, q. 77, a. 1, resp.) between a particular buyer and seller who are familiar to each other and, as a result, sufficiently aware of the conditions under which such an object is sold or bought to be morally involved in the transaction, so allowing the actual price to depart from the just price on the basis of these specific conditions. Thomas Aquinas argued:

[I]f the one man derive a great advantage by becoming possessed of the other man's property and the seller be not at a loss through being without that thing, the latter ought not to raise the price, because the advantage accruing to the buyer, is not due to the seller, but to a circumstance affecting the buyer. (*Summa Theologica*, II^a–II^ae, q. 77, a. 1, resp.)

Such a representation of the way a transaction is concluded did not lead to any condemnation of the trade which gives birth to profit in itself, and Thomas's position might be viewed as a continuation of Augustine's, which he quotes as follows: "The greedy tradesman blasphemes over his losses; he lies and perjures himself over the price of his wares. But these are vices of the man, not of the craft, which can be exercised without these vices." The conclusion is straightforward: "Therefore trading is not in itself unlawful" (*Summa Theologica*, II^a–II^ae, q. 77, a. 4, sed contra). Consequently, the regulation process, which aims at excluding vicious behaviour, does not concern profitable trade in itself, but the existence of opportunities of fraud. Both information-providing and information-seeking are clearly encouraged: such is the case of the virtuous buyer of a book, who is expected to inform his seller of its high value (*Summa Theologica*, II^a–II^ae, q. 77, a. 1, ad 2); or of the brass that the seller mistakes for gold (*Summa Theologica*, II^a–II^ae, q. 77, a. 2, resp.). But Thomas's solution can be more indirect, in particular when vicious behaviour not only arises from the possibility to manipulate the information, but also from the dominating position of one of the parties in the negotiation. In such a situation, a virtuous seller is allowed to protect himself from the potential vicious behaviour of a powerful buyer by keeping for himself some easily available information. A significant example is given in *Summa Theologica*, II^a–II^ae, q. 77, a. 3, resp., with the case of the "one-eyed horse". Thomas Aquinas comes to such a conclusion at the end of a comparative analysis of hidden and evident vices that may affect a commodity:

But when the defect is evident, as for a one-eyed horse; . . . if, as a result of this defect, he [the seller] decides on his own to lower the price, he is not bound to reveal the defect of the thing. For it is possible that as a result of this defect a buyer might want to reduce the price to lower than it should be. In this case, the seller can licitly wish to protect himself against any loss by not disclosing the fact that the thing is defective. (*Summa Theologica*, II^a–II^ae, q. 77, a. 3, resp.)

Price and individual behaviour: alternatives to Thomistic issues
In spite of its importance, Thomas Aquinas's teaching did not remain unchallenged. From the beginning of the fourteenth century, such challenges seem to have jeopardized the elegant construction he had achieved, giving more room to individual behaviour. This was clearly linked to the growing distance between the analysis of price and the organicist understanding of society, which followed Thomas Aquinas's death in 1274. An outstanding symptom of this period of intellectual upheaval was the condemnation of the so-called "Averroist theses" by the Bishop of the University of Paris in 1277: Thomas Aquinas's influence within these theses was clear to everyone concerned. From a philosophical, religious, and political point of view, this period is now well known (see Gilson 1944 [1955]: chs 8 and 9). The ensuring development of alternatives to Aristotle's authority, at least in its Thomistic version, made possible the birth of individualistic approaches, mainly among the Franciscan order, with John Duns Scotus or the nominalist authors, for instance. Now, however, the puzzling observation can be made that the resulting theory of price was not so remote from its Thomistic predecessor.

It seems clear today that most authors fell into the same logical trap, generated by the lack of a demand function relating a list of prices and a list of quantities, which results from the demands formulated by all those who are interested in the good. Such a representation would be consistent with the idea that people usually have different needs, since this difference does not lead to a difference in prices, but to a difference in the quantities demanded. Within the nominalist tradition, this is evident, for instance, from John Buridan's comments on Aristotle's claim in the *Ethics* that need is a measure of price. If individual (and, therefore, different) needs do constitute a measure of price, "the poor should buy corn at higher price than the rich, since he needs corn more than the rich" (Buridan 1637, V, q.16, doubt 1). The famous Rector of the University of Paris at the beginning of the fourteenth century tried to bypass his own objection by arguing that each one gives what he has in excess – money for the rich, and labour for the poor. Nonetheless, this might explain how the poor should get money to buy grain, but not why both the poor and the rich should pay the same amount for the same quantity of corn. The same could be said, for instance, about Henry of Langenstein (Henry of Hesse), at the end of the fourteenth century. In his *Tractatus de Contractibus*, he is also faced with the idea that if individual needs are related to prices, this would mean that no one would pay the same price, and that the poor would be charged more than the rich.

The difficulty was the same and, to some extent, Buridan's and Langenstein's solutions were convergent. Whereas Buridan argued that the kind of need which measures the price of corn is the "common need" (*indigentia communis*) of those who are able to perform such exchanges, Langenstein also favoured the "common need", now understood as the part of individual need which is similar for each of us, since it rests on moral grounds and not on fancy or passions (*voluptas* or *cupiditas*). The resulting device was quite close to the main features of Thomas's theory of price, in spite of the attempt to give it a more individualistic foundation (on Buridan and Langenstein's analysis and, for other examples, see Lapidus 1992: 37–42). A referential norm is introduced as a just price: this fulfils the requirements of commutative and distributive justice as in Thomas Aquinas, and departures from this norm might be explained from a moral or informational point of view.

Interestingly, such a logical trap – making it difficult to conceive a unique price as a result from unequal individual needs – constituted an obstacle to the development of what is known as a subjective theory of value, at least until the concept of a demand function was unambiguously accepted among the predecessors of the marginalist revolution.

Interest and Usury

The great period of the medieval theory of interest and of the associated doctrine of usury might be viewed as a long thirteenth century, beginning in the mid-twelfth century with the *Decretum* by Gratian and ending in the first years of the fourteenth century with the *Tractatus de Usuris* by Alexander Lombard. Historically, it might be viewed as one aspect of a broader history concerning the three great monotheisms (see Ege 2014). Analytically, as in the case of the conception of price, the problem of interest rests on an entanglement of its positive and its normative side: properly speaking, the theory of interest and the doctrine of usury. For a modern reader, this entails the methodological prerequisite of dis-entanglement, although the neglect of such prerequisite also has a relevant history – namely, the history of economists who have sought precursors of their theories in the thought of the Middle Ages. We find, for instance, a most suggestive prefiguration of the idea that only business profit raises interest above zero (Schumpeter 1954: 105) or that underemployment could be efficiently fought by increasing the incentive to invest, which means lowering interest rates (the argument, found in Sommerville 1931, is taken up by Keynes 1936 [1973]: 351–2).

Hereafter, we will try not only to separate positive and normative statements, but also to explain how and why they were embedded. On the one hand, we can consider as granted that the schoolmen did have explanations of a possible difference between the amount lent on the occasion of a money loan and the amount paid back by the borrower. On the other hand, all explanations were not equally acceptable on moral grounds. From this point of view, this seems similar to what we have already encountered in the case of the analysis of price: a play with three characters – the two participants in the transaction (here, a creditor and a debtor) and the moralist (for instance, a priest, or a judge at an ecclesiastical court).

During this period, the explanations given for the difference between the money lent and the money paid back looked very much like those we are familiar with today: they favoured, not exclusively, time preference, technical productivity, risk-taking, liquidity preference, and negotiation power. Nonetheless, from a moral point of view, at least one of them was clearly not admissible: the use of greater power in negotiation in order to obtain this difference, which today we would naturally view as interest. However, the mere factual existence of interest does not by itself show how it should be explained. The creditor and the debtor might know it, but the moralist does not.

Such a perspective, which views the problem faced by the moralist as a variant of a classical asymmetric information problem, constitutes an efficient reading guide for controversies which ran throughout the long thirteenth century, and helps dispel the impression of confused, if not indeed contradictory, statements. The various positions of the schoolmen regarding usury can be understood as so many attempts to avoid the committing of a major sin, and to obtain the relevant information on the actual interpretation of interest which should prevail.

These discussions on interest and usury dealt with money, either directly in the case of money-lending, or indirectly in the case of other operations regarded as possible substitutes for money-lending. In these discussions, the focus was on the morality of the lender and of the borrower, on their respective negotiation power, and on their information, with the question of the value of the money lent remaining in the background.

The value of money: conventionalist versus metalist view
At first sight, the medieval conception of money, typically seen as running from Thomas Aquinas to John Buridan and Nicholas Oresme (at the beginning and in the middle of the fourteenth century), draws on the same sources: Aristotle's *Politics* book I and, to a lesser degree, *Ethics* book V (see Langholm 1983). However, this common Aristotelian legacy had been interpreted and developed in two different ways: a conventionalist conception of money for Thomas Aquinas (the *valor impositus*), and a metalist conception for John Buridan and Nicholas Oresme (see Lapidus 1997; this distinction can be traced back in the secondary literature to Bridrey 1906 and to Gordon 1961).

At first sight, the conceptions share a similar starting point. Thomas Aquinas considered that the rise of money was "ordered by nature" out of a barter situation, as a means of exchange and of measure (*Politicorum*, I, 7). Something similar can be read in Buridan's comments on book V of the *Ethics*, when he impressively argued that money is an appropriate solution to the scattering of sellers and buyers, to the non-simultaneity of needs, to the gap between possessions and needs, and to the indivisibility of goods (*Ethicorum*, V, q. 17, a. 1, proofs 1, 2, 3, and 4). Though based on a reflection on the destiny of Adam's posterity after the Fall, the same analysis could be found in the first chapter of Oresme's influential book on monetary matters, *Treatise on Money*.

However, on closer examination it becomes clear that the paths followed by Thomas Aquinas, on the one hand, and by Buridan and Oresme, on the other, depart from one another.

According to Thomas Aquinas, money, as the highest form of exchange, though ordered by nature, is separated from it: "[I]t is convenient that there be a single thing which could measure everything, and this thing does not measure according to its nature, but because men decided for it to be" (*Ethicorum*, V, 9).

As a measure, Thomas Aquinas explained, money does not depend on the nature of things but on the will of men. This gives rise to the recurrent etymological observation that "specie is called *numisma*, which comes from *nomos*, the law, because specie is not measured by nature, but by law. It is our power to transform it or to make it useless" (*Ethicorum*, V, 9). Or, in the words of the commentaries on the *Politics*, it "will be of price nil if the King or the community decides that it is worthless" (*Politicorum*, I, 7).

On the contrary, for Buridan, as for Oresme, the link between the natural origin of money, the metal it is made of, and its value, cannot be broken. For instance, when commenting on the *Ethics*, Buridan clearly aimed at challenging the Thomistic interpretation of Aristotle's conception of money as *valor impositus*: "Some people [like Thomas Aquinas; I.C. and A.L.] say that the prince imposes the quantity of value of the money, and that, according to the imposed value, it measures the exchanges: this is why Aristotle said that money is not by nature, but by name, and it is up to us to make it useless" (*Ethicorum*, V, q. 17, a. 2). However, Buridan continued, this only means that whereas the prince can impose the name of the money (call it, for instance, "*denier*" or "*obole*"), he may not commit the injustice of imposing its value. This is because the property of money to be a measure of value depends on its being constituted by a material which is, itself, the object of human needs and, therefore, measured by them. In Buridan's words, this amounts to saying that money is not an immediate but an intermediary measure of values (*Ethicorum*, V, q. 17, a. 2). Buridan echoes Thomas Aquinas's idea of a double measure, natural (need) and artificial (money). See also Oresme (*Traduction et Glose de l'*Ethique *d'Aristote*, V, ch. 11) who used a Thomistic vocabulary for a Buridan-like purpose. As a measure of value, money therefore remains anchored in the metal from which it is made.

Oresme's writings especially took into account the effects of the link between money and metal. Again reading the *Politics*, he transposed to money the Aristotelian difference between the "principal use" and the "secondary use" of a good, namely consumption and exchange (*Traduction et Glose de la* Politique *d'Aristote*, I, 10), claiming that the specificity of money is an inversion of content between its principal and its secondary use. As a result, the same precious metal could be viewed alternatively as a good properly speaking, whose principal use is consumption, and as money, whose principal use is from now on exchange. Interestingly, Oresme hierarchized these two uses: employing metal for monetary purpose takes for granted that it is available in a quantity sufficient to guarantee that the satisfaction of its use as a good leaves a large enough surplus. Such a sequential mechanism was suggested when, for instance, Oresme claimed:

> [T]here must be enough of such material. That is why, if there is not enough gold, money is also made of silver; but if one does not have these two metals or not in sufficient quantity, it is necessary to make an alloy or a simple money in another pure metal: thus it was formerly made of copper. . . . [A] large quantity of these metals must not be allowed to be put to other use, to the extent that there is not enough left for money. (*Treatise on Money*: ch. 2)

An important consequence of this sequential mechanism is that money cannot draw its value from its use in exchange, but that it is inherited from the secondary use, as a good, of the metal it is made of. Again in the *Treatise*, when discussing the genealogy of monetary transactions, Oresme argued: "[W]hen men first began to trade, or to compare wealth through the use of money, there was not yet any stamp or image on money; but a certain amount of silver or copper was given for a drink or food" (*Treatise on Money*: ch. 4).

Oresme's conception of money, whose value is determined by that of the metal as a commodity, and whose quantity depends on the importance of the transactions, should be regarded with circumspection. A classical interpretation of the first aspect, by Roscher (1862) to whom we are indebted for the rediscovery of Oresme's *Treatise*, and also taken up by Bridrey (1906), considered it as a prefiguration of the idea that the price of a good is determined by its rarity. However, discussions of the amount of silver "in proportion to natural wealth" (*Treatise on Money*: ch. 3), or of the relative values of gold and silver money (ibid.: ch. 10), show that the value of metal which is transferred to money is not related to its rarity but, in a quite common way, to its just price (see Gillard 1990; Lapidus 1997) – which explains the emphasis laid on the question of debasement of money, regarded as an injustice. Besides, the second aspect of Oresme's conception of money – the link between the quantity of money and the transactions it is used for – suggests some kind of prefiguration of a quantity theory of money (see, for instance, Arena 1987). However, here again, Oresme seems to have been more interested in structural adjustments between various kinds of money (gold, silver or black –that is, copper – money) which are imperfectly substitutable, and the corresponding types of commerce, than on simple quantitative relations between the overall stock of money and the overall volume of trade (Lapidus 1997: 32–4).

It is obvious that such a nuanced monetary analysis is worth considering directly through the contrast between a conventionalist and a metalist conception. It is also obvious that it is worth considering through its various policy implications, whether money does not constitute a limit to the power of the prince (Thomas Aquinas), or does constitute such a limit (Buridan and Oresme) – typically in the case of the debasement of money (see Lapidus 1997: 34–52). Nonetheless, where money was viewed as the possible object of a loan, the question of knowing whether its value is the consequence of a convention established by the prince or of the value of the metal it is made with, fades in favour of other issues concerning its ability to give birth to a specific income, and the possibility to separate its use from its ownership.

Where does interest come from and why is it judged so badly?
The Civil Law (*Corpus Juris Civilis*), built on the great texts of Roman law which were rediscovered during the first half of the eleventh century, provided an analytical framework which seems to have left no room for the possibility of interest. This was influential on Canon Law, especially for Gratian around 1140, who in his *Decretum* introduced the various decisions of the popes and of the Councils on usury, as well as for popes such as Gregory IX, Boniface VIII and Clement V, who completed the *Corpus Juris Canonici*. Moreover, the prohibition of usury reached its climax at the beginning of the fourteenth century, when Clement V promulgated a decretal at the Council of Vienna in 1311, according to which those who claimed that usury was not a sin should be punished as heretics. Numerous texts by theologians, including William of Auxerre, Robert of Courçon, Thomas Aquinas, Giles of Lessines, and Raymond of Peñaforte, supplemented this literature. All this shows the variety of the influences on the doctrine of usury: the Patristic literature came first, drawing on the teaching of the Scriptures. It was on this already well-established basis that both the Roman law and the rediscovery of Aristotle's moral and political philosophy gave the doctrine of usury the shape of the classical argument which Thomas Aquinas developed in the *Summa Theologica* (II^a–II^{ae}, q. 78).

The decisive elements could be traced back to Christian antiquity, to the Greek and Latin Church Fathers who told, in various ways, the same instructive story: that of a consumption loan by a rich man who is widely provided for in all necessities, given to a poor man for whom obtaining the loan is a condition of survival (typical examples from the fourth century can be found in Gregory of Nazianzus or John Chrysostom). This story remained a reference point for centuries, and, later, most scholastic thinkers considered that in such a situation the "voluntary agreement" of both parties was not enough to prevent the loan from being usurious (see, for instance, Robert of Courçon at the beginning of the thirteenth century, for whom a poor man is not guilty of usury when he is obliged to borrow and pay interest (*De Usura*: 17–19): this voluntary agreement was called "absolute" for the lender, but "conditioned" for the borrower.

This distinction, concerning the nature of an agreement, rests on a positive state-ment: the money loan can be understood as a particular case of voluntary exchange, after which neither the lender's nor the borrower's situation gets worse (and the lender's is clearly much better). This is a way to say that scholastic thinkers conceded that exchange is mutually advantageous. Of course, this was not specific to the analysis of a money loan: it clearly comes from the theory of the just price. Such was, for instance, Thomas Aquinas's position when, commenting on Aristotle's *Politics*, he wrote that "purchasing and selling were instituted for the common good of both parties, for each one needs the other's products and reciprocally" (*Ethicorum*, l.V, lect.9, c; see also *Summa Theologica*, II^a–II^{ae}, q.77, a.1, resp.). This is a way to argue that some kind of surplus arises from a money loan as it does from every more standard type of voluntary exchange. Analytically, this also explains why interest is a withdrawal from this exchange surplus to the benefit of the lender. However, the story of the consumption loan has another consequence: it emphasizes the difference between the negotiating power of the lender and of the borrower. The lender is supposed to be vested with a much greater power than the borrower, so that he is able to appropriate most of the surplus emerging from exchange. We know that such a picture is highly disputable, at least in its practical relevance. The fourteenth century, for instance, presents several examples of loans where the borrower is the prince, so that the greater power of negotiation is on his side, the lenders being threatened with the loss of their capital – if not their lives. Nonetheless, the normative conclusion is straightforward: the condemnation of usury amounts to the condemnation of the appropriation of a part of the surplus arising from a loan.

Now, what is the proportion of the surplus above which a licit transaction, morally acceptable, would turn into a usurious transaction? Curiously, the primary impression produced by the literature on usury gives rise to two opposite answers. The story of the consumption loan is one where the total amount of the surplus falls into the hands of the lender: the loan has not helped the borrower escape misery. His situation after the loan is by no means better. The loan has just given him the opportunity to survive, as he did before. Usury might therefore be viewed as a situation in which the negotiating power of the lender is high enough to allow him to appropriate the whole surplus. By contrast, both the severity of the Church Fathers, and the popular knowledge based on the *exempla* to which Jacques Le Goff (1986) had devoted special attention, suggest that the slightest amount perceived above what is paid back would be usurious.

The contradiction is only apparent. The consumption loan story expresses constant suspicion of the lender, and the belief that his negotiation power usually gives him all that is possible under the condition of voluntary agreement by the borrower. The church shows such a strong aversion against this asymmetry of power that it finds it more appropriate to forbid any kind of supplement paid on a loan by the borrower.

The basis of such suspicion against the lender comes from the fact that usury as a sin is a sin of intention, which means that far from being self-evident from its factual existence, it depends on an intention, which is usually not observable to the moralist. In the early thirteenth century, for instance, William of Auxerre defined usury as "the intention to receive something more in a loan than the capital" (*Summa Aurea*, t.48, c.1, q.1). Though the formulation insists on the materiality of usury, a similar idea can be found in Robert of Courçon: "usury is a sin resulting from the fact of receiving or aiming at receiving something above the principal" (*De Usura*: 3; see also ibid.: 13, 57, 61, and 78).

Thomas Aquinas's classical argument

Thomas Aquinas's argument against usury gave a rigorous basis to the prohibition of usury, in the sense of the payment of an income in reason of the loan itself. It might be considered as a development of three topics, coming from Roman law, from Canon law, and from the Aristotelian tradition, respectively. The first borrowed from the *Digesta* the contractual framework of the money loan; the second skilfully justified the choice of this framework by reversing the way the *Decretum* explains how an income is generated by a stock; the third draws on the Aristotelian analysis of the causes of exchange.

The contractual framework of the money loan: the mutuum   Even before Thomas Aquinas, the legal framework for money loans was a free contract for fungible goods, the *mutuum* (see *Digesta*, 44, 7, f.1, n.2, 4). When the underlying contract for a transaction is a *mutuum*, the nature of this contract itself precludes any interest being paid. Robert of Courçon, for example, at the very beginning of the thirteenth century, explained the mechanism by writing:

[T]he name of the *mutuum* comes, indeed, from that which was mine [*meum*] becomes yours [*tuum*] or inversely. As soon as the five shillings that you lent me become mine, property passes from you to me. It would then be an injustice if, for a good which is mine, you were to receive something; for you are not entitled to any return from that which is my possession. (*De Usura*: 15)

In the *mutuum*, the prohibition of interest is linked to the fact that the money lent and the money paid back is not, physically, the same object, so that the ownership of the lender has to be interrupted at the beginning of the loan. Conversely, if they had been the same object, interest could have been charged on it because the lender would have kept his ownership throughout the duration of the loan while selling the use of it. This case was known as *mutuum ad pompam*. For Thomas Aquinas, the argument ran as follows: "silver money could have a secondary use: for instance, if money is conceded to somebody in order to make a display of it or to pawn it. And one can licitly sell such a use of money" (*Summa Theologica*, II^a–II^{ae}, q.78, a.1, ad 6).

Such a position was challenged throughout the Middle Ages, and even condemned by Pope Nicholas III in a decretal incorporated in Canon law (*Decretales*, Liber Sextus, V, tit.11, c.3, *Exiit qui seminat*), thus supporting nonThomistic interpretations of usury. This clearly contradicts our current way of representing economic categories. We would accept that the money lent and the money paid back are not the same in the case of the *mutuum*, but because they are money at different dates, not because they are physically different objects. Thus, the case of the *mutuum* would be equivalent to that of the *mutuum ad pompam*. But we would also admit that the ownership of money is not interrupted by the loan since, apart from the time dimension, the money lent and the money paid back are perfect substitutes in both the *mutuum* and the *mutuum ad pompam* (Lapidus 1987, 1992). This disagreement is not easy to settle, because it is an ontological (and not an analytical) disagreement concerning the conception of economic categories. Nonetheless, the argument based on the *mutuum* is consistent, and leaves no room for a payment to the lender.

However, Roman law also acknowledged other contractual arrangements which would allow such a payment: the *locatio*, for instance, in which only the use of a thing is transferred from the lender to the borrower, its possession remaining unchanged; or the *foenus*, in which possession is transferred, but where such transfer is not free. This was far from entirely new at the time of Thomas Aquinas. But the effect of his contribution was to remove the possible arbitrariness of the choice of the *mutuum* as the contractual framework for money loans.

The nature of money   This was made possible by reversing an argument concerning the reasons why a stock can be a source of income. This argument was presented in a well-known palea called *Ejiciens*, wrongly attributed to John Chrysostom, and integrated by Gratian in Canon law. The author of *Ejiciens* asked whether "the one who rents a field to receive its fruits or a house to receive an income is not similar to the one who lends money at usury" (*Decretum*, dist.88, can.11). The negative answer favoured three reasons:

First, because the only function of money is the payment of a purchase price. Then, because the farmer makes the earth fructify, the tenant takes advantage of inhabiting the house: in both cases, the owner seems to give use of his thing to receive money and, in a certain way, he exchanges gain for gain, whilst from money which is stored up, you make no use. At last, its use gradually exhausts the earth, deteriorates the house, whilst the money lent suffers neither diminishing nor ageing. (Ibid.)

The first reason recalls the Aristotelian argument about the sterility of money. The second argues that the income should arise from a pre-existing surplus, like that which comes from production. The third reason is decisive: it asserts that a stock is a source of income from the moment the stock begins to depreciate. This income is then defined as the counterpart of this depreciation. Now, the great skilfulness of Thomas Aquinas was to reverse *Ejiciens'* third reason (see Noonan 1957: 54–5). His argument was expounded in *De Malo* (q.13, a.4c) or in the *Summa Theologica*:

> One must know that the use of certain things is identical with their consumption . . . In such [exchanges], one must not count the use of the thing apart from the thing itself but, as a result of conceding the use, the thing itself is conceded. And this is why, for such things, the loan transfers property. Thus, if someone wanted to sell wine on the one hand and the use of wine on the other hand, he would sell twice the same thing or sell what is not . . . Conversely, there are things the use of which is not their consumption. So, the use of a house is to live in, not to destroy it. Therefore, one can concede separately use and property. (*Summa Theologica*, IIᵃ–IIᵃᵉ, q.78, a.1, resp.)

As a result, interest as an income no longer proceeded from the depreciation of a stock but from the possibility of separating property and use – the sale of the latter producing the income. Therefore, a house or a field could – as in *Ejiciens*, but for another reason – be the source of an income, while bread, wine and, of course, money could not.

The material and the formal causes of exchange   Far from being a consequence of a possibly arbitrary decision of a moralist or a lawyer, the choice of the *mutuum* for a money loan now came from the nature of the object of the transaction: this means that the nature of money itself, as a thing whose possession cannot be separated from its use, determined the nature of the contract. This conception of money was explained by Thomas Aquinas chiefly in his commentaries on Aristotle, from whom he claimed he had borrowed it.

It was when commenting on Aristotle's *Politics* that Thomas Aquinas stressed the conventional nature of money (*Politicorum*, I, 7). For Thomas, this meant that it was a product of human reason, as the most complete form of exchange. In this respect, he pointed out two functions of money, which he discussed at length when commenting on Peter Lombard's *Sentences*, on the *Politics* or on the *Ethics* and, of course, in the *Summa*. The first function of money stood in the Aristotelian tradition – it is a medium of exchange: "But money, according to the Philosopher [Aristotle] in the *Ethics* (V, 5) and in the *Politics* (I, 3), was principally invented to facilitate exchanges: and so, the proper and principal use of money is to be consumed without diversion, because it is spent in exchanges" (*Summa Theologica*, IIᵃ–IIᵃᵉ, q.78, a.1, resp.). In this regard, usurious activity is considered as distorting the nature of money (*Politicorum*, I, 8).

Thomas Aquinas was not so faithful to Aristotle when introducing the second function of money – the unit of account:

All other things have from themselves some utility: however, this is not the same for money. But it is the measure of the utility of other things, as it is clear from the Philosopher in the *Ethics* (V, 9). And therefore the use of money does not hold the measure of its utility from this money itself but from the things which are measured by money according to the various people who exchange money for goods. Hence, receiving more money for less seems nothing else than differentiating the measure in giving and receiving, which obviously brings inequity. (*In IV Libros Sententiarum*, l.III, dist.37, a.1, q.16)

This contrasts with Aristotle's original position, according to which "money itself is submitted to depreciations, for it has not always the same purchasing power" (*Ethics*, V, 5:14). However, this emphasis on money as a unit of account, therefore free from either appreciations or depreciations, meant that it could not give rise to any supplementary income.

In spite of their discrepancies, the various sources of Scholastic thought continued along the same lines as Thomas Aquinas's construction: the nature of money and the contractual framework thereby induced rendered impossible the charging of interest on a money loan. This impossibility is, first of all, a positive one: interest, as generated by the money loan itself, can simply not exist. So that, if interest happens to be associated with a money loan, its amount must be explained on another basis than the money loan itself.

Interest without usury

The literature on usury shows that the range of analytically acceptable explanations of the existence of interest was limited. Each attempt to give an alternative explanation therefore reveals to the moralist that the income perceived by the lender was only due to his negotiation advantage, and had to be viewed as usurious.

The starting point was the widespread idea that for both the lender and the borrower, a present and a future good are not worth the same. "One harms one's neighbour", wrote Thomas Aquinas, "when preventing him from collecting what he legitimately hoped to possess. And then, the compensation should not be founded on equality because a future possession is not worth a present possession" (*Summa Theologica*, II^a–II^{ae}, q. 62, a. 4, resp. 2; see also his disciple, Giles of Lessines, *De Usuris*, c.9). This was a way to say that although the legitimacy of interest paid on a loan does not depend on the loan itself, it might depend on the harm generated by the loan. Also, when interest compensates the harm suffered by the lender, the operation is not usurious. Extrinsic titles aim, precisely, at identifying this harm.

The same intertemporal framework of the loan contract opens the path to another issue. It is obvious – both for us today, as it was as for medieval merchants, lawyers or theologians – that several intertemporal operations (credit sale or *census*, for example) stand as close substitutes for an interest loan. Disregarding the possibility of a compensation for the harm suffered by the lender, this would mean that the strict prohibition of usury might be bypassed through a close substitute for an interest loan. Noticeable efforts were devoted to the attempt to identify the conditions under which an intertemporal operation, giving rise to interest, counts as (or doesn't count as) a usurious transaction.

Anyway, in both cases (the compensation of harm, or an intertemporal operation generating an income), the practical difficulty is the same: how can we be sure that the income gained by one of the partners of the transaction does not result from his superior power in the negotiation?

Extrinsic titles   Exterior to the loan contract and providing reasons for a compensating payment, the so-called "extrinsic titles" might be viewed as attempts to account for the harm suffered by the lender, according to its nature. These extrinsic titles, such as *poena conventionalis*, *damnum emergens* or *lucrum cessans*, existed separately from the *mutuum*, and gave, for each of them, reasons for the payment received by the lender. A general problem linked to extrinsic titles is that although some of them became widely accepted, the harm often remained unobservable, so that the possibility of a usurious transaction could not be totally avoided. The level of acceptation or refusal of the extrinsic title therefore depended less on the nature of the alleged harm than on the trust or distrust on the effectiveness of this harm.

Designed to protect the creditor from a possible failure of the debtor to repay the loan in time, the *poena conventionalis* stipulated a daily indemnity in case the expiry date was not respected. Through the *damnum emergens*, the prejudice to the lender was described as his sacrifice, in terms of consumption, in order to keep his money available for lending. The *lucrum cessans* widened the perspective to the profitable operations which would have to be given up in order to carry out the loan, so that the prejudice was the sacrifice of a possibility of profit.

The *damnum emergens* and the *lucrum cessans* make obvious the working of the harm-compensation mechanism. As Noonan (1957: 116) pointed out, these two titles were not really discussed before the mid-thirteenth century (with the exception of Robert of Courçon, who condemned the *lucrum cessans*; *De Usura*: 61–3) since they needed, as a prerequisite, a general agreement about the use of the *mutuum* for a money loan. Thomas Aquinas, despite showing a certain mistrust – chiefly aimed at the *lucrum cessans* – clearly stated the principles on which they were founded:

> In his contract with the borrower, the lender may, without any sin, stipulate an indemnity to be paid for the prejudice he suffers while being deprived of what was his possession; this is not to sell the use of money, but to receive a compensation. Besides, the loan may spare the borrower a greater loss than the one to which the lender is exposed. It is thus with his benefit that the first makes up the loss of the second. (*Summa Theologica*, II^a–II^{ae}, q.78, a.2, ad. 1)

In spite of an earlier and more general acceptance, the *poena conventionalis* also illustrates the possibilities for manipulation that the extrinsic titles afforded the lender. This could be done in two different ways. First, the duration of the loan might have been so short that the borrower could by no means pay back in time. Naturally, this practice was clearly condemned, but the fault was not that easy to establish. Second, the lender could increase the indemnity mentioned at the beginning of the contract so that it was higher than the loss he suffered because of the non-availability of his money at the expiry date. Some scholastic authors expressed this last argument quite systematically, such as Raymond of Peñaforte who claimed that "if the penalty proceeds from a convention, that is from a common agreement between the parties mentioned in the contract, so that at least the fear of this penalty forced payment at the expiry date, there is no usury" (*Summa de Casibus Conscientiae*, II, par.5; see also Robert of Courçon, *De Usura*: 65–7). John Duns Scotus, some 60 years later, was even more precise when writing: "An obvious sign that a penalty is not usurious is the following: the merchant prefers to have his money back at the expiry date rather than the day after, accompanied by a penalty" (*In Quattuor Libros Sententiarum*, Opus oxoniensis, IV, dist.15, q.2, 18).

The principle of an interest that was both analytically and morally acceptable therefore appeared as an outcome of the discussions on the *mutuum* and the major extrinsic titles. The emphasis laid on the fact that the interest was a compensation for the specific harm suffered by the lender, and not a product of the loan itself, shows that it might be understood as the opportunity cost of the loan. This opportunity cost is the key to the distribution of the surplus of exchange between the lender and the borrower: after the payment of an interest equal to the cost of opportunity of the loan, the respective situations of the lender and of the borrower have improved.

Naturally, this requires the credibility, for the moralist, of the harm alleged by the lender. In case the fear of a mortal sin was not sufficient to move the latter away from a usurious transaction, this might constitute an evident weakness of the system. This explains the importance granted, in the discussions between schoolmen, to the nature of the harm associated with each extrinsic title. For instance, it justifies the quite general mistrust about the *lucrum cessans* (when compared to the *damnum emergens*): not because this kind of prejudice was inexistent, but because it concerns, by nature, professional merchants who are always suspected of taking advantage of their superior power of negotiation. This also explains the poor confidence, even during the sixteenth century, in a loan where the interest paid is supposed to compensate an insufficiently specified harm: the late extrinsic title called *carentia pecuniae*.

Substitutes for an interest loan   Whereas the extrinsic titles added something more to the main loan contract, a complementary possibility for a potential lender to draw an income was to replace the interest money loan by another intertemporal operation for which it was a close substitute.

The difficulty of the problem faced by the moralists came from the ability of the merchants to construct such close substitutes: credit sale, anticipated payment, *census*, *societas*, triple contract, *mohatra*, mortgage, *foenus nauticum*, bank deposit, etc. The case of the *census*, which appeared in the thirteenth century, is significant. Initially, it had nothing to do with a loan since it consisted in the sale of a productive good – land, for instance, or cattle – bought with the products of its exploitation. As such, this is a sale, and apparently the only disputed question concerns knowing how many times the annual product had to be paid for a *census*. However, if the seller of the *census* had already bought it for cash from his buyer, he clearly becomes the equivalent of a lender receiving interest. As a simple sale, the *census* would be licit, as Giles of Lessines (*De Usuris*, c.9) acknowledged. But alternatively, it could also be the basis of a usurious loan, as Robert of Courçon explained (*De Usura*: 63).

The solution for separating usurious from legitimate transactions in the presence of these kinds of substitutes was to find among them a characteristic which allowed such a separation. Property could be viewed as such a characteristic: in the *mutuum*, the interruption in property made impossible the receipt of an income by the lender; continuous property might, on the contrary, support a claim for such income. However, the institutional arrangements of the transaction can conceal the reality of the ownership. The *societas* illustrates this point. In Roman law, this is an association between persons who engaged their labour, money or goods in a profitable operation. The income of each member of the *societas* depends, naturally, on the issue of the operation. Every modality of sharing was allowed. However, in the Middle Ages, this excluded the modality in which one partner would bear the entire responsibility in case of loss. Robert of Courçon expressed this by writing that "every merchant contracting with another for trading must, if he wishes in particular to profit, show that he participates in the danger and expenses which attend all buying and selling" (*De Usura*: 73).

This shows that, in turn, the claim for property was not enough to ensure its reality, and that beyond its formal existence, a supplementary characteristic of this property was required in order to consider it as able to produce non-usurious income for the owner. Robert of Courçon's reference to the participation "in the dangers" accounts for the commonly held idea that risk-taking was this supplementary characteristic. Furthermore, the general principle was stated by Thomas Aquinas as follows:

> The one committing his money to a merchant or a craftsman by means of some kind of partnership does not transfer the property of his money to him, but it remains his possession; so that at his [the lender's] risk, the merchant trades or the craftsman works with it; and he can thus licitly seek a part of the profit as coming from his own property. (*Summa Theologica*, II^a–II^{ae}, q.78, a.2, obj.5)

A significant expression of the role granted to risk for assessing the legitimacy of a transaction was the well-known decretal *Naviganti* by Pope Gregory IX:

> Somebody lending a certain quantity of money to one sailing or going to a fair in order to receive something beyond the capital, for he takes the risk upon himself, is to be thought a usurer. Also the one who gives ten shillings to receive after a certain time the same measure of grain, wine or oil, though it is then worth more, when one really doubts whether it will be worth more or less at the date of delivery, must not, for that, be considered a usurer. Because of this doubt again, the one who sells bread, grain, wine, oil or other commodities so that he receives after a certain period of time more than they are worth then, is excused if, in lack of a forward contract, they would not have been sold. (*Decretales*, 15, tit. 19, c. 19, *Naviganti*)

This decretal is highly questionable (see Mc Laughlin 1939: 103–4 or Noonan 1957: 137 ff.). At first glance, it seems to adopt successively two opposite positions concerning the effects of risk: the first sentence condemns the sea loan (*foenus nauticum*) while the concluding sentences allow a reduction in price in the case of anticipated payment – and an increase in the case of a credit sale – if the future value of the sold commodity is uncertain. The difference in treatment is large enough to have led some commentators to imagine that the condemnation of the *foenus nauticum* could have proceeded from an error of transcription by the Pope's secretary, Raymond of Peñaforte.

However, a careful examination suggests more consistent interpretations. The first rests on the expression "is to be thought a usurer" (*usurarius est censendus*). Usury being a sin of intention, this means that, in the *foenus nauticum*, receiving an income is not in itself usurious, but an external observer will be far from certain that the lender is not overestimating the risk of the operation to disguise a usurious benefit as a legitimate income.

Such a "moral hazard" interpretation of *Naviganti* was suggested by Goffredus of Trani (see McLaughlin 1939: 103, or Noonan 1957: 139). Besides this, it may also be noticed that the *foenus nauticum* is not such a simple operation, where only two states of the world can occur – the freight arrives safe and sound or perishes at sea. Actually, if the freight is intact, the merchant will run another risk when selling it. This last risk is not taken into account in the contract between the lender and his borrower. So that, in the event of the ship not sinking, one party has to assume the entire responsibility if a loss occurs. As the possibility of selling overseas is submitted to the advance of capital which belongs to the lender for the duration of the crossing, there is no reason for this ownership to be transferred to the borrower during the second phase of the operation. In spite of its name, the *foenus nauticum* is clearly not a loan, but rather similar to a kind of partnership (a *societas*) which allows common ownership of money invested in a presumably profitable operation. This strictly forbids any partner from escaping, at any moment, from the risk of loss.

This shows the utmost importance of risk-bearing as sign of a lender's continuous property during an intertemporal operation, therefore allowing the payment of a non-usurious income (see, for instance, the cases of *venditio sub dubio*, where a real doubt concerns a credit sale or an anticipated payment). Nonetheless, this did not nullify the suspicion concerning the lender's intention, despite the imaginative conditions imposed by some theologians (see, for example, Giles of Lessines for whom the same doubt should exist for both the lender and the borrower, *De Usuris*, c.9), or the typical medieval solution of the resort to an expert, a wise man, already advocated by William of Auxerre in the *Summa Aurea* (*De Usura*, c.3, q.2).

Concluding Remarks

In the two questions from Thomas Aquinas's *Summa Theologica* respectively devoted to them, both price and the interest loan were taken up as special applications of a theory of justice. An outstanding and obvious consequence is that understanding these two economic categories rests on the coexistence of a norm which satisfied the requirements of justice, and of a departure from this norm which explains actual behaviour, usually from a moral point of view. Their respective futures were nevertheless quite different.

The construction of a theory of price drawing on a comparative approach between hierarchized concepts of valuation clearly survived the initial concerns expressed by theologians and lawyers from the Middle Ages. Their legacy can be followed (see Lapidus 1986), from the revival of Thomism within the School of Salamanca during the sixteenth century, to the foundation of what was later called "modern" theories of natural law in the works of Grotius and Pufendorf, one century later, and, at last, to the dissemination of their ideas in Great Britain, at the very origin of the School of Glasgow, by Gershon Carmichael and Francis Hutcheson – Adam Smith's most admired predecessor. So when Smith explained to his students (*Lectures on Jurisprudence*, LJB: 494; see also LJA: 353) that "[o]f every commodity there are two different prices, which tho' apparently independent will be found to have a necessary connection, viz. the natural price and the market price", he made use of the same comparative approach as his predecessors did, but now free from its submission to moral ends. Though the market price is interpreted, in the *Lectures* and, later, in the *Wealth of Nations*, in relation to the natural price, as the current price was interpreted in relation to the just price, the possible differences are no longer considered in terms of the morality of the partners to the transaction.

Economic matters had become worthy of being studied in themselves. However, the way price was understood by most classical economists, from Smith to Marx, retained the hallmark of the intellectual device originated by schoolmen several centuries earlier.

The difficulties facing the understanding of interest at the turn of the thirteenth century were different. From Augustine, for instance, the authors of this period already knew what was later forgotten by Bernard of Mandeville: that trade is not, by nature, dishonest. However, the proliferation of substitutes for money interest loans and of the institutional possibilities for a lender to manipulate the information about the harm he suffers as a result of a loan, increased both the suspicion of trade in general, and the obsolescence of the various mechanisms used to avoid usury loans: the reinforcement of the prohibition of usury came along with a lessening of its efficiency.

The reason for this dead end was the lack of information, on the part of the theologians or the lawyers, concerning the precise conditions under which such a loan would be non-usurious. Whereas for price the problem concerned the moral assessment of a possible departure from the norm of the just price, this very norm was only imperfectly known in the case of a money loan. The intellectual conditions for a renewal of economic ideas about interest therefore came from a transformation of the norm and of its role, making its identification easier, and progressively superfluous.

The first actual deviation from the Thomistic representation was a consequence of the growing awareness of the unexpected effects of a strict attitude toward interest loans – an attitude which prohibited most of them on the basis of the slightest suspicion of a usurious intention. John of Gerson, Chancellor of the University of Paris, noticed in the 1420s that such an attitude might result in increased poverty and crime. From a moral point of view, this amounted to the provocative claim that, in some cases, a good might result in an evil. Gerson's provocative solution was that a good might arise from a moderate evil. In other words, that light usuries help the indigent and prevent him from sliding into crime. Obviously, this did not completely dismiss the Thomistic representation of the money loan: it only led to considering that the lender's appropriation of the exchange surplus above the non-usurious part might constitute a referential norm, evidently more distant from an evangelical ideal, but more in accordance with usual economic practices.

Much later, at the beginning of the seventeenth century, the Jesuit Leonardus Lessius proposed the introduction of a new extrinsic title, named *carentia pecuniae*, according to which the harm suffered by the lender would depend not on what he was prevented from doing with his money but, more generally, on the fact that this money was missing (see Van Houdt 1998). The *carentia pecuniae* had a far-from-favourable reception: suspicion of potential lenders was too high to exempt them from giving detailed information about the harm associated with a loan. However, this was also a way to increase the gap with the classical argument on usury: it could be admitted that a money loan did not bring any income to the lender by reason of the loan itself, but only because of the harm that it generated. Now, what remains of the classical argument when the nature of the harm was only that the money lent was missing? One step more and the same analyses could be extended to the case where money is desirable in itself and where the rate of interest is its price. Through their diversity, the mercantilist and classical analyses showed that the giving up of the moral imperatives inherited from the Middle Ages allowed a recomposition of the medieval ingredients of the theory of interest. John of Gerson and

Leonardus Lessius had paved the way. The resulting theoretical elaborations were, of course, different, but the constitutive elements needed no substantial change.

IRINA CHAPLYGINA AND ANDRÉ LAPIDUS

See also:

Economics and philosophy (III); Money and banking (III); Value and price (III).

References and further reading

Arena, R. (1987), 'Réflexions sur la Théorie Monétaire de Nicole Oresme', in *Actes du Colloque Oresme*, Paris: Belles Lettres and Beltrame: Uno piu Uno.

Aristotle (1934), *Ethics*, London: J.M. Dent and New York: E.P. Dutton.

Aristotle (1981), *Politics*, Harmondsworth: Penguin.

Baldwin, J.W. (1959), 'The medieval theories of the just price' (monograph), *Transactions of the American Philosophical Society*, **49** (4).

Barath, D. (1960), 'The just price and costs of production according to Thomas Aquinas', *New Scholasticism*, **34** (4), 413–30.

Bridrey, E. (1906), *La Théorie de la Monnaie au XIVe siècle – Nicole Oresme*, Paris: Giard et Brière, reprinted 1978, Geneva: Slatkine.

Buridan, J. (1637), *Quaestiones in Decem Libros Ethicorum Aristotelis ad Nichomachum*, Oxford: H. Cripps.

Buridan, J. (1640), *Quaestiones in Octo Libros Politicorum Aristotelis*, Oxford: G. Turner.

De Roover, R. (1958), 'The concept of the just price: theory and economic policy', *Journal of Economic History*, **18** (4), 418–34.

De Roover, R. (1971), *La Pensée Economique des Scolastiques*, Montreal and Paris: Vrin.

Decretum, in *Corpus Juris Canonici* (1879–81), 2 vols, vol. 1, Leipzig: B. Tauchnitz.

Digesta, in *Corpus Juris Civilis*, vol. 1, reprinted 1968, Dublin and Zurich, Weidmann.

Ege, R. (2014), 'La question de l'interdiction de l'intérêt dans l'histoire européenne: un essai d'analyse institutionnelle', *Revue Economique*, **65** (2), 391–417.

Fau, J. (ed.) (1990), *Nicolas Oresme [1355], Traité Monétaire – Treatise on Money*, Paris: Cujas.

Friedman, D.D. (1980), 'In defense of Thomas Aquinas and the just price', *History of Political Economy*, **12** (2), 234–42.

Giles of Lessines (1871–80), *De Usuris*, in T. Aquinas, *Opera Omnia*, eds P. Mare and S.E. Frette, vol. 28, Paris: Vivès.

Gillard, L. (1990), 'Nicole Oresme, Economiste', *Revue Historique*, **279** (1), 3–39.

Gilson, E. (1944), *History of Christian Philosophy in the Middle Ages*, reprinted 1955, London: Sheed & Ward.

Gordon, B. (1961), 'Aristotle, Schumpeter, and the metalist tradition', *Quarterly Journal of Economics*, **75** (4), 608–14.

Grice-Hutchinson, M. (1952), *The School of Salamanca – Readings in Spanish Monetary Economy, 1544–1605*, Oxford: Clarendon Press.

Grice-Hutchinson, M. (1978), *Early Economic Thought in Spain: 1177–1740*, London: George Allen & Unwin.

Henry of Langenstein (Henry of Hesse) (s.d.), *Tractatus de Contractibus et Origine Censuum*, in John of Gerson (1484), *Opera Omnia*, vol. 4, Cologne: Johannes Koelhoff, pp. 185–224.

Hollander, S. (1965), 'On the interpretation of the just price', *Kyklos*, **18** (4), 615–34.

John of Gerson (1483–84), *Opera Omnia*, 4 vols, Cologne: Johann Koelhoff.

Johnson, C. (1956), *The 'De Moneta' of Nicholas Oresme*, London: Nelson.

Keynes, J.M. (1936), *General Theory of Unemployment, Interest and Money*, in E. Johnson and D. Moggridge (eds) (1973), *The Collected Writings of John Maynard Keynes*, vol. 7, London: Royal Economic Society.

Langholm, O. (1983), *Wealth and Money in the Aristotelian Tradition*, Bergen, Oslo, Stavanger and Tromsø: Universitetsforlaget.

Langholm, O. (1984), *The Aristotelian Analysis of Usury*, Bergen and Oslo: Universitetsforlaget.

Langholm, O. (1987), 'Scholastics Economics', in S.T. Lowry (ed.), *PreClassical Economic Thought*, Boston, Dordrecht and Lancaster: Kluwer Academic, pp. 115–35.

Langholm, O. (1992), *Economics in the Medieval Schools*, Leiden, New York and Cologne: E.J. Brill.

Lapidus, A. (1986), *Le Détour de Valeur*, Paris: Economica.

Lapidus, A. (1987), 'La Propriété de la Monnaie: Doctrine de l'Usure et Théorie de l'Intérêt', *Revue Economique*, **38** (6), 1095–110.

Lapidus, A. (1991), 'Information and risk in the medieval doctrine of usury during the thirteenth century', in W. Barber (ed.), *Perspectives in the History of Economic Thought*, vol. 5, Aldershot, UK and Brookfield, VT, USA: Edward Elgar, pp. 23–38.

Lapidus, A. (1992), 'Introduction à la Pensée Economique Médiévale,' in A. Béraud and G. Faccarello (eds), *Nouvelle Histoire de la Pensée Economique*, vol. 1, *Des scolastiques aux classiques*, Paris: La Découverte, pp. 24–70.

Lapidus, A. (1994), 'Norm, virtue and information: the just price and individual behaviour in Thomas Aquinas' *Summa Theologiae*', *European Journal of the History of Economic Thought*, **1** (3), 435–73.

Lapidus, A. (1997), 'Metal, money, and the prince: John Buridan and Nicholas Oresme after Thomas Aquinas', *History of Political Economy*, **29** (1), 21–53.

Le Bras, G. (1950), 'La Doctrine Ecclésiastique de l'Usure à l'Epoque Classique (XIIème–XIVème siècles)', in A. Vacant, E. Mangenot and E. Amann (ed.), *Dictionnaire de Théologie Catholique*, vol. 15 (2), Paris: Letouzey et Ané, col. 2336–72.

Le Goff, J. (1986), *Your Money or Your Life: Economy and Religion in the Middle Ages*, New York: Zone Books.

Lombard, A. (Alexander of Alexandria) (1962), *Tractatus de Usuris*, in A.-M. Hamelin (ed.), *Un Traité de Morale Economique au XIVe Siècle*, Leuven: Nauwelaerts, Montreal: Librairie Franciscaine and Lille: Giard.

McLaughlin, T.P. (1939), 'The teaching of the canonists on usury (XIIth, XIIIth and XIVth centuries)', pt 1, *Mediaeval Studies*, **1**, 81–147.

Noonan, J.T. Jr (1957), *The Scholastic Analysis of Usury*, Cambridge, MA: Harvard University Press.

Oresme, N., *Traduction et Glose de l'Ethique à Nicomaque d'Aristote*, in A.D. Menut (1940), *Maître Nicole Oresme: Le Livre de Ethique d'Aristote*, New York: Stechert.

Oresme, N., *Traduction et Glose de la Politique d'Aristote*, in A.D. Menut (1970), *Maître Nicole Oresme: Le Livre des Politiques d'Aristote*, *Transactions of the American Philosophical Society*, **60** (6), 1–392.

Oresme, N., *Treatise on Money*, in J. Fau (1990), *Nicolas Oresme [1355], Traité Monétaire – Treatise on Money*, Paris: Cujas, Latin–French–English edn based on a Latin version constituted from five Latin manuscripts, published in C. Johnson (1956), the original French version being published as *Traictie de la Première Invention des Monnoies*, by L. Wolowski (ed.) (1864).

Raymond of Peñaforte (1744), *Summa de Casibus Conscientiae*, Verona.

Robert of Courçon (1902), *De Usura*, in G. Lefevre (ed), *Le Traité 'De Usura' de Robert de Courçon*, Travaux et Mémoires de l'Université de Lille, vol. 10, m. 30, Lille: University of Lille.

Roscher, W. (1862), 'Un Grand Economiste Français du XIVème Siècle', *Compte-Rendus de l'Académie des Sciences Morales et Politiques*, reprinted in L. Wolowski (ed.) (1864), *Traictie de la Première Invention des Monnoies de Nicole Oresme et Traité de la Monnoie de Copernic*, Paris: Guillaumin, reprinted 1969, Rome: Bizzarri.

Schumpeter, J.A. (1954), *History of Economic Analysis*, London: Allen & Unwin.

Scotus, J.D. (1891–95), *In Quattuor Libros Sententiarum*, op. oxoniensis, in *Opera Omnia*, vol. 18, reprint of L. Wadding (ed.) 1639 edn, Paris: Vivès.

Smith, A. (1762–63), *Lectures on Jurisprudence* (LJA), reprinted 1978, Oxford: Clarendon Press.

Smith, A. (1766), *Lectures on Jurisprudence* (LJB), reprinted 1978, Oxford: Clarendon Press.

Sommerville, H. (1931), 'Interest and usury in a new light', *Economic Journal*, **41** (December), 646–9.

Thomas Aquinas (1871–80), *Opera Omnia*, eds P. Mare and S.E. Frette, Paris: Vivès.

Thomas Aquinas, *De Malo*, in *Opera Omnia*, eds P. Mare and S.E. Frette (1871–80), Paris: Vivès, vol. 13.

Thomas Aquinas, *In IV Libros Sententiarum*, in *Opera Omnia*, eds P. Mare and S.E. Frette, vol. 10, Paris: Vivè.

Thomas Aquinas, *In VIII Libros Politicorum*, in *Opera Omnia*, eds P. Mare and S.E. Frette, vol. 26, Paris: Vivè.

Thomas Aquinas, *In X Libros Ethicorum ad Nichomachum*, in *Opera Omnia*, eds P. Mare and S.E. Frette, vol. 25, Paris: Vivè.

Thomas Aquinas, *Summa Theologica*, in *Opera Omnia*, eds P. Mare and S.E. Frette, vol. 3, Paris: Vivè.

Tortajada, R. (1992), 'La Renaissance de la Scolastique, la Réforme et les Théories du Droit Naturel', in A. Béraud and G. Faccarello (eds), *Nouvelle Histoire de la Pensée Economique*, vol. 1, Paris: La Découverte, pp. 71–91.

Van Houdt, T. (1998), '"Lack of money": a reappraisal of *Lessius*' contribution to the scholastic analysis of money-lending and interest-taking', *European Journal of the History of Economic Thought*, **5** (1), 1–35.

William of Auxerre (1986), *Summa Aurea*, Paris: CNRS.

Wilson, G.W. (1975), 'The economics of the just price', *History of Political Economy*, **7** (1), 56–74.

Wolowski, L. (ed.) (1864), *Traictie de la Première Invention des Monnoies de Nicole Oresme et Traité de la Monnoie de Copernic*, Paris: Guillaumin, reprinted 1969, Rome: Bizzarri.

Worland, S.G. (1977), '*Justum pretium*: one more round in an endless series', *History of Political Economy*, **9** (4), 504–21.

Cameralism

During the seventeenth and eighteenth centuries a new discourse of wealth and welfare developed in the German territorial states: the power and wealth of a ruler and his Court was directly related to that of his people. This new discourse originated as a language of counsel, presented in pamphlets and books to the Court and its officials – those whose workplace was the *Kammer*. In the early eighteenth century it was transformed into a university science, introduced chiefly in northern, Protestant universities as a means to improve the training of administrators. Only in isolated cases did this new science – *Kameralwissenschaft* – displace law as the basis for administrative training, and in any case the subject was taught in faculties of philosophy as part of the general education that these offered – contrasting with the vocational education offered by the other three superior faculties of law, medicine and theology. Nonetheless, the idea that a flourishing state was based on principles of good order, and that these principles should be taught to young men in a systematic way, persisted through the eighteenth century, until the vogue for critical philosophy and the rise of a new natural law undercut the ideas of state and society upon which the discourse of cameralism had been based. Early in the nineteenth century the literature transmuted into a new doctrine of economic order which, while still conceiving the wealth of a nation as founded upon the activity of a labouring population, now took its point of departure from the needs of the individual. This was referred to variously as a *Volkswirtschaftslehre*, a *Nationalökonomie*, or indeed a *Politische Ökonomie*. The new discourse was gradually adopted by incumbent professors, and as elsewhere in continental Europe it found its place as a compulsory part of the training in law, and so was almost everywhere taught in faculties of law.

Court and Counsel

There are therefore three main phases to the story of cameralism, to which must also be added a very substantial practical literature upon mines, forestry, agriculture, money, finance and commerce from which it drew. It is generally accepted that its origins lie in the mid-seventeenth century, following the devastation to land and people brought about by the Thirty Years' War (1618–48). This was mirrored in the reduced circumstances of the rulers of German territorial states. Their fiscal base eroded, and their own domainal lands laid waste, if nothing else the experience of war had taught them that the road to power and plenty certainly did not lead directly through conquest or annexation. As the political history of eighteenth century Europe was to demonstrate, the idea that the strength of a ruler was augmented by judicious marriages, shifting alliances and recurrent warfare still prevailed. It nevertheless became widely accepted during the second half of the seventeenth century that the foundation for this necessarily lay in sound finances and a flourishing population. Quite how this foundation might be created became the theme of a new kind of writing, presented to dukes and princes by "practical men" who sold themselves on their knowledge, not of politics and diplomacy, but of the means to wealth.

The addressee of these "practical men" was the ruler of the territorial state who, if his lands were to flourish, had much to do. The state was for them conceived in neo-Aristotelian terms as a giant household; at its head, the ruler overseeing the wise

43

disposition of resources and the proper conduct of affairs. The subjects of this ruler were, they argued, his means to wealth, and hence power: the greater the number of subjects and the wealthier they became, the more powerful the ruler. This is a post-Machiavellian conception of power: the ruler becomes powerful not through the exercise of guile, but by promoting the welfare of his subjects. The ruler becomes wealthier with the increase in number and well-being of his subjects, for these provide him both with an army and with revenues. Even though there developed a problem with the latter, as the *Stände* (the various orders and ranks) contested the ruler's right to extend the taxation of his subjects, the ruler still possessed substantial territories in his own right, which with improved management were likewise an important source of revenue to the Court.

The *Fürstenspiegel*, a "mirror for princes" representing an ideal, virtuous and righteous ruler, was already well established in courtly discourse by the seventeenth century. The precepts for such an ideal were contained in *Politica*, a genre of writing comprehending proper action for a ruler, as well as for the citizens and subject (Sellin 1978: 815). Brought together as a system of virtues or a *Tugendlehre*, to act in accordance with these doctrines was to show *Klugheit,* prudence, in Latin *prudentia civilis* or *prudentia politica* – in this context then *Regierkunst*, the art of ruling. At this time *Politicus* as a substantive was linked both to writers of *Klugheitslehre* and to the active statesman, whether ruler or counsellor. The Germanisation of this term did not take it directly to the modern conception of *Politik*, but instead to the early modern conception of *Polizei*, a conception of social order as derivative of good and vigilant government (Knemeyer 1980). The rules of right conduct in this social order were anchored in a natural law tradition capable of countering the Machiavellian idea of *reason of state.* In this way natural law could become the basis for good government, its principles ensuring the harmony between the actions of the ruler and the will of God.

During the course of the seventeenth century a shift took place in the relationship between the state and the work of government. Hitherto traditional teaching had dealt with the state as a given and then inquired how this state should be governed. In the latter half of the century there was a reversal, so that the state became a construction built according to the rules of good government; the ruler became a technical planner pursuing the increase of his powers. No longer was the common good the point of departure, but rather the welfare of the ruler. This did not however mean that the ideal of the common good was abandoned; instead it shifted position, so that the welfare of the ruler became indissolubly linked to the welfare of his subjects. This worked both ways: without a *glückliche* population, a "happy" population, the ruler could not become powerful, while without power the ruler was not in a position to secure the welfare of his subjects. So economic advice became of importance in the Courts of later seventeenth-century Central Europe.

A leading example of this genre is Hörnigk's *Österreich über alles, wann es nur will* (1684). The novelty of this and similar contemporary texts lies in the manner in which a specific form of economic management is recommended as the path to wealth and hence power. Hörnigk emphasised the importance of money as a means of circulation that promoted activity, and so the augmentation of the money supply results in an expansion of activity in general. Other measures which Hörnigk suggests increase the level of economic activity by stimulating marginal areas of production, and hence consumption. However, in the absence, or shortage, of money, this linkage of money, production and circulation will not enhance the wealth of the territory. His recommendations remain strictly limited to those areas over which a ruler could exercise command. The manufacturing activity which he identifies is closely linked to existing domestic agricultural production; there is no suggestion that we might here have an expansion programme for manufacturing instead of agriculture. Trading is said to be beneficial only so long as it serves the existing domestic economy. Central to his thinking is the general stimulation of the existing range of economic activity in Austria through the securing of an adequate money supply; and so attracting money (bullion) is a means to the stimulation of this activity, and not in itself the means to wealth and power.

This linkage of wealth to power was perhaps expressed most pithily in Schröder's affirmation that there were just two key principles that a ruler had to observe: the maintenance of a standing army and the knowledge that there was "viel geld im kasten", that the treasury was well-stocked with money (Schröder 1686 [1752]: Vorrede s. 9) How the ruler might come by the required hoard of money was what Schröder set out to describe, just as von Hörnigk seeks to persuade the Austrian emperor that the country can be made wealthy and strong, and a model to all other territories. The addressee in this mode of argument was the ruler and his Court; and coupled with the explicit concern for the ruler's well-being was an implicit concern with personal advancement. Those who live by proffering advice require clients who will become their patrons; and all these writings betray an interest in gaining entry to Court, or securing preferment at Court, or, as is evident in the second edition of Becher's treatise, constructing a defence against the machinations of detractors (Becher 1688: "Vorrede an den Leser").

Cameralist discourse through the seventeenth and eighteenth centuries places very little emphasis on trade and exchange; it argues instead for the proper use of resources in the production and consumption of goods. However, one of the more disconcerting features of cameralistic writings is the resolute manner in which the human subject is constructed as a work of administrative activity. The wealth of the ruler depends upon the happiness and welfare of his subjects, so the argument goes; but these subjects cannot find their own way to such happiness, they require deliberate, external guidance. It is this which distinguishes German writing from the contemporary political discourse of France, England and Scotland, where the contraposition of state and civil society involved a conception, however constructed, of a distinct human nature whose qualities were relevant to the conduct of state affairs. In the German language, however, the distinction of a *bürgerliche Gesellschaft* from that of the *Staat* was purely nominal; both terms were in use, but were used interchangeably to denote political order. The *Bürger* lived therefore indifferently in civil society and the state – and hence is no *citizen* in the sense developed from the French *citoyen*. This political order underlying cameralism was nonetheless conceived as natural, but its character required that it be in a permanent condition of construction – practically in the *Polizeiordnungen* of principality and town, discursively in the burgeoning literature of the *Polizei- und Staatswissenschaften*, the sciences of police and state.

The fiscal structure of the territorial state was also important to this mode of thinking, for the ability of a ruler to increase his revenue through increases of taxation was severely limited by the power of the estates, the *Stände*. The early literature of economic advice to a ruler consequently directed his attention elsewhere, to those areas more directly under his control: to agricultural management, manufacture and mining, since improvement of the ruler's own domain land or the creation of new forms of economic activity would augment his income without the need to negotiate new taxes with the *Stände*. In time, however, the expanding financial needs of the territorial states propelled a transformation of its fiscal base from the ruler's own domainal resources to the entire territory and its population. The transition from cameralism as a literature of counsel to a pedagogic regime implied therefore the eclipse of the political power of the *Stände* and the assumption of a general right of taxation on the part of the territorial ruler.

The foundations for this conception of natural order and good government can be found in Wolffian philosophy, where we find "general welfare" identified as the highest good attainable on earth, with happiness as it corollary, thus linking welfare and happiness together as the chief objectives of wise administration. It was the action of government that promoted or hindered the achievement of a state of happiness; and in the absence of such activity no good could be achieved.

> By contrast one can easily see that this salutary objective cannot be attained if everybody, the populace (*Pöbel*) as a whole, need to agree with what has been decided. For the understanding of the common man is inadequate to judge what is useful or harmful, being insufficiently farsighted; and neither is he steady enough in virtue or the love of others to find his own intended advantage for any eventuality in that of the common good. . . (Wolff 1736 [1975]: 190, s. 253)

There are, consequently, a number of factors which have to be taken into account if the ruler and his people are to flourish: the state should be populous with means sufficient for the maintenance of its inhabitants; there should be adequate schools and academies; the prices of goods bought and sold should be regulated; wages should likewise be controlled; the cheapest possible food, drink and clothing should be available, commensurate with the social standing of the person concerned; poorhouses should be made available to the unemployed, and begging outlawed; not to mention the need to punish drunkenness, the need for clean air, the harmfulness of duelling, the plague and of infectious diseases in general. Quite evidently this list is long, and perpetually open to extension, so that the conclusion could well be drawn that this endless task of regulation represents simply a relentless pragmatism concerning all the things which might go wrong in a well-ordered polity. However, underlying this diffuse endlessness there lies a fundamental conception of human nature: that human capacities, if they were to achieve the maximum of perfectibility attainable on earth, had to be deliberately guided there by a prudent and wise ruler.

The Transition from Court to University

It was in 1727 that this discourse first entered the university: Friedrich Wilhelm I of Prussia decreed that two chairs be established, in "Oeconomie, Policey und Cammersachen" at the University of Halle, and in "Kameral-Ökonomie und Polizeiwissenschaft" at the University of Frankfurt on the Oder. At the same time he proposed that all future recruits to state administration be required to study these subjects, although this was not, it seems, ever enforced. The tripartite distinction made in the titles was primarily a formal one. Nominally these can be construed as denoting agriculture (oeconomy), police (in the sense of ordered administration still used by Adam Smith in his lectures at Glasgow in the 1750s), and "court finance". In practice, or at any rate in the books which the occupants of these chairs eventually published, these distinct realms tend to converge. At Halle the appointee was Simon Peter Gasser, previously rewarded for domainal administration in Cleves with an appointment to a chair in Law at Halle in 1721. The text which Gasser nominated for his lectures was Seckendorff's *Fürsten-Stat* (1656), a leading example of the seventeenth century genre of economic counsel, written by the first Chancellor of the newly founded University of Halle. In 1729 Gasser published his own textbook, which is little more than a compendium of domainal tasks such as the valuation of fields, breweries and mills, the making of inventories for cattle and land, the determination of hunting and fishing rights, and so forth – nothing like Seckendorff's account of prudent government and the need for a ruler to care for his subjects and heed the advice of his officials.

Comparison with the textbook written by the Frankfurt appointee, Justus Christoph Dithmar, suggests that he had a better grasp of the relationship between administration and the economy, and his work was subsequently twice republished. When Dithmar died in 1737, however, his post remained vacant – as in so many cases, Dithmar is worth noting because of the book that he wrote (Dithmar 1731), and not for the effectiveness of his teaching.

Institutional initiatives to mid-century were indeed sporadic and short lived; one account suggests that out of 32 German, Scandinavian, Dutch, Swiss and Austrian universities only three had cameralistic chairs – Åbo (that is, Turku), Göttingen and Rinteln. This is certainly inaccurate, for a chair had been founded at Uppsala in 1741 by Anders Berch, and a number of academies existed where the subject was taught; but it serves to bring up an important feature: that cameralism was a new subject that emerged in the curriculum of northern, Protestant universities. Little is known about Rinteln (a small university near Hanover that was entirely destroyed by the invading French forces in 1809) besides the fact that Johann Hermann Fürstenau was appointed professor of agriculture there in 1730, and he subsequently published the third cameralistic textbook, *Gründliche Anleitung Zu der Haushaltungs-Kunst*, in 1736. By contrast, Göttingen's importance as a new university directed at the training of public officials of all kinds is well-known, but an independent chair of cameralistic science was never founded there. Instead, various parts of the broadly defined *Staatswissenschaften* were taught by Gottfried Achenwall, Johann Beckmann and August Ludwig Schlözer. However, in 1755 Johann Heinrich Gottlob von Justi was appointed Councillor for Mines and Police Director, with the right to lecture in the university.

Justi made his name by writing, not teaching. He was vehemently opposed to the role of "projectors" in the formulation of policy for the territorial state, but was himself one of the last representatives of this genre, a prolific writer who lived from his writing, both in the sense of selling his books to readers and selling himself to clients – to Haugwitz and the reformers in mid-century Vienna, to agricultural reformers in Copenhagen and, finally, to the Prussian administration. His periods as a teacher in Vienna and in Göttingen were both relatively brief. His eventual appointment in 1765 as Prussian Inspector of Mines, Glass and Steelworks ended a seven-year campaign of pro-Prussian writing, but it was an appointment that was to come undone in accusations of fraud and mismanagement, ending in imprisonment, followed by his death in 1771 (Wakefield 2009: ch. 4).

In the same year as his appointment in Göttingen, Justi published his *Staatswirthschaft*, subtitled "On the maintenance and increase of the entire property of the state, for which the principles of *Staatskunst*, *Polizei* and commercial science, as well as oeconomy, are necessary". At this time, *Staat* and *bürgerliche Gesellschaft* were used synonymously – and so while we today would translate the title of Justi's book as "state economy", "state" includes what we would today understand as "society". Justi's book accordingly deals not only with the work of political and economic management, but also includes provisions for the good order of social life, excluding only the conduct of private households. The object of management, according to Justi, is state property – defined as including not simply all moveable and immoveable goods within the frontiers of the land, but also the capacities and skills of its inhabitants – and the purpose of management is the augmentation of state property to the greatest extent possible.

Justi's book was neither concise nor brief – it ran to 1245 pages in the first edition, and his later works varied the same themes at greater length, relying to a great extent on self-plagiarism and thereby betraying his reliance on an income directly from his writing rather than his teaching. *Staatswirthschaft* and its successors provided a foundation for a rapid expansion in cameralistic literature in the latter half of the eighteenth century, the most prominent exponent of which was Josef von Sonnenfels, appointed in 1763 to the newly founded chair of police and cameralistic sciences at the University of Vienna. His own three-volume textbook, *Sätze aus der Polizey, Handlung und Finanz*, began publication in 1765 and was quickly reprinted, appearing in at least eight editions, together with a Latin version published in 1808 for use in non-German speaking areas of the empire, together with several concise versions compiled by teachers in other Austrian universities, one of which in turn reached a third edition in 1820. An image of the centrality of "nutrition" in the body economic plays a dominant role in Sonnenfels's *Principles*, and he identified economic development with the "multiplication of the means of subsistence", an extension of the means to wealth and welfare which is echoed some 50 years later by Hegel's treatment of needs in the *Philosophy of Right* (1821).

The reproduction of cameralistic discourse upon the foundations outlined above was halted by the rise of a critical philosophy founded upon a new anthropology, in which the interaction of free human beings exercising their reason created order, not the statesman. In all the cameralistic textbooks published during the 1760s to the early 1790s we encounter the same assumptions and assertions concerning the nature of the state as the embodiment of social and political order. Also, in the initial phases of the cameralistic reception of critical philosophy we find a tendency to take up the new slogans and categorisations, without these however displacing the established conceptual framework and order of exposition, for the older tradition did retain some scope for flexible response. Johann Christian Christoph Rüdiger, Professor at Halle and Assessor in the Prussian Salt Office, began for example his *Introductory Foundations for a General Doctrine of the State* by noting that "every cultivated person lives as a citizen in the state, and he must find agreeable the ability to judge, correctly and according to principles, basic arrangements and relations, government and its institutions" (Rüdiger 1795: 1, s. 1).

This suggests that, contrary to the view of Wolff, the subject was a citizen capable of exercising good judgement. However, since Rüdiger then proceeded to define *Politik* as true knowledge of all the means by which the institutions of the greater civil society could be purposively arranged to meet the common good of the individual members, a way back to the older conception of economic order remained open. Elsewhere a distinction between "pure" and "applied" parts of the cameralistic sciences became especially popular in titles and in general declarations of intent. Thus we can read in an outline of lectures at Giessen in 1795 that "Oeconomy is simply an empirical science, but its ultimate foundations, deriving from logic and moral philosophy, belong to pure reason. . . . Oeconomy is the science of the purposeful determination of external means of subsistence to our needs" (Walther 1795: 5, "Vorbericht", and 7, s. 1).

The "dictate of reason" commands that every proper means be employed to enhance external perfection in order to sustain inner perfection – for "*Ein unwirthschaftlicher Mann ist immer ein sehr unglücklicher Mensch*" ("a man lacking in economy is always a very unhappy man") (Walther 1795: 16, s. 18). Reversing this, it might be said that a happy person was "economic man", for as Bensen noted a little later, "Thanks to his reason the person is an absolutely self-acting (*selbstthätiges*) being." (Bensen 1798: 25, s. 27). These and other texts continued to refer to the older literature, but inflected it through the new anthropological principles.

The Transition to Needs and their Satisfaction

The vogue for critical philosophy had at first a largely superficial impact on cameralistic discourse; the terminology was adopted, but the older literature to which reference was made sustained an older understanding of state and subject, in which the reasoning action of a subject was not directly considered. By 1797 it had penetrated deeper; those teachers whose task it was to represent the subject matter of cameralism to students begin to revamp systematically their lectures and textbooks. The typical result of this is at first a degenerated form of philosophical discourse which bears only marginally on the practical business of administration which had always been the subject matter for cameralist writers. However, there are two important features of this: first, the source upon which these writers draw is not Kantian epistemology as such, but the implications of this for natural law and a theory of personality; and secondly, the new terminology begins, despite its posturing, to effect a reorganisation of the conventions of cameralistic teaching.

Translated into the new natural law, this principle can be generalised into what Schmalz calls "the first original right of man, *his right to autonomy*" (Schmalz 1792: 29, s. 39, original emphasis). Accordingly, the conceptions of welfare and happiness that prevailed in the conventional cameralistic literature are decisively rebutted. It is no longer the activity of government which creates and maintains order, the welfare of the subject being constantly overseen and organised by the state. The seat of reason has shifted to a knowledgeable citizen capable of making judgements and acting upon them; and instead of a *Staatswirthschaft*, a new *Wirtschaftslehre* begins to emerge. This constructs a conception of economic processes around the needs of the person. Instead of the endless work of economic administration that typifies the conventions of cameralistic discourse, the economy itself becomes a self-constituting process and the form of order of civil society.

Economic activity is initiated in the process of appropriation of nature by human beings – this transforms the natural world into one of goods: "Goods in the most *general* sense are those things *over which the person is capable of exercising property. . . . Actual* goods are constituted in the hands of man only through the *application of his physical and moral powers*, or, what is the same thing, through *labour*" (Schlözer 1805: 14–15, ss.15, 17, original emphasis).

In succession, then, the surplus of goods obtained through production enables a process of exchange to develop, and thereby the accumulation of capital in the world of goods (as distinct from personal capital). This capital, argues Schlözer, is consumed in use, and it is therefore necessary to renew and replace capital out of the revenue to which it gives rises. The rate at which this is done depends on the productivity of labour, itself dependent on the varying composition of capital and labour in the process of production. Likewise, out of the process of exchange there arises (on the basis of use value) exchange value, which although subjectively assessed, is ultimately based upon the amount of labour embodied in it. The doctrines of wealth elaborated around the ruler and his people has been definitively replaced by one oriented to an economic subject who creates his own wealth through his activity.

KEITH TRIBE

References and further reading

The classic work in English remains Small (1909). Interest in this area was first revived by Pierangelo Schiera's analysis of Prussian economic administration and the literature of cameralism (1968). My own book (1988) is primarily focused upon the development of university teaching from the early eighteenth century, while my 2006 essay provides a more concise survey. Guillaume Garner (2005) is the only detailed account in French of cameralism, developing an argument about the spatial reorganisation of early modern economies. Ulrich Adam (2006) has written a monograph on Justi which draws attention to the more general political implications of his diverse activities, while Andre Wakefield (2009) directs attention to the more practical aspects of "wealth creation" in eighteenth century Germany.

Adam, U. (2006), *The Political Economy of J.H.G. Justi*, Bern: Peter Lang.
Becher, J.J. (1688), *Politische Discurs, von den eigentlichen Ursachen/ deß Auff- und Abnehmes der Stadt/Länder und Republicken*, 3rd edn, Frankfurt.
Bensen, H. (1798), *Versuch eines systematischen Grundrisses der reinen und angewandten Staatslehre für Kameralisten*, vol. 1, Erlangen.
Dithmar, J.C. (1731), *Einleitung in die Oeconomische-, Policey- und Cameralwissenschaften*, Frankfurt an der Oder.
Garner, G. (2005), *État, économie, territoire en Allemagne. L'espace dans le caméralisme et l'économie politique 1740–1820*, Paris: Éditions de l'École des Hautes Études en Sciences Sociales.
Gasser, S.P. (1729), *Einleitung zu den Oeconomischen Politischen und Cameral-Wissenschaften*, Halle.
Hörnigk, P. von (1684), *Österreich über alles, wann es nur will*, n.p.
Knemeyer, F.-L. (1980), 'Polizei', *Economy and Society*, 9 (2), 172–96.
Rüdiger, J.C.C. (1795), *Anfangsgründe der allgemeinen Statslehre*, Halle.
Schiera, Pi. (1968), *Dall'arte di governo alle Scienzo dello Stato. Il Cameralismo e l'assolutismo Tedesco*, Milan: Antonino Giuffrè.
Schlözer, C. von (1805), *Anfangsgründe der Staatswirthschaft oder die Lehre von dem Nationalreichthume*, vol. 1, Riga.
Schmalz, T. (1792), *Das reine Naturrecht*, Königsberg.
Schröder, W. von (1686), *Fürstliche Schatz- und Rentkammer*, reprinted 1752, Leipzig: J.H. Hartung.
Sellin, V. (1978), 'Politik', in O. Brunner, W. Conze and R. Koselleck (eds), *Geschichtliche Grundbegriffe*, vol. 4, Stuttgart: Klett Cotta Verlag, pp. 789–874.
Small, A. (1909), *The Cameralists*, Chicago, IL: University of Chicago Press.
Sonnenfels, J. von (1765–76), *Sätze aus der Polizey, Handlung und Finanz*, 3 vols, Vienna.
Tribe, K. (1988), *Governing Economy. The Reformation of German Economic Discourse 1750–1840*, Cambridge: Cambridge University Press.

Tribe, K. (2006), 'Cameralism and the sciences of the state', in M. Goldie and R. Wokler (eds), *The Cambridge History of Eighteenth-Century Political Thought*, Cambridge: Cambridge University Press, pp. 525–46.

Wakefield, A. (2009), *The Disordered Police State. German Cameralism as Science and Practice*, Chicago, IL: University of Chicago Press.

Walther, F.L. (1795), *Versuch eines Grundrisses der allgemeinen Oekonomie für Vorlesungen*, Giessen.

Wolff, C. (1736), *Vernünfftige Gedancken von dem Gesellschaftlichen Leben der Menschen und insonderheit Dem gemeinen Wesen*, 4th edn, reprinted 1975 in *Gesammelte Werke I. Abt. Deutsche Schriften*, vol. 5, Hildesheim: Georg Olms Verlag.

Mercantilism and the science of trade

Introduction

Setting the stage

Gathering under a single name the great diversity of authors who wrote on economic matters from the early seventeenth century until the second third of the eighteenth century seems to be an impossible task. However, this is what has been done in the past. Many economists and economic historians have called these writers "mercantilists", a generic term which gave rise to discussions but was widely adopted (see Wilson 1957; Herlitz 1964; Rashid 1980; Magnusson 1994, 1995, 2008; Pincus 2012; Stern and Wennerlind 2014).

The history of mercantilism appears as a series of "disconnected still pictures" (Herlitz 1964: 101): initially considered as an inconsistent doctrine, mercantilism was later presented as a coherent system and then sometimes as an imaginary or uninfluential construction. The debate on mercantilism has been deeply entangled in the discussion on "liberty" versus "protection". Many scholars questioned the traditional boundary delimited by Smith's work and corrected "Smith's caricature" of this literature (Rashid 1980: 5), adding to the picture "late" or "moderate" or "liberal mercantilists" (see Ingram 1888; Cossa 1892; Schatz and Caillemer 1906; Grampp 1952; Hutchison 1982). The fact remains that to some extent scholars accepted the designation, the description suggested by the writings of Smith, Quesnay or Mirabeau (below), and the subsequent idea of a more or less common body of doctrines beyond the particularities of national economies and commercial empires. For most of them, mercantilism was a truly modern policy, not a remnant of the Middle Ages, and a body of doctrine sufficiently homogeneous and unified to be compared to that of laissez-faire. What unified the doctrine was the great emphasis put on foreign trade as a means of national enrichment and an expression of rivalry between nations, leading to a discussion whether the wealth of a nation tended towards a limit if it came only from internal resources, namely, land and raw materials, and whether this limit could be pushed as far as possible with the deployment of labour.

Few commentators disputed the idea of the unity and coherence of mercantilism. James Bonar (1893: 130) had serious doubts that such a school existed. This was also the conclusion reached by Arthur Judges (1939 [1969]: 35) and a few years later by David Coleman (1969: 117). During the same period, Joseph Schumpeter, while describing mercantilism as an "imaginary organon . . . of traditional teaching" (1954: 335) that constituted neither a school nor a scientific theory, highlighted nevertheless a main current from the 1680s onwards characterised by "analytic progress" (ibid.: 362). The progress was supposed to be threefold. First, these writers turned to an analysis of money as a quasi-ordinary commodity, capable of being exported profitably for the nation and whose importation did not add more to wealth than that of raw material. Second, they gradually accepted the idea that there is a mechanism which, under certain conditions, leads in the long run to "an equilibrium relation between the money stocks, prices, incomes and interest rates of different nations" (ibid.: 365). Third, they laid the basis for a general theory of international trade. This approach presupposed that protectionism should be abandoned and supported the idea that a nation is not necessarily a rival to its neighbours and can benefit from their prosperity.

A "science of trade"?

What Schumpeter alluded to was the possibility of a science of trade or commerce. If we now read the more recent assessment by Lars Magnusson (1994), we find a similar view. Two moments are outlined, characterised by two discussions: the 1620s discussion on the causes of the English trade crisis, whose protagonists were Gerard de Malynes (*fl.* 1586–1641), Edward Misselden (*fl.* 1616–54), Thomas Mun (1571–41) and Thomas Culpepper (1578–1642); and that of the 1690s on the recoinage project, the creation of the Bank of England and the funding of the war with France, which involved Josiah Child (1630–99), John Locke (1632–1704), Nicholas Barbon (*c.*1640–98), Dudley North (1641–91), John Cary (*c.*1649–1717–22), Charles Davenant (1656–1714) and Henry Martyn (*c.*1665–1721) among others. This second debate gave rise to what Magnusson (1994: 116) calls a "science of trade". He defines it as a reflection (1) on the creation and distribution of wealth; (2) endowed with some elements of the "Baconian scientific programme"; (3) based upon a materialist conception of man and society; (4) considering the economy as a system regulated by its own laws; (5) which focuses on the supply and demand in markets and their connection with economic progress or decline. Magnusson (2008, I: xii–xiv) adds that it would be wrong to consider the proponents of that discourse as practical men incapable of formulating analytical principles on a number of economic issues – the coherence of their writings is rooted in the same political thinking which examines the links between economic means and political ends and praises patriotism, the reason of state and the commercial strength of nations.

As opposed to "mercantilism", the term "science of trade" can be found in the writings of the authors of the time. Magnusson (1994: 116) refers to the association of the words "trade", "science", and "principles" in John Cary (1717: 1): "In order to discover whether a Nation gets or loses by its Trade, 'tis necessary first to inquire into the Principles whereon it is built; for Trade hath its Principles as other Sciences have, and as difficult to understand". Well before Cary, Misselden (1623 [1973]: epistle, 130) also used the word "science" when analysing the decline in English foreign trade. While frequently used, these words were rarely placed side by side in a single phrase during the seventeenth century. An exception seems to be the scientific populariser Edward Hatton (*c.*1664–after 1733), who used "science of trade and commerce" in the introduction to his work on quantification and measurement (Hatton 1728: vi). At the end of the preceding century, Child (1693 [1698]: 108) spoke of the "art or science of merchandizing". Slightly later, Isaac Gervaise (1680–1739) referred to a "system or theory of trade" (1720 [1995]: 1).

"Science of commerce" was also used later and became widespread in the second half of the eighteenth century. The phrase is used for example by Josiah Tucker (1753: 153) who focused on the following elements: (1) a definition of commerce or trade as a means of satisfying various needs; (2) a distinction between domestic and foreign trade; (3) a definition of the balance between nations by comparing the flows of precious metals; (4) the assertion "that labour (not money) is the riches of a People" (ibid.: iv); and, finally, (5) the idea that commerce follows principles that are "clear and certain in themselves", on which traders are however divided. The French expression "science du commerce", however, is older. It is already to be found in the mid-sixteenth century in Sully (1745: 444), and refers to a "method by which a state is rendered flourishing". However, as in Britain, the expression was more widely used in the second half of the eighteenth century.

Eli Heckscher (1931 [1955]) and Magnusson (1994, 1995, 2008) provide accounts of who were the alleged "mercantilists" and which questions they tackled. In the following only some main topics addressed by the commercial writers, mostly English or British, can be dealt with. The focus will be on the importance of commerce for the state, on natural and artificial wealth, freedom of trade and monopoly, "trade in general" and the doctrines of the balance of trade. Some other topics cannot be covered due to space constraint.

Domestic and Foreign Trade and the State

The works on trade published from the end of the sixteenth century onwards primarily relate to foreign trade, considered to be the true way of increasing the wealth of a nation. This trade is not exempt from political concerns. Jean Bodin (1520–96) ranked it among the seven ways in which a prince can establish the finances of the republic (Bodin 1576 [1986]: 36–7.) Antoine de Montchrétien (1575–1621) made it directly connected to politics:

> Thus the exercise of traffic, which represents a large part of political action, has always been practised between the peoples, who have thriven with glory and power. And now more diligently than ever by those who seek their strength and enlargement. It is also the shortest way to become rich. And through wealth, to rise to the height of honour and authority. (Montchrétien 1615 [1999]: 288–9)

The same author wrote a little later that if domestic trade is "more secure, more common, more constant, and universally more useful", foreign trade is in return "larger, more famous, more hazardous, both in loss or in profit" (ibid.: 291). The idea that domestic trade looks after the preservation of a country's economy, while foreign trade (or war) looks after its expansion runs through the French literature (for example, Colbert 1663 [2000]: 101; Richelieu 1668 [1995]: 333; and later Melon 1735: 92; Forbonnais 1758 I: 1–2).

This view recurs in the English writers (see Steiner 1992: 111–16). They also frequently used other antinomies which, although not strictly equivalent, clarified and reinforced the distinction: natural/artificial, matter/form, natural exchange/political exchange, native/foreign, internal/external, inland/abroad, inward/outward. When it is internal, trade is generally considered from the viewpoint of its effect on civil peace and the preservation of common wealth. When it is carried out with foreign countries, it comes under international relations and is discussed alongside war and conquest.

There is also a clear link with political thought. Niccolò Machiavelli (1469–1527) discussed the case in which small republics in a world of political instability were facing the alternative of "manternersi" or "fare un imperio" (Machiavelli 1531 [1984]: 74), that is, the preservation of what was acquired – land, riches and the liberty of citizens – or the policy of empire, expansion and acquisition of new territories, increasing wealth, greatness and glory. These policies were based on two distinct arguments: that of reason which rather indicated preservation, and that of necessity which justified expansion (ibid.: 78). These two objectives referred to two characteristics of human nature: the desire for liberty ("affezione del vivere libero") and the desire to acquire, to conquer ("desiderare di acquistare"). Machiavelli's conclusion was the following: assuming instability in international relations, it may be an advantage, or a necessity, for a republic to expand rather than develop internally and be transformed into a tyranny. Hence, the imperialist strategy is not incompatible with the desire for liberty and security.

Machiavelli assumed that international relations were shaped by jealousy and war, however he did not deal with trade. This is what Nicholas Barbon objected to him (1690 [1905]: 5), proposing a more commercial version of the problem of preservation and expansion, partly inspired by Machiavelli but applied to the English case, in which the desire for greatness was transposed from the land – as it became impossible to establish a territorial empire in Europe – to the sea, which remained a free area. Also, he explicitly linked the desire for wealth and greatness to the growth in foreign trade and navigation.

Giovanni Botero (1544–1617) responded to the Machiavellian alternative differently (Botero 1598 [1956]: 6): it is better to preserve the state, once it has been territorially enlarged. This politics of preservation is justified by the primacy of the internal economy: the strength of a nation lies in its population, because where it is numerous, goods abound, the genius of man and industry are deployed, money pours in and the Treasury becomes rich (ibid.: 144–6). Spain became poorer because it neglected its land and manufacturing and preferred arms.

This politics of preservation is also apparent in Thomas Hobbes (1588–1679). In *Leviathan* (1651 [1991]: 230), he pointed out that one of the causes of the dissolution of a Commonwealth was that a sovereign or an assembly was prey to an "insatiable appetite, or *Bulimia*, of enlarging dominion". He criticised international merchants on the grounds that their interests were separate: "the end of their incorporating, is to make their gaine the greater; which is done two wayes; by sole buying, and sole selling, both at home, and abroad" (ibid.: 160). This tendency towards monopoly made them harmful both to national and to foreign consumers, and could lead them to form a state within a state. This was the reason why these merchants should be placed under the authority and the supervision of the state (ibid.: 173–4).

This position of Hobbes in favour of preservation did, of course, not please the supporters of foreign trade. William Petyt (1636–1707) ranked Hobbes among the defenders of the "meer absoluteness of monarchy" (1680 [1856]: 384), a kind of predatory government, hostile to trade, depreciating individuals and instilling fear in them. He contrasted this with the government of "legal liberty and property" (ibid.: 385), the main feature of which was to use liberty as a means to promote foreign trade. Jacob Vanderlint (d.1740) insisted on the distinction between the state of nature and the civil state – a state in which individuals give up their natural right to possess land and their natural equality in return for greater happiness. He argued that the latter was only legitimate if it achieved the dual objective of "peace and plenty". And since peace was a more probable condition in the eighteenth century, a civil state that did not achieve wealth, because of the sluggishness in trade and agriculture, would have been "worse than a State of Nature itself" (Vanderlint 1734 [1914]: 159), as in the state of nature at least the individual still had a right to possess land.

Wealth: Natural and Artificial, Certain and Uncertain

Another distinction of the English authors is that between natural and artificial wealth. "Natural wealth" consists of the products of the land, mines and sea. Some products can be reproduced through the action of nature itself (fish, forests, wild fruits), others are so through man's action (cereals, livestock and vegetables), while still others are more or less exhaustible (mines and quarries). "Artificial wealth" consists of the products of labour, the "arts" and "industry". This kind of wealth is supposed to be superior to natural wealth, not only because of its ability to be reproduced – that is assumed to be almost infinite as opposed to certain elements of natural wealth – but also because it stimulates invention, ingenuity, curiosity, frugality, while natural wealth may cultivate indifference and laziness.

Some remarks on the distinction between natural and artificial wealth are apposite. First, the writers generally thought that it was better to preserve one's natural wealth than to export it. Edgar Johnson (1937) provides the example of the "staple system", namely, the English export policy, in force until the sixteenth century, of native raw products: wool, tin, wheat, leather, and so on. This system was based on the concession of privileges to the Merchants of Staples, in particular that of exporting these products to Hanseatic markets. This was challenged by a rival body, the Merchant Adventurers, on the grounds that this system was unfavourable to England. The latter argued in favour of another policy discouraging the export of native raw products and encouraging that of manufactured products. Paramount in the seventeenth century, this new policy was based on the "principle of conservation" (Johnson 1937: 302) by which foreign manufactured goods were burdened with duties while foreign raw materials were allowed to enter with no or almost no duties.

Second, the assumed superiority of artificial wealth highlights the key role of the foreign trade. The literature on trade underrates domestic trade because of its assumed limited capacity to enrich the nation. Mun writes: "for we may exchange amongst our selves, or with strangers; if amongst our selves, the Commonwealth cannot be enriched thereby; for the gain of one subject is the loss of another. And if we exchange with strangers, then our profit is the gain of the Commonwealth" (Mun 1664 [1986]: 52). The superiority of foreign trade is stressed, for example, by Petyt (1680 [1856]: 289–90), Petty (1690 [1986], 295) and Child (1693 [1698]: preface, 25, 152).

Third, many authors noted the uncertainty in foreign trade and the unpredictable nature of the wealth it brings. John Wheeler (1560–1617) emphasised the irregularity of a foreign trade which would operate without great trading companies (Wheeler 1601 [1931]: 363), and Barbon (1690 [1905]: 11) stressed that the foreign staples, whether or not reworked, are "uncertain wealth" if the country only establishes a single kind of trade with another country. If this trade ceases, the country is in difficulty. This uncertainty correlated to the inevitable rivalry between nations instilled in minds the idea of trade as a sort of zero-sum game. This idea we encounter, for example, in John Hales (1581 [1907]: 96), Francis Bacon (1597 [1740]: 322), Montchrétien (1615 [1999]: 303), William Temple (1673 [1705]: 245) and, in a way, in Mun (1664 [1986]: 52). However, the metaphor can accommodate some variations. For example, Petyt writes (1680 [1856]: 487): "it does not follow that everything which will prejudice the Trade of one Nation, shall better the Trade of another" (see also Child 1693 [1698]: 174–5). The commonly held belief at the end of the seventeenth century is rather that world trade represents a volume of business or an amount of gains relatively fixed, which does not *ipso facto* mean that this trade cannot produce effects which are mutually beneficial (see Irwin 1996: 31).

Free Trade and Monopoly: The Legacy of Scholasticism and Jusnaturalism

Trade, the universal economy, natural law and the law of nations

In dealing with trade, the commercial writers, at least some of them, were liable to be influenced by the theories of natural law and the law of nations. In the seventeenth-century political thinking, the natural law expresses the principles that govern human beings placed in their natural condition, namely, the rights that are universally and perpetually attached to them. These principles or rights, established by natural reason, are considered to be the foundations for relations between individuals within a commonwealth. They mainly relate to self-preservation and independence or liberty. The law of nations expresses the preceding principles or rights that are applicable to the relations among commonwealths. It concerns the knowledge of the interest of the commonwealth itself.

The commercial writers were thus led to think of commerce as an element of a general and all-encompassing trade, which Jacob Viner called the "doctrine of universal economy" (1959 [1991]: 41). Christian belief does not radically condemn trade in general (as in the case of the merchants of the Temple); it rather accepts foreign trade on the grounds that this activity allows resources that are unequally distributed amongst nations to be circulated throughout the world and thus meet the needs of the different peoples. God or Providence has arranged for an unequal distribution of resources precisely in order to enable them to be circulated between men and to encourage peaceful cooperation. Trade can thus be mutually beneficial to mankind as a whole. This doctrine is found *inter alios* in Bodin (1568 [1997]: 86) and Thomas Smith (1581 [1969]: 62).

The idea of a universal economy does not necessarily call for free trade. English writers invoked Providence to explain the specific situation of the nation (Viner 1937: 101–3). Endowed with wool, England's vocation was to manufacture and export it and not to import wool products (see also Henry Martyn 1701 [1856]: 585).

The doctrine of the universal economy finds a particular expression in the writings of Francisco de Vitoria (*c.* 1483–1546), Hugo Grotius (1586–1645) and Samuel von Pufendorf (1632–1694). In *De Indis*, Vitoria proposed an interesting combination of this doctrine and the theories of natural law and the law of nations, whose purpose was to legitimise Spanish foreign trade. Among the seven proposals he developed to this end, three are of special interest: (1) "That the Spaniards have the right to travel and dwell in those countries, so long as they do no harm to the barbarians, and cannot be prevented by them from doing so"; (2) "That the Spaniards may lawfully trade among the barbarians, so long as they do no harm to their homeland"; (3) "That if there are any things among the barbarians which are held in common both by their own people and by strangers, it is not lawful to prohibit the Spaniards from sharing and enjoying them" (Vitoria 1537 [1991]: 278–80). The logical conclusion was that, if the Indians prohibited the Spanish from exercising their indisputable right to trade, Spaniards had the right to defend themselves and wage a just war.

In *Mare liberum* (1609 [2004]: 10), Grotius made international trade an element of the law of nations just as explicitly. Presenting international trade as an effect of the division of labour – God did not want men from every place and every nation to be self-sufficient in their consumption of goods but wanted them to specialise where they excel and to communicate with each other – he inferred that most conflicts between nations arose from the obstacles that one or the other nation put in the way of this communication by practising commercial exclusions. Yet, unlike the shore, the sea was not tied to the land, consequently it belonged to no one by virtue of some right of occupation and its use should remain free, "common unto all" (ibid.: 28), in navigation as in fishing and trade.

In *De jure naturae et gentium* (1672 [1710]), Pufendorf modified the doctrine of universal economy. He started from the same point: it is a human duty that everyone can obtain for himself the commodities which he lacks in another country by exchanges or other lawful contracts, and it is good that these exchanges or contracts are not prevented "by any civil ordinance, or by any unlawful combination, or monopoly" (ibid.: 199). This statement is in accordance with one of the provisos of natural law, namely, the right of everyone to basic necessities of life, but not necessarily to the proviso of independence and liberty that "any one may sell his own when and to whom he pleases" (ibid.: 396). The solution therefore is to distinguish the "necessities of life" from the "pleasure and superfluity of life" (ibid.: 199): everyone is naturally free to sell to whom he pleases, unless the commodity is so vital that one cannot do without it. It would be an offence against humanity to deprive others from the right to procure for themselves the necessities of life.

From the viewpoint of the laws of nations, the reasoning is much the same: as trade promotes the interests of all nations, forbidding or restricting the international circulation of commodities would be contrary to the law of nations. However, in so far as the preservation and the independence of a nation are at stake, some exceptions are acceptable. For example, a state has no obligation to bring to a foreign nation its necessities of life when its subjects lack them. It can quite legally prohibit their exportation, but it has no right to forbid that of luxuries. In the same way, it can favour its subjects more than foreigners (Pufendorf 1672 [1710]: 200) by granting the former a preferential right or by imposing higher taxes on the latter. It can also establish a treaty in favour of one single nation or private company. Along the same lines, as the seas do not belong to anyone, everyone is, by natural law, free to sail and to trade and nothing must prevent him from keeping his goods or selling them to a single buyer; likewise a nation (ibid.: 309–10).

Free access versus monopoly

This examination of trade, of economic liberty and monopoly through the philosophy of natural law and the law of nations reveals the influence of scholasticism and, through the latter, that of Roman law – what Odd Langholm calls the "liberalistic principles of Roman law" (1982: 260). These principles permeate the literature on trade. Barbon illustrates this well: "the Market is the best Judge of Value; for by the Concourse of Buyers and Sellers, the Quantity of Wares, and the Occasion for them are Best known: Things are just worth so much, as they can be sold for, according to the Old Rule, *Valet Quantum Vendi potest*" (Barbon 1690 [1905]: 16).

This "old rule" goes back to the *Digest* of Justinian and to its successive rewordings in medieval scholastic glosses. According to Langholm, this rule "embodies the very essence of a free exchange economy" (1982: 262). It means that "a thing is worth what it can be sold for" or what can be obtained, and it implies that consenting to this price amounts to justice. What is important here is to consider that this consent should result from free bargaining for the contract in order to be valid. It is in this area that economic freedom lies.

This rule, which appears in a very simple form in Barbon, allows the market mechanism to wrap itself in the morality that it is apparently lacking. The scholastic doctors have of course added restrictive clauses to this rule, for example, the condition that the buyer should be properly informed and act in full knowledge of the facts. In their mind, it was a question of making the consent conditional. The decision on price should be free and reflect equal power in negotiations – that is, the non-exploitation of the buyer – and the limit of this freedom should only be the result of the impersonal force of circumstances – constraints such as the wants and needs of a community (the rich members as well as the poor) – and not personal powers. This explains the different treatment of markets for necessary goods and markets for luxury goods where freedom is inevitably more extensive.

Nevertheless, a market logic is at work that certainly does not correspond to the logic which prevailed later, that of the market as an impersonal force imposing itself on individual actors. In the scholastic vision, the market should be governed by trading rules that are compatible with the common good and which mean that nobody should profit from another. This leads Langholm (1982: 283) to state that for the scholastics "liberty is duty". Consequently, this free bargaining is not incompatible with some regulation of prices by the political authority. The literature on trade proceeds in same way, except that it under-estimates the moral and ethical aspects. It demands a sort of minimal freedom that is needed for all trading activity, and simultaneously certain forms of regulation compatible with this freedom, particularly as regards foreign trade. Like the scholastics, the commercial writers were marked by Roman law and therefore accepted a certain idea of liberty which implied a criticism of the monopoly, not an abandonment of regulations. However, morals and ethics were no longer the reason for the combination of liberty and regulations. Misselden and Malynes, for example, explicitly invoked free trade in their work, meaning free access to a given trade.

As Viner observed (1937: 91ff.), free trade is not laissez-faire, as we understand this expression today (see also Perrotta 1991: 303–11; Steiner 1992: 107–10). The example of monopoly can help to understand this. The scholastic argument, derived from Aristotle, distinguishes between two kinds of monopoly, namely, two cases of collusion or of conspiracy between sellers: (1) when they seek to establish a single seller, or (2) when they seek to create a cartel. In the second case, it is a pact between sellers aimed at charging excessive prices. In the sixteenth century, this is what led Martin de Azpilcueta (1491–1586) to add a clause to the rule of the *Digest: res tantum valet quantum vendi potest, cessent omne monopolium, fraus et dolis* ("a thing is worth as much as it can be sold for in the absence of every monopoly, fraud and deceit"; see Langholm 1998: 98 n.).

Let us now look at the argument by John Wheeler (1601 [1931]: 333), a member of the Merchant Adventurers. He presented his company as both an association of free traders and a privileged association. At the same time, having to defend himself against the accusation of monopoly, he used this definition: "*Monopoly* is when one man alone buyeth up all that is to be got of one kind of merchandise, to the end that he alone may sell at his own lust and pleasure" (ibid.: 427, original emphasis). It is the Romanist and scholastic definition: the fact of being the only buyer and the only seller of a commodity. Wheeler (ibid.: 427) could therefore conclude that his company was not a monopoly: "What soever is free and at liberty to buy and sell, the same by no reason or right construction can be accounted a *Monopoly*."

Following this tradition, Pufendorf (1672 [1710]: 395) defined the monopoly as a trade to which the access is voluntarily closed. Monopoly is objectionable, not because there is only one seller, but because this single seller prevents others from enjoying the same right to sell. More importantly, Pufendorf made a distinction between monopoly of the state in charge of the interests of the commonwealth and "monopoly among citizens" (ibid.: 396). By treaty, a state can legally bring certain goods to one foreign nation, with the exception of necessary goods that its subjects may lack. It may entrust foreign trade to an individual or a company on the grounds that this trade is far away and that establishing it is costly and risky. Private monopolies are objectionable, because these are breaches of the law of nature that are not always justified by the law of nations. One must keep in mind the maxim that "the *monopolies* of private men are spurious and illegal, and do not depend upon rights and privileges, but are generally carried on by clandestine frauds and combinations" (ibid., original emphasis): for example, traders who prevent access to certain foreign goods and their resale in the country, or who buy and store great quantities to speculate on their scarcity and resell them at an exorbitant price.

Trade in General and in Particular

Particular and general interests
At the beginning of the seventeenth century, Montchrétien (1615 [1999]: 287) again tried to justify the gains made by merchants by separating honest gain linked with social usefulness from dishonest gain linked with covetousness. He subsequently recommended, from a political viewpoint, not ostracising the honest merchants and trade in general. Indeed, the first characteristic of the science of trade is to refer to that trade, and not to trade in particular. This science is assumed to consist of writings which no longer present themselves just as *pro domo* pleas, defending particular interests in particular markets, but as writings whose conclusions can be applied to different sectors or nations and which can be put into practice by a sovereign.

Mun (1664 [1986]: 1–3) had already observed that the merchant was the "stewart of the Kingdom stock" and it was in this capacity that he should certainly be "a good penman, a good arithmetician and a good accountant", know all the details of his profession, the institutions and the customs of the markets, but also have followed Latin tuition. Child (1681 [1995]: 27) added that to deal with trade in general the merchant had to be experienced and educated, but also retired from business. It was with this proviso that he would consider trade, not from the sole viewpoint of his private, but from the higher viewpoint of the public interest. In this, Child was inspired by the Dutch model, as described by Temple, according to which practising merchants were in a minority in the trade councils, which were made up of "Civilians or Sons of Merchants, that have long since left off their active Trades". In the same period, Barbon (1690 [1905]: 6) admitted that the merchants had not given their activities any purpose other than that of promoting their interests, and that they had rarely embraced the knowledge of trade in general. Treating a particular trade as part of trade in general is indeed to make the latter a fully political subject and to assert that merchants' particular interests are identical to those of trade in general, and therefore to those of the nation. But the demonstration of this identity is far from being self-evident (see Malynes 1622 [1971]: 3–4).

Thus there are disadvantageous trades from a nation's point of view, and particular interests that do not work in favour of the public interest. Towards the end of the seventeenth century, Petyt (1680 [1856]: 289), echoed by Child (1681 [1995]: 26), again pointed out this questionable congruity of interests. A few decades later, Tucker (1753: iv–v) observed that the science of commerce had been misunderstood, judged to be "dark and crabbed" and lacking in "fixed and certain principles". The conclusions of this science fluctuated depending on the divergent interests of the merchants, so much so that it was preferable that its study was entrusted to people "of a *liberal* and *learned* education, *not concerned* in trade", "*freer* from the prejudice of *self-interest*" (ibid.: vi, original emphases). General trade was something that was too serious to be entrusted only to merchants, even if they were removed from business. From then on, it was taken care of by politics and also placed under the gaze of philosophers, lawyers, literati and polygraph writers.

Trade, mores and empire

Another characteristic of the science of commerce is to understand general trade as an element of the international politics of States, including war and peace. Barbon (1690 [1905]: 5) coupled this activity with achieving two political objectives: "Trade is now become as necessary to preserve governments, as it is useful to make them rich." Hume (1741 [1985]: 88) wrote slightly later: "Trade was never esteemed as an affair of state till the last century." By affair of state, Hume meant a political concern. Trade became an affair of state during the seventeenth century as it became a stake for rival nations. If Hume saw in this activity a means of civilisation and refinement, Barbon first noticed the ambivalent means of power: foreign trade strengthens the power of government by financing war, but also diverts it from the objective of territorial expansion and directs it towards peace, as this activity only prospers with peace. The two authors logically emphasised the ties which link trade and freedom (see Hont 2005: 8–11).

Child had observed that trade in general was political and was dealt with through political institutions. Consequently, he regarded an assembly of "noblemen, gentlemen, and merchants" as the best constitution "for the carrying on any trade for the publick utility of the Kingdom" (Child 1681 [1995]: 26–7). In the same way, Barbon maintained that foreign trade is better suited to free governments than to absolute monarchies. To that end, he developed a kind of theory of climate and of "doux commerce" – generally associated with the name of Montesquieu – which stated that the warlike people of the cold regions of northern Europe were finally conquered by the trading people of the milder regions of the south that they invaded. Through contact with them, they softened their manners by engaging in trade and preferred to peacefully preserve their possessions (Barbon 1690 [1905]: 37–8). Trade was profitable for the merchant, the landlord and, by derivation, for any man whom the latter employed, but also for the government, in so far as it increases its revenues and strengthens its power: "if an Universal Empire, or Dominion of a very Large Extent can be raised in the World, It seems more probable to be done by the Help of Trade" (ibid.: 24).

What Barbon meant by "universal empire" was an empire of the sea, the only one that it was still possible to achieve. An empire on land corresponded to a plan for the establishment of a universal monarchy, so powerful that it would rule over Europe and would be the only arbiter of conflicts between minor nations. Such a plan was no longer feasible, given that the land had been conquered for a long time, governments had generally been formed on the basis of "liberty and property of land", populations had become more educated and too numerous to be subdued. Thus, any new conquest of territory became pointless; it would reduce the population, which was the source of wealth, and would destroy the towns. The two forms of government were therefore envisaged, the first was the absolute monarchy, Spanish and French, "best fitted to raise Dominion by Armies", the other was the English mixed monarchy, "Best for *Trade*; for men are most industrious, where they are most free, and secure to injoy the Effects of their Labours" (ibid.: 27–8, original emphasis). The latter was also the better adapted to the new form of enrichment and expansion, namely, the empire of the sea (ibid.: 31).

Towards the mid-eighteenth century, Hume rejected the doctrine of the universal monarchy, but also the plan for an empire of the sea. He admitted that international relations had been based on jealousy since the seventeenth century, but that they could also prove to be mutually beneficial. Jealousy could indeed be overcome on condition that the relationship between domestic trade and foreign trade was reversed, which led to a depreciation of the notions of empire and territorial expansion. The most important element in the *Essays* is the strengthening of the relationship between trade and economic, political and religious freedom. Hume considered that, as truths were drawn from history, the arts, the sciences and trade were born in free nations, that they diminished with the decline of freedom, and that a free nation lived under a popular government – namely, non-absolute government – with trade increasing where property is guaranteed.

The Doctrine of the Balance of Trade

Earlier formulations and internal criticisms
The science of trade invents neither the expression nor the idea of a balance of trade. Price (1905) traces the idea from the Middle Ages onwards, and, more clearly, from the modern era in Hales (1581 [1907]). He points to the development of a more precise vocabulary at the beginning of the seventeenth century, in particular, the use by Malynes of the terms "overbalance" (1601 [1977]: 2) and "balance" (1603 [1972]: 87). The complete expression "balance of trade" appeared shortly afterwards, notably in Bacon (1616 [1740]: 586) and in Misselden (1623 [1973]: 116–17) who is generally regarded as the provider of the first expression in print. In *A Discourse of Trade* (1621 [1930]: 27) Mun only used the term "overbalance" twice, while in *England's Treasure by Forraign Trade* (prior to 1630, 1664 [1986]) he used "overbalance" twice, "overplus" three times, "balance" nineteen times and the complete expression once, inserting an adjective: "balance of our forraign trade". The French expression "balance du commerce" is almost absent in France in the seventeenth century.

Frank Fetter (1935: 623) notes that the expressions "favourable balance" and "unfavourable balance" are also of late occurrence. They are most often attributed to James Steuart (1713–80). Previously other expressions were current: "against us", "in our favour", "to our advantage", "wrong balance", "advantageous", "lucrative", "on our side", and so on. Like Viner, Fetter also emphasises that quite early on, the English writers were aware of the different constituent elements of the balance, in particular, the "invisibles". Consequently, they referred to the costs, traders' profits, war expenses, insurance payments and so on. Petty (1623–87) writes, for example: "The labour of seamen, and freight of ships, is always of the nature of an exported commodity, the overplus whereof, above what is imported, brings home money, etc." (Petty 1690 [1986]: 260).

As for the balance, favourable or unfavourable, and the inflow or outflow of money and bullion as a counterpart, these were interpreted as an indicator of gain or loss in international trade. An inflow of bullion can be sought for different reasons, such as financing wars or increasing domestic liquidity in order to stimulate trade and employment (see Viner 1937: ch. 1, s. iv).

The *locus classicus* of the doctrine of the favourable trade balance is this sentence by Mun: "The ordinary means therefore to increase our wealth and treasure is by *Forraign Trade*, wherein wee must observe this rule; to sell more to strangers yearly than wee consume of theirs in value" (Mun 1664 [1986]: 5; author's emphasis). The generally accepted argument was that public benefits came from exports rather than from imports, or that the former were considered to be more positive for the nation. The good policy that resulted from this contrast consisted, then, in encouraging exports by making them more secure and quicker, thanks to public infrastructure, by supporting them with a strong navy and garrisons, by reducing taxes on them, by subsidising them and by establishing free ports where goods were stored for re-exportation. As for imports, the writers complained in general that they were mainly satisfying a demand for luxury goods and suggested limiting them or imposing high duties on them. This suspicion concurred with scholastic or Protestant positions on the harmful effects of corrupting luxury and the benefits of parsimony, but the prosaic interest had here partly replaced the moral and ethical arguments. Imports of luxuries actually related to goods that national manufacturing did not rework and which consequently increased national consumption without increasing national production. Hence the proposals aimed at reducing or abolishing duties on exports, prohibiting imports or imposing high duties on them if they were not intended for re-export (ibid.: 12).

Thereafter some authors considered other measures to achieve a positive balance, for example, encouraging domestic production intended for export. Others considered the opposition between export and import to be excessive and criticised the idea of a favourable balance but never thought of abandoning it permanently. This idea is controversial, at least because of the argument that, in a world where trade between nations becomes widespread, there are fewer and fewer reasons to consider that the only rule possible for enrichment is to gain at the expense of one's neighbours. Moreover, Child (1693 [1698]: 173, original emphasis) established as one of the rules of trade: "*To make it the Interest of other Nations to Trade with us.*" However, it should be noted that Mun (1621 [1930]: 56) himself did not draw the most categorical conclusions of his sentence when he wrote: "we ought not to avoid the importation of forraine wares, but rather willingly to bridle our own affections to the moderate consuming of the same". It was not a question of banning, but of containing in the name of parsimony the consumption of imported goods, especially luxuries, that is judged to be excessive.

However, in the mind of Child there was no doubt that an examination of foreign trade went through a measurement of the balance of trade. It was rather the method usually retained to evaluate this balance that he questioned, that is, the comparison of the value of goods exported by a nation and that of goods imported. The difficulty, according to Child (1693 [1698]: 153), was that this valuation was imperfect, although it had "much of truth in it". The concept of balance was difficult to put into practice from the viewpoint of general as well as particular trade, because the measures drawn from customs ledgers were not very reliable (ibid.: 154). It was therefore difficult to draw any

general political conclusion, as was shown by the "paradox" (ibid.: 156) of Ireland –
which Child took from Petty (1662 [1986]: 46) – which exported more than it imported
and yet grew poorer. What applied to trade in general also applied to particular trades.
Indeed, one trade sector could be an importer without necessarily being "destructive"
(Child 1693 [1698]: 158) for wealth. This was the case, for example, with regard to
imports from Denmark and Norway of wood for construction, tar and pitch, used by the
English navy. Child concluded:

> The best and most certain discovery . . . is to be made from the Encrease or diminution of our
> *Trade* and *Shiping* in general. . . *if our Trade and Shiping encrease*, how small or low soever the
> profits are to private Men, it is an infallible Indication that the Nation in general thrives. (Ibid.:
> original emphases)

Barbon took up the argument of the low reliability of measuring by means of customs
records, which he reinforced through the argument of the vagaries of international trade,
whose effects on the nation's wealth were sometimes positive and sometimes negative.
His explanation of enrichment was as follows: "the only way to know what sort of Goods
and Trade are most profitable to a Nation, is, by examining which sort of Goods employ
most hands by importing and manufacturing. For every man that works, is paid for his
time; and the more they are employ'd in a Nation, the richer the Nation grows" (1696
[1995]: 178).

Thus it is the merchants who enrich the nation, in particular, because they provide
work for the people. The "fear of importation" vanishes and it even becomes useful to
import raw materials, if the country does not possess them naturally, to rework and then
export them with higher value. If imports were to be in competition with domestic goods
and hinder their consumption, a customs policy well calculated to limit these would be
enough (Barbon 1696 [1995]: 179). Finally, the consumption of foreign products depends
on opinion, mood and fashion. The French want to buy goods manufactured in England
and vice versa. All this creates a trade that can be "beneficial to all Nations" (ibid.).

Restating the doctrine
Thus, from the end of the seventeenth century, some authors advocated foreign trade
as a means to promote the domestic economy, through its effect of stimulating national
manufacturing and promoting national employment.

The doctrine of a favourable balance was supported by new political recommendations. As it is positive to import raw materials and inputs in order to rework and export
them, it is preferable to tax these imports lightly and, in contrast, to tax imports of
finished products heavily. Conversely, it is necessary to impose high taxes on exports of
national raw materials to encourage their processing at home. This doctrine was formulated very early on by Samuel Fortrey (1663 [1744]: 29).

These policies have acquired the names of "foreign-paid incomes doctrine", or
"balance of labour theory" (see Johnson 1937: ch. 15). Taking into account the two
trades, domestic and foreign, and seeing them as interdependent, rather than just as
a single trade, is a characteristic of the science of trade in the eighteenth century. The
advantage provided by national manufactures is not only the gain derived from the
exchange of goods of the great value against goods of lower value; it is also the ability
of this manufacture to generate national employment. From this emerges the idea that

wages paid in the production of manufactures destined for export are ultimately paid by foreign consumers:

> If the value of the matter imported be greater than the value of what is exported, the country gains. If a greater value of labour be imported than exported, the country loses. Why? Because in the first case, strangers must have paid, *in matter*, the surplus of the labour exported; and in the second case, because the country must have paid to strangers, *in matter*, the surplus of labour imported. It is therefore a general maxim, to discourage the importation of work, and to encourage the exportation of it. (Steuart 1767 [1966], I: 291; original emphases)

The "gain from exchange doctrine" or "eighteenth century rule" is a doctrine that is somewhat different from the previous one. According to Viner (1937: 440), it is the rule "that it pays to import commodities from abroad whenever they can be obtained in exchange for exports at a smaller real cost than their production at home would entail". This doctrine is understood as an explicit call for free trade: indeed, on the assumption of freedom, commodities that circulate between trading nations are those which are produced at the lowest cost. Viner notes this doctrine of the international division of labour in Martyn, and Irwin wisely points out that Martyn is a defender of free trade in the following meanings of this expression: opposition to monopoly (particularly that of trade with the Indies) and opposition to restrictions on imports (particularly goods coming from India):

> The Kingdom is not more impoverish'd by the consumption of *Indian* than of *English* Manufactures. Indeed whatsoever is consum'd in *England* is loss, it can be no profit to the Nation; but yet to permit the consumption of the *Indian* is not the way to lose so much as if we shall restrain our selves to only *English* Manufactures. Things may be imported from *India* by fewer hands than as good wou'd be made in *England*; so that to permit the consumption of *Indian* Manufactures, is that to permit the loss of few Men's labour; to restrain us to only *English*, is to oblige us to lose the labour of many; the loss of few Men's labour must needs be less than that of many: Wherefore, if we suffer our selves to consume the *Indian*, we are not so much impoverish'd as if we were restraind to the consumption of only *English* Manufactures. (Martyn 1701 [1856]: 578, original emphases)

However, Martyn's plea for free trade cannot be adequately assimilated to the plea for a "system of natural liberty" or of laissez-faire in the nineteenth-century meaning. As for many writers on the science of trade, Martyn's position in favour of freedom of trade is as much influenced by general principles as by circumstances. Thus, in *Considerations* dated from 1701, Martyn defended the free trade argument, not as an ideal, but with the aim of preventing the formation of a monopoly, while in the columns of the *British Merchant* of 1713, he was opposed to the Treaty of Utrecht with France for reasons of domestic politics. He was, in fact, commissioned by the Whig party to oppose the arguments of free-traders in the Tory party who were in favour of this treaty (see MacLeod 1983: 226; Maneschi 2002: 247).

What is true for Martyn is also true for North. The latter was unquestionably an advocate of free trade (North 1691 [1907]: 33) and probably the writer who had the clearest vision of the self-regulating mechanisms of the economy, in any case the vision that was most based on the supply and demand mechanisms, and even more on supply than demand (see Finkelstein 2000: ch. 12). Nevertheless, Douglas Vickers (1959: 103) remarks that North still makes wealth dependent on foreign trade and finally on maintaining a favourable balance of trade, apart, of course, from any policy of restriction.

Vanderlint (1734 [1914]: 33) also placed the arguments in favour of free trade within the doctrine of the favourable balance, stating that free trade means the absence of restrictions and of losses due to them. In particular, he raised the well-known question of retaliations: restrictions in one country lead to restrictions in another, and employment suffers on both sides (ibid.: 81–2).

All the preceding arguments are found in Matthew Decker (1744 [1995]: 56), but again, the impact of the demand for free trade should not be exaggerated. This leads to differentiating several levels of demand for economic freedom. The first level is the association of freedom and protection or regulation; in this case, freedom is minimal, it is a demand for free access to the market and is grounded on the Romanist, scholastic or natural law tradition. The second level is that of free trade, namely, a demand that brings together two aspects, free access and opposition to severe restrictions. The third level is that of laissez-faire or natural liberty, when a more individualistic vision of society is superimposed.

The Science of Trade as the "Système des commerçants" or "Mercantile System": From Quesnay and Smith to McCulloch

The idea that writers in the period between the early seventeenth century and the second third of the eighteenth century shared a common doctrine was put forward by Quesnay, Mirabeau and Smith. In "Hommes" (1757 [2005], I: 302), François Quesnay wrote of a "système des commerçants" which he condemned for two main reasons: first, this system was committed to supporting the interests of particular trades; second, its conclusions were detrimental to trade in general and to the interests of agriculture and the nation. In *Philosophie rurale* (1763 [1764], III: 91, 211), the Marquis of Mirabeau used the phrase "mercantile system" in the same way, blaming its "absurd inconsistency" and its propensity to take hold of all sorts of trades.

In the *Annual Register*, Edmund Burke (1762 [1787]: 179–80) still referred to a "science of trade", albeit in a critical way. He opposed two visions of trade, the first which perceived it as a "science of individuals", namely, an understanding of "the interests and connexions of individuals, together with the quality and value of each commodity", and the second, the so-called "science of trade", whose aim was to establish the "general direction of trade" at government level. Defined in a negative way, the latter was nothing more than an incorrect systematisation of wrong principles, whose consequences were harmful for individuals and their economic freedom. While Burke repeated the vocabulary in common use, Smith (1776 [1976], IV.i.2) used the expression "commercial or mercantile system" and more rarely "system of commerce".

Smith devoted eight chapters of the *Wealth of Nations* to this system. It was, of course, the alleged confusion between money and wealth, which, *prima facie*, characterised it. He (1776 [1976], IV.i.3) pointed first of all to John Locke's alleged fixation on bullion and that of some unspecified writers who were in favour of the accumulation of precious metals (to finance war) and the prohibition of their export. However, it was Mun on whom he focused his attention, and secondarily on Joshua Gee (1667–1730). It was Mun who established the mercantile system, took it to a high level of elaboration, reconciled it with a certain degree of freedom – that of the export of precious metals – related it to the doctrine of a favourable balance and made it the instrument of the interests of the merchant. Smith gave little credit to this claim of freedom. Merchants pleaded for the cause of freedom when it was favourable to their interests.

Smith thus put forward three ideas. First, merchants can be expected to act in their own interests, but they strive to persuade politicians and public opinion that these interests are identical to the interests of the nation. Second, merchants' knowledge rests on an erroneous identification of the causes of private enrichment with the causes of public enrichment and pretends that the wealth of a nation depends mainly on foreign trade. Moreover, this knowledge is established as a system, entirely constructed from Mun's work (Smith 1776 [1976], IV.i.10). Third, there is reason to doubt the merchants' aspirations for freedom. While Mun tolerates a degree of freedom regarding the export of precious metals, this is insufficient according to Smith, who advocates a more comprehensive "system of natural liberty" (ibid., IV.ix.51).

Alfred Coats (1976: 222) notes that Smith was both very suspicious of the merchants and full of praise for the fourth commercial stage of the history of mankind, considered to be the most civilised, the most beneficial and which offers the best governments (1776 [1976], III.iv.4). This implies that trade promotes two attitudes: to act through a "love for freedom" or through a "love for commerce and gain" (see also Cropsey 1957: 95). If, despite everything, the mercantile system suggests a progress towards the commercial society, why does Smith denigrate it? The reason is that this system cannot fully achieve this society, in the Smithian meaning of the word, namely, a society governed by natural liberty alone. The difficulty is that the system of natural liberty, too utopian, cannot do this either, which brings to mind Solon's argument: "When he [the legislator] cannot establish the right he will not disdain to ameliorate the wrong; but like Solon, when he cannot establish the best system of laws, he will endeavour to establish the best that the people can bear" (Smith 1759–90 [1976], VI.ii.2.16).

The flaw of the mercantile system was not so much that it confused money and wealth, but that it corrupted commercial society through its insistent demands for privileges and monopolies. Yet Smith did not seem to exclude on principle the merchants from the government, since "every man thus lives by exchanging, or become in some measure a merchant" (1776 [1976], I.iv.1). But the question of government was not asked in the same way for all the nations that have reached the commercial stage. Britain was not Holland. He admitted (ibid., V.ii.k.80) that Holland was ruled by merchants since it was largely made up of merchants. He conceded that its form of the government was rather oligarchic, plutocratic, and had a very distant relationship with the ancient republic, for the reason – a commonplace of English republicanism in the seventeenth century – that the ancient republic was not fully compatible with commerce. Furthermore, Smith thought that this modern republic declined if its ruling class did not manage to have a solid public ethos, promoting a certain rejection of immediate private interests and the commitment to a moderate and thrifty behaviour. The danger was the development of the "sneaking arts of underling tradesmen" and the "monopolizing spirit of merchants and manufacturers" (ibid., IV.ii.c.9). Britain fortunately had another constitution in which powers balanced each other out, and also a landed aristocracy, which was loyal to its country and in fact governed, at least partly. However, the difficulty with the British constitution was that the balance of powers, which was so virtuous, allowed the interplay of lobbies, parties and separate interests within the House of Commons, particularly those of the wholesale merchants and manufacturers. Those whom Smith would like to see removed from public decision-making were international traders.

Thus Smith retained only one of the two criticisms expressed by Quesnay and Mirabeau. For it seemed indisputable for him that the mercantile system favoured the accumulation of capital and contributed to the rise of the modern trading society. On the other hand, it clearly reflected the conspiracy of international merchants and manufacturers against the nation's interest. It is this defective side of the system that forms the core of the interpretation of Robert Ekelund and Robert Tollison (1981) who define it as the expression of rent-seeking behaviour inside government institutions.

Smith (1776 [1976], IV.iii.c.2, 9) pointed out another absurdity of the mercantile system besides the confusion between money and wealth: the belief that trade is a zero-sum game. These absurdities, these prejudices and an ambivalent use of the concept of freedom that mark this system were also criticised by Smith's successors, notably John Ramsay McCulloch (1828 [1863]: xxix). McCulloch presented it less as a system than as a series of opinions that matched the spirit of the times and he hastened to exempt a few authors from this erroneous alleged system in order to make them the predecessors of Smith. This is the case of Dudley North who first demonstrated the benefits of free-trade for all the nations (ibid.: xxix) and Locke who clearly understood that labour is the source of the greatest part of the value and of increasing wealth, thus anticipating the conditions of a potentially indefinite growth. However, McCulloch added (ibid.: xxxii), Locke did not fully perceive the consequences of his assertion, especially that an increase in wealth may be maintained indefinitely thanks to the division of labour. He was still reasoning in a world of scarcity – of land and natural resources – and consequently of rivalries.

Mercantilism as a Coherent System, from Schmoller to Schumpeter's Criticism

The term "mercantilism" appeared in British economic literature over the two last decades of the nineteenth century. Scholars used it together with the term "mercantile system" (see, for instance, Ingram 1888). The same pattern occurred in Italy and France, as illustrated by the writings of Luigi Cossa or Émile Levasseur. The origin of the use of this term by the economists is to be found in the German economic literature. "Mercantilismus" was ascertained in the 1830s and thereafter popularised by the Historical School. Wilhelm Roscher (1851) defined it as a system aimed at the acquisition of precious metals and therefore distinct from Colbertism and the agricultural system.

At the end of the nineteenth century and in the first third of the twentieth century, Gustav Schmoller, William Cunningham and Eli Heckscher advocated the idea of a common doctrine. But for these scholars the question was not to bring together a certain number of economic writers who were assumed to share the same absurdity – an "obsession with bullion" (Wilson 1957: 182) and a faulty conception of wealth – but, on the contrary, to seek the coherence of these writers' contributions in an area other than economic theory.

Gustav Schmoller's account

According to Schmoller, what makes this system coherent and explains the support that it generated was that it was the response best adapted to the historical circumstances that characterised Europe at the end of the Middle Ages. This response was extremely modern. Between the fifteenth and the seventeenth centuries, he observed, Europe moved from a particularist and local phase, organised around towns, districts or small territories, to a national phase that itself was based, from the seventeenth and eighteenth centuries, on establishing national states and national economies. This process of unifying a large territory, one illustration of which is Frederick II's Prussia, was inseparable from a "selfish national policy of a harsh and rude kind" (Schmoller 1884 [1902]: 77). Reacting to these new circumstances, the young nations, driven by a "strong and exclusive feeling of community" and a "spirit of violent rivalry" (ibid.: 62), were led in their search for self-sufficiency, independence or supremacy to imitate and expand at the international level the policy of small trading entities of the Middle Ages (ibid.: 63–4, 73). The doctrine of the balance of trade was just a consequence of this process of expanding trade between these new nations. The essence of mercantilism lay neither in this doctrine, nor in a particular doctrine of money, or even in protectionism, but in "something far greater" (ibid.: 51), namely, the transformation of national political communities into national economic communities. Considered as a "state-building system", mercantilism connected the establishment of political institutions and the search for the means of prosperity and national power in a coherent way.

However, Schmoller did not cling to the stereotype of the subordination of economic objectives to political or strategic objectives. On the contrary, he thought that the two objectives were achieved simultaneously (Schmoller 1884 [1902]: 50) and sometimes he even inverted the relationship of subordination (ibid.: 69). As for the idea of trade as competition between nations and possibly as a zero-sum game, Schmoller did not make this a question of principle, but of context: historical circumstances were that international trade had been reduced to a series of opposing interests between states that had recently emerged, all eager to maintain or to improve their position in the "circle of European nations" (ibid.: 50). The doctrine of the natural harmony of national interests was no more justified than that of the conflict of these same interests. The second simply prevailed more in a context of the formation of colonial empires (ibid.: 63).

William Cunningham

Compared with Schmoller, Cunningham proposes a description of mercantilism focused on British political history where the two objectives of this system are quite clearly ranked: plenty is an element or a condition of power (Cunningham 1882–92 [1910], I: 471).

Mercantilism is a constituent part of modernity in so far as it is the expression of a patriotic spirit and a national ambition unlike the medieval municipal spirit. The emergence of this system was promoted by "the rise of nationalities and the increasing bitterness of national rivalries, the discoveries of the New World and the struggle for the possession of its treasures" (ibid.). Cunningham (ibid., II: 20, 25) placed the mercantilist period between the beginning of the reign of Elizabeth and the accession to power of William Pitt. This period is itself divided into three sub-periods corresponding to English political chronology: first, the Elizabethan period that was more concerned with the need to manage the national economy, to control some of its production and to become a leading maritime power than the need to increase finances and attract precious metals; then the Stuart period, which favoured the growth in privileged companies and had a dual objective, both to obtain goods that were lacking from abroad and to procure the means to acquire money; finally, the period of the Whig ascendency, which favoured the development of credit and no longer made the accumulation of precious metals its primary purpose.

This periodisation allows Cunningham to distinguish "bullionism", namely, the doctrine that wealth consists in precious metals and subsequently the policy of accumulating them, from mercantilism *stricto sensu*, namely, the doctrine of a positive balance of trade (Cunningham 1882–92 [1910], II: 177, 195, 260, 601–2). Mercantilism *lato sensu* was no more and no less than the extension of the regulatory action of the State in the maritime sector (Navigation Acts), in industry (protective tariffs), and agriculture (Corn Laws) (ibid., II: 829–30). This system was advocated by politicians until Smith's time, until public opinion noticed the failings of this system as implemented by the politics of the Whig ascendency. Thus it was by rejecting collusion between the monied interest and the Whig oligarchy in power that public opinion became favourable to laissez-faire.

Eli Heckscher

However, in the interwar period, the most influential work was Heckscher's *Mercantilism*. In it he explained that mercantilism was but an "instrumental concept" that gave meaning to a particular period in the history of economic policy, that of the transition between medieval municipal policies and the policy of laissez-faire. This presupposed a certain uniformity of thought among the writers of the period (Heckscher 1931 [1955], I: 27). Smith saw mercantilism mainly as a protectionist and a monetary system, Schmoller as a system of unification and reorganisation of the economy and society around a state and a national market, and Cunningham as a system of power in a context of national rivalries. In a way, Heckscher tried to bring together these three interpretations by arguing that Smith's criticism, although theoretically sound, lacks historical relativity, a failing that could be compensated for by the Historical School.

At the heart of Heckscher's synthesis was the idea that the specificity and coherence of mercantilism lay in its perfect adequacy with the early modern period, just as with laissez-faire in the following period. As the Historical School noted, the specificity of the first modernity was to make the State the subject of economic policy and consecutively to make wealth a "basis for state power" (Heckscher 1931 [1955], I: 21, 25), while laissez-faire understood wealth as a mainly individual subject. Thus, on the question of objectives, Heckscher followed Cunningham: mercantilism placed the objective of power before that of plenty, while laissez-faire reversed their relationship. The reason for this ranking derived mainly from a "static" and finite vision of world economic resources that inevitably led to conflicts over their allocation, as each nation can only improve its position "through acquisitions from other countries". This led to frequent trade wars in the seventeenth and eighteenth centuries that often turned into military wars (ibid., I: 25–6; see also Heckscher 1936–37 [1969]: 25).

Mercantilist policy broke with medieval policy. It was no longer based on the dominant feeling of the "love of goods", but on the "fear of goods", namely, the fear of not selling goods justifying a policy of exporting goods rather than importing them and of protection rather than provision. As for the "monetary aspect", which according to Heckscher was less important than the "commodity aspect", the main element of mercantilism was the doctrine of the balance of trade and the dominant feeling would tend to be that of the love of money, although he did not use this expression in his book.

Ultimately, what unified and particularised the mercantilists and divided them from economic liberals were the different beliefs and "conceptions of society" (Heckscher 1931 [1955], I: 28). It was not freedom of trade that the mercantilists "harped upon", but the doubt that there was "a pre-established harmony" and therefore the free play of economic forces (Heckscher 1936–37 [1969]: 32).

Joseph Schumpeter's criticism

From early on, Schumpeter (1912 [1954]: 40–41) had supported the idea that, analytically, the mercantilists did not form a school of thought, or a scientific theory, and that, consequently, the charge of incoherence raised against them was largely unfair. Their importance could be found again, first, in their doctrine of the balance of trade, which could be considered as the "first step towards an analysis of economic factors", and, secondly, in the "lucid definition of national interests as distinguished from private ones and the recognition of a clash between the two". But unfortunately they did not perceive the "nature of the circular flow of economic life, even less the interaction of the various spheres of individual economies within the framework of the national economy".

In *History of Economic Analysis* (1954: 143), Schumpeter retained the same idea, but partly changed his comments. While he had no doubts that the economic literature of the seventeenth and eighteenth centuries had no "logical or historical unit", he distinguished a sociological category of economic authors linked to the rise of the national states and conscious of their rivalries. They are the "consultant administrators" whose literary production – Schumpeter used the British case as a reference – reflects not the general, but the specific conditions of their nation, focusing on foreign trade rather than on agriculture, on the legitimacy of the great financial or navigation companies, and of monopolistic practices.

This category of actors is itself subdivided into three groups (Schumpeter 1954: 159–60): the "teachers and writers of more or less systematic treatises", whose aim was to form the emerging bureaucracy of civil servants; the "public administrators", less cultured than the previous group and also called "practitioners"; and the "businessmen". These sociological subdivisions aim at avoiding using the word mercantilism as far as possible, allowing a distinction between systems and quasi-systems. The systems came from academic professions and public administrators. Most often they are by-products of the philosophy of natural law and political theory. The quasi-systems came from businessmen, but also from civil servants. These are less complete systematisations, in fact "programs of industrial and commercial development" (ibid.: 295). The model is the *Discourse of Trade* by Child, who deals with practical problems "in the light of clearly adumbrated 'laws' of the mechanism of capitalist markets" (ibid.: 196).

THIERRY DEMALS

See also:

Balance of payments and exchange rates (III); Cameralism (II); Richard Cantillon (I); John Law (I); Charles-Louis de Secondat de Montesquieu (I); Money and banking (III); James Steuart [James Denham-Steuart] (I).

References and further reading

Bacon, F. (1597), 'Essays', reprinted in F. Bacon (1740), *Works*, vol. 3, London: J. Walthoe et al.

Bacon, F. (1616), 'Advice to George Villiers', reprinted in F. Bacon (1740), *Works*, vol. 3, London: J. Walthoe et al.

Barbon, N. (1690), *A Discourse of Trade*, reprinted 1905, Baltimore, MD: Johns Hopkins Press.

Barbon, N. (1696), *A Discourse Concerning Coining the New Money Lighter*, reprinted in L. Magnusson (ed.) (1995), *Mercantilism. Critical Concepts in the History of Economics*, vol. 3, London: Routledge.

Bodin, J. (1568), *Réponse de maître Jean Bodin au paradoxe de Monsieur de Malestroict touchant à l'enchérissement de toutes choses, et le moyens d'y remédier*, English trans. 1997, *Response to the Paradoxes of Malestroit*, Bristol: Thoemmes Press.

Bodin, J. (1576), *Les six livres de la République*, book 6, reprinted 1986, Paris: Fayard.

Bonar, J. (1893), *Philosophy and Political Economy in Some of their Historical Relations*, London: Macmillan.

Botero, G. (1598), *Della ragione di stato*, English trans. 1956, *The Reason of State*, London: Routledge and Kegan Paul.

Burke, E. (1762), 'A letter concerning the Marquis de Belloni's dissertation upon commerce', *The Annual Register*, 5th edn 1787, London: R. and J. Dodsley, pp. 177–80.

Cary, J. (1717), *An Essay Towards Regulating the Trade and Employing the Poor of this Kingdom*, London: S. Collins.

Child, J. (1681), *A Treatise Concerning the East-India Trade*, reprinted in L. Magnusson (ed.) (1995), *Mercantilism. Critical Concepts in the History of Economics*, vol. 2, London: Routledge.

Child, J. (1693), *A New Discourse of Trade*, reprinted 1698, London: T. Sowle.

Coats, A.W. (1976), 'Adam Smith and the mercantile system', in A. Skinner and T. Wilson (eds), *Essays on Adam Smith*, Oxford: Clarendon Press, pp. 218–36.

Colbert, J.-B. (1663), 'Mémoires sur les affaires de finances de la France pour servir à l'histoire', reprinted in D. Dessert (ed.) (2000), *Colbert ou le serpent venimeux*, Paris: Éditions complexe, pp. 99–166.

Coleman, D.C. (ed.) (1969), *Revisions in Mercantilism*, London: Methuen.

Cossa, L. (1892), *Introduzione allo studio dell' economia politica*, 3rd edn, Milan: Ulrico Hoepli.

Cropsey, J. (1957), *Polity and Economy. An Interpretation of the Principles of Adam Smith*, The Hague: Martinus Nijhoff.

Cunningham, W. (1882–92), *The Growth of English Industry and Commerce*, 3 vols, reprinted 1910, Cambridge: Cambridge University Press.

Decker, M. (1744), *An Essay on the Causes of the Decline of the Foreign Trade*, in L. Magnusson (ed.) (1995), *Mercantilism. Critical Concepts in the History of Economics*, vol. 4, London: Routledge.

Ekelund, R.B. and R.D. Tollison (1981), *Mercantilism as a Rent-Seeking Society. Economic Regulation in Historical Perspective*, College Station, TX: Texas A & M University Press.

Fetter, F.W. (1935), 'The term favourable balance of trade', *Quarterly Journal of Economics*, **49** (4), 621–45.

Finkelstein, A. (2000), *Harmony and the Balance*, Ann Arbor, MI: University of Michigan Press.

Forbonnais, F. Véron de (1758), *Recherches et considérations sur les finances de France*, vol. 1, Liège.

Fortrey, S. (1663), *England's Interest and Improvement*, reprinted 1744, London: W. Bickerton.

Gervaise, I. (1720), *The System or Theory of the Trade of the World*, in L. Magnusson (ed.) (1995), *Mercantilism. Critical Concepts in the History of Economics*, vol. 4, London: Routledge.

Grampp, W.D. (1952), 'The liberal elements in English mercantilism', *Quarterly Journal of Economics*, **66** (4), 465–501.

Grotius, H. (1609), *Mare liberum*, English trans. 2004, *The Free Sea*, Indianapolis, IN: Liberty Fund.

Hales, J. (1581), *A Discourse of the Common Weal of this Realm of England*, reprinted 1907, Avallon: Imprimerie Paul Grand.

Hatton, E. (1728). *A Mathematical Manual: Or Delightful Associate*, vol. 4, London: Illidge.

Heckscher, E.F. (1931), *Mercantilismen*, English trans. 1955, *Mercantilism*, 2 vols, 2nd edn, London: George Allen and Unwin.

Heckscher, E.F. (1936–37), 'Mercantilism', in D.C. Coleman (ed.) (1969), *Revisions in Mercantilism*, London: Methuen.

Herlitz, L. (1964), 'The concept of mercantilism', *Scandinavian Economic History Review*, **12** (2), 101–20.

Hobbes, T. (1651), *Leviathan*, reprinted 1996, Cambridge: Cambridge University Press.

Hont, I. (2005), *Jealousy of Trade International Competition and the Nation-State in Historical Perspective*, Cambridge, MA: Harvard University Press.

Hume, D. (1741), 'Of civil liberty', in E.F. Miller (ed.) (1985), *Essays Moral, Political and Literary*, Indianapolis, IN: Liberty Fund.

Hutchison, T. (1982), *Before Adam Smith. The Emergence of Political Economy 1662–1776*, Oxford: Blackwell.

Ingram, J.K. (1888), *A History of Political Economy*, New York: Macmillan.

Irwin, D. (1996), *Against the Tide. An Intellectual History of Free Trade*, Princeton, NJ: Princeton University Press.

Johnson, E.A.J. (1937), *Predecessors of Adam Smith*, New York: Prentice Hall.

Judges, A.V. (1939), 'The idea of mercantilism', in D.C. Coleman (ed.) (1969), *Revisions in Mercantilism*. London: Methuen.

Langholm, O. (1982), 'Economic freedom in scholastic thought', *History of Political Economy*, **14** (2), 260–83.

Langholm, O. (1998), *The Legacy of Scholasticism in Economic Thought*, Cambridge: Cambridge University Press.

Machiavelli, N. (1531), *Discorsi sopra la prima deca di Tito Livio*, reprinted 1984, Milan: Rizzoli.

MacLeod, C. (1983), 'Henry Martin and the authorship of considerations upon the East-India Trade', *Bulletin of the Institute of Historical Research*, **56** (November), 222–9.

Magnusson, L. (1994), *Mercantilism. The Shaping of an Economic Language*, London: Routledge.

Magnusson, L. (1995), *Mercantilism. Critical Concepts in the History of Economics*, 4 vols, London: Routledge.

Magnusson, L. (2008), *Mercantilist Theory and Practice: The History of British Mercantilism*, 4 vols, London: Pickering and Chatto.

Malynes, G. de (1601), *The Canker of England's Commonwealth*, reprinted 1977, Amsterdam: Theatrum Orbis Terrarum.

Malynes, G. de (1603), *England's View, in the Unmasking of Two Paradoxes*, reprinted 1972, New York: Arno Press.

Malynes, G. de (1622), *The Maintenance of Free Trade*, reprinted 1971, New York: Augustus M. Kelley.

Maneschi, A. (2002), 'The tercentenary of Henry Martyn's considerations upon the East-India Trade', *Journal of the History of Economic Thought*, **24** (2), 234–49.

Martyn, H. (1701), *Considerations on the East-India Trade*, reprinted in J.R. McCulloch (ed.) (1856), *A Select Collection of Early English Tracts on Commerce*, London: Political Economy Club.

McCulloch, J.R. (1828), 'Introductory discourse', reprinted in A. Smith (1863), *An Inquiry into the Nature and Causes of Wealth of Nations*, Edinburgh: Adam and Charles Black, pp. xv–lxi.

Melon, J.-F. (1735), *Essai politique sur le commerce*, 2nd edn, Amsterdam: Changuion.

Mirabeau, V.R. de (1763), *Philosophie rurale*, reprinted 1764, Amsterdam.

Misselden, E. (1622), *Free Trade or the Meanes to Make Trade Flourish*, reprinted 1971, New York: Augustus M. Kelley.

Misselden, E. (1623), *The Center of the Circle of Commerce*, reprinted 1973, Clifton, NJ: Augustus M. Kelley.

Montchrétien, A. de (1615), *Traicté de l'œconomie politique*, reprinted 1999, Geneva: Droz.

Mun, T. (1621) *A Discourse of Trade*, reprinted 1930, New York: Facsimile Text Society.

Mun, T. (1664), *England's Treasure by Forraign Trade*, reprinted 1986, Fairfield, NJ: Augustus M. Kelley.

North, D. (1691), *Discourses Upon Trade*, reprinted 1907, Baltimore, MD: Johns Hopkins Press.

Perrota, C. (1991), 'Is the mercantilist theory of favourable trade really erroneous?', *History of Political Economy*, **23** (2), 301–36.

Petty, W. (1662), *Treatise of Taxes and Contributions*, reprinted in C. Hull (ed.) (1986), *The Economic Writings of Sir William Petty*, Fairfield, NJ: Augustus M. Kelley, pp. 1–97.

Petty, W. (1690), *Political Arithmetick*, reprinted in C. Hull (ed.) (1986), *The Economic Writings of Sir William Petty*, Fairfield, NJ: Augustus M. Kelley, pp. 233–313.

Petyt, W. (1680), *Britannia Languens*, reprinted in J.R. McCulloch (ed.) (1856), *A Select Collection of Early English Tracts on Commerce*, London: Political Economy Club.

Pincus, S. (2012), 'Rethinking mercantilism: political economy, the British Empire, and the Atlantic world in the seventeenth and eighteenth centuries', *William and Mary Quarterly*, 3rd series, **69** (1), 3–34.

Price, W.H. (1905), 'The origin of the phrase balance of trade', *Quarterly Journal of Economics*, **20** (1), 157–67.

Pufendorf, S. von (1672), *De jure naturae et gentium*, English trans. 1710, *Of the Law of Nature and Nations*, Oxford: A. and J. Churchill et al.

Quesnay, F. (1757), 'Hommes', reprinted 2005, in *Œuvres économiques complètes et autres textes*, vol. 1, Paris: INED, pp. 259–323.

Rashid, S. (1980), 'Economists, economic historians and mercantilism', *Scandinavian Economic History Review*, **28** (1), 1–14.

Richelieu, A.J. du Plessis, Cardinal de (1668), *Testament politique*, reprinted 1995, Paris: Champion.

Roscher, W. (1851), *Zur Geschichte der Englischen Volkswirthschafstlehre*, Leipzig: Weidmannsche Buchhandlung.

Schatz, A. and R. Caillemer (1906), *Le mercantilisme libéral de la fin du xviie siècle. Les idées économiques de M. de Belesbat*, Paris: Sirey.

Schmoller, G. (1884), *The Mercantile System and its Historical Significance*, reprinted 1902, New York and London: Macmillan.

Schumpeter, J.A. (1912), *Epochen den Dogmen und Methodengeschichte*, English trans. 1954, *Economic Doctrine and Method*, London: Allen and Unwin.

Schumpeter, J.A. (1954), *History of Economic Analysis*, London: Allen and Unwin.

Smith, A. (1759–90), *Theory of Moral Sentiments*, reprinted 1976, Oxford: Oxford University Press.

Smith, A. (1776), *An Inquiry into the Nature and Causes of The Wealth of* Nations, 2 vols, reprinted 1976, Oxford: Oxford University Press.

Smith, T. (attributed to) (1581), *A Discourse of the Commonweal of this Realm of England*, reprinted 1969, Charlottesville, VA: University Press of Virginia.

Steiner, P. (1992), 'L'émergence des catégories économiques', in A. Béraud and G. Faccarello (eds), *Nouvelle histoire de la pensée économique*, vol. 1, Paris: La découverte, pp. 103–10.

Stern, P.J. and C. Wennerlind (eds) (2014), *Mercantilism Reimagined. Political Economy in Early Modern Britain and its Empire*, Oxford: Oxford University Press.

Steuart, J. (1767), *An Inquiry into the Principles of Political Economy*, 2 vols, reprinted 1966, Edinburgh: Oliver and Boyd.

Sully, M. de Béthune, Duke of (1745), *Mémoires*, vol. 1, London.

Temple, W. (1673), *Observations upon the United Provinces of the Netherlands*, reprinted 1705, London: J. Tonson, A. and J. Churchill.

Tucker, J. (1753), *A Brief Essay on the Advantages and Disadvantages which Respectively attend France and Great Britain, with Regard to Trade*, 3rd edn, London: Trye.

Vanderlint, J. (1734), *Money Answers all Things*, reprinted 1914, Baltimore, MD: Johns Hopkins Press.

Vickers, D. (1959), *Studies in the Theory of Money, 1690–1776*. Philadelphia, PA: Chilton.

Viner, J. (1937), *Studies in the Theory of International Trade*, London: Allen and Unwin.

Viner, J. (1959), 'Five lectures on economics and freedom', reprinted 1991 in *Essays on the Intellectual History of Economics*, Princeton, NJ: Princeton University Press, pp. 39–81.

Vitoria, F. de (1537), 'De Indis', reprinted in A. Pagden and J. Lawrance (eds) (1991), *Political Writings*, Cambridge: Cambridge University Press, pp. 231–92.

Wheeler, J. (1601), *A Treatise of Commerce*, reprinted 1991, New York: New York University Press.

Wilson, C. (1957), 'Mercantilism: some vicissitudes of an idea', *Economic History Review*, 2nd series, **9** (2), 181–8.

French Enlightenment

Setting the Stage

The age of Enlightenment is certainly one of the most exciting periods in the history of sciences and philosophy (see, for example, the classic studies of Hazard 1935, 1946; Gay 1966, 1969). This is especially true in France where the number of first-rank philosophers and scientists, the so-called "philosophes", is astonishing – from Pierre Bayle (1647–1706) to Marie-Jean-Antoine-Nicolas Caritat de Condorcet (1743–1794), including Bernard Le Bovier de Fontenelle (1657–1757), Charles-Louis de Secondat de Montesquieu (1689–1755), François-Marie Arouet (Voltaire) (1694–1778), Pierre Louis Moreau de Maupertuis (1698–1759), Jean-Jacques Rousseau (1712–1778), Denis Diderot (1713–1784), Claude-Adrien Helvétius (1715–1771), Étienne Bonnot de Condillac (1715–1780), Jean Le Rond d'Alembert (1717–1783), Paul Henri Thiry d'Holbach (1723–1789) and Antoine Laurent Lavoisier (1743–1794), to mention only some of the most celebrated among them. The age extends from the second half of the seventeenth century right up to the French Revolution, which epitomises its climax. Building on the development of modern sciences started in the early seventeenth century, it brought progressively a radical change in all the fields of knowledge and thought. Not surprisingly, this intellectual groundswell also provoked numerous reactions, both during and after the period, which formed the various Anti- or Counter-Enlightenment traditions still active today (see, for example, Monod 1916; Masseau 2000; McMahon 2001; Sternhell 2006 [2009]).

A European movement of ideas, the Enlightenment naturally presented a great diversity of writings and opinions, accentuated by the different national contexts, and gave rise to sometimes diverging interpretations – the more recent debates dealing with the distinction between a "radical" and a "moderate" Enlightenment (see Jacob 1981 [2006]; Israel 2001, 2006, 2010, and some related discussion – for example, Fœssel 2009; Bove et al. 2007; Lilti 2009; Miklaszewska and Tomaszewska 2014). In spite of this, during this period, authors broadly shared some fundamental values of autonomy and freedom, universality and toleration, experimentation and the "reign of reason", perfectibility – all that is supposed to aim at the happiness of humankind and to found modernity. The *Encyclopédie, ou Dictionnaire raisonné des sciences, des arts et des métiers*, edited by Diderot and d'Alembert from 1751 to 1772, is considered the flagship of this period, the best testimony of a revolution in thought and attitudes. There, in the entry "Philosophe", the "philosophe" is depicted as firmly having his feet on the ground, acting for the benefit of all human beings:

> Our *philosophe* does not believe . . . to be in exile in this world; . . . he wishes to enjoy as a wise *œconome* the gifts that nature offers him . . . For him, civil society is like an earthy divinity: he praises it, honours it with integrity, with exact attention to his duties and with a sincere desire to be a member neither worthless nor a cause of embarrassment.

Towards the end of the period, the spirit of Enlightenment was well defined by Immanuel Kant in his celebrated answer to a question asked by the *Berlinische Monatsschrift*: "Was ist Aufklärung?" – what is Enlightenment?

Enlightenment is man's release from his self-incurred tutelage. Tutelage is man's inability to make use of his understanding without direction from another. Self-incurred is this tutelage when its cause lies not in lack of reason but in lack of resolution and courage to use it without direction from another. *Sapere aude!* "Have courage to use your own reason!" – that is the motto of enlightenment. (Kant 1784 [1963]: 3)

The economic field was not left aside, from the second half of the reign of Louis XIV to the Revolution. It even progressively became a central topic in politics, with unwavering fight in favour of laissez-faire – first at the end of the seventeenth century, with Pierre Le Pesant de Boisguilbert (1646–1714), and then in the second half of the eighteenth, with the main figures of François Quesnay (1694–1774), Anne-Robert-Jacques Turgot (1727–1781) and Condorcet. It entailed also many lively controversies over taxes, public expenditure, foreign trade, or over money and banking from the collapse of John Law's (1671–1729) system to Richard Cantillon (*c.*1680–1734) and the circle of J.C.M. Vincent de Gournay (1712–1759). The number of publications of books and pamphlets on economic matters increased dramatically during the second half of the eighteenth century (Théré 1998) – the *Encyclopédie* also included contributions in the field by Quesnay, Turgot, François Véron de Forbonnais (1722–1800), and so on – and authors became aware to deal with a new field of knowledge. In 1755, for example, on the occasion of the death of Montesquieu who had devoted some books of his celebrated treatise *De l'esprit des lois* (1748) to economic subjects, the mathematician, physicist and philosopher Maupertuis made his eulogy at the Royal Academy of Sciences in Berlin. Stressing Montesquieu's interest in the "principles of the system of wealth", he remarked that this system lacked an appropriate name: "this science is so novel among us . . . that it still has no name" (Moreau de Maupertuis 1755 [1768]: 416). In 1763, Quesnay and Victor Riqueti de Mirabeau (1715–1789) in France, and Pietro Verri (1728–1797) in Italy, spoke of "economic science", in the modern meaning of the phrase, to designate the new field. In 1767, Jean-Joseph-Louis Graslin (1728–1790) – an enemy of the Physiocrats – quoted Maupertuis's remark and declared that "the science of political economy . . . has just been born among us" (Graslin 1767 [1911]: 1). One year later, Pierre-Samuel Dupont (later known as Dupont de Nemours) (1739–1817) published *De l'origine et des progrès d'une science nouvelle* (Dupont 1768).

This is not to say that the developments in economic thought were homogenous. Among the wealth of the literature of the time, it is however possible to distinguish two main currents of thought: "commerce politique" and "philosophie économique". (For more precise developments, see the other entries of this *Handbook*, mentioned in the "See also" section at the end of the present text.)

The first consists in a French adaptation of the English "science of trade" and is illustrated by such different authors as Jean-François Melon (1675–1738), Nicolas Dutot (also spelled Du Tot, 1684–1741), Montesquieu, or the members of the circle of Vincent de Gournay (see, for example, Murphy 1986, 1998; Skornicki 2006; Charles et al. 2011), the main figure of which was Véron de Forbonnais. The second (see, for example, Faccarello 1986 [1999], 1998, 2006, 2009; Steiner 1998; Charles and Théré 2008, 2011; Faccarello and Steiner, 2008a, 2012) includes those who fought in favour of the "liberté du commerce", from Boisguilbert and the foundation of "laissez-faire" at the end of the seventeenth century, to the developments of Quesnay, Turgot and Condorcet – to whom some independent authors such as Graslin can be added. Both currents of thought aimed at a deep change in French politics and proposed new political philosophies centred on economic policies for a prosperous economy, mainly in the context, first of the great economic difficulties during the reign of Louis XIV and the Régence, and then of a mounting rivalry with Great Britain, the Seven Years War (1756–63) and the loss by France of some parts of its overseas empire – with, permanently, the structural question of the financing of the state and the huge public debt.

From the Science of Trade to "Commerce politique"

"Commerce politique" is a French phrase that was widespread in diplomacy. Towards the end of the seventeenth century, it referred to the code of conduct which applied to public discussion, more particularly when negotiating treaties and alliances between nations. The expression thereafter acquired a broader meaning of political sociability or court ceremonial. Véron de Forbonnais introduced the expression into economic language by giving it most of the attributes of the science of trade. He made systematic use of it in the 1750s, contrasting the "practical merchant [who] sees in trade nothing but his fortune" with the "political merchant [who] considers the wealth of all, that is, the wealth of the State" (Véron de Forbonnais 1753: 114). This distinction also appears in Dutot (1738 [1739]: 257), who uses it as a way of asserting the primacy of "general trade" over "particular trade". "Commerce politique" is therefore trade observed and analysed from the viewpoint of the political body, that is, the national interest. It is an adaptation to the French intellectual context of the British "science of trade". A sign of the greater sophistication of the analyses of British writers, the references, the borrowings of ideas and the translations increased in the middle of the eighteenth century. The climax of this British vogue is Vincent de Gournay's intendance (1751–58). It is under the latter's administration that works of John Cary, *The British Merchant* (edited by C. King), Charles Davenant, David Hume, Josiah Child, Thomas Culpepper, Lord Bolingbroke, Josiah Tucker and Matthew Decker were translated.

However, a feature of the British literature was the contrast between, on the one hand, Britain and the free States of Holland, and, on the other hand, the absolute monarchies of France and Spain. Moreover, William Petyt, Nicholas Barbon and Davenant described France as an absolute monarchy with pretentions to be a universal monarchy. What concerned therefore the French writers was to prove that France, even with an agricultural territory and neither a mixed constitution nor a Republican government, could be a trading nation just as Britain and Holland and even commercially dominate the other nations in Europe. Three main attempts were made in this direction: Melon's parable of the islands, the "doux commerce" thesis and the developments proposed by the Vincent de Gournay circle.

The islands parable
In his *Essai politique sur le commerce*, Melon imagines a system of nations formed of three or four islands of the same area and identical population, and confronted successively with three different situations. In the first situation, each island produces, with the same number of workers, a single kind of commodity adapted to its territory – corn in the first, wool in the second, and so on – in sufficient quantities to meet its own needs and the needs of the other islands. With each one trading its surplus for

the other goods, an equal balance of trade emerges between the islands (Melon 1734a [1735]: 2).

In the second situation, the island that produces corn is assumed to be more fertile than the others and can exist without any kind of specialisation. This island produces not only its own commodity in abundance, but also the commodities produced by the other islands in quantities sufficient for its consumption. The other islands' soil, poorly fertile, does not allow their inhabitants to produce the amount of corn necessary for their subsistence. The latter are therefore dependent on the corn island for their subsistence and find it impossible to sell their surplus for the corn they need. As their commodity is no longer an object of trade, they are confronted with the alternative, either to leave their island and to be employed on the corn island in order to obtain this basic commodity, or to force the corn island, through a "just war", to produce corn for them and to sell it to them. The second alternative implies that the other islands unite and invoke the "law of nations" to force the corn island to cultivate for them again and to prohibit it from producing what they produce themselves (Melon 1734a [1735]: 3). In this second situation the law of nations is a "balance of power" that the corn island can influence in its favour, since it has the monopoly of a commodity that is absolutely necessary.

In the third situation, all the islands are equally fertile and self-sufficient in corn or in necessary goods, so that none of them can now either dominate the others because of the fertility of its soil, nor claim a "just war". The islands then enter into more intense, but also more uncertain, trading relations, as it becomes difficult to "know which of the islands becomes the most powerful" (Melon 1734a [1735]: 6). Melon draws several consequences from this situation. First, the more islands there are which produce a diversity of manufactured goods, the more the needs of all will be varied, the more trade there will be between them and, consequently, the less an island will dominate by trading corn alone. Second, this extensive trade only works if the islands adopt the principle of competition, that is, if they seek a hegemonic position without resorting to monopoly. Third, the more the circulation of goods increases, the more money and instruments of credit are needed. Three principles therefore emerge to increase the power of an island: to possess a fertile territory that permits an increase in the production of corn, to develop a manufacturing policy suitable to employ a growing population, and to proportion monetary instruments to the circulation of goods. "With these advantages, an island will soon end the balance of equality, achieve superiority of power, and give its laws to the other islands" (Melon 1734a [1735]: 10): trade appears to be a more confrontational than harmonious relation. Essentially reciprocal, it rapidly becomes a way of tilting the balance of power in its favour.

Of these three situations, the first recalls the old doctrine of the "universal economy" that the modern era has made obsolete. The second, assuming a decline in international trade, concludes that war is the primary means of wealth and power: it is a possible expression of the doctrine of the "universal monarchy". The third, separating trade from war and replacing the latter with competition in times of peace, makes trade the main cause of wealth and power: it expresses a doctrine, not of harmony, but of the balance of trading nations.

The doctrine appears as a derivation of the English doctrine of favourable balance of trade. Melon (1734b [1736]: 283–4) faithfully repeats the four ways of making a positive balance that Child (1693 [1698]: 168–9) had listed: "encrease the hands in trade", "encrease the stock in trade", "make trade easie and necessary", "make it the interest of other nations to trade with us". He also takes from Child the plea for a low rate of interest. Finally, as in the British science of trade, he associates this doctrine with a policy combining freedom and protection (Melon 1734a [1735]: 29–30). The demand for freedom is the assertion of the principle of competition and free access, against that of monopoly and privilege. However, two situations justify the concession of privileges: in a newly established trade when a privilege is granted "either to reward the discovery, or to encourage entrepreneurs", and in the case of a strong commercial rivalry when international competition harms the interests of the nation (Melon 1734a [1735]: 69–70).

This theme of the compatibility of freedom of trade and protection can also be found in Henri de Boulainvilliers (1727: 219–20) and Montesquieu (1748, bk XX.: ch. 12). Melon, for example, writes that freedom is measured by its contribution to the common good. This primacy of the common good over the individual good is a central topic of "commerce politique" and the British science of trade: the interest of the merchant is not necessarily the same as the interest of trade in general. Freedom of trade is not the right to trade without rules and limits, but to "negotiate under . . . established laws" (Melon 1734b [1736]: 165). A policy of freedom and protection thus aims at guaranteeing a nation a dominant position in international trade, but certainly not a monopoly position. Yet, Melon writes, it is towards such a position that Petty inclines when he writes that the English are the only ones to have enough funds and ability to "drive the trade of the whole commercial world" (ibid.: 354). Melon interprets this quest for a single emporium, or "universal trade" (Petty 1690 [1899]: 312), as symmetrically the same flaw as the quest for a universal monarchy, and emphasises the doctrine of preservation, competition and the balance of nations: that is, the doctrine of the preservation of the territories and wealth already acquired, as opposed to the doctrine of expansion to new territories and appropriation of their wealth (Melon 1734a [1735]: 102).

The "doux commerce" approach

While Melon stressed the English inclination in favour of "universal trade" and the empire of the sea, English writers of a republican culture, such as Charles Davenant, John Trenchard and Thomas Gordon, emphasised the tendency of the French monarchy towards universal domination, leading to the successive restriction of all kinds of freedoms. They set against this the multiplicity of free and trading nations. Montesquieu also maintained that the hegemony of a superpower threatens the balance of European nations. He therefore assumed that these nations, considered as "members of a great republic" and "undertaking all the trade and navigation in the universe" (Montesquieu 1727 [1964]: 192–3), should mediate their conflicts through the mechanism of the balance of powers and not by relying on a single sovereign. He also knows, like the English republicans, that trade is at the same time a restraint on the excesses of power – what is called "doux commerce" or civilising trade – and an agent for the corruption of values.

The notion of "doux commerce" has been commented on (see Hirschman 1977). It generally means a certain number of effects caused by the expansion of trade, such as gentle manners, religious tolerance, freedom of opinion, security of property, a trade policy that is not arbitrary, and so on, but also an interest-oriented behaviour, particularly that of the trader, which should be assumed here neither reducible to the love of gain, nor identical to the public interest.

The effects of trade are, first, moral and political. They make themselves felt in different ways, depending on the kind of government and territories. Montesquieu distinguishes two cases. On the one hand, the "commerce du luxe", typical of the spending of the higher ranks, is appropriate to a vast and fertile territory ruled by a monarchical government; on the other hand, the "commerce d'œconomie" (carriage and re-export) is fitted to a small and poor territory ruled by a republican government. In the light of this distinction, trade certainly refines the manners of monarchical governments, but corrupts those of military republics, which are grounded in freedom – that of the ancients. As for trading republics, these are only based on (modern) freedom because it is necessary for trade and the establishment of trust between traders. Freedom is therefore defined as "this tranquillity of mind arising from the opinion that everyone has of his security" (Montesquieu 1748, bk XI: ch. 6), which implies, by extension, the compliance with legal rules (exchange contracts, commitments, and so on) that guarantee the security of people and goods. These rules have the same effects in a monarchy that is open to luxury goods trade: they put people and goods beyond the reach of government.

However, trade produces a second kind of effect on the functioning of the economy. The more it expands and the international circulation of goods is free, the less the initiative of government is arbitrary – commerce is incompatible with despotism. This does not mean however a reduction in the legal and political activity of the government. On the one hand, Montesquieu (1748, bk XX: ch. 9, bk XXII: chs 10, 14) maintains that international competition – in the sense of free access – sets a just price for things and that foreign exchange sets a just price for money. He thus suggests that on the international markets there is an adjustment mechanism for quantities and prices which ultimately escapes the arbitrariness of territorial governments and prevents despotism. This is the same idea that explains his support for the quantity theory of money. Montesquieu's position therefore leans towards cosmopolitanism, the criticism of privileges, monopolies and customs restrictions. On the other hand, like Melon, Montesquieu (ibid., bk XX: ch. 12) states that traders' interest is not the national interest in trade, in the same way as the national interest in trade is not that of competing nations. The result is the necessity to limit trade or to control its expansion. He (ibid., bk VII: ch. 5) thus justifies the prohibition of foreign goods, which would be exchanged, because of their high price, against a too important quantity of domestic goods. He emphasises also that some nations do not have an interest in trade, for example, those who, lacking any kind of goods, become poorer by obtaining these, and those who, having everything, are self-sufficient and expect nothing from it (ibid., bk X: ch. 13). Finally, he affirms that the expansion of the carrying and re-exporting trade in a monarchy constitutes a threat of corruption of the monarchy and of this kind of trade itself (ibid., bk V: ch. 8).

Moreover, practising trade is for noblemen the equivalent to abandoning their military function and losing their rank, and leads to unfair competition with the lower rank of traders. Hence, commerce would no longer be the "profession of equals". This position of hostility to the "noblesse commerçante" is, in a way, running counter to the trend. A few years earlier, Dutot (1738 [1739]: 263–4) defended a contrary position. Vincent de Gournay (1993: 11) considers the emergence of such a nobility as one of the reasons for England's economic success, and Forbonnais (Véron de Forbonnais 1753: 117), without denying that the function of the nobility is firstly military, sees no disparagement in the fact this nobility could maintain its rank thanks to income from commercial activity. This debate on the trading nobility ("noblesse commerçante") is an element in a wider debate on whether France is a monarchy sufficiently free to promote commerce with as much success as in the trading republics, namely, whether this nation has broken with the politics of the empire on land and committed itself to the politics of freedom and protection. There are therefore two questions raised by Melon and Montesquieu: that of the compatibility of commerce and monarchy, and that of freedom and protection, namely, the substitution, as much as possible, of competition for war.

The circle of Vincent de Gournay

Vincent de Gournay and his circle make no mystery of their aim: to propel France to the rank of a major trading nation, equal or superior to Britain, and to direct its policy towards establishing an empire, not on land, but on sea. Forbonnais (Véron de Forbonnais 1755b: 67) similarly says that one of the purposes of *commerce politique* is not only to seek a maritime empire, that is, to control navigation and some trade flows from the colonies, but also a "balance of power on sea" not subject to any despotism. Montesquieu had explained England's success with the fact that this nation is engaged in both luxury trade and carrying trade, while France is engaged only in the former and Holland only in the latter. He had made commerce as a whole a matter of constitution, linking carrying trade to republics, luxury trade to monarchies, and the two forms to the countries with mixed constitutions based on the separation of powers. The members of Vincent de Gournay's circle, on the contrary, sought to demonstrate that, while commerce retains its relationship with politics, it has no constitutional dimension.

The question of the compatibility of commerce and the monarchy is not new. Law (1715 [1934]: 18, 48) clearly supported this in relation to credit and banking, and Melon (1734a [1735]: 75) responded to this positively by trying to show that there was no close link between exclusive commerce and monarchical government, because the former was to be found just as much in republican governments. Vincent de Gournay thinks in the same way. Child had asserted that the French colonies of the Indies had not progressed as quickly as their English counterparts because they had been established by a government that was purely monarchical and originally not well versed in commerce and navigation. Vincent de Gournay conceded that the monarchs were certainly less susceptible to the spirit of commerce. However, he replied, "when the principles of commerce have once broken through to the counsel of Monarchs, and it is seen . . . as a major affair, as the real source of wealth and power, these Princes will find it even easier than the Republics to expand and support their commerce" (Vincent de Gournay *c.*1752 [1983]: 352–3).

Véron de Forbonnais's identical position is aimed more directly at Montesquieu. It is the circumstances, he writes (1753: 21), and not the constitutions of Holland and France themselves which make a success of such a branch of commerce in the first country and its failure in the second. A monarchy certainly inclines naturally towards luxury, but this commerce, limited by the size of its market, only employs a small part of the population. The supernumerary part turns necessarily towards the carrying and re-exporting trade, which it expects to be as profitable as the luxury goods trade (Véron de Forbonnais 1753: 111). Véron de Forbonnais interprets Montesquieu's restrictive conception not only as a belittling of the monarchy which was supposed to tolerate only one form of commerce, but also a heightening of the English mixed constitution which tolerates both of them. Within Vincent de Gournay's circle, Louis-Joseph Plumard de Dangeul

(1722–1777) appears to be the strongest defender of the mixed constitution. Indeed, he devotes a whole chapter in his *Remarques sur les avantages et les désavantages de la France et de l'Angleterre par rapport au commerce et aux autres sources de la puissance des États* to show that the constitution of Great Britain is one of the reasons which explain the commercial advantage this nation has over France. Rather than entrusting the laws and administration of commerce to the "individual legislators", he stresses, this nation has set up a legislative assembly which contributes to the public interest, and has thus managed private actions "through the principles of the common good": "The nation. . . governs itself", instead of the monarch dealing with everything (Plumard de Dangeul 1754: 150–1, 170).

The second above-mentioned question concerns the politics of freedom and protection. To Vincent de Gournay, this politics comes directly from Child: freedom applies to the nation's subjects in relation to domestic trade, protection to the nation's subjects in relation to foreign trade. As regards protection, Vincent de Gournay initially supported the policy of the Navigation Act, considered to be the most efficient way of promoting shipments, but he replaced it later by a policy of encouragement and direction of exports, more pragmatic and more compatible with the idea of freedom of trade. The opinions of the members of the circle on this Act are mixed.

Like the British writers, the members of the circle thought in terms of balance (see, for example, Demals and Hyard 2015) and used expressions that are similar to the doctrine of foreign-paid incomes or the export of wrought products. For example, Forbonnais (Véron de Forbonnais 1754, 1: 51–2) summarises in the following way the principles established by the English science of commerce: export the surplus; export raw materials once they have been wrought; import raw materials with a view to reworking them rather than wrought products; exchange goods for goods; avoid imports of foreign goods that can be substituted for domestic goods; avoid imports of "pure luxury foreign goods"; avoid as far as possible imports of goods of absolute necessity; encourage the commerce of storage and re-export; carry goods for other nations. The policy of tariffs and restrictions must be moderate to avoid retaliations, and take account of the quantity of goods, as well as the quantity of labour (Véron de Forbonnais 1755a: 112–13). A reader of Tucker, Plumard de Dangeul takes up the "balance of labour" doctrine perhaps even more than Forbonnais, aiming at an increase in employment and national manufacturing.

Vincent de Gournay concludes his memorandum on smuggling with a well-known phrase: "These two expressions, *laisser faire* and *laisser passer*, being two continuous sources of action, would therefore be for us two continuous sources of wealth" (1993: 34). But the phrase "laissez-faire" is nothing else than the equivalent of "liberty and protection" and had not yet acquired the meaning which can be found in Boisguilbert and inspired Quesnay and Turgot, that is, in "philosophie économique".

"Philosophie économique" and the Foundations of Laissez-Faire

From the 1760s onwards, the Physiocrats and their friends were known as the "économistes", the "écrivains économistes" or the "philosophes économistes". The current of thought they represent came thus to be naturally called "philosophie économique". This phrase was in particular used by Condillac's brother, Gabriel Bonnot de Mably

(1709–1785), in his 1768 *Doutes proposés aux philosophes économistes sur l'ordre naturel et essentiel des sociétés politiques* – a book criticising the political magnum opus of the physiocratic school, Pierre-Paul Le Mercier de la Rivière's *L'ordre naturel et essentiel des sociétés politiques* (1767 [2001]). It was accepted by his adversaries: one of the foremost members of the school, Nicolas Baudeau (1730–1792), used it in the title of his 1771 theoretical synthesis, *Première introduction à la philosophie économique, ou analyse des États policés*. The appellation however fits all the authors of the laissez-faire approach, from Boisguilbert to Jean-Baptiste Say (1767–1832): they all proposed a new political philosophy centred on the working of markets in competitive conditions, developed around three main axes: a theory of knowledge based on sensationism, a theory of self-interested action in society, and a peculiar conception of the efficient action of the legislator (Faccarello and Steiner 2008a, 2012). The point is well perceived by Mably, who blamed Quesnay of having begun "his political studies with agriculture, the nature of tax and commerce, and consequently considered these quite secondary objects of administration to be the fundamental principles for society" (Bonnot de Mably 1768 [1795]: 144) – Rousseau's opinion was not different.

Knowledge and action: the role of sensationist philosophy

The reference to sensationism is an important element of "philosophie économique" – Boisguilbert had of course no contact with this philosophy but his theological point of departure leads to the same conclusions as regards individuals' behaviour and political economy. It represented an important line of development for the old discourse on the passions, interest and self-love. On the one hand, sensationism allowed them to be harmonised. One passion might create good or evil, pleasure or pain: passions can therefore be dealt with in terms of their positive or negative consequences, both individually and collectively. On the other hand, the power of human reason, while praised, was also recognised to be imperfect – if only, as Boisguilbert insisted in a traditional way, because original sin enfeebled its powers and enslaved people to their self-love. Knowledge consequently became problematic: it was impossible to know the essential nature of things. To escape this situation, however, it was possible to be guided by clear rules which were supposed to prevent reason from being led astray – the philosophy of Descartes and the Port-Royal *La logique, ou l'art de penser* (Arnaud and Nicole 1662), for example, provided such rules. However, it was also possible to resort to experience and experimentation, and limit oneself to the knowledge of more or less regular phenomena and their relationships, in the traditional sciences such as physics and astronomy, for example, as well as in the novel "moral and political sciences": "we only know relationships. Wishing to say more is to confuse the limits of our spirit with that of nature" (Turgot 1750 [1913]: 168). In this perspective, the development of probability theory (to which the Port Royal *Logique* also contributed) and a probabilistic vision of science – from Christiaan Huygens (1629–1695) and Blaise Pascal (1623–1662) to Condorcet and Pierre-Simon de Laplace (1749–1827) – marked the eighteenth century. So did sensationism: based on John Locke's *Essay Concerning Human Understanding* (1690), which was translated into the French language by Pierre Coste and saw many editions throughout the century, sensationist philosophy was developed by Condillac in *Essai sur l'origine des connaissances humaines* (Bonnot de Condillac 1746) and *Traité des sensations* (1754). This approach generated the sensationist political economy of

Quesnay, Turgot and Condorcet, and the so-called French materialistic thought of Helvétius and d'Holbach.

Quesnay's article "Evidence" in the *Encyclopédie* showed that sensationism served as the foundation for an empirical theory of knowledge unencumbered by the mind/body dualism of the Cartesians. This new sensationism led to the idea that it is the utility of an action (the agreeable or disagreeable sensations) which determined behaviour (Quesnay 1756: para. 24); nevertheless, for Quesnay and the Physiocrats this approach was associated with the idea of a natural order. This meant that seeking the useful is not the criterion for the discovery of the good, but only the means of reaching it. In the socio-political construction of "legal despotism", the norm of economic government is fixed in the natural order, but it is the harmony of interests between different classes that permitted its realisation.

Turgot and Condorcet's approach is different: they rejected the idea of legal despotism. In their view, sensationism establishes fundamental natural human rights – liberty, security and property. It also serves to found a theory of subjective value based on utility and explain the determination of equilibrium prices in free markets. Upon the same foundation there also rested notions of justice and morality which, with the effective realisation of free trade, must guide the political and administrative organisation of the country.

The position of Helvétius and of d'Holbach is also different. They did not develop a theory of self-interested behaviour in markets under competitive conditions, but traced all behaviour to a calculation of pleasures and pains. In a society where economic activity played a significant part, this calculation involved a love of money which, since it permitted the reduction of pain and the increase of pleasure, became the most common passion of all. Deprivation of such a passion in such a society would remove any principle of action (Helvétius 1773, II: 580).

A theory of self-interested action and the "liberté du commerce"
For our authors, a natural and optimal political order must rest upon the harmony that economic activities spontaneously create in a regime of "liberté du commerce". Boisguilbert was the first to mark out this position at the end of the seventeenth century. He argued that if one was to uncover an order within economic activity it was enough to consider the motivations of agents, which are nothing but the translation into economic life of the selfish conduct of men, a form of conduct generated by original sin and the fall of man: "each thinks of attaining his own personal interest to the highest degree and with the greatest possible ease", he writes in 1705 in his first *Factum de la France* (Le Pesant de Boisguilbert 1695–1707 [1966]: 749). This order is characterised by what Boisguilbert calls "equilibrium" or "harmony", that is, a situation in which a specific system of relative prices prevails: the "prix de proportion". Also if, in *Le Détail de la France* (1695), he can emphasise "the harmony of the Republic, invisibly ruled by a superior power" (Le Pesant de Boisguilbert 1695–1707 [1966]: 621), this is because, in his opinion, this "superior power" consists of nothing other than free trade which forces people to be reasonable in markets and secure the realisation of these "prix de proportion". The basic passion of cupidity is thus neutralised. By confronting each individual's cupidity with the cupidity of all other people, competition eliminates socially harmful effects and enables one to obtain an orderly society, a harmony, as if each individual were motivated by charity.

Boisguilbert's ideas were of particular importance in the development of "philosophie économique" during the eighteenth century: Quesnay and Turgot developed them in various complementary ways. For example, the idea of a "maximising" behaviour based on interest was adopted and considered as natural. In Boisguilbert this attitude was connected with the fall of man and embedded in his Augustinian Jansenist approach. After him, the religious point of departure faded away and was substituted: it was replaced by the sensationist explanation of the behaviour of individuals, with the same consequences however in favour of "liberté du commerce" – as it is obvious, for example, from Turgot's writings. During the eighteenth century, the maximising behaviour of men was also metaphorically linked to the mathematical theory of "maximis et minimis" first developed by Pascal's friend Pierre de Fermat (who died in 1665) and then by Gottfried Wilhelm Leibniz (1646–1716), and the image was so pervasive that even critiques of "philosophie économique" – Ferdinando Galiani (1728–1787), for example – referred to it. All these developments, together with some ideas taken from the theologian Nicolas Malebranche (1638–1715) and Leibniz (Steiner 2005 [2010]: ch. 8), led to the progressive emergence of a new kind of rationality and cost–benefit calculations, even at the practical level of engineers who, during the eighteenth century, built roads, canals and bridges.

The efficiency of competition in markets is also forcefully asserted. Competition, it is stressed, allows the realisation of a system of equilibrium relative prices – Quesnay's "bon prix", Turgot's "valeurs appréciatives", or even Graslin's labour values. The social link between individuals and the equilibrium structure of the economy is fundamentally grasped in real terms, leading, at the end of the period, to Turgot and Graslin's respective theories of values. Money is however not unimportant. Prices are money prices: exchanges in markets are monetary and the flows of money between classes have to respect certain proportions to generate a state of "harmony". Even for Turgot, who grasps value in terms of utility, value cannot be expressed as such: only the "valeur appréciative" (equilibrium relative price) can be known. It is expressed, in an isolated transaction, by the quantity of the good against which a commodity is exchanged; or in general by each of the quantities of every other commodity against which it can be exchanged. Thanks to its intrinsic qualities, related to the requirements of the functions of measure of values and medium of exchange, one commodity detaches itself from the rest, and all the other commodities, by convention, express their value in terms of it, which therefore becomes the unique form of expression of value: money. What is basically unimportant are the quantity of (metallic) circulating money and absolute prices. For Boisguilbert and Turgot, for example – but the idea is also to be found in Quesnay and later in Say – the economy automatically generates the quantity of money it needs for transactions, by means of the circulation of bills of exchange or credit money.

> It is very certain . . . that the quantity [of money] does nothing for the opulence of a country in general . . .: [money] does not prevent those countries in possession of mines from being very impoverished. One man in that kind of country can spend two *écus* a day and pass his life in greater difficulty than someone who, in Languedoc, has no more than six *sols* to support himself. One can indeed say that the richer a country is, the more it is capable of doing without specie, for there are then more people prepared to accept instead a piece of paper, called a bill of exchange." (Le Pesant de Boisguilbert 1695–1707 [1966]: 617)

The quantity of circulating money is never the cause of an economic depression: that an economy "lacks money" is only an erroneous impression, the effect and not the cause of a crisis. Moreover, the interest rate is never considered as a monetary variable: it is a price determined between lenders and borrowers in the loanable funds market. These points run counter to the balance of trade doctrine. It is useless and absurd for the countries that do not possess mines to import precious metals through a surplus in foreign trade, because the quantity of money is irrelevant and does not impact on the interest rate.

A last important point must be stressed. While laissez-faire is an essential feature of "philosophie économique", authors also insist in linking free trade at home to free foreign trade: "liberté du commerce" at home, they argue, can only stabilise the price of corn and generate a harmonious system of relative prices if it is supported by freedom in foreign exchanges. The importance of free foreign trade is first qualitative through its action on the expectations of economic agents: the size of the flows of imports or exports, and their possible balance or imbalance, are of almost no significance in this regard. This new view of foreign trade, initiated by Boisguilbert, naturally conflicts with the balance of trade doctrine. However, it also provided a solution to the problem caused by the material interests of different countries, contesting the political solutions traditionally advanced in the field. The material interests of nations, the authors stressed, can be peacefully harmonised provided the merchants are able to trade freely in international markets, pursuing their own private interests, thus establishing the conditions for economic prosperity and stability. This policy of external free trade was presented by Le Mercier de la Rivière or Guillaume-François Le Trosne (1728–1780) as a political alternative to the policy of the "balance of powers in Europe" – considered as a source of disagreement and warfare between nations – whatever the attitude of the other countries.

> The principle of fraternity of nations is not ... only dictated by justice, but it is also in agreement with the interest of each nation, independently from the behaviour of the others. It should not simply be regarded as a beautiful moral idea, a worthy conception to be taught in schools of philosophy, but also as a practical maxim of government from which we can only detach ourselves to our own detriment. (Le Trosne 1777: 413–14)

Shaping economic policy: the role of the legislator
How can the new policy be implemented? How can the legislator be influenced if, unlike Turgot in 1774–76, the "philosophes économistes" are not themselves in power? Starting our period with Boisguilbert, the "philosophe économiste" had to act by gaining access to the king or his ministers. Boisguilbert had the traditional role that the monarchy offered the king's advisers: informing the king and proposing solutions. By the middle of the eighteenth century this changed, especially in the case of the Physiocrats and Turgot, with the idea of reforming the monarchy. Here there was a clear movement towards the "public sphere" and an appeal to "public opinion" or "the tribunal of opinion". Instead of papers and memoranda addressed to the royal authority, authors turned to printed works and even articles in journals intended for the public and for debate. As an ideal it functioned as a new way of thinking about politics and the legitimising of political action, seeking to convince the "reading and thinking public" – a good example of this can be found in the preliminary declarations of Turgot's edicts. Additionally, Turgot

and Baudeau began to define the social category that formed the basis of this new public opinion: the middle class. This can also be found in the writings of d'Holbach and Pierre-Louis Rœderer.

"Philosophie économique" also treated politics as a pedagogic practice: clear explanations must be given so that the opinions of the reasonable members of the public might be guided – Turgot's edicts are preceded with developed pedagogical preliminary declarations – thus defining the conditions of acceptability and legitimacy for the measures taken by the legislator. This pedagogical dimension is associated with various institutional structures. In some cases (Quesnay and Le Mercier de la Rivière for example) the importance assigned to public opinion, strongly associated with public education, went hand in hand with the role of the "philosophe économiste" as an expert. In other cases (for example, Dupont, Turgot and Condorcet), projects for the representation of interests through a system of assemblies were developed so that the interests of the landowners might be discovered and channelled – these interests being considered identical to the interests of the nation. In all cases, the importance of education and teaching was recognised.

However, what is the specific task of the legislator as regards markets and the economy? A first task concerns the functioning of markets in free competition. In this case the harmonisation of the self-interested behaviours of individuals was supposed to occur without any specific regulation – whether it be political like the regulation of the grain trade or religious like the ban on the lending at interest. In some cases, however, the legislator and the political power had to intervene, when the conditions for a smooth working of competition were not fulfilled. For example, according to Boisguilbert, when free foreign trade could not take place because of a war, the government was supposed to intervene in markets, and, through announcements of some sale or purchase of grain, according to the circumstances, influence agents' expectations in order to stabilise them and, via them, prices.

In some cases also, in the opinions of the authors, the mechanism of competition can never work and the legislator must intervene accordingly. This is the domain of market failures and of the so-called artificial harmonisation of interests, the main example of which is the problem of the financing of public goods (justice, police, defence, and so on), and taxation. Turgot, Graslin, Condorcet, Rœderer were perfectly aware of this. Facing the central question of free riding, they developed theories of state intervention and, in the quid pro quo perspective, mainly considered taxes as the (compulsory) prices of the services provided by the State. In addition, the legislator has also to decide on merit goods, such as instruction and education, and questions related to externalities.

One aspect of the public service of protection is worth mentioning because it is particularly symptomatic of the mentalities of the time. A traditional and widespread idea was that the merchant was dangerous because he was motivated by greed, and that the population therefore needed protection, especially during periods of grain shortage (requisitioning of grains, regulated price of bread, and so on). "Philosophie économique" saw instead the merchant in competitive markets as equal to Providence in regard to food distribution: it was therefore the merchant who needed protection from the irrational passions and ignorance of the people. Turgot ordered such a protection.

Conclusion

French Enlightenment saw an incredible amount of publications in each field of political economy and authors almost always stressed the links with and implications on political and moral philosophy. They almost all were aware that the age was aiming at deep reforms of structures, behaviours and minds, both in private and social life. This chapter has depicted the main currents of thought that in a sense monopolised attention at the time. These did not, of course, coexist peacefully. Lively polemics took place between them, for example, between Forbonnais and the Physiocrats. One of the most famous was launched by Galiani's attack, on the part of "commerce politique", against "philosophie économique", with the publication of his 1770 *Dialogues sur le commerce des blés* and the reaction of Turgot (Faccarello 1998). However, many attacks on the laissez-faire approach came also from other corners, for example, from Mably or Simon-Nicolas-Henri Linguet (1736–1794) (see, for example, Orain 2015). Individual positions sometimes evolved. Diderot, for example, praised the Physiocrats before supporting Galiani, and Turgot, one of the most important theoretician of laissez-faire, was a former member of the Vincent de Gournay circle – his 1759 "Eulogy of Vincent de Gournay" powerfully contributed to create the erroneous picture of Vincent de Gournay as an adept of laissez-faire. And while "philosophie économique" can be considered as the origin of the subjective theory of value, which developed later in France with Dupuit and Walras, an author such as Graslin (Graslin 1767 [1911], 1768 [2008]) also proposed a Rousseauist approach involving a labour theory of normal prices and distribution and the idea of a gravitation of market prices around natural prices that, a decade before Smith, led the foundations of (British) classical political economy (Faccarello 2009).

The period of the Revolution was also not sterile, especially on the institutional ground. The need for textbooks was felt, in parallel to the reorganisation of the national school system – Say published his *Traité d'économie politique* in 1803. An attempt to establish political economy as an academic discipline was also made in the ephemeral 1795 École Normale – the mathematician Alexandre Vandermonde (1735–1796) being in charge of the course (Faccarello 1989). Vandermonde's lectures were rather confused, but he stressed utility and the fact that labour is productive whenever it produces utility, an idea developed a few years later by Say and Antoine-Louis-Claude Destutt de Tracy (1754–1836). Two other mathematicians were of particular interest during the period: Nicolas-François Canard (1750–1833) and Charles François de Bicquilley (1738–1814). In 1799, each of them submitted independently a manuscript to the recently established Institut – Canard to the second section (moral and political sciences) and Bicquilley to the first (mathematics and physics). Both texts were published later, respectively as *Principes d'économie politique* (Canard 1801) and *Théorie élémentaire du commerce* (Bicquilley 1804), and both are outstanding attempts to formalise economic theory (Crépel 1998), Turgot's theory of prices in particular.

The French Revolution, however, marked in many fields the end of the period of the Enlightenment in France, with, in particular, Condorcet's emblematic philosophical testament, *Tableau historique des progrès de l'esprit humain* (Caritat de Condorcet 1794 [2004]). Since then the debates never ceased over the causes of the Revolution and the role that the politico-economic writings of the time played in it (the literature on the subject is abundant: for some recent views, see, for example, Charles and Steiner 2000;

Shovlin 2006; or Sonenscher 2007). The two main currents of thought outlined in this entry faded away with the end of the century, even if "philosophie économique" survived for some decades with J.-B. Say (Faccarello and Steiner 2008a, 2008b).

THIERRY DEMALS AND GILBERT FACCARELLO

See also:

Daniel Bernoulli (I); Pierre Le Pesant de Boisguilbert (I); Richard Cantillon (I); Marie-Jean-Antoine-Nicolas Caritat de Condorcet (I); Achilles-Nicolas Isnard (I); John Law (I); Mercantilism and the science of trade (II); Charles-Louis de Secondat de Montesquieu (I); François Quesnay and Physiocracy (I); Anne-Robert-Jacques Turgot (I).

References and further reading

Arnaud, A. and P. Nicole (1662), *La logique ou l'art de penser*, Paris: J. Guignart.
Baudeau, N. (1771), *Première introduction à la philosophie économique ou analyse des États policés*, reprinted 1910, Paris: Paul Geuthner.
Bicquilley, C.-F. (1804), *Théorie élémentaire du commerce*, Toul: Veuve Carez.
Bonnot de Condillac, É. (1746), *Essai sur l'origine des connaissances humaines*, Amsterdam: Pierre Mortier.
Bonnot de Condillac, É. (1754), *Traité des sensations*, Paris: Debure.
Bonnot de Mably, G. (1768), *Doutes proposés aux philosophes économistes sur l'ordre naturel et essentiel des sociétés politiques*, The Hague and Paris: Nyon & Veuve Durand, reprinted 1795 in *Collection complète des œuvres de l'abbé de Mably*, Paris: Desbrière, vol. 11, pp. 1–256.
Bonnot de Mably, G. (1795), 'Du commerce des grains', posthumously published in *Collection complète des œuvres de l'abbé de Mably*, Paris: Desbrière, vol. 13, pp. 242–98.
Boulainvilliers, H. de (1727), *Mémoires présentés à Monseigneur le Duc d'Orléans, régent de France*, vol 1, La Haye and Amsterdam: Aux dépends de la Compagnie.
Bove, L., T. Dagon and C. Secrétan (eds) (2007), *Qu'est-ce que les Lumières radicales? Libertinage, athéisme et spinozisme dans le tournant philosophique de l'âge classique*, Paris: Éditions Amsterdam.
Canard, N.F. (1801), *Principes d'économie politique*, Paris: Buisson.
Caritat de Condorcet, M.-J.-A.-N. (1794), *Tableau historique des progrès de l'esprit humain. Projets, esquisse, fragments et notes (1772–1794)*, ed. with comments by J.-P. Schandeler, P. Crépel and the Groupe Condorcet, 2004, Paris: INED.
Cary, J. (1717), *An Essay Towards Regulating the Trade and Employing the Poor of this Kingdom*, London: S. Collins.
Charles, L. and P. Steiner (2000), 'Entre Montesquieu et Rousseau. La Physiocratie parmi les origines intellectuelles de la Révolution française', *Études Jean-Jacques Rousseau*, **11**, 83–160.
Charles, L. and C. Théré (2008), 'The writing workshop of François Quesnay and the making of physiocracy', *History of Political Economy*, **40** (1), 1–42.
Charles, L, and C. Théré (2011), 'From Versailles to Paris: the creative communities of the physiocratic movement', *History of Political Economy*, **43** (1), 25–58.
Charles, L., F. Lefebvre and C. Théré (eds) (2011), *Le cercle de Vincent de Gournay. Savoirs économiques et pratiques administratives en France au milieu du XVIIIe siècle*, Paris: INED.
Cheney, P. (2010), *Revolutionary Commerce*, Cambridge, MA: Harvard University Press.
Child, J. (1693), *A New Discourse of Trade*, reprinted 1698, London: T. Sowle.
Crépel, P. (1998), 'Mathematical economics and probability theory: Charles-François Bicquilley's daring contribution', in G. Faccarello (ed.), *Studies in the History of French Political Economy*, London: Routledge, pp. 78–119.
Demals, T. (2004), 'Une économie politique de la nation agricole sous la Constituante?', *Revue française d'histoire des idées politiques*, **20**, 2nd semester, 307–33.
Demals, T. and A. Hyard (2015), 'Forbonnais, the two balances and the Économistes', *European Journal of the History of Economic Thought*, **22** (3), 445–72.
Diderot, D. and J. Le Rond d'Alembert (eds) (1751–72), *Encyclopédie, ou Dictionnaire raisonné des sciences, des arts et des métiers, par une société de gens de lettres*, 17 vols, Paris: Briasson, David, Le Breton and Durand.
Dupont, P.-S. (1768), *De l'origine et des progrès d'une science nouvelle*, London and Paris: Dessaint.
Dutot, N. (1738), *Réflexions politiques sur les finances et le commerce*, English trans. 1739, *Political Reflections upon the Finances and Commerce of France*, London: A. Millar.
Faccarello, G. (1986), *Aux origines de l'économie politique libérale: Pierre de Boisguilbert*, Paris: Anthropos, revised edn. 1999, *The Foundations of Laissez-faire*, London: Routledge.
Faccarello, G. (1989), 'L'évolution de la pensée économique pendant la Révolution: Alexandre Vandermonde

ou la croisée des chemins', in various authors, *Politische Ökonomie und Französische Revolution*, Trier: Schriften aus dem Karl-Marx-Haus, pp. 75–121.

Faccarello, G. (1998), 'Galiani, Necker and Turgot: a debate on economic reforms and policies in eighteenth century France', in G. Faccarello (ed.), *Studies in the History of French Political Economy*, London: Routledge, pp. 120–95.

Faccarello, G. (2006), 'An "exception culturelle"? French sensationist political economy and the shaping of public economics', *European Journal of the History of Economic Thought*, **13** (1), 1–38.

Faccarello, G. (2009), 'The enigmatic Mr Graslin. A Rousseauist bedrock for classical economics?', *European Journal of the History of Economic Thought*, **16** (1), 1–40.

Faccarello, G. and P. Steiner (eds) (1990), *La pensée économique pendant la Révolution française*, Grenoble: Presses Universitaires de Grenoble.

Faccarello, G. and P. Steiner (2008a), 'Interests, sensationism and the science of the legislator: French *Philosophie économique*, 1695–1830', *European Journal of the History of Economic Thought*, **15** (1), 1–23.

Faccarello, G. and P. Steiner (2008b), 'Religion and political economy in early-nineteenth-century France', *History of Political Economy*, **40** (annual supplement), 26–61.

Faccarello, G. and P. Steiner (2012), '"Philosophie économique" and money in France, 1750–1776: the stakes of a transformation', *European Journal of the History of Economic Thought*, **19** (3), 325–53.

Fœssel, M. (ed.) (2009), 'Refaire les lumières?', *Esprit*, special issue (August–September), Paris: Le Seuil.

Gay, P. (1966), *The Enlightenment: An Interpretation*, vol. 1, *The Rise of Modern Paganism*, New York and London: W.W. Norton.

Gay, P. (1969), *The Enlightenment: An Interpretation*, vol. 2, *The Science of Freedom*, New York and London: W.W. Norton.

Graslin, J.-J.-L. (1767), *Essai analytique sur la richesse et sur l'impôt*, reprinted 1911, Paris: Geuthner.

Graslin, J.-J.-L. (1768), 'Dissertation sur la question proposée par la Société économique de St. Pétersbourg', new edn with introduction and notes by G. Faccarello, in P. Le Pichon and A. Orain (eds) (2008), *Jean-Joseph-Louis Graslin (1727–1790): le temps des Lumières à Nantes*, Rennes: Presses Universitaires de Rennes, pp. 293–317 (where the original pagination is indicated).

Hazard, P. (1935), *La crise de la conscience européenne, 1680–1715*, Paris: Boivin.

Hazard, P. (1946), *La pensée européenne au XVIIIe siècle, de Montesquieu à Lessing*, Paris: Boivin.

Helvétius, C.-A. (1773), *De l'homme, de ses facultés intellectuelles et de son éducation*, 2 vols, reprinted 1989, Paris: Fayard.

Hirschman, A.O. (1977), *The Passions and the Interests. Political Arguments for Capitalism Before its Triumph*, Princeton, NJ: Princeton University Press.

Israel, J. (2001), *Radical Enlightenment: Philosophy and the Making of Modernity, 1650–1750*, Oxford: Oxford University Press.

Israel, J. (2006), *Enlightenment Contested: Philosophy, Modernity, and the Emancipation of Man, 1670–1752*, Oxford: Oxford University Press.

Israel, J. (2010), *A Revolution of the Mind: Radical Enlightenment and the Intellectual Origins of Modern Democracy*, Princeton, NJ: Princeton University Press.

Jacob, M.C. (1981), *The Radical Enlightenment: Pantheists, Freemasons and Republicans*, Baltimore, MD: Johns Hopkins University Press, revised edn 2006, Lafayette, LA: Cornerstone.

Kant, I. (1784), 'Beantwortung der Frage, Was ist Aufklärung?', English trans. in I. Kant (1963), *On History*, ed. L.W. Beck, New York: Macmillan, pp. 3–10.

King, C. (ed.) (1713), *The British Merchant, or Commerce Preserv'd*, 2nd edn 1721, 3 vols, London: John Darby, reprinted 1968, 2 vols, New York: A.M. Kelley.

Law, J. (1715), 'Mémoire sur les banques', in P. Harsin (ed.) (1934), *Œuvres complètes*, vol. 2, Paris: Sirey, pp. 5–39.

Le Mercier de la Rivière, P.-P. (1767), *L'ordre naturel et essentiel des sociétés politiques*, reprinted 2001, Paris: Fayard.

Le Pesant de Boisguilbert, P. ([1695–1707] 1966), 'Œuvres manuscrites et imprimées de Boisguilbert', in J. Hecht (ed), *Pierre de Boisguilbert ou la naissance de l'économie politique*, vol. 2, Paris: INED.

Le Trosne, G.-F. (1777), *De l'ordre social*, Paris: Debure.

Lilti, A. (2009), 'Comment écrit-on l'histoire des Lumières? Spinozisme, radicalisme et philosophie', *Annales – Histoire, Sciences Sociales*, January–February, 171–206.

Locke, J. (1690), *An Essay Concerning Human Understanding*, London: Thomas Baffet.

Manin, B. (2001), 'Montesquieu, la république et le commerce', *European Journal of Sociology/Archives européennes de sociologie*, **42** (3), 573–602.

Martin, T. (ed.) (2003), *Arithmétique politique dans la France du XVIIIe siècle*, Paris: INED.

Masseau, D. (2000), *Les ennemis des philosophes. L'antiphilosophie au temps des Lumières*, Paris: Albin Michel.

McMahon, D.M. (2001), *Enemies of the Enlightenment. The French Counter-Enlightenment and the Making of Modernity*, Oxford: Oxford University Press.

Melon, J.-F. (1734a), *Essai politique sur le commerce*, 2nd edn 1735, Amsterdam: Changuion.
Melon, J.-F. (1734b), *Essai politique sur le commerce*, 3rd edn 1736, Amsterdam: Changuion.
Miklaszewska, J. and A. Tomaszewska (eds) (2014), *The Radical Enlightenment*, *Diametros. An Online Journal of Philosophy*, **40** (June), special issue, accessed September 2015 at http://www.diametros.iphils.uj.edu.pl/index.php/diametros/issue/view/42.
Monod, A. (1916), *De Pascal à Chateaubriand. Les défenseurs français du Christianisme de 1670 à 1802*, Paris: Librairie Félix Alcan.
Montesquieu, C.-L. de Secondat de (1727), *Réflexions sur la monarchie universelle en Europe*, reprinted 1964 in *Œuvres complètes*, Paris: Le Seuil.
Montesquieu, C.-L. de Secondat de (1748), *De l'esprit des lois*, reprinted 1964 in *Œuvres complètes*, Paris: Le Seuil.
Moreau de Maupertuis, P.-L. (1755), 'Éloge de M. de Montesquieu', reprinted 1768 in *Œuvres de Maupertuis*, vol. 3, Lyon: Jean-Marie Bruyset, pp. 386–433.
Murphy, A. (1986), 'Le développement des idées économiques en France', *Revue d'histoire moderne et contemporaine*, **33** (October–December), 521–41.
Murphy, A. (1998), 'The enigmatic Monsieur du Tot', in G. Faccarello (ed.), *Studies in the History of French Political Economy*, London: Routledge, pp. 57–77.
Orain, A. (ed.) (2015), *Antiphysiocratic Perspectives in Eighteenth-Century France*, *European Journal of the History of Economic Thought*, **22** (3), special issue.
Petty, W. (1690), 'Political arithmetick', in C.H. Hull (ed.) (1899), *The Economic Writings of Sir William Petty*, vol. 1, Cambridge, Cambridge University Press, pp. 233–313.
Plumard de Dangeul, L.-J. (1754), *Remarques sur les avantages et les désavantages de la France et de l'Angleterre par rapport au commerce et aux autres sources de la puissance des États*, 3rd edn, Dresden.
Quesnay, F. (1756), 'Évidence', in C. Théré, L. Charles and J.-C. Perrot (eds) (2005), *Œuvres économiques complètes et autres textes*, vol. 1, Paris: INED, pp. 61–90.
Say, J.-B. (1803), *Traité d'économie politique*, 2 vols, Paris: Deterville.
Shovlin, J. (2006), *The Political Economy of Virtue. Luxury, Patriotism, and the Origins of the French Revolution*, Ithaca, NY: Cornell University Press.
Skornicki, A. (2006), 'L'État, l'expert et le négociant: le réseau de la science du commerce sous Louis XV', *Genèses*, **4** (65), 4–26.
Sonenscher, M. (2007), *Before the Deluge. Public Debt, Inequality, and the Intellectual Origins of the French Revolution*, Princeton, NJ and Oxford: Princeton University Press.
Steiner, P. (1998), *La 'science nouvelle' de l'économie politique*, Paris: Presses Universitaires de France.
Steiner, P. (2005), *L'école durkheimienne et l'économie. Sociologie, religion et connaissance*, Geneva: Droz, English trans. 2010, *Durkheim and the Birth of Economic Sociology*, Princeton, NJ: Princeton University Press.
Sternhell, Z. (2006), *Les Anti-Lumières. Du XVIIIe siècle à la Guerre froide*, Paris: Fayard, revised edn, 2010, Paris: Gallimard, English trans. D. Maisel (2009), *The Anti-Enlightenment Tradition*, New Haven, CT: Yale University Press.
Théré, C. (1998), 'Economic publishing and authors: 1566–1789', in G. Faccarello (ed.), *Studies in the History of French Political Economy. From Bodin to Walras*, London: Routledge, pp. 1–56.
Turgot, A.-R.-J. (1750), 'Remarques critiques sur les *Réflexions philosophiques* de Maupertuis sur l'origine des langues et la signification des mots', in G. Schelle (ed) (1913), *Œuvres de Turgot et documents le concernant*, vol. 1, Paris: Félix Alcan, pp. 157–79.
Turgot, A.-R.-J. (1759), 'Éloge de Vincent de Gournay', in G. Schelle (ed.) (1913), *Œuvres de Turgot et documents le concernant*, vol. 1, Paris: Félix Alcan, pp. 595–623.
Velde, F.R. (2012), 'The life and time of Nicolas Dutot', *Journal of the History of Economic Thought*, **34** (1), 67–107.
Véron de Forbonnais, F. (1753), *Un Extrait chapitre par chapitre du livre de l'Esprit des Loix*, Amsterdam: Arktée and Merkus.
Véron de Forbonnais, F. (1754), *Elémens du commerce*, 2 vols, Leiden: Briasson.
Véron de Forbonnais, F. (1755a), *Examen des avantages et des désavantages de la prohibition des toiles peintes*, Marseille: Carapatria.
Véron de Forbonnais, F. (1755b), *Questions sur le commerce des François au Levant*, Marseille: Carapatria.
Véron de Forbonnais, F. (1767), *Principes et observations œconomiques*, Amsterdam: Marc Michel Rey.
Vincent de Gournay, J.C.M. (c.1752), *Traité sur le commerce de Josiah Child avec les remarques inédites de Vincent de Gournay*, reprinted 1983, T. Tsuda (ed.), Tokyo: Kinokuniya.
Vincent de Gournay, J.C.M. (1993), *Mémoires et lettres*, T. Tsuda (ed.), Tokyo: Kinokuniya.

Italian Enlightenment

The Italian Enlightenment is one of the great intellectual achievements of Europe's *siècle des Lumières*. Both its Southern (Naples) and its Northern (Milan) branches cooperate to produce perhaps the greatest contribution of Italian culture to the development of a modern European tradition of civil rights and enlightened governance. After the Second World War, there was an intense flourishing of studies, particularly in Italy (with a worldwide readership, though), on the Italian Enlightenment. Much of the post-war Italian production on the Enlightenment has been a response to the emerging need for deeper research on the roots of western culture and on the civic values of our societies so much shattered by the traumatic experiences of a new kind of war ravaging our cities in Europe and in other parts of the world. A single name, among many others, will be enough to give the idea: Franco Venturi's studies on the eighteenth-century's reforms.

Much less has been done by economists and historians of economics but economic analysis is the core issue of the Italian Enlightenment, as illustrated by Schumpeter (see below). The economic discipline – originally called civil economy in eighteenth-century Naples and Cameral science (or public economy) in Milan – was indeed prominent in the historical experience of the Italian Enlightenment, although the salience of the discipline still is, to the present day, only imperfectly reflected in much of the recent historiography. A new line of research on the Italian Enlightenment, rooted in a retrieval of the economic discipline of the time, is currently developing (for an overview, see Porta and Scazzieri 2014). It is not surprising that Italy is the country where the first university Chairs in the world were created for the discipline during the second half of the eighteenth century.

Schumpeter's classic *History of Economic Analysis* (1954: 177) is outspoken in his assessment of the high level of the Italian contribution. Italian economists, Schumpeter observes, deserve "the honours of the field of pre-Smithian system production". He adds: "The regionalism of Italian life divides them into groups. But I can discern only two 'schools' in the strict sense of the term . . . the Neapolitan and the Milanese." This entry presents a comparison and discusses the reciprocal integration of these two main schools in Italy, taking into account also the teaching and influence of the two incumbents to the respective Chairs, Antonio Genovesi (1712–1769) in Naples, from 1754, and Cesare Beccaria (1738–1794) in Milan, from 1769, especially through their respective textbooks, the *Lezioni di economia civile* of Genovesi (1765–67 [2013]) and the *Elementi di economia pubblica* of Beccaria (1984–2014). The two professors do share an economic perspective, which appears to be at the root of the whole of their literary production.

In general terms the Italian Enlightenment shares the French Enlightenment's interest in rational governance and the Scottish Enlightenment's interest in civil society. However, it is different from both in its close attention to the interplay between legislation and moral sentiments, civic culture and economic development, fiscal technique and social structure.

The Italian Enlightenment largely focuses on sociability embedded in the country's civic traditions. Both the Neapolitan and the Milanese branches of the Italian Enlightenment address social co-ordination and analyse existing civil arrangements by comparing those arrangements with suitable prototypes derived from ethics and philosophy. That is conducive to a characteristic combination of theoretical ambition and practical outlook, which leads the Italian Enlightenment to be interested in a detailed investigation of the institutional context of rights, entitlements and reform policies.

After a general overview ("A Civil Enlightenment"), the two subsequent sections deal with the historical contexts of the Milanese and Neapolitan Enlightenments respectively. Those sections also discuss the key figures of the Italian civil Enlightenment, from the Milanese economists, legal theorists and administrators such as Cesare Beccaria and Pietro Verri (1728–1797) to the Tuscan economist Pompeo Neri (1706–1776) and the Neapolitan philosophers, economists and legal theorists among whom Paolo Mattia Doria (1667–1746), Ferdinando Galiani (1728–1787), Antonio Genovesi, Gaetano Filangieri (1752–1788) and Francesco Mario Pagano (1748–1799) are particularly important. A section summarizing the core contributions of the Italian Enlightenment to the history of economic thought and their influence on subsequent stages of the developments of political economy in Italy concludes.

A Civil Enlightenment

Recent analyses (particularly Bruni and Zamagni 2007; Quadrio Curzio 2007) argue that the tradition of economic thought in Italy has a characteristic expression in the form of "economia civile", which is the result of the combination of three different elements: (1) a conception of the economic order based on civil society rather than based on state authority; (2) a setting based on the evolution of institutions through continuing reform; (3) a scientific and cultural emphasis on practical applications or policy issues. Those three elements acquire, as we shall see, a special sense in the context of the Italian *vita civile*.

The resulting discipline has been showing since the start the strong tendency to cluster around the following points: (1) a social and ethical concern, leading to a close analysis of institutions and more generally the link of economic with extra-economic elements; (2) a close interest into dynamic economics; (3) the adoption of an *ante-litteram* history-of-economic-analysis approach.

That the idea of "vita civile", or "civil life", is a staple reference in the Italian tradition since the Middle Age and through the Renaissance is shown by classic examples of authors from the fourteenth to the seventeenth century such as Coluccio Salutati, Leonardo Bruni, Matteo Palmieri, Paolo Mattia Doria. They are some of the scholars discussed by the intellectual historians of humanism: Eugenio Garin, Jacob Burckhardt and Hans Baron. Expressions such as "vita civile" and "umanesimo civile" go together. Eugenio Garin's book (1952) on Italian humanism – first published in Bern as *Der italienische Humanismus* in 1942 and translated into other languages after the war – probably provides the best source for the interested reader. As Hans Baron (1955: 92) writes, Italian humanism is civic humanism precisely because it sympathizes with the ideals of the "vita activa et politica" of the citizen of the ancient republics. At the same time there is an important influence of the Christian tradition and of Catholic faith in the whole process. That is hardly surprising; as Peter Brown (1978) has shown, the very rise of Christianity through late antiquity has to be explained precisely as the result of a special attitude of the Christian communities in Italy to develop new styles of human and social relations.

Coluccio Salutati, for example, was the mentor of Bernardino da Siena (1380–1444), one of the greatest representatives of the Franciscan world and a refined intellectual, who extolled civil life and had a view of social and economic development as the main focus of his whole approach. (On the active and creative role of the Franciscans, see Negri Zamagni and Porta 2012.)

A "glacial period", as it were, would very soon follow historically and produce a time of "civil darkness". Contradictory to appearances, that was a necessary passage to be understood in the reconstruction of the Italian Enlightenment as civil enlightenment. While the economic discipline through modern times in Europe reflects the diverse attempts of different schools to resolve the question of the nature and the causes of the wealth of nations, the debate on the foundations of social order gradually turns into a vital crossroad in economic research. That is, the perspective where the Italians are outstanding. Machiavelli and Hobbes respectively – though at a distance in time – both disseminate a pessimistic view on the nature of man and on the chances of a spontaneous social order, thus opening the way to a whole breed of thinkers who were strongly inclined to rely on some kind of demiurgic intervention as the unavoidable condition for a civil order to come about and survive. Their influence shakes the faith in civic virtues as the foundation of civil life. A further turning point occurs early in the eighteenth century, when Mandeville's *Fable of the Bees* (1705 [1714]) argues convincingly that virtue is not necessarily conducive to social order and prosperity. Virtue, in Mandeville's view, may well be a hindrance for that purpose and thereby a source of misery and distress. The idea (if not the name, which came about later) of heterogenesis of ends thus surfaces with Mandeville early in the eighteenth century, although we should not forget the French Jansenist tradition with Jean Domat, Pierre Nicole and Pierre de Boisguilbert. The same idea would come forth, as a full and constructive argument leading to a new idea of the social order, with the Italians, before re-appearing as one of the building blocks of the British classical school of economists. The contributions of the Neapolitan philosopher Giambattista Vico (1668–1744) are fundamental at this point and give evidence of the continuity of civil enlightenment with respect to the tradition of *vita civile*.

From that angle, the British classical school owes something to the Italian Enlightenment, perhaps even more than it owes to the Physiocrats, although, admittedly, the Italian influence was largely an indirect one and it is not explicitly discussed, for example, by Adam Smith. The Italian Enlightenment is no longer naively civil (in the humanists' sense), but it is civil in a more sophisticated sense. As Bruni and Zamagni argue (2007: 68 ff.), the Italian economists develop and share the persuasion that "without civil virtues there is no room for market economy", thus paving the way to "laying down a new anthropological and ethical foundation for a new commercial society". The competitive market must be conceived as a form of co-operation based on trust. The novelty introduced by the Italian authors, with respect to Mandeville, is that the work of the principle of the heterogenesis of ends is not seen to be opposed to civic virtues (as it is in Mandeville), but it is subsidiary to them. This is clear, at least since the work of Giambattista Vico (see Bruni and Zamagni 2007: 84–5), and Vico "was a universal reference point in Naples in eighteenth-century philosophy" (ibid.).

Giambattista Vico (*Scienza nuova*, 1725) writes of a "divine legislative mind", which "takes man's passions . . . and turns them into civil orders". Smith would later speak of an "invisible hand" (see Roncaglia, 2005), particularly in the *Theory of Moral Sentiments*

(1759 [1976]) and later in the *Wealth of Nations* (1776 [1976]). The Italian tradition is at the source of such developments: the old civic tradition of Italian Humanism re-surfaces in a new, more sophisticated form. That is the basis of the Italian Enlightenment.

The Neapolitan School

Antonio Genovesi

The earliest school of economic principles, which develops the theoretical and practical implications of the Civil Enlightenment in Italy, is the Neapolitan school. The phrase "economia civile" was first used by its leader, Antonio Genovesi. He is the genuine heir of the previous generation of intellectuals in Naples, including Giambattista Vico, Pietro Giannone, and Paolo Mattia Doria, who had lived under the spell of Cartesianism and Neo-Platonism. Genovesi instead lived in an age of reforms with a strong drive to achieve economic independence through economic and civil development. At the same time the scholastic notion of natural law and of "bonum commune" largely loom behind his work.

Genovesi, the first incumbent to a Chair of political economy in the world, taught "economia civile", from 1753, at the University of Naples and he was universally recognized as the leading figure of the Italian School. To him our discipline was, in fact, "economia civile", with the special approach to which historians of economic thought are returning today. His *Lezioni di economia civile* (1765–67 [2013]) remain his main work.

To Genovesi an idea of well-being is fundamental to explain the functioning of civil economy with its frame of relationships created by informal norms and conventions. That includes reciprocity, mutual friendship, confidence and trust. Thus the idea of civil economy exhibits perfect continuity with respect to the humanist civic ideal. In Genovesi's system there are three levels of agency in society: the individual, civil society and the state, whereas, for example, in Hobbes civil society and the state are not distinct but coincident. This tripartite scheme is, among other sources, reminiscent of Montesquieu's insistence on the significance of the *corps intermédiaires*: Montesquieu had a very large influence on the Italian Enlightenment.

The presence of a strong civil society is for Genovesi a precondition for economic development. That is why it remains all important to increase and support civil virtues, and particularly (especially echoing Paolo Mattia Doria) reciprocal trust. Genovesi is distinctly Aristotelian on happiness as *eudaimonia*, while his attachment to the idea of spontaneous order clearly echoes Vico. He appreciates the advantages of luxury, he thinks highly of free trade, and he perfectly understands the whole hidden work of the dispersed knowledge, which would later be named "invisible hand" particularly (but not only) in the Scottish Enlightenment. It is no doubt true – Genovesi writes (1765–67 [2013], I: ch. 17, s. xii) – that "people endeavouring to enrich aim only at their own self interest", but "it is no less true that enriching they promote the public advantage by enriching the whole nation". Little wonder that the economic discipline, in the Italian tradition, would later (1845) be called by Ludovico Bianchini "scienza del ben vivere sociale", or the science of "good social living", a label which would probably be deemed appropriate for Smith as well, though clearly much less so for Ricardo or Marx, who only had an indirect interest into public happiness as such. It must be added, however, that Bianchini himself did not realize all the implications of Genovesi's approach. It is only nowadays that we come to realize all that in full, in a new scientific climate leading to a generalized historiographic revision of the sources of the economic thought of the Enlightenment. That happens also outside Italy although each branch of the Enlightenment has its own *Sonderweg* (exceptionalism). For the French Enlightenment, for example, the work on Boisguilbert (1646–1714) was especially significant along parallel lines with the case of Italy, although with differences owing in particular to the influence of Port Royal in France with Blaise Pascal (1623–1662), Pierre Nicole (1625–1695), Jean Domat (1625–1696) and others. The best known case of an explicit historiographic revision concerns Adam Smith (see Winch 1978). For the Italian case, and particularly for the reading of Genovesi, Bruni and Sudgen (2000) was an important milestone.

Since 1724 the Kingdom of Naples had acquired some degree of independence under the Bourbon rule and the decades following that event were an era of new hopes for a civil and enlightened government. Genovesi was in fact, together with his direct sponsor Bartolomeo Intieri (1678–1757), one of a group of thinkers who tried to understand the failures of the old regime and to find new routes to economic and social development. Ten years older than Smith, he parallels the latter's experience in the transition from philosophy to the economic discipline. Genovesi himself described the transition as a passage from *metafisico* to *mercatante*, from metaphysicist to merchant (see Bellamy, 1987).

Genovesi was convinced that culture, philosophy and science must serve the improvement of society and produce public happiness. As we have seen above, the Italian Enlightenment puts the emphasis on linking together ethics, institutions and the common weal. Thus Genovesi's *Discorso sopra il vero fine delle lettere e delle scienze* (1753 [1962]) – the opening lecture of his Chair – has been considered the manifesto of the Italian Enlightenment. It is here that he expresses most clearly his ideas on development, philosophy and the economic science. The purpose of letters and sciences is to improve the well-being, the happiness, of the people.

In his anthropology, Genovesi distinctly shuns reducing human motivations to self-interest. In his *Diceosìna* (1766 [1973]), he argues that some passions express self-love ("forza concentriva"), but others reflect "love of the species" ("forza espansiva"). Genovesi accepts the Newtonian idea that any phenomenon (human, social and physical) can be explained as an "equilibrium" between two opposite forces, the attractive and the repulsive. More precisely, in the Newtonian system of planets the key idea is that the real force is the gravitational one (the attractive), the repulsive (the centrifugal) being a "fictive force". Likewise, the large majority of human actions depend, in Genovesi's view, basically on the attractive force. From such a standpoint he offers criticisms on Mandeville's *Fable of the Bees* and on Hobbes's *Leviathan* (Bruni and Porta 2003; also Bianchini 1982).

In chapter 10 of the *Lezioni* (Genovesi 1765–67 [2013]) Genovesi argues that solitary men are wild, cruel, unforgiving, since in solitude there is no room for the diffusive force of the human heart, and only the concentrative force works, which makes men hypochondriac and brutal. In other words Genovesi's thought is based on "sociality", that is, the desire for relationships with our fellows, coming from a natural (or "ontological") character of the human being. Sociality is "an indelible feature of our nature".

More precisely, Genovesi argues that what is really typical of man as an animal species is "reciprocal assistance". He does heed the natural law tradition, as he maintains (Genovesi 1765–67 [2013]: ch. 1) that each person has a natural right to the benefits of reciprocal assistance and a corresponding duty to provide them to others. In agreement with the Italian civic tradition, Genovesi understands economic relations, such as exchange and production, as relations of reciprocal assistance: in an economic system, each agent is helping others to satisfy their wants. On this conception of the economy, engagement in economic relations is turned into an exercise of virtue based on reciprocal trust, which is both virtuous and rational: this, as an idea of rationality, is quite different from the idea surviving in latter-day rational choice theory. The difference is mainly due to an emphasis on sociality and we-thinking. Social relations, in other words, cannot be explained by instrumental rationality; for they are not just means by which, or constraints within which, we pursue self-interest. In Genovesi's work there is a strong sense that interpersonal relationships are valuable for their own sake: the main advantage of society is not so much to be found in its production of material goods, but in the enjoyment of social relationships.

Finally, Genovesi puts forward a theory of spontaneous order, which can be summarized in the following steps: (1) human beings naturally look for their interest; (2) their true interest is happiness; (3) happiness means *eudaimonia*, full self-realization by means of virtue, that is, the promotion of the happiness of others – he accepts as a universal law that it is impossible to make our happiness without granting the happiness of others; and (4) if all people act with a view to happiness, they will be virtuous and public happiness will result and increase.

These and similar concepts are echoed in other economic works belonging to the Neapolitan school in the latter half of the eighteenth century. One of the best examples is afforded by Gaetano Filangieri (1753–1788), who gives an effective idea of the relationship of commerce and wealth and develops Genovesi's own emphasis on trust or "fede pubblica".

Ferdinando Galiani

Parallel to Genovesi, though considerably younger, Ferdinando Galiani is the other outstanding economist of the Neapolitan school. The problem of monetary reform is one of the main issues, together with laissez-faire and free markets (particularly free market of staple food, the so-called problem of "annona", the Latin and Italian word for provisions), in the economy by the mid-eighteenth century. The author who best illustrates the case among the Neapolitans at the time is Galiani. His main works are *Della moneta* (*Money*, 1751, see Galiani 1975), on one side, and the *Dialogues sur le commerce des bleds* (*Dialogues on Grain Trade*) published in French in 1770, on the other. Although Galiani does include a passing mention in *Della moneta* to the "cunning of reason", as the work of a superior hand (or providence), his main interests turn distinctly more technical.

Galiani's early treatise *Della moneta* is quite often quoted by historians of economics as a forerunner of the marginal utility theory of value, although both labour cost and utility are extant in his analysis on the foundations of value (see Pasinetti 1984). Galiani is outstanding in putting forward the solution to the famous paradox of value (or "water-diamond paradox"), by giving a rigorous form to the argument based on a combination of utility with scarcity (or rarity), an argument which is so often resorted to in the writings of the Italians, at least since Bernardo Davanzati's *Lezione delle monete*

(*Discourse upon Coins*) of 1588. Hutchison (1988) offers a rigorous reconstruction of the utility-cum-scarcity approach to value before Smith.

The craving for value theory among economists of many generations, together with the use of the French language in the *Dialogues*, has had the effect of making Galiani a much better known author compared with Genovesi. Galiani had many connections in Paris, where he lived, and his *Dialogues* were elegantly put in French by his close friends, among whom were Louise d'Épinay and, in particular, Denis Diderot. Concerning *Della moneta*, it was Galiani's main purpose to establish a natural value for money, a value which would not be subject to artificial influences and manipulations. That also corresponded with the main purpose of the monetary reforms of the time, designed to get rid of (or at least limit) all forms of "ideal" or "imaginary" money, quite often used as "account money" in current transactions. The metallist philosophy lurks behind the monetary reforms. What is at stake, along with the practical question of the widespread "monetary disorder", so often talked about at the time, is the proper scientific standing of the new science of political economy as such. Indeed, the two principles of metallism and cartalism (in Knapp's language, notoriously retrieved by Schumpeter) are both present in Galiani: which has given rise to a number of disputes about the real meaning of his monetary theory (see, in particular, Cesarano 2012; Costabile 2016).

Unlike Genovesi, Galiani was not an academic. He was a learned intellectual who entered public administration and ended up (as just hinted) spending a number of years (1759–69) in Paris as the Secretary to the Embassy of the King of Naples. That was during the 1760s when Paris was the cultural capital of the world and the physiocratic school, or the *économistes* (as they were called), was at the height of its success. The *Dialogues*, for example, discuss the hot issue of free trade of grains. Galiani offers an example of his opportunistic character by changing sides (with respect to previous treatments) and by producing a scathing onslaught on the physiocratic doctrine, with his criticism of free trade in the *Dialogues*. Also, in his first treatise of 1751, Galiani was to a large extent the sort of pragmatic economist who does not abide by any principle of sorts. He is thereby much less impressive, compared with Genovesi, as a social philosopher and reformer. At the same time he is more effective and brilliant in style and his works are full of insights and they have in general conquered a wider readership and larger space in any syllabus of history of economic thought. It should be noted, however, that some authors have pointed out that Galiani's method is not reducible to mere pragmatism, but it is reminiscent of Montesquieu's methods applied to economic matters (see Faccarello 1994, 1998).

The Milanese School

The "School of Milan", as Voltaire called it at the time of Beccaria's visit to Paris in the mid-1760s, gives an opportunity to examine political economy during the time span from the mercantilist to the "classical" era. That is the age to which the "Italian school" belongs. Within the "Italian school", Pietro Verri is the main leader and mentor of the Milanese branch of the school. The notion of "felicità pubblica", or public happiness, is probably the best phrase to convey the meaning and significance of the contribution of the Milanese. Their concern was first about happiness in a utilitarian vein. Genovesi and Galiani were also making use of a utilitarian frame of reasoning; however, the utilitarian language becomes more explicit and richer in Milan. At the same time the public dimension becomes more prominent and intertwined with the practical needs of the reforms. Economists here are directly involved with the design and practical implementation of the Maria-Theresian Reforms in the Milanese territories. The predecessors of the generation of the Verris (Pietro and his brother Alessandro, 1741–1816) and their associates are Ludovico Antonio Muratori (1672–1750), who had put forward the ideal of public happiness, and Pompeo Neri, the Tuscan economist and administrator, who had worked on the practical side of the promotion of public happiness with his decisive contribution to the cadastral reform of the 1750s.

Pietro Verri was born in Milan into a noble family. During a short military career through the 1750s, he developed a lifelong friendship with Henry Lloyd, the Welsh officer who has some place in the history of economic thought for his work on money and as an early mathematical economist. Verri soon became convinced that political economy had to be at the centre of all serious social and political interests. He never conceived, though, of political economy as a separate scientific subject, but as part of a more elaborate and multi-level scientific enterprise, which largely parallels what Genovesi called "economia civile". Compared with Genovesi, Verri and his followers were more inclined to take an active part in the administration under the Habsburg monarchy in Vienna, but also with considerable autonomies affecting the whole of the Lombard region, of which Milan is the centre. Verri's project to build a new science led him to found the Accademia dei Pugni – the punching academy, a curious name – and the periodical *Il Caffè* (*The Coffee House*), sometimes described as the Italian *Spectator*, published between 1764 and 1766. These initiatives served the purpose of gathering together a number of friends who shared a common scientific spirit, in a number of different fields, and the need for cultural exchange through conversation and work in common. Cesare Beccaria, by far the best-known name of the Italian economic school at the time of the rise of the Italian Enlightenment, was one of Verri's younger associates.

Pietro Verri

The Italian school of economists was active, at the time, in close coincidence with a turning point concerning practical or policy issues, including, in particular, the significance to be attributed to monetary and financial phenomena and magnitudes vis-à-vis real magnitudes, and the advantages (over the disadvantages) of free trade. Four points emerge from Verri's scientific work: (1) the question of money, including the link between money supply and growth; (2) free trade, especially in staple food (whether this should be admitted and defended or should be conceived as inimical to the interests of the state); (3) pain and pleasure, scientifically considered, with a view to the definition and measure of happiness and public happiness in particular; (4) developing quantitative tools to analyse the economy and draw policy conclusions.

Among the early works of Pietro Verri we find the *Meditazioni sulla felicità* (*Reflections on Happiness*) of 1763. As far as economics is concerned, the main contribution of Verri comes forth with the *Meditazioni sulla economia politica* in 1771: an English edition was published (Verri 1986 [1993]) by Kelley edited by Peter Groenewegen. Both of these works had a number of reprints and editions: finally, Verri decided to re-publish them together with a new work on the nature of pain and pleasure (*Dell'indole del piacere e del dolore*) in a volume of *Discorsi* in 1781, which is now vol. 3 of the National Edition, that is, the *Opere di Pietro Verri*. In the volume the treatments on pleasure and pain and on happiness are clearly designed to provide the necessary background for the section on political economy, which focuses on public happiness.

Verri's *Meditazioni sulla felicità* – usually classified as a philosophical pamphlet – spells out the foundational pieces of his approach to civil life and he argues that the excess of desires over and above possibilities or "power" is a measure of unhappiness. The search for happiness in the form of the removal of unhappiness is a core issue in Pietro Verri's political philosophy. He appears from the start as one of the leading representatives of eighteenth-century eudemonistic views.

The great object of happiness – Verri argues – can be pursued in two ways. Happiness consists in the reduction of the difference between the two elements of desires and power; achieving such a reduction can be effected by acting upon either one or the other of the two elements. It can be said, therefore, that, the object of happiness being reduced to a difference, it can be conquered either by "addition" or by "subtraction": addition of power or subtraction of desires. Verri declares, in a typical utilitarian vein, addition to be superior. An addition in the form of the enlargement of power provides the main route to happiness as compared with a check on desires. He however lays a special emphasis upon creativity rather than mere enjoyment of what is already in our possession as a condition for happiness. Therefore, sheer enjoyment is to be distinguished from creative enjoyment or the pleasure to make and create. Virtuous, Verri states, is every useful act. His definition of utility is that of a disposition to perform good acts: "*utilità*' è '*attitudine a far del bene*'". This is an active concept, quite different from the idea of utility that would later prevail. Thus utility has an active meaning which provides the basis for his view of society in its formative steps as an industrious gathering of cooperating forces, founded upon a compact the end of which is the participants' well-being or public happiness. What is meant by this is, of course, the greatest possible happiness distributed with the greatest possible equality. Verri invites a reflection on how "la beneficenza puramente umana sia una emanazione dell'amore del piacere" ("purely human beneficence is a by-product of our love for pleasure"). Love for pleasure, in turn, operates through the "secret connection" – la *secreta connessione* – between our own pain and the pain of others. Good arises from evil, sterility produces abundance, poverty generates wealth, burning needs spur ingenuity, blunt injustice arouses courage. Pain excites labour, leads to the perfection of trades, teaches us to think and reflect: it creates sciences, induces to imagine arts and refine them.

All the above also sets the stage for Verri's main book on political economy. Through the 40 sections of the *Meditazioni sulla economia politica* of 1771, Pietro Verri lays great stress on creativity as the source and origin of the formation of wealth and the real object of the science of political economy.

> In a country made rich through industry machines and tools are perfected to such a degree that the workman in a single day will produce an article which in a less industrious nation would take several days to make; such are the resources available to a country which has grown rich through its industry, resources that are lacking in a country whose riches have come spontaneously from the land. (Verri 1986: 44)

Of course (Verri 1986, s. I: 4), "Need or, in other words, the sensation of pain is the goad used by nature to arouse man from the indolent state of stagnation in which he would otherwise languish. . . . *Need* – he continues – sometimes leads men to plunder, sometimes to trade. For trade to exist, there must be both *want* and *plenty*". Concerning plenty – Verri explains (ibid., s. III: 9), outspokenly contentious with the "sect of the economists" – "[r]eproduction applies as much to manufacture as it does to work in the fields", so that we should speak of "this highly fruitful *sterile class*" (original emphasis), on the product of which entire cities and states survive. Such and similar concepts crop up time and again through Verri's writings. Particularly noticeable is the unity of these three works, all of them originally drafted by him during the 1770s and later collected by the author himself under the heading of *Discorsi*: his work on happiness, on the nature of pleasure and pain, and on political economy.

Verri is also generally noted for his theory of price (see Porta and Scazzieri 2002). Verri's theory can be summarized in the well-known proposition that "[i]f the number of *sellers* increases (other things being equal), *plenty* will increase and the *price* will fall; if the number of *buyers* increases (again, other things being equal), so will the *want* grow and the *price* increase. Thus the *price* is deduced from the *number of sellers* in comparison to the *number of buyers*". In Verri's own words, "*the price of things will be in direct proportion to the number of buyers and in inverse proportion to the number of sellers*" (Verri 1986, s. IV: 17–18, original emphasis). Verri tried to give a mathematical treatment of his formula also with the aid of the mathematician Paolo Frisi, who was a member of the Pugni Academy. The so-called sixth edition of Verri's *Meditazioni* (now in vol. II.2 of the National Edition of his works) has especial significance, not only as it reflects Verri's reaction to the annotations of his authoritative opponent Gian Rinaldo Carli, but also as it includes a series of notes on the theory of price by the mathematician Paolo Frisi, besides an abstract of Henry Lloyd's 1771 book on the theory of money. In general terms it is *il moto dell'industria*, or "active industry", which forms the *primum mobile* of a virtuous circle in the economy. Schumpeter rightly singles out Verri as "the most important pre-Smithian author on Cheapness-and-Plenty" (1954: 287). Cheapness, or low price, as the result of industry, can well be brought about via an increase of the quantity of money. This seems paradoxical in terms of a Humean quantity theory; in fact it is not, as Verri is precisely a critic of Hume's analysis and he interprets the quantity equation (as it were) as a theory of the income level. That was not new, but he made an original application of the argument.

Concerning social and political order, it is only natural that some of the most typical features of his experience as a practical reformer should surface.

> Let any man be free to practise his business wherever he chooses. Let the legislator permit sellers in every category to multiply, and in a very short time he will see competition and the desire for a better life reawaken creative capacities and quicken the hands of his people; he will witness a refinement of all the arts, a fall in price levels and the spread of plenty everywhere in the wake of competition its inseparable companion. (Verri 1986, s. VII: 26)

Verri's political economy comes at a stage when the economic discipline is transformed from a theory on possessive acquisitiveness, based on commerce in a zero-sum game (mercantilism), to one of productivity, based on primary production and on circulation (physiocracy), to approach, as a further step, a line of thinking based on creativity, founded on learning and on human and social capital: the novelty of the last approach is the unusually larger space given to the analysis of the motivations to action and to institutions.

The Italian school, of course, worked in parallel with the physiocratic school. At the same time those authors, belonging to the Italian School, overcome the limitations of physiocracy, as we have seen above. While they follow physiocracy on free trade (with some qualifications), they do not confine positive economic productivity to the produce of agriculture only. It is the result of a special sense of sociality which puts the emphasis on productive relations as a source of creativity.

Cesare Beccaria

Among the main followers of Verri, Cesare Beccaria must be singled out. He is by far the best known figure of the Italian Enlightenment. Schumpeter dubs him "the Italian Adam Smith", which appears at face value to be an appreciation of the economist. However, Beccaria is very often not perceived as an economist, but as a jurist. He is also sometimes considered as a moral philosopher of a utilitarian breed, as Bentham would later acknowledge. His immense reputation is almost entirely due to the pamphlet *Dei delitti e delle pene* (*Of Crimes and Punishments*), which appeared in 1764. The pamphlet was widely read and highly praised in the climate of enthusiasm for the *Lumières*, even if the application of its principles (against torture and the death penalty) would come to suffer considerable restraint, particularly later in the century, as a number of the children of the *Lumières* started (under the French lead) to indulge in the practice of revolutions.

Cesare Beccaria, ten years Verri's junior, had made his first significant contributions (published in *Il Caffè*) as a mathematical economist on the theory of smuggling. His *Tentativo analitico sui contrabbandi*, originally appeared in *Il Caffè* in 1764, is a remarkable piece of mathematical economics (see Theocharis 1961). The idea that Beccaria's original attraction was to the economic discipline is not only proven by his early works, but is also the substance of his 1764 pamphlet, which must therefore be rated as an economic work. Beccaria was still in his twenties when he acquired a superior worldwide reputation and his celebrated pamphlet on crimes and punishment became an explosive success. An extraordinarily brilliant mind, combined with a distinctly lazy and ineffective character, he was himself surprised by his own success. Invited in great honour to Paris, the centre of the world, he completely bungled the announcement he could have given about the nature and quality of the research going on within the Accademia dei Pugni, or the "School of Milan". That famous negative episode shocked the French *philosophes* and caused a serious rift with Verri. The mark left on history is still there to be seen and it has to be reckoned among the factors that have made it difficult, thus far, to give full justice to the Italian Enlightenment. As just hinted, it is only recently that Beccaria has been appreciated as the economist that he actually was (see Audegean 2010; Bruni and Porta 2014; Porta and Scazzieri 2014). However, it should be noted that such appreciation was anticipated by Franco Venturi, who had argued that Beccaria was among those who saw in political economy the key factor of the political thought of the *Lumières* (Venturi 1969: 449).

Beccaria's pamphlet is entirely a product of the Accademia and it is an economic pamphlet, more precisely a contribution to the economics of law. The gist of the contribution of the Milanese school goes towards paving the way for Adam Smith's conception, whereby political economy is considered as "a branch of the science of a statesman or legislator".

A professorship of "Scienze Camerali" or "Kameralwissenschaft", meaning political economy through German-speaking Europe, was created for Beccaria in Milan (to Verri's dismay) in 1769. Beccaria moreover, very much like Verri, was also a consultant administrator and a member of the local Economic Council ("Supremo Consiglio di Economia") since 1771. Both Beccaria and Verri contributed a number of reports, or "Consulte", within the council, giving advice to the government. There is no doubt that Pietro was the founder, leader and intelligence of the group, and the real mentor behind Beccaria, but in the public imagination he stood, and still stays, behind the first rank, while lazy Beccaria (shamefully, to Verri's mind) was in the limelight.

Beccaria also left a volume of *Lezioni*, his lectures in Milan at the Scuole Palatine. He never published them, however; they were only first published in Milan in the Custodi Collection in 1804. They are now being prepared for publishing in a critical edition in volume III of the National Edition of Beccaria's works.

The Significance of the Italian Enlightenment in the History of Economic Thought

The privileged place of the economic problem in the political views of the Italian Enlightenment is one of the historical preconditions to the rise of the classical school with the work of Adam Smith. As is well known, Adam Smith's thought has been made the object of a great variety of readings by historians of economic thought. In particular, in recent years a historiographic revision (as Winch 1978, called it) has set in, leading to a complete reversal of previous perspectives on Smith. That revision is a complex issue, which includes a number of aspects. Certainly a salient aspect concerns the more precise and stronger link that has been demonstrated between Adam Smith's thought as a whole and the Enlightenment, particularly the Scottish Enlightenment. The result of a whole series of contributions has been to weaken the link of Adam Smith and the physiocratic school, on the one side, and to emphasize, on the other, the close connections of Smith's economic thought with other branches of the Enlightenment movement.

What has been left out in the revision is the important fact that the resulting image of Adam Smith owes something to the Italian Enlightenment, so that it is plausible to talk of some special connection between the Italian and the Scottish Enlightenments. A prolonged overemphasis on the theory of value (particularly on the labour theory of value) together with a widespread retrieval of the surplus approach under the spell of Sraffa's work had, for a long time, created a standard image of the classical school based on the sequence Smith–Ricardo–Marx, with the Physiocrats as forerunners. That conception has merits, but it is at the same time lopsided and, in particular, it is singularly prone to pushing aside interest in the Italian tradition. It is among the characters of the Italian tradition that it generally stands aloof from a close involvement with the theory of value: this is a point that must be mentioned even if it cannot be treated here (see Bruni and Porta 2007; also Porta 1982).

What the Smithian revision today really amounts to is a reconsideration of the Enlightenment and its role in the history of economic ideas. It is a characteristic of much of the recent literature on Smith that an increasing restraint is being applied to the traditional, almost exclusive, emphasis on self-interest as the motive for action. That Smith was familiar with the Italian language and politico-economic literature transpires from a number of passages in his works. Smith carefully followed the developments of the economic discipline in Italy, as is proved by Luigi Einaudi's analysis of the Italian section of Smith's library (Einaudi 1953). There is an objective connection between the teachings of the Italian tradition and the public-spirited attitude which Smith attributes to the legislator. That extends from the legislator to the economist, in Smith's view, and he explicitly conceives of political economy as a branch of the science of a statesman or legislator.

It is interesting to note that the Italian tradition has repeatedly echoed, through the nineteenth and twentieth centuries, ideas of the same kind as the civil economy of the eighteenth century. Examples of that are afforded by Gian Domenico Romagnosi's (1761–1835) emphasis on "incivilimento" and "civile concorrenza". That also links up with the approach to industry and creativity: the spur of ingenuity is prominent particularly in Verri and it would later find significant developments through the nineteenth century in the work of Carlo Cattaneo (1801–1869). Both Francesco Ferrara (1810–1900), on the one hand, and the Italian historical school, on the other, are sources of many more examples. However, even in the marginalist and neoclassical camp, where the Italians were pioneers, public economics came to prominence with the rise of the "Scienza delle finanze", as a special kind of public economics. In the twentieth century we should single out the case of Luigi Einaudi (1874–1961) as an example of a mid-way theorist, linking institutionalism, historicism and marginalism. That special blend gives rise to a line of social economy, which must, in many respects, be considered the child of the Enlightenment as it grew in Italy during the eighteenth century.

Pier Luigi Porta

See also:

Formalization and mathematical modelling (III); French Enlightenment (II); Scottish Enlightenment (II); Adam Smith (I).

References and further reading

Audegean, P. (2010), *La philosophie de Beccaria: savoir punir, savoir écrire, savoir produire*, Paris: J. Vrin.

Baron, H. (1955), *The Crisis of the Early Italian Renaissance*, Princeton, NJ: Princeton University Press.

Beccaria, C. (1764), *Dei delitti e delle pene*, ed. F. Venturi, reprinted 1994, Turin: Einaudi.

Beccaria, C. (1764), '*On Crimes and Punishments' and Other Writings*, ed. R. Bellamy, reprinted 1995, Cambridge: Cambridge University Press.

Beccaria, C. (1984–2014), *Edizione Nazionale delle Opere di Cesare Beccaria*, eds L. Firpo and G. Francioni, Milan: Mediobanca, esp. vol. III, *Scritti economici*, ed. G. Gaspari, 2014, which contains the first diplomatic edition of Beccaria's *Elementi di economia pubblica*.

Beccaria, C. (n.d.), *Lezioni di economia pubblica*, reprinted in G. Francioni (ed.) (in preparation), *Edizione Nazionale delle Opere di Cesare Beccaria*, vol. 3, *Scritti economici*, Milan: Mediobanca.

Bellamy, R. (1987), '"Da metafisico a mercatante". Antonio Genovesi and the development of a new language on commerce in 18th century Naples', in A. Pagden (ed.), *The Languages of Political Theory in Early Modern Europe*, Cambridge: Cambridge University Press, pp. 277–99.

Bianchini, L. (1845), *Della scienza del ben vivere sociale e della economia degli stati: parte storica e di preliminari dottrine*, 2nd edn 1855, Palermo: Dalla stamperia di Francesco Lao.

Bianchini, M. (1982), *Alle origini della scienza economica*, Parma: Studium Parmense, French trans. 2002, *Bonheur public et méthode géométrique: enquête sur les économistes italiens (1711–1803)*, Paris: INED.

Brown, P. (1978), *The Making of Late Antiquity*, Cambridge, MA: Harvard University Press.

Bruni, L. and P.L. Porta (2003), '*Economia civile* and *pubblica felicità* in the Italian Enlightenment', in N. De Marchi and M. Schabas (eds), *Œconomies in the Age of Newton, History of Political Economy*, **34**, annual supplement, Durham, NC: Duke University Press, 261–86.

Bruni, L. and P.L. Porta (2007), 'La rivoluzione mancata: la teoria del valore nei manuali degli economisti italiani', in M.M. Augello and M. Guidi (eds), *L'economia divulgata. Stili e percorsi italiani (1840–1922)*, Milan: Angeli, pp. 3–20.

Bruni, L. and P.L. Porta (2014), 'Cesare Beccaria's *On Crimes and Punishments*', *History of Economics Review*, **60** (Summer), 64–74.

Bruni, L. and R. Sugden (2000), 'Moral Canals: trust and social capital in the work of Hume, Smith and Genovesi', *Economics and Philosophy*, **16** (April), 21–45.

Bruni, L. and S. Zamagni (2007), *Civil Economy. Efficiency, Equity, Public Happiness*, Oxford: Peter Lang.

Cesarano, F. (2012), *Monetary Theory in Retrospect. The Selected Essays of Filippo Cesarano*, London: Routledge.

Costabile, L. (2016), 'The value and security of money. Metallic and fiduciary media in Ferdinando Galiani's *Della Moneta*', *European Journal of the History of Economic Thought*, **23** (3), 400–424.

Custodi, P. (ed.) (1803–16), *Scrittori Classici Italiani di Economia Politica: Parte Moderna*, 50 vols, Milan: Destefanis, esp. vols. 3–17 for the Enlightenment.

Davanzati, B. (1588), *Lezione delle monete*, Florence, in P. Custodi (ed.) (1804), *Scrittori classici italiani di economia politica*, 'Parte Antica', vol. 2, Milan: G.G. Destefanis, pp. 15–50.

Einaudi, L. (1953), 'Dei libri italiani posseduti da Adam Smith', in L. Einaudi, *Saggi bibliorafici e storici intorno alle dottrine economiche*, Roma: Edizioni di storia e letteratura, pp. 71–89.

Faccarello, G. (1994), 'Nil repente: Galiani and Necker on economic reforms', *European Journal of the History of Economic Thought*, **1** (3), 519–50.

Faccarello, G. (1998), 'Galiani, Necker and Turgot. A debate on economic reforms and policy in 18th century France', in G. Faccarello (ed.), *Studies in the History of French Political Economy. From Bodin to Walras*, London: Routledge, pp. 120–85.

Faccarello, G. (1999), *The Foundations of 'Laissez-Faire': The Economics of Pierre de Boisguilbert*, London: Routledge, French edn published 1986.

Galiani, F. (1769), *Dialogues entre M. Marquis de Roquemaure, et M. le Chevalier Zanobi: the Autograph Manuscript of the 'Dialogues sur le commerce des bleds'*, posthumously published in 1968, P. Koch (ed.) (*Analecta Romanica*, bk 21), Frankfurt-am-Main: Vittorio Klostermann.

Galiani, F. (1770), *Dialogues sur le commerce des bleds*, Paris.

Galiani. F. (1975), *Opere*, ed. F. Diaz, Milan and Naples: Ricciardi, includes both *Della Moneta* and the *Dialogues sur le commerce des bleds*.

Garin, E. (1952), *L'Umanesimo italiano. Filosofia e vita civile nel Rinascimento*, Bari: Laterza.

Genovesi, A. (1753), *Discorso sopra il vero fine delle lettere e delle scienze*, reprinted 1962, Milan: Feltrinelli.

Genovesi, A. (1765–67), *Lezioni di economia civile*, reprinted 2013, ed. F. Dal Degan, Milan: Vita & Pensiero.

Genovesi, A. (1766), *Diceosìna, o sia della filosofia del giusto e dell'onesto*, reprinted 1973, Milan: Marzorati.

Hutchison, T. (1988), *Before Adam Smith. The Emergence of Political Economy 1662–1776*, Oxford: Blackwell.

Il Caffè (1764–66), reprinted 1993, eds G. Francioni and S. Romagnoli, Turin: Bollati Boringhieri.

Mandeville, B. de (1705), *The Grumbling Hive, or Knaves turn'd Honest*, London, enlarged edn 1714, *The Fable of the Bees, or Private Vices, Publick Benefits*, London: Edmund Parker.

Negri Zamagni, V. and P.L. Porta (eds) (2012), *Il Contributo Italiano alla Storia del Pensiero: Economia*, Encyclopedia Italiana di Scienze, Lettere e Arti, Appendice VIII, Rome: Istituto della Enciclopedia Italiana.

Pasinetti, L.L. (1986), 'Theory of value – a source of alternative paradigms in economic analysis', in M. Baranzini and R. Scazzieri (eds), *Foundations of Economics*, Oxford: Blackwell, pp. 409–31.

Pocock, J.G.A. (1975), *The Machiavellian Moment. Florentine Political Thought and the Atlantic Republican Tradition*, Princeton, NJ: Princeton University Press.

Porta, P.L. (1982), 'I fondamenti ricardiani del marxismo', *Giornale degli economisti e annali di economia*, **41** (11–12), 721–39.

Porta, P.L. (2011), 'Lombard enlightenment and classical political economy', *European Journal of the History of Economic Thought*, **18** (4), 521–50.

Porta, P.L. (2012), 'Ferdinando Galiani', in V. Negri Zamagni and P.L. Porta (eds), *Il Contributo Italiano alla Storia del Pensiero: Economia*, Rome: Istituto della Enciclopedia Italiana, pp. 352–7.

Porta, P.L. and R. Scazzieri (2002), 'Pietro Verri's political economy: commercial society, civil society, and the science of the legislator', *History of Political Economy*, **34** (1), 81–108.

Porta, P.L. and R. Scazzieri (eds) (2014), *L'Illuminismo delle riforme civili: il contributo degli economisti lombardi*, Milan: Istituto Lombardo di Scienze e Lettere.

Quadrio Curzio, A. (2007), *Economisti ed economia. Per un'Italia europea: paradigmi tra il XVIII e il XX secolo*, Bologna: Il Mulino.

Robertson, J. (2005), *The Case for the Enlightenment. Scotland and Naples 1680–1760*, Cambridge: Cambridge University Press.

Roncaglia, A. (ed.) (1995), *Moneta e sviluppo negli economisti napoletani dei secoli XVII–XVIII*, Bologna: Mulino.

Roncaglia, A. (2005), *Il mito della mano invisibile*, Rome and Bari: Laterza.

Schumpeter, J.A. (1954), *History of Economic Analysis*, New York: Oxford University Press.

Smith, A. (1759), *The Theory of Moral Sentiments*, London: Millar and Edinburgh: Kincaid and Bell, reprinted in D.D. Raphael and A.L. Macfie (eds) (1976), *Adam Smith. The Theory of Moral Sentiments* (Glasgow Edition of the Works and Correspondence of Adam Smith, vol. 1), Oxford: Clarendon Press.

Smith, A. (1776), *An Inquiry into the Nature and Causes of the Wealth of Nations*, 2 vols, London, Strahan and Cadell, reprinted in R.H. Campbell, A.S. Skinner and W.B. Todd (eds) (1976), *Adam Smith. An Inquiry into the Nature and Causes of the Wealth of Nations* (Glasgow Edition of the Works and Correspondence of Adam Smith, vol. 2), 2 vols, Oxford: Clarendon Press.

Theocharis, R.D. (1961), *Early Developments in Mathematical Economics*, London: Macmillan.

Venturi, F. (1969), *Settecento riformatore*, vol. V, *L'Italia dei lumi*, Turin: Einaudi.

Verri, P. (1760), *Meditazioni mie sul commercio*, in G. Bognetti, A. Moioli, P.L. Porta, G. Tonelli (eds) (2007), *Edizione Nazionale delle Opere di Pietro Verri*, vol. II: *Scritti di economia, finanza e amministrazione*, Rome: Edizioni di Storia e Letteratura.

Verri, P. (1763), *Meditazioni sulla felicità*, London (Livorno): anon., reprinted in 1997 from the 1765 impression, Milan: Fondazione Feltrinelli.

Verri, P. (1771), *Meditazioni sulla economia politica*, English trans. by B. McGilvray (of final, 1781, edn) (1986), *Reflections on Political Economy*, ed. P.D. Groenewegen, Reprints of Economic Classics, Series 2, vol. 4, Sydney: University of Sydney, reprinted 1993, New York: Augustus M. Kelley.

Verri, P. (2003–15), *Edizione Nazionale delle Opere di Pietro Verri*, gen. ed. C. Capra, Rome: Edizioni di Storia e Letteratura, in particular vol. 2, *Scritti di economia, finanza e amministrazione*, eds G. Bognetti, A. Moioli, P.L. Porta and G. Tonelli, and vol. 3, *Discorsi del Conte Pietro Verri*, ed. G. Panizza.

Vico, G. (1725), *Principi di una scienza nuova d'intorno alla natura delle nazioni*, revised edns 1730 and 1744, Napoli: Felice Mosca.

Winch, D. (1978), *Adam Smith's Politics. An Essay on Historiographic Revision*, Cambridge: Cambridge University Press.

Scottish Enlightenment

The second half of the eighteenth century saw an astonishing outburst of intellectual creativity in Scotland covering a great range of disciplines, from the physical sciences to economic and social studies and the humanities – this is what is now called the Scottish Enlightenment. As far as economics is concerned, the main figures in the Scottish Enlightenment are David Hume (1711–1776; his main economic work was included in his *Essays, Moral, Political, and Literary*, 1752), James Steuart (1712–1780; *Inquiry into the Principles of Political Oeconomy*, 1767) and Adam Smith (1723–1790; *Inquiry into the Nature and Causes of the Wealth of Nations*, 1776). Other figures who played a lesser but still significant role in the development of economic thinking in Scotland include Francis Hutcheson, Adam Ferguson, John Dalrymple and Lord Kames (Henry Home).

A major theme of enlightenment thinking was progress, including, but not limited to, economic progress. A major theme of Hume's economic writings is an analysis of the emergence and development of a commercial society, that is, a society producing, consuming and trading in a wide variety of manufactured goods. This is an analysis of what we might now call economic development. It is primarily qualitative, not quantitative, and it is not clear whether it is a once-and-for-all process, so that it is not necessarily going to continue into the future. Smith took the next critical step, incorporating capital and capital accumulation as essential elements of a theory of growth. We now take continued economic growth for granted. This way of thinking was largely a product of the Scottish Enlightenment.

One example will give an impression of the concentration of talent in Scotland in those years. In Edinburgh in the 1770s four men, David Hume, Adam Smith, Joseph Black and James Hutton, agreed to meet regularly for dinner and discussion. They called themselves the Oyster club. They make a remarkable quartet. Hume is undoubtedly one of the greatest philosophers of all time and is sometimes described as the founder of the sceptical school of philosophy, or of British empiricism; Smith is often called the founder of economics, Black the founder of modern chemistry, and Hutton the founder of modern geology. Without taking the appellation "founder" too seriously, it is clear that all four were doing seminal, foundational work in their different fields. It is hard to think of any other place and time which could match a group like that. Also, they were not the only intellectual stars in Edinburgh at the time. There were others, across a range of disciplines. There were larger groups, such as the Edinburgh Philosophical Society. There was close contact with other centres such as London and Paris but, for a generation or so, Edinburgh was among the most important centres, perhaps *the* most important centre of new ideas in Europe.

This is the more remarkable in that Scotland was a small and relatively poor country on the far edge of Europe. Historians no longer accept Trevor-Roper's rather extreme judgement that "at the end of the seventeenth century, Scotland was a by-word for irredeemable poverty, social backwardness, political faction. The universities were the unreformed seminaries of a fanatical clergy" (1967: 1636). That said, Trevor-Roper's critics have shown that a variety of elements of economic, social and intellectual progress can be traced back to the mid- or late-seventeenth century, but it remains the case that seventeenth-century Scotland played no significant role in the wider intellectual scene.

The dramatic contrast between the Scottish Enlightenment and the context from which it arose remains.

The Enlightenment as a whole was a Europe-wide movement. The term was not used at the time (though the German equivalent, *Aufklärung*, was) but many of those involved were conscious of themselves as part of an intellectual and (in some cases) political transformation. It is not easy to define, but the one thing that all attempts to pin the term down have in common is that Enlightenment writers wanted to base themselves on reason and on evidence, and that they rejected religious dogma when it came into conflict with the evidence (though many remained religious believers, and those who did not, generally had to conceal the fact for safety's sake). The Enlightenment was much influenced by the scientific revolution of the late seventeenth century, perhaps particularly by the success of Newton's physics.

The starting and ending dates of the Enlightenment in the wider sense are also difficult to pin down. Many scholars simply identify it with the eighteenth century, though some would set the starting date a little earlier, and many would set an end-date at or before the start of the French revolution. The concern here is with the Scottish Enlightenment and specifically with its contribution to economic thinking, and in this case the question is easier. In the first half of the eighteenth century there were some signs of what was to come (Hutcheson 1726 and some parts of Hume's *Treatise of Human Nature*), but the main works which are discussed here date from (approximately) the third quarter of the century, from Hume's *Essays* of 1752 to Adam Smith's *Wealth of Nations* of 1776.

As noted above, economics (or political economy) was not recognized as a subject in its own right at the beginning of the period. James Steuart's *Inquiry into the Principles of Political Oeconomy* of 1767 was the first comprehensive work on the subject in English, but it was overshadowed by Adam Smith's *Wealth of Nations* which came out only nine years later. It was the *Wealth of Nations* that set the pattern for the development of what is called classical political economy in the first half of the nineteenth century. Before Steuart and Smith, economic issues appeared in a variety of forms. Hume's collections of essays were one example. There was a very large pamphlet literature relating to immediate policy issues but often touching on wider issues, especially in London and especially in the late seventeenth century.

More relevant in Scotland in the earlier stages of the Scottish Enlightenment was the teaching and related literature on moral philosophy and jurisprudence, epitomized by Adam Smith's *Theory of Moral Sentiments*, which was based on his lectures at Glasgow, and the student notes of his *Lectures on Jurisprudence*, which have been discovered and published. In an earlier generation one could point to the work of Smith's teacher, Francis Hutcheson. The focus here must be on the emergence of economic ideas rather than on wider aspects of the Scottish Enlightenment (on which see, for example, Brodie 2003; Hont and Ignatieff 1983).

History and the Four Stages

The Scottish Enlightenment was particularly distinguished by an interest in history, and the theory of the four stages of development of society is a distinctively eighteenth-century Scottish view of historical development. The theory postulates that there are four different types of society defined by the primary source of subsistence or income:

hunting, pastoral (animal rearing), agricultural (cultivating the soil to grow crops), and commercial (engaged in internal and external trade, manufacturing, and so on). In the early- to mid-eighteenth century this classification of societies was anthropological rather than historical – the four were seen as different types of society existing alongside each other in different parts of the world. Corresponding to the different sources of income are different social systems and forms of the state, and different conceptions of property. So, for example, hunting societies can only support a low density of population, hence small social units, a limited notion of property, and so on. Smith made extensive use of this classification in his lectures on jurisprudence.

John Locke had argued that "in the beginning all the world was America" (1988: 301), referring, of course, to native American hunter-gatherer societies. The next step was to link that insight to the fourfold typology to argue that the four types of society were successive stages of development – human societies had all started by hunting, before advancing (or not) via the pastoral and agricultural stages, with some, finally, reaching the commercial stage. Link this to the idea that government and law depend on the stage reached, and it could provide, at least in principle, a comprehensive framework for economic and social history. The theory of the four stages, as a theory of history, was developed mainly in Scotland. Good examples are John Dalrymple, *Essay toward a General History of Feudal Property in Great Britain* (1757; arguably the first mention in print of the four stages as stages of history) and Lord Kames's *Historical Law Tracts* (1761). As a result Kames, Ferguson and others are seen as pioneers of sociology and of the social explanation of institutions and laws. The four stages are also developed in Adam Smith's *Lectures on Jurisprudence* (1762–63 [1978]) which were delivered in the early 1760s but not, of course, published at the time.

The analytical economic content of the stages in themselves is limited. The main economic interest attaches to the character and development of the final stage, that of commerce. Note here that the commercial stage differs from the rest in that it does not represent a new source of food, and that the evolution of commerce within the agricultural stage is a matter of degree.

Luxury, Commerce and Economic Development

The moral standing and social effects of "commerce" were a live issue in the eighteenth century, and especially so for the writers of the Scottish Enlightenment, who were in the main committed to an open economy and society, but who were at the same time deeply concerned about issues of moral philosophy. This connected to a long-running debate about luxury which went back to Plato and Aristotle and before.

In modern English, "luxury" is a bland and rather positive word, but that was not so in the early modern period. The basic meaning, that luxuries are things which are desired without being necessary, is the same, but the word then had strongly negative overtones of excess, greed, and the like. Until about the seventeenth century, the literature was almost entirely hostile – in practice, of course, rich people often revelled in what any reasonable person would describe as luxury, but they did not like to say so. The case against luxury was in fact rather vague, though one fairly constant element, going back at least to Plato, was that the desire for luxuries, unlike that for necessities, is in principle unlimited, leading to an unending struggle for increased wealth.

Hostility to luxury, at least in its more extreme forms, is not quite the same as hostility to commerce, but it could not be denied that trade, especially the more profitable forms of long-distance trade, was frequently trade in luxuries. In pre-modern times it was easy to present trade in luxuries as pandering to a minority at the expense of the rest of society. By the seventeenth and eighteenth centuries things were changing, with expanded trade in a wider range of goods and more people able to afford at least some modest luxuries. London was displacing Amsterdam as the primary centre of trade in northern Europe. Small wonder that the old view came under fire in the London-centred pamphlet literature.

The Scottish response was particularly stimulated by Bernard Mandeville's deliberately provocative *Fable of the Bees, or Private Vices, Publick Benefits* of 1707. Economic success, he claimed, depends on "vice". The trick is to define vice very broadly and virtue correspondingly narrowly. In particular, any self-interested, market-oriented behaviour, and any consumption over and above bare necessities, were implicitly counted as vice. People were not sure how to react to this. Rousseau, in France, took it seriously and agreed – to him, a commercial society was indeed immoral. Most Enlightenment thinkers, wherever they came from, challenged Mandeville's definitions of virtue and vice, but the Scots, with their focus on moral philosophy and on social and economic questions, seem particularly to have felt the challenge.

There were two elements to the Scottish response. First, it was argued that spending on luxuries was only a vice if it went beyond the individual's means. There were differences of emphasis. Hume, for example, robustly dismissed criticisms of luxury. "To imagine, that the gratifying of any sense, or the indulging of any delicacy in meat, drink, or apparel, is of itself a vice, can never enter into a head, that is not disordered by the frenzies of enthusiasm" (1752 [1987]: 268). Adam Smith, by contrast, described the "baubles and trinkets" of the rich with contempt, but argued that they did no harm.

More important to the history of economics is the second element, the analysis of a commercial society and, in particular, of the economic effects of a demand for luxuries. Francis Hutcheson, Smith's teacher, sketched an argument which was to be developed by Hume and Smith: if the land were equally divided and used only to produce necessities there would be "no knowledge of arts [and] no agreeable amusements or diversions" (1726 [1971]: 139). Demand for unnecessary but agreeable products and services led to a better society.

This line of argument was developed by Hume, Steuart and Smith into a description of the process of development of commerce, starting from a simple (agricultural) society. Hume set out the argument in 1752 in an essay on luxury (the title was changed in 1760 to "on refinement in the arts", presumably because supporting "luxury" as such was asking too much of his readers). James Steuart followed much of Hume's argument, with a less gung-ho style. Smith also accepted the main line of argument, although in the *Wealth of Nations* it is secondary to an account of growth driven by capital accumulation.

The common-sense case for commerce had been, very reasonably, that it led to an increase in employment and income in urban manufacture and trade. The essential step forward made by the Scots was to bring agriculture into the picture as a necessary complement to urban activities. Agriculture is essential because both farmers and non-farmers have to eat. Fortunately, as Hume noted: "The land may easily maintain a much greater number of men, than those who are immediately employed in its culture, or who furnish the more necessary manufactures to such as are so employed" (1752 [1987]: 256).

Steuart had exactly the same idea in different words (for example, 1776 [1966]: 42). This notion is of course a sort of surplus arising in agriculture (though Hume did not use the word "surplus"). It is a marketable surplus of food, and it arises in agriculture simply because agriculture is the sector which produces food. It is not necessarily all available to be paid to landlords or to be taken in taxation (although it sets an upper limit to the amount that can be taken from the sector). It has little or nothing in common with the notion of a "net product" which was developed by the Physiocrats in France a little later. The idea of a marketable surplus arising in agriculture, or more generally of a surplus of necessities, was not entirely new – it is to be found in Petty and Cantillon – but the use Hume made of it was new.

The key point was that farmers could not just produce more food than they need to survive, but that they could produce more than the (perhaps larger?) amount they want to eat. If farmers do not themselves want the surplus but cannot trade it for something they want, and if they are not forced to produce it for someone else, they will simply not produce it at all:

> Where manufactures and mechanic arts are not cultivated, the bulk of the people must apply themselves to agriculture; and if their skill and industry encrease, there must arise a great superfluity from their labour beyond what suffices to maintain them. They have no temptation, therefore, to encrease their skill and industry; since they cannot exchange that superfluity for any commodities . . . A habit of indolence naturally prevails. The greater part of the land lies uncultivated. (Hume 1752 [1987]: 260–61)

Taken on its own, this might look hypothetical, but Hume's historical writings show that he was entirely serious. A poor or relatively underdeveloped country may be held back by the absence of attractive goods to stimulate effort, or by habits and tastes that favour leisure rather than purchase of luxuries. "In the first and more uncultivated ages of any state, ere fancy has confounded her wants with those of nature, men, content with the produce of their own fields, or with those rude improvements which they themselves can work upon them, have little occasion for exchange" (Hume 1752 [1987]: 290–91).

Steuart followed the same line of argument and reached much the same conclusions. Considering the effect of an increase in agricultural productivity ("the scheme of agriculture"), he claimed:

> where the inhabitants are lazy; or where they live in such simplicity of manners, as to have few wants which labour and industry can serve . . . the laziest part of the farmers, disgusted with a labour which produces a plenty superfluous to themselves, which they cannot dispose of for any equivalent, will give over working, and return to their ancient simplicity. . . . Thus . . . a part of the country . . . will again become uncultivated. (Steuart 1767 [1966]: 41)
> Experience every where shews the possible existence of such a case, since no country in Europe is cultivated to the utmost: and that there are many still, where cultivation, and consequently multiplication, is at a stop. These nations I consider as in *moral incapacity* of multiplying. (Ibid.: 42, original emphasis)

Agricultural development is the key, but it is promoted by the supply of attractive non-agricultural goods. In Hume's words: "Every thing in the world is purchased by labour; and our passions are the only cause of labour. When a nation abounds in manufactures and mechanic arts, the proprietors of land, as well as the farmers, study agriculture as a science, and redouble their industry and attention" (1752 [1987]: 261).

The overall effects are entirely desirable to a man of the Enlightenment (though one can imagine that many traditional rulers and religious leaders might not agree):

> The spirit of the age affects all the arts; and the minds of men, being once roused from their lethargy, and put into a fermentation, turn themselves on all sides, and carry improvements into every art and science. Profound ignorance is totally banished, and men enjoy the privilege of rational creatures, to think as well as to act, to cultivate the pleasures of the mind as well as those of the body. (Hume 1752 [1987]: 271)

How does the process get started? In an isolated agricultural state in which manufactures are only produced on a small scale for local use, better products do not come into view and farmers have no incentive to enter the market at all. Hume's *History of England* explains the state of Britain before the Romans, and again after the Anglo-Saxon conquest in those terms. Trade with outsiders is the answer. Imports show what can be done and induce farmers to enter the market as sellers of food and buyers of manufactures, while local manufacturing has something to copy and improve on: "In most nations, foreign trade has preceded any refinement in home manufactures. . . . Thus men become acquainted with the *pleasures* of luxury and the *profits* of commerce" (Hume 1752 [1987]: 264, original emphasis).

Steuart followed Hume. In one example, he described a hypothetical country "of great simplicity of manners". Traders arrive with "instruments of luxury and refinement", show off their wares, sell a little at first (because there is little to trade it for), and promise to return. To have something to sell, the inhabitants set to work, "those who formerly lived in simplicity become industrious", and output increases (1767 [1966]: 166–71; cf. 38–41). Unlike Hume, Steuart did not insist that the initial impulse has to come from outside. Elsewhere (1767 [1966]: 215–16) he claimed that trade and industry owed their establishment to ambitious princes, who encouraged development in order to strengthen their position against rival states.

Military power was an issue in the eighteenth century. Hume posed the question: was there a conflict between the happiness of individuals and the power of the state? He answered that there was not. Suppose a commercial state with a substantial luxury sector was threatened by a rival. Taxes could be increased and demand for luxuries would fall as a result, forcing those previously employed in luxury production to take new jobs in the army (Hume 1752 [1987]: 261–2). A simple agricultural state, by contrast, could not afford to raise a substantial army since the whole labour force would be needed to grow food at the prevailing low levels of productivity. (This clearly assumes that agricultural methods cannot be changed overnight.) It would admittedly be possible to extract a surplus from peasants by force, but that would be ineffective: "It is a violent method, and in most cases impracticable, to oblige the labourer to toil, in order to raise from the land more than what subsists himself and family. Furnish him with manufactures and commodities, and he will do it of himself" (ibid.: 262).

That said, Hume knew perfectly well that feudal lords had extracted a surplus from their tenants, even if they had done so very inefficiently. Either because there were few luxury manufactures to spend on, or because military strength was more important, feudal lords used their surplus to maintain gangs of retainers and soldiers. As tastes changed and more attractive manufactures became available, rich landlords cut down on retainers and switched to buying luxuries from independent merchants and manufacturers, living a better life but sacrificing their personal power. The decline of feudalism was thus the result of the rise of commerce and of the demand for luxuries. Smith shared this analysis, as we shall see. More generally, a commercial society might not be equal – the Scottish Enlightenment writers were very well aware of the huge wealth of leading aristocrats – but it did entail a large, relatively independent, middle class.

Here it is worth mentioning Adam Ferguson. His *Essay on the History of Civil Society* (1767 [1967]) has attracted little attention from historians of economics (it is, instead, regarded as a pioneer work in sociology) but it contains a surprisingly coherent, if sketchy, account of economic development. Like others at the time, he supported the four stages framework. More to the point, he discussed human motivation, arguing that the animal instinct to seek one's own survival and to produce descendents is combined with the human characteristics of reflection and foresight to make us constantly seek material wealth and security. Humans, he claims, always seek to improve, so we are always aiming to raise the efficiency and quality of production.

This amounts at least to the beginning of an account of economic development which has much in common with Hume's but with the emphasis more on improved methods of production, and an implication, at least, that growth should be normal (since it is the result of normal human instincts), and that any end to growth is far away. Sketchy though it is, Ferguson's account of growth is in some ways more modern than Hume's or, in fact, Smith's.

Money and the Balance of Payments

A commercial society is a money-using society. Indeed, any trade or exchange beyond the simplest requires money, so any analysis of a commercial society had to deal with money. What is more, monetary questions had a prominent place in the policy debates of the time, and the "mercantilist" pamphlet literature of the late seventeenth and eighteenth centuries was frequently focused on money and the balance of payments. Clearly the Enlightenment writers could not ignore the interaction between money, prices and the balance of trade.

Hume's magisterial analysis of metallic money in an open economy largely settled the matter, and became the starting point for work in the mainstream of monetary theory for more than a century. It is perhaps his main contribution to the development of economic analysis.

The basic argument was simple. In a closed economy, the quantity of money is of no importance since prices adjust proportionately. (Locke had already argued this point.) In an open economy, a change in the money supply causes a corresponding price change, which in turn affects competitiveness:

Suppose four-fifths of all the money in Great Britain to be annihilated in one night . . . Must not the price of all labour and commodities sink in proportion? . . . What nation could then dispute with us in any foreign market? . . . In how little time, therefore, must this bring back the money which we had lost, and raise us to the level of all the neighbouring nations? Where, after we have arrived, we immediately lose the advantage of the cheapness of labour and commodities; and the farther flowing in of money is stopped. (Hume 1752 [1987]: 311)

Similarly, any excess of money flows out. The conclusion is simple. There is no need to worry about the balance of trade or about a scarcity of money. The system is self-adjusting. The essential elements of the theory – the link between prices and the quantity of money in circulation (now called the quantity theory of money) and the automatic adjustment of the quantity of money to imbalances in the balance of payments (now called the specie-flow mechanism) – were not wholly original, but they had never been stated so clearly, nor had their full consequences been worked out and presented in the way that Hume did. He effectively settled the issue for a century or more.

He was the master of the killer example. Thus, a Mr Gee had presented detailed calculations to show that the British trade balance was "against them for so considerable a sum as must leave them without a single shilling in five or six years" (Hume 1752 [1987]: 310). Fortunately, that prediction had been made 25 years before, and money still seemed to be plentiful, as Hume's theory predicted. The data relating to trade was notoriously inaccurate, so attempts such as Gee's to measure the balance of trade were a waste of time and effort. Hume's arguments showed that there was no need to rely on such unreliable calculations.

Europe was a single system with a system-wide general price level. India and China were only loosely connected to the European price level because transport costs between Europe and South or East Asia were high and trade was restricted by monopolistic companies. Within the European system, money was more or less abundant in different areas according to demand. Austria, for example, had a small money stock because it was relatively underdeveloped (not the other way around). Within a country, the capital and the major ports will have a larger share of the money stock because more business is done there.

Hume's treatment of paper currency is an interesting application of his theory. Money, at that date, was primarily precious metal. (The British currency was legally based on silver, but was close to a de facto gold standard.) Banknotes, the relevant form of paper money, were convertible into metal. The creation of additional banknotes would initially increase the money stock, but that would lead to increased prices and an outflow of metallic money, the only kind of money acceptable internationally. Hence, the introduction of paper money would not in the end increase the money stock within the country concerned (except to the extent that it increased the Europe-wide money stock) but would simply displace metallic money within a total determined by real factors. Hume's arguments provided an important, if implicit, methodological lesson in the use of the conditions of equilibrium to derive a series of conclusions.

Hume conceded that there would be some stimulus to economic activity during the process of monetary expansion, because prices and wages are slow to adjust. Extra spending is initially perceived as an increase in real demand. Output and employment rise, but when the price increases have fully worked their way through the system, everything returns to normal. Similarly, monetary contraction causes a temporary depression:

> [I]t is of no manner of consequence, with regard to the domestic happiness of a state, whether money be in a greater or less quantity. The good policy of the magistrate consists only in keeping it, if possible, still encreasing; because, by that means, he keeps alive a spirit of industry in the nation, and encreases the stock of labour, in which consists all real power and riches. (Hume 1752 [1987]: 288)

This concession has attracted much attention. Hume hardly elaborated on it, leaving it unclear whether he should be counted as an inflationist, encouraging the magistrate to inflate the currency without end. Against this reading of Hume, note that it is not possible to inflate a metallic currency to any significant extent in an open country (or, without unlimited supplies of precious metals, in a closed economy), while adding paper money, as we have seen, simply drives out metal money. Hume's advice to the magistrate (in modern terms, the government) seems impossible. Mainstream economists have generally averted their eyes from this paragraph in Hume's essay, though some Keynesians have rather optimistically claimed that it puts Hume on their side.

A second problematic aspect of Hume's economics is his treatment of what has come to be called the rich country/poor country debate. Does trade between rich and poor countries tend to widen or narrow the gap between them? Hume's most frequently quoted comment on the question is to be found in the essay *On Money* of 1752, but the essay *On the Jealousy of Trade*, added to the collection when it was reissued a few years later, must also be taken into account. In the earlier essay, Hume claimed that "a happy concurrence of causes . . . checks the growth of trade and riches, and hinders them from being confined entirely to one people" (1752 [1987]: 283). Admittedly, a country which has got ahead of others in trade has many advantages – superior skill, larger stocks, and so on – but these advantages can be counter-balanced by the low price and wage levels (and hence low costs) in a relatively less developed country with a smaller money stock. Hence manufacturing will tend to move, as time goes by, "leaving those countries and provinces which they have already enriched, and flying to others, whither they are allured by the cheapness of provisions and labour" (ibid.: 283).

The essay *On the Jealousy of Trade* was added to counteract the temptation for trading nations to "look on the progress of their neighbours with a suspicious eye and to consider all trading states as their rivals" (Hume 1752 [1987]: 328). Hume's main line of argument against this zero-sum view is to reassert the arguments in favour of a commercial society, and particularly the argument that imports provide us with opportunities and incentives to learn and copy, while our exports have the same effect in other places. We all benefit from wider trade. The implication in the rich country/poor country context is surely that there is no reason why both should not gain. Hume probably regretted the argument presented in the earlier essay since it portrayed the relation between trading states, rich or poor, as one of rivalry rather than complementarity.

Hume's essay on interest complements his treatment of money. His main purpose was to refute the common belief that interest rates are determined by the abundance or scarcity of money. This, he argued, was false because prices vary in line with the quantity of money, so (in modern terms) the real quantity of money is not affected by changes in the nominal quantity. Suppose gold were as common as silver, would interest rates be lower? No, he argued, "our shillings should then be yellow" (Hume 1752 [1987]: 296) instead of silver.

What then determines the interest rate? Essentially, the demand and supply for borrowing or, in Hume's terms (1752 [1987]: 298), the demand for borrowing, the riches to supply that demand, and the profits of commerce. (The last of these perhaps could be included in the first.) Note, too, it is the profits of commerce, not the profits made in production, which Hume cites. The key role of capital in production, and hence the role of accumulation in growth, did not come fully into the story until Smith, a few years later.

As determinants of demand and supply for borrowing, Hume emphasized the makeup of the population and the behaviour of different kinds of people. Landlords are more often prodigals than misers, so a society of landlords and peasants will have high interest rates. Commerce, on the other hand, promotes frugality, tending to lower rates, and so on.

Steuart rejected Hume's quantity theory of money, and hence the automatic adjustment of the balance of payments. His argument was that the prices of commodities depend on competition and on the demand for each good separately:

> Let the specie of a country, therefore, be augmented or diminished, in ever so great a proportion, commodities will still rise and fall according to the principles of demand and competition . . . Let the quantity of the coin be ever so much increased, it is the desire of spending it alone, which will raise prices. (1767 [1966]: 345)

In general terms, Steuart had little faith in unregulated markets and saw potential difficulties everywhere. Political economy should provide guidance to what he called a "statesman", an idealized, altruistic, ruler. The balance of payments is an example. It would not adjust itself, but needed the attention of the statesman – a very mercantilist point of view.

Steuart had a very ambivalent attitude to luxury and to international trade. A taste for (modest) luxuries is needed to stimulate development, examples from outside are needed to arouse demand in the first place, and demand from foreign markets increases employment. However, success in trade leads to wealth, which induces a demand for foreign luxuries, laziness, and high prices. The balance of trade will turn against a rich country in the end. "No trading state has ever been of long duration, after arriving at a certain height of prosperity" (Steuart 1767 [1966]: 195). At this stage, the statesman must turn away from foreign trade and guide the country towards "inland commerce", that is, production for the home market, but only in order to preserve industry until it can be directed to some new foreign market "under the direction of an able statesman" (ibid.: 229).

Adam Smith on Commerce and Luxury

Adam Smith and David Hume came to be very good friends, and agreed about most things (though not everything). Smith was a dozen years younger than Hume, so it is reasonable to think of Hume as something of a mentor to the younger man, at least to begin with. It is natural, then, to ask how far Smith's economics was based on Hume's, especially when the focus is on the collective achievements of the Scottish Enlightenment, of which they were such prominent members. At a very simple level the answer seems to be that Smith largely took over Hume's qualitative account of the formation of a commercial society, but transformed the story of continuing growth in an already developed commercial society by focusing on the need for capital accumulation.

This section looks at the development of Smith's economic thinking and at the elements in his mature work that derive from (or are shared with) Hume. Subsequent sections deal with the main thrust of the *Wealth of Nations*, and the legacy that Smith left to his "classical" successors.

We have some evidence about early versions of his economics from his *Theory of Moral Sentiments* of 1759 and from student reports of his lectures dating from the early 1760s. These sources have to be used with care, of course. The *Theory of Moral Sentiments* is a work of moral philosophy, not economics, although, as we shall see, it contains one brief but brilliant passage devoted to growth, luxuries and inequality, exactly the things that Enlightenment writers like Hume had discussed. The student notes on the lectures are just that, and are therefore subject to obvious limitations. Even so, the absence of anything like Smith's mature theory of capital and accumulation in these early works tells us something about the development of his thinking.

In the *Theory of Moral Sentiments*, Smith tackled the question of luxury (without using the word) as a motivation. Even what he called the "oeconomy of greatness", the lifestyle of the great landed magnates with their liveried servants, their wigs, coaches, and all the rest of it guaranteed no real happiness. To Smith these were no more than "baubles and trinkets". To drive the point home, he told a story about a poor but ambitious boy who struggles throughout his life to become rich and successful, but finds that it was pointless. Our desire for wealth and success is a deception, but:

> The pleasures of wealth and greatness . . . strike the imagination as something grand and beautiful and noble. . . . And it is well that nature imposes upon us in this manner. It is this deception which rouses and keeps in continual motion the industry of mankind. It is this which first prompted them to cultivate the ground, to build houses, to found cities and commonwealths, and to invent and improve all the sciences and arts, which ennoble and embellish human life. (Smith 1759 [1976]: 183)

This is Hume (even perhaps Mandeville) – luxury is the motive to produce more, to invent new products, and so on – but with a distinctive Smithian twist, in that the rich get no real benefit from their wealth.

Smith went further:

> It is to no purpose, that the proud and unfeeling landlord views his extensive fields . . . The capacity of his stomach bears no proportion to the immensity of his desires, and will receive no more than that of the meanest peasant. The rest he is obliged to distribute among those, who prepare, . . . that little which he himself makes use of, . . . among those who provide and keep in order all the different baubles and trinkets, which are employed in the oeconomy of greatness; all of whom thus derive from his luxury and caprice, that share of the necessaries of life, which they would in vain have expected from his humanity or his justice. The produce of the soil maintains at all times nearly that number of inhabitants which it is capable of maintaining. The rich . . . consume little more than the poor, and in spite of their natural selfishness and rapacity, though they mean only their own conveniency . . . they divide with the poor the produce of all their improvements. (1759 [1976]: 184)

So, the selfish desire for luxuries extracts a surplus from agriculture (via the rents of landlords) which is distributed again to the makers of luxuries, servants, and so on. The landlords "are led by an invisible hand" to distribute the necessaries of life to those who need them (ibid.: 184). Smith used the famous phrase "invisible hand" once only in the *Theory of Moral Sentiments*, in the passage under discussion, and once only in the *Wealth of Nations*.

The role of luxuries in stimulating agricultural (and non-agricultural) production continues in Smith's lectures and in the *Wealth of Nations*:

> When by the improvement and cultivation of the land the labour of one family can provide food for two, the labour of half the society becomes sufficient to provide food for the whole.

> The other half, therefore, or at least the greater part of them, can be employed in providing other things, or in satisfying the other wants and fancies of mankind. (1776 [1976]: 180)
> The desire of food is limited in every man by the narrow capacity of the human stomach; but the desire of the conveniences and ornaments of building, dress, equipage, and household furniture, seems to have no limit or certain boundary. Those, therefore, who have the command of more food than they themselves can consume, are always willing to exchange the surplus, or, what is the same thing, the price of it, for gratifications of this other kind. (1776 [1976]: 181)

Smith differed from Hume in that he was rather unwilling to admit that undeveloped countries may be held back by a lack of desire for luxuries. For Smith, some wants are unlimited.

Hume's explanation of the decline of feudalism, in which feudal lords cut back on their (armed) retinues in favour of luxury consumption, was taken over by Smith in his lectures and in the *Wealth of Nations*, with his typical contempt for the rich:

> the silent and insensible operation of foreign commerce and manufactures gradually . . . furnished the great proprietors with something for which they could exchange the whole surplus produce of their lands . . . and thus, for the gratification of the most childish, the meanest, and the most sordid of all vanities, they gradually bartered their whole power and authority. (1776 [1976]: 418–99)

The four stage theory of history is developed and used at length in Smith's lectures. At the time when the notes we have were taken (probably 1762–64), others had already published versions of the theory, but it is possible, perhaps probable, that Smith had been using similar material in his lectures for years. The four stages are implicit in a number of places in the *Wealth of Nations*, though in a secondary role because the book is almost wholly about modern commercial societies.

There are, then, many echoes of Hume and of the Scottish Enlightenment generally in Smith's economics, but it is time to turn to what is different in the *Wealth of Nations*.

Capital Accumulation and Growth

The *Wealth of Nations* introduced a new way of thinking in which economic growth over indefinite periods of time is normal, provided there is reasonable security and a reasonable degree of freedom to produce and trade. Growth, in this view, requires no special intervention by the government, other than to avoid policies which interfere with the natural process of growth (see Brewer, 2010: ch. 2).

Smith did not use the word "growth" or the phrase "economic growth" in the way that we do today. Closest, perhaps, are a couple of places where he wrote of the "growth of a new colony" and one example of "the growth of public opulence". Most often, the word "growth" refers to the biological process of growth, for example, of corn. Talking about what we would call economic growth, he used a variety of phrases such as "progress of opulence", the "continual increase of national wealth", and so on. For the sake of clarity, in this discussion the word "growth" will be used to mean a continuous increase in total output over indefinitely long periods of time, as opposed to once-and-for-all bursts of expansion in response to changed conditions. It is important to distinguish between total output and per-capita output, and it will be convenient to start the discussion here by focusing on growth in total output, even though Smith started the *Wealth of Nations* with per-capita output. Growth in total output may be accompanied by changes in the composition of output (because of changes in the relative prices of agricultural and non-agricultural goods or differing income elasticities of demand). Smith's optimistic account of the division of labour implies that growth in total output is accompanied by increases in per-capita output, at least in manufacturing.

The key elements of this new analysis of growth are, first, that saving is normal, second, that saving is normally invested as additional capital, and that the capital market is sufficiently effective to direct investment to where it is needed and, third, that investment (capital accumulation) is the key factor in the growth of output. All of these are clearly developed in the *Wealth of Nations*.

It will help to say, first, that population is endogenous in Smith's analysis, and in most other eighteenth- (and nineteenth-) century analysis. If the economy can support more people, then population will grow accordingly (given, of course, time). This argument was developed more fully by Malthus, a generation after Smith, but it had already been spelled out by a variety of writers (Scottish and otherwise) well before Smith. The "Malthusian" analysis of population was simply part of the intellectual background. The consequence is that capital accumulation can induce population growth and a general increase in the scale of the economy or it can induce an increase in capital per head.

Saving is normal. Here is Smith's (very well known) explanation:

> the principle which prompts to save is the desire of bettering our condition, a desire which, though generally calm and dispassionate, comes with us from the womb, and never leaves us till we go into the grave. . . . An augmentation of fortune is the means by which the greater part of men propose and wish to better their condition . . . and the most likely way of augmenting their fortune is to save and accumulate some part of what they acquire. . . in the greater part of men, taking the whole course of their life at an average, the principle of frugality seems not only to predominate, but to predominate very greatly. (1776 [1976]: 341–2)

The "uniform, constant, and uninterrupted effort of every man to better his condition" is "the principle from which public and national, as well as private opulence is originally derived" (Smith 1776 [1976]: 343). Capital accumulation is necessary for economic growth, defined explicitly as an increase in the "annual produce of the land and labour" (ibid.: 343), since increased output requires either increased employment of productive labourers or increased productivity, and both require additional capital. Saving and the resulting accumulation are therefore necessary to growth. Smith, at least implicitly, assumes that saving is also sufficient to ensure accumulation and hence growth. The saver either invests himself, in his own business, or lends to someone who invests (ibid.: 337).

He went on to describe the resulting process of growth, in which the annual produce of a nation increases over time, "its lands are better cultivated, its manufactures more numerous and flourishing, and its trade more extensive" than before, adding "we shall find this to have been the case of almost all nations, in all tolerably quiet and peaceable times" (Smith 1776 [1976]: 343). He further went on, as if he were merely stating the obvious, to claim that "the annual produce of the land and labour of England, for example," had increased in the previous century, in the period before that, and so on, back to the Norman conquest and to the invasion by Julius Caesar (ibid.: 344). Similarly, he claimed that "since [at least] the time of Henry VIII. the wealth and revenue of the country have been continually advancing, and . . . their pace seems rather to have been gradually accelerated than retarded" (ibid.: 106). It was not just England: most of Europe was "advancing in industry and improvement" (ibid.: 211), and had been advancing for many centuries (for example, ibid.: 199, 211, 220, 258).

Smith chose to start the *Wealth of Nations* with the division of labour, as the main explanation of the (per-capita) wealth of the nation, defined as the ratio of output to the number of people who consume it. His first example, the famous pin factory has led some readers to emphasize the division of labour in the factory, but Smith's more general discussion of the importance of the division of labour emphasizes the division of labour across the whole system, what has been called the social division of labour.

In terms of some of the main concerns of the eighteenth century and of the Scottish Enlightenment, an extensive division of labour, permitted by extensive markets, is the characteristic of a highly developed commercial society, exemplified by Smith's example (1776 [1976]: 22–3) of "the accommodation of the most common artificer or day-labourer", where Smith devotes something over a page to the beginnings of a list of the occupations (and hence specialized workers) whose work goes into the simple consumption of a common worker.

The point here is that a productive division of labour requires investment to provide the worker with materials and tools to work with and with goods to maintain him (Smith 1776 [1976]: 276). Hence "labour can be more and more subdivided in proportion only as stock is previously more and more accumulated" (ibid.: 277). Accumulation increases total output in two ways: it increases the number employed and also, by permitting a wider division of labour, increases per-capita output.

Note here that Smith's emphasis on the division of labour corresponds to a certain playing down of invention, of technical change, as a source of growth and of increased output per capita. Smith mentions, as third of three advantages of the division of labour, that "the invention of all those machines by which labour is so much facilitated and abridged seems to have been originally owing to the division of labour (Smith 1776 [1976]: 20). The logic seems to be that accumulation gives rise to a division of labour, which in turn gives rise to the corresponding inventions. Technical change need not be considered as an independent causal factor. A relevant factor in interpreting Smith's intentions here is that in the eighteenth century "machine" or "machinery" meant any kind of tool, however simple, so that Smith's (brief) comments on invention need not imply the sorts of development which we now associate with the industrial revolution. Thus, for example, the use of different types of hammer for different tasks would count as an example of the invention of machines as a result of the division of labour. He did, it is true, describe the introduction of a valve linkage for steam engines, but that is presented as a simple cost saving, no more. Adam Ferguson had little in the way of substantive economic analysis, certainly nothing to compare with the *Wealth of Nations*, but he did stress the almost unlimited potential of new inventions.

The idea of continuing growth as the normal result of everyday behaviour was substantially new. The earlier generation of Scottish writers, led by Hume, had celebrated the fact of growth at least in England (both Hume and Smith most often drew on England for examples, without wholly ignoring their native Scotland), but their accounts can perhaps be read as a description of a once-for-all event rather than a continuing process. Smith recognized the series of once-for-all qualitative transformations that had occurred, such as the fall of feudalism, but added the quantitative process driven by accumulation summarized above. Quesnay, in France, recognized the need for investment, at least in agriculture, but thought that the French economy had declined catastrophically in the previous century or so, and emphasized a short- or medium-run process of recovery from this position. Neither Hume nor Quesnay considered the possibility of very-long-run growth and rejected it. They simply did not consider it at all.

The one writer who can be said to have anticipated Smith's growth theory is A.-R.-J. Turgot in France. His *Reflections on the Formation and Distribution of Wealth*, written in 1766 [1977], contains all the key elements of Smith's theory as set out above – saving as normal, capital allocated by the market and output constrained by capital and increasing as a result of saving. That said, the growth theory is really quite well hidden and its implications are not spelled out. Almost all his readers missed the point (or, rather, missed that particular point while finding much else in what is a brilliant book) and the *Reflections* were in any case never widely circulated. There is, then, little doubt that this fundamental shift in economic thinking came primarily from Scotland and from Adam Smith.

Markets, Prices and Profits

The essential complement of Smith's macroeconomic account of growth is a corresponding treatment of capital and profit at the microeconomic level. Before Smith (and Turgot) profit was regarded as a special kind of wage, a reward for risk taking, or a form of exploitation resulting (say) from a monopoly position. Quesnay recognized the need for capital investment but not the need for a corresponding return on investment. Smith (and Turgot) were the first to include a return on investment as a normal form of income alongside wages and rent.

Smith distinguished between market prices and natural prices. Market prices are the actual prices at any moment, determined by supply and demand. He did not use curves in diagrams or supply and demand functions subject to market clearing equations, but it is clear from the examples that he worked through that he understood how markets work. The natural price of anything is the price that will just pay the going rate to the various inputs required, including the going return on capital. If the market price of something is below its natural price then at least one input must be getting less than it could earn elsewhere, so supply will be cut, pushing the price up, while if the market price is above the natural price, the reverse will hold. It is clear that Smith saw competition in the market as a process in which changes in conditions on the supply or demand sides have a succession of repercussions – see, for example, the discussion of a public mourning (Smith 1776 [1976]: 76–7 and elsewhere) or of the effect of the acquisition of new, profitable, branches of trade on existing trades (ibid.: 110), among many others.

In Smith's system there are three types of income arising in production and corresponding to three elements of cost in determining natural prices: wages, profits and rent. This framework dominated the mainstream of economics for about a century. Smith's treatment of wages also lasted well, but his analysis of rent and profit did not.

Wages are determined by supply and demand. Recall that population is endogenous, so that wages above subsistence induce population growth as more children survive to reach working age and swell the supply of labour. In a stationary economy, that is, an economy with a constant demand for labour, wages would be forced down to subsistence by growth of the supply of labour. In a growing economy, by contrast, wages can remain significantly above subsistence as the labour force grows in step with the growth of the economy. "The progressive state is in reality the cheerful and the hearty state to all the different orders of the society. The stationary is dull; the declining, melancholy" (Smith 1776 [1976]: 99). Since growth is normal in a commercial society, it is normal for wages to be above subsistence. Indeed, "a workman, even of the lowest and poorest order, if he is frugal and industrious, may enjoy a greater share of the necessaries and conveniences of life than it is possible for any savage to acquire" (ibid.: 10). This, then, is the case for a commercial society – even the worst paid are better off than in a primitive society, better off by far than the "master . . . of ten thousand naked savages" (ibid.: 24).

Smith's treatment of profit and rent has been less highly rated by subsequent writers. In his defence, simply to provide the category of profit, or return on investment, calculated as a percentage or proportional return on the value invested, distinct both from wages (per hour's work) and rent (per unit of land) was an important step forward. Smith had a great deal that was interesting to say about the determinants of profits or rent in particular cases as, for example, in the long digression on the value of silver (Smith 1776 [1976]: 195–275) which includes a discussion of the different uses of land and how they change, and how rents change, during the process of development. However, it has to be admitted that his treatment of the overall level of profit is less than satisfactory.

Although Smith treated growth as normal, he did imply an ultimate limit to growth in each country, its "full complement of riches". In a country which had reached that level, and "which could, therefore, advance no further", both wages and profits would be low, wages reduced to subsistence for reasons already explained and profits, in an analogous way, reduced to a level such that no new investment would be forthcoming (Smith 1776 [1976]: 111). Smith seems to have thought of this stage as far away. China, perhaps, had reached the full complement that its laws and institutions permitted (ibid.: 89), but that is far from what might be possible with appropriate reforms. Overall the full complement seems almost a formality, not to be taken seriously.

Smith did recognize that continuing growth would lead to structural changes, primarily because land becomes relatively scarce as population and capital grow. Hence the "natural progress of opulence", exemplified by the American colonies, in which agriculture comes first when land is plentiful, but "where there is either no uncultivated land, or none that can be had upon easy terms" (Smith 1776 [1976]: 379) the emphasis shifts to manufactures for distant sale, and so on. Note, incidentally, that Smith, like all his contemporaries, assumes an open economy engaged in some sort of foreign trade throughout. It would be odd to do otherwise – a commercial economy is a trading economy.

Natural Liberty

Most of those who have heard of Adam Smith probably think of him as an advocate of free markets. There is a great deal to be said for this reading of the *Wealth of Nations*. Smith did not use the French phrase *laisser faire* and he only mentioned a free market once, in a specific case, not as a general principle. However, he did advocate what he called natural liberty:

All systems either of preference or of restraint, therefore, being thus completely taken away, the obvious and simple system of natural liberty establishes itself of its own accord. Every man, as long as he does not violate the laws of justice, is left perfectly free to pursue his own interest his own way, and to bring both his industry and capital into competition with those of any other man, or order of men . . . According to the system of natural liberty, the sovereign has only three duties to attend to . . . first, the duty of protecting the society from violence and invasion of other independent societies; secondly, . . . the duty of establishing an exact administration of justice; and, thirdly, the duty of erecting and maintaining certain public works and certain public institutions which it can never be for the interest of any individual, or small number of individuals, to erect and maintain; because the profit could never repay the expense to any individual or small number of individuals, though it may frequently do much more than repay it to a great society. (Smith 1776 [1976]: 687)

That seems pretty clear. On the other hand, many scholars have pointed out that Smith advocated or at least accepted quite a few violations of this principle. Typical examples are his acceptance of the Act of Navigation, which restricted foreign shipping, on the grounds that protecting English shipping would be good for the navy, and that defence is more important than opulence (Smith 1776 [1976]: 464–5), and his support for restrictions on the issue of small notes by Scottish banks, which were designed to reduce the risks of collapse of the banking system (ibid.: 324). The latter restriction is, according to Smith, similar in principle to requiring builders to build party walls between houses to prevent fire from spreading. What we can say is that Smith seems to have had a very strong presumption against state intervention except where there were strong and specific reasons for it – many modern economists adopt a similar stance.

It would be inappropriate here to follow the convoluted debates about Smith's invisible hand in any detail, but some simple points may be worth making. First, it is clear that Smith thought that natural liberty was good in itself, quite apart from the economic arguments for or against. Thus, for example, Smith considered two laws which restricted trade in opposite ways and rejected both. "Both laws were evident violations of natural liberty, and therefore unjust" (1776 [1976]: 530), although he also argued that both would be impolitic as well. Second, the claim that Smith is in some simple sense the ancestor of modern mathematical welfare economics needs to be very heavily qualified, on several grounds. One such ground would be that it is fundamental to modern welfare economics that, of two alternatives, it is better for an individual to have the one that he or she chooses or prefers. That is the significance of market demands – they show what people prefer. This is quite incompatible with Smith's account of the deceptive attraction of wealth (mostly, admittedly, in the *Theory of Moral Sentiments*).

The Scottish Enlightenment and the Modern World

We now take for granted the normality of economic growth, that is, of quantitative growth in output, population and other economic variables, and of what we might call economic development, meaning qualitative and structural change over time involving changing institutions and changing products and methods of production. It was the Scots of the Enlightenment who first taught us to think in this way. The four stages theory was, perhaps, of little practical value but it provided a very long-run framework for thought. Hume's account of development provided a causal analysis, in which changing "manners" and opportunities led to the development of a commercial society, and it also defused some of the political and moral fear of luxury and commerce, which still existed in the eighteenth century. Smith had the greatest impact – the *Wealth of Nations* remained standard reading for a century or more. He was able to combine Hume's qualitative and historical approach with a quantitative theory of growth driven by continued accumulation and hence by saving. The missing element in Smith is a full appreciation of the importance of technical change. Ferguson had pointed the way, but without winning over the mainstream.

ANTHONY BREWER

See also:

David Hume (I); French Enlightenment (II); Italian Enlightenment (II); Adam Smith (I); James Steuart [James Denham-Steuart] (I).

References and further reading

Brewer, A. (2007), 'Surplus', in S.N. Durlauf and L.E. Blume (eds), *The New Palgrave Dictionary of Economics*, 2nd edn, London: Palgrave Macmillan.

Brewer, A. (2010), *The Making of the Classical Theory of Economic Growth*, Abingdon: Routledge.

Broadie, A. (ed.) (2003), *The Cambridge Companion to the Scottish Enlightenment*, Cambridge: Cambridge University Press.

Dalrymple, J. (1757), *Essay toward a General History of Feudal Property in Great Britain*, London: A. Millar.

Ferguson, A. (1767), *An Essay on the History of Civil Society*, reprinted 1967, ed. D. Forbes. Edinburgh: Edinburgh University Press.

Hont, I. and M. Ignatieff (eds) (1983), *Wealth and Virtue. The Shaping of Political Economy in the Scottish Enlightenment*, Cambridge: Cambridge University Press.

Hume, D. (1752), *Essays Moral, Political, and Literary*, reprinted 1987, ed. E. Miller, Indianapolis: Liberty Classics.

Hume, D. (2007), *Treatise of Human Nature*, eds D.F. Norton and M.J. Norton, Oxford: Clarendon Press.

Hutcheson, F. (1726), 'Letter to Hibernicus', *Dublin Weekly Journal*, 4 February (signed P.M.), reprinted 1971 in *Collected Works of Francis Hutcheson*, vol. 7, Hildesheim: Georg Olms Verlagsbuchhandlung, pp. 132–44.

Kames, Lord (H. Home) (1761), *Historical Law Tracts*, reprinted 2000, Union, NJ: Lawbook Exchange.

Locke, J. (1988), *Two Treatises of Government*, ed. P. Laslett, Cambridge: Cambridge University Press.

Mandeville, B. (1707), *The Fable of the Bees, or Private Vices, Publick Benefits*, reprinted 1988, ed. F. Kaye, Indianapolis, IN: Liberty Press.

Smith, A. (1759), *The Theory of Moral Sentiments*, reprinted 1976, eds D. Raphael and A. Macfie, Oxford: Clarendon Press.

Smith, A. (1762–63), *Lectures on Jurisprudence*, reprinted 1978, eds R. Meek, D. Raphael, and P. Stein, Oxford: Clarendon Press.

Smith, A. (1776), *An Inquiry into the Nature and Causes of the Wealth of Nations*, reprinted 1976, eds A.H. Campbell, A.S. Skinner and W.B. Todd, Oxford: Clarendon Press.

Steuart, J. (1767), *An Inquiry into the Principles of Political Oeconomy*, reprinted 1966, ed. A. Skinner, Edinburgh: Oliver and Boyd.

Trevor-Roper, H. (1967), 'The Scottish Enlightenment', *Studies on Voltaire and the Eighteenth Century*, **58**, 1635–58.

Turgot, A.-R.-J. (1766), *Reflections on the Formation and Distribution of Wealth*, reprinted in P.D. Groenewegen (ed.) (1977), *The Economics of A.R.J. Turgot*, The Hague: Martinus Nijhoff, pp. 43–95.

British classical political economy

Introduction

The notion of a "classical political economy" was first used by Karl Marx in *A Contribution to the Critique of Political Economy*, where he related it to "the research carried on for over a century and a half . . . beginning with William Petty in Britain and Boisguilbert in France, and ending with Ricardo in Britain and Sismondi in France" (1859 [1970]: 52). It was given a more precise meaning in Marx's manuscript on *Theories of Surplus Value* (1861–63 [1988]: 358), and in vol. 1 of *Capital*, where he observed that "by classical Political Economy, I understand that economy which, since the time of W. Petty, has investigated the real relations of production in bourgeois society, in contra-distinction to vulgar economy, which deals with appearances only" (1867 [1954]: 85 n.). Marx referred to David Ricardo as "the last great representative of classical economics" (1867 [1954]: 24) – a view that was endorsed also by Joseph A. Schumpeter (1912 [1954]: 62–7) – and from his discussion in *Theories of Surplus Value* it is clear that he associated such well-known figures as John Ramsay McCulloch and John Stuart Mill, often regarded as the British classical economists par excellence, with the decline of classical political economy.

A different characterization of "classical economics" is frequently used in the second-ary literature, and accordingly a different demarcation also of the "classical" period: the latter is associated with (roughly) 1776–1848, placing at the centre of classical eco-nomics Smith, Ricardo, and John Stuart Mill. This definition, introduced by authors such as Cannan (1893) and Bonar (1894), and employed more recently, for instance, by Blaug (1987 [2008]) and O'Brien (1975, 2004), is based on an understanding of "classical economics" as an early and rude type of supply and demand analysis, with the demand side still in its infancy. However, this "Marshallian" interpretation of classical economic theory does not stand up to close scrutiny. As the reconstruction of the surplus approach to value and distribution, initiated by Piero Sraffa (1951, 1960), and then followed up in numerous contributions including, *inter alia*, Dobb (1972), Walsh and Gram (1980), Garegnani (1983, 1984, 1987), De Vivo (1984), Bharadwaj (1978), Aspromourgos (1996, 2009), and Kurz and Salvadori (1995), has clearly shown, there has been a distinctive alternative approach to the theory of value and distribution. Characteristic features of the classical approach are the determination of relative prices and income distribution from the following set of data: (1) the size and composition of the social product; (2) a given real wage rate; and (3) the available methods of production from which cost-minimizing producers can choose (see Kurz and Salvadori 1995: ch. 1).

In this entry, classical political economy is understood accordingly as denoting the period from *c*.1660 to *c*.1825, and the major British representatives are William Petty, Richard Cantillon, James Steuart, Adam Smith, Robert Torrens, and David Ricardo. Because of its central importance for all economic theory, attention focuses exclusively on the theory of value and distribution. The idea is to reconstruct some major lines in the development of the surplus approach and to assess the contributions made by the British classical political economists. Since there are several, though partly intertwined, aspects involved in this development, it seems appropriate to state them here briefly in terms of four main strings that run through it.

The first string to be followed up consists in the changing conception of the surplus, which was first regarded, by Petty, Cantillon, and the French Physiocrats, to emerge from agricultural production alone and to be realized in income form only as rent. Profits were not yet identified as a separate and distinctive form of income and not related systematically to capital advances, and the workers' wages were regarded as being confined to what is strictly necessary for subsistence. With the emergence and rising importance of capital and profits, the latter came to be regarded as forming an important part of the "net income" of society. That the workers may also participate in the sharing out of the surplus was first acknowledged by James Steuart and then particularly emphasized by Adam Smith, though not so much as an empirical fact but as a desirable goal. In Ricardo, we then find the idea that a part of the surplus might also be obtained by the workers as wages, over and above their subsistence requirements, and could be saved or expended by them.

A second important string is the development of the circular flow concept and its role in the analysis of distribution and prices. This concept was first introduced by Petty and then further refined by Cantillon, from whom it was passed on to François Quesnay and the French Physiocrats. The circular nature of the social production process implies that the commodities produced in the different sectors must be regularly exchanged in order for each sector to obtain the necessary inputs needed in its own production. A major problem for the classical political economists was the determination of the exchange ratios in conditions of circular production relations. Following Cantillon's lead, Quesnay had provided a clear conception of the circular flow, but the physiocratic analyses of prices and distribution were unsatisfactory. Smith and Ricardo, on the other hand, although they were aware of the circular nature of the social production process, had recourse to simplifying assumptions in their analyses of distribution and prices by which production circularity was effectively assumed away.

A third line of development (which is closely related to the second string) concerns the attempts of the classical political economists to find some "common measure of value", such as "food", "land" or "labour", which could be measured in physical units and would allow them to determine relative prices and the distributive variables without circular reasoning, that is, without explaining prices in terms of prices. The fourth line of development that is analysed in some detail below concerns the changing conceptualization of "natural" or "normal prices". Here, the development was fairly linear and straightforward, leading from an early exposition by William Petty to an ever more sophisticated but basically unchanged conceptualization in Smith and Ricardo.

(Apart from the theory of value and distribution, the British classical political economists have of course made many other important contributions in such diverse fields as international trade theory, monetary theory and policy, the theory of growth and technological change, the analysis of taxation and public debt, and so on. For summary accounts and assessments of those contributions the reader is referred to the entries on the major British classical political economists in this *Handbook*, as well as to those in Kurz and Salvadori (1998, 2015). For assessments of the contributions of less well-known British classical economists, see O'Brien (2004).)

The Origins of Classical Political Economy: William Petty

In Marx's judgement the contributions of William Petty mark the beginning not only of classical political economy but also of systematic economic analysis on a scientific basis more generally (for a similar view, see Hutchison 1988: 6). Petty was conscious of founding a new science and variously discussed questions of method in his writings. As a physician, he was keen to adopt an objectivist or natural science point of view, and he called the new science he set out to establish "political anatomy", or "political arithmetic" (1690 [1986]: 244). Petty proposed to adopt a strictly objectivist approach to political economy; he intended to analyse the "body politick" like a physician analyses the human body, basing himself on the principles of anatomy. Petty's economic thought accordingly was directed at finding relations between quantifiable, measurable objects.

Surplus, distribution, and prices
Petty conceived of the production process of the economic system as a whole as a circular process, in which commodities are produced by means of commodities. The circular character of production processes is immediately evident in agricultural production, where corn is produced by means of corn (as seed), but according to Petty the concept of an economic circular flow was applicable also to the system as a whole. Deducting from the annual gross produce, which consists of a heterogeneous set of commodities, the amounts of the various commodities used up in its production gives the annual net product, or surplus produce. The wage goods used up by (productive) workers Petty reckoned as part of the necessary annual production advances. In his *Treatise on Taxes and Contributions* of 1662 he illustrated the concept of the surplus by means of the production of corn:

> Suppose a man could with his own hands plant a certain scope of Land with Corn, that is, could Digg, or Plough, Harrow, Weed, Reap, Carry home, Thresh, and Winnow so much as the Husbandry of his Land requires; and had withal Seed wherewith to sow the same. I say, that when this man has subducted his seed out of the proceed of the Harvest, and also, what he himself has both eaten and given to others in exchange for Clothes, and other Natural necessaries; that the remainder of Corn is the natural and true Rent of the Land for that year; and the *medium* of seven years, or rather of so many years as makes up the Cycle, within which Dearths and Plenties make their revolution, doth give the ordinary Rent of the Land in Corn. (Petty 1662 [1986]: 43)

Corn rents are explained as a surplus that remains after deducting the amount of seed corn and the corn consumption of the workers, as well as corn exchanged for "Clothes, and other Natural necessaries". Petty here ran up against the problem of finding a rule for determining the exchange ratios between different commodities (in this case between corn and clothing and other necessaries) so as to make the heterogeneous inputs commensurate – a problem that was to occupy the classical political economists for a long time. In the case of corn production the problem could be avoided by boldly supposing no material inputs apart from seed corn were required and the workers' subsistence requirements consisted of corn alone, or else by conceiving of the latter as a catch-all for a heterogeneous commodity bundle, as Petty indeed explicitly did when he referred to "Corn, which we will suppose to contain all necessaries for life, as in the Lords Prayer we suppose the word Bread doth" (1662 [1986]: 89).

Petty stressed that the surplus can also be expressed in terms of the additional number of persons who can be maintained, given the amount of corn needed per person for subsistence, by a given number of workers engaged in the production of necessaries, taking as given the prevailing production methods and the length of the working day (1662 [1986]: 30). The size of the corn surplus then determines the number of persons who can be maintained beyond those engaged in producing corn, that is, "helpless and impotent Persons", "supernumeraries" (unemployed persons) and "Divines, Lawyers, Physicians, Merchants, and Retailers" (1662 [1986]: 29–30). Petty was particularly interested in ascertaining the number of "supernumeraries", whom he proposed to engage in military service and public works (building of roads, bridges, canals, and so on), to be financed out of taxes on rents (ibid.). His main concern in the *Treatise* was thus with explaining how taxation can finance surplus employment by extracting and redistributing the surplus product from necessary consumption.

Petty clearly identified the concept of the surplus, although he conceived of it only in the specific form of rent (and taxes), and of "rent on money capital" (interest), as derived from the former. His object of analysis was a pre-capitalist society, in which economic (and political) power was still related to landed property, and although he knew money lending, he had no notion of profit as a separate income category, and also no proper notion of capital. Petty also failed to develop a systematic analysis of the determination of wages, but he noted that for given technical conditions of production there is an inverse relationship between wages and rents: If "Wages . . . rise . . . consequently the Rents of Land must fall" (1690 [1986]: 267). Moreover, he also suggested that the common wage is given by the average amount of food that a worker needs to eat "so as to Live, Labour, and Generate" (1691 [1986]: 181). This can be regarded as an early formulation of the classical concept of the "natural wage", which keeps the supply of labour constant without either increase or diminution, which can be encountered later in more elaborate form in Smith and Ricardo. He also noted that with rapid economic growth the increased demand for labour could raise wages above subsistence, and thus stimulate population growth or immigration. Accordingly, we find foreshadowed in Petty also the idea of labour supply adapting to the demand for labour.

Prices and exchange ratios

In his attempts at developing a theory of value Petty introduced the distinction between "natural values" and "accidental values". The former are taken to reflect the "permanent Causes" governing the relative values of commodities; they are determined by difficulty of production, or production costs, whereas "accidental values" are also affected by "contingent Causes", such as ship wrecks or bad harvests (1662 [1986]: 51, 90). For Petty only the former can be the object of systematic economic analysis. Petty's approach to the determination of "natural values" starts out from his famous dictum: "Labour is the father and active principle of Wealth, as Lands are the Mother" (1662 [1986]: 68). In fact, Petty proclaimed that

> All things ought to be valued by two natural Denominations, which is Land and Labour, that is, we ought to say, a Ship or garment is worth such a measure of Land, with such another measure of Labour, forasmuch as both Ships and Garments were the creatures of Lands and mens Labours thereupon. (1662 [1986]: 44)

Although with both measures values are expressed in natural denominations he considered this insufficient and suggested reducing them further to a *common* measure of value: "the most important Consideration in Political Oeconomies" is "how to make a *Par* and *Equation* between Lands and Labour, so as to express the Value of any thing by either alone" (1691 [1986]: 181, original emphases). In Petty's example to illustrate this it is assumed that land alone (without any labour) yields an annual produce in the amount of 50 days' food, whereas labour alone (or rather, labour in addition to land) generates an (additional) annual produce in the amount of at least ten days' food. In Petty's view, the amounts of days' food thus provide the sought-after "common measure", and the ratio between the amounts of days' food generated by land and labour respectively can be used for transforming the amounts of embodied land units into amounts of embodied labour units, or vice versa. After explaining that the amounts of days' food used in the equation always refer to those which can be procured most easily in each country (as, for instance, rice in India, or oatmeal in Ireland), Petty succinctly summarized his method in the following terms: "the days food of an adult Man, at a Medium, and not the days labour, is the common measure of Value . . . Wherefore I valued an *Irish* Cabbin at the number of days food, which the Maker spent in building of it" ([1691] 1986: 181–2, original emphasis).

Petty thus proposed as a common measure of the physical costs of production the total amount of the means of subsistence, summarily expressed in terms of his notion of "food". The value of each commodity could be ascertained, Petty maintained, by the total amount of "food" required, directly and indirectly, in producing it. However, although Petty formulated a theory of natural values, which he also construed as a kind of centre of gravity for relative prices, "this theoretical construction finds almost no operational role in Petty's economic writings" (Aspromourgos 1996: 49). In fact, it is not needed in the case of Petty's corn model reasoning in the strict sense, that is, in a one-commodity model, and not applied by him when he accounts for heterogeneous inputs in the production of corn. There he argues as if the measure for expressing non-corn inputs in corn units were already known.

In conclusion, it may be said that Petty's economic thought, although concerned with the analysis of a pre-capitalist social economy, was the original stimulus for further developments around the notion of surplus in classical political economy. However, many elements were still missing: Petty had no theory of profits (and, therefore, no theory of capital), no theory of competition, and no method for ascertaining the surplus when inputs and outputs consisted of heterogeneous commodities. Except for the simplifying case of the one-commodity or "corn" model, Petty could not properly determine the size of the surplus, and could determine "natural values" only by assuming the "amounts of days' food" as known.

From Political Arithmetick to Circular Flow: Richard Cantillon

Richard Cantillon's *Essai sur la Nature du Commerce en Général* (*Essay on the Nature of Trade in General*, 1755 [1964]), probably written in 1728–34 in English, but published only posthumously in 1755 in French, provided the theoretical bridge between seventeenth-century British economics and French physiocracy – between William Petty and François Quesnay. From Petty, Cantillon took over a number of elements, most importantly, the idea of a "body politick" that is able to obtain a surplus produce over and above the requirements of the means of production and subsistence. However, unlike Petty, who tended to analyse the generation, distribution, and disposition of the surplus on the assumption of a powerful state directing it, Cantillon gave far more emphasis to the allocative functions of competitive markets. In Cantillon's *Essay*, the processes of the circulation of commodities are linked up with those of production and of distribution, so that the conception of the economic system as a circular flow comes out much clearer. In addition, Cantillon also introduced the notion of entrepreneurial profits and refined Petty's analysis of natural values by means of his concept of "intrinsic values".

The generation and distribution of the surplus

Cantillon's *Essay* opens with a statement on the creation of wealth which is immediately reminiscent of Petty's formulation cited above, except for the asymmetrical roles attributed to land and labour: "The Land is the Source or Matter from whence all Wealth is produced. The Labour of man is the Form which produces it: and Wealth in itself is nothing but the Maintenance, Conveniencies, and Superfluities of Life" (1755 [1964]: 1). Cantillon's division of society into classes and sectors is closely related to the primary role he attributed to land in the creation of wealth, and has also a geographical dimension. Since land is considered to be the source of all wealth, social stratification in Cantillon is based on land ownership. Accordingly, one class consists of the owners of land (the "prince" and the nobility), who are entitled to dispose of the surplus produce even though they have not participated in its generation. The other class, which includes farmers, merchants and artisans as well as wage labourers, is made up of all those who do not own land. While wage labourers subsist on incomes that are fixed by wage contracts in advance, the incomes of farmers, merchants and artisans are subject to uncertainty; they are "undertakers" or entrepreneurs. Geographically, the distinction is between the "country" and the "cities", the former including villages and market towns, in which "there must . . . be enough Farriers and Wheelwrights for the Instruments, Ploughs, and Carts which are needed" (1755 [1964]: 4). For Cantillon, then, the "country" (or the "rural" part of the economy) includes production of manufactured inputs needed in agricultural production; conceptually, this sector is equivalent to a vertically integrated sector that produces agricultural surplus for the "cities", where the proprietors of the land live and dispose of the surplus as they see fit: "[T]he overplus of the Land is at the disposition of the Owner" (1755 [1964]: 3). As in Petty, surplus is taken to be realized in income form essentially as rents (and taxes), with its commodity composition being explained by the modes of living of the landlords and the nobility.

Prices and income distribution

In his theory of value Cantillon referred explicitly to Petty's thought, of which he embraced the main idea: "The Price and Intrinsic Value of a Thing in general is the measure of the Land and Labour which enter into its Production" (1755 [1964]: 27). His notion of "intrinsic value" is synonymous with Petty's "natural value" as referring to production costs under normal or average conditions and, as in Petty, is complemented by the concept of "market value". With regard to the determination of "intrinsic values" Cantillon had recourse to a "three rents" conception, which he seems to have adopted from Bellers (1714), but in which he newly introduced profit or "entrepreneurial income" as a separate income category:

> It is the general opinion in England that a Farmer must make three Rents (1) The principal and true Rent which he pays to the Proprietor, supposed equal in value to the produce of one third of his Farm, a second Rent for his maintenance and that of the Men and Horses he employs to cultivate the Farm, and a third which ought to remain with him to make his undertaking profitable. (1755 [1964]: 121)

The three "rents" of the farmer thus need to cover his production costs, including replacement of the used-up means of production and the farm workers' (and the farmer's own) subsistence requirements, the "true" rent he has to pay to the landlord, and his remuneration for agricultural entrepreneurship. The profits of the farmer-entrepreneur were conceived by Cantillon merely as remuneration for risk taking, and not systematically related to capital advances. Hence the notion of a rate of profits, and the idea of a tendency towards a uniform rate of profits under competitive conditions, is still absent from Cantillon's analysis.

With regard to the determination of a "par" between labour and land, Cantillon dismissed the method proposed by Petty as "fanciful and remote from natural laws"; in his view, Petty had "attached himself not to causes and principles but only to effects" (1755 [1964]: 43). In Cantillon's understanding, the workers' means of subsistence (that is, Petty's "food") enter as a cost element into the production costs of all commodities (besides other cost elements such as raw materials), and thus are merely a component part of "intrinsic values", but not their cause. In order to find this underlying "cause" or "source", Cantillon insisted, the amount of food required for subsistence must be further reduced to the amount of land that was needed for generating it. He accordingly proposed another method, different from Petty's, which to most interpreters has been suggestive of a land theory of value (1755 [1964]: 41).

The method proposed consisted in reducing labour, or rather the amounts of "food" needed for performing this labour, to (what Cantillon considered to be) its ultimate source in nature: the amounts of land needed to generate this "food". As in Petty, the value of labour is given by the daily amount of food required for subsistence by the worker and his offspring (1755 [1964]: 35). This amount of food is then further reduced to the amount of land needed in its production. Accordingly, the "intrinsic values" of commodities are given by the amounts of land needed directly and indirectly in their production.

James Steuart's Contributions, in Relation to those of the French Physiocrats

Cantillon's analysis of the circular flow of income and expenditure was to serve as the basic conceptual model from which François Quesnay was to develop his *Tableau économique* in the late 1750s. Quesnay clearly depicted the social production process as a circular process based on sectoral interdependencies, and he also emphasized the role of capital advances in the production process, introducing (in terms of his "avances annuelles", "avances primitives" and "avances foncieres") also the distinction between circulating and fixed capital (see Gehrke and Kurz 1995).

Contemporaneous with the contributions of the French Physiocrats was James

Steuart's *Inquiry into the Principles of Political Oeconomy*, which was published in 1767 (although the parts relevant here had been drafted by 1759). Compared with the French contributions, Steuart's work lacked a clear conception of the circular flow and, in particular, a notion of profits in relation to advanced capital. This latter concept had not been present in Quesnay's writings either, but in Anne-Robert-Jacques Turgot's *Reflections* of 1766, where the role of competition in equalizing rates of return on capital (net of differential risk and other returns for entrepreneurship) was for the first time clearly stated. Steuart rather related profits to the income of the farmer or master manufacturer over and above his subsistence, that is, he amalgamated profits with surplus wages. He also had no satisfactory principle for determining the distribution of the surplus and no clear conception of capital advances and profitability in relation to price determination. His main contributions to the further development of British classical political economy consisted in going beyond Cantillon's notion of entrepreneurial profit and in introducing habit formation elements into the subsistence wage concept.

Steuart's notion of agricultural surplus or "net product" refers to "the quantity of food and necessaries remaining over and above the nourishment, consumption and expence of those engaged in agriculture" (1767 [1966]: 54). Similar to Petty and Cantillon, surplus is supposed to be realized in income form as rent, and in a passage reminiscent of Cantillon's "three rents" conception, Steuart observed:

> It is very certain, that all rents are in a pretty just proportion to the gross produce, after deducting three principal articles. First, The nourishment of the farmer, his family, and servants, Secondly, The necessary expences of his family, for manufactures, and instruments for cultivation of the ground. Thirdly, His reasonable profits, according to the custom of every country. (1767 [1966]: 53)

The novel elements are, first, that necessary expenses explicitly included manufactured commodities, and, second, the inclusion of "reasonable profits" amongst the expenses to be deducted. However, since profits were not systematically related to capital advances, it remained unclear what was meant by "reasonable".

In his explanation of the concept of subsistence Steuart introduced the distinction between "physical-necessary" and "political-necessary", defining the former as providing "ample subsistence where no degree of superfluity is implied" (1767 [1966]: 269–70). As opposed to this, "political-necessary" subsistence comprises provision for "desires" which "proceed from the affections of [the] mind, are formed by habit and education, and when once regularly established, create another kind of necessary" (Steuart 1767 [1966]: 270). In Steuart, subsistence wages can thus also contain surplus elements which have been rendered necessary from habit and custom. The size of profits he sought to explain with reference to the conditions of "supply" and "demand" – which meant that it was left indeterminate in normal conditions. (This indeterminacy comes out also in the reference to "reasonable profits, according to the custom of every country" in the above quotation.)

Closely related to what has just been said, Steuart's treatment of prices was also unsatisfactory, primarily because the idea of capitalist competition as an organizing principle of price formation was missing. Here also Turgot's exposition, or Graslin's contributions (see Faccarello 2009), were more advanced than Steuart's. Prices were conceived by

Steuart as being regulated by "real values", understood as costs of production (exclusive of profits) with an element of "profit upon alienation" added on (1767 [1966]: 159). He also noted the possibility of profits being "consolidated" into the "real value" of commodities (1767 [1966]: 192–3); this perhaps reflects an attempt to make profits a permanent component part of price in normal conditions. Steuart recognized that the reference to "costs of production" as price-determining involved him in circular reasoning, but was unable to provide any remedy for this.

The agricultural sector occupies a central position in Steuart's economic system because it generates demand for the manufacturing sector and determines the size of the population that can be sustained. Although Steuart's formulations are somewhat ambiguous, there is also a construction similar to the Petty–Cantillon notion of surplus labour in corn model or integrated rural sector terms, that is, the ratio between total employment in the agricultural sector and the quantity of labour directly and indirectly required to produce the necessary food or subsistence. Like Petty and Cantillon, Steuart also discussed the relation between necessary and total employment in the economy as a whole, and related population size to agricultural surplus (1767 [1966]: 36). However, Steuart was well aware that, by including "clothing" and other manufactures among the means of subsistence, the two sectors are mutually providing each other with necessary inputs. And he variously reversed the causality, arguing that the activity level of the agricultural sector is determined by the demand from those employed in manufacturing and trade, rather than the other way around.

Developing a Comprehensive Conceptual Framework for the Analysis of Capitalist Economic Systems: Adam Smith

Adam Smith's *Wealth of Nations* (1776 [1976], hereafter cited as *WN*) marked the advent of "mature classical economics" (Walsh and Gram 1980: 48). Smith provided a clear conception of long-period prices that included a general rate of profit on capital as an element of normal production prices. He thus based the theory of value and distribution firmly on capitalist market relations. In addition, Smith also made some decisive steps towards integrating manufacturing and trade into the theory of production and growth, although he continued to attribute a special role to agriculture, and, in particular, to "food" or "corn" production, in the generation of the surplus.

Market prices and natural prices

Smith's distinction between "market prices" and "natural prices" takes up the conceptualization introduced by his predecessors. The market price of a commodity refers to the actual price, as it can be observed in a given time and place. It is influenced by a variety of factors, both of a permanent and of an accidental or temporary nature. In Smith's conception, market prices are defined with reference to the associated natural price, that is, by confronting the supply of a commodity in a given historical situation with the corresponding "effectual demand":

> The market price of every particular commodity is regulated by the proportion between the quantity which is actually brought to market, and the demand of those who are willing to pay the natural price of the commodity, or the whole value of the rent, labour, and profit, which must be paid in order to bring it thither. (*WN* I.vii.8)

In the usual price–quantity diagram Smith's notions of "supply" and "effectual demand" correspond to single points (see Garegnani 1983). If the supply exceeds (falls short of) the effectual demand for the commodity, competition among sellers (buyers) will lower (raise) the market price below (above) its natural value. In both cases adjustment processes are triggered by which the supply is adapted to the "effectual demand":

> If at any time it [the quantity brought to market] exceeds the effectual demand, some of the component parts of its price must be paid below their natural rate. If it is rent, the interests of the landlords will immediately prompt them to withdraw a part of their land; and if it is wages or profit, the interest of the labourers in the one case, and of their employers in the other, will prompt them to withdraw a part of their labour or stock from this employment. The quantity brought to market will soon be no more than sufficient to supply the effectual demand. (*WN* I.vii.13)

A similar reasoning applies in the converse case, so that the natural levels of the three rates of income are restored through the reactions of land-owners, workers, and capitalists to above- or below-normal rates of remuneration. Accordingly, natural prices can be conceived as "attractors" of market prices, which according to Smith always gravitate towards or oscillate around them (*WN* I.vii.15).

How, then, are the natural prices determined? Smith approached this problem with reference to two different stages in the development of societies – a distinction which can be interpreted as reflecting a mere thought experiment or also a real historical sequence. In the "early and rude state of society which precedes both the accumulation of stock and the appropriation of land" (*WN* I.vi.1) the entire produce of labour belongs to the labourer, and the exchange ratios of commodities are determined by the ratio of the quantities of direct labour employed in their production. The amount of labour "embodied" in a commodity is then equal to the amount of labour "commanded" by it. However, in an "improved society", where land has been privately appropriated and capital has been accumulated, the labourers have to share the produce of their labour with the owners of capital and land. Since profits and rents now enter into the prices of commodities as component parts, besides wages, the amount of labour "commanded" by a commodity must necessarily exceed the amount of labour "embodied" in it. In Smith's view, the labour theory of value must then be dispensed with, and he suggested replacing it by defining the "natural prices" of commodities as the sum of three components: wages, profits, and rents, all remunerated at the corresponding "natural rates" (*WN* I.vi). Smith contended that the price of every commodity can always be entirely resolved into these three income components, because the means of production which have been used in the commodity's production have themselves been produced in the preceding period by means of land, labour, and produced means of production, and the latter in turn have been produced, in the previous production period, by land, labour, and produced means of production, and so on. Smith also suggested that the "natural price varies with the natural rate of each of its component parts, of wages, profit, and rent" (*WN* I.vii.33). He thus missed the constraint binding changes in the three distributive variables in a given technical environment.

It is clear that Smith's "adding-up theory of prices" (Sraffa 1951: xxxv) involves circular reasoning: it transfers the problem of price determination to that of determining the natural rates of wages, profits, and rents; and the level of the natural wage was made to depend by Smith on the prices of the workers' means of subsistence (see Garegnani 1984). In addition, for commodity prices to be completely resolvable into the three income components there must be a production stage at which only labour and land are required as inputs, that is, the reduction series to dated quantities of labour and dated quantities of land would have to be of finite duration.

Profits and wages

The natural level of the real wage is made to depend by Smith on the workers' bargaining position and their subsistence requirements, which are determined not merely by physiological needs but also comprise wants rendered necessary from habit and custom. In economies which are stationary or retrogressing, the common real wage is said to be usually low or declining, while in fast growing ones, due to the better bargaining position of the workers, it is high or increasing (*WN* I.viii.16–17). Increases or decreases in real wages are taken to lead, however, to increases or decreases in the growth rate of population, and thereby of labour supply (*WN* I.viii.40).

The idea that the supply of labour is adapting endogenously to the demand for it is encountered in many classical writers, but rather than invoking the population mechanism, authors such as Ricardo, Torrens, and Marx placed more emphasis on other factors, such as labour displacement due to labour-saving technical progress or international labour migration.

When the price is at the natural level the producer obtains the normal or natural rate of profits on the advanced capital. Smith is very clear about the fact that the popular belief that profits are "only a different name for the wages of a particular sort of labour, the labour of inspection and direction" is a misconception: "They are regulated altogether by the value of the stock employed, and are greater or smaller in proportion to the extent of this stock." (*WN* I.vi.6). In competitive conditions, the rate of profits obtained in different lines of production must be the same (except for profit rate differentials that can be explained by differences in risk, agreeableness, and so on) and must equal the normal or "natural" rate. Its level is said to be low in societies that are stationary and retrogressing, and high in newly advancing ones. However, according to Smith there is a tendency towards a secular decline in the rate of profits also in advancing societies due to the "increasing competition of capitals" (*WN* I.ix.2) – but the arguments he put forward in support of this view cannot be sustained.

Surplus, gross and net revenue

Smith took over the concept of surplus from his precursors, but introduced a novel element which is reflected in his ambiguous definition of gross and net revenue:

> The gross revenue of all the inhabitants of a great country, comprehends the whole annual produce of their land and labour; the neat revenue, what remains free to them after deducting the expense of maintaining . . . their . . . capital; or what, without encroaching upon their capital, they can place in their stock reserved for immediate consumption, or spend upon their subsistence, conveniencies, and amusements. (*WN* II.ii.5)

Smith's notion of "national revenue", in both gross and net terms, refers to the income of "all the inhabitants" of a country. But Smith reckoned the wages of "productive" labourers as part of the capital so that his notion of "net revenue" can only comprise those wages which are destined to support either "unproductive" labourers or *additional* "productive" labourers. Smith's treatment of wages in his social accounting scheme differed significantly from that of his precursors, most notably the French Physiocrats, whose conceptualization had been unambiguous: defining the "net revenue" (or "produit net") as the annually produced wealth ("reproduction totale") minus the advances required to repeat the process on the same scale, they included the workers' subsistence, to which wages were assumed to be strictly confined, among the necessary production expenses, on the same footing as the feed of the cattle. Smith seems to have vacillated between adopting this treatment and dispensing with it in favour of a conceptualization of wages as a share in net income: he considered it adequate, when measuring the wealth and prosperity of a nation, to include the workers' wages in the national income. His measure of "wealth", which he established definitely for subsequent economic analysis, was income per head.

The accumulation of capital was seen by Smith as a precondition for increasing the division of labour and raising aggregate wealth or income per head. It consists in re-investing part of the surplus in additional means of production and wage advances for "productive" workers. Smith's distinction between "productive" and "unproductive" labour has given rise to much debate, because he offered several, and partly contradictory, definitions. Thus he defined "productive" labour as that labour which is paid from capital (and not from income), that which gives rise to physical goods (and not to services), and that which recoups the value of the capital advances and in addition generates profits (and rents). The latter definition perhaps captures best what seems to have been the main point Smith wanted to emphasize: productive labour is surplus-generating labour, whereas unproductive labour is surplus-consuming labour. In this reading, Smith's concept of "net revenue" was meant to serve as a measure of the upper bound for net capital accumulation (Aspromourgos 2009: 196).

With regard to the question of the origin of the surplus Smith emphatically rejected the physiocratic idea that the agricultural sector alone is capable of generating a surplus, and in fact emphasized the "impropriety" of designating manufacturing and trade and transport activities as unproductive (*WN* IV.ix.29). However, Smith nowhere stated, and indeed did not properly perceive, that in a system of production of commodities by means of commodities it simply makes no sense to say that the surplus emanates from one sector alone. Because with a social division of labour manufactures are used as inputs in agriculture and vice versa, it is the economic system as a whole that either is, or is not, capable of generating a surplus. That Smith failed to understand this, and more generally did not succeed in liberating himself from physiocratic modes of thought, becomes apparent from his theory of rent, his statements on the "natural course" of economic development, and from his adoption of corn-ratio reasoning in determining the size of the surplus. Let us consider these in turn.

Rent and corn

Smith possessed several elements for the development of a consistent theory of rent, but failed to use them adequately. He noted that the rent of land "is naturally a monopoly price" which "is not at all proportioned to what the landlord may have laid out upon the improvement of the land" (*WN* I.xi.a.5). He also observed that "high or low rent" is not the cause but rather "the effect" of a high price of agricultural products (*WN*

I.xi.a.8), but the arguments he put forward in explaining this proposition, which David Ricardo was later to confirm on the basis of his theory of differential rent, are not sound. Although Smith in one place referred to cost differentials in connection with rent, he failed to grasp the principle of differential rent and its underlying rationale. The main shortcoming of his theory of rent, however, was his adherence to the physiocratic idea that "rent may be considered as the produce of those powers of nature, the use of which the landlord lends to the farmer. . . . It is the work of nature" (*WN* II.v.12). In fact, in the final analysis Smith appears to have seen the source of rent not in the "work of nature" in general, but in its "work" specifically in the production of "food" or "corn" (*WN* I.xi.c.8). When "the labour of half the society becomes sufficient to provide food for the whole . . . [the] other half . . . can be employed in providing other things" (*WN* I.xi.6–7). Also, since the "desire of food is limited in every man by the narrow capacity of the human stomach", Smith is confident that "those, who have the command of more food than they themselves can consume, are always willing to exchange the surplus" for "conveniences and ornaments of building, dress, equipage, and household furniture" (*WN* I.xi.7). These passages show that the circular character of the social process of production, which had been brought out so clearly in the *Tableau économique*, was perceived by Smith only partially. In Smith's *Wealth of Nations* circular production relations are in fact confined to the agricultural sector alone, where the products are envisaged as being produced by means of themselves as inputs. However, the agricultural sector is depicted as requiring no necessary inputs from the manufacturing sector. The latter is rather envisaged as producing more refined consumption goods and luxury commodities ("conveniences and ornaments"), using as inputs the "raw produce" and the foodstuff received from the agricultural sector. The social production process is thus envisaged as a one-way avenue or unidirectional process with a clear hierarchical structure.

That Smith was, in this regard, more agrocentric than the Physiocrats can also be seen in his discussion of the natural course of development. In chapter V of book II, Smith argued that the employment of capital in the different sectors "puts into motion . . . different quantities of productive labour" and adds "different values . . . to the annual produce of the land and labour of the society" (*WN* II.v.37). Both with regard to the employment effects and the generation of value added he envisaged a clear sectoral hierarchy, leading from agriculture (and mining) to manufacturing and, finally, to wholesale and retail trade (see Jeck 1994). If undisturbed by (mercantilist) policy interventions, capital would therefore first be employed in the agricultural sector, thereafter in manufacturing and domestic trade, and finally in the distant foreign trade (*WN* III.i.2). Interestingly, it is not agriculture in general, but more specifically the production of food or "corn", which Smith regarded as of central importance. In Smith's thinking "corn" (as a catch-all for means of subsistence) has a special role, owing to his belief that there exists a "great and essential difference which nature has established between corn and almost every other sorts of goods" (*WN* IV.v.a.23): in its capacity as the principal wage good corn enters into the production of all commodities.

The special position which "corn" occupied in Smith's thinking comes out also in his development of (some elements of) a corn-ratio theory, similar to the one put forward later by Ricardo in his *Essay on Profits*. This was used by Smith, however, unlike it was used later by Ricardo, not in order to determine the general rate of profits, but rather the entire surplus, shared out between profits and rents (see Vianello 2011). Smith's argument, which seems to have provided the original stimulus for Ricardo's later adoption of a corn-ratio theory in his *Essay on Profits*, is to be found in book IV of the *Wealth of Nations*. There, Smith maintained that "the money price of corn regulates the money price of labour" (*WN* IV.v.a.12). Money wages depend chiefly on the price of corn, Smith contended, because corn is the principal wage good (*WN* I.xi.e.29), and also because the money prices of other agricultural products that might enter into the workers' wage basket are also regulated by it (see *WN* IV.v.a.13). Through its influence on the money wage and on the money prices of other agricultural products the money price of corn then also regulates the money prices of manufactures (*WN* IV.v.a.14). While Smith thus clearly suggested that the price of corn regulates all other prices, he did not derive from this a determining role of the agricultural rate of profits for the general rate of profits (which he rather considered to be determined by the intensity of competition in the economy as a whole).

Determining the Laws which Regulate the Distribution of Income: David Ricardo

The contributions of David Ricardo to the further elaboration of the surplus approach are so important that his role in British classical political economy can hardly be overstated. As he explained in the Preface to his *Principles of Political Economy and Taxation*, published in 1817, he shared in the "great admiration, . . . in common with all those who acknowledge the importance of the science of Political Economy", which the "profound work" of Adam Smith "so justly excites" (Ricardo 1951–73, I: 6). His work focuses attention particularly on those passages in the writings of Smith "from which he sees reason to differ" (1951–73, I: 6).

Net income and natural prices
Ricardo returned to the clear-cut, pre-Smithian conceptualization of wages and systematically used the expression "net revenue" (or "net income") to denote the sum of profits and rents – although he noted, and indeed emphasized, that the workers generally participate in the sharing out of the surplus (1951–73, I: 348 n.). However, in most of his analysis Ricardo nevertheless identified the net income with profits and rents only, treating the entire wages as advanced capital. The net produce he identified with the gross produce minus replacement of the advanced wage goods and means of production. However, in his analysis of income distribution he frequently treated the produced means of production as if they could be reduced to indirect wages in a finite number of steps.

Ricardo fully endorsed Smith's distinction between natural and market prices and expressed his general agreement with the analysis provided by the Scotsman. However, he gave more emphasis to the decisions of profit-seeking capitalists in general and to those of "monied men", that is, financial capitalists, in particular. The "restless desire on the part of all the employers of stock, to quit a less profitable for a more advantageous business, has a strong tendency to equalize the rate of profits for all" (Ricardo 1951–73, I: 88). This adjustment process does not require capitalists to change their business, because bankers and "monied men" with large amounts of "floating capital" are always ready to finance investments in different lines of production. For Ricardo, then, it is first and foremost the capitalists who bring about the adaptation of the quantities supplied to those effectually demanded, together with the related tendency towards a uniform rate of profits and the gravitation of market prices towards natural prices (1951–73, I: 91).

Most of the passages in Smith's writings from which Ricardo saw "reason to differ" concern issues that are directly related to, or followed from, Smith's "original error respecting value" (Ricardo 1951–73, VII: 100), that is, his "adding-up" theory of value. In chapter 1 of his *Principles* Ricardo showed that the transition from the "early and rude" to the "advanced" state of society does not per se imply that the labour theory of value must be dispensed with: it is not necessarily invalidated by private land ownership and by the fact that commodities are produced capitalistically. It is only because commodities are produced with different proportions of labour and means of production, or different proportions of direct and indirect labour, that relative prices deviate from the relative quantities of direct and indirect labour embodied in them.

Income distribution

"The principal problem in Political Economy", Ricardo famously stated in the Preface to his *Principles*, is "to determine the laws which regulate . . . the proportions of the whole produce . . . which will be allotted to . . . rent, profit, and wages" (1951–73, I: 5). The main task he set himself thus consisted in finding the laws governing the income shares and their development over time. The theory of differential rent, which he first adopted in the *Essay on Profits* of February 1815, allowed him to separate this problem into two parts: "By getting rid of rent . . . the distribution between capitalist and labourer becomes a much more simple consideration" (1951–73, VIII: 194).

In the *Essay on Profits*, and then more extensively in chapter 2 of the *Principles*, Ricardo expounded the principles of extensive and intensive diminishing returns in agriculture due to the scarcity of land. The clarity of his exposition has led to the identification of this theory with his name, although he acknowledged earlier expositions by authors such as James Anderson, Edward West, and Thomas Robert Malthus. Unlike those authors, Ricardo integrated the theory of differential rent into a system of political economy whose main aim was the determination of the general rate of profits. He first focused attention on extensively diminishing returns and assumed that the available plots of land can be brought into a ranking of natural "fertility", reflecting the unit costs incurred in the production of the agricultural product, which for simplicity he supposed to consist of corn only. In the first settling of a country, where the total demand for corn is low, only land of the highest fertility will be cultivated and there will be no rent, because land, even that of the best quality, is not scarce (Ricardo 1951–73, I: 69). As capital accumulates and the population grows, recourse must be had to less and less fertile land in order to satisfy the growing social demand for corn. As a consequence, the costs of production and hence the price of corn will have to rise. For a given level of demand and hence gross output, the price of corn will equal unit costs (including profits at the normal rate) on the marginal land, for which the proprietors under competitive conditions obtain no rent, because this quality of land is not scarce. Accordingly, on the marginal land the product is shared out only between wages and profits. On the intra-marginal lands the landowners obtain rents that correspond to the cost differential between the unit costs on the quality of land owned by them and the marginal land. This implies that, contrary to the views of Smith and the Physiocrats, rent arises not because of the generosity of nature, but rather because of its "niggardliness"; that it is not the cause of a high price of corn, but rather its effect; and that rent "cannot enter in the least degree as a component part of its price" (1951–73, I: 77).

For Ricardo it was clear that "profits come out of the surplus produce" (1951–73, II: 130–31; also I: 95); the problem was to determine the size of the share of profits (relative to those of wages and rents) and the level of the rate of profits. In his early monetary writings, Ricardo followed Smith in maintaining that the rate of profits depends on the "competition of capitals", but in spring 1813 he began to doubt the correctness of this doctrine. In correspondence with Malthus he stressed the importance of the production conditions in agriculture for the level of the general rate of profits, and he already referred to "my theory" without however explicating it in any detail (Ricardo 1951–73, VI: 95). In March 1814 he composed "some papers on the profits of capital", which however have been lost, and to Trower he wrote in the same month:

> The profits of the farmer . . . regulate the profits of all other trades,– and as the profits of the farmer must necessarily decrease with every augmentation of capital employed on the land, provided no improvements be at the same time made in husbandry, all other profits must diminish and therefore the rate of interest must fall. (1951–73, VI: 104)

According to Sraffa's interpretation, the "rational foundation" of the determining role of the profits of agriculture was that:

> in agriculture the same commodity, namely corn, forms both the capital (conceived as composed of the subsistence necessary for workers) and the product; so that the determination of profit by the difference between total product and capital advanced, and also the determination of the ratio of this profit to the capital, is done directly between quantities of corn without any question of valuation. (1951: xxxi)

Sraffa stressed that the corn model was "never stated by Ricardo in any of his extant letters and papers" (1951: xxxi), but concluded from the available indirect evidence that Ricardo "must have formulated it either in his lost "papers on the profits of capital" of March 1814 or in conversation" (1951: xxxi). The proposition that the profits of the farmer regulate the profits of all other trades recurs in the *Essay on Profits* (Ricardo 1951–73, IV: 23), together with the statement that "the rate of profits . . . must depend on the proportion of production to the consumption necessary to such production" (1951–73, IV: 108). In the *Essay*, however, the advanced capital in agriculture is assumed to consist not only of corn but of several commodities, including also manufactures, so that Ricardo's reasoning in the *Essay* only "reflects" the corn-ratio argument, since "both capital and the 'neat produce' are *expressed* in corn, and thus the profit per cent is calculated without need to mention price" (Sraffa 1951: xxxii, emphasis added).

It has not been much noticed that in the *Essay on Profits* the "rate of rent" was calculated by Ricardo also as a percentage of the advanced capital, that is, as the ratio of the amount of rent (in corn) to the amount of capital advanced (also expressed in corn). This misled several commentators, including Marx (1861–63 [1989]: 73–4, 308), into wrongly supposing that it had been a proposition of Ricardo that the accumulation process was bound up with a fall in the rate of profits and a rise in the rate of rent (so defined). In the *Principles*, and more explicitly in one of his *Notes on Malthus* (1951–73, II: 196–7), Ricardo later clarified that no such inverse relationship between the rates of rent and profits exists (see Gehrke 2012: 60–61). What Ricardo had maintained in the *Essay*, and had indeed demonstrated on the basis of his corn-ratio theory, was that in a given technical environment real wages (that is, corn wages) and the rate of profits are inversely related to one another.

However, Ricardo soon realized that the corn-ratio theory was not general enough, although he was convinced that the basic idea underlying it was correct. Therefore the same principle recurs in a different and more general form in the *Principles*. But whereas the rate of profits was conceived in his early theory as a material ratio between two quantities of corn, it was now determined as a ratio between two quantities of labour: the amount of labour embodied in the surplus product (at the agricultural margin, and thus exclusive of rent) and the amount of labour embodied in the social capital (where Ricardo frequently identified capital with wages, setting aside all other items of circulating and fixed capital). This novel conceptualization was made possible by adopting the labour theory of value, that is, by introducing the hypothesis (in section 1 of chapter 1, "On Value") that the exchange values of commodities are governed by the relative amounts of direct and indirect labour embodied in them, which allowed Ricardo to make bundles of heterogeneous commodities commensurable, and thus to determine the general rate of profits for the system as a whole. It also allowed him to state that "in proportion . . . as wages rose, would profits fall" (Ricardo 1951–73, I: 111), that is, to confirm in the more general framework his earlier finding that the two distributive variables are inversely related to one another. The labour theory of value thus enabled him to dispel the wrong idea, deriving from Smith's "adding-up theory" of prices, that real wages and the rate of profits could move independently of one another.

However, Ricardo knew that the labour theory of value was "not rigidly true" (1951–73, VII: 279). In sections 4 and 5 of the chapter "On Value" he noted that *"the principle that value does not vary with the rise of fall of wages"* is *"considerably modified by the employment of machinery and other fixed and durable capital"* and *"modified also by the unequal durability of capital, and the unequal rapidity with which it returns to its employer"* (1951–73, I: 30, 38, original emphases). Different proportions between capital laid out in advanced wages (direct labour) and in means of production (indirect labour), as well as different durabilities of the means of production, made the relative prices of commodities depend on income distribution: the higher the rate of profits (and, correspondingly, the lower the real wage rate), the relatively more costly are commodities produced with a high proportion of indirect to direct labour. Except for the unrealistic case of equal proportions, the relative prices of two commodities will therefore "deviate" from the relative amounts of direct and indirect labour embodied in them. Ricardo first tried to play down this problem, by adopting a standard of value which minimized the magnitude of these deviations, and to argue that the "modifications" were small in magnitude and thus could be neglected. He then tried to cope with the problem in terms of his concept of an "invariable measure of value". Originally, and following Adam Smith, this concept was only meant to allow for interspatial and intertemporal value comparisons, that is, comparisons relating to different technical environments. For the standard to be invariable it had to be a commodity produced with an unvarying quantity of labour. However, Ricardo was then facing also the different problem that even in the same technical environment two commodities could vary in relative value from a change in income distribution. In a manuscript on "Absolute value and exchangeable value", written shortly before his death, Ricardo tried to investigate how the prices of commodities produced under different production conditions vary with changes in income distribution, and concluded that for the standard to be invariable it would have to be a "medium between the extremes" (1951–73, IV: 372). Subsequent research has shown that the two requirements cannot be met simultaneously (see Kurz and Salvadori 1993).

The inverse wage–profit relationship

When Ricardo first exposed the fallacy of Smith's "adding-up theory" in his *Essay on Profits*, the argument was conducted in terms of commodity (corn) wages, and the inverse relationship between the wage rate and the general rate of profits was derived by assuming a given technical environment, explicitly setting aside improvements in production methods (Ricardo 1951–73, IV: 12). Prompted by objections raised by Malthus in subsequent debates, Ricardo developed a novel conceptualization of "real wages", and in the first edition of the *Principles* presented the proposition that the rate of profits must always vary inversely with *proportional wages*. (A first allusion to the new concept can be found in a letter to Malthus of 14 October 1816; 1951–73, VII: 81).) Ricardo adopted this concept precisely because it enabled him, or so he thought, to demonstrate an inverse relationship between wages and the rate of profits even in a changing technical environment. Suppose, he argued, that with the same amount of labour annually expended, "by improvements in machinery and agriculture", the whole produce of society is doubled, but that the portions going to rents, profits and wages are not increased proportionately:

Of every hundred hats, coats, and quarters of corn produced, if

The labourers had before . . .	25
The landlords . . .	25
And the capitalists . . .	50
	100:

And if, after these commodities were double the quantity, of every 100

The labourers had only . . .	22
The landlords . . .	22
And the capitalists . . .	56
	100:

In that case I should say, that wage and rent had fallen and profits risen; though, in consequence of the abundance of commodities, the quantity paid to the labourer and landlord would have increased in the proportion of 25 to 44. Wages are to be estimated by their real value, viz. by the quantity of labour and capital employed in producing them, and not by their nominal value either in coats, hats, money, or corn. (Ricardo 1951–73, I: 50)

As Ricardo stressed, his conceptualization of the "real value of wages" relied on the possibility of measuring the total produce in terms of a standard which is invariant with regard to changes in the distribution of income and in the productivity of labour. In terms of such a standard, Ricardo argued, the value of the social product is given by the total amount of labour expended (that is, by the total annual labour of society), and wages can accordingly be expressed as the proportion of the annual labour of the country which is devoted to the support of the labourers. This device was not merely another way of expressing the relative distribution of income. Ricardo rather conceived of it as an analytical concept that allowed him to assert, or so he thought, that the rate of profits depends only on proportional wages, even in changing technical environments (Ricardo 1951–73, I: 126, II: 252).

Ricardo's numerical example quoted above is of interest also from another viewpoint, because it also contains a novel device by means of which the rate of profits can be ascertained as a physical ratio. Instead of supposing homogeneity between the capital advanced and the product in a single industry, as in the corn-ratio theory of the *Essay on Profits*, Ricardo now assumed homogeneity between product and capital in aggregate terms: the commodity composition of the surplus product is the same as the commodity composition of the social capital if the latter is assumed to consist only of the real wages bill. In this case the general rate of profits may again be conceived of in purely physical terms. In the example, of every 100 units produced of the three commodities – hats, coats, and quarters of corn – workers are paid 25 (or 22) units of each of them and landlords are also assumed to receive 25 (or 22) units; accordingly, profits consist of 50 (56) units of each commodity. If capital is assumed to consist only of the real wages bill, the rate of profits can be determined independently of the problem of the valuation of the different commodities. It amounts to $50/25 = 2$ (or $56/22 \approx 2.55$).

By adopting the simplifying assumption that the advanced capital consists only of wages, or can be reduced to direct and indirect wages in a finite number of steps, Ricardo had abandoned the conceptualization of social production as a circular flow. This made him lose sight of the fact that the price of a commodity can never be fully resolved into wages and profits: however far back one carries the reduction to dated quantities of labour, there will always remain a commodity residue. Therefore the rate of profits will not tend towards infinity when wages are hypothetically reduced to zero, as it is the case with a unidirectional view of the production process. There is rather a finite maximum level of the rate of profits corresponding to zero wages. This implies that the rate of profits depends on two magnitudes instead of on only one – it depends on proportional wages *and* on the maximum rate of profits (for further details, see Gehrke and Kurz, 2006).

Torrens's Criticisms of Ricardo's Theory of Value and Distribution

One of Ricardo's ablest critics among his contemporaries was Robert Torrens. His thinking on the theory of value and distribution developed in close relation to that of Ricardo, and comprised phases and elements of acknowledging, adopting, opposing, and rejecting Ricardo's ideas. Starting out from Smith's "adding-up" theory of value, in his *Essay on the External Corn Trade* (1815 [2000]) Torrens then adopted some of Ricardo's ideas. In particular, he picked up from Ricardo's *Essay on Profits* the idea of determining the rate of profits by assuming homogeneity between product and capital, and also endorsed Ricardo's proposition regarding the inverse wage–profit relationship. However, in his "Strictures on Mr Ricardo's doctrine respecting exchangeable value" (1818 [2000]), a review of Ricardo's *Principles*, Torrens then put forward a criticism of the labour theory of value and to propose instead a "capital theory of value": that "it is always the amount of capital, and never the quantity of labour, which determines the value of commodities" (1818 [2000], VIII: 5). However, he had to admit that this "theory" had serious weaknesses, which eventually forced him to abandon it – and to have recourse to labour value reasoning again. First, there was the problem of defining "equal amounts of capital", as Ricardo (1951–73: IX, 359–60) was quick to point out. When Torrens specified this in his *Essay on the Production of Wealth* (1821 [2000]) in terms of "equal amounts of accumulated labour", the whole conception was seen to involve him in circular reasoning: "to disproof that commodities exchange according to labour embodied, Torrens starts from assuming that the commodities which constitute their capitals do so exchange" (De Vivo 2000, III: x–xi). Secondly, as opposed to Ricardo's labour-value based reasoning, this theory did not allow for a determination of the general rate of profits (except by assuming the particular conditions of production for which homogeneity between product and capital obtains, that is, except when no theory of value was necessary to determine the rate of profits). Nonetheless, the numerical examples Torrens produced were sufficient to demonstrate the incompatibility between exchange in proportion to labour embodied and a uniform rate of profits.

The main interest of Torrens's contribution lies in his attempts to determine the general rate of profits without following Ricardo in adopting the labour theory of value. In the second edition (1820) of his *Essay on the External Corn Trade* he provided a clear statement of the corn-ratio theory of profits (1820 [2000], II: 362). In the *Essay on the Production of Wealth*, published in 1821, Torrens then generalized the idea of homogeneity between product and capital by formulating numerical examples in which the commodities enter into the net social product in the same composition in which they enter into the aggregate social capital, so that the general rate of profits is determined as a physical ratio between two different quantities of a composite commodity, with no need to determine relative prices. Torrens's example comprised two industries, one producing corn, the other suits of clothing, and both industries use both products in the same proportions (and actually in the same absolute amounts) as inputs (1821 [2000], III: 372–3).

Torrens was aware of the fact that physical homogeneity of product, surplus, and capital cannot be expected to hold in any real economy other than in highly special cases. In his attempt to deal with more general cases he was thus of necessity confronted with the complexity of the relationship between income distribution and relative prices. In yet another attempt to contain this complexity and arrive at a simple determination of the general rate of profits, Torrens resorted to the special assumption we just encountered, namely, that in all lines of production the same commodity input proportions apply. With a uniform real wage rate this assumption implies, of course, that relative prices are correctly explained by the labour theory of value. More specifically, commodities exchange for one another according to the quantities of labour contained in the (circulating) capitals (means of production and means of subsistence) used up in the course of their production.

In the Preface to the third edition (1826) of the *Essay on the External Corn Trade* Torrens then constructed numerical examples which showed that Ricardo's inverse wage–profit relationship need not necessarily hold true if non-wage capital was properly taken into account: productivity-enhancing technical change could raise the general rate of profits without a fall of proportional wages (see Torrens 1826 [2000], II: xv–xvi; see also De Vivo 2000: II, xxviii–xxix). Torrens's demonstration anticipated Marx's later criticism of Ricardo for his neglect of non-wage capital in his observations on profits and wages. Unlike Marx, however, Torrens made no reference to the notion of a maximum rate of profits in his argument.

The Decline of British Classical Political Economy

After Ricardo's death the task of elaborating on his theory of value and distribution and defending it against the criticisms of Malthus, Torrens, and others fell to his self-proclaimed disciples John Ramsey McCulloch and James and John Stuart Mill. None of them was up to this task, and the "corrections" and "amendments" to Ricardo's theory which they introduced amounted in effect to its abandonment, and its eventual replacement with a cost of production theory of value (Meek, 1950).

McCulloch, who propagated Ricardian ideas in his *Principles of Political Economy* (1825) and edited Ricardo's *Works* in 1844, posited himself as one of the closest associates of Ricardo and staunchest advocates of his theories. However, in subsequent writings (and in later editions of his *Principles*) he distorted Ricardo's theory of value, and thereby paved the way towards the establishment of the notion of "real cost" of J.S. Mill and Alfred Marshall (see O'Brien 1970; De Vivo 1984). Already in the first edition of his *Principles* McCulloch had introduced the notion of "accumulated labour", as including a "wage" that remunerated the capitalist for the time during which the embodied labour remained stored up. By means of this device he believed he could render the labour theory of value compatible with the complications, already noted by Ricardo, which arise from different production periods, different ratios of fixed and circulating capital, and different durabilities of fixed capitals. McCulloch's re-definition of the notion of "embodied labour" provided no solution, but transformed Ricardo's labour theory of value into a "real cost" theory consisting of wages paid plus profits accrued on advanced wages: "It was precisely this element of "real cost" that gradually acquired importance, to the point of transforming the Ricardian theory of value, related to the difficulty of production, into a theory of the cost of production" (Roncaglia 2001: 220).

In his *Critical Dissertation on the Nature, Measure and Causes of Value* (1825 [1967]) Samuel Bailey criticized Ricardo's concept of "absolute value" on the ground that value was something essentially relative that denotes nothing positive or real. The Smith–Ricardo–Malthus search for an invariable measure of value he dismissed as a pointless exercise. Bailey made some valid criticisms of the Ricardian theory of value, which prompted James Mill and McCulloch to reformulations and amendments. The *Critical Dissertation* also provoked extensive responses from Malthus (1827 [1971]) and from De Quincey (1844 [1970]). The importance that is sometimes attributed to Bailey's *Critical Dissertation* as a landmark contribution to value theory owes much to the fact that Torrens had declared, in 1831, that this treatise had been decisive for the abandonment of Ricardo's doctrines. However, this was as much an overstatement as the claims that have been made later by Seligman and others, who depicted Bailey as a precursor of "modern", that is, marginal utility value theory and as an early exponent of the abstinence theory. Bailey's remarks on the causes of value fell far short of anything that could be called an alternative theory, and indeed did not get beyond the vague suggestion that a theory of value must take into account "mental states" and "estimations". If Bailey contributed to the abandonment of the surplus approach and its gradual replacement by the marginalist approach, then this did not so much concern the demand side, but rather the supply side. More specifically, with his division of reproducible commodities into those which can be supplied at constant costs and those which are only producible at increasing costs, Bailey introduced the idea of a relationship between cost and quantity produced. It was this idea which eventually paved the way to Marshall's attempted reconciliation of "cost of production" and "marginal utility" in the determination of prices (see De Vivo 1984: 133–5).

Subjectivist elements were also introduced into the theory of value by authors such as Nassau W. Senior and Mountifort Longfield; and various other writers, such as Thomas Read and George Poulett Scrope, advocated cost of production theories in some form or another. A combination of utility and cost of production elements in price determination was proposed also by Thomas De Quincey, who in 1824 had published an excellent exposition and defence of Ricardo's theory of value and distribution, entitled "Dialogues of three templars on political economy". However, in his later work, *The Logic of Political Economy* (1844), he made some decisive steps towards a theory of prices based on demand and supply and a subjective theory of value. On the one hand, he stressed the role of utility in the determination of the value of scarce, non-reproducible commodities. On the other, he introduced the concept of "actual prices", and thereby deprived the Smithian notion of "market prices" of the role previously assigned to it. He thus paved the way to the Marshallian conceptualization of different levels of analysis in terms of the length of time allowed for adjustment processes, with utility and cost of production, or demand and supply, both acting simultaneously on the determination of prices, with the former being of primary importance in ultra-short and short periods, and the latter in long periods.

John Stuart Mill completed the abandonment of the surplus approach to the theory of value and distribution of the British classical political economists. His *Essays on Some Unsettled Questions in Political Economy*, written in 1829–30 but published only in 1844, contained an essay on the theory of foreign trade (Mill 1844a [1967]), in which he introduced the concept of "reciprocal demand", and an essay on profit (Mill 1844b [1967]), in which he set out to correct Ricardo's formulation of the wage–profit relationship. Mill's reciprocal demand theory was later taken up by Marshall in the elaboration of his theory of value. In his *Principles of Political Economy* (1848 [1965]) Mill then merged Senior's theory of abstinence with the Ricardian theory of distribution. Mill also introduced the wage fund theory (which he later famously recanted) and in his value theory transformed Ricardo's theory into a cost of production theory. Moreover, he introduced the distinction between commodities the supply of which is fixed, those of which the supply can be increased without an increase in costs, and those of which the supply can only be increased at increasing costs, and suggested that the classical theory applies only to the second class of commodities, whose natural prices are given by their costs of production, which consist of wages, profits (considered as remuneration for abstinence) and rent (considered as an opportunity cost).

CHRISTIAN GEHRKE

See also:

Balance of payments and exchange rates (III); Pierre Le Pesant de Boisguilbert (I); Capital theory (III); Richard Cantillon (I); French classical political economy (II); Thomas Robert Malthus (I); Karl Heinrich Marx (I); John Stuart Mill (I); Money and banking (III); William Petty (I); François Quesnay and Physiocracy (I); David Ricardo (I); Adam Smith (I); Piero Sraffa (I); James Steuart [James Denham-Steuart] (I); Robert Torrens (I); Anne-Robert-Jacques Turgot (I); Value and price (III).

References and further reading

Aspromourgos, T. (1996), *On the Origins of Classical Economics. Distribution and Value from William Petty to Adam Smith*, London and New York: Routledge.

Aspromourgos, T. (2009), *The Science of Wealth. Adam Smith and the Framing of Political Economy*, London and New York: Routledge.

Bailey, S. (1825), *A Critical Dissertation on the Nature, Measures, and Causes of Value; Chiefly in Reference to the Writings of Mr. Ricardo and his Followers*, London: Hunter, reprinted 1967, New York: A.M. Kelley.

Bellers, J. (1714), *An Essay towards the Improvement of Physick*, London: J. Sole.

Bharadwaj, K. (1978), *Classical Political Economy and the Rise to Dominance of Supply and Demand Theories*, Calcutta: Orient Longman.

Blaug, M. (1987), 'British classical economics', in J. Eatwell, M. Milgate and P. Newman (eds), *The New Palgrave. A Dictionary of Economics*, vol. 1, Basingstoke: Palgrave Macmillan, reprinted in S.N. Durlauf and L.E. Blume (eds) (2008), *The New Palgrave. A Dictionary of Economics*, 2nd edn, Basingstoke: Palgrave Macmillan.

Bonar, J. (1894), 'Classical economics', in R.H.I. Palgrave (ed.), *Dictionary of Political Economy*, vol. 1, London: Macmillan, p. 303.

Cannan, E. (1893), *A History of the Theories of Production and Distribution in English Political Economy from 1776 to 1848*, London: Perceval & Co.

Cantillon, R. (1755), *Essai sur la nature du commerce en général*, London: Fletcher Gyles, English trans. H. Higgs (ed.) (1931), *Essay on the Nature of Trade in General*, London: Macmillan, reprinted 1964, New York: A.M. Kelley.

De Quincey, T. (1824), 'Dialogues of three templars on political economy', *London Magazine*, reprinted in T. De Quincey (1887), *Collected Writings*, ed. D. Masson, Edinburgh: A. and C. Black, vol. 9, reprinted 1970 as *Political Economy and Politics*, New York: A.M. Kelley, pp. 37–112.

De Quincey, T. (1844), *The Logic of Political Economy*, London and Edinburgh: Blackwood, reprinted in T. De Quincey (1887), *Collected Writings*, ed. D. Masson, Edinburgh: A. and C. Black, vol. 9, reprinted 1970 as *Political Economy and Politics*, New York: A.M. Kelley, pp. 118–294.

De Vivo, G. (1984), *Ricardo and His Critics. A Study of Classical Theories of Value and Distribution*, Studie ricerche dell'Istituto Economico no. 23, Modena.

De Vivo, G. (2000), 'Introductions', *Collected Works of Robert Torrens*, 8 vols, ed. G. de Vivo, London: Thoemmes Press.

Dobb, M. (1972), *Theories of Value and Distribution since Adam Smith. Ideology and Economic Theory*, Cambridge: Cambridge University Press.

Faccarello, G. (2009), 'The enigmatic Mr Graslin. A Rousseauist bedrock for classical economics?', *European Journal of the History of Economic Thought*, **16** (1), 1–40.

Garegnani, P. (1983), 'The classical theory of wages and the role of demand schedules in the determination of relative prices', *American Economic Review (Papers and Proceedings)*, **73** (2), 309–13.

Garegnani, P. (1984), 'Value and distribution in the classical economists and Marx', *Oxford Economic Papers*, **36** (2), 291–325.

Garegnani, P. (1987), 'Surplus approach to value and distribution', in J. Eatwell, M. Milgate and P. Newman (eds), *The New Palgrave. A Dictionary of Economics*, vol. 4, London: Macmillan.

Gehrke, C. (2011), '"Price of wages": a curious phrase', in R. Ciccone, C. Gehrke and G. Mongiovi (eds), *Sraffa and Modern Economics*, vol. 1, London: Routledge, pp. 405–22.

Gehrke, C. (2012), 'Marx's critique of Ricardo's theory of rent: a reassessment', in C. Gehrke, N. Salvadori, I. Steedman and R. Sturn (eds), *Classical Political Economy and Modern Theory. Essays in Honour of Heinz D. Kurz*, London: Routledge, pp. 51–84.

Gehrke, C. and H.D. Kurz (1995), 'Karl Marx on physiocracy', *European Journal of the History of Economic Thought*, **2** (1), 54–92.

Gehrke, C. and H.D. Kurz (2006), 'Sraffa on von Bortkiewicz: reconstructing the classical theory of value and distribution', *History of Political Economy*, **38** (1), 91–149.

Hutcheson, T. (1988), *Before Adam Smith: The Emergence of Political Economy 1662–1776*, Oxford: Blackwell.

Jeck, A. (1994), 'The macrostructure of Adam Smith's theoretical system: a reconstruction', *European Journal of the History of Economic Thought*, **1** (3), 551–76.

Kurz, H.D. and N. Salvadori (1993), 'The "standard commodity" and Ricardo's search for an invariable measure of value', in M. Baranzini and G.C. Harcourt (eds), *The Dynamics of the Wealth of Nations. Growth, Distribution and Structural Change: Essays in Honour of Luigi Pasinetti*, Basingstoke: Macmillan, pp. 95–123.

Kurz, H.D. and N. Salvadori (1995), *Theory of Production. A Long-Period Analysis*, Cambridge: Cambridge University Press.

Kurz, H.D. and N. Salvadori (eds) (1998), *The Elgar Companion to Classical Economics*, 2 vols, Cheltenham, UK and Northampton, MA, USA: Edward Elgar.

Kurz, H.D. and N. Salvadori (eds) (2015), *The Elgar Companion to David Ricardo*, Cheltenham, UK and Northampton, MA, USA: Edward Elgar.

Malthus, T.R. (1820), *Principles of Political Economy*, reprinted 1989, variorum edition, 2 vols, ed. J. Pullen, Cambridge: Cambridge University Press.

Malthus, T.R. (1827), *Definitions in Political Economy. Preceded by an Inquiry into Rules That Ought to Guide Political Economists in the Definition and Use of their Terms; With Remarks on the Deviations from These Rules in Their Writings*, London: J. Murray, reprinted 1971, New York: A.M. Kelley.

Marx, K. (1859), *A Contribution to the Critique of Political Economy*, reprinted 1970, New York: International.

Marx, K. (1861–63), *Economic Manuscript of 1861–63. A Contribution to the Critique of Political Economy ["Theories of Surplus Value"]*, reprinted 1988 in *Karl Marx, Frederick Engels: Collected Works*, vol. 30, New York: International.

Marx, K. (1861–63), *Economic Manuscript of 1861–63. A Contribution to the Critique of Political Economy ["Theories of Surplus Value"]*, reprinted 1989 in *Karl Marx, Frederick Engels: Collected Works*, vol. 32, New York: International.

Marx, K. (1867), *Capital. A Critique of Political Economy*, vol. I, reprinted 1954, Moscow: Progress.

McCulloch, J.R. (1825), *The Principles of Political Economy: With a Sketch of the Rise and Progress of the Science*, Edinburgh: Adam and Charles Black.

Meek, R.L. (1950), 'The decline of Ricardian economics in England', *Economica*, **17** (65), 43–62.

Mill, J.S. (1844a), 'Of the laws of interchange between nations', in *Essays on Some Unsettled Questions of Political Economy*, London: John W. Parker, reprinted in J.M. Robson (ed.) (1967), *Collected Works of John Stuart Mill*, vol. IV, *Essays on Economics and Society, 1824–1845*, Toronto: University of Toronto Press, pp. 232–61.

Mill, J.S. (1844b), 'On profits, and interest', in *Essays on Some Unsettled Questions of Political Economy*, London: John W. Parker, reprinted in J.M. Robson (ed.) (1967), *Collected Works of John Stuart Mill*, vol. IV, *Essays on Economics and Society, 1824–1845*, Toronto: University of Toronto Press, pp. 290–308.

Mill, J.S. (1848), *Principles of Political Economy with Some of their Applications to Social Philosophy*, reprinted 1965, Toronto: University of Toronto Press.

O'Brien, D.P. (1970), *J.R. McCulloch: A Study in Classical Economics*, London and New York: Routledge.

O'Brien, D.P. (1975), *The Classical Economists*, London: Oxford University Press.

O'Brien, D.P. (2004), *The Classical Economists Revisited*, Princeton, NJ and Oxford: Princeton University Press.

Petty, W. (1662), *A Treatise of Taxes and Contributions*, London: Brokes, reprinted in C. Hull (ed.) (1899), *The Economic Writings of Sir William Petty*, vol. 1, reprinted 1986 (in one volume), New York: A.M. Kelley, pp. 1–97.

Petty, W. (1690), *Political Arithmetick*, London: Robert Clarel, reprinted in C. Hull (ed.) (1899), *The Economic Writings of Sir William Petty*, vol. 1, reprinted 1986 (in one volume), New York: A.M. Kelley, pp. 232–313.

Petty, W. (1691), *The Political Anatomy of Ireland*, London: D. Brown and W. Rogers, reprinted in C. Hull (ed.) (1899), *The Economic Writings of Sir William Petty*, vol. 1, reprinted 1986 (in one volume), New York: A.M. Kelley, pp. 121–231.

Ricardo, D. (1951–73), *The Works and Correspondence of David Ricardo*, 11 vols, ed. P. Sraffa with the collaboration of M.H. Dobb, Cambridge: Cambridge University Press.

Roncaglia, A. (2001), *The Wealth of Ideas. A History of Economic Thought*, Cambridge: Cambridge University Press.

Schumpeter, J.A. (1912), 'Epochen der Dogmen- und Methodengeschichte', in M. Weber (ed.), *Grundriß der Sozialökonomie*, Tübingen: J.C.B. Mohr. English trans. 1954, *Economic Doctrine and Method: A Historical Sketch*, London: Allen & Unwin.

Smith, A. (1776), *An Inquiry into the Nature and Causes of the Wealth of Nations*, 2 vols, reprinted 1976, eds R.H. Campbell, A.S. Skinner and W.B. Todd, Oxford: Clarendon Press.

Sraffa, P. (1951), 'Introduction', in D. Ricardo (1951–73), *The Works and Correspondence of David Ricardo*, vol. 1, ed. P. Sraffa with the collaboration of M.H. Dobb, Cambridge: Cambridge University Press, pp. xiii–lxii.

Sraffa, P. (1960), *Production of Commodities by Means of Commodities. Prelude to a Critique of Economic Theory*, Cambridge: Cambridge University Press.

Steuart, J. (1767), *An Inquiry into the Principles of Political Oeconomy*, reprinted 1966, ed. with Introduction by A.S. Skinner, 2 vols, Edinburgh and London: Oliver and Boyd.

Torrens, R. (1815), *Essay on the External Corn Trade*, reprinted in R. Torrens (2000), *Collected Works of Robert Torrens*, ed. and introduction by G. de Vivo, vol. II, London: Thoemmes Press.

Torrens, R. (1818), 'Strictures on Mr Ricardo's doctrine respecting exchangeable value', reprinted in R. Torrens (2000), *Collected Works of Robert Torrens*, ed. and introduction by G. de Vivo, vol. VIII, London: Thoemmes Press.

Torrens, R. (1820), *Essay on the External Corn Trade*, 2nd edn, reprinted in R. Torrens (2000), *Collected Works of Robert Torrens*, ed. and introduction by G. de Vivo, vol. II, London: Thoemmes Press.

Torrens, R. (1821), *Essay on the Production of Wealth*, reprinted in R. Torrens (2000), *Collected Works of Robert Torrens*, ed. and introduction by G. de Vivo, vol. III, London: Thoemmes Press.

Torrens, R. (1826), *Essay on the External Corn Trade*, 3rd edn, reprinted in R. Torrens (2000), *Collected Works of Robert Torrens*, ed. and introduction by G. de Vivo, vol. II, London: Thoemmes Press.

Torrens, R. (2000), *Collected Works of Robert Torrens*, ed. and introduction by G. de Vivo, 8 vols, London: Thoemmes Press.

Turgot, A.-R.-J. (1766), *Réflexions sur la formation et la distribution des richesses*, English trans. 1971, *Reflections on the Formation and Distribution of Riches*, New York: A.M. Kelley.

Vianello, F. (2011), 'The Smithian origin of Ricardo's corn-ratio theory of profits. A suggested interpretation', in R. Ciccone, C. Gehrke and G. Mongiovi (eds), *Sraffa and Modern Economics*, vol. 2, London: Routledge, pp. 239–69.

Walsh, V. and H. Gram (1980), *Classical and Neoclassical Theories of General Equilibrium: Historical Origins and Mathematical Structure*, Oxford and New York: Oxford University Press.

French classical political economy

Setting the Stage

Defining French classical political economy

It is usually asserted that French classical political economy vaguely refers to liberal authors who wrote during the first three-quarters of the nineteenth century. This tradition will be followed here with some reluctance, because it should be remembered that these economists have never properly been a school: their opinions were diverse and many of them criticized the ideas put forward by the English classical economists – especially those of David Ricardo (see, for example, Béraud and Faccarello 2014; see also Gehrke and Kurz 2001). The vague link that connects them is that they all start from the works of Jean-Baptiste Say. They are not necessarily Say's disciples in the strict sense of the word: they differ from his views on important points, but they are influenced by him. They are liberals because they insist, with him, that the interests of men and nations do not conflict with each other. They therefore condemn any kind of protection or state intervention which would, they say, disrupt the competitive market mechanism. However, gradually, the memories of Say faded and towards the end of the nineteenth century French liberal economists became critical of the ideas defended by their predecessors. The liberal tradition continues but economists such as Paul Leroy-Beaulieu or Clément Colson can hardly be considered "classical" in the sense entertained here.

In 1803, Jean-Baptiste Say (1767–1832) and Jean-Charles Léonard Simonde de Sismondi (1773–1842) published respectively the *Traité d'économie politique* and *De la richesse commerciale*: both books are at the origin of the development of classical political economy in France. In this first generation also, Antoine Destutt de Tracy (1754–1836) – the leader of the *idéologues* – deserves to be mentioned. His writings pertain to philosophy, economics and political science, and were highly influential in France and abroad.

In the second generation are Charles Comte (1782–1837) – Say's son in law – and Charles Dunoyer (1786–1862), both disciples of Say, on the one hand, and Pellegrino Rossi (1787–1848), who was more influenced by Ricardo, on the other. During the 1840s, the main topics under discussion changed. Jules Dupuit (1804–1866), Frédéric Bastiat (1801–1850) and Michel Chevalier (1806–1879) – a former Saint-Simonian – were all in favour of free trade, but their approaches differed in important respects. While Dupuit is well known for his analysis of utility, Bastiat had to break with the classical analysis of the distribution of income – whether Ricardo's or Say's – in order to state that the interests of the different social classes are "harmonious" ("harmoniques"). Chevalier and Charles Coquelin (1802–1852) are especially known for their writings on money and their defence of the freedom of issuance, thus opposing Louis Wolowski (1810–1876) who was in favour of the monopoly of issue by the Banque de France.

Joseph Garnier (1813–1881) and Jean-Gustave Courcelle-Seneuil (1813–1892) published successful textbooks. Gustave de Molinari (1819–1912), a long-time editor of the *Journal des économistes*, was a fierce advocate of an uncompromising liberalism and is considered today one of the first libertarians. French classical economists, in particular Say and Sismondi, had tried to explain economic crises. Clément Juglar (1819–1905) proposed a different approach to the problem with his theory of business cycles. To conclude this brief review of the "troops", the influence of two prominent political philosophers – Benjamin Constant (1767–1830) and Alexis de Tocqueville (1805–1859) – on French liberal economists must be stressed.

Analytical underpinnings
Say (1828 [2010]: 1271) argued that the evolution of the ideas of the French economists in the early nineteenth century was the product of two major political events – "the revolution of North America and that of France. Speculative politics and political economy have harvested a significant number of exact notions, and these same two events have dethroned more than a mistake". The influences of Montesquieu, Voltaire and Rousseau continue, but their successors do not hesitate to dismiss some of their ideas. The figures of the enlightened despot and benevolent state faded when Napoleon Bonaparte became Emperor and Benjamin Constant criticized Filangieri for having incessantly considered:

> the legislator as a separate being, above the rest, necessarily better and more informed than them: and filled with enthusiasm for this phantom created by his imagination, he grants him authority on the people subjected to his orders – an authority which he only thinks sometimes to limit . . . Pretending to extend the jurisdiction of the law on all subjects is just organising tyranny, and returning . . . to the state of slavery from which one hoped to be freed . . . The functions of the State are purely negative. (Constant 1822: 36–44)

From the first edition of his *Traité*, Say breaks away from his predecessors. He recognizes much to the benefit of the Physiocrats, that "all were in favour . . . of the freedom that men must dispose of to do as they please with their persons and their property, freedom without which social happiness and property are empty words" (Say 1803 [2006]: 30). However, he reproaches them for having considered agriculture as the sole productive activity. He also criticizes Turgot and Condorcet for not having clearly broken away from the physiocratic theses. In short, for him, there was no political economy before Smith, even if he parted company with Smith on two essential points.

The first point regards Smith's (1776 [1976]: 10) assertion that "the annual labour of every nation is the fund which originally supplies it with all the necessaries and conveniences of life". However, goods are not the products of human labour alone – the latter is combined with the actions of natural agents and capitals. Say's readers were not all convinced however. Destutt de Tracy, for example, argued that "actions subjected to our will are absolutely the only means we have to provide for our needs" (1815 [1818]: 84), and "our work is our only original wealth" (ibid.: 159). Similarly, Dunoyer regretted that Say "had assigned several causes to production and presented riches as produced not only with human industry, but with industry, capitals and natural agents" (Dunoyer 1827: 75). The idea is the same: human activity is certainly not the only force that exists in nature, but land and machines can serve human happiness only as labour forces them to produce.

Second, Say also criticizes Smith for having stated that one could speak of production in a material sense only, and for having opposed productive and unproductive labour. For Say, the labour that produces immaterial goods ("produits immatériels") is just as productive as that which produces material goods. "Production is no *creation*; it is production of utility" (Say 1803 [2006]: 78, original emphasis). Dunoyer (1827: 68) criticized

Say for not having drawn all the consequences from this principle: as production is a production of utility, the expenses of the state are productive.

In 1814, in the second edition of the *Traité*, Say asserts that the foundation of the value of a good is not the amount of labour required to produce it, but its utility, and he thus questions the Smithian distinction between the natural and the market prices of commodities. Say admits that competition tends to bring about the equality between prices and costs of production, but as the prices of productive services themselves depend on supply and demand, calling "natural price" the cost of production seemed unnecessary to him (Say 1819 [2006]: 1132).

During the First Empire, and then the Restoration, the Liberals were opponents to the government, whose activities were closely watched by the police. The government did everything in its power to prevent the spread of their subversive ideas. When they started a newspaper – *Le Censeur* in 1814 and then *Le Censeur Européen* in 1817 – they ran into the worst difficulties: Charles Comte was forced into exile and Charles Dunoyer was imprisoned. The reputation Say had acquired allowed him to continue to teach economics – an essential task in his eyes. From 1815 to 1819, he taught at a private institution, the Athénée. In 1820, a position in "industrial economics" was created for him at the Conservatoire National des Arts et Métiers which he held until his death in 1832.

With the revolution of 1830 the situation changed, although it did not bring the radical change the Liberals had hoped for. A new position in political economy was founded at the College de France in 1831. Say was the first to occupy the chair. Pellegrino Rossi (from 1833 to 1840) and Michel Chevalier (from 1840 to 1871) succeeded him. In 1832, the Académie des sciences morales et politiques having been restored by the minister François Guizot, the Liberals dominated the section devoted to political economy. While not included in the teaching programme, political economy had somehow received some official recognition.

In 1841, the liberal economist and publisher Gilbert-Urbain Guillaumin founded the *Journal des économistes* with Jérôme-Adolphe Blanqui becoming the editor in 1842. The following year Guillaumin was behind the creation of the Société des économistes – the name was changed into Société d'économie politique in 1847 – together with Eugène Daire, Joseph Garnier, Adolphe Blaise des Vosges and Pierre Bos. Finally, he started to publish works of contemporary and classical economists. The Liberals thus had a journal, a publisher and a society.

At around the same time, in the 1840s, the influence of the socialists was growing in France, especially with the publication of works by Louis Blanc and Pierre-Joseph Proudhon. As stated by Molinari (1855 [1863], vol. 1: XII): "it is no longer a question of fighting the beneficiaries of the injustices of the Ancien Régime, who claim . . . the preservation of their privileges, but the socialists who denounce industrial liberty by invoking the interest of the masses and asking for an organisation of labour".

Two types of responses were developed. On the one hand, Bastiat (1850 [1851]: 1) stressed, as did Carey, that "all the interests are harmonious". In support of his view, he had to dismiss three propositions that played a crucial role in classical theory: the Ricardian theory of rent, the Malthusian theory of population and the idea that natural resources have a value. This amounted to rewriting economic theory and only few liberals agreed with him.

On the other hand, Molinari's project was even more ambitious. He thought that economics suffered from an important shortcoming, that is, "the absence of a demonstration . . . of the general law which, establishing . . . a balance between the various branches of production as well as between the remunerations of the productive agents, maintains order in the economic world" (Molinari 1855 [1863], vol. 1: xl). The mechanism of gravitation of classical economics assumes that the agents have perfect information, but such an assumption is not self-evident. Molinari wanted to show how the organization of the economy was evolving to solve these information problems.

In the second half of the nineteenth century, the political context changed profoundly with the fall of the Second Empire, the Paris Commune and the establishment of the Third Republic. The Free Trade treaty, which was signed in 1860 between France and Britain, was questioned. The government willingly intervened in economic affairs and sought to establish a colonial empire. Economic liberalism was unfashionable and liberal economists gradually lost some of their influence. For a long time, they retracted to academic life. However, when the government introduced political economy in the faculties of law, they failed to control the selection of teachers. Professors in charge of the lectures in economics were in fact specialists in law. The academic world was deeply disturbed. The *Journal des économistes* had long been the only journal in economics. It was now in competition with *L'économiste* that Leroy-Beaulieu started in 1873, and with the *Revue d'économie politique* that Charles Gide started in 1887 with the support of his colleagues from the faculties of law. The *Journal des économistes* continued to be published until 1940 but it quickly lost influence.

During this period liberalism did not disappear, rather it evolved. The "new" liberals defended the same individualistic conception of the state as their predecessors, but they discarded the classical analysis of price and distribution. The case of Edmond Villey is typical in this respect. When dealing with the natural law or the role of the state, he developed ideas similar to those of the Liberals in the early nineteenth century. However, when he discussed the issue of wages, he clearly broke away from received ideas. He considered the "classical" theory of wages to be radically false. The natural wage is not a subsistence wage and the market wage is not determined by the wage fund. At the end of the nineteenth century, French liberals thus discarded a series of propositions that had been advocated not only by Smith and Ricardo but also by Say and Garnier. This was the end of the French classical political economy even though many economists still cherished the liberal tradition in France.

This entry cannot offer a complete overview of the ideas of the French classical economists. It focuses instead on three prominent themes: price theory, income distribution and the relationship between money and business cycles.

Value and Price

In spite of many differences, and with the notable exception of Bastiat, most French classical economists share the same approach to price determination: natural price, like the market price, depends on supply and demand. This consensus was only formed gradually.

Natural prices and demand
Say and Sismondi started from Smith's analysis of gravitation. The natural value of goods – Sismondi preferred to speak of their intrinsic price – consists of profits, wages and rents, calculated at market prices ("prix courants"), which is necessary to pay for their production and to bring them to markets (Sismondi 1803, vol. 1: 287–8). The market price "depends on the proportion between the amount of the commodity that is . . . for sale and the quantity . . . one is willing to buy" (Say 1803 [2006]: 598). When the market price of a good exceeds the natural price, the quantity supplied increases, and it decreases when the market price falls below the natural price. This is the mechanism that regulates the system where "*the market price* of a commodity always tends to be on par with its *natural price*" (ibid.: 600, original emphases). Destutt de Tracy (1815 [1818]: 160) gave a different version of this idea by opposing the "conventional" or "venal" value – that which the general opinion gives to a thing – and the "required" value defined as "the sum of needs whose satisfaction is necessary for the existence of the one who does the work, while he performs it". That is, when he calculates the required value, Destutt acknowledges that wage is a subsistence wage and he thus considers labour like any other commodity.

However, after having read Ricardo's *Principles of Political Economy* first published in 1817 and after some discussions with the author, Say was led to believe that using the concept of natural price could be ambiguous. As a consequence he deleted every reference to this concept in the *Épitomé sommaire* appended to the fourth edition of the *Traité* (1819 [2006]: 1132). The idea that in equilibrium the price is equal to the cost of production does not mean that demand does not affect the price. In his *Cours d'économie politique pratique*, Say admits that Ricardo is right when he argues that the market price of commodities is always determined by the cost of production, but that he is wrong when he asserts that the demand does not affect the price, because in fact demand affects the prices of the services used in production. When the demand for a good increases, "the product becomes more expensive, although it does not exceed the cost of production" (Say 1828 [2010]: 373).

Rossi: the value and the cost of production
Say's contribution to the theory of value was often referred to and discussed by his successors. It differs in some respects from the analyses of Smith and Ricardo. In the lectures he gave at the Collège de France from 1836 to 1838, Pellegrino Rossi came back to these differences and proposed a synthesis. Say had argued that utility is the foundation of value. You may wonder to what extent this assertion is consistent with the way in which Smith and Ricardo analysed exchangeable value, with utility only playing a passive role: goods that are not useful in any way would not have an exchangeable value however rare they are and no matter the amount of work it would cost to obtain them. Rossi argued, however, that use value is a relationship – between human needs and goods – which plays a fundamental role in political economy. Smith wrote that an object – he uses the example of a diamond – could have an exchangeable value that is out of proportion of its use value. According to Rossi, this cannot be so (1836–38 [1865], vol. 1: 68) because the exchangeable value of the diamond, like that of any good, is in proportion to the service that it is supposed to provide to the person who possesses it, that is, in proportion to its use value. If, taking up the Smithian terminology, he contrasted use value and

exchangeable value, Rossi gives the opposition a new meaning. Use value is the value of a good that directly satisfies our needs. But the value of a good may be indirect: we have no use for it, but through trade, it allows us to procure other goods that meet our needs. The utility of such a good is its exchange value. Exchangeable value thus appears as a form derived from use value.

To account for the causes that determine exchangeable value, two principles have been mentioned: the cost of production and supply and demand. Rossi asserts that they should not be opposed but rather considered as complementary to one another. However, he ranks them in a strange way. "The law of supply and demand . . . contains the true, complete and *subjective* explanation of all variations of the exchangeable value" (1836–38 [1865], vol. 1: 89; original emphasis). However, Rossi stresses, it is necessary to clarify what is meant here by supply and demand. It is therefore necessary to find a more adapted phrasing: "the regulating factor of the exchangeable value of goods is the amount of labour required to produce them; and, more generally, the determining factor of the value of goods lies in their . . . costs of production" (ibid.: 89–90). Rossi is convinced that this idea does not contradict the principle of supply and demand, but expresses it accurately. As a basis for his argument, he simply relies on the idea that market prices gravitate around production prices. It is only when the market price coincides with the natural price that the oscillations in production stop. At equilibrium, at the natural price, supply and demand are equal, and it is this assertion that allows two principles, which were sometimes considered rivals, to be taken as equivalent.

Prices and utility: from Say to Dupuit

Say (1814 [2006]: 83) asserted that "the price is the measure of the value of things". From this two conclusions were derived: (1) since in exchange we always swap things of equal value, he argued, against Condillac, that "exchanges do not produce wealth, no matter the price one obtains" (Say 1828 [2010]: 314); (2) in order to estimate the usefulness of a public work, a road, for example, one should evaluate the cost reductions that the users of the road enjoy.

Dupuit (1844 [2009]: 208) pointed out that the usefulness a buyer attributes to a product he buys cannot be lower than the price he pays for it, but that it can be higher: the buyer thus gets a "kind of profit". The construction of a public work results in the lowering of the cost of transport and circulation of new products. Say, suggesting that consideration be given to these products as well as to those which circulated during the time when the work did not yet exist, significantly overestimates the utility of the work. If some products were not in circulation before the construction of the work, it is because they could not bear the high costs. The same reasoning applies to trade. In general, the utility of the acquired good exceeds the utility of the good given in exchange: the seller and the buyer both benefit from exchange and the total wealth is increased. The criticism Ricardo levelled at Say for neglecting the essential difference between value in use and exchangeable value – and worse, for assessing one in terms of the other – is well justified.

Say (1819 [2006]: 110) argued that "natural resources . . . that are likely to be owned . . . do not give their cooperation without remuneration". To justify the existence of such income, he put forward a utilitarian argument: land is productive only if it is privately owned and, in this sense, rent is an indispensable expense which, like wages and profits, must be included in the price of commodities. Proudhon (1840 [1873]: 73–4) had little difficulty in showing that even if Say's explanation were satisfactory it "would remain to know who has the right to charge for land use, for this wealth which is not produced by man. Whom do we owe the rent of land to? The creator of the land, no doubt. Who created the land? God. Therefore owner, stand back". The Liberals had to respond to him. Bastiat did, relying not on utilitarianism, as Say did, but on natural law.

Bastiat, the effort saved and the value of things
Bastiat criticizes the classical economists for having attributed a value to natural resources and having admitted that they were only given up for a remuneration. "So men, and especially landowners, sell God's blessings for actual work, and receiving a reward for utilities in the production of which their labour took no part" (Bastiat 1850 [1851]: 6). Economists have analysed exchange as an exchange of goods, and they sought the origin of value in the utility of these goods or in the time required to produce them. However, the often used example of the diamond shows that the value of a commodity can be unrelated to its usefulness or the effort necessary for its production. What we exchange are not goods but services produced by labour and nature, most often together. The cooperation of nature is free; that of labour is costly because it requires effort. However, it should not be concluded that the value is determined by the amount of labour spent by the person producing the service: it is proportional to the labour saved by the person who receives it. The labour commanded conceived as a measure of value, as in Smith's *Wealth of Nations* (1776 [1976]), is seen by Bastiat as the cause of value: it is the labour one saves when buying a service that determines its value.

This attempt to reconstruct the theory of value was met with many reservations. The long review of *Harmonies économiques* that Ambroise Clément (1850) published in the *Journal des économistes* is very critical. Bastiat's starting point was, in his view, erroneous: the cooperation of natural resources is not always free. It would be free only if they are abundant enough to be at the disposal of any agent who needs them, and if they are not susceptible of private and exclusive ownership. To answer Proudhon, the obvious must not be denied: the services of scarce natural resources are costly. However, it does not follow that the landowners should be evicted, because they bought the property they own and paid for the value of the natural service of land, regardless of the capital invested.

The role of prices in coordinating economic activities
When the debate about the possibility of general crises of overproduction began, Sismondi discussed the regulatory function of the market. He explained that when the production of an industry is disrupted – for example by the introduction of new technologies – the adjustment, while theoretically possible, is difficult because of the many factors that hinder the mobility of labour and capital and by the imperfect knowledge that entrepreneurs have of the markets for commodities. To be certain to sell, the producer "should know two things of which the most capable can only have a very vague idea: the quantity of the good he produces which is required by the public, and the quantity which could be produced by those who are in the same trade" (Sismondi 1838, vol. 1: 120–21). According to Sismondi, the low mobility of factors and the fragmentary nature of the available information explain why improved techniques in a particular activity can lead to a general glut in markets. In these circumstances, he

concluded, it is up to the legislator to intervene to ensure that the social interest prevails over individual interests.

For Molinari (Benkemoune 2008) Sismondi's arguments should be taken seriously: an analysis should be made of how the problem of the balance between consumption and production is solved in a system based on the division of labour and exchange. To answer this question, economists have relied on the mechanism of gravitation. Molinari argued that this mechanism is all the more effective when a small change in the quantity of the product brought to or removed from the market significantly changes the price. In this case each manufacturer has an incentive to produce and bring to the market what is demanded. The pricing mechanism can be relied upon as solving the problem of the balance between consumption and production.

However, various phenomena could disturb the natural order. One phenomenon, stressed by Molinari, is the lack or insufficiency of knowledge, and this case is typical of systems based on the division of labour and exchange. In his *Cours* (1855 [1863], vol. 1: 172), Molinari sees the solution in the development of "industrial and commercial advertising". In *Les notions fondamentales d'économie politique* he is more specific. It is the intervention of intermediaries – such as traders and speculators – who, by circulating products across space and over time, disseminate information and stabilize prices. Unlike Sismondi, Molinari does not ask the state to intervene to ensure equilibrium: "The markets, at one time isolated . . . now regularly and permanently communicate with one another. Products and capitals . . . move from one country to another with the same ease they once moved from one district to another in the same town" (1891: 398). The problem is that this trend has not yet also transformed the labour market. The worker combines two naturally distinct functions: he is the producer and merchant of his labour. In fact, he needs an intermediary to sell his commodity. To overcome this absence, workers have formed unions or syndicates but these associations have neither the capital nor the credit for the development of their activities. According to Molinari, the solution lies in the development of private businesses, with sufficient capital, to transfer the labour from markets where it is in excess supply to those where it is in excess demand. In short, it is necessary for the labour market to evolve like the other markets that have evolved, and create Labour exchanges in the image of the model of the Stock or Commodity exchanges.

Income Distribution

Regarding the controversies around value, the starting point of the French classical economists was the opposition between Say and Ricardo. The same opposition is to be found about distribution of income. However, on this last point what is at stake is different. The liberals are reluctant to accept Say's assertion that rent is a monopoly income, and they refuse Ricardo's idea that a rise in wages lowers the profit rate: it is their opinion that both assertions undermine the idea of an harmony of interests between men.

A first difficulty arises when it comes to defining the different kinds of income. In Say's works, the entrepreneur is central. Regardless of whether or not he has a share of the capital of the firm, what matters is that he manages the business, buying productive services to provide the goods as requested. It is thus necessary to distinguish the income that pays for his work from the interest he draws from his capital. To state this idea, Say abandoned the Smithian trilogy of wages, profits and rents. He contrasted the "profits of industry" – that is, labour incomes – with territorial incomes and capital incomes. He also put the incomes of the entrepreneur, the scientist and the worker at the same level: they are all rewards of labour. Labour is not simply nor primarily a physical activity. It requires different abilities, skills, intelligence or organizational talent. It is fundamentally heterogeneous and the theory of distribution must explain the rewards of these different types of workers.

Supply and demand determine the prices of the productive services

The solution is simple. The prices of the productive services are determined by supply and demand. This demand is indirect however: "when a good is in demand, all the services susceptible to produce it are in demand" (Say 1828 [2010]: 705). Their supplies may depend on different causes. Say, for example, explains that the supply of services by entrepreneurs is limited because of the moral qualities necessary to this kind of labour, the necessity of having a sufficient capital and the uncertainty of the gains in this activity.

The phrase "natural wage" does not appear in Say's works. He admits, however, that "it is difficult that the price of labour of the simple worker rises above or falls below the rate needed to maintain the number of this class of workers at the required level" (ibid.:735). Sismondi (1819, vol. 1: 89) put forward a similar idea. However, this necessary rate does not play the same role as that of the natural rate in Smith and Ricardo's analyses as it only determines the price of a particular category of labour.

Say takes up Smith's idea: rent is a monopoly income. "Land . . . is not the only natural resource which has productive power but is the only one man could own and consequently, from which he could appropriate the benefits" (Say 1803 [2006]: 793). He thus opposed economists who, like Ricardo and Destutt de Tracy, consider rent as a differential income, which is not a component of the price of commodities. He disagrees with the idea that marginal land does not yield any rent: any cultivated land necessarily yields a rent because no owner would ever allow the cultivation of his land for nothing.

Back to Ricardo?

French liberal classical economists inherited a set of heterogeneous ideas. On many points, Say had opposed the views defended by Ricardo. In his lectures at the Collège de France from 1836 to 1838, Rossi tried to develop a synthesis incorporating some of the Ricardian propositions in a theoretical framework inherited from Say. Bastiat (1850 [1851]), however, rejected both Ricardo and Say's ideas. Molinari, who was critical of Bastiat's *Harmonies économiques*, took up in his *Cours* (1855) Rossi's approach, but in a slightly different way. Defending some of Ricardo's propositions, he implicitly responded to Bastiat.

Rossi (1836–38 [1865], vol. 3: 121) argued that despite the heterogeneity of workers, there are laws governing the level and evolution of the wage rates. His starting point is the idea that the workers' incomes may, according to circumstances, simply reward their labour, or also their capital and talents. These incomes should be broken down into wages proper, profits and rents. However, even if these distinctions are taken into account, there are differences between the wages in various occupations that may seem to be irreducible. Rossi argued that it is legitimate for pure science – rational political economy – to disregard these differences and to suppose a uniform wage rate.

He does not use the phrase "natural wage" but prefers to speak of a "necessary wage" defined as the indispensable remuneration to the worker in order to survive and support his family (Rossi 1836–38 [1865], vol. 3: 153). He admits, however, that the worker is not a commodity, that his salary is not technically determined. The use of this concept was criticized by Garnier (1847: 208) who stressed that this terminology is misleading because it suggests that any change in the price of wage goods immediately affects the wage rate. It is not so: it is only through its action on the supply of labour that the price change affects the wage rate. If the prices rise, the real wage declines prompting a decrease in the population. Then, but only then, the monetary wage increases in order to restore the real wage rate to its original level.

Rossi took up some aspects of the Ricardian theory of intensive rent. For example, he stressed that if the amount of labour and capital employed on a given plot of land increases, the product increases less than proportionally. This assertion allowed him to dismiss Say's criticism (Rossi 1836–38 [1865], vol. 3: 140) that Ricardo's theory of rent was based on the assumption that the marginal land does not get a rent. However, this vindication of Ricardo remains equivocal because Rossi criticized him for having disregarded that the rent on a piece of land not only depends on its relative productivity, as compared to other lands, but also on its absolute productivity; and – neglecting the analysis that Ricardo made of the effects of technical progress on rent – he argued that improving land productivity increases their rent in all cases.

Bastiat believed that all previous theories on rent were based on the same mistake: they attribute "a specific *value*, independent of any human service, either to the elements of labour, or to the forces of nature. Hence, property is as unjustifiable as unintelligible" (Bastiat 1850 [1851]: 248, original emphasis). Bastiat argued in two steps. When there is still land to clear, the landowner enjoys no monopoly, and if he receives a rent, this may only be because of the labour he spent to render it cultivable and to improve it. If, on the contrary, all the land is cultivated, "the value of land . . . depends not only on the labour spent but moreover on the power which lies in society to pay for this labour; [it depends] on demand as well as supply" (ibid.: 288). Bastiat thus seems to go back to Rossi's opinion that rent is the difference between the market price and the natural price of the products of land. Bastiat's assertion provoked a lasting controversy. Mathieu Wolkoff explained that land rent cannot be considered the remuneration of past labour, even in the simple case of an economy where an uniformly fertile land is not fully cultivated. The value of land is not equal to what was spent clearing it "but to the capital which currently suffices to produce the same result; that is to say, to the service that the initial land clearing permits to provide now" (Wolkoff 1854: 176).

The second problem is the analysis of the evolution of distribution in a growing economy. Ricardo explained that as capital accumulates and population grows, it is necessary to cultivate less fertile qualities of land: man must spend an increasing amount of work to get an equal amount of subsistence. Rent increases while the rates of wages and profits decline if technical progress is set aside. To the Ricardian theory, Bastiat opposes the idea that the accumulation of capital makes for better use of natural resources and increases the production more than proportionally. When capital accumulates, profits increase but their share in the product decreases. The share of labour and the sum total of wages increase. Bastiat (1850 [1851]: 12) thought that he has thus shown the "harmony of interests between workers and their employers".

Molinari's analysis of distribution is based on the concept of net product defined as the difference between the gross product and what is needed "to replace the share of productive factors that had been completely destroyed or consumed, [and] to repair and renew that which was partly destroyed" (Molinari 1855 [1863], vol. 1: 49–50). The necessary price of the various services – of land, capitals and the various kinds of labour – is the amount necessary to maintain and replace them. The gross profits of capital must, for example, cover the replacement cost and provide a premium sufficient to compensate for the deprivation of immediate enjoyment which the owner consent to. When the net product is nil, the quantity produced remains the same through time. Similarly, if the payment for a service is equal to its necessary price, the amount available remains constant. If the net product is positive, production will increase if each service receives a "proportional" share thereof. The natural price of a service includes, beyond its necessary price, a share of the net product sufficient to grow at the required rate. The market prices of services gravitate around this natural price. If one of them received a payment greater than its natural price, its quantity would increase more rapidly than that of the other services and the relative excess would lead to a decline in its current price.

The end of French classical school

In his *Essai sur la répartition des richesses*, Leroy-Beaulieu argued that what characterizes the economies in the late nineteenth century is a trend towards less inequality. The world has changed and we can no longer argue like Turgot, Malthus or Ricardo. The Ricardian theory of rent is devoid of any practical significance because the advancement of knowledge and competition from new countries led to a decline in rents in France and England. The Malthusian theory of population does not find application in a largely uninhabited world where the production of food is increasing to the point where the price of the products of land is more likely to fall than to rise. The analyses of the classical economists, which highlighted that in wage bargaining, the employers were always in a strong position, are now obsolete in countries where the right of association is recognized for the workers. All this is not radically new because the French liberals, especially Bastiat, had often criticized the "pessimism" of the English classical economists. What is new is the conclusion that Leroy-Beaulieu (1881: vi) draws from this observation: "From a theoretical point of view, we are led to the conclusion that almost all accepted doctrines of political economy on the distribution of wealth are to be reworked or at least corrected." He thus tried to put forward a new theory of distribution, seeking to understand the factors that determine the supply and demand of productive services. He explained, for example, that technical progress has reduced rents because its effects were greater on land that was initially less fertile. On the other hand, he argues that capital accumulation simultaneously has the effect of increasing the average productivity of labour and reducing that of capital; and that, for this reason, it tends to increase the wage rate and reduce the rate of profit. French classical political economy has come to an end. To explain the distribution of income, the French liberals no longer refer to Ricardo, Malthus and Say; instead, they seek to build a new theory.

Money and Crises

In monetary analysis, once again we do not find the opposition between Ricardo and Say that was at the centre of the debates around value and income distribution. The main point is here to understand the role that money and credit play in capital accumulation and commercial crises. However, on this main question, some other topics are also debated: how to organize the financial system? Must the issuing of banknotes be free? Should the standard of money be unique or should bimetallism be adopted?

When dealing with monetary questions, the French liberals were first concerned with the issue of commercial crises and the role played by money and credit. They were also concerned with the organization of the monetary regime, the freedom of issuance and bimetallism. They did not participate in the debate between the currency and banking schools: nobody proposed to subject the Bank of France to rules as strict as those the Bank of England had to follow. However, they were interested in them: the *Journal des économistes* published the speech that Robert Peel delivered in Parliament to present his bill, and reviewed Tooke's book, *An Inquiry into the currency principle*. Later, the supporters of free banking often used, in support of their view, some arguments the banking school had advanced. Thus Courcelle-Seneuil (1867: 335) argued that "a bank can never issue too many banknotes no matter what are the efforts it makes or the confidence it inspires". In contrast, the supporters of the monopoly of the Bank of France availed themselves of the currency school but they maintained that it was not appropriate to establish a strict link between the quantity of notes and the metallic reserves: when deemed necessary, the central bank should have the opportunity to issue banknotes needed for circulation. However, we must be careful to not confound the two debates. Wolowski (1869: 348) pointed out that in *The History of Prices*, Tooke argued that allowing competition from issuing banks in London would have had disastrous consequences and that, more generally, the principle of freedom of action to the issuing banks could not be extended without restriction.

When the Bank of France was established, it was given the monopoly of issue in Paris but banks issued their own notes in the provinces. In 1848, the Bank of France absorbed them. Coquelin (1848) defended the freedom of issuance but without success. In 1860, France annexed Savoy where there was an issuing bank. In 1865, the Bank of France absorbed it. The Liberals, but also the Saint-Simonians, raised again the question of the freedom of issuance.

The French monetary system was organized by the Law of 28 March 1803. It combined two standards – gold and silver – exchanged at the ratio of 15.5 grams of silver for 1 gram of gold. The coins were minted by the state at the request of individuals and were endowed with the power of unlimited acceptability. In 1870, following the discovery of new mines, the market value of silver fell. Thus, with the quantity of metal that could be acquired for 16 francs, one could mint four coins of 5 francs and exchange them for a gold coin of 20 francs. The result was a massive outflow of gold. In 1876, the free coinage of silver was withdrawn. This was the end of bimetallism, if not in law, at least in practice.

The freedom of issuance and bimetallism: Say's answers

Say had proposed answers to these questions. His starting point is Smith's idea: the introduction of money is a precondition to the development of exchanges because it allows overcoming the problem of double coincidence of needs implied in direct barter. Money is defined as a medium of exchange – even if it is also a measure and store of value. Its value, like that of any other good, is determined by its quantity and our need for it. Hence there follow two consequences. If gold and silver coins are accepted as payment, they cannot keep a fixed relative value. The factors that affect the prices of these two metals are different. When the governments declared constant what is variable, they simply excluded gold or silver from the circulation. He therefore discarded bimetallism.

After much hesitation, Say came to believe that paper money does not derive its value from an unlikely repayment, but from the need of a medium of exchange: a commodity without intrinsic value can play the role of money. The case of convertible banknotes is different. These are tokens of money like promissory notes and bills of exchange. They do not derive their value from our need for them but from the need of the amount of which they guarantee the payment. However, tokens of money replace it in the circulation and depreciate its value. The issue which then arises is "to know how far the power can be left to individuals or individual companies to change at their discretion the value of a good in which the obligations between individuals are stipulated" (Say 1826a [2006]: 587). Say concludes that the government may impose to the issuing of banknotes some restrictions dictated by caution, without clearly ruling out that several banks be allowed to issue promissory notes as was the case at the time he was writing.

If money is a medium of exchange, it is tempting to think that its scarcity makes selling difficult. In order to rule fight this idea Say wrote the chapter "Des debouches" of the *Traité*; however, his arguments changed across the various editions of the book. In 1803, he put forward the idea that everyone finds himself with more or less the same amount of money at the end of the year as at the beginning even if large amounts of money have changed hands. He thus justifies what will later be called Say's identity: the sum of excess demands for goods, money excluded, is identically nil. In the second edition, he abandoned this assumption and asserted that "when money runs out at the mass of business, it is easily compensated" (Say 1814 [2006]: 248). In the absence of gold and silver, bills, checks or bills of exchange will be used as medium of exchange. The quantity of the means of payment is endogenous and therefore there cannot exist an excess demand for it.

Nevertheless, Say argued that the origin of the crises in the excess issuance of banknotes must be sought. Studying the crisis of 1825 in England, he wrote that "the spirit of speculation was aroused in an exaggerated manner by the banks that have all, in England, the power to issue notes payable to the bearer" (Say 1826b: 43). The abundant circulation provoked the decrease of the value of coins as compared to the ingot; there was a run to banks to change notes for gold coins that were melted to get ingots. Bank reserves were exhausted and banks found themselves incapable of discounting commercial bills presented to them. Unable to meet their commitments, entrepreneurs found themselves bankrupt.

A critical reappraisal

Say's successors challenged certain of his proposals commencing with his starting point. For Chevalier, the problem in barter is that the value of a good is expressed in the value of all other goods. It is in the multiplicity of these expressions that he sees the initial obstacle to the development of trade. To overcome this, we must choose among the goods by joint agreement, the one to which all the others are compared. Money is first a measure of value. Of course it has other functions, but this one characterizes it. Chevalier concluded that money can only be a commodity that has value, a commodity that would satisfy a number of our needs. Banknotes are not money; they are paper credit like promissory notes and bills of exchange.

In this perspective Coquelin explained the effects of the development of the banking system – and thus the distribution of banknotes – on the real economy and asserted that the abolition of the privilege of the Bank of France would accelerate capital accumulation and stabilize the economic system. He maintained that Say committed two errors that led him to underestimate the effects of the introduction of banknotes. In the first place Say (1803 [2006]: 577), like Smith, thought that notes replace coins whose value can be used to increase the national capital. Coquelin asserted instead that banknotes replace advantageously bills of exchange: issued by powerful banks, they are circulated everywhere while bills of exchange, issued by individuals, are only accepted reluctantly. The dissemination of banknotes enables credit expansion. Then comes Say's second error. He (1817 [2006]: 767) argued that credit does not create capital but simply transfers a capital from the lender to the borrower. However, Say considers only the case where a capitalist lends his money to an entrepreneur. For Coquelin, however, credit is most often an inter-company credit: it allows the borrower to make productive use of goods which, in the absence of credit, would have remained unused in the stores of their producers.

The opponents of the freedom of issuance stressed the fact that it could lead to an excessive growth in the quantity of the means of payment and a rise in domestic prices, which would destabilize foreign trade. When the depletion of metallic reserves of the banks would encourage them to reduce their credits, firms would no longer be able to refinance themselves and a crisis would inevitably occur. Coquelin stated instead that it is the monopoly of issuance which is causing crises. A bank with a privilege allows its shareholders to make excessive profits while other capitalists are inclined to choose riskier investments in order to maintain their profits. The monopoly of issuance increases the instability of the system for this reason.

To criticize bimetallism, the Liberals often relied on Say. For example, Chevalier (1850 [1866]: 148–9) argued that the system of a double standard leads to a gradual alteration of currencies. In fact, any circumstance that sustainably decreases the relative value of one of the precious metals causes the outflow of the other. To maintain the circulation of the two metals, it would be necessary to modify the metallic content of the coins whose value is appreciated. The currency would depreciate and creditors would be stripped in favour of their debtors. However, Wolowski (1869) asserted that bimetallism can limit the magnitude of fluctuations in the value of money. In fact, this system allows paying a debt with one or the other metal. Thus, when the price of a metal decreases, it is sought after to make payments, its demand increases and slows down the fall of its price.

Credit and crisis

Juglar's analysis of crises is new because of his method – the systematic use of statistical data – the idea that crises are not accidents but periodic events and the analysis of the role played by credit in their development. His thesis deviates both from Say's ideas as well as what the free banking followers advocated. Say argued that a crisis finds its origins in an over-issue of notes; supporters of free banking thought it was the result of the behaviour of the privileged bank. Juglar's (1863: 11) response is that the study of the circulation of the banknotes issued by the Bank of France and the Bank of England shows that it is not excessive in times of crisis and thus cannot be the cause of the latter. His starting point is the contrast between cash transactions, which necessitate payments in specie, and operations of credit, which only involve fiduciary money (bills of exchange, banknotes and cheques). He consequently rejected the idea that notes can be substituted for specie in cash transactions. For this reason, he rejected also the analysis of the currency school and the provisions of the Peel Act. For him, it is impossible to judge of the excess or the lack of circulation after the number of notes issued and the level of the metallic reserve. Only the foreign exchange indicates it.

There is a crisis, Juglar wrote, when payments in specie are necessary in order to balance the credit market. In times of prosperity, when the bills they issued expire, traders can repay them with the bills they received. In case of a disequilibrium, they must resort to rediscount. Similarly, bills of exchange on foreign countries usually compensate those on the country. The movements of precious metals only intervene if this is not the case. It is thus possible to describe the origin of the crisis. During the period of prosperity, producers easily sell their products to traders who pay for their purchases by issuing bills of exchange. This easy access to credit allows an increase in wholesale prices, which makes it difficult to sell goods on the spot market.

This description of the cycle suggests three questions: What is the origin of the initial disequilibrium? How could this imbalance be detected? How could it be addressed? Based on statistical data concerning England, Juglar thought that price changes are independent from the issuance of banknotes. "Credit is what promotes business development and rising prices: trade itself is the first provider of credit, banks can only help to circulate it by substituting their promises to pay for those of the public. In whichever case, the issuance of notes is always secondary and results in the conclusion of the transaction, far from giving it birth" (Juglar 1868: 31). What is important in the triggering of the crisis is not the quantity of banknotes but the entire fiduciary circulation including bills of exchange. There is no measurement of this circulation. The sole criterion for the over-issue of paper money is therefore found in the comparison of its value with the value of precious metals. This is not without problems because a drain of species and the depreciation of money can have multiple causes that call for different answers. In case of a panic, the solution is the suspension of payments. When demands for species are intended to feed internal circulation, an increase in the issuance by the central bank is the right response. When the drain of species is the effect of an unfavourable foreign exchange, the discount rate should be increased. This analysis does not lead Juglar to dismiss the principle of free banking. He however admits that in such a system, each bank is not immediately aware of the consequences of the foreign exchange on its balance and does not take timely measures. The system must be regulated by a central bank, which would be in charge of clearing transactions and would be able to establish a strict control on all banks.

Conclusion

The readers of French liberal economists have often focused on the political aspects of their writings, and their theoretical contributions were regarded with some condescension, but this does not do justice to them. The analyses of the French liberals owe much to the careful reading of the English classical economists – Smith, Ricardo, Malthus, Mill and Tooke in particular. However, they deviate from them in a variety of respects. In particular, they emphasize the role of utility in the formation of prices, and they even propose how to measure it. In many other areas, especially in the theory of economic crises, they contributed new insights into the functioning of the economic system.

ALAIN BÉRAUD

See also:

Banking and currency schools (II); Frédéric Bastiat (I); British classical political economy (II); Barthélemy-Charles Dunoyer de Segonzac (I); Jules Dupuit (I); French Enlightenment (II); Gustave de Molinari (I); Pierre-Joseph Proudhon (I); François Quesnay and Physiocracy (I); David Ricardo (I); Jean-Baptiste Say (I); Adam Smith (I); Anne-Robert-Jacques Turgot (I); Marie-Esprit-Léon Walras (I).

References and further reading

Bastiat, F. (1850), *Harmonies économiques*, 2nd edn 1851, Paris: Guillaumin.
Benkemoune, R. (2008), 'Gustave de Molinari's Bourse network theory: a liberal response to Sismondi's informational problem', *History of Political Economy*, **40** (2), 243–63.
Béraud, A. (2003), 'Jean-Baptiste Say et la théorie quantitative de la monnaie', in J.-P. Potier and A. Tiran (eds), *Jean-Baptiste Say, nouveaux regards sur son œuvre*, Paris: Economica, pp. 447–70.
Béraud, A. and G. Faccarello (2014), '"Nous marchons sur un autre terrain." The reception of Ricardo in the French language: episodes from a complex history', in G. Faccarello and M. Izumo (eds), *The Reception of David Ricardo in Continental Europe and Japan*, London: Routledge, pp. 10–75.
Béraud, A., J.-J. Gislain and P. Steiner (2004), 'L'économie néo-smithienne en France, 1803–1848', *Cahiers de l'ISMÉA, série PE*, **34** (February) 325–418.
Béraud, A. and P. Steiner (2008), 'France, economics in (before 1870)', in S.N. Durlauf and L.E. Blume (eds), *The New Palgrave Dictionary of Economics*, 2nd edn, London: Palgrave Macmillan.
Blanc, L. (1839), *Organisation du travail*, Paris: La Revue du Progrès, 5th edn 1847, Paris: Au bureau de la société d'industrie fraternelle.
Bonnet, V. (1859), *Questions économiques et financières à propos des crises*, Paris: Guillaumin.
Breton, Y. and M. Lutfalla (eds) (1991), *L'économie politique en France au 19ème siècle*, Paris: Economica.
Chevalier, M. (1850), *Cours d'économie politique fait au Collège de France*, vol. 3: *La monnaie*, 1866, Paris: Capelle.
Clément, A. (1850), 'Harmonies économiques par Frédéric Bastiat', *Journal des économistes*, **26** (111), 235–47.
Constant, B. (1822), *Commentaire sur l'ouvrage de Filangieri*, Paris: Dufart.
Coquelin, C. (1848), *Du crédit et des banques*, Paris: Guillaumin.
Courcelle-Seneuil, J.-G. (1867), *Traité d'économie théorique et pratique*, Paris: F. Amyot.
Courtois, A. (1889), 'Notice historique sur la société d'économie politique', *Annales de la Société d'économie politique*, **1**, 1–19, Paris: Guillaumin.
Destutt de Tracy, A. (1815), *Éléments d'idéologie*, 4th and 5th parts, *Traité de la volonté et de ses effets*, 2nd edn 1818, Paris: Courcier.
Dunoyer, C. (1827), 'Traité d'économie politique par Jean-Baptiste Say', *Revue Encyclopédique*, **34** (May), 63–90.
Dupuit, J. (1844), 'De la mesure de l'utilité des travaux publics', *Annales des Ponts et Chaussées*, 2nd séries: mémoires et documents, **8**, 332–75, reprinted in Y. Breton and G. Klotz (eds) (2009), *Jules Dupuit, Œuvres économiques complètes*, Paris: Economica, pp. 203–41.
Faccarello, G. (2010), 'Bold ideas. French liberal economists and the state: Say to Leroy-Beaulieu', *European Journal of the History of Economic Thought*, **17** (4), 719–58.
Garnier, J. (1847), 'Études sur la répartition de la richesse: profits et salaires', *Journal des économistes*, **18** (71), 201–23.
Gehrke, C. and H.D. Kurz (2001), 'Say and Ricardo on value and distribution', *European Journal of Economic Thought*, **8** (4), 449–86.
Juglar, C. (1862), *Des crises commerciales et de leur retour périodique en France, en Angleterre et aux États-Unis*, Paris: Guillaumin.
Juglar, C. (1863), 'Crises commerciales', in M. Block (ed.), *Dictionnaire général de la politique*, Strasburg: Berger-Levrault.
Juglar, C. (1868), *Du Change et de la liberté d'émission*, Paris: Guillaumin.

Le Van-Lemesle, L. (2004), *Le Juste ou le Riche, l'enseignement de l'économie politique 1815–1950*, Paris: Comité pour l'histoire économique et financière de la France.

Leroy-Beaulieu, P. (1881), *Essai sur la répartition des richesses et sur la tendance à la moindre inégalité des conditions*, Paris: Guillaumin.

Molinari, G. de (1855), *Cours d'économie politique*, Brussels and Leipzig: A. Lacroix, Verboeckhoven, 2nd edn 1863, Paris: Guillaumin.

Molinari, G. de (1891), *Les notions fondamentales d'économie politique et programme économique*, Paris: Guillaumin.

Proudhon, P.-J. (1840), *Qu'est-ce-que la propriété? Ou recherche sur le principe du droit et du gouvernement*, Premier mémoire, Paris, reprinted 1873 in *Œuvres Complètes*, vol. 1, Paris: Lacroix.

Proudhon, P.-J. (1846), *Système des contradictions économiques ou philosophie de la misère*, Paris: Garnier frères.

Ricardo, D. (1817), *On the Principles of Political Economy and Taxation*, London, John Murray.

Rossi, P. (1836–38), *Cours d'économie politique*, vols 1 and 2, Paris: Joubert, Thorel, 1840–41, vol. 3, Thorel, 1851, vol. 4, Paris: Guillaumin, 1854, reprinted 1865 in *Œuvres Complètes de P. Rossi*, Paris: Guillaumin.

Say, J.-B. (1803), *Traité d'économie politique*, Paris: Deterville, reprinted in J.-B. Say (2006), *Œuvres complètes*, vol. 1, Paris: Economica.

Say, J.-B. (1814), *Traité d'économie politique*, 2nd edn, Paris: Antoine-Augustin Renouard, reprinted in J.-B. Say (2006), *Œuvres complètes*, vol. 1, Paris: Economica.

Say, J.-B. (1817), *Traité d'économie politique*, 3rd edn, Paris: Deterville, reprinted in J.-B. Say (2006), *Œuvres complètes*, vol. 1, Paris: Economica.

Say, J.-B. (1819), *Traité d'économie politique*, 4th edn, Paris: Deterville, reprinted in J.-B. Say (2006), *Œuvres complètes*, vol. 1, Paris: Economica.

Say, J.-B. (1826a), *Traité d'économie politique*, 5th edn, Paris: Rapilly, reprinted in J.-B. Say (2006), *Œuvres complètes*, vol. 1, Paris: Economica.

Say, J.-B. (1826b), 'De la crise commerciale en Angleterre', *Revue Encyclopédique*, **32** (October), 40–45.

Say, J.-B. (1828), *Cours complet d'économie politique pratique*, Paris: Rapilly, 3rd edn with notes by Horace Say, 1852, Paris: Guillaumin, reprinted in J.-B. Say (2010), *Œuvres complètes*, vol. 2, Paris: Economica.

Sismondi, J.C.L.S. de (1803), *De la richesse commerciale ou principes d'économie politique appliqués à la législation du commerce*, Geneva: Paschoud.

Sismondi, J.C.L.S. de (1819), *Nouveaux principes d'économie politique ou de la richesse dans ses rapports avec la population*, Paris: Delaunay, Treuttel and Wurtz.

Sismondi, J.C.L.S. de (1824), 'Sur la balance des consommations avec les productions', *Revue Encyclopédique*, **22** (May), 264–98.

Sismondi, J.C.L.S. de (1838), *Études sur l'économie politique*, Paris: Treuttel and Wurtz.

Smith, A. ([1776] 1976), *An Inquiry into the Nature and Causes of the Wealth of Nations*, London: Strahan and Cadell, reprinted 1976 in *The Glasgow Edition of the Works and Correspondence of Adam Smith*, Oxford: Oxford University Press.

Villey, E. (1887), *La question des salaires ou la question sociale*, Paris: Larose and Porcel.

Wolkoff, M. (1854), *Opuscules sur la rente foncière*, Paris: Guillaumin.

Wolowski, L. (1864), *La question des banques*, Paris: Guillaumin.

Wolowski, L. (1869), *La question monétaire*, 2nd edn, Paris: Guillaumin.

Bullionist and anti-bullionist schools

The bullionist controversy refers to the series of debates about monetary and banking issues that took place in England from 1797 to 1821. It arose in very particular circumstances, namely, the suspension of the specie convertibility of Bank of England notes, on 26 February 1797, after fears of a French invasion had caused a run on the banks. Great Britain had declared war on France in February 1793, and in 1797 a small French force did actually land on the Welsh coast. The Bank of England explained that the suspension was a temporary measure necessary to avoid the loss of its reserves. However, what was supposed to be a brief suspension of convertibility lasted 24 years, until six years after Napoleon's defeat. The reasons and mechanisms of the increase in the market prices of gold and silver bullion that appeared as a consequence of this suspension were the main subject under discussion and gave the controversy its name.

The bullionists criticized the Bank of England for taking advantage of the suspension of convertibility to finance the government's military engagements and to over-issue banknotes. They argued that this excess pushed up the prices of commodities, bullion, and foreign currencies, and that the solution to these problems lay in an immediate return to the convertibility of notes into gold and silver coin, that is, into legal tender. On the opposite side, anti-bullionists justified the suspension. Their main argument was twofold. First, the high price of bullion was not linked to the inflation of money and prices but to real and financial causes that brought about a decrease of the exchange rate. Second, the suspension of payments of Bank of England banknotes in legal tender was necessary to guarantee the liquidity of the money market. According to them, the high price of bullion was the consequence of a combination of factors: the disruption of trade by the war, foreign war expenditure by the British government and the particular position of the Bank of England as the country's central reserve. The bullionist thesis was first introduced in 1801 by Walter Boyd, to whom Francis Baring replied in the same year and Henry Thornton a year later. The bullionists were close to the Whigs' Parliamentary opposition; among them, the most famous were Boyd, Francis Horner, Lord King, John Wheatley and David Ricardo. The anti-bullionists were close to the Bank of England and the Tory government; they included Baring, Thornton, Charles Bosanquet, John Hill, Nicolas Vansittart and Thomas Malthus. From an analytic point of view, the bullionists were more homogeneous than their opponents; they adhered to the quantity theory of money and favoured Hume's balance of trade theory. Although all anti-bullionists emphasized the importance of the balance of payments, they had differences of opinion when it came to money and credit; Baring, Bosanquet and Hill agreed with Smith's real bills doctrine, while Thornton rejected it. Rigid anti-bullionists contested the idea that the Bank of England could issue notes in excess, whereas moderate anti-bullionists thought it could. Thornton and Ricardo were the two great figures of this controversy, which considerably influenced nineteenth century English monetary and banking analysis.

Historical Context and Debates

Banknotes and market prices of gold and silver
Prior to the suspension of payments, the British monetary and banking system was characterized by the functioning of the Bank of England as a central bank, that is, lender of

last resort, under a standard gold–silver bimetallism regime. Since Isaac Newton's monetary reform of 1717, the British official coinage price of gold bullion was £3 17s 10½d per ounce. This meant that £1 was equivalent to 123¼ grains of 22 carat (standard gold) or 7.988 grams of standard gold. The gold "guinea" coin had a weight of 8.3874 grams and its price was 21 shillings. The silver "shilling" coin had a weight in metal of 6 grams and its price was 1 shilling. Coins were the only legal tender and could not be legally melted and exported. Bank of England notes were not legal tender but were widely used as a means of payment on the money market. As long as the bank redeemed its notes in coins, the market price of bullion in banknotes could not vary from the mint price.

The British banking system had at its centre the biggest issuing bank of the country and the only one in London with the right to have more than six partners: the Bank of England, founded in 1694. Its notes were the only paper money circulating in London. In this city there were also 60–70 bankers who played the role of intermediary between the "country" banks and the Bank of England. Outside London, the country banks (over 200 institutions) issued their own notes. The notes and deposits subject to check made up almost the entire supply of means of payment. There was no legal tender paper money. All banks were required to redeem their notes in coin, but the country banks used to pay them in Bank of England notes. The Bank of England, which centralized the reserves of the system, redeemed them in cash. These notes and the deposits in the Bank of England were used as reserve by the country banks. This meant that each bank in particular, as well as the banking system as a whole, operated on a fractional reserve basis, thus incurring a liquidity risk: the possibility of being unable to pay their notes and demand deposits. By lending its notes, the Bank of England helped the banks to manage their liquidity. In 1793, for the first time in history, the bank prevented a systemic bank liquidity crisis by issuing its notes.

Thanks to the Bank Restriction Act of February 1797, the Bank of England maintained its capacity to provide banks with liquidity, but the functioning of the monetary system changed. The suspension of the bank's obligation to pay its notes in coins left the market price of gold and silver dependent on variations in supply and demand. The same conclusion applied to foreign exchanges. However, the prophecy that the Bank of England notes would go the way of French *assignats* was not fulfilled. The prices of most commodities did not rise substantially and there was no sign of banknotes being distrusted during the first years of suspension. In 1799, food prices rose, but nobody mentioned a monetary cause. In 1800 the situation deteriorated: the market price of gold reached a level of 9 per cent above the mint price. In 1805, the price was 10 per cent above the mint price and in 1809 it was 15.5 per cent higher. Thereafter the situation worsened until 1814–15. See Figure 1.

The first bullionist pamphlet, Boyd (1801)

After the rise in the price of gold in 1800, a first debate was triggered by the publication of Boyd's pamphlet *Letter to the Right Honourable William Pitt, on the influence of the stoppage of issues in specie at the Bank of England: on the prices of provisions, and other commodities*, published in 1801. According to Boyd, the over-issue of banknotes permitted by the suspension of convertibility caused a rise in the prices of commodities, including gold and silver, and a fall in the exchange rates.

He argued that depreciation of the pound sterling has several effects on the balance of

Source: Hawtrey (1919: 464–5).

Figure 1   *Prices of gold, of silver and exchange rate*

trade: on the one hand, it increases the foreign demand for national goods, thus favour-ing exports; on the other hand, it increases the prices of imported goods, and therefore domestic prices. While this second effect reduces the demand for foreign goods, it also increases the value of a given volume of imports. By raising prices, it also counteracts the first effect. The total effect on the balance of trade of the decline in the exchange rates is therefore indeterminate. This is an anticipation of the Marshall–Lerner elasticities approach. In the end, Boyd favoured the effect of the increase in banknotes on the rising price of foods.

Concerning the issue of banknotes, Boyd estimated that from February 1797 to 1800 there had been an increase in circulation of £3.5 million, in other words an augmentation of nearly one-third of the former amount of banknotes. However, he stressed that there "exists no positive proof" of this increase because it is "a fact necessarily secret in itself" (quoted by Arnon 2011: 77). In Boyd's view, the existence of the fact is established "by reasoning from effect to cause" (ibid.): the proof relies on the low rate of exchange and the high prices of commodities in general, including gold. The natural tendency of money (that is, banknotes and gold) to depreciation from the increase of it, or of its representa-tive signs, is admitted to be a principle invariable "as the law of gravitation" (quoted by Arnon 2011: 78). Concerning the responsibility for this increase, Boyd thought that the Bank of England was the only bank to blame, because the situation of the country banks had not changed after the Bank Restriction Act.

> Every note which the country banker issues is payable on demand either in specie or in notes
> of the Bank of England. It may therefore be inferred, that no part of these issues can possibly

remain in circulation, beyond what the increasing prosperity and industry of the country where they circulate, can fairly absorb and digest. (Quoted by Arnon 2011: 80)

During the suspension, the amount of country banknotes rose and fell in proportion to the abundance or scarcity of the Bank of England notes.

Baring's and Thornton's replies; King's and Wheatley's developments (1801–03)

Baring, a private banker in London, answered Boyd's pamphlet by publishing *Observations on the publication of Walter Boyd* (1801). He agreed that the suspension of payments could permit the Bank to over-issue, but denied that this had yet been the case. In an earlier article, *Observations on the Establishment of the Bank of England and on Paper circulation in the Country* (1797), where the French phrase "dernier ressort" (last resort) was used for the first time to qualify the working of the Bank of England, Baring advocated the suspension of payments and at the same time warned that excessive monetary expansion would be inflationary. In 1801, he agreed with Boyd that the Bank of England, and not the country banks, would be solely to blame in the event of over-issue, but drawing on Adam Smith's banking analysis, he claimed that the paper money issued by the Bank after 1797 never exceeded the wants and needs of the public, and that the Bank did not operate to produce any increase in the price of goods. According to Baring, the increase of £3.5 million in the circulation of Bank of England notes mentioned by Boyd was the result of the growing prosperity of the country.

Above all, Baring contested Boyd's theory of the effect of the exchange rate on prices and emphasized the absence of any premium on guineas. First, he contrasted the relatively small deterioration in the exchange with Hamburg with the sharp rise in commodity prices. According to him, Boyd's argument could not explain this contrast. Although he agreed that a fall in the exchange rate "produces a good effect, by furnishing the means of exporting a larger quantity of goods and merchandise", he believed it to have "no influence or effect upon the price of corn grown in this country [England]" (Baring 1801: 20). Second, he pointed out that the prices of goods in paper money were no higher than the prices in gold, and that this was proof of "perfect and entire" confidence in the Bank. According to Baring, banknotes circulating at par cannot cause a rise in the price of corn.

In April 1802, there was a parliamentary debate on a bill aiming to extend the restriction until 1803. The same year, Thornton, a Member of Parliament allied with the Tories, and also a private banker in London and supporter of the Bank of England's policy, published his *Inquiry into the Nature and Effect of the Paper Credit of Great Britain*. Thornton began to write the book after the suspension of payments, in order to justify it, but before the market prices of bullion began to rise. The publication of Boyd's pamphlet convinced him to complete his inquiry by dealing with the subject of exchange and precious metal prices. In reply to Boyd, Thornton explained that a high price of bullion can occur even when there is no over-issue of notes pushing up the prices of goods; that the high price of bullion is the effect of falling exchange rates, and that exchange rates may fall as a consequence of financial outflows or bad harvests. His conclusion was that the high price of bullion was linked to the foreign war expenditures.

However, when the book was published, the debate about Boyd's pamphlet was over. In fact, Thornton participated in the controversy about the Irish currency exchange rate, when in 1803 it became unfavourable to the unprecedented degree of over 10 per cent, abandoning the old parity of 108.33 Dublin pounds to 100 English pounds. These fluctuations provoked a new discussion both in Parliament and in pamphlets about the relation between prices and exchange rates. In March 1804, the House of Commons appointed a committee to investigate the state of the Irish currency and the exchange relations between Ireland and England. Henry Thornton played a leading role on the committee.

Before the Irish crisis, King had published several pamphlets in accordance with the bullionist thesis, one of them entitled *Thoughts on the Restriction of Payments in Specie at the Banks of England and Ireland* (London 1803). King left aside Boyd's theory of the effect on food prices of the excess of banknotes, and considered that the high market price of bullion and the low exchange rate are "in conjunction the most accurate criterion of . . . [the] depreciated state of the currency" (quoted by Fetter 1965: 37). King affirmed that there was an excess of banknotes but did not describe any mechanism that could explain the relationship between this excess, the depreciating exchange rate and the high price of bullion. At about the same time, Wheatley entered the controversy with his *Remarks on Currency and Commerce* (1803). He later published his *Essay on the Theory of Money and Principles of Commerce* (1805). Wheatley anticipated Ricardo's bullionist argument that the depreciation of exchange rates cannot be caused by foreign payments alone, but can only occur in the context of, and as a consequence of, the falling value of money. This arises in the event of over-issue, which leads to the departure of specie.

The Bullion Committee and Bullion Report
After the Irish controversy and the publication of the *Report, from the Committee on the Circulation Paper, the Specie, and the Current Coin of Ireland; and also, on the Exchange between that part of the United Kingdom and Great Britain* (1804), the exchange rate between Dublin and London returned to its parity level. Bank of England notes remained almost at par in Hamburg for nearly five years. In 1809, the price of gold rose to about 15 per cent above the mint price and there was a considerable loss on the exchanges. David Ricardo published a letter in the *Morning Chronicle* of 29 August 1809 on "The Price of Gold," in which he attributed the responsibility for both problems to over-issuing by the Bank of England. On 1 February 1810, Francis Horner, a Whig member of the Parliament close to Ricardo, called for a committee to inquire into the subject. Horner was a specialist in financial questions; in 1802, he had written a favourable review article of Thornton's *Paper Credit* in the first issue of the *Edinburgh Review*. On 19 February of 1810 he was appointed Chairman of the Select Committee on the High Price of Gold Bullion, known as the Bullion Committee. Willam Huskisson, a Tory Member of Parliament and also a specialist in financial questions, and Thornton helped him to chair the sessions until 25 May and then to write the report, known as the Bullion Report, published on 8 June. According to Horner in a letter of 26 June 1810, the report:

> is a motley composition by Huskisson, Thornton, and myself; each having written parts which are tacked together without any care to give them an uniform style or a very exact connection. One great merit of the Report, however, possesses; that it declares, in very plain and pointed terms, both the true doctrine and the existence of a great evil growing out of the neglect of that doctrine. (Quoted in Cannan 1919 [1969]: xxii.)

The "true doctrine" was that a market price of bullion above its mint price is proof of the depreciation of paper money – that is, the great evil – and can only be rectified by reducing the quantity of banknotes. According to Horner, it was unfortunate that the opposing doctrine, according to which the high price of bullion was the consequence of a depreciation in exchange rates due to the war, and irrespective of excess issues, was also present in the report.

The report – discussed by Ricardo (1810 [1962]), Bosanquet (1810 [1994]), Vansittart (1811 [1994]) and Malthus (1811 [1994]) – went to Parliament for consideration and voting in May 1811. It was presented by Horner and introduced for vote in 16 resolutions, including the fourteenth, stipulating that the Bank of England had to refer to the state of the foreign exchanges and the price of bullion to regulate its issues as long as the suspension continued. On 6 May, the first 15 resolutions, asserting that excess issues were causing the high price of bullion, were rejected by 151 to 75. The sixteenth, which determined that the suspension should end within two years, whether the war was over or not, was rejected by 180 to 45. On 13 May, Vansittart presented 17 anti-bullionist resolutions which were adopted by a large majority. The Parliament disagreed with bullionism.

The resumption of payments

Five years after the publication of the Bullion Report, in June 1815, Napoleon was defeated at Waterloo. Thereafter the price of gold gradually declined. On 2 July 1819, Parliament voted the resumption of payments of banknotes in gold at the old mint price (£3 17s 10 ½d per ounce) in two steps: first in bullion from 1 May 1821, and then in gold coin from 1 May 1823. However, as early as 3 August 1819, the market price of gold fell to £3 18s, so that the Bank of England returned easily to full payments in gold coin and bullion on 1 May 1821.

During 1815–19, the controversy was no longer about the causes of the high price of bullion, but the terms and requirements for the resumption of payments. A first debate concerned the mint price at which it would be desirable to re-establish payments. The Attwood brothers, Matthias and Thomas, and Henry James, from Birmingham, a town of arms manufacturers strongly affected by peace, lobbied for a devaluation of the pound to avoid the consequences of the deflation of prices. They were quantity theorists and thought that a return to the old mint parity would be synonymous with the deflation of banknotes. However, the great deflation of banknotes did not happen. A second debate was about bimetallism. Since Newton's reform and up until the suspension of payments, the mint ratio between gold and silver had been above the international ratio, therefore above the market price in London. As a consequence, the English standard system was mainly a gold standard. There was a consensus for the adoption of monometallism, but the question of the choice of the precious metal arose. Since the exchange with Hamburg was primordial and most foreign countries were on a silver standard regime, some people, including Ricardo, argued in favour of silver. In the end, the return to the old British gold standard was preferred. A third debate concerned the establishment of a gold bullion standard instead of a return to the gold specie standard. With the exception of Ricardo, the consensual opinion was that the maintenance of gold coin as legal tender and the return to payment in gold coin were desirable to restore confidence and eliminate forgery in small banknotes (Fetter 1965). The first step in the resumption of payments, that is, in gold bullion, two years before payments in gold coin, was understood to be provisory. In order to prepare the full resumption, the Bank of England bought gold with a view to sending it to the Royal Mint for coinage. Ricardo criticized these purchases.

Thornton's Anti-Bullionism

When the suspension of payments occurred, the prevailing knowledge about money and banking was that developed by Adam Smith. Smith was in favour of the Bank of England, whose stability "is equal to that of the British government" (Smith 1776 [1981]: 320), and he emphasized its contribution to the reduction of interest rates through the circulation of Exchequer bills. At the same time, he developed the real bills theory, rejected the quantity theory and expounded an analysis of international precious metal flows that did not rely on any price mechanism. Following Smith's doctrine, public opinion did not adhere to the bullionist thesis. However, Smith was a theorist of the gold standard, and he did not anticipate either the central bank function of the Bank of England or the phenomenon of the high price of bullion. During the bullionist controversy, most of his followers, Bosanquet among them, did not consider that the situation might render some Smithian recommendations obsolete. Thus they could not understand that Smith's real bills theory, whereby the banking system responds to the needs of circulation and cannot over-issue banknotes, was a fallacy in the context of inconvertibility. Thomas Tooke explained this later, during the Banking versus Currency Schools controversy. So in 1810–11, Smithian anti-bullionism was at the same time politically strong but analytically weak.

Thornton's position was distinct. He supported neither the bullionism of the Whigs nor the anti-bullionism of the Bank of England directors. His 1802 work *An Enquiry into the Nature and Effects of the Paper Credit of Great Britain* criticized Smith's real bills theory and issuing rules; he introduced original developments in quantity theory but rejected Boyd's bullionism; he expounded the gold points mechanism which explains how a high price of bullion may occur irrespective of any fall in the value of money. In his most influential pamphlet, *The high price of bullion, proof of the depreciation of banknotes*, Ricardo (1810 [1962), who would subsequently embody bullionism, concentrated his criticism on Thornton. Thornton did not respond to Ricardo, but Malthus did. Although Thornton participated in the drafting of the Bullion Report and voted in favour of it, his analytical disagreement with bullionists about the main subject under discussion – that is, the mechanism that creates the high price of bullion – leads us to place him among the anti-bullionists. We do not share the tradition introduced by Viner (1937) of considering Thornton as a moderate bullionist.

The Bank of England as lender of last resort

Thornton linked the suspension of payments with the need to preserve the lender-of-last-resort function of the Bank of England. He considered the situation in 1797 with respect to the 1793 financial crisis. At that time, the banking system experienced liquidity difficulties which ended in a systemic crisis after the Bank's refusal to discount bills and issue banknotes because its reserve was at a very low level; a refusal in accordance with Smith's theory. According to Thornton, the banking system had suffered a flight to quality resulting from the public distrust of business, and, in such circumstances, the solution lies in the capacity of the Bank of England to restore confidence by increasing the supply of money, which means issuing its debt. The crisis was resolved by issuing 5 million sterling Exchequer bills which were lent to the merchants by the Treasury, and which the bank had to circulate (since 1707). Although the Bank of England was not the lender in 1793, it supported the Treasury's lending by issuing its notes. It is important to note that the Treasury took the credit risk, and the Bank took the liquidity risk. By assuming a higher liquidity risk in this way, the Bank of England helped the banks to manage their own liquidity, and resolved the crisis. Although its notes were not legal tender, the bank guaranteed the liquidity in the money market. However, if the bank succeeded in restoring confidence, in the circumstances of 1793, without having to suspend the payment of its notes, in the circumstances of 1797 – the fear of a French invasion – the suspension of payments was unavoidable. According to Thornton:

> The law authorizing the suspension of cash payments of the bank seems, therefore, to have only given effect to what must have been the general wish of the nation in the new and extraordinary circumstances in which it found itself. If every bill and engagement is a contract to pay money, the two parties to the contract may be understood as agreeing, for the sake of a common and almost universal interest, to relax as to the literal interpretation of it, and as consenting that "money should mean money's worth," and not the very pieces of metal: and the parliament may be considered as interposing in order to execute this common wish of the public. (Thornton 1802 [1939]: 139)

Explaining the lender-of-last-resort function of the Bank of England led Thornton to criticize Smith's credit and monetary theory. Contrary to the real bills theory, he considered that the credit risk is linked to the solvency of the debtor rather than the reality of the merchandises traded, and that credit granting and money issuing have effects on prices that depend on the price anticipations of debtors. Against Smith's issuing rule – that issues should be reduced when the reserve falls – Thornton introduced the concept of circulating medium (which includes different kinds of credit instruments, the notes of different banks, the notes of the Bank of England and the legal tender coins) and pointed out the solvency hierarchy existing between the different issuers of debt, with the Bank of England at the top. He demonstrated that the various components of the circulating medium have different velocities of circulation according to particular interest rates and degrees of confidence. Thornton considered that the instruments forming the circulation medium vary with the general level of confidence. In the case of distrust, the velocity of circulation of paper credit at the bottom of the hierarchical solvency structure increases, although it decreases at the top; there is an increasing demand for guineas and Bank of England notes, then an increasing supply of paper credit to be discounted on the money market, and then rising interest rates. By lending its notes irrespective of its reserve, the bank stops this process. This function must be performed whether there is convertibility of England banknotes or not, as was the case during the war. Ricardo never commented on this part of Thornton's contribution to monetary theory.

Balance of payments and the price of gold: the gold points mechanism
Thornton's explanation of the high price of bullion through the functioning of the currency market and gold points mechanism (GPM) was Thornton's second main contribution to monetary theory. This part of his work was strongly criticized by Ricardo.

According to Thornton, international trade lies at the origin of debts. If imports to England are higher than its exports, then the supply of English bank debt exceeds demand on the currency market, and the exchange rate falls. An arbitrage opportunity appears when the fall in the exchange rate reaches the point at which it is profitable for gold dealers to demand English bank debt in order to buy gold on the British market at the market price, or to request their reimbursement in coins at the mint price. The arbitrage between market and mint prices induces the draining of the banks' gold reserves. The level of exchange rate that causes an external drain of gold is called the "gold export point". Through this mechanism, by seeking "like [other commodities] that country in which it is the dearest" (Thornton 1802 [1939]: 145), gold fulfils the function of international means of payment. Here, gold outflows are the effect of the low exchange rate. This can occur as a consequence of a trade deficit caused by British inflation, but it can also happen if the trade deficit is caused by bad harvests, which lead to more imports, irrespective of any inflation in the prices of British exports. The excess supply of bank debts on the currency market may also occur when capitalists export capital in order to invest in foreign countries, or when the government supports foreign governments by sending them important sums of money in time of war. In this case, the exchange rate can fall to the level of the "gold export point" even though there is no trade deficit in goods. The conclusion is that gold flows are not linked to the balance of trade, but to the balance of payments.

Now, what happens when the obligation for the Bank of England to pay its notes in gold is suspended? Then, if the exchange rate falls below the gold export point, the international arbitrageurs continue to buy bank debt on the currency market with a view to transforming it into gold in London. However, under the suspension of specie payments, they can only buy the metal on the gold market, creating an excess demand that pushes up the market price of gold. Consequently, because the bank no longer supplies gold at the mint price, the price of bullion reaches a level far above its mint price. This level is proportional to the fall in the exchange rate. Neither Boyd, nor King, nor Wheatley envisioned this causality mechanism between exchange rate and high price of bullion. The originality and main contribution of Ricardo was that he contradicted Thornton by reversing the causality between exchange rate and price of bullion:

> Here, and in many other parts of the same article, the fall in the exchange, or the unfavourable balance of trade, is stated to be the *cause* of the excess of the market above the mint price of gold, but to me it appears to be the *effect* of such excess. (Ricardo 1810, vol. III: 64, original emphases)

Ricardo's Bullionism

Ricardo shared Boyd's and Wheatley's conclusions: excess issues of unconvertible banknotes are the sole cause of the high price of bullion. However, he did not share the vague idea that the price of bullion increases with the prices of other goods and of foreign currencies. Ricardo presented an innovative argumentation, criticized Smith's real bill doctrine, referred to Hume and gave an explanation of the high price of bullion in terms of arbitrage which resembled that of Thornton on some points, and opposed it on others. The way he justified bullionism laid the foundations of the British monetary orthodoxy that would prevail from 1844 until the First World War and, more generally, provided quantity theory with durable foundations.

The value of gold and the high price of bullion

Ricardo's explanation of the high price of bullion is based on two distinct arbitrages. The first, described in *The Price of Gold* (1809), concerns the domestic arbitrage between the face value of banknotes and the mint and market prices of gold. At first sight, Ricardo's approach is similar to Thornton's: under convertibility, if any difference appears between the mint and market price of gold, there will be an arbitrage which will close this gap. If the market price is higher than the mint price, the agents will find it profitable to sell gold bullion on the market and, with the banknotes received, buy guineas at the Bank of England at the mint price, melt the guineas, and then sell the bullion again, thus making a profit. The opposite will happen if the market price of bullion is lower than the mint price. These arbitrage processes continue until the market price reaches the level of the mint price. This conclusion is the same as that proposed by Thornton, although we must emphasize that Ricardo's explanation of the process is different. According to Thornton, it is the increase in the supply (demand) of bullion on the market that produces the decrease (increase) in its price. According to Ricardo, the bank brings the market price to the level of the mint price by withdrawing "the superfluous quantity of their notes from circulation". He uses the quantity principle to explain the variation in the market price of gold: "No efforts of the Bank could keep more than a certain quantity of notes in circulation, and if that quantity was exceeded, its effects on the price of gold always brought the excess back to the Bank for specie" (1809 [1962]: 16). A high price of bullion reflects a low value of money, resulting from a high quantity of banknotes.

The second arbitrage, described in *The High Price of Bullion* (1810 [1962]), operates at the international level. Ricardo assumed an open economy without banknotes, therefore without a currency market, and without international capital flows. Money is gold. Ricardo considered Hume's price-specie flow mechanism, and established that a country in which a gold mine is discovered will experience an increase in the quantity of money in circulation. Its value decreases, and in so far as its value abroad remains at the same level, an arbitrage opportunity appears. Because it is "cheap", the gold, "whether in coin or in bullion . . . leave[s] the country . . . for those countries where [it is] dear" (Ricardo 1810 [1962]: 54). Exportation of gold results from the arbitrage between the domestic and foreign values of the metal. Consequently, the quantity of gold diminishes in the country, and its value therefore increases, removing the arbitrage opportunity. Ricardo explained that the creation of a bank with the right to issue convertible notes has the same effect as the discovery of a gold mine on the value of money (gold and banknotes) and on the export of gold to other countries. Furthermore, in the domestic circulation, the banknotes take the place left by the exported gold coins. Under the suspension of specie payments, the adjustments will be the same as long as there are gold coins in circulation to be sent abroad. However, if gold disappears from circulation and notes can no longer buy it, then because banknotes have no intrinsic value so that they are not exportable, the adjustment mechanism between the quantity of money and its value ceases to function. There is no way to remedy the depreciation of banknotes when they are the only money in circulation. Then, an arbitrage opportunity appears: as a consequence of the legal fixed price of coins, the internal value of gold coin has decreased along with the depreciation of the banknotes, whereas the international value of gold bullion still remains the same. This situation creates the opportunity to melt the coins and export the bullion. Ricardo did not describe this arbitrage, but concluded that the existence of an equilibrium with no arbitrage opportunities requires an increase in the internal market price of gold that reflects the depreciation of banknotes: "An increase of paper currency. . . lowers the value of gold bullion but rises its money price" (Ricardo 1810 [1962]: 64). This conclusion is used as the keystone for the analysis of exchange rates.

The high price of bullion and the exchange rate

Ricardo wrote *The High Price of Bullion, a Proof of the Depreciation of Bank Notes*. He added that it is the high price of bullion that causes the fall in the exchange rate. The latter proposition is the foundation of the former. Ricardo did not accept Thornton's thesis that the fall in the exchange rate can be at the root of the arbitrage that pushes up the market price of gold. He developed the second proposition.

The price-specie flow mechanism shows that the value of gold money varies according to variations in its quantity and in the quantity of goods that (money helps to) circulate. The same mechanism also shows that the quantity of gold money varies to adjust its value to the international level. This double mechanism is described with gold coins that are in good shape. However, what happens when coins are debased, which means that the quantity of gold contained in the coin is lower than the mint one, that is, lower than the quantity in the bullion? What happens in an intermediary situation when the coins are not debased but the payment of banknotes is suspended? The same law explains all the possible cases: the surplus of gold money will leave the country as long as the value of the coins resulting from their weight is lower than their value abroad. The coins debased in a proportion of 20 per cent will be exported as long as their domestic value is more than 20 per cent lower than the foreign value of the non-debased coins, which means that the outflow will continue until this difference disappears; as soon as this point of equilibrium is reached the arbitrage with debased coins stops. However, there remains an arbitrage opportunity with bullion whose foreign value is 25 per cent higher than the domestic value of debased coins. The equilibrium with no arbitrage opportunity supposes that the market price of bullion rises 25 per cent; that is, the increase in the market price over the mint price is proportional to the debasement of coins. The same conclusion is reached with an amount of inconvertible banknotes 25 per cent higher than the equilibrium amount of non-debased coins. Ricardo established analogies between these various cases.

From the "gold points mechanism" point of view, the circulation of debased coins means a fall in the par of exchange. The arbitrageurs will send the exchange rate down. The same effect comes from a market price of gold above the mint price of gold, supposed to be caused by an excess of inconvertible banknotes. On the currency market, nobody will buy sterling pounds at the legal parity if it is necessary to pay an additional 25 per cent to buy gold in London, in the form of either debased coins at mint price or bullion at market price. As long as the exchange rate of the pound sterling has not fallen 25 per cent, it is profitable to send gold from the continent to London. The equilibrium with no arbitrage opportunities supposes this 25 per cent fall in the exchange rate. However, it is important to note that again, Ricardo did not describe these arbitrages. He did not expound the arbitrage that leads to the increase in the market price of bullion. Nor did he talk about the arbitrage that provokes the fall in the exchange rate. But he was convinced that the high price of bullion, which is the proof of the depreciation of debased coins or unconvertible banknotes, was also at the root of the fall in the exchange rate.

According to Malthus in 1811, and the Banking School authors 30 years later, Ricardo was wrong. They argued that the high price of bullion was not the cause but an effect of the fall in the exchange rate, in the same way that Thornton explained the arbitrages involved. However, these authors were not able to persuade their contemporaries. In fact, in spite of the strength of Thornton's theory of the arbitrages at work in the currency markets, Ricardo overshadowed him. Thereafter, the Currency School won the battle against the Banking School, and the price-specie flow mechanism dimmed the brightness of the GPM. We would have to wait until the end of the First World War for new light to be shed on the GPM, thanks to the disciples of Frank William Taussig, in particular Jacob Viner (1924) and James Angell (1926).

JÉRÔME DE BOYER DES ROCHES AND RICARDO SOLIS ROSALES

See also:

Balance of payments and exchange rates (III); Banking and currency schools (II); British classical political economy (II); Ralph George Hawtrey (I); Thomas Robert Malthus (I); Mercantilism and the science of trade (II); Monetarism (II); Money and banking (III); Open economy macroeconomics (III); David Ricardo (I); Adam Smith (I); Henry Thornton (I); Thomas Tooke (I); Value and price (III).

References and further reading

Angell, J.W. (1926), *The Theory of International Prices – History, Criticism and Restatement*, Cambridge, MA: Harvard University Press.
Arnon, A. (2011), *Monetary Theory and Policy from Hume and Smith to Wicksell: Money, Credit, and the Economy*, Cambridge: Cambridge University Press.
Baring, F. (1797), *Observations on the Establishment of the Bank of England and on Paper Circulation of the Country*, London: Minerba.
Baring, F. (1801), *Observations on the Publication of Walter Boyd*, London: Minerba.
Bosanquet, C. (1810), *Practical Observations on the Report of the Bullion-Committee*, London: J.M. Richardson, reprinted in D.P. O' Brien (ed.) (1994), *Foundations of Monetary Economics*, vol. 3, *The Anti-Bullionists*, London: William Pickering, pp. 39–82.
Boyd, W. (1801), *Letter to the Right Honourable William Pitt, on the Influence of the Stoppage of Issues in Specie at the Bank of England on the Prices of Provisions, and Other Commodities*, London: Wright.
Boyer des Roches, J. de (2003), *La pensée monétaire, histoire et analyse*, Paris: Les Solos.
Boyer des Roches, J. de (2013), 'Prices, value and seigniorage in Ricardo's monetary economics', in Y. Sato and S. Takenaga (eds), *Ricardo on Money and Finance – A Bicentenary Reappraisal*, London: Routledge, pp. 30–52.
Cannan, E. (1919), *The Paper Pound of 1797–1821 – The Bullion Report, 8th June 1810*, reprinted 1969, New York: Augustus M. Kelley.
Fetter, F.W. (1965), *Development of British monetary orthodoxy, 1797–1875*, Cambridge, MA: Harvard University Press.
Hawtrey, R.G. (1919), *Currency and Credit*, London: Longmans, Green.
Horner, F. (1802), 'Review of "An Inquiry into the Nature and Effects of the Paper Credit of Great Britain by Henry Thornton"', *Edinburgh Review*, **1** (1), pp. 172–201, reprinted 1957 in *The Economic Writings of Francis Horner in the Edinburgh Review*, New York: Kelley & Millman.
King, P. (Lord) (1803), *Thoughts on the Restriction of Payments in Specie at the Banks of England and Ireland*, London: J. Taylor.
Laidler, D. (1992), 'Bullionist controversy', in P. Newman, M. Milgate and J. Eatwell (eds), *The New Palgrave Dictionary of Money and Finance*, vol. 1, London: Macmillan, pp. 255–61.
Malthus, T.R. (1811), 'Depreciation of paper currency', *Edinburgh Review*, **17** (November 1810–February 1811, pp. 339–72, reprinted in D.P. O' Brien (ed.) (1994), *Foundations of Monetary Economics*, vol. 2, *The Bullionists*, London: William Pickering, pp. 253–88.
Marcuzzo, M.C. and A. Rosselli (1991), *Ricardo and the Gold Standard, The Foundations of the International Monetary Order*, London: Macmillan.
O'Brien, D.P. (1994), *Foundations of Monetary Economics*, vols 2 and 3, London: Pickering & Chatto.
Report, from the Committee on the Circulation Paper, the Specie, and the Current Coin of Ireland; and also, on the Exchange between that Part of the United Kingdom and Great Britain (1804), ordered, by the House

of Commons to be reprinted, 26 May 1826; reprinted in F.W. Fetter (1955), *The Irish Pound, 1797–1826*, London: Allen & Unwin.

Ricardo, D. (1809), 'The price of gold', *Morning Chronicle*, 29 August, reprinted 1962 in *The Works and Correspondence of David Ricardo*, vol. 3, *Pamphlets and Papers 1809–1811*, ed. P. Sraffa with the collaboration of M.H. Dobb, Cambridge: University Press.

Ricardo, D. (1810), *The High Price of Bullion, a Proof of the Depreciation of Bank Notes*, London: John Murray, reprinted 1962 in *The Works and Correspondence of David Ricardo*, vol. 3, *Pamphlets and Papers 1809–1811*, ed. P. Sraffa with the collaboration of M.H. Dobb, Cambridge: University Press.

Ricardo, D. (1951–62), *The Works and Correspondence of David Ricardo*, vols III and IV, ed. P. Sraffa with the collaboration of M.H. Dobb, Cambridge: Cambridge University Press.

Rist, C. (1938), *Histoire des doctrines relatives au crédit et à la monnaie depuis John Law jusqu'à nos jours*, Paris: Sirey, English trans. 1940, *History of Monetary and Credit Theory, from John Law to the Present Day*, London: Thoemmes Press.

Sember, F. (2013), 'Interwar reflections on the balance of payments – Taussig and the influence of the Ricardian bullionist tradition', in Y. Sato and S. Takenaga (eds), *Ricardo on Money and Finance – A Bicentenary Reappraisal*, London: Routledge, pp. 198–218.

Smith, A. (1776), *An Inquiry into the Nature and Causes of the Wealth of Nations*, reprinted 1976, eds R.H. Campbell and A.S. Skinner, Oxford University Press, reprinted 1981 by Indianapolis, IN: Liberty Classics.

Solis Rosales, R. (1999), *Banco central y tasas de interes: un ensayo sobre las teorias de Wicksell, Thornton y Hawtrey*, Mexico City: Universidad Autonimia Metropolitana.

Thornton, H. (1802), *An Enquiry into the Nature and Effects of the Paper Credit of Great Britain (1802): together with his evidence given before the Committees of Secretary of the two Houses of Parliament in the Bank of England, March and April, 1797, some manuscript notes, and his speeches on the bullion report, May 1811*, ed. with an introduction by F.A. von Hayek 1939, London: Allen & Unwin.

Tooke, T. (1838–56), *A History of Prices and of the State of the Circulation from 1792 to 1856*, 5 vols, London: Longman, Brown, Green, and Longmans, reprinted 1928 London: P.S. King, reprinted 1972 in New York: Johnson Reprint.

Vansittart, N. (1811), *Substance of Two Speeches made by the Right Honour. N. Vansittart on the 7th and 13th of May, 1811, in the Committee of the Whole House of Commons, to which the report of the Bullion Committee was referred*, London: J. Hatchard, reprinted in D.P. O' Brien (ed.) (1994), *Foundations of Monetary Economics*, vol. 3, *The Anti-Bullionists*, London: William Pickering, pp. 147–76.

Viner, J. (1924), *Canada's Balance of International Indebtedness*, Cambridge: Harvard University Press, reprinted 1978, Philadelphia, PA: Porcupine Press.

Viner, J. (1937), *Studies in the Theory of International Trade*, London: Allen & Unwin.

Wheatley, J. (1803), *Remarks on Currency and Commerce*, London: Burton.

Wheatley, J. (1805), *Theory of Money and Principles of Commerce*, London: W. Bulmer & Company.

Banking and currency schools

The Banking School/Currency School controversy is typically viewed as the second major British monetary controversy of the nineteenth century. Perhaps a more just assessment of the controversy sees it as a long-running debate between the followers of the two great monetary theorists of the first two decades of the century: Henry Thornton and David Ricardo. Although the controversy came to a head in 1844, when a parliamentary committee was formed to take evidence from a wide variety of British bankers and businessmen on the occasion of the renewal of the Bank of England's charter, in reality, the controversy had cropped up repeatedly, from the time of the Bullion Committee hearings in 1810. The crisis of 1825 re-ignited the controversy. A variety of writers then began contesting the question of how the British banking system – and the Bank of England – should be organized and regulated in the wake of the banking crisis of 1825.

The crisis of 1825 came on the heels of an economic boom in 1824. Agricultural and commodity prices rose sharply, and speculation in the stock market drove share prices sharply higher. Commercial banks, seeking higher earnings, loaned freely, as did the Bank of England, and commodity prices began to rise, while the pound sterling fell against foreign currencies. The fall in the exchange was accompanied by an outflow of capital, which generated fears that some banks would not be able to pay in specie on demand. In an attempt to prop up the British banking system, the Bank of England loaned freely, putting itself in some danger of having to suspend payments in gold. In the event, the bank managed to weather the storm without suspending payments in gold, but had the drain on the bank been only a little larger, or had it lasted only a little longer, suspension would have been required.

Although the Bank of England managed to survive the storm without resorting to a suspension of cash payments, the episode triggered a new round in the controversy over how the Bank of England should conduct its affairs. Monetary pamphleteers began writing on the topic with renewed vigour. The memory of this episode guaranteed that the Government's Bank Charter Committee would hold hearings on the renewal of the bank's charter at its earliest opportunity, which came in 1832, before the bank's current charter was to expire in 1833. These hearings were the most extensive ever held on the renewal of the bank's charter up to that point. Although the committee determined that it was unable to state a "unified opinion" on the questions at hand (Fetter 1965 [1978]: 145), a number of principles were widely agreed upon. In particular, the committee was firm in its adherence to the gold standard, rejecting any return to a paper currency.

During the hearings, the Bank Charter Committee called J. Horsley Palmer, the Governor of the Bank of England, who spent most of his life at the bank, beginning his first term as a director in 1825–26. He remained on the Court until 1857, except for the usual break every third year (Horsefield 1944 [1953]: 143). Palmer testified regarding the rules or guidelines utilized by the governor and directors in deciding how large the bank's note issue should be. Governor Palmer, speaking for the bank's directors, described the "Palmer rule" to the committee. According to the rule, when the circulation was "full", that is, when the exchanges were just on the brink of turning against Great Britain, the bank should hold a gold reserve of "about one third" against the bank's outstanding notes and deposits, except under unspecified "special conditions" (Fetter 1965 [1978]: 132–3). The absence of specific quantitative standards meant that the bank's directors were not constrained by rigid rules but had the discretion to manage the currency as they saw fit, at least within limits that were quite broad. Thus, the Palmer rule was far less restrictive than the proposition suggested several years earlier by James Pennington. In 1827, Pennington, who shortly thereafter was made a member of the Political Economy Club, laid out the first formal statement of the Currency Principle: the bank's notes circulation should vary with the bank's holdings of gold coin and bullion. It is possible that Pennington was encouraged to write his manuscript by Thomas Tooke, whose views on monetary theory and policy later underwent a dramatic change. It is certain that Pennington's idea became widely known and discussed by the members of the Political Economy Club, who disseminated it through their frequent interactions among themselves and with others interested in the monetary question.

However, despite the bank's adherence to a rule that purportedly ensured, to a significant degree, that the convertibility of the bank's notes into gold on demand would be guaranteed, the Bank of England faced crises in 1835–36 and, much more violently, in 1839. So great was the 1839 crisis that the Bank of England had no recourse but to appeal to the Bank of France for help in order to maintain the convertibility of bank notes (Horsefield 1944 [1953]: 109). Not surprisingly the bank's directors were subjected to withering criticism, and the public came to expect that the bank would exercise its "break clause" whenever monetary stringency emerged. Subsequently, a Secret Committee on Joint-Stock Banks, which held hearings from 1836 to 1838, and a Select Committee on Banks of Issue, which operated from 1840 to 1841, "produced only masses of evidence, from which the conscientious student of banking reforms could have deduced almost any remedy he cared, but which the Committees themselves found impossible to digest" (Horsefield 1944 [1953]: 109). However confused the Members of Parliament may have been, by the end of 1843, Prime Minister Robert Peel had a well-formulated plan in mind. Early in 1844, Peel met with William Cotton and J.B. Heath, the Governor and Deputy Governor of the Bank of England, to discuss the changes that he wished to see implemented when hearings were held later in the year. Peel was well prepared for the meeting: his memorandum contained "almost all the essential features of the 1844 Act": the prohibition of any further banks of issue; the limitation of existing note-issues to their then size; the division of the structure of the Bank between an Issue Department and a Banking Department; and the limitation of the notes issued against securities to a fixed sum, any further issues to be backed by bullion. Peel added only one proposal that did not become part of the Act: that "extensions of the fiduciary issue should be permitted, if and when the need arose, on the sanction of three Ministers of the Crown" (Horsefield 1944 [1953]: 110–11). As Horsefield (ibid.: 113) has noted, this would not have come as a surprise to anyone familiar with Peel's voting record as a Member of Parliament

Peel's proposal set forth a pure currency-school approach to the regulation of the money supply. In accordance with the currency principle, bank notes were treated as money, but Bank deposits were not. This opened the door for the bank to expand credit excessively, even if its note issue were held within reasonable bounds.

The Controversy of 1844

Although Prime Minister Peel's intentions regarding the restructuring of the Bank of England and the restriction of the issuance of bank notes were well known among those in the financial community, opposition to the Currency Plan surfaced only as the hearings on the renewal of the bank's charter were about to begin. The primary opponents of the Act were Thomas Tooke, well-known monetary economist and collector of economic data; John Fullarton, who recently had returned to England from India; John Stuart Mill, economist and philosopher; James Wilson, founding editor of *The Economist* magazine, and James Gilbart, a well-known banker and advocate of free banking. In no sense did the Banking School project a coordinated front in their opposition to the Bank Act; their only common purpose was to defeat the proposed changes in the structure and operations of the Bank of England.

Tooke was the standard-bearer for the Banking School. He laid out his opposition to the Act in *An Inquiry into the Currency Principle* (Tooke 1844), one of two book-length critiques of the Currency Principle and the Bank Act. The second was Fullarton's *On the Regulation of Currencies* (Fullarton 1844), its title specifying one of the major complaints of the Banking School advocates: that the currency of Great Britain did not consist solely of coin and bank notes. In fact, a large portion of the transactions in the wholesale trade were carried out with bills of exchange, just as Henry Thornton had observed more than four decades earlier in *An Enquiry into the Nature and Effects of the Paper Credit of Great Britain* (1802).

Tooke's *Inquiry into the Currency Principle*

Even before writing the *Inquiry into the Currency Principle* Tooke had been a critic of the Currency School's theory, arguing that implementation of the Act would increase monetary instability and increase the danger of periods of inconvertibility.

Tooke began his *Inquiry into the Currency Principle* with a statement of the Banking Principle:

> It was held by most writers of any authority on the subject of the Currency, till within the last few years, that the purposes of a mixed circulation of coin and paper were sufficiently answered, as long as the coin was perfect, and the paper constantly convertible into coin; and that the only evils to be guarded against by regulation were those attending suspension of payment and insolvency of the banks, a large proportion of which blend an issue of promissory notes with their other business. This, in point of fact, is what is understood in general terms as the banking principle, and is that upon which our system of currency is constructed and conducted. (Tooke 1844: 1)

However, according to Tooke, a "new canon of currency" had been promulgated by the members of the Currency School. The convertibility of the paper currency into gold had always been the criterion of the soundness of banknotes, but according to the currency theory, the "bank notes in circulation should be made to conform to the gold, into which they are convertible, not only in value, but in amount" (Tooke 1844: 2). The purpose of Tooke's *Inquiry* was to examine the wisdom of requiring the quantity of bank notes outstanding, above the fiduciary issue of £14 million, to be limited by the quantity of gold held by the Issuing Department.

Tooke provided a summary of his conclusions in the *Inquiry* in the form of 17 points (1844: 121–4). For our purpose, let us stress the first twelve of them. First, he argued that if the currency consisted entirely of precious metals, large inflows and outflows of bullion, up to "at least" £5 million to £6 million could take place without affecting the amount or the value of the British currency. Second, this implied that the belief that the currency would necessarily be affected by such bullion flows was false. Third, Tooke argued that the distinction between banknotes and other forms of paper credit over-stated their differences; only small banknotes, used in retail trade, were essentially differ-ent. Fourth, if "the obstacle of stamp duties" were removed from bills of exchange, bills could be used to transact nearly all business in the wholesale trade. Fifth, checks were widely used in retail trade and were generally as convenient as bank notes, if not more so. Sixth, higher denomination notes were generally used for "peculiar" purposes, such as clearinghouse settlements, provision markets, and purchases of fixed property. Bills of exchange could easily substitute for banknotes in such uses.

Seventh, "the amount of bank notes in the hands of the public is determined by the purposes for which they are required, in circulating the capital, and in distributing the revenues of the different orders of the community, valued in gold" (Tooke 1844: 122). Eighth, banks of issue, including the Bank of England, cannot increase the quantity of notes in circulation unless the public wish to hold more notes, though one bank might expand its note issue at the expense of another bank. Ninth, banks lack the power to diminish the total quantity of notes in circulation; a reduction of the note issue of one bank will be offset by an increase of the notes circulated by other banks. Tenth:

> That it is consequently an error to suppose that, however well informed the country bankers might be of the state of the foreign exchanges, and disposed to follow those indications, they would be disposed to regulate their circulation in conformity with such views. And that it is equally an error to suppose that the Bank of England can exercise a *direct* power over the exchanges, through the medium of its circulation. (Tooke 1844: 123, original emphasis)

Eleventh, neither country banks nor the Bank of England have the power to enlarge their note circulation unless more notes are demanded by the public. Forcing notes into cir-culation reduces bank capital. Twelfth and finally, the quantity of money in circulation does not determine prices; rather, prices determine the quantity of notes in circulation; that is, the money supply is endogenous, with the general level of prices tied to gold.

Tooke's theoretical system
The Currency School, following the lead of David Ricardo, adopted the quantity theory of money as their basic model of how prices react to changes in the money supply. However, Ricardo developed his monetary theory during the restriction of cash pay-ments, when the pound sterling was not convertible. The Currency School continued to use the quantity theory as their basic model of how changes in the supply of convertible currency would affect prices. Tooke and other members of the Banking School rejected the quantity theory as a valid approach to understanding how a convertible currency actually worked. In sharp contrast to the Currency School's approach, Tooke argued that the quantity of money, consisting of all different kinds of monies, was endog-enously determined by the price level and the level of output. Hence, causation ran from the price level to the quantity of money, including the quantity of banknotes. Tooke also maintained that short-run changes in the interest rate had little effect on the level of expenditures, but that the "long-run average" rate of interest – which governed the normal rate of profit – was determined in the financial market by politico-institutional and conventional factors, largely independent of Bank of England policy (Smith 2003:

46–7). Tooke's theory drew on Adam Smith's concept of two circulations: wholesale and retail.

John Fullarton's law of reflux

The most effective attack on the proposed Bank Act and the Currency School system came not from Tooke but from John Fullarton. Unlike the Currency School adherents, such as Robert Torrens and Lord Overstone, Fullarton (and other Banking School theorists) were careful to differentiate between "money" and "credit." Proponents of the Currency School routinely referred to ordinary banknotes as "money," though such notes were in fact credit instruments: they represented both an asset to the holder and a liability to the issuer, whereas gold coins (and the bank's fiduciary issue) were money, since no liability attached to them. Banking School writers uniformly treated the notes of both the Bank of England (except for the fiduciary issue) and of ordinary banks as credit instruments.

The debate over what was money and what was credit was not merely semantic. A pure paper currency represents no liability to the issuer. Thus, if the entire money supply of Great Britain had consisted of inconvertible bank notes, the Currency School would have been fully justified in arguing for a quantity-theoretic approach to the control of the money supply – or for a bank-managed proto-Keynesian policy (as Henry Thornton had described in the *Paper Credit of Great Britain* in 1802), for that matter. The problem, as the Banking School writers saw it, was that the Currency School wanted to impose a quantity-theoretic approach on an economy whose money supply was endogenous, by virtue of its commitment to tie the pound sterling to the international gold standard. While the Bank of England could and did sterilize specie flows to some extent, there were limits beyond which the Bank of England could not go in its attempt to force the currency to behave according to Currency Principle.

Fullarton understood that the British money supply was endogenous: "There is this broad and clear distinction between all currencies of value and currencies of credit, that the quantity of the former is in no degree regulated by the public demand, whereas the quantity of the latter is regulated by nothing else" (Fullarton 1844b [1845]: 63).

Fullarton insisted that the equilibrium price level was determined by the relative cost of gold production. However, that did not prevent him from recognizing that an increase or decrease of the amount of credit supplied could temporarily drive prices up or down. In Fullarton's opinion, speculation in commodity markets, supported by an extension of bank credit, enabled the speculators to drive prices higher than they could have if working only with their own capital. On this issue, Fullarton's views were not so different from those of Lord Overstone, although Fullarton did not focus so narrowly on the activities of country banks as did Overstone, who believed that a contraction of banknotes was typically offset by an increase in the circulation of country-banknotes, thereby prolonging the process of adjustment undertaken by the Bank of England.

Although Fullarton recognized the necessity of the Bank of England doing what it could to counteract speculative bubbles, he was not particularly optimistic that the Bank would have much success if speculation were excessive. In Fullarton's view:

> [T]he part which seems to me most befitting the Bank, and the most consistent with the duties of circumspection and forbearance prescribed by its position, is to hold itself aloof from all

transactions of a speculative character, and refuse the aid of its credit in any shape to those who are avowedly or notoriously engaged in them. And, when it finds the balance of foreign payments becoming unsettled, from the multitude and magnitude of such projects, the exchange depressed, and its treasure menaced with exhaustion, if it does not immediately exert itself, to the full extent of its power, to break up the speculation, and compel as many of the parties as it can control to bring their securities or their commodities (as the case may be) to market, it ought not to be from any particular tenderness to the individuals, but from a desire to spare, if possible, the number of innocent sufferers who would be involved in the catastrophe, and I may say, indeed, the public at large. (Fullarton 1844b [1845]: 163–4)

Fullarton feared that the Currency School's adherence to the price-specie-flow theory would lead bank officials to take harmful measures to prevent large losses of bullion, when in fact all that was necessary to stem an outflow of bullion was to raise the bank rate, thereby putting upward pressure on market rates. If interest rates in Britain rose significantly above those in other economies, gold would begin flowing into the London market. Fullarton argued that large hoards of gold were held in many countries, hoards that migrated to the market offering the highest rate of return. If the Bank of England would commit to holding a large bullion reserve, on average, and to use a high Bank rate to attract foreign capital, the Bank could prevent major collapses in the British economy. Besides, Fullarton argued, gold drains are not interminable: drains caused by crop shortages or war expenditures had clear limits. In addition, Fullarton argued that anything approaching a "perpetual drain would soon become as intolerable to the recipient as to the disbursing party" (Fullarton 1844: 151).

The outcome of the debate, of course, had been settled before the hearings of 1844 commenced. The Currency School held the political power, and the Bank Act of 1844 became law with little opposition in Parliament. The Bank of England was reorganized, with the Issue Department separated from the Banking Department. The bank was permitted to extend its issue of banknotes beyond the fiduciary limit of £14 million only as it obtained more bullion. That is, the Issuing Department faced a marginal reserve requirement of 100 per cent.

The crisis of 1847
How the bank would respond, if it once again came under great pressure, was not stated in the Act of 1844. When the proponents of the Act were queried as to how the bank would react to a threat to convertibility, they responded that the Act itself provided assurance that such pressure would not appear, since the possibility of over-issuance of bank notes had been eliminated (Fetter 1965 [1978]: 201). Unfortunately, the bank's officers adopted the attitude that implementation of the Bank Act freed the bank from any necessity of taking extraordinary actions (as it had done multiple times before) because the Act itself eliminated the improper behaviour that had led to previous crises. This attitude, quite naturally, led the bank to seek to garner a larger share of the discount business. The bank reduced its discount rate from 4.0 to 2.5 per cent, thereby matching the market rate and confirming the predictions of London's private bankers that the Bank of England would become much more aggressive in its pursuit of profits (Fetter 1965 [1978]: 202). The bank's new policy certainly produced more income. By February 1845, the value of bills discounted by the bank had risen by nearly two thirds, and the bank's total assets had risen by 64 per cent (based on data in Fetter 1965 [1978]: 204).

Commercial deposits began growing rapidly in 1845, with the bulk of the growth being driven by special "railway deposits linked to payments for new securities, while the bank of England continued to expand its lending apace. The ratio of the Banking Department's cash reserves to assets plunged throughout 1845. An improvement of the bank's reserve ratio in the first half of 1846 gave way to a sharp drop later in the year, culminating in the suspension of the Bank Act in October 1847 (Fetter 1965 [1978]: 203).

Although the suspension took a great deal of pressure off the bank, it did not solve all its problems. One issue that bedevilled the bank was the fact that more than a fifth of the bank's reserves were in silver. Since most European nations, as well as Asian countries, were on the silver standard, holding substantial silver reserves was appropriate. However, the bank could not redeem its notes in silver; banknotes were redeemable only in gold, which had the effect of reducing the bank's effective reserve (Fetter 1965 [1978]: 206–7). Fearing that it would fall afoul of the law, the bank refused to lend on silver at all.

The British economy gradually recovered over the course of 1848, though the debate over how best to regulate the note issued continued for some time.

Assessing the Intellectual Controversy

Although the Banking School writers considered themselves the victors in the intellectual battle over how to manage the bank's note issue, Currency School partisans could justifiably retort that, had the bank's officials not engaged in an all-out effort to expand lending and increase earnings, thereby violating the most basic tenet of the Currency Principle, it would have provided a useful guide to issuing notes in an orderly manner; the note issue would not be a source of economic disturbance.

However, unfortunately for both banking and currency schools, it is probable that neither approach to issuing notes would have produced the expected results, for a very basic reason: neither school of thinkers really grasped how the British monetary system had changed over the preceding decades. The Currency School placed altogether too much emphasis on the notes of the Bank of England, while ignoring deposits and other financial instruments. They learned, to their sorrow, that controlling credit conditions was crucial to a successful monetary policy. They also learned that rigid rules can generate problems that require that the rules be suspended, at least temporarily. The Banking School learned that having a better theory of credit markets and how to manage them was of little importance when the political cards are stacked against you. However, in fact, the banking theory was nearly as out of touch with the workings of the British financial system as was the currency theory.

In a paper entitled "Monetary base control and the Bank Charter Act" (1997), Denis O'Brien used such data as were available to test a number of hypotheses that focused on the changes in the British banking system that emerged between two periods: 1832–44 and 1844–1857. O'Brien's intention was to gauge the ability of the Bank of England to control the price level through its control over the note issues of the Bank of England. While data deficiencies constrained him from answering all the questions posed, the data were sufficient to shed light on several issues. O'Brien's major conclusion was that "the Act of 1844 did not succeed in its aims of introducing monetary base control for the British economy and of stabilizing the price level and the monetary aggregates" (O'Brien 1997: 628). Instead, data support a viewpoint set out by Thomas Joplin (who died before the banking–currency controversy began), that the country-banknote issues for England and Wales "had the dominant influence on the price level" (ibid.: 628). Although the Bank Act failed to bring the country issues under the bank's control, the statutory limitations placed on the note issues of the country banks prevented the country-bank note issues from being an important source of monetary instability.

NEIL T. SKAGGS

See also:

Bullionist and anti-bullionist schools (II); Money and banking (III); David Ricardo (I); Henry Thornton (I); Thomas Tooke (I).

References and further reading

Arnon, A. (2011), *Monetary Theory and Policy from Hume and Smith to Wicksell. Money, Credit and the Economy*, Cambridge: Cambridge University Press.

Fetter, F.W. (1965), *Development of British Monetary Orthodoxy: 1797–1875*, Cambridge, MA: Cambridge University Press, reprinted 1978, Fairfield, NJ: A.M. Kelley.

Fullarton, J. (1844), *On the Regulation of Currencies; being an Examination of the Principles on which it is Proposed to Restrict, within Certain Fixed Limits, the Future Issue on Credit of the Bank of England, and of the Other Banking Establishments throughout the Country*, London: John Murray.

Horsefield, J.K. (1944), 'The origins of the Bank Charter Act, 1844', *Economica*, reprinted in T.S. Ashton and R.S. Sayers (eds) (1953), *Papers in English Monetary History*, Oxford: Clarendon Press, pp. 109–25.

O'Brien, D.P. (1997), 'Monetary base control and the Bank Charter Act of 1844', *History of Political Economy*, **29** (4), 593–633.

Skaggs, N.T. (1991), 'John Fullarton's law of reflux and central bank policy', *History of Political Economy*, **23** (Fall), 457–80.

Smith, M. (2003), 'Central banking rules: Tooke's critique of the Bank Charter Act of 1844', *Journal of the History of Economic Thought*, **25** (1), 39–61.

Smith, M. (2011), *Thomas Tooke and the Monetary Thought of Classical Economics*, London: Routledge.

Thornton, H. (1802), *An Enquiry into the Nature and Effects of the Paper Credit of Great Britain*, London: J. Hatchard.

Tooke, T. (1838–57), *History of Prices and of the State of the Circulation during the Years 1703–1856*, 6 vols, vols 1–3, London: Longman, Orme, Brown, Green and Longmans, vol. 4, London: Longman, Brown, Green and Longmans, vols 5–6, with W. Newmarch, London: Longman, Brown, Green, Longmans and Roberts.

Tooke, T. (1844), *An Inquiry into the Currency Principle: The Connection of the Currency with Prices and the Expediency of a Separation of Issue from Banking*, London: Longman, Brown, Green, and Longmans.

Non-Marxian socialist ideas in France

Non-Marxian socialist ideas in France emerged in a political movement, which progressively constituted itself in the early nineteenth century, and are inextricably linked with an enhanced political, syndical, cooperative and cultural awareness and identification among workers or a working class within industrial society. This movement progressively built up a provenance for itself, prior to, and when faced with, the influence of Karl Marx (1818–1883), the full diversity of which remains largely unrecognized. The works of Claude Henri de Saint-Simon (1760–1825) and François Marie Charles Fourier (1772–1837) are at the origin of the movement and were highly influential in the 1820–30s. Each of the two ensuing schools of thought had their own followers: the Saint-Simonian school with Barthélemy Prosper Enfantin (1796–1864), Saint-Amand Bazard (1791–1832), Michel Chevalier (1806–1879) or Émile Pereire (1800–1875) and his brother Isaac (1806–1880); and the Fourierist school with Victor Considerant (1808–1893), for example.

There were also dissident authors – mainly Pierre Leroux, who is well known for having provided one of the first definitions of socialism in 1833, but also Philippe Buchez (1796–1865) or Constantin Pecqueur (1801–1887). Leaving aside the communist utopias of Étienne Cabet's (1788–1856) (Sutton 1994) and Alexandre Théodore Dezamy (1808–1850) (Maillard 1999), the second phase of French socialism is intrinsically linked with the names of Pecqueur, François Vidal (1812–1872), Louis Blanc (1811–1882), Auguste Blanqui (1805–1881) and Pierre-Joseph Proudhon (1809–1865), who all played a role in the 1848 Revolution but also in the constitution of the First International in 1864.

The influence of these schools of thought can clearly be felt in the third key phase which is marked by the institutionalization and success of French socialist movements and their ideas (for example, access to parliamentary representation). This phase then carried over to the Third Republic after the end of the Paris Commune and the fierce repression that followed. At this point, the intellectual and political context changed, and French socialism became confronted with the considerable influence of German Marxian socialism in France and the First International (whose theorist, as a matter of fact, was Marx). A voluntarist movement emerged, from Benoît Malon (1841–1893) to Jean Jaurès (1859–1914), to constitute a French filiation of socialism with a specific profile ("integral socialism"), in particular as regards the economy ("collectivism"). However, this third phase remained diverse despite an effort to bolster ideological and political unity.

The main focus here is on the economic contents of these socialist ideas, which, while suffering from various shortcomings, contain important ideas. The period examined ranges from 1820 to 1914. After this, everything changed. A long series of causes gradually ate away at the diversity of socialist ideas: that is, the downslide of the Second International into nationalism, the part taken by non-Marxian socialists in the French "Union sacrée" in 1914 and the ravages caused by the war, the upheavals brought about by the Third International, the historical divide brought about by the majority decision to create a communist party which broke up the SFIO (French Section of the Worker's International), and finally the Bolshevik interpretation of Marxism and state socialism.

Two Approaches of the Economy and Industrial Society in the Early Nineteenth Century

Saint-Simon and the Saint-Simonians

Saint-Simonianism was initially part of a broad industrialist movement, founded on French neo-Smithianism, which developed considerably from 1816 to1820. Claude Henri de Saint-Simon placed particular emphasis on the role of work, the division of labour, and supported full development of an industrial society. This society was designed to become the culmination of the perfectibility of mankind. The historical development, Saint-Simon asserted, was hampered by an opposition between two classes: workers and idlers. However, the term worker in this case encompasses foremen, active capitalists as well as the "working class" or "proletariat" – all terms used by Saint-Simon. The idlers are inactive capitalists who consume without producing. Saint-Simonianism is thus a theory that is critical of the rentier system and not, as it is often thought, a theory of exploitation in the Marxian sense. Salaries and profits are not distinguished by Saint-Simonians and an unjustified monopoly over the land and means of production lie in the way of closer productive affinity between workers and these means of production. A historical trend was supposed to bring gradually these two components closer together (with a gradual drop in rent and interest) with the aim of achieving worldwide production.

The reforms suggested were thus intended to match workers and means of production: new "constitution of property", that is, property more easily transferable, inheritance called into question, progressive taxation, contestation regarding indirect taxation on consumption, development of material and immaterial infrastructure (credit, canals and railways). This new society was analysed as if it were a social workshop – association was substituted for competition, administration for government – and criticism was voiced against poverty and the precarious situation of non-owners (influenced in part by Sismondi's work). The social objective was based on a triptych associating three human functions within a social entity (feelings, ideas and interests) combined with three dimensions of the social workshop (morality and religion, science and industry). It became the "improvement of the condition of the last and largest class" (Saint-Simon 2012: 2505), associated with two rules of justice which in one form or another proved to be an inspiration for all future socialism: a rule of distribution of the means of production (according to ability), and a rule concerning material and immaterial remuneration (according to performance). Saint-Simon thus argued in favour of a non-egalitarian and meritocratic society linked to industrial capacity.

Disciples developed the historic typology of societies with a distinction between "critical" and "organic" phases, leading to the suppression of the "exploitation of man by man". Enfantin and É. Pereire formulated an economic analysis of the progressive transformation of society while pushing for centralized and state organization – revolving mainly around the crucial role of the banking system but also centralization by the state of part of the inheritance. Despite social conflict arising from use of machines, tariffs and wages (and in particular the first revolt of the Lyon silk workers, the "Canuts", in 1831), as well as the failed July 1830 Revolution, the definition of "workers" is maintained, as are profit sharing schemes between workers and industrialists.

In spite of the break-up of the Saint-Simonian school of thought after 1832, brought about by official repression and in-fighting, crucial developments took place on the economic front well into the Second Empire – developments of the banking sector, railways, industry, creation of companies (something Marx later called imperial socialism) on a national and international level from Suez to Algeria. Saint-Simonians showed a remarkable aptitude for reconversion in business and political life, the clearest example certainly being Michel Chevalier (1849). This propensity for reconversion is almost certainly due to the ambiguity of Saint-Simonian ideas and the fact that various interpretations were possible (technocracy, corporatism, and even socialism). While it remained profoundly attached to the integration of the proletariat within industrial society and to a series of significant and anticipatory reforms, this school of thought mainly advocated enhanced industrial organization and non-rentier capitalism which guaranteed a position for the working class in proportion with abilities and performance in the social workshop.

Fourier and the Fourierists

Charles Fourier's intent was to describe a universal system of social organization whose presentation was never completed (Beecher 1986) and which differs considerably from the Saint-Simonian approach. While Saint-Simonians argued in favour of an extensive development of industrial society, Fourier was critical of "false industry" characterized by indigence of the population, treachery and revolutions: industry, he thought, brings about poverty as a result of abundance itself. Fourier provided a parody of the hypocritical "appeal" of free competition, commerce, free trade and the stock exchange. He was also critical of the principle of the division of labour, and also of the subordination of agriculture to the manufacturing industry.

While the Saint-Simonians argued in favour of the perfectibility of mankind, Fourier rejected this hypothesis and advanced a cyclic and non-linear approach. Humanity would pass through eight stages (from primitive stage to the highest stage of harmony); however, he suggested that mankind might end up straying away from its destiny and fall into a social trap. This fall would be the consequence of a philosophy of progress that had failed to recognize the intentions of the deity and to identify the social code that governs the organization of human societies.

While Saint-Simonians strove to establish a framework for human behaviour through a global view of functions and their coordination revolving around a social objective, Fourier radically based social and economic order on individual desire, passions and "passionate attraction" (Fourier 1829). This attraction pushes individuals to freely join agricultural and domestic groups which are built up in a precise manner, vary over time and enable the expression and development of passions. The economic and social approach proposed by the Saint-Simonians came with a call for strict industrial hierarchy, administration by those with the ability and, in the case of Enfantin, a religious and sectarian order. Fourier's approach is closely associated with cosmological speculations (Beecher 1986: ch. 17) and a theory of "destinies" mainly based on the satisfaction of personal well-being: repressing or even modifying natural passions is impossible. In this way, any new organization of production must accept that "the main issue in social mechanics is getting people to rise to the role of proprietor" (Fourier 1836 [2013]: 15): no solution can be based on a revolutionary working class which positions itself as the enemy of the wealthy classes and a wealthy class which is the enemy of the people. Every individual must be proportionally enriched according to three criteria based on work, capital and skill. In this way, Fourier argued in favour of a combined industry and "phalanxes" (with 1620 members in each phalanx, or twice the number of people depict-ing the 810 passional personality types) bringing together the full range of male and female passions and leading to a "quadrupling of production". The main characteristics of this organization are the following: (1) work units which are specialized or make use of a specific means of production; (2) the flourishing of individuals' instincts which develop each and everyone's productive values and vocations, as opposed to the industrial system in civilization which stifles and alters instincts via education and domestic violence; (3) universal attraction, linked to attractiveness and emulation, once tasks are distributed among a series of special groups with short work sessions and each individual participat-ing in various groups; and (4) converging participation based on an unequal share distri-bution within the group. This distribution is supposed to grant access to dividends and varied and refined types of gratification, which in turn stimulates consumption, the latter being the basis for production. Thus, the hallmarks of the phalanx – the community which Fourier proposes as the basis from which to launch the new social organization – are the refusal of equality, a respect for property, an increase in the wealth of all classes of society without spoliation, the absence of a centralizing and federating body between communities, an increase of production which is strictly dependent on the intensity and refinement of passions, and free and voluntary participation.

While Saint-Simonians went ahead with concrete applications of their utopian system and set up industrial and banking projects within industrial society itself, the disciples of Fourier – Considérant in particular – established Fourierist communities or phalanxes which experimented with the concept of ideal society as a whole in virgin locations (for example, near Dallas in Texas as from 1857 after the two French experiments in 1833 and 1842 and numerous American experiments). However, the influence of the Fourierists was not limited to the creation of phalanxes: from 1831, part of the Saint-Simonians switched to Fourierism and joined what was to become the "École sociétaire". Having made certain adjustments to the doctrine, its leader, Considérant, played a major role in its diffusion (Beecher 2001) and, opposed to Fourier, tried to bring together theory and politics by establishing connections with a republican program (right to vote and elec-toral reform in particular). Considérant (1839 [1848]) continued to defend the natural right to individual property, free inheritance without state intervention, and the idea of harmony between the classes within a community. However, he introduced a right to work compensating for spoliation of usufruct rights pertaining to land with the guaran-tee of paid work enabling the disinherited to live on. The degree of uncertainty regarding the position adopted by Considérant from the late 1840s mirrors the difficulty in grasp-ing the changes brought about by the entry of the working classes into politics (revolu-tion of February 1848), even though the Fourierist movement has often been interpreted as anticipating associative socialism.

Socialist Ideas around 1848

The term "socialism" was first created and used by its supporters and opponents in the 1830s and 1840s. This period was marked by a proliferation of socialist ideas, a variety of definitions and attempts to set out political rights (recognized by the revolution of February 1848, the provisional government and the Second Republic) as well as social and economic rights (can a social republic see the light of day?), in particular subsequent to the repression of the insurrection of June 1848 and the putsch of Louis-Napoléon Bonaparte in December 1851.

Pierre Leroux

Leroux, an ex-Saint-Simonian, showed signs of dissidence as early as 1831 and openly challenged Saint-Simonian ideas in 1832 with the *Revue encyclopédique* which he had just taken over, by pointing to direct opposition between (1) the proletariat class producing the wealth of the nation and only possessing the daily wage by means of labour and working conditions they have no control over, and (2) the bourgeois class who owns the means of production, that is, proprietors and manufacturers who are the "feudal lords" of industry and pilot production only to match their own interests. In this way, Leroux clearly identified a direct opposition between workers and capitalists in terms that are far less ambiguous than before. When it comes to economic activity, equality is not guaranteed, even though everyone's right to industry and property is proclaimed (Leroux 1834–49 [1996]: 18–19). The interests of these two classes differ.

According to Leroux, however, they are by no means contradictory as long as a regime of association and true equality is ensured. This would be done by a democratic government, whose aim is to elevate the proletariat – a republic which addresses social issues and strives to achieve real equality through legislative progress (multiplicity of legislators, representation of the proletariat, economic measures such as socialization of means of production, extension of the right of property to all, right to time off work, and restoration of the role of agriculture). As the main focus is not on economic measures (Frobert 2010), Leroux had to outline his definition of socialism. Having drawn attention to a contradiction between freedom and equality, he placed two extremes head to head (Leroux 1834 [1996]): on the one hand, individualism, which conceives society merely from the standpoint of individual contracts and cannot ensure real equality, and on the other, socialism, which he qualified as "absolute", which is a sectarian aberration giving society total rights over the consciousness of its members (as advocated by the Enfantin variant of Saint-Simonianism). The form of socialism defended by Leroux is a compromise between the individual and society. From an economic point of view, Leroux perceived equality as the possibility of enjoying access to the same goods and the acquisition of a universal right to information and knowledge. Equality should give its real meaning to sentiment (fraternity) and to the right to act (freedom), through a transformation of the Saint-Simonian trinitarian formula. This economic equality thus challenges the first Saint-Simonian principle based on ability – it points instead to a more Fourierist qualitative principle – but accepts the second principle (remuneration according to performance, hence meritocracy). Socialism is thus inseparable from a democratic republican context and from a tutelary state which, however, is not authoritarian (and not an abolition of the state as revealed by the debates between Blanc, Proudhon and Leroux). But it also depends on the non-institutionalization of a religion of humanity which is necessary to establish solidarity and the effectualness of society as a "mystical body".

Philippe Buchez

Buchez, a physician and ex-Saint-Simonian, was certainly the most prominent proponent of a conciliation between socialism and Christianity while rejecting paternalism. He accepted the Saint-Simonian analysis of the misery of the working class (critique of conventional economic policies based on individualistic principles, class analysis opposing a minority of idle proprietors and producers, and role of competition) and wished to continue the ideas Saint-Simon expressed in his 1825 *Nouveau Christianisme* by providing an outline of morality reflecting present day world. Although a partisan of a "République dans l'atelier", he nevertheless developed (Buchez 1833) a three-tier implementation of the associative principle (or collectivism): the creation of joint bodies with State representation in factories (the main aim being to set wages), smaller sized associations of skilled workers, and access to public (state-run) credit funds based on taxation and placements. The latter would support the creation of skilled workers' associations and make up for any initial shortage of individual capital (Frobert 2014b). These economic measures would however first require a moral revolution through an education based on devotion, in accordance with the Gospel principles.

Constantin Pecqueur

Pecqueur was also a Saint-Simonian dissident who later temporarily joined the Fourierist school. His works and influence in the 1830s and 1840s are of pivotal importance to socialist economic ideas in France. He was keen to establish an economic law of a tendency towards a socialization of the means of production. Pecqueur took the Saint-Simonian analysis of transportation networks one step further by suggesting that machines coupled with steam provide the material conditions for the association. The "regulating centripetal action of the association" (Pecqueur 1839: 271) thus gains a firm foothold and puts an end to the fragmentation of production. This analysis establishes a connection between an underlying trend towards socialization and the establishment of a new approach to economic organization (association). In Pecqueur's view, this trend was not merely material; it also encompasses economics (concentration of production and consumption, fusion of individual capitals, bringing together of agricultural and industrial activities), politics (universality and association of classes, communication, democracy) and morality (new lifestyles, sociability). From an institutional standpoint, it could be expressed either by the development of new versions of feudality, which this time are industrial, or by systematic association (key intermediary role of the middle classes, establishment of numerous interconnected urban hubs which challenges the imbalance between Paris and the countryside).

In terms of the associative model, Pecqueur defended the model of the Christian republic, which is based on socialization together with sovereignty of the people at each level of production. When it comes to the transition phase, Pecqueur argues in favour of a Fourierist model of productive communities but supported by the state, which exerts an indirect influence on the economy and ensures that there is no return to private coalitions. The right of ownership (Pecqueur 1842) is transformed into the right to a function (that is, a coherent type of activities) but also righteous involvement of state officials or citizen-magistrates. The state defines the various functions with a balanced calculation of the quantity of labour, and verifies the aptitude of individuals to fulfil these tasks and appoints those who are apt to judge the results of their implementation. In accordance with a Christian standpoint, there should be absolute equality in terms of remuneration when work is carried out correctly – even though the equivalence of all functions within the economy is hard to achieve during the transition phase, hence a degree of inequality may prevail. Within the context of the 1848 revolution and pressure to create a Ministry of Labour, Pecqueur, together with Vidal and Blanc, played a crucial role in the work of the so-called "Luxembourg commission" concerning the implementation of national workshops (Frobert, 2014a).

Louis Blanc

Louis Blanc played a significant role in the first phase of the 1848 revolution, and in particular while president of the Luxembourg commission. His contribution to socialist ideas is often under-estimated and very frequently associated with arguments in favour of economic statism. His role, however, is far more complex (Demier 2005). The work organization he suggested aims to address the issue of deprivation and not merely the right to work. This right to work – which was already put forward by Considérant – is dependent on a right to live, a claim initially made during the revolution and used by Leroux. Blanc placed considerable emphasis on both principles, rejected a simple right to assistance and explicitly supported the power of the state to establish this right: "The State is the banker of the poor" ([1839] 1840: 14). He was a proponent of the association principle and opposed competition by granting access to instruction and means of production to all. Social workshops – and not the famous national workshops established by the government in 1848 – in the industrial as well as agricultural sectors were destined to gradually substitute themselves for individual workshops and were thus production cooperatives launched by the state (via credit in particular) for the first year only, and then managed by the members of the workshop themselves.

The state is a backer and legislator but not a producer in its own right. Blanc clearly believed that a state bank was required because the Banque de France established in 1803 and controlled by private shareholders did not have a long-term strategy, especially in times of crisis. Credit provided to the workshops had to be interest-free but reimbursed. The state had also to be involved in the commercial side of things by providing warehouses and bazaars to ensure free trade – acknowledgements of receipt of the deposit of products was supposed to be transferable by endorsement and thus could fulfil the role of paper money. When it came to remuneration, Blanc argued in favour of a distribution of profits in three parts: one part to be distributed between the members of the workshop, another for the upkeep of the old, the sick and the infirm and the third to be used to ease the burden in other industries. As regards individual remuneration, Blanc remained hesitant: wages could be set equal, or proportional to the work performed, but ideally: "Equality is proportionality and it will only really exist when everyone . . . will produce according to his faculties and consume according to his wants". The latter formula will remain associated with him for years. It is only later that it is attributed to Marx. Blanc's socialist system (Blanc 1848) thus combines interconnected production cooperatives, which are destined to eventually take over most of the production, and tight state regulation concerning banking and trade. His state is a republican state under universal suffrage but Blanc opposes the tyranny of the majority through the Thomas Hare single transferable vote system. This state is also unified and its sovereignty is indivisible (political centralization with administrative decentralization in municipalities only), as opposed to the views of Proudhon. On a more general level, this state establishes a common interest, which is beneficial for capitalists themselves and thus is not based on the hypothesis of a class struggle.

Auguste Blanqui

Blanqui is reputed for being an unwavering activist: he participated in three revolutions, in 1830, 1848 and 1871, several failed insurrections (1839 in particular), and a considerable part of his life was spent in prison. However, placing excessive focus on this reputation would be to over-simplify his contribution as Blanqui bears witness to the diversity of socialist ideas and the existence of a variety of persuasions. Blanqui (1805–81 [1993]) believed in upholding socialism without accepting any reference to progress while remaining perpetually in doubt as to whether socialism can blossom under the Republic. First, he rejected any positivist law of progress, which according to him paves the way for a fatalistic view of history. He argued that there can be no laws when it comes to social issues as action breaks the law. History is thus an open book that remains uncertain by nature with critical points in time which can alter its course. Socialist positivism produced "admirers of the accomplished fact" (1869 [1993]: 22) but there is nothing fatalistic about the advance of socialism. The characteristic traits of Blanquism are that history can be written on a daily basis through rupture, violent uprisings and the use of weapons and via class war or what Blanqui referred to as regular anarchy. Political concerns thus take the upper hand over economic policies.

Despite a critical or ironical analysis (Blanqui 1885 [2012]) of certain concepts (usury, capital) and of various political economists (Frédéric Bastiat, Auguste Walras and Henri Baudrillart), Blanqui placed little emphasis on utopian programmes or transitional strategies, apart from some general thoughts regarding substitution of the association for individual ownership of land and other means of production and arguments in favour of the necessity of universal education. According to Blanqui, these issues could only be addressed once the initial hurdle had been overcome, contrary to the practice of communists and Proudhonists. A focus on the exploitive nature of the state and a call for a temporary dictatorship in order to trigger the free development of socialism echoed the 1796 "Conspiration des Égaux" ("conspiracy of equals"), and placed more emphasis on insurrectional creativity than on examining socialist republicanism in greater depth (Vigier 1986).

Pierre-Joseph Proudhon

Proudhon's contribution was of the utmost importance to socialist ideas, due above all to his influence during the period 1840–60, but also his in-depth theoretical analysis – economic philosophy and theory of value – and the originality of several of his arguments. Rather than providing a full description of his ideas (see Haubtmann 1982, 1988; Vincent 1985), we shall focus on two key points: (1) the issue of the state and of mutualism, and (2) the issue of socialist economic organization. Proudhon is the main contributor to a socialist tradition that puts the state radically into question. In a society characterized by the exploitation of labour by capital, the state, in the same way as capital, had established itself as an autonomous power. Emancipation of society and of labour thus occurs through an upheaval, which establishes an unalienable and spontaneous right overriding any state legislation: the right of direct and reciprocal exchange between workers which guarantees both autonomy and solidarity. Mutualism is the application of this right within society and the socialist economic system.

According to Proudhon and in the same way as for other socialist schools of thought, this requires the workers to gain access to the means of production and thus a shake-up of the ownership rules: private property restrains natural and reciprocal exchange thus enables the exploitation of man by man which is theft and thus immoral, because property is sacrosanct. While his views on the subject evolved over time (Proudhon 1846), Proudhon fundamentally opposed private property. However, private property could be maintained in the transition period during which the state remains present albeit within a contractual framework, and could also be used as a counterweight to the power of the state. The new model also advocates associations similar to those suggested by Saint-Simonians between sponsors and partners in a public limited liability company, and the use of promissory notes (instead of metal coins and bank notes) but with a federative structure: an exchange bank should provide everyone with the means to produce when clients have declared their intention to buy the products (proposal of a "Banque du Peuple", made to the 1848 Luxembourg Commission). Furthermore, no interest is paid in this mutual credit system. Finally, the Proudhonian model advocates federalism on an agricultural and industrial level, which must progressively dissolve the state and is based on workers' associations. Abolition of the exploitation of man by man comes with abolition of the exploitation of the government of man and development of an economically and politically decentralized system (hence the deep contention with Blanc and Leroux).

The last important point concerns Proudhon's view on equality. Proudhon argued that the Saint-Simonian position (from each according to his abilities and to each according to his performance) and Fourierian position (from each according to his capital, his work and his skill) are both false and unjust. Capital cannot justify payment: if property or possession can only be justified as being the result of labour, then receiving farm rent would inevitably turn the farmer into a proprietor. As far as remuneration of labour is concerned, Proudhon returns to his theory of "collective force": payment proportional to work performed is unjust as society on the whole only exchanges products of equal value – individual differences are abolished. Workers are associates and equal, so wages must be equal. Natural inequality is gradually neutralized as the association develops. Property is the only thing that can bring back inequality. When labourers are associated, the right of each is limited by the right of all. As soil is limited, the law of absolute equality takes effect (Proudhon 1840 [1867]: ch. 3, s. 6). With this anti-state mutualism, Proudhon thus developed an "anarchist" line of thought (Knowles 2004), but very different from that of Blanqui. His egalitarian ideas also contrast considerably with the Saint-Simonian and Fourierian approaches – with the exception of their stance on women.

The Institutionalization of Socialist Ideas in France: 1880–1914

After the 1851 coup d'état, and after the failure and harsh repression of the Paris Commune in 1871, the socialist movement regains momentum (Réberioux 1997). A process of institutionalization gets under way with tangible outcomes as from the 1890s: political institutionalization with unprecedented national and municipal elective representation and the creation of a united socialist party in 1905; ties established with trade unions (first syndical confederation in 1886 under Guesdist domination, followed in 1896 by the Confédération Générale du Travail, as well as the federation of Labour Exchanges under libertarian influence); ties with the cooperative movement and Charles Gide (1847–1932) in particular (see Gide 1894, 1924), concerning the role of consumer cooperatives; and a broadening of the ideological scope, with intellectuals such as Émile Durkheim (1858–1917), or graduates from the École normale supérieure.

The socialist ideas of this period are influenced by Marx but also by French "revisionism" (which does not exclude the Marxian contribution) and by the constitution and defense of a French socialist heritage in the face of the German Marxian influence (Prochasson 2004) and its French Guesdist representatives (Derfler 2009): Jules Guesde, Gabriel Deville and Paul Lafargue. In this way, French socialism strives to construe a united base for itself around Benoît Malon and then Jean Jaurès, with a focus on defining the economic content of socialism ("collectivism"), and on defining socialism itself ("integral socialism"). Some differences do subsist though within and outside this context, exemplified by the writings of Georges Sorel (1847–1922) and Charles Andler (1866–1933) or the "marginalist socialism" of Adolphe Landry (1874–1956) and of Léon Walras (1834–1910).

The attempt to form a coherent doctrine of socialism: the Malonians and Jaurès

Benoît Malon played a central role in this project, being both the founder and director of a pluralistic publication entitled *La Revue socialiste*, as well as an advocate of a unified and integral version of socialism, which would be the product of the socialist movement's evolution. The economic content of what was then considered to be the modern stage of socialism, "collectivism", is central. Collectivism, from an economic standpoint, is the gradual socialization of main production resources and credit (railway, mines, canals and Banque de France), used by associations under the control of the state (but not used directly by the state). It is also the substitution of associative work for the wage system, first in industry, then in commerce and agriculture. Finally, it implies that workers should be allowed to dispose freely of their remuneration. This was the French implementation of the orientations of the International at the Marseille congress of 1879 – prior to the creation of the Second International in 1889 – which saw the victory of the "collectivists" over the mutualists and cooperativists.

This economic content was presented as stemming from a French filiation, first proposed, before Marx, by Pecqueur in particular. According to Malon, modern collectivist socialism, as opposed to what was referred to as utopian communism, restricts socialization to productive forces: common goods and labour incomes are not to be socialized. State intervention is supported and a republican strategy of conquest of power is validated. This orientation challenged mutualism and the heritage of Proudhon, which according to Malon had negative repercussions on the socialist movement in the 1860s: cooperatives, in particular, proved incapable of bringing about emancipation from the wage system and replacing it with the associative model. Malon supported the economic content of this model of socialism with (1) a somewhat confused interpretation of the Marxist theory of value, based on Rodbertus and mainly Lassalle's views on Marx; (2) the perception of a logical and historical sequence of events – a tendency to capitalist concentration, a transition to monopoly and constitution of industrial, banking and commercial feudal powers and finally the necessity for socialization of property by the state, with reference to Brousse's communal public utilities approach (Brousse 1883 [1910]); (3) the iron law of wages, with the underlying influence of the Malthusian law of population; (4) and finally the influence of Spencerian evolution (Bellet 2000).

Malon placed emphasis on the practical dimension of this socialism, which he described as reformist, non-utopian, pragmatic and aiming for concrete outcomes. In this way, it appears to be compatible with Marx's philosophy of history and historical materialism but rules out any fatalistic interpretation.

Finally, Malon's conception of socialism included the concept of morality: collectivism is presented as a synthetic and integral socialism (Malon 1890), in the sense that man is an individual and a social being that must emancipate itself from state authority. This emancipation must be both intellectual and political while the state keeps acting as a collectivist from an economic standpoint, regulating production and distribution of wealth (not consumption). Malon also placed emphasis on morality and the emergence of an "altruistic" era of humanity. This approach was also a way of bolstering the French filiation of socialism in the face of German socialism. It was followed by the group of Malonians – Fournière (1901, 1904a), Rouanet (1887) and Renard (1887–88), the successive directors of the *Revue socialiste* – with varying degrees of inflection concerning Marx's contribution to socialism, historical determinism, the rejection of catastrophism, the individualist filiation of socialism, the integration of federalist elements or the role of moral progress (Bellet 2016).

Jean Jaurès was himself intrinsically linked with this collectivist line of thought and played a prominent role in the difficult constitution of a united socialist party in 1905. His *Histoire socialiste de la Révolution française*, with several Malonians participating in it, bolstered the process of revitalization of French socialism. Jaurès' views are relatively flexible and weakly theorized economically, but do display some hallmarks of a "socialist method" (Jaurès 1902 [2013]). The notion of revolutionary development is taken from Marx and is used to analyse the relationship between reform and revolution, the decline of capitalism brought about by the state, or the decline of the state, and the gradualism of revolutionary transformation. However, while borrowing from Marx, he was also critical of the *Communist Manifesto* and Book I of *Capital* (the only book to be read directly at the time, apart from a few exceptions). Jaurès upheld that property is defined by the law and is thus alienable even though he recognized the right of ownership as such. He clearly argued in favour of a state collective property so as to abolish capitalist exploitation and the wage system. Furthermore, he was critical of the German state socialism system, which restricted itself to merely correcting capitalism. He also voiced criticism against proposals which advocated the fragmentation of property and the general defence of individual property (linked to the Radical party), when the state had already set up limitations to private ownership (expropriation laws, tax on inheritance and so on). He was sceptical as regards production cooperatives as a way of achieving socialization since they failed in 1848; but he advocated corporative property under delegation of the state to regrouped workers, with a national board representing the groups and elected under universal suffrage. Finally, he upheld that socialism is the continuation of revolutionary individualism of the French Revolution and had to clearly address the issue of property. Strikes are legitimate as a permanent form of class struggle linked to the private ownership of the means of production, as a way for workers to defend their economic rights (wages, working hours and hygiene), and are opposed to general strikes as a political tool, defended by revolutionary syndicalism. The state cannot be assimilated with a bourgeois state and partial reforms within the capitalist system could lead to a transition to a socialist republic – Jaurès on the whole supported Millerand's contentious ministerial socialism as from 1899. Democracy, freedom and social Republic are thus associated with socialist ideas.

Two dissidents: Sorel and Andler

Georges Sorel is a controversial figure but is highly representative of the ongoing diversity of socialist ideas (Charzat 1986; Gervasoni 1997). His thoughts owe much to his reading of Proudhon, and he remained highly critical of the process of unification peculiar to collectivism and integral socialism, being for a while a supporter of the influential revolutionary syndicalism socialist movement. Sorel's economic ideas stem mainly from an acerbic criticism of Marx, but also occasionally from a more respectful interpretation. First, he argued that there is no real theory of value in Marxism (Sorel 1897). This theory stems from the first sphere of value, whereas in a second sphere, which includes variable capital and competition, prices establish themselves to level out profit rates. Basing himself on Italian critiques of Marxism (Benedetto Croce and Antonio Labriola), Sorel argued that Marx had only come up with a theory of economic equilibrium, which is reduced to the case of an overly simplified economy, or a kind of pure economy (in a Paretian sense) found in a homogenous form of capitalism. Once the theory is applied to a real and more complex economic system, simple values representing labour time are no longer equivalent to prices. Marx made a methodological error by applying the method which was used in an abstract context, and none of his conclusions was confirmed when he had to analyse actual facts. According to Sorel there is an ambiguity as regards the notion of labour, due to a confusion between the work of society with its tools – in which case it is justified to claim that wealth is produced by work – and the labour of a worker without tools, in which case it is unjustified to claim that wealth is produced by their work. The notions of paid and unpaid work are also obscure and this is even more pronounced among readers of Marx (Jaurès, Guesde, and so on), since the thoroughly non-Marxist concept of theft reappears. Marx's economic concepts should thus be interpreted as being hypotheses for further deliberation. From a more general standpoint, Sorel challenged the evolutionary reading of Marx inherent to Malonian and Jauresian socialism and its sole focus on the economic aspects of social issues.

His attempt to construe an economic analysis of a concrete economic system (Sorel 1903 [1924]) uses the rural economy as a field study to reveal the errors, ambiguities and superficial pragmatism of the socialist vision of collectivism, such as the mistaken assumptions regarding the growing proletarization in the countryside, the role of the large property or mechanization. The line between private property and state administration must be based on the Proudhonian approach, which distinguishes production from its economic environment. The issue of property in the agricultural sector must be addressed by socialization of the exchange process of products, but not of production. The latter would call into question the very nature of the producer, their spirit of ownership, their myths (images which have the power to instinctively trigger feelings) within a whole encompassing production, the family, habits, social authority, which Sorel called juridical consciousness of the people. In this way, authors who have understood the rural economy and voice criticism against state or federalist solutions could attempt to apply the same kind of approach to industrial production and to workers in order to gain a better understanding of possible socialization.

Sorel did not identify himself with the historiography produced by Malonian socialists.

In his view, prior to 1848, socialist thinking (from Saint-Simon to Pecqueur) was largely based on a vision of the economy founded on kindness, enthusiasm, religion, with declarations of rights and invocation of the spirit of association. Proudhon and Marx were the only authors to oppose this line of thought and argued that the division of labour and exchange represents the only truly collective force. The Second Empire and the Third Republic led to the development of a sophisticated industrial sector, with exchange and credit as well as state support: that period confirmed the role of material and economic forces and condemned the sentimental socialism. However, different from Marxist predictions, capitalism did not collapse. Socialism was lagging behind once again: it was busy debating Marx and the crisis of Marxism in a society which saw Marx already as an outdated thinker. Socialism thus needed to become rooted in struggle. Filiation with the Proudhonian school of thought led Sorel to argue in favour of a struggle against the state and the transfer of state functions to workers' unions, independently of political socialism. According to Sorel, general strikes and violence are a legitimate response to the extension of the state's functions, and meet the working class' need for a socialist myth (Sand 1985). This belief is at the basis of his support of revolutionary syndicalism which was influential in the years 1903–07 – with, in particular, Hubert Lagardelle and Édouard Berth – and which led to some anarcho-syndicalist echoes being carried forward to the 1906 trade union charter.

Charles Andler was an eminent germanist and one of the rare readers of Marx's works that had not yet been translated into French, and contributed to the collectivist school of thought. He provided a subtle appraisal of the crisis of Marxism and, in his well-informed commentary of the *Communist Manifesto* (Andler 1901), he stressed the French influence (mainly Saint-Simonianism and Pecqueur) on the text, without avoiding thorny issues, for example, the role of the middle class, sustainability of the petty bourgeoisie, relationships between material improvement and alteration of morality and mentality under capitalism. However, in the same way as Sorel, he challenged an approach that focused merely on the economic dimension of social issues and drew attention to juridical and moral dimensions. Furthermore, the non-deterministic nature of the link between infrastructure and superstructure had to be considered. From an analytical standpoint, Andler was critical of Marx's theory of value. He initially sided with Otto Effertz – labour is not the only source of value, land is a second one, which is not produced – but seemed to finally settle for a theory of value determined by social opinion (Andler 1911 [2010]). Most often, Andler (1900 in particular) abandoned the theory of exploitation and returned to a conception in which capitalists are rentiers who do not pay a fair wage to the workers, in which landowners and traders have an advantageous situation compared with consumers. Andler, inspired by the reading of Proudhon, advocated the establishment of a social Republic of cooperators (Andler 1900), which would be capable of tackling that "triple surplus value abuse" (ibid.: 127). As this triple profit is accomplished through sale, and as, contrary to Marx's doctrine, the surplus is created through exchange and ends up impacting the worker-consumer, the collectivist cause can only truly be served, as in Gide's recommendation (Gide 1924), by setting up a complete network of consumption cooperatives connecting towns and the countryside and setting up purchase cooperatives and production workshops. This peaceful revolution can occur without bringing about any moral transformation in mankind, and will simply serve to satisfy the legitimate requirements of "poor quality human materials" (Andler

1900: 500). Nonetheless, Andler then echoed Nietzsche and claimed that the morality of producers needed to be enhanced in order to establish a socialist civilization – that is, solidarity, joy brought about by selfless attitude to work, not turned towards production but towards an ideal which is both ethical and aesthetic.

Marginalist socialism

Two economists who had adopted a theory of value different from the labour theory of value did however attempt to uphold a vision of socialism using marginalist tools (Arena 1995; Herland 1996).

Léon Walras was exposed to socialist ideas from an early age as his father Auguste Walras participated in a Saint-Simonian circle from 1829 to 1831. In an article he wrote for the *Revue socialiste* in 1896, Léon Walras challenged Marx's theory of value and pointed to the difficulty of coordinating agents in a single state system of exchange and production. He was himself temporarily drawn to Saint-Simonianism and was in direct contact with Malon and other socialists; between 1895 and 1909, he published seven articles in the *Revue socialiste* and was seen and supported as a socialist economist by Gustave Rouanet (1894) and Charles Péguy (1897). However, having established a theory of value with no connection to the labour theory of value, his relationship with socialist ideas came under strain owing to a significantly modified scientific backdrop heavily critical of the usual socialist doctrines.

According to Léon Walras, economics covers three domains. The first, that is, pure economics, is the cornerstone: it studies the value of social wealth in conditions of hypothetical and ideal competition, and defines general equilibrium; in it, the determination of value and price stems from natural economic forces. The second domain, applied economics or the theory of economic production of social wealth, defines the rules of efficient conditions of production: organization of production, free competition organized by the state, end of scarcity. The third domain, social economics, is the science of social wealth dealing with the distribution of wealth between individuals and the state. It is based on the principle of justice (theory of property, taxation). According to Walras (1860), when it comes to distribution, the organization of production and justice are not dependent on natural forces but instead on human will. Different from Proudhon, the Walrasian formula of justice is: "equality of conditions within the state, inequality of positions between individuals" (Walras 1860: 172, 179). Land must not be privately owned because it is something that has been given to everyone by nature. Walras thus advocated the gradual purchase of land by the state (nationalization of land) in order to ensure equality of conditions. However, this does not hold true for inheritance when it results from private resources. Inequality of positions is linked to inequality of personal abilities and thus inequality of the service provided in a working environment, with a natural inequality of wages. State intervention through state run organizations, concessions or nationalizations are also justified due to the presence of market failures stemming from collective functions or goods: public services and natural monopolies (railways). Walras accepted the term "semi-collectivist" proposed by Renard (Potier 2012) to argue that the theoretical regime of absolute free competition proves, in applied and social economics, the necessity of fighting laissez-faire. According to Walras, socialism has scientific legitimacy when it raises the social issue, even though it is politically misguided when authoritarian solutions involving the suppression of private property are chosen to address this issue. The hypothesis of "scientific socialism" is therefore legitimate if the trilogy between pure economics, applied economics and social economics is respected.

Adolphe Landry strived to use marginalism to prove the superiority of socialism over capitalism (Soriot 2001), albeit differently from Walras, who attempted to conciliate liberalism and socialism within an economic regime of free exchange and private property – with the exception of land. In his non-conformist thesis of 1901, Landry used an Austrian marginalist theory of value and showed that there is a conflict between profitability and productivity in the capitalist system, itself linked to an opposition between entrepreneur and capitalist. If the growth of future collective wealth is the aim of the economy, capitalization, hence renunciation of something in the present to obtain more in the future is decisive. The existence of a positive rate of interest creates undercapitalization because the demands of the lender are over and beyond the reimbursement and payment of an insurance premium. A fall in interest rates could be possible but lead to major behavioral reactions from private capital owners. The opposition between productivity and profitability, which is taken in part from the works of Effertz (Arena and Hagemann 1997), may produce entrepreneurial default. This may provoke underproduction or under-utilization of labour in order to preserve entrepreneurial profitability or rent. Furthermore, the private system may lead to an uneven distribution of wealth by using means of production which are only able to satisfy the needs of the most fortunate. Personal interests in a system of private property are thus not susceptible to promoting the general interest. In this way, albeit in a very general and weakly argued fashion (Maupertuis and Romani 2000), Landry advocated substituting collective property for individual property. This progressive transformation would make up for the shortcomings of production and lead to a state of equality among workers.

Conclusion

Prior to World War I, a body of rich and diverse non-Marxian socialist ideas was formed in France. This diversity can never really come across when examined through the prism of any single aspect – for example, reform versus revolution, or statism versus cooperativism and federalism, or liberal individualist socialism vs collectivist socialism, and so on. An analysis of the content of these approaches often reveals standpoints that are highly subtle and transcend various preconceived conceptions one might have of these authors (Bouchet et al. 2015). The crossover between socialism and Republic (the "république sociale") and the way in which social issues were addressed reinforce the variety of possible interpretations (Bouglé 1932: conclusion) – role of universal suffrage, Republic in the workshop, welfare reforms, new forms of property, and so on. However, economic analysis remained relatively underdeveloped, apart from a few exceptions. The analysis of the market as an institution of coordination remained weak and its importance was underestimated relative to the debate about free competition between men and activities. Furthermore, the economic arguments, which support the central concepts – first of association and then of cooperation and socialization or even public utilities – often remained relatively superficial. Social and political struggles, violent uprisings (in 1830, 1848 and 1871) and repressions of social conflicts often led to a simplification of the battle of ideas both from the point of view of socialist ideas and of their liberal opponents: a caricatured battle between individualism and communism. However, subsequent to the emergence of Saint-Simonianism, a recurring attempt was made by socialism to establish economic theories, which did not merely boil down to political economy, but touched instead on "social economics" or "sociology", thus encompassing human relationships over and beyond the issues of production and distribution of wealth (Fournière 1904b). This call for a positive science of human relationships also took on very diverse forms, which sometimes hardly proved compatible (Pecqueur, Leroux, Malon, Fournière and Walras, but also the projects of Durkheim 1895–96 [1992], and of Simiand). Paradoxically, it is this ambition that played a role in the analytical limitations of socialist ideas in the field of economics. One of the key characteristics of socialist ideas in France was this desire to depict a broader picture that might sometimes be relatively composite but integrates a powerful moral dimension, which will then be left aside (Grange 2011: 107). This moral dimension took on a religious and Christian form, or was sometimes substituted for Christianity, or in some cases took on a secular form. It played a central role in Saint-Simon's 1825 *Nouveau christianisme*, Buchez's "Androgénie" (see Buchez 1833, pt VI), Pecqueur's 1844 *De la république de Dieu*, Blanqui's 1872 *L'éternité par les astres* or the socialist morality described by Malon or Andler.

World War I marked a new era for socialist ideas. These ideas become less diverse due to the pre-eminence of the Bolshevik reading of Marxism. Revolutionary cooperative socialism tended to become Marxist state socialism (Moss 1976: epilogue) and a non-Marxist socialism of rationalization of the economy carried out through state control (Moch 1927; Philip 1935).

MICHEL BELLET

See also:

Karl Heinrich Marx (I); Non-Marxian socialist ideas in Britain and the United States (II); Non-Marxist socialist ideas in Germany and Austria (II); Pierre-Joseph Proudhon (I); Jean-Charles Léonard Simonde de Sismondi (I); Marie-Esprit-Léon Walras (I).

References and further reading

Andler, C. (1900), 'Le rôle social des coopératives', *Revue de métaphysique et de morale*, **8** (1) 121–34 and **8** (4), 485–501.
Andler, C. (1901), *Introduction historique et commentaire du Manifeste communiste, II*, Paris: Bibliothèque socialiste, Société nouvelle de Librairie.
Andler, C. (1911), *La civilisation socialiste*, reprinted 2010, Paris: Bord de l'Eau.
Arena, R. (1995), 'French socialists and theories of value', in I. Steedman (ed.), *Socialism and Marginalism in Economics. 1879–1930*, London and New York: Routledge, pp. 188–202.
Arena, R. and H. Hagemann (1997), 'Adolphe Landry et Otto Effertz: les leçons d'un débat', paper presented at Colloque international 'Adolphe Landry, économiste, démographe et législateur', Corte-Calvi, 3–6 September.
Beecher, J. (1986), *Charles Fourier, the Visionary and his World*, Berkeley, CA: University of California Press.
Beecher, J. (2001), *Victor Considerant and the Rise and Fall of French Romantic Socialism*, Berkeley, CA: University of California Press.
Bellet, M. (2000), 'B. Malon, un économiste autodidacte du mouvement ouvrier', in C. Latta, M. Vuilleumier and G. Gâcon (eds), *Du Forez à la Revue socialiste. Benoît Malon (1841–1893)*, Saint-Étienne: Publications de l'Université de Saint-Étienne.
Bellet, M. (2016), 'La réception de l'œuvre de Pecqueur par le milieu de *La revue socialiste* (1885–1914) et l'enjeu de l'économie', in C. Coste, L. Frobert and M. Lauricella (eds), *De la République de Constantin Pecqueur (1801–1888)*, Besançon: Presses Universitaires de Franche-Comté.
Blanc, L. (1839), *Organisation du travail*, reprinted 1840, Paris: Bureau de la société fraternelle.
Blanc, L. (1848), *Le socialisme. Droit au travail, réponse à M. Thiers*, 2nd edn, Paris: Michel Levy Frères.

Blanqui, L.A. (1805–1881), *Œuvres 1, Des origines à la Révolution de 1848*, ed. D. Le Nuz, reprinted 1993, Nancy: Presses Universitaires de Nancy.
Blanqui, L.A. (1869), *Contre le positivisme*, in *Œuvres, Des origines à la Révolution de 1848*, vol. 1, ed. D. Le Nuz, reprinted 1993, Nancy: Presses Universitaires de Nancy.
Blanqui, L.A. (1872), *L'éternité par les astres*, Paris: Librairie Germer Baillière.
Blanqui, L.A. (1885), *Critique sociale*, reprinted 2012, Paris: Dittmar.
Bouchet, T., V. Bourdeau, E. Castleton, L. Frobert and F. Jarrige (2015), *Quand les socialistes inventaient l'avenir. Presse, théories et expériences 1825–1860*, Paris: La Découverte.
Bouglé, C. (1932), *Socialismes français. Du 'Socialisme utopique' à la 'Démocratie industrielle'*, Paris, Armand Colin.
Brousse, P. (1883), *La propriété collective et les services publics*, reprinted 1910, Paris, Bureaux du *Prolétaire*.
Buchez, P. (1833), *Introduction à la science de l'histoire ou science du développement de l'humanité*, Paris: Paulin.
Charzat, G. (ed.) (1986), *George Sorel*, Paris: Cahier de l'Herne.
Chevalier, M. (1849), *L'économie politique et le socialisme, discours prononcé au Collège de France*, Paris: Capelle.
Considérant, V. (1839), 'Théorie du droit de propriété et du Droit au travail', *La Phalange*, 1 May, reprinted 1848, Paris: Librairie Phalanstèrienne.
Demier, F. (2005), 'Louis Blanc face à l'économie de marché', in F. Demier (ed.), *Louis Blanc, un socialiste en république*, Paris: Creaphis, pp. 133–50.
Derfler, L. (2009), *Paul Lafargue and the Flowering of French Socialism, 1882–1911*, Cambridge, MA: Harvard University Press.
Durkheim, E. (1895–96), *Le socialisme. Sa définition. Ses débuts. La doctrine saint-simonienne*, first part of a (non-completed) course on the history of socialism, reprinted 1992, Paris: Presses Universitaires de France.
Fourier, C. (1829), *Le nouveau monde industriel et sociétaire, ou invention du procédé d'industrie attrayante et naturelle distribuée en séries passionnées*, Paris: Bossange, Mongie.
Fourier, C. (1836), *La fausse industrie, morcelée, répugnante, mensongère, et l'antidote l'industrie naturelle, combinée, attrayante, véridique, donnant quadruple produit*, reprinted 2013, Paris: Presses du réel.
Fournière, E. (1901), *Essai sur l'individualisme*, Paris: Alcan.
Fournière, E. (1904a), *Les théories socialistes au XIXème siècle de Babeuf à Proudhon*, Paris: Alcan.
Fournière, E. (1904b), 'Les caractères scientifiques de l'économie sociale', *La Revue socialiste*, **39** (231), 257–72.
Frobert, L. (2014a), 'What is a just society? The answer according to the *Socialistes Fraternitaires* Louis Blanc, Constantin Pecqueur, and François Vidal', *History of Political Economy*, **46** (2), 281–306.
Frobert, L. (2014b), 'Christianisme, socialisme et économie politique: Ballanche-Buchez-Ott', in C. Giurintano (ed.), *Pensiero cristiano, questione sociale e liberalismo in Francia nel XIX secolo*, Palermo: Edizioni dell'Università di Palermo, pp. 87–116.
Frobert, L. (2010), 'Politique et économie politique chez Pierre et Jules Leroux', *Revue d'Histoire du XIXème siècle*, **40**, 77–94.
Gervasoni, M. (1997), *Georges Sorel. Una biographia intellettuale. Socialismo e liberalismo nella Francia della Belle époque*, Milan: Unicopli.
Gide, C. (1894), 'Le néo-collectivisme', *Revue d'économie politique*, **8** (5), 423–40.
Gide, C. (1924), *Le programme coopératiste et les écoles socialistes. Trois leçons du cours sur la cooperation au Collège de France*, Paris: Association pour l'enseignement de la coopération.
Grange, J. (2011), 'L'esprit du socialisme, de Saint-Simon à Jaurès', in J. Grange and P. Musso (eds), *Les socialismes*, Paris: Le bord de l'eau, pp. 107–17.
Haubtmann, P. (1982), *Pierre-Joseph Proudhon, sa vie et sa pensée, 1809–1849*, Paris: Beauchesne.
Haubtmann, P. (1988), *Pierre Joseph Proudhon, sa vie et sa pensée 1849–1865*, vol. 1 1849–1855, vol. 2 1855–1865, Paris: Desclée de Brouwer.
Herland, M. (1996), 'Three French socialist economists: Leroux, Proudhon, Walras', *Journal of the History of Economic Thought*, **18** (1), 133–53.
Jaurès, J. (1902), *Etudes socialistes*, 2nd edn, reprinted 2013 in *Œuvres de Jean Jaurès*, vol. 8, *Défense républicaine et participation ministérielle*, Paris: Fayard, pp. 501–648.
Jaurès, J. (1999–), *Œuvres*, eds Société d'études jaurèsiennes, M. Rébérioux and G. Candar, Paris: Fayard (17 planned, 8 published to date).
Knowles, R. (2004), *Political Economy from Below. Economic Thought in Communitarian Anarchism 1840–1914*, New York: Routledge.
Landry, A. (1901), *De l'utilité sociale de la propriété privée*, Paris: Société nouvelle de librairie et d'édition.
Le Bras-Chopard, A. (1986), *De l'égalité dans la différence. Le socialisme de Pierre Leroux*, Paris: Presses de la Fondation Nationale des Sciences Politiques.
Leroux, P. (1834–49), 'De l'individualisme et du socialisme', in P. Leroux (1996), *De l'Egalité (1849), précédé de De l'individualisme et du socialisme (1834)*, Paris and Geneva: Slatkine.
Leroux, P. (1840), *De l'Humanité*, Paris: Perrotin.

Maillard, A. (1999), *La communauté des Égaux. Le communisme néo-babouviste dans la France des années 1840*, Paris: Kimé.

Malon, B. (1890), *Le socialisme intégral*, Paris: Alcan.

Maupertuis, M.-A. and P.-M. Romani (2000), 'Des antagonismes entre rentabilité et rentabilité chez Adolphe Landry. Quand le marginalisme sert la critique du capitalisme', in P. Dockès, L. Frobert, G. Klotz, J.-P. Potier and A. Tiran (eds), *Les traditions économiques françaises. 1848–1939*, Paris: CNRS Éditions.

Moch, J. (1927), *Socialisme et rationalisation*, Brussels: L'Églantine.

Moss, B.H. (1976), *The Origins of the French Labor Movement. The Socialism of Skilled Workers, 1830–1914*, Berkeley, CA: University of California Press.

Pecqueur, C. (1839), *Économie sociale. Des intérêts du commerce, de l'industrie, de l'agriculture sous l'influence des applications de la vapeur*, 2 vols, Paris: Desessart.

Pecqueur, C. (1842), *Théorie nouvelle de l'économie sociale et politique ou Etudes sur l'organisation des sociétés*, Paris: Capelle.

Pecqueur, C. (1844), *De la république de Dieu. Union religieuse pour la pratique immédiate de l'égalité et de la fraternité universelles*, Paris: Charpentier, Ebrard and Masgana.

Péguy, C. (1897), 'Un économiste socialiste: M. Léon Walras', *La Revue socialiste*, **25** (146), 174–86.

Philip, A. (1935), *La crise de l'économie dirigée*, Paris: ed. De Cluny.

Potier, J.-P. (2012), 'Léon Walras, un économiste socialiste libéral', in J.-L. Fournel, J. Guilhaumou, and J.-P. Potier, *Libertés et libéralismes. Formation et circulation des concepts*, Lyon: ENS éditions, pp. 259–82.

Prochasson, C. (2004), *Saint-Simon ou l'anti-Marx. Figures du saint-simonisme français XIXe–XXe siècles*, Paris: Perrin.

Proudhon, P.-J. (1840), *Qu'est ce que la propriété?*, in P.-J. Proudhon (1867), *Œuvres completes*, vol. 1, Paris: Librairie internationale.

Proudhon, P.-J. (1846), *Système des contradictions économiques ou Philosophie de la misère*, 2 vols, Paris: Guillaumin.

Rebérioux, M. (1997), 'Le socialisme français de 1871 à 1914', in J. Droz (ed.), *Histoire générale du socialisme de 1875 à 1918*, vol. 2, Paris: Presses Universitaires de France, Quadrige, pp. 133–236.

Renard, G. (1887–88), 'Le socialisme actuel en France', *La Revue socialiste*, 1887, **6** (33), 225–48, **6** (35), 456–80, **6** (36), 583–600, 1888, **7** (37), 21–39.

Rouanet, G. (1887), 'Le matérialisme de Marx et le socialisme français', *La Revue socialiste,* **5** (29), 395–422, **5** (30), 579–602, **6** (31), 76–86, **6** (33), 278–94.

Rouanet, G. (1894), 'Un économiste socialiste (Léon Walras)', in G. Rouanet, *Critique de combat*, Paris, Dentu, pp. 143–52.

Saint-Simon, C.H. de (2012), *Œuvres complètes*, eds J. Grange, P. Musso, Ph. Régnier and F. Yonnet, 4 vols, Paris: Presses Universitaires de France.

Saint-Simon, H. (1825), *Nouveau christianisme, Dialogues entre un conservateur et un novateur*, Paris: Lachevardière, in J. Grange, P. Musso, Ph. Régnier and F. Yonnet (eds) (2012), *Œuvres completes*, vol. 4, Paris: P.U.F.

Sand, S. (1985), *L'illusion du politique. Georges Sorel et le débat intellectuel 1900*, Paris: La Découverte.

Sorel, G. (1897), 'Sur la théorie marxiste de la valeur', *Journal des économistes*, **30** (2), 222–31.

Sorel, G. (1903), *Introduction à l'économie moderne*, in 2nd edn 1924, revised and expanded, Paris: Marcel Rivière.

Soriot, A. (2001), 'Le "socialisme marginaliste" d'Adolphe Landry', *Économie et Sociétés*, **35** (11–12), 1677–701.

Sutton, R.P. (1994), *Les Icariens. The Utopian Dream in Europe and America*, Urbana, IL: University of Illinois Press.

Vigier, P. (1986), *Blanqui et les blanquistes*, Société d'Histoire de la Révolution de 1848 et des révolutions au XIXème siècle, Paris: SEDES.

Vincent, K.S. (1985), *Pierre-Joseph Proudhon and the Rise of French Republican Socialism*, Oxford: Oxford University Press.

Walras, L. (1860), 'L'économie politique et la justice. Examen critique et réfutation des doctrines économiques de M. P.-J. Proudhon', in *Oeuvres d'Auguste et Léon Walras*, vol. 5, *L'économie politique et la justice*, Paris: Economica, pp. 87–340.

Non-Marxian socialist ideas in Britain and the United States

The non-Marxian socialist political economies of Britain and the United States represent rich and multifaceted traditions of economic thinking. These had their origins in what it is now unfashionable to term the industrial revolution but which was, by any standards, a period of profound economic and social change. In Britain the first three decades of the nineteenth century saw the proportion of the population involved in manufacture, mining and industry rise from 29.7 per cent to 40.8 per cent and from 1.3 million to 3 million. The socialist political economies which emerged in Britain can be seen as a response to these developments that in consequence saw a working population increasingly exposed to the vagaries of market forces. For these were political economies which sought to elucidate the causes of impoverishment, as labour was increasingly commodified, and of economic crises, as it was rendered periodically redundant and which sought to establish too the lineaments of a different economic and social order from which impoverishment and instability had been removed and where the principles of liberty, equality and fellowship prevailed.

Early-Nineteenth-Century Socialist Political Economy in Britain and the United States

In Britain the most potent strand of socialist political economy was that of communitarianism, to which the key contributors were Robert Owen (1771–1858), William Thompson (1775–1833), John Francis Bray (1809–97) and John Gray (1799–1883); writers whose works furnished both a critique of contemporary capitalism, while articulating the principles and practice of those co-operative communities which, by their example, would effect the transition to a new moral world.

The magnum opus of communitarian political economy was Thompson's *An Inquiry into the Principles of the Distribution of Wealth* (1824). Similar to other communitarian socialists, a rendition of the labour theory of value formed the theoretical foundation of his critique of capitalism; something which has led to his, and others, misleading categorisation as Ricardian socialists. So, for Thompson, as for Gray and Owen, "labour was the sole parent of wealth" and commodities should therefore exchange according to the labour they embodied (Thompson 1824: 7). Further, it was through the violation of this "natural", labour-embodied law of value that economic injustice and material impoverishment entered the world; a violation perpetrated by capitalists, landowners and the state. Thus, for William Thompson, in *Labor Rewarded* (1827: 12), it was:

> by unjust exchanges . . . supported by force or fraud, whether by direct operation of law, or by indirect operation of unwise social arrangements . . . [that] the products of the labor of the industrious classes [are] taken out of their hands . . . It is not the differences of production of different laborers, but the complicated system of exchanges of those productions when made, that gives rise to . . . frightful inequality of wealth.

Also "it [was] capital . . . dextrous in the mere tricks and over-reaching of exchanges, in the turns of the market, that now wallow[ed] . . . in enormously unequal shares of the national product" (Thompson 1827: 12).

It was this understanding of labour exploitation in terms of unequal exchanges that led writers such as Owen to advocate the formation of so-called "labour exchanges", where goods would be exchanged through the medium of labour notes denominated in hours of labour time. Indeed, such exchanges were established in the early 1830s in Birmingham and London, though these were seen as essentially transient entities that might mitigate but could not eliminate the iniquities of contemporary economic arrangements.

As to Thompson, he conceded theoretically that a system of free labour and voluntary exchanges in a truly competitive economic system might go some considerable way to eliminate the exploitation and impoverishment of the working class. However, it would not eliminate the social, psychological and ethical diseconomies that inhered to such individualistic, market-organised economic activity; diseconomies which he was to discuss at greater length in *Labor Rewarded*, 1827, than in his *Inquiry*.

What was needed, therefore, was the creation of new moral worlds in microcosm; co-operative communities which gave their members access to the means of producing and from which the evil of unequal exchanges was banished; with goods being distributed on the basis of need, social relations resting on an equitable basis and with their rationale being the realisation of human potentialities rather than the accumulation and acquisition of wealth. Such "communities of mutual co-operation", as Thompson termed them, would also end the social or class antagonism that was an inevitable feature of a system where those with economic power derived from ownership exploited it, through unequal exchanges, to the detriment of a working class kept at a bare subsistence level of existence.

However, this aspiration to create socialism in microcosm, the concomitant emphasis on self-sufficiency and its autarchic implications meant that, as conceived and as realised, these communities were essentially agrarian. So, for Owen, they would: "hav[e] their basis in agriculture", "with manufactures as an appendage" and this meant that they, and the communitarian political economy that provided their theoretical underpinning, were singularly ill-equipped to address the challenges of an increasingly industrialised economic world (Owen 1821 [1927]: 259).

Nevertheless, the ideals of these communitarian socialists were put into practice in both Britain and the United States: in Britain most notably in the community of Queenwood, near Tytherley in Hampshire, 1839–45 and in the United States in the Owenite community of New Harmony on the banks of the Wabash in Indiana, 1825–27. Such communities, as were most of their brethren, were short-lived but the political economy of communitarian socialism nonetheless enjoyed considerable support amongst the working class, particularly in the period 1820–50.

Gray's major contribution to communitarian political economy was his *Lecture on Human Happiness*, 1825 and a subsequent work, *The Social System, a Treatise on the Principle of Exchange*, 1831, was to replicate the *Lecture*'s critique of competitive capitalism as a system that skewed the distribution of wealth in favour of the unproductive as a consequence of unequal exchanges. However, there was in the latter volume a significant shift in emphasis towards explicating the macroeconomic crises that characterised capitalism in terms of the role played by money. So, for Gray, a deficient demand resulting from a medium of exchange which failed to increase *pari passu* with output, together with a system of unequal exchanges that skewed the distribution of wealth in favour of those with a relatively lower propensity to consume, made for glutted markets and thence a powerful check upon production.

To rectify this state of affairs, Gray proposed radical systemic change which took the form of the purposive planning and direction of economic activity as the foundation of a new "social" system of exchange. Here Gray contrasted the contemporary micro and macro economies. Thus "whilst contrivance, arrangement, plan are indispensably necessary to every part, the aggregate of the parts is left to work as best it can, ungoverned" (Gray 1831: 331). The prerequisite of such planning was to be the possession of the economic power to do so, which in turn required the collective ownership of the means of production. Gray's expectation was that such a transition from private to public ownership would occur voluntarily, with owners of capital and land recognising the macroeconomic imperatives for acceding to this. However there was to be a financial inducement with owners "receiv[ing] a fixed annual remuneration for the use [of their property], proportionate to its value, in lieu of retaining in their hands, the chance of gain or loss by its cultivation or employment". This would help realise the ultimate aim of creating "a national capital, consisting of land, mines, manufactories, warehouses, shipping, machinery, implements, and, in short, of every thing required in the production, exchange and distribution of commodities" (Gray 1831: 32, 108–9).

As to those involved in the business of economic planning, Gray's view was that the key planning authority – the National Chamber of Commerce – should be drawn from those who already wielded economic power and had experience of the organisation and direction of economic activity. Economic leadership in Gray's planned economy was therefore decidedly meritocratic and technocratic in character.

The social ownership of the means of production as the basis for the more effective and equitable organisation of economic activity was also at the heart of the political economy of another early nineteenth-century socialist, John Francis Bray (1809–97), a writer whose major work, *Labour Wrongs and Labour's Remedy*, was published in Leeds in 1839 but who also had strong links with socialism in the United States; in particular, in the latter part of the century, through the neo-syndicalist Knights of Labor.

With Bray we have a writer who saw the distribution of economic power as the key determinant of the material condition of the labouring classes. The skewed distribution of this made for unequal exchanges and it was these that made for labour's wrongs and labour's impoverishment. So,

> the wealth which the capitalist appears to give in exchange for the workman's labour was generated neither by the labour nor the riches of the capitalist, but it was originally obtained by the labour of the workman . . . the whole transaction therefore between the labourer and the capitalist, is a palpable deception, a mere farce. (Bray 1839: 49)

Consistent with this he believed that the reforms proposed by political radicalism would do little or nothing to improve the position of the masses. The fact was that the major exactions from labour derived from the exploitative exercise of economic not political power and could only be remedied by measures which fundamentally altered the distribution of the former. So "if we would end our [labour's] wrongs . . . THE PRESENT ARRANGEMENTS OF SOCIETY MUST BE TOTALLY SUBVERTED", and it was therefore "necessary . . . to the success of any social change that the real capital of the country should be possessed by society at large" (Bray 1839: 17).

However if ownership of the means of production was to be vested in society as a whole, Bray clearly envisaged a kind of decentralised socialism where considerable decision-making power would reside with the workforces of socially owned, joint stock enterprises; though with an overarching planning structure that would involve "general and local boards which would regulate production and distribution in gross" (Bray 1839: 160). As with Gray, therefore, the idea of planning, the conscious social control of economic activity, was central to Bray's conception of the organisation of a socialist economy.

In significant measure, socialist political economy in early and mid-century America mirrored that in Britain; not least because of the ideological influence of Owen and the Owenites and their practical activity in the formation of communities, such as New Harmony. In the period 1820–40 it has been estimated that more than 100 communities were established and the United States had its own communitarian theoreticians, in part influenced by Owenism but also by the thinking of the French socialist, Charles Fourier (1772–1837).

As to the former, specific mention should be made of Cornelius Blatchly (1773–1831), founder of the Owenite New York Society for Promoting Commonwealths and author of *An Essay on Common Wealths*, 1822. This Society was also responsible for publishing no fewer than three American editions of John Gray's *Lecture on Human Happiness* and an edition of Thompson's *Inquiry*. Further, with Langdon Byllesby (1789–1871), we have another American socialist influenced by Owenism but who, in works such as *Observations on the Sources and Effects of Unequal Wealth* (1826), used such ideas to underpin the notion of producer co-operatives and articulate a political economy in which some have seen the roots of American syndicalism.

As to Fourierism, a key figure in its dissemination was Albert Brisbane (1809–90), whose *Social Destiny of Man* (1840) advocated the restructuring of American society on the basis of essentially agricultural phalanxes. Horace Greeley (1811–72), too, was to play an important role in both the dissemination of Fourierist ideas and the formation of Brook Farm, 1841–46, a Fourierist-inspired community which was established on a 200-acre site at West Roxbury, a suburb of Boston. As with the Owenites, the American Fourierists believed that it was necessary to withdraw from a competitive, socially fragmented and individually acquisitive society and create one informed by communitarian values and a social ethos.

Fin de Siècle Socialism in Britain and the United States

The last quarter of the nineteenth century saw an efflorescence of socialism and socialist literature in both Britain and the United States. In Britain it may be seen, in part, as a response to the economic difficulties experienced in that period, but it was also a product of an ideological ferment to which the ideas of Karl Marx, Henry George's (1839–97) *Progress and Poverty*, 1879, the philosophical idealism of writers such as T.H. Green (1836–82) and F.H. Bradley (1846–1924), the positivism of Frederic Harrison (1831–1923) and E.S. Beesly (1831–1915), the social investigations of Seebohm Rowntree (1871–1954) and Charles Booth (1840–1916), and the social criticism of writers such as Andrew Mearns (1837–1925) and G.R. Sims (1847–1922) all contributed.

Statist socialism in Britain and the United States

In this period capitalism came under sustained critical fire from a number of quarters. For some, such as the Fabian socialists, the focus was on the anarchic nature of a system characterised by wasted resources, most obviously the unemployment of labour; by its instability, as evidenced by the periodic economic crises which afflicted it; and by the growth of monopoly power, which disadvantaged both labour and the consumer. Fabians, such as Sidney and Beatrice Webb (1859–1947 and 1858–1943, respectively), therefore stressed the need for rational economic planning of what had previously been left to chance.

As to the growth of monopoly power, it was the particular Fabian view that any system which involved private ownership of the means of production necessarily entailed its exercise. This was so because the supply of all productive factors was finite and, generalising from the principles of Ricardian land rent theory to capital and labour, this made for an economic surplus on all intra-marginal factors accruing to their owners; a surplus denominated a "rent of ability" in the case of highly skilled and educated labour and "interest" in the case of capital. As Sidney Webb put it in a Fabian Tract, *English Progress towards Social Democracy* (1892), "the additional product determined by the relative differences in the productive efficiency of the different sites, soils, capital and forms of skill above the margin of cultivation has gone to those exercising control over those valuable but scarce productive factors" (Webb 1892: 5).

Such a view of things led on logically to a critique of the contemporary allocation of resources, with a skewed distribution of income and wealth, resulting from the exercise of monopoly power, producing for Webb "a flagrantly 'wrong production' of commodities": "the unequal value of money to our paupers and our millionaires depriving the test of "effective demand" of all value as an index to social requirements" (Webb 1892: 11).

By way of remedy, Fabians such as William Clarke (1852–1901) supported the idea of a radically redistributive fiscal policy "of a socialistic character, involving collective checking of individual greed and the paring of slices off the profits of capital in the interests of the working community" (Clarke 1889: 110). However, it was recognised that this, of itself, would be insufficient. For, as Sidney Webb put it, "the purpose of socialism is not the division of wealth among the poor but the assertion of the right of the community to the complete control over the means of production" (Webb 1892: 9). Or as George Bernard Shaw (1856–1950) phrased it, "socialism, as understood by the Fabian Society, means the organisation and conduct of the necessary industries of the country and the appropriation of all forms of economic rent of land and capital by the nation as a whole through the most suitable public authorities" (Shaw 1896: 5). Socialism required, therefore, the public ownership of a substantial part of the means of production, distribution and exchange. Only then would the collective planning and organisation of economic activity eliminate the exploitation, economic anarchy and waste which characterised contemporary capitalism.

Here, with the growth of industrial monopolies, history seemed to be moving in a Fabian direction, laying the basis for what Annie Besant (1847–1933) anticipated would be "the taking over of the great centralized industries, centralized for us by the capitalists, who thus unconsciously pave the way for their own supersession" (Besant 1889 [1962]: 190). (This is a very Marxist idea – it is also a very Fabian idea as they too saw the march of economic history in these "progressive" terms.) In effect the choice now lay between public and private monopoly and the Fabians looked to the former, with the gradual emergence of state and municipally owned and controlled enterprises, after the appropriate compensation of their existing owners.

Statist socialism also flourished in the United States in this period, in part as a consequence of the influx of European immigrants who brought with them the doctrines of Marx and other European socialists. There were, though, indigenous writers whose thinking proved influential, not just in the United States but also in Britain, most notably Laurence Gronlund (1846–99) and Edward Bellamy (1850–98).

Bellamy's (1888 [1982]) utopian fantasy, *Looking Backward, 2000–1887*, was set in a twenty-first century Boston whose essentially socialist organisation of society contrasted with that prevailing in contemporary America. The work was one of the most widely read and influential in the history of American socialism, in large measure because it spoke to the challenges and discontents of the turbulent and dynamic experience of a rapidly industrialising *fin-de-siècle* United States.

For Bellamy that turbulence was manifested in the abandonment of production to the "haphazard efforts of individuals" who had "no means of knowing what demand there was for any class of products or what was the rate of supply" (Bellamy 1888 [1982]: 223). And in the absence of any "common control of the different industries and the consequent impossibility of their orderly and co-ordinated development", disastrous micro and macroeconomic consequences were inevitable. Specifically, there was "waste by mistaken undertakings . . . waste from competition and mutual hostility . . . waste by periodical gluts and crises, with . . . consequent interruptions of industry . . . waste from idle capital and labour at all times". As "the industries of the world multiplied and became complex and the volume of capital was increased . . . business cataclysms [also] became more frequent" (Bellamy 1888 [1982]: 169, 171).

For Gronlund too, in *The Co-operative Commonwealth* (1886), "production by . . . [capitalist] manufacturers . . . must necessarily be absolutely planless. It depends altogether on chance . . . All their production, all their commerce is thus in the nature of gambling. A thoughtful observer will see that this planless production must end in overproduction". The economic crises which characterised contemporary capitalism were therefore "the result of planless work" and "the absolute Social Anarchy" which pervaded "our whole economic sphere", with idle capital and labour an inevitable consequence (Gronlund 1886: 33, 34, 41).

The solution to all this was public ownership as the basis for a scientific ordering of economic life. Prices were to be objectively determined by reference to the expenditure of labour time, and the allocation of resources would have reference to accurate statistical information on the extent of communal needs and thence the particular social utilities of different goods and services. At a macroeconomic level, crises would be eliminated by a calculated matching of aggregate demand with the aggregate capacity to supply and this would spell an end to the waste of unemployment and underutilised productive capacity. In short, the anarchy and planlessness of competitive market capitalism was to give way to the rational, social control and administration of economic activity.

In Britain writers such as Robert Blatchford (1851–1943) and Marxists such as H.M. Hyndman (1842–1921) saw things in a similar light and advanced comparable solutions. As to Blatchford, if Bellamy's *Looking Backward* was the most popular work of socialist literature published in the late nineteenth and early twentieth-century United States, then the former's *Merrie England* (1893) had a comparable standing in Britain. Blatchford professed himself "to have been a communist of the William Morris type" (Blatchford 1899: 10), but in truth his conception of the infrastructure of socialism, en route to the realisation of a Morrisian vision, was very different.

As with Gronlund and Bellamy, Blatchford believed that at root many of the failings of contemporary capitalism derived from its unplanned and anarchic nature, with private ownership of the means of production entailing individualistic and unco-ordinated economic decision-making. As he wrote in *Britain for the British* (1902), "today the industries of England are not ordered nor arranged but are left to be disordered by chance and by the ups and downs of trade" (Blatchford 1902: 87). Like Gronlund and Bellamy too, Blatchford took a statist view of the initial economic organisation of a future socialist commonwealth. Thus "the land and all the machines, tools and buildings used in making needful things, together with all the canals, rivers, roads, railways, ships and trains used in moving . . . needful things shall be the property of the whole people" (Blatchford 1898: 13). On this basis and under what he termed "ideal socialism", "the industry of the country would be organised and managed by the state" and "goods of all kinds would be produced and distributed for use, and not for sale, in such quantities as were needed" (Blatchford 1894: 103).

Decentralised socialism and anarcho-communism in Britain and the United States
However, if Gronlund, Bellamy and Blatchford advanced what might be termed a statist socialism, a very different vision was articulated by William Morris (1834–96), whose political economy was influenced by Marx but, more profoundly, by John Ruskin (1819–1900). Morris did take on board some of the central components of Marx's critique of capitalism – the exploitation and increasing impoverishment of labour, the growing reserve army of the unemployed, the tendency to periodic crises of increasing severity and the growing intensity of class conflict – but the whole was informed by an aesthetic and moral critique which was distinctively Ruskinian. In particular for Morris, as for Ruskin, capitalism not only exploited labour, it also corrupted its nature. For the creative capacities of humanity were subordinated under capitalism to the desire for pecuniary gain. Instead, therefore, of "the intelligent production of beautiful things", labour was condemned to produce "vulgarities and shabby gentilities" that "pandered to degraded follies". And with this, "joyful labour" degenerated into "useless toil" (Morris 1883 [1966]: 383; 1895 [1910–15]: 21).

However, in contrast to the statist socialists, Morris looked ultimately to a decentralised socialism where power resided with communes and where that of the state withered away. His vision was therefore an essentially anarcho-communist one; a vision that was to receive its fullest expression in *News from Nowhere* (1890 [1920]). In that work he painted the picture of an economy characterised by small-scale, relatively unmechanised units of production, where the values of craftsmanship were prioritised, where "useless toil" had been transformed into "useful labour" and where the creative impulse was no longer constrained and corrupted by the pressures of commercialism; a society in which labour would be transmuted into artistry and characterised by fellowship and social equality.

A communitarian anarcho-communism was also to have its counterpart in the United States; though here the inspiration was largely drawn from Marx and was to assume, on occasion, a violent revolutionary form. While the spirit of communitarianism that had characterised the mid-century period was sustained and socialist communities and colonies continued to be established into the early twentieth century, the late nineteenth and early twentieth centuries in both Britain and the United States saw the emergence of a more militant, non-statist, decentralised and often syndicalist socialist political economy, with movements pressing for workers' ownership and control of productive capacity. In the United States syndicalism was embraced by the Socialist Labor Party under the leadership of Daniel de Leon (1852–1914), who advocated the overthrow of capitalism by militant industrial action and its supercession by a trade-union based organisation of economic activity, to which end the syndicalist International Workers of the World was established in 1905.

In Britain, prior to 1914, figures such as Tom Mann (1856–1941) and James Connolly (1868–1916) played an important part in spreading syndicalist ideas to Britain. The years prior to the outbreak of the Great War saw the growth of rank and file movements, one of which, the South Wales Miners' Federation Unofficial Reform Committee, produced one of the classic texts of British syndicalism, *The Miners' Next Step* (1912).

Further, if out of step with an increasingly complex, urban, industrial economy, the Morrisian political economy noted above also proved influential on other British thinkers who took a decentralist view of the economic organisation of socialism. Most obviously, Morris's emphasis on creative labour, fellowship and the decentralisation of power left its imprint on the political economy of guild socialist writers such as S.G. Hobson (1870–1940) and G.D.H. Cole (1889–1959). For them, what the Fabians offered smacked more of "state commercialism" than socialism; prioritising the needs of the consumer for cheapness and efficiency over the interests of the producer. For Hobson, *per contra*, the primary objective should be the destruction of the wages system which involved the alienation of the worker's creative powers and laid the basis not just for exploitation but for mindless and repetitive labour.

As Hobson saw it, the way forward was through the creation of guilds of producers which he believed would emerge out of an increasingly puissant trade union movement. Once established these would be responsible for all aspects of production in a particular industry and they "would [also] assume, instead of the State, complete responsibility for the material well-being of their members" (Hobson 1914: 135). These entities would therefore enjoy considerable autonomy. That said, ownership of the means of production was to be vested in the state which would have a role, alongside the guilds, in co-managing the economy. So while, for Hobson, guild socialism "rejects State bureaucracy . . . it [also] rejects Syndicalism because it accepts co-management with the State . . . subject to the principle of industrial democracy" (Hobson 1914: 132).

Cole's critique of both contemporary capitalism and the Fabian socialist alternative was very similar to that of Hobson and, similar to the latter, his emphasis was on economic arrangements that allowed the liberation, not the attenuation, of the creative impulse. Again, in works such as *Self-Government in Industry* (1917) and *Guild Socialism Restated* (1920), his vision was predicated on the decentralisation of economic decision-making to worker-controlled units of production; though with the state still having a substantial role to play in terms of representing and defending the interests of consumers. For while the national guilds, and a National Guilds' Congress, would assume responsibility for "the organisation of supply and demand . . . [and] the control of prices", this function would be performed "in consultation with the consumer", represented either by the state or specific institutions representative of consumer interests (Cole 1917: 272).

Socialist Political Economy in Inter-War Britain and the United States

However, in the post-Great War period decentralised socialism, in its many and varied forms, lost traction. In part this was a consequence of the profound macroeconomic difficulties which characterised the period and that put on the back foot those organisations that were frequently seen as the harbingers of workers' control. In part it was also because communitarianism was regarded as providing a narrowly defensive and microcosmic response to capitalism's ills and in part it was because the experience of the Great War suggested that the state was the effective vehicle for the delivery of fundamental economic and social change.

The inter-war period was one during which, after the economic turbulence of the immediate post-war period and a measure of recovery in the 1920s, Britain, as other industrialised economies, experienced a decade of mass unemployment which called into question the sustainability of the capitalist system. In such circumstances it might have been expected that socialist thinking would flourish and in many respects it did. That said, the 1930s were characterised more by the efflorescence of Marxist rather than non-Marxist political economy, with the work of writers such as John Strachey (1901–63) having a particular purchase on the minds of the Left through works such as *The Nature of Capitalist Crisis* (1935) and *The Theory and Practice of Socialism* (1936).

On the social democratic Left, Fabian political economy continued to exert a profound influence through writers such as the Webbs, G.D.H. Cole and Barbara Wootton (1897–1988). However, in this period too there emerged a new generation of professionally trained socialist economists, often profoundly influenced by the work of Keynes and, in particular, his *General Theory of Employment, Interest and Money* (1936). Among their number were Hugh Gaitskell (1906–1963), E.F.M. Durbin (1906–1948) and James Meade (1907–1995); writers who addressed the fundamental question as to whether it was possible to stabilise capitalism in a manner that laid the basis for socialist progress.

Not all, of course, derived their inspiration from Keynes, and the influence of the liberal socialist J.A. Hobson (1858–1940) should not be discounted. However, it is also interesting to note that in his analysis of the 1930s' depression Evan Durbin drew on the work of Hayek, in particular, his *Prices and Production* (1930). This led him, initially, to the conclusion that expansionary policies if tentatively pursued would do "nothing or very little to improve things", while if they were pursued more vigorously they would, by generating inflationary pressures, "merely repeat the trade cycle and lead to a new crisis" (Durbin 1933: 163). However, under the influence of James Meade, Durbin jettisoned this negativity, suggesting in *The Problem of Credit Policy* (1935) that a combination of monetary and fiscal policy would "banish unemployment forever" and "double the standard of living in thirty years" (Durbin 1935: 239–40). This would though require closer public control over the conduct of monetary policy through "the initiation of the fundamental institutions of a Planned Money". While that need not necessarily entail the nationalisation of the banking system, it would necessitate "a monetary system planned under unified control" (Durbin 1935: 219). As to the specifics of the immediate strategy, Durbin advocated cheap money pursued in conjunction with open market operations to increase the liquidity of the banking system, government guarantees to underpin private investment, public works schemes and direct government investment.

For James Meade the primary influence was that of Keynes and the younger generation of Cambridge economists. Indeed Meade took an important part in the discussion of Keynes's work that preceded and followed the publication of the *General Theory*. His *Introduction to Economic Analysis* (1936 [1937]) is certainly redolent of Keynesian optimism, stating at the outset that "we can start by dismissing the theory that there is some fundamental flaw in the existing monetary and pricing system . . . the problem of unemployment is capable of solution without any revolutionary changes in our economic system" (Meade 1936 [1937]: 2). Thus pump-priming public expenditure, together with a reduction of interest rates by the banking system, would be sufficient to stimulate private investment and move the economy back towards full employment.

Yet if public investment and a cheap money policy could do the trick, what would take effect even more rapidly was an increase of purchasing power in the hands of the populace. Here Meade suggested a contra-cyclical use of the existing unemployment insurance scheme and personal taxation. As to the latter, "consumer credits" would be built up in times of prosperity, when tax revenue exceeded expenditure, to be repaid in less prosperous times to boost consumer demand.

The ideas of both the Keynesian socialists and those of the Fabians raised the issue of how a socialist economy would be organised, which in turn posed the question of whether rational economic planning and decision-making were possible where the market played a negligible or heavily circumscribed role. In relation to this, Ludwig von Mises (1881–1973) had raised the whole problem of "Economic calculation in a socialist commonwealth" in an article published in 1920, arguing that in the absence of the information gathering and dissemination mechanism of the market such calculation could not proceed on a rational basis: a view that was to provoke a response in Britain from writers such as H.D. Dickinson (1899–1969), Durbin and Meade and, in the United States, from F.M. Taylor (1855–1932). It is beyond the scope of this chapter to trace their contributions to the socialist calculation debate but it was the case that while much of what they wrote would have been unintelligible outside the ranks of professional economists, and had little relevance to the practical task of building a socialist economy, their preparedness and their capacity to meet the challenge emanating from Mises, Hayek, Lionel Robbins (1898–1984) and others helped to instil a belief that socialist planning could deliver on its promises for a more ordered and equitable economy than that which characterised capitalism.

In the United States too dramatic economic collapse in the aftermath of the Wall Street Crash, with roughly 12–15 million unemployed by 1932, called into question for many both the rationality and viability of capitalism. If this was grist to the mill of American Marxists, it also precipitated a crisis of confidence amongst professional economists as to capitalism's vitality, with many embracing ideas which, if not avowedly socialist, certainly put them on the centre-left of the political spectrum and led them to adhere to positions not manifestly different from those of British social democracy.

Moreover, it made some economists, such as Lauchlin Currie (1902–1993), Leon Henderson (1895–1986) and Harry White (1892–1948), receptive not just to Keynesian ideas on macroeconomic management and the liberal socialist underconsumptism of J.A. Hobson (1858–1940), but also to indigenous heterodox traditions of institutionalism and progressivism and led them to question the relationship between the state and industry and the nature and future dynamism of industrial corporations. In relation to the latter,

Adolf Berle's (1895–1971) and Gardner Means's (1896–1988) *The Modern Corporation and Private Property* (Berle and Means 1932) was also important in articulating the need for greater social control of the modern, monopoly power-wielding private corporation, while the work of Rexford Tugwell (1891–1979), pointed to a greater economic role for the state and looked to the more scientific management of economic activity.

Further, the embrace by writers such as Alvin Hansen (1887–1975) of the notion of "stagnationism", in part deriving from Keynes's pessimism about the long-term dynamism of capitalism and in part from an indigenous tradition linked to the notion of an exhausted land frontier, led in a similar direction, with those developing this idea looking to the federal government to assume a more active role within the economy in relation to the activities of large corporations and public utilities and to intervene in new areas of economic activity. In effect, as Donald Winch (b. 1935) has put it, the radical reformism of stagnationist political economy meant that "for many it was the American equivalent of the non-Marxist left-wing movements in Europe in the thirties" (Winch 1972: 25).

All this, of course, contributed to the *pot pourri* of ideas underpinning Roosevelt's New Deal; itself an attempt to define and redefine the relationship between the state, society and the economy in a period of profound economic difficulty.

Socialist Political Economy in Britain and the United States since 1945

The post-Second World War period posed new and qualitatively different challenges for socialism and socialist theorists. In Britain, with the Labour Party winning a decisive victory in the 1945 General Election, there was the particular and pressing one of translating social democratic ideas into practice. Specifically, this concentrated the minds of policymakers on just what was meant by socialist planning and whether this involved simply macroeconomic management or if it was something that necessitated a level of state intervention that significantly circumscribed, if it did not altogether supplant, the market. Either way there was at least a consensus on the need to take the "commanding heights" of the economy into public ownership, even if it was not always agreed exactly what the commanding heights encompassed.

At an ideological level, though, there was the profound challenge for the Left posed by the unparalleled prosperity that characterised the 1950s and 1960s. This was the golden age of post-war capitalism; a period of affluence that transformed the material circumstances of a substantial proportion of the populations of both Britain and the United States. The challenge for socialist theorists was to reconcile this rejuvenated capitalism that was delivering a generalised material prosperity with the view that such an economic system was inherently flawed and lacked the capacity to effect a significant material transformation in people's lives.

Tony Crosland's (1918–1977) *The Future of Socialism* (1956) represented one such response, challenging Fabian and other views that the road to a socialist society lay through a further extension of public ownership and state control of economic activity. Moreover, he celebrated the affluence which characterised the post-war period, seeing it as opening up possibilities for individual self-fulfilment and egalitarian social expenditure which socialists should embrace. In effect Crosland saw a Keynesian social democratic capitalism as having gone some considerable way to eliminating the impoverishment and instability that had previously characterised the capitalist system, thereby allowing socialists to concentrate on other issues; issues that might involve increased social expenditure but also those of a less material nature. Thus he envisaged "sociological and cultural issues" coming "increasingly to the forefront as traditional economic problems recede" (Crosland 1956: 128–9).

Crosland challenged too the efficacy of a redistributive fiscal strategy as a means of promoting social equality, believing that "the classless society cannot be reached simply by more redistribution of wealth" (Crosland 1956: 124). Rather what was necessary was the elimination of what he saw as the profoundly divisive social effects of occupational prestige, accent, vocabulary and differing "lifestyles". These would remain largely untouched by redistribution but would respond to expedients such as the introduction of the greater egalitarianism of American management practices, the widening of educational opportunity and the greater uniformity of lifestyles likely to emerge in the wake of the rising tide of contemporary affluence.

However others, such as Michael Harrington (1928–1989) in the United States (*The Other America, Poverty in the United States*, 1963) and Peter Townsend (1928–2009) in Britain (*Poverty in the United Kingdom, A Survey of Household Resources and Living Standards*, 1979) took a different view of things. Affluence there might be but poverty was still the experience of a significant proportion of the British and American populations; consumer durable consumption might rise inexorably but public squalor frequently proceeded *pari passu* with such private affluence.

Moreover, in the case of Britain, while there might be economic progress, the nation was nonetheless experiencing the golden age of capitalism as one of relative decline, with an economy, for many writers, characterised by manifest waste and inefficiency. Further, although Britain might now possess a mixed economy, the power of the capitalist class remained unbroken.

As to the undiminished power of the capitalist class, John Strachey's *Contemporary capitalism* (1956) argued the case for a further extension of public ownership. The advances that had been made since the war were the product of a democratic polity establishing its authority over an anarchic and self-interested concentration of private economic power. To ensure that these gains were retained; to ensure that macroeconomic stability and the momentum of socialist progress was sustained, the economic powerbase of democracy had to be extended. For Strachey, given the power still wielded by the capitalist class, there had arisen a "state of antagonistic balance" between "democracy and last stage capitalism"; one that must be resolved in favour of the former by a continued transference of economic power to the state (Strachey 1953: 17).

Richard Crossman (1907–74), in *Labour and the Affluent Society* (1960), similarly argued the need for an extension of public ownership as the basis for more effective economic planning and questioned the proportion of the national product that was going to private consumption rather than public investment. For Crossman it was the contemporary predilection for consumerist indulgence that had skewed resources away from the investment necessary to sustain high rates of economic growth and it was this that explained Britain's relative economic underperformance. He therefore looked to "a socialist programme" that would "involve transferring gigantic powers, which are now dispersed amongst the oligopolists, to the central government and the planning authorities" and, more generally, considered that socialists should refuse in any way to come to terms with the affluent society (Crossman 1960: 23).

Such socialist fundamentalism was to acquire greater currency and purchase within the Labour Party in the period of economic turbulence that characterised the 1970s and early 1980s. In policy terms this took the form of the so-called "Alternative Economic Strategy" (AES), the central aim of which was to effect a "fundamental shift in the balance of power in favour of working people and their families" (Labour Party 1982: 4); something that in turn would require, as Stuart Holland (b. 1940) saw it, "a substantial addition [to the public sector] of companies from the present private sector ... spread across leading firms throughout the different sectors of industry ... For the range of tasks suggested some twenty-five of our largest manufacturers would be required" (Holland 1979: 159).

For adherents to the AES, Keynesian social democracy had failed to deliver what its proponents had anticipated. Macroeconomic management, together with enhanced social expenditure in the context of a mixed economy, had run into the sands. This was so because the power of governments to pursue saw a strategy was diminishing in line with the increasing power of transnational capital. As Stuart Holland, one of those whose work gave theoretical underpinning to the AES, put it:

> [R]ecent acceleration in the trend to monopoly and multi-national capital has eroded Keynesian economic policies and undermined the sovereignty of the capitalist nation state. The trend has resulted in a new mesoeconomic power between conventional macroeconomics and microeconomics. In compromising Keynesian economic management, the new economic power has compromised the gradualism of Keynesian social democracy. (Holland 1975: 9)

In terms of the values it inculcated, the behaviour it encouraged and the aspirations it engendered, critical concern with the emergence of an affluent society was even more strongly articulated in the United States. J.K. Galbraith's (1908–2006) coruscating eponymous critique highlighted the dangers of a society that privileged private over public consumption; private affluence and public squalor being seen as a necessary consequence of a marketing industry expanding exponentially in terms of expenditure and sophistication in the decades that followed the end of the Second World War. So, courtesy of that industry, "we view the production of some of the most frivolous goods with pride" and "we regard the production of some of the most significant and civilizing services with regret" (Galbraith 1958 [1962]: 115–16). The result of this hedonistic materialism was, in particular, underfunded public services; with all that that meant in terms of social fragmentation and material deprivation for a significant minority of the population.

Galbraith's critique of affluence also resonated with that emanating from the New Left in Britain and the United States in this period. Though, to a greater extent or lesser extent, this also had as a common core the work of Frankfurt School writers such as Herbert Marcuse (1898–1979) whose *One Dimensional Man* (1964 [1972]) and *Eros and Civilization* (1955) had a profound impact on New Left thinking. For Marcuse contemporary capitalism was characterised by the creation of false needs by those who had an interest in the repression of liberty. "Such needs have a societal content and function which are determined by external powers over which the individual has no control; they continue to be what they were from the beginning, products of a society whose dominant interest demands repression" (Marcuse 1964 [1972]: 19). Ideally individuals should be able to distinguish the true from the false but could do so only if they were truly "free to give their own answer". However, "as long as they are kept incapable of being autonomous, as long as they are indoctrinated and manipulated down to their very instincts, their answer to this question cannot be taken to be their own" (Marcuse 1964 [1972]: 20). The possibility of a rational, autonomous consumer was therefore vitiated by the very nature of capitalist society.

Moreover, for Marcuse, "free choice among a wide variety of goods and services does not signify freedom if these goods and services sustain social controls over a life of toil and fear, that is if they sustain alienation" (Marcuse 1964 [1972]: 21). So not only did the malleability of consumers mean their decisions were a consequence of a false consciousness; those decisions resulted in consumption the nature of which reinforced the existing forces making for social control; geared as they were to "the kind of consumption that soothe[s] and prolong[s] stupefaction" (Marcuse 1964 [1972]: 20). Domination, the denial of the possibility of human liberation, paradoxically therefore took the form of affluence and the putative freedom of consumer choice that came with it.

In the 1960s and 1970s the New Left in Britain echoed at least some of the substance and sentiments of this. Thus writers such as Stuart Hall (1932–2014), Raymond Williams (1921–1988), Richard Hoggart (1918–2014) and other contributors to the *New Left Review* focused on the extent to which a consumerist society was eroding working class communal values and an appetite for radical social change. Here the threat was not that "working-class people take hold of the new goods, washing machines, television and the rest" (Hoggart and Williams 1960: 28). For Hoggart and Williams, this was neither "necessarily regrettable or reprehensible". The danger was rather "the type of persuasion which accompanies these sales, since its assumptions are shallower than many of those people already have" (Hoggart and Williams 1960: 28). In terms of values and culture Williams's concern was therefore with what people were being persuaded to buy into, rather than with what they actually bought; namely, into a set of vapid aspirations that precluded or substituted for the ideals of fellowship, solidarity and that rounded development of human beings which social democracy should embrace.

As to the United States, there were also those who, if more in a radical, anti-capitalist than socialist tradition, expressed similar concerns about the impact of consumerism, both on society but also on the environment. Thus the work of late-twentieth-century American writers, such as Daniel Bell (1919–2011), Christopher Lasch (1932–1994), Robert Bellah (1927–2013) and Rachel Carson (1907–1964), underpinned an ethical critique of a consumer society characterised by self-indulgent, self-gratifying, self-regarding and self-seeking behaviour that fuelled a rampant egoism or, in Lasch's formulation, a compelling "narcissism"; a narcissism which threatened to undermine the possibility of sustaining those social and civic sensibilities which made possible a tolerant, democratic and relatively equitable society. Juxtaposed with this critique of late-twentieth-century consumerism went a concomitant aspiration for a more socially responsible, socially cohesive, moral and environmentally sensitive consumption. In this vein were Lasch's *Culture of Narcissism* (1979), Bell's *Contradictions of Capitalism* (1976), Carson's *Silent Spring* (1962) and Bellah's *The Broken Covenant* (1975).

Recent Developments in the Political Economy of British Social Democracy

In Britain, the ascendancy of AES socialist fundamentalism in the 1970s and early 1980s was relatively short lived. The rise and ultimate triumph of Thatcherism, the Labour

Party's subsequent years in the political wilderness, an increasing globalisation of economic activity that militated against the pursuit of socialism in one country and an increasing willingness of many on the Left to make their peace with the market, spelt its demise by the mid-1980s.

In its place there emerged in Britain a Leftist political economy to which many would hesitate to apply the epithet of socialism and whose proponents were fundamentally influenced by the seeming dynamism of the Anglo-American model of capitalism. As two New Labour theorists put it, "all the big new companies of the 1990s such as Microsoft, Netscape and Oracle" came from "the entrepreneurial culture of the United States". So, "rather than forlornly searching the Rhineland or suburban Nagoya for models of the future, British [social democratic] policymakers would do better to look at the fleet-footed, information, entertainment and software companies on the US West Coast" (Leadbeater and Mulgan 1996). This was the kind of business culture which social democracy should embrace and, where possible, replicate across the public sector.

In tandem with this went a New Labour emphasis on the need for investment in human capital; something that, on the surface, seemed to resonate with a tradition of socialist political economy that prioritised the development of labour's creative faculties. However, in the hands of New Labour theorists this ambition assumed a different character, with emphasis put on the individual's responsibility to acquire the requisite marketable skills to make him or her attractive to potential employers. To this end, and in keeping with the spirit of this, New Labour proposed an individually based knowledge investment fund and stressed the need for the greater flexibility of a less-regulated labour market to make highly skilled labour more freely and readily available.

So, as one commentator put it, New Labour therefore saw work "not in . . . socialist terms of human creativity, not even in social liberal terms as a quid pro quo for services granted . . . but as the far starker assumption of individual responsibility for financial independence, and as an activity subservient to the goals established by market forces" (Freeden 1999: 47). Education in this context became something good for an individual's marketability, rather than their self-development.

As for New Labour's approach to the public sector, this was consistent with Gordon Brown's (b. 1951) general injunction to the Labour Party that "instead of being suspicious of competition we should embrace it . . . Instead of being suspicious of entrepreneurs, we should celebrate an entrepreneurial culture" (Brown 2003: 271); an ethos that was to be extended to public services which should view their users as customers not supplicants and embrace quasi-market disciplines to ensure efficiency and responsiveness to service users' needs. As a Labour Minister, Alan Milburn (b. 1958), put it in a speech in 2002:

> [T]hirty years ago the one size fits all approach of the 1940s was still in the ascendant. Public services were monolithic. The public were supposed to be truly grateful for what they were about to receive. People had little say and precious little choice. Today we live in a quite different world. *We live in a consumer age.* People demand services tailor made to their individual needs. (Milburn 2002 [2006]: 195, emphasis added)

For some this evocation of "models of consumer empowerment" could be seen as an attempt to "revitalize the languages of representative democracy", particularly with respect to public services (Newman and Vidler 2006: 195). For others it was an attempt to re-connect with the middle classes, both for reasons of political expediency but also to secure their buy-in to public provision, "by ensuring a more personalised, consumer-friendly and choice-oriented service." So, as one commentator saw it, "by promising choice in valued public services . . . the defection of the affluent to privately purchased choices could be averted" (Clarke et al. 2007: 41). From a more critical perspective, however, New Labour was seen as using a language which conceptualised "the voter as a consumer to be pleased rather than a citizen to be enlightened"; though New Labour theorists would have responded that there was no fundamental tension here between the two (Needham 2003: 18). Whatever the motivation, the narrative of consumer empowerment altered conceptions of the nature of public provision and the relationship between user and provider, the citizen and the state. It has also fundamentally altered the character of the ascendant ideological strains within social democracy in Britain.

NOEL THOMPSON

See also:

John Atkinson Hobson (I); Nicholas Kaldor (I); John Maynard Keynes (I); James Edward Meade (I); Non-Marxian socialist ideas in France (II); Non-Marxist socialist ideas in Germany and Austria (II); Poverty (III); Philip Henry Wicksteed (I).

References and further reading

The literature on this theme is huge. The reader who wishes to dig deeper into the topic is especially recommended to consult Diggins (1992), Harrington (1993), Johnpoll and Johnpoll (1981) and Thompson (2006, 2014).

Bell, D. (1976), *Contradictions of Capitalism*, London: Heinemann.
Bellah, R. (1975), *The Broken Covenant*, New York: Seabury Press, originally presented as lectures in 1971.
Bellamy, E. (1888), *Looking Backward, 2000–1887*, reprinted in 1982, ed. V. Tichi, Harmondsworth: Penguin.
Berle, A. and G. Means (1932), *The Modern Corporation and Private Property*, New York: Macmillan.
Besant, A. (1889), 'Industry under socialism', reprinted in G.B. Shaw (ed.) (1962), *Fabian Essays*, London: Allen and Unwin.
Blatchly, C. (1822), *An Essay on Common Wealths*, New York: New York Society for Promoting Communities.
Blatchford, R. (1893), *Merrie England*, London: Clarion Press.
Blatchford, R. (1898), *Real Socialism: What Socialism is and What Socialism is Not*, London: Clarion Press.
Blatchford, R. (1899), 'Editorial', *Clarion*, 10 June.
Blatchford, R. (1902), *Britain for the British*, London: Clarion Press.
Bray, J. (1839), *Labour's Wrongs and Labour's Remedy, or the Age of Might and the Age of Right*, Leeds: David Green.
Brisbane, A. (1840), *Social Destiny of Man, Or Association and Reorganization of Industry*, Philadelphia, PA: Stollmeyer.
Brown, G. (2003), 'State and market: towards a public interest test', *Political Quarterly*, **74** (3), 266–84.
Byllesby, L. (1826), *Observations on the Sources and Effects of Unequal Wealth*, New York: Nichols.
Carson, R. (1962), *Silent Spring*, reprinted 1964, London: Readers' Union.
Clarke, J., J. Newman, N. Smith, E. Vidler and L. Westmarland (2007), *Creating Citizen-Consumers, Changing Publics and Changing Public Services*, London: Sage.
Clarke, W. (1889), 'The industrial basis of socialism', in G. Shaw (ed.), *Fabian Essays*, London: Allen & Unwin.
Cole, G. (1917), *Self-Government in Industry*, London: Bell.
Cole, G. (1920), *Guild Socialism Restated*, London: Bell.
Crosland, A. (1956), *The Future of Socialism*, London: Jonathan Cape.
Crossman, R. (1960), *Labour and the Affluent Society*, Fabian Tract, 325, London: Fabian Society.
Diggins, J. (1992), *Rise and Fall of the American Left*, New York: Norton.
Durbin, E. (1933), *Purchasing Power and Trade Depression: A Critique of Underconsumption Theories*, London: Jonathan Cape.
Durbin, E. (1935), *The Problem of Credit Policy*, London: Chapman and Hall.
Freeden, M. (1999), 'The ideology of New Labour', *Political Quarterly*, **70** (1), 42–52.
Galbraith, J. (1958), *The Affluent Society*, reprinted 1962, Harmondsworth: Penguin.

George, H. (1879), *Progress and Poverty*, New York: D. Appleton and Co.

Gray, J. (1825), *Lecture on Human Happiness*, London: Sherwood Jones and Co.

Gray, J. (1831), *The Social System, A Treatise on the Principle of Exchange*, Edinburgh: Tait.

Gronlund, L. (1886), *The Co-operative Commonwealth, An Exposition of Modern Socialism*, London: Sonnenschein and Co.

Harrington, M. (1963), *The Other America, Poverty in the United States*, London: Macmillan.

Harrington, M. (1993), *Socialism, Past and Future*, London: Pluto.

Hayek, F. (1931), *Prices and Production*, London: Routledge.

Hobson, S. (1914), *National Guilds, An Inquiry into the Wage System and the Way Out*, London: Bell.

Hoggart, R. and R. Williams (1960), 'Working-class attitudes', *New Left Review*, **1** (1), 26–30.

Holland, S. (1975), *The Socialist Challenge*, London: Quartet.

Johnpoll, L. and B. Johnpoll (1981), *The Impossible Dream: The Rise and Demise of the American Left*, Westport, CT: Greenwood Press.

Keynes, J. (1936), *The General Theory of Employment, Interest and Money*, vol. VII, *The Collected Writings of John Maynard Keynes*, London: Macmillan.

Labour Party (1982), *Labour's Programme, 1982*, London: Labour Party.

Lasch, C. (1979), *Culture of Narcissism: American Life in an Age of Diminishing Expectations*, New York: Norton.

Leadbeater, C. and G. Mulgan (1996), 'Labour's forgotten idea', *Financial Times*, 2 October, p. 16.

Marcuse, H. (1955), *Eros and Civilization, A Philosophical Inquiry into Freud*, reprinted 1961, Boston, MA: Beacon Press.

Marcuse, H. (1964), *One Dimensional Man*, reprinted 1972, London: Abacus.

Meade, J. (1936), *Introduction to Economic Analysis and Policy*, 2nd edn 1937, Oxford: Oxford University Press.

Milburn, A. (2002), Speech to the Annual Social Services Conference in Cardiff, 16 October, quoted in J. Newman and E. Vidler (2006), 'Discriminating customers, responsible patients, empowered users: consumerism and the modernisation of health care', *Journal of Social Policy*, **35** (2), 193–209.

Mises, L. (1920), 'Economic calculation in a socialist commonwealth', in F. Hayek (ed.) (1935), *Collectivist Economic Planning*, London: Routledge.

Morris, W. ([1883], 'Art and the people, a socialist's protest against capitalist brutality', in M. Morris (ed.) (1966), *William Morris, Artist, Writer, Socialist*, vol. 2, New York: Russell and Russell.

Morris, W. (1885), 'Useful work and useless toil', M. Morris (ed.) (1910–15), *The Collected Works of William Morris*, vol. 23, London, Longmans Green, pp. 3–26.

Morris, W. (1890), *News from Nowhere, An Epoch at Rest*, reprinted 1923, London, Longmans: Green and Co.

Needham, C. (2003), *Citizen Consumers: New Labour's Marketplace Democracy*, London: Catalyst Forum.

Newman, J. and E. Vidler (2006), 'More than a matter of choice? Consumerism and the modernization of health care', *Journal of Social Policy*, **35**.

Owen, R. (1821), *A Report to the County of Lanark of a Plan for Relieving Public Distress*, in G. Cole (ed.) (1927), *A New View of Society and Other Writings*, London: Dent.

Shaw, G. 1896), *Report on Fabian Policy*, Fabian Tract, 70, London: Fabian Society.

South Wales Miners' Federation, Unofficial Reform Committee (1912), *The Miners' Next Step*, Tonypandy: Robert Davies and Co.

Strachey, J. (1935), *The Nature of Capitalist Crisis*, London: Gollancz.

Strachey, J. (1936), *The Theory and Practice of Socialism*, London: Gollancz.

Strachey, J. (1953), 'Marxism revisited II', *New Statesman*, 23 May.

Strachey, J. (1956), *Contemporary Capitalism*, London: Gollancz.

Thompson, N. (2006), *Political Economy and the Labour Party, The Economics of Democratic Socialism, 1884–2005*, 2nd edn, London: Routledge.

Thompson, N. (2014), *The Market and its Critics, Socialist Political Economy in Nineteenth Century Britain*, London: Routledge.

Thompson, W. (1824), *An Inquiry into the Principles of the Distribution of Wealth*, London: Longman, Hurst, Rees, Orme, Brown and Green.

Thompson, W. (1827), *Labor Rewarded, the Claims of Labor and Capital Conciliated or, How to Secure to Labor the Whole Product of its Exertions*, London: Hunt and Clarke.

Townsend, P. (1979), *Poverty in the United Kingdom, a Survey of Household Resources and Living Standards*, Harmondsworth: Penguin.

Webb, S. (1892), *English Progress towards Social Democracy*, Fabian Tract, 15, London: Fabian Society.

Webb, S. (1896), *The Difficulties of Individualism*, Fabian Tract 69, London: Fabian Society.

Winch, D. (1972), *Economics and Policy: An Historical Study*, London: Fontana.

Non-Marxist socialist ideas in Germany and Austria

The term "socialist" conveys a variety of meanings that are shaped by national contexts (German, French, and English speaking countries). To limit the range of coverage in view of given space constraints, the main focus will be non-Marxist economic contributions to the concept of a socialist economic order. From the viewpoint of economics, a socialist economic order has two essential elements: social ownership of the means of production, and coordination of economic activities through a central plan instead of private ownership and coordination via independent markets. Authors who deal with measures of social policy to improve the living conditions of the working class, but not under the perspective of a socialist order, will be mentioned but given less attention.

In contrast to Britain, in Germany and in Austria socialism as a political movement was dominated by Marxist theory from the 1870s onward to 1914. This implied adherence to the labour theory of value which was vigorously defended by Karl Kautsky and Rudolf Hilferding. As a consequence, marginalist thinking was rejected as "Vulgärökonomie" – "vulgar economics" (Chaloupek 1987). Rodbertus's version of socialism, developed independently of Marx, is of theoretical interest only, while the so-called "Kathedersozialisten" (socialists of the chair) were opposed to socialism and did not support the Social-Democratic Party. Lassalle was recognized as co-founder of the party. If his theory of the state could not be harmonized with Marx's approach, it became evident before World War I that it was in many cases better suited as a basis of concrete policy demands, when the Social-Democratic Party gained strength as a political force in the parliamentary system.

When the debate about socialization erupted at the end of World War I, Marxists – theoreticians as well as politicians – were helpless. They turned to concepts offered by non-Marxist socialists or even bourgeois theoreticians and practitioners. The theoretical background of non-Marxist socialist economists in Germany and Austria was marginalist economics, mostly of the Austrian School type. Unlike most Marxists, they did not consider the capitalist market economy an "anarchic" system without social purpose. In their understanding of the functioning of the market system, there were important elements which had to be preserved for a functioning socialist system.

The challenges posed by the Great Depression of the 1930s were even more difficult to meet than those of the post-World War I situation. National economic planning, which emerged as a central concept of economic policy debates, would have required socialization which was practically unfeasible and/or politically impossible. Keynesianism which provided the foundations for a new approach to economic policy came too late for Social Democrats in Germany and Austria.

Even after World War II, the Social Democrats in Germany and Austria were hesitant to embrace Keynesianism, which they adopted only in the 1950s as a theoretical basis, combining elements of a market economy and state control.

Nineteenth Century

Carl Rodbertus von Jagetzow

For Rodbertus (1805–1875) the social misery of the working class was the prime motive of his economic and social studies. Following Ricardo, Rodbertus started from the postulate that all goods are the result of human labour and that, therefore, labour is the sole source of economic value. He explained the existence of rent, profit and interest by means of a surplus theory. In the modern economy which is characterized by a highly developed division of labour it is the system of property rights that enables the owners of capital and land to acquire the results of the production process and reserve part of the product of labour for themselves. Rodbertus put great emphasis on the distinction between "capital" in itself, in the sense of produced means of production, and the "ownership of capital" ("Kapitalbesitz") (Kozak 1882: 194). Private ownership of capital and land is the legal institution through which capitalists and landowners can rob workers of part of their product ("surplus theory" of profit). Profit and rent are essentially the same phenomenon, based on the ownership of capital and land by the propertied class.

Based on his surplus theory of profit, Rodbertus developed a dynamic theory of increasing relative exploitation of workers in the process of industrialization. Rodbertus saw very clearly that national product not only grew due to increasing population and labour force, but also due to increasing productivity per worker. As a consequence of the working of "natural laws" of market exchange, the share of the wage in the product declined while the productivity of labour increased (Kozak 1882: 213). Explicitly rejecting Say's law, Rodbertus also attributed the recurrent crises of production to the increasing income gap between capitalists and workers during the upswing of the trade cycle. In the long run, the severity of crises is increasing, whereas the duration of the upswing-phase is shortening. In Rodbertus's words, the welfare losses of the capitalist system are "immeasurable", compared with a production system organized by the state (1850 [1979]: 128 ff.). The central idea of Rodbertus's reform socialism was to ensure regular and full participation of workers in the increase of productivity. This would not only lead to a gradual improvement of living standards of the working class, but also save the economy from recurrent economic crises. He also proposed a new system of money based on the unit of labour. However, workers cannot receive the full amount of their labour, since part of the total social product must be reserved for collective needs. (Kozak 1882: 238 ff.)

Rodbertus located the fundamental flaw of this "economic system" in the pursuit of their own interest by the systems' agents. Therefore, it is the central task of the state to establish a legal framework that provides an alternative mechanism for the functioning of the economy. The division of labour within the national economy is essentially a social phenomenon, based on the "unity of the social organism, and not on its atoms, the individual organisms". This unity of the social organism is adequately represented by a system which Rodbertus called "national economy" in the sense of "state economy" ("Nationalökonomie oder Staatswirthschaft"). To divide the ownership of capital and land among workers would be a regression from the high degree of the division of labour and productivity of the economy achieved under the capitalist system. Hence, Rodbertus rejected models for the organization of production in co-operatives (Schulze-Delitzsch) as a principal approach to social reform. In the long run, Rodbertus envisaged a socialist economic system in which all capital and land is owned by the state, while consumption remains essentially private.

Rodbertus identified several tendencies within the existing capitalist system which prepare a transformation towards socialism (concentration of production, separation of entrepreneurial function from capital ownership). He proposed to establish institutions through which the existing "defunct state system" could be gradually transformed into "a higher order of the state" (Kozak 1882: 220). Transition could be achieved "in a rather painless way, without inflicting injustice to the owners of land and capital", through redemption of their claims to rent and profit by the state (Kozak 1882: 252). It would take centuries rather than decades to complete the transformation process. Rodbertus warned against revolution and strongly argued for "continuity of the law". As a firm monarchist, Rodbertus expected a strong government that stands above conflicting parties to take the initiative.

Occasionally, Rodbertus's socialism takes a nationalistic turn. He considered it the mission of Germany and the German people to develop a solution of the "Social Question" (Kozak 1882: 192) and to save the world from the "Smithian system". He considered the internationalist orientation of the proletarian movement as a challenge of the "national autonomy of state organisms" (Thier 1940: 176).

Ferdinand Lassalle

Lassalle (1825–1864) was an active participant in the revolution of 1848. He came in intensive contact with Marx and Engels through his contributions to the *Neue Rheinische Zeitung*. As one of only a few revolutionaries, Lassalle remained in Prussia after having served a prison sentence for subversive activities. He died after a duel in 1864, at the age of 39.

As with Marx, Lassalle started from the writings of Hegel and the Hegelian school. He devoted his main theoretical interest to the study of the philosophy of law and the evolution of the legal system. In his main theoretical work, *Das System der erworbenen Rechte* (1861), he tried to present a philosophical-empirical history of law which – similar to the development of the economy – displayed a tendency towards socialism as a final state. Lassalle was convinced that the progress in the history of law essentially consisted in "imposing ever more restrictions on the sphere of property of the private individual, in moving an increasing number of objects outside of the sphere of private property" (Lassalle 1919–20, vol. 9: 390).

In economics, Lassalle considered himself a follower of Marx. However, in the preface to the first edition of *Das Kapital*, Marx criticized Lassalle for having misunderstood essential elements of his economic doctrine (Marx 1867 [1969]: 11). As has been shown (Grigorovici 1910), Lassalle had only superficially adopted Marx's theory of value. Even if Lassalle generally accepted that all prices and values are determined by the "socially necessary labour" expended in the production of a commodity, implicitly he attributed to "social demand" the role of an additional determinant of value under certain circumstances.

More importantly, Lassalle's theory of the state was different from that of Marx. For Marx, the state was essentially an executive committee of the ruling class – "nothing more than the form of organization which the bourgeois necessarily adopt both for internal and external purposes, for the mutual guarantee of their property and interest" (Marx and Engels 1939: 59). This view precluded any expectation of using the state as an instrument for transforming the capitalist system into a socialist one. Lassalle thought quite differently. In a speech to workers in Berlin, Lassalle said that it was the state that has to assume the function to unite the powers of individuals in order to enable each individual to achieve a level of existence which the individual can never achieve by acting on its own (Lassalle 1862 [1919]: 32). He advocated a political strategy in which the state played a central role in improving the conditions of the working class. Following Ricardo and Marx, Lassalle postulated an "iron law of wages" ("ehernes Lohngesetz") which would keep the wage at the low level of a socially determined minimum of subsistence as long as workers were separated from the ownership of the means of production. The central idea of Lassalle's economic programme was to break this iron law by using the institution of co-operatives to enable workers to participate in the ownership of capital. The state had to play an essential role by providing money capital necessary for financing the co-operatives. In Lassalle's view, the state-supported co-operative economy was an important step towards the new social order which remained the distant goal of the movement. With respect to trade unions and consumer co-operatives Lassalle took a sceptical attitude.

In Germany, the co-operative movement had been pioneered by Hermann Schulze-Delitzsch and gained momentum after the failed revolution of 1848. Lassalle parted with this movement in 1863 when he founded the Allgemeiner deutscher Arbeiterverein (General German Workers' Association) which propagated the formation of producer co-operatives, an idea which Lassalle had borrowed from Louis Blanc. He tried to convince Bismarck, who was at that time struggling for survival as chancellor of the Prussian state, to grant financial state support for the formation of worker co-operatives in exchange for political support from workers against the liberal-bourgeois Progressive Party.

With respect to taxation Lassalle dissented from the Marxian position that indirect taxes do not reduce real wages. Lassalle argued that the increase or the introduction of special excises have a diminishing effect on workers' incomes and cannot be shifted forward to the employers (Gerloff 1922: 16 ff.).

The German Social Democratic Party, and its Austrian sister organization, always held Lassalle in high esteem as one of its founders. If, nonetheless, its majority remained distinctly Marxist until 1914, after World War I, when the Social Democrats shared responsibility for the government, it became obvious that Lassalle's approach to the function of the state was a better foundation of their political program than Marx's negative position.

On the surface, Lassalle's concern with German unification makes his state socialism appear as "German socialism". Yet his concern with the unity of Germany is fundamentally different from that of other German state socialists. Lassalle does not advocate this unity for its own sake, that is, for nationalistic aims, but to form an organizational unit within which the socialist society can be established.

Socialists of the chair
The economists of the German Historical School who founded the Verein für Socialpolitik (Association for Social Policy) in 1872 were called *Kathedersozialisten* (socialists of the chair) by their political adversaries. They rejected the negative attitude of the Manchester School according to which "the state was a necessary evil which should be restricted to a minimum" and advocated an active role of the state by improving the living conditions of the working class and the poor. On the other hand, they opposed "socialist experiments" and revolutionary ambitions (Schmoller 1998: 70 ff.). Most of their policy proposals contented themselves with preventing or modifying undesired social effects

of industrial development by introducing compulsory accident and health insurance, pension systems, and factory laws to improve working conditions, and were thus essentially of an interventionist character. The most far reaching proposals were presented by Adolph Wagner in his "Program of State Socialism". Wagner called for comprehensive participation of the working classes "in the material and cultural fruit to the maximum extent which is made possible by the increase of productive powers". This implies raising the share of wages, limiting daily working hours, introducing occupational health and safety standards, workers' insurance, and so on. Wagner also proposed to use the provision of public services for redistribution through nationalization or communalization. He also called for changes in the system of taxation to shift the burden of financing state expenditure in favour of the working class and the lower income groups (Wagner 1887 [1940]: 279 ff.). Wagner's programme does not aim at a fundamental change of the economic order since in principle private ownership of the means of production, and market coordination are maintained. Therefore, Adolph Wagner is not a socialist in the sense of Carl Rodbertus's long-term vision. With Rodbertus, Wagner shared the preference for the monarchist rule in the form of a "social kingship".

Austrian economists
In comparison with the German Reich, the support for measures of social policy from academic economists was more limited in Austria. Among the members of the Austrian School of economics a sceptical attitude prevailed, with Friedrich von Wieser as the main exception. Wieser expressed sympathy for measures of social legislation and concern about increasing dominance of giant capitalist enterprise. Searching instruments to "elevate workers from their hopelessly dependent position and to give them a share in the profit of the enterprise" more effective than trade unions, Wieser considered producers' co-operatives the most promising alternative (Wieser 1892 [1929]: 290).

Anton Menger, Carl Menger's younger brother, professor of law at the University of Vienna, developed his socialist ideas from a legal science perspective. He criticized civil law codes for their failure to protect the interests of the propertyless classes. He called for a peaceful transformation of the "individualistic power state" into a "popular worker's state" by transferring the law of property rights and contract law from the sphere of civil law to public law, in order to model the legal system according to the needs of the majority of the population (Menger 1890 [1908], 1903). Among Anton Menger's students was Theodor Hertzka, whose utopian novel *Freiland* envisages a market-socialist model of a Jewish colony in Kenya where land is freely available.

"Deutscher Sozialismus"
The idea of a specifically German socialism, "Deutscher Sozialismus", has its roots in German philosophy and social theory, especially that of Lorenz von Stein (Vogel 1925). Stein's idealistic version defines socialism by the ethical relationship between the individual and society, conceived either as *Volk* (people), or state. German socialism rejected Marxist and other "materialist" approaches. There is a romanticist current in German socialism which admired the spirit of corporatism which permeates the urban societies of the Middle Ages.

An extreme idealistic, non-economic version of socialism was presented under the impression of Germany's defeat in World War I by Oswald Spengler with his Prussian socialism (*Preußentum und Sozialismus*, 1919 [1932]). Spengler's concept of socialism rested on the idea of an identity of state and people. Whereas in Britain – and also in Marxist thinking – the state in its essential meaning does not appear, the Prussian state is essentially a socialist state since it represents the whole people, with all social formations within the population being integral parts of the state. In the Prussian socialist state, labour is not a commodity but a social duty, wages are impartially set by the state, not by bargaining between trade unions and employers, rivalry between political parties of the type of British parliamentary democracy is alien to German socialism (Spengler 1919 [1932]: 80 ff.).

Sombart's concept of *Deutscher Sozialismus* (1934) was rejected by the Nazis mainly due to its anti-industrialist, anti-modern-growth orientation. Efforts from the side of academic economists to further elaborate German socialism as a basis of National-socialist economic and social policies were more or less neglected. Most academic sympathizers of Nazi Germany tried to play down the socialist element in the economic policy of the Nazi state (Hausmann 2011: 840–72).

Twentieth Century

In 1918, when the social-democratic parties of Germany and of the newly founded Austrian state came to power, and for brief periods dominated parliaments and governments of these countries, the idea of "socialization" was the central concept of the economic policy debate. Yet Social Democrats in both countries were ill equipped for this task due to their close orientation towards the teachings of Marx and Engels, who had displayed a strong distaste for any "utopian" attempts to devise a blueprint of the type of economy which they expected to succeed capitalism. As a consequence, most concrete proposals for how to proceed with socialization came from non-Marxist socialists or even bourgeois authors (Weissel 1976).

Walther Rathenau
The most prominent example of the latter is Rathenau (1867–1922) whose influential pamphlet *Die neue Wirtschaft* was published in early 1918. In one of his central propositions Rathenau followed the ideas of German state socialism: that it is the task of the state to take charge of the organization of production as well as of income distribution. Similar to the concept provided by British guild socialism, Rathenau proposed the formation of associations of production establishments for all branches of the industrial sector of the economy ("Berufsverbände") through which production and investment would be organized within a comprehensive overall national plan. However, Rathenau's ultimate aim was not a socialist economy with state or workers' ownership of enterprises, but rather to preserve private ownership within a "mixed economy". The socialization concept of Rudolf Wissel (1920) who was minister of economic affairs in the first Social-Democratic government of the Weimar Republic followed Rathenau's principal ideas. A national economic plan ("Reichswirtschaftsplan") should have exercised control over the economy as a whole. Wissel conceived his planned economy as a state of transition during which the masses would be educated for a new way of thinking and behaving adequately in a socialist economy.

Rathenau also introduced "rationalization" of the production apparatus as a key concept for the reorganization of the industrial sector and of economic activities as a whole to cope with post-war problems. A large part of the proliferous literature on socialization was concerned with elimination of "wasteful activity" of the capitalist system (unnecessary transport routes, excessive sales efforts, advertising, and so on).

The alternative between partial and total socialization was another hotly debated issue in Germany. Drawing on his experience as a member of Germany's and Austria's committees for socialization ("Sozialisierungskommission") in 1919, Emil Lederer (1920) presented an economic concept for socialization of "key industries" such as coal, iron and steel, and parts of the chemical industry. Lederer acknowledged that total socialization was out of reach, while Wissel's *Reichswirtschaftsplan* was ineffective in practice. In Lederer's view, partial socialization was urgent to stop the sell-out of key German industrial enterprises to foreign companies. Socialization of enterprises should be achieved through organizing companies of the identified branches in "trusts".

Rudolf Goldscheid

Goldscheid's (1870–1931) book, *Staatssozialismus oder Staatskapitalismus*, published in 1917, is probably the best known contribution from a non-Marxist socialist in Austria, mainly due to Schumpeter's essay *Die Krise des Steuerstaates* (1918) which was a reply to Goldscheid's theses (Peukert 2009). A capital levy of one-third which had to be paid in kind was the core idea of Goldscheid's socialization concept, from which he expected a double effect: first, state ownership of one third of the productive capital would approximately balance state debt accumulated during the war, and enable the state to service its debt without further increase in taxes; secondly, in the mixed private/state economy, the state would be in a better position to enforce social priorities such as investment in infrastructure, the provision of public goods and social insurance, and also to exercise control over external trade (Goldscheid 1917 [1976]: 128 ff.).

Goldscheid's socialization program was embedded in a more fundamental concept of state socialism, or "social capitalism". Even pre-war experience had shown that without ownership of the means of production the state was permanently constrained by excessive indebtedness. To become independent from capitalist dominance the state has to be recapitalized, freed of its debt and made independent from the need of gathering tax revenues. Goldscheid's general thesis against which Schumpeter objected was that the tax state was a thing of the past, and that the future belonged to the debt-free "owner-state" ("Besitzstaat").

Otto Neurath

The design of an appropriate accounting system posed a difficult problem for Marxist economists which they tried to cope with by using the labour hour as an accounting unit (Chaloupek 1990). In this context, the most radical, but also most controversial contribution to the post-war socialization debate came from the Austrian philosopher and social scientist Otto Neurath (1882–1945) (1919 [1979]: 14) with his proposition that production in a socialist economy would be carried out according to a central plan based on accounting in kind ("Naturalrechnung" – accounting in natural terms). Neurath thought that the war economy was sufficient proof for the feasibility of his natural economy. On the basis of utilitarian economic reasoning, "the maximum degree of happiness, of life disposition of the population, of utility as the goal of a socialist economy" (Neurath

1925: 394) could be chosen among alternatives only by a democratic decision, based on detailed comparisons of a variety of alternatives, showing possible combinations of inputs and outcomes in natural terms. Despite its practical irrelevance, Neurath's idea attracted considerable attention, though the reactions were overwhelmingly negative. If Ludwig von Mises (1922: 79) cited Neurath as a witness of the impossibility of rational calculation in a socialist economy, the socialists hastened to reject the idea of accounting in kind in order to ward off damage for their political seriousness (Kautsky 1922: 308; Leichter 1923: 77).

Karl Polanyi
Karl Polanyi (1886–1964) who was an editor of the Austrian weekly *Der österreichische Volkswirt* developed his model of a socialist economy (Polanyi 1922) in response to Mises to whom he conceded that the problem of economic calculation was insoluble in a centrally administered socialist economy. Institutionally, Polanyi proposed an economy based on guild-socialist principles. Polanyi also took great effort in elaborating a system of economic accounting. Costs and prices are calculated in the decentralized production units. He introduced a basic distinction between purely technical costs caused by nature and costs imposed on production by society, in order to make clear that the setting of social standards and minimum wages must be reflected in the cost of production. According to Polanyi, there is a constant conflict between technical productivity and the social purpose of production, which must be solved politically through bargaining, compromise, and also majority decision. In an article published in 1925 Polanyi cautiously tried to dissuade Austria's Social Democrats from their preference for centralism and administrative-bureaucratic procedures in their economic proposals. He pointed to the examples of trade unions and the party as alternative procedures for generating information.

Market socialism: Eduard Heimann
Building on Rathenau's model of *Neue Wirtschaft*, and taking up of Ludwig Mises's fundamental critique of the *Gemeinwirtschaft* as an economic system, Eduard Heimann (1889–1967) developed a model of market socialism (Heimann 1922) for which the author has been given credit as "the first economist who proposed a model of a socialist market economy, ten years before Taylor, Dickinson and Lange" (Lowe 1967).

Heimann envisaged a socialist order with a rational system of "free and independent formation of prices". At the same time, he emphasized that even more important was to change the rules of the system in such a way that "the field should not be left to the conflict of interests, but to ensure that the mutuality of labour as a service to the community is raised to general awareness" (Heimann 1922: 180). For Heimann, socialization was not primarily an economic matter, but an element of his philosophical idea of ethical socialism which in the last instance rested on religious belief (Rieter 1999: 245 f.).

Freedom of consumers' choice provides the basis for a rational mechanism of price formation. On the supply side, all production units are organized in monopolistic associations, which, however, refrain from any profit maximizing price fixing, but strictly adhere to the principle of cost pricing. Thus, in the case of a change in the demand for their product, the producer (the association) passively follows the price signal by offering the desired quantity at the new price which covers its costs until a new equilibrium is reached in the particular product market. To establish overall equilibrium, changes in the demand for a certain product entail the need for compensating changes somewhere else. To accomplish these changes, similar to the market mechanism in a private economy, the central planning body applies a procedure of trial and error. Heimann thought that the search for a new equilibrium could be more effective if there is a central authority with a complete oversight of all markets, compared to private producers who do not make information on their moves available to competitors (Heimann 1922: 186 f.).

If Heimann's model of a market anticipates important elements of Oscar Lange's (1936–37) "On the economic theory of socialism", especially the use of the trial and error-method for determination of prices and quantities, it lacks the theoretical rigour of Lange's neoclassical construction.

National planning against the crisis

During the Great Depression "Planwirtschaft" ("planned economy, national planning") became the favourite concept of socialist economists in their search for strategies against economic crisis. Also non-socialist economists advocated some sort of overall planning of the economic process. For example, Werner Sombart embraced the idea of "Planwirtschaft" as an element of his theory of "late capitalism" ("Spätkapitalismus").

According to Carl Landauer (1931), "planned capitalism" could last only for a limited period. In his view, socialization of corporate enterprises, especially of industry, was the key to transformation of the existing economic order into a socialist economic system. He proposes a gradual take-over of corporate enterprises by the state with full compensation of private owners, wherever possible through the purchase of shares on the stock exchange. That the state can draw up an investment programme for the economy as a whole constitutes a decisive advantage of the planned economy over the market system (Landauer 1931: 122).

In his brochure of 1932 titled *Planwirtschaft* Emil Lederer reflects on the difference between the post-war situation and the situation of the economy in 1932. Lederer argues that partial socialization of certain industries would not have been an impossible task as long as the market economy was functioning reasonably well. In the depression of the 1930s, the capitalist system was paralyzed. A "revival of productive energies" could only be initiated by a comprehensive plan for the economy as a whole – a much more demanding task which could be accomplished in a fully planned economy (Lederer 1932: 41). Turning to the planning experiment that was undertaken in the Soviet Union, Lederer did not deny that there could be large-scale investment failures owing to planning errors. Such failures would result in losses of general welfare, which would, however, be less severe than the welfare losses in a capitalist market economy of a depression as severe as the one of the 1930s.

Epilogue

Socialist economic theorizing came to a sudden end with the take-over of the Nazi government in Germany in 1933 and the establishment of authoritarian rule in Austria 1934. When the debate resumed in 1945, many contributions came from scholars who had been forced to emigrate after 1933. The introduction of a system of national planning of the type discussed before 1933 still dominated contributions of the late 1940s, with a mix of public and private ownership of the means of production (Ortlieb 1947; Sering 1948; in Austria: Bayer 1947). Towards the end of the 1950s, the economies of Germany and Austria reached a state of full employment. Return to normal economic conditions was faster than anticipated. In the 1950s, growth of the economy surpassed even the most optimistic expectations. Keynesian macroeconomics became the theoretical foundation of a new regime of managing broad economic aggregates.

GÜNTHER CHALOUPEK

See also:

Oskar Ryszard Lange (I); Karl Heinrich Marx (I); Marxism(s) (II); Ludwig Heinrich von Mises (I); Non-Marxian socialist ideas in France (II); Non-Marxian socialist ideas in Britain and the United States (II); Karl Polanyi (I); Gustav Friedrich von Schmoller (I); Adolph Heinrich Gotthilf Wagner (I); Friedrich von Wieser (I).

References and further reading

Bayer, H. (1947), *Sozialisierung und Planwirtschaft*, Vienna: Manz Verlag.
Chaloupek, G. (1987), 'Die Österreichische Schule und der Austromarxismus', *Wirtschaft und Gesellschaft*, **13** (4), 469–86.
Chaloupek, G. (1990), 'The Austrian debate on economic calculation in a socialist economy', *History of Political Economy*, **22** (4), 659–75.
Gerloff, W. (1922), *Steuerwirtschaft und Sozialismus*, Leipzig: Verlag C.L. Hirschfeld.
Goldscheid, R. (1917), *Staatssozialismus oder Staatskapitalismus*, reprinted in R. Hickel (ed.) (1976), *Rudolf Goldscheid/Joseph Schumpeter, Die Finanzkrise des Steuerstaats*, Frankfurt: Suhrkamp Verlag, pp. 40–252.
Grigorovici, T. (1910), *Die Wertlehre bei Marx und Lassalle*, Vienna: Verlag der Wiener Volksbuchhandlung.
Hausmann, F.-R. (2011), *Die Geisteswissenschaften im 'Dritten Reich'*, Frankfurt am Main: Vittorio Klostermann.
Heimann, E. (1922), *Mehrwert und Gemeinwirtschaft*, Berlin: Engelmann Verlag.
Hertzka, T. (1890), *Freiland. Ein soziales Zukunftsbild*, Dresden and Leipzig: E. Pierson's Verlag.
Kautsky, K. (1922), *Die proletarische Revolution und ihr Programm*, Stuttgart and Berlin: J.H.W Dietz-Verlag.
Kozak, T. (1882), *Rodbertus-Jagetzows socialökonomische Ansichten*, Jena: Gustav Fischer Verlag.
Landauer, C.L. (1931), *Planwirtschaft und Verkehrswirtschaft*, Munich and Leipzig: Duncker & Humblot.
Lange, O. (1936–37), 'On the economic theory of socialism', *Review of Economic Studies*, **3** (1/2), 72–98.
Lassalle, F. (1862), *Arbeiterprogramm*, in W. Sombart (ed.) (1919), *Grundlagen und Kritik des Sozialismus*, Zweiter Teil, Berlin: Askanischer Verlag, pp. 3–37.
Lassalle, F. (1919–20), *Gesammelte Reden und Schriften*, ed. E. Bernstein, 12 vols, Berlin: Paul Cassirer Verlag.
Lederer, E. (1920), *Deutschlands Wiederaufbau und weltwirtschaftliche Neueingliederung durch Sozialisierung*, Tübingen: J.C.B. Mohr Verlag.
Lederer, E. (1932), *Planwirtschaft*, Tübingen: J.C.B. Mohr Verlag.
Leichter, O. (1923), *Die Wirtschaftsrechnung in der sozialistischen Gesellschaft*, Vienna: Verlag der Wiener Volksbuchhandlung.
Lowe, A. (1967), 'In memoriam: Eduard Heimann', *Social Research*, **34** (4), 609–12.
Marx, K. (1867), *Das Kapital*, vol. 1, reprinted 1969 in *Marx/Engels Werke*, vol. 23, Berlin: Dietz Verlag.
Marx, K. and F. Engels (1939), *The German Ideology*, pts I and III, New York: International Publishers.
Menger, A. (1890), *Das bürgerliche Recht und die besitzlosen Volksklassen*, 3rd edn 1908, Tübingen: J.C.B. Mohr Verlag.
Menger, A. (1903), *Neue Staatslehre*, Jena: Gustav Fischer-Verlag.
Mises, L. (1922), *Die Gemeinwirtschaft*, Jena: Gustav Fischer-Verlag.
Neurath, O. (1919), 'Wesen und Weg der Sozialisierung', reprinted 1979 in *Wissenschaftliche Weltauffassung, Sozialismus und Logischer Empirismus*, Frankfurt: Suhrkamp Verlag, pp. 242–61.
Neurath, O. (1925), Sozialistische Nützlichkeitsrechnung und kapitalistische Reingewinnrechnung, *Der Kampf*, **18** (10), 391–95.
Ortlieb, H.-D. (1947), *Wandlungen des Sozialismus*, Hamburg: Phönix Verlag.
Peukert, H. (2009), *Rudolf Goldscheid und die Finanzkrise des Steuerstaates*, Graz: Leykam Verlag.
Polanyi, K. (1922), 'Sozialistische Rechnungslegung', *Archiv für Sozialwissenschaft und Sozialpolitik*, **49** (2), 377–420.
Polanyi, K. (1925), 'Neue Erwägungen zu unserer Theorie und Praxis', *Der Kampf*, **18** (1), 18–24.
Rathenau, W. (1918), *Die neue Wirtschaft*, Berlin: S. Fischer Verlag.

Rieter, H. (1999), Entry on *Eduard Heimann*, in H. Hagemann and C.-D. Krohn (eds), *Biographisches Handbuch der deutschsprachigen wirtschaftswissenschaftlichen Emigration nach 1933*, 2 vols, Munich: K.G. Saur Verlag.

Rodbertus, C. (1850), *Sociale Briefe an von Kirchmann, Erster Brief: Die sociale Bedeutung der Staatswirtschaft*, reprinted in K. Diehl and P. Mombert (eds) (1979), *Wirtschaftskrisen*, Berlin: Ullstein Verlag.

Schmoller, G. (1998), *Historisch-ethische Nationalökonomie als Kulturwissenschaft*, Marburg: Metropolis Verlag.

Schumpeter, J.A. (1918), *Die Krise des Steuerstaates*, reprinted in R. Hickel (ed.) (1976), *Rudolf Goldscheid/ Joseph Schumpeter, Die Finanzkrise des Steuerstaats*, Frankfurt: Suhrkamp Verlag, pp. 329–79.

Sering, P. (1948), *Jenseits des Kapitalismus Ein Beitrag zur sozialistischen Neuorientierung*, Vienna: Verlag der Wiener Volksbuchhandlung.

Sombart, W. (1932), *Die Zukunft des Kapitalismus*, Berlin: Buchholz & Weißwange.

Sombart, W. (1934), *Deutscher Sozialismus*, Berlin: Buchholz & Weißwange.

Spengler, O. (1919), *Preußentum und Sozialismus*, reprinted 1932 in *Politische Schriften*, Munich: C.H. Beck-Verlag, pp. 1–105.

Thier, E. (ed.) (1940), *Wegbereiter des deutschen Sozialismus*, Stuttgart: Kröner Verlag.

Vogel, P. (1925), *Hegels Gesellschaftsbegriff und seine geschichtliche Fortbildung durch Lorenz Stein, Marx, Engels und Lassalle*, Berlin: Pan Verlag.

Wagner, A. (1887), *Staatssozialistisches Programm*, in E. Thier (ed.) (1940), *Wegbereiter des deutschen Sozialismus*, Stuttgart: Kröner Verlag, p. 278 ff.

Weissel, E. (1976), *Die Ohnmacht des Sieges*, Vienna: Europaverlag.

Wieser, F. von (1892), 'Großbetrieb und Produktivgenossenschaft', in F.A. Hayek (ed.) (1929), *Gesammelte Abhandlungen*, Tübingen: J.C.B. Mohr, pp. 278–334.

Wissel, R. (1920), *Die Planwirtschaft*, Hamburg: Auer Verlag.

Marxism(s)

Marx and Engels

Marx saw himself as the heir and critic of classical political economy, which concentrated its attention on the production and distribution of the means of subsistence (Dobb 1973). Ricardo and his followers explained the evolution of modern economies in terms of the fundamental conflict between the different social classes in a predominantly agricultural society where the producers enjoyed a bare minimum standard of living and the surplus product was shared between landlords and capitalist farmers. The size of the surplus, relative to total output, set a maximum limit on the rate of growth; actual growth depended on the relative shares of thrifty capitalists and prodigal landlords. Marx himself defined the subject matter of the political economy of capitalism as the production, distribution, consumption and exchange of commodities, which are useful products of human labour destined for sale on markets rather than for direct use. He privileged production over the other categories, not only in the explanation of distribution, consumption and exchange, but also in accounting for the nature of the state and forms of social consciousness.

According to the principle of historical materialism, the relations that define the economic system, and the institutions of politics and the law, as well as the dominant forms of social consciousness, are all ultimately determined by the requirements of the productive forces, which consist of means of production and human labour power. The productive relations are relations of power, and usually also of ownership, over the productive forces. Three propositions are central to historical materialism. The development thesis states that human creative intelligence, reacting to scarcity, makes the productive forces develop over time. The primacy thesis asserts that it is the level of development reached by the productive forces that explains the nature of the productive relations, which in turn account for the nature of the superstructure (non-economic institutions such as the legal system and the state). Most important for the dynamic of history, the fettering thesis states that, when the productive relations become a shackle on the development of the productive forces, they will change in order to break the fetters (Marx 1859 [1971]; Cohen 1978).

Marx distinguished several modes of production, characterised by the different ways in which surplus labour was performed and the resulting surplus product was appropriated. In primitive communism there was little or no surplus and no class stratification. In classical antiquity the critical social relation was that between slaves and slave-owners, while under the feudal mode of production surplus labour was extracted through the serf's obligation to work, without remuneration, for several days each week on the lord's land. In none of these early modes of production were market relations of over-riding importance; the production of commodities was not central to the way in which they operated. In classical antiquity and feudalism, the exploitation of the producers was directly observable. Capitalism, by contrast, is defined by the dominance of commodity production, and above all by the fact that human labour power has itself become a commodity. This gives rise to the appearance that every hour of work is paid for, concealing the underlying reality of surplus labour, which is now produced in the form of surplus value.

The theory of historical materialism maintains that the classical, feudal and capitalist modes of production followed each other in chronological sequence, each serving at first to develop the forces of production but eventually becoming a fetter upon them. Capitalism would in its turn give way to socialism/communism, which, Marx believed, constituted the final stage in the unfettering of human productive potential, with the eventual abolition of the market and the direct regulation of production by society in accordance with genuine human needs. Another typology that Marx used was a three-fold distinction between relations of personal dependence, as in slavery and serfdom, material dependence, in which impersonal market relations concealed the producers' continuing dependence on their own products, and free individuality, a future society where people would control their own lives and cooperate freely with others inside and outside of production (Marx 1857 [1973]: 158).

Most of the central features of the capitalist mode of production were identified by Marx and Engels as early as 1848 in the *Communist Manifesto*, and their analysis has formed the basis for all subsequent developments in Marxian political economy (Hobsbawm 1998). These core features are: exploitation; alienation and fetishism; compulsion to accumulate; concentration and centralisation of capital; constant revolutionising of the means of production; global expansion; social and economic polarisation; intensification of class conflict; increasingly severe economic crises, accompanied by the growth of a reserve army of unemployed workers; development of socialist relations within capitalism; and the eventual replacement of capitalism by socialism/communism through proletarian revolution.

Marx's masterpiece was, of course, his *Capital*, the first volume published in 1867 and the second and third (edited by Engels) only after his death, in 1885 and 1894 respectively (Fine and Saad-Filho 2010; Harvey 2010; Howard and King 1985). For Marx the defining characteristic of capitalism is the relationship between wage labourers and capitalists: capital is defined as a social relation, not primarily as a sum of value or a collection of machines and buildings. In this relationship workers are not only exploited, that is, forced to perform surplus labour or required to work for longer than would be necessary to produce the means of subsistence that they need to keep them alive and able to work. They are also alienated, since the products of their labour have escaped their control and have instead become external forces that increasingly dominate their own producers. Marx sometimes referred to alienation as human self-estrangement, meaning by this that although people exist in a social world of their own collective making they relate to it only as strangers. Alienation is an objective social condition; its reflection in human consciousness is commodity fetishism, a distorted view of the economic world in which historically contingent social relations are seen as the natural properties of things.

All pre-modern legal, political, religious and cultural constraints on competition are progressively eliminated as capitalism develops, and the pressure on individual capitalists intensifies. Machine production drives out the earlier technology of manufacturing (literally, making things by hand), so that the economic advantages of large-scale production are increasingly evident and the processes of concentration and centralisation of capital accelerate. Individual units of capital become larger and the number of capitalists able to survive in any branch of industry diminishes. Peasants, petty traders and small handicraft producers disappear as the polarisation of society between large capitalists and propertyless wage labourers becomes more and more extreme. Increasingly this occurs on a global scale, as capitalists pursue a world market for their commodities.

Hours of work increase, as do the intensity of labour and the workers' experience of alienation. Real wages may fall, remain constant or even rise somewhat, but relative to profits they continually decline, and the insecurity of proletarian existence grows. This is the material basis for increasingly acute class conflict, which is accentuated by the socialising effects of the factory system. Working-class radicalism is further provoked by periodic economic crises, which throw many of them out of work and demonstrate that capitalism has itself now become a fetter on the development of the productive forces. Its own technology and social organisation point unerringly towards the socialist/communist future that will be realised, sooner rather than later, through proletarian revolution.

Marx attempted to formalise his vision of capitalism into a systematic model of accumulation and crisis. For this he needed a theory of value so that the fundamental relationships could be expressed in a clear and coherent manner. The qualitative dimension of Marx's value theory expresses the profound but frequently neglected truth that a social division of labour underpins each individual act of market exchange. People relate to each other not merely through buying and selling in the market place but also, and more fundamentally, by cooperating in a social process of production. Since the physical properties of commodities differ, the only quality that they have in common is that they are products of human labour, and this defines their value. The quantitative dimension of Marx's theory of value is concerned with the magnitude of value. This, he argued, depends on the amount of labour embodied in a commodity, although this need not and in fact normally will not equal the price at which the commodity is actually sold.

Marx distinguished dead from living labour, where dead labour is contained in the produced means of production (machinery and raw materials) that are used in the course of production. Only part of the workers' living labour is paid for; their unpaid or surplus labour is what produces surplus value (s), which is in turn the source of profit, interest and rent. Capital has two components. The first is constant capital (c), the value of which is merely transferred from the means of production to the final product without increasing in quantity. The second is variable capital (v), embodied in the wage-goods consumed by the workers, which expands its value during production because of the performance of surplus labour. Thus the value of any particular commodity has three components, c, v and s, and the same is true of the total product of society as a whole.

Some of the difficulties with this quantitative labour theory of value were acknowledged by Marx himself, in particular the problems associated with the payment of rent, the distinction between productive and unproductive activities, the application of the law of value to the market for labour power, and the continuing diversity of the working class in terms of its skills and capabilities. Even more troublesome was the transformation problem, which required Marx was to distinguish the labour value of a commodity from the price of production at which it was actually sold, and also to distinguish the profit accruing to individual capitalists from the surplus value produced by their workers. However, he concluded that value determined price, and surplus value determined profit, even though competition inevitably transformed the first of these categories into the second.

In volume II of *Capital*, Marx used his value categories to set out a formal model of capital accumulation and to explain why the process of accumulation necessarily involved cyclical crises. He distinguished two sectors, one producing capital goods and the other consumer goods; sometimes he drew a further distinction between wage-goods and luxuries. His models of simple reproduction (zero growth) and expanded reproduction (positive growth) reveal that the rate of accumulation depends on the proportion of surplus value that capitalists decide (or are compelled) to devote to accumulation, and also on the rate of profit. Marx's objective here was not to demonstrate that smooth growth was likely but precisely the opposite: to show why it is not likely to occur. In volume III of *Capital* he developed a model of the falling rate of profit in which rising productivity in industrial production was reflected in a tendency for the organic composition of capital (c/v) to increase more rapidly than the rate of exploitation (s/v). This, he argued, would eventually result in a falling rate of accumulation, and this would vindicate the fettering thesis that is central to historical materialism.

The Marxism of the Second International, *c.* 1890–1914

In the 1890s the revisionist Eduard Bernstein challenged many of the fundamental tenets of Marx's system. He was opposed by more orthodox Marxists, some of the most important of whom, including Karl Kautsky and Rudolf Hilferding, later came to accept much of the revisionist position (Howard and King 1989: chs 4–6, 14). Bernstein argued that capitalism had changed, and its internal contradictions had become much less sharp. German society was becoming less polarised, he claimed, not more so as the orthodox Marxists maintained, and there was real scope for an alliance between the working class and the liberal bourgeoisie to implement economic and social reforms in the interests of the workers. In *Finance Capital*, published in 1910 but largely completed four years earlier, Hilferding defended Marx's classic vision of capitalism against Bernstein and the revisionists; this, and not its detailed analysis of money and finance, is the core message of the book. He argued that the contradictions of capitalism were becoming more acute, not less. As a result of the growing centralisation and concentration of capital and the increased power of finance, social polarisation was increasing. Middle-class liberalism in Germany was both weak and in rapid decline, as the growth of finance capital and its imperialist policies strengthened authoritarian, militarist and racist views among the middle class. The revisionists were deluding themselves that piecemeal reform of the system through a class alliance was feasible.

For Hilferding the term finance capital had several layers of meaning, denoting not only one form taken by capital but also a phase in the circulation of capital and an increasingly powerful sectional interest within the capitalist class. Finally, and most importantly, finance capital represented a stage in the development of the capitalist mode of production, and hence also a stage on the road to socialism. Finance was becoming more important, and those who controlled it were becoming more powerful, owing to increased economies of scale in industry and the growing need for bank finance to carry out the centralisation of productive capital. Financial capitalists therefore became more influential, relative to industrial and commercial capitalists. As a stage of capitalism, Hilferding maintained, finance capital had its own distinctive properties and its own laws of development, above all the rise of monopoly, growing state involvement in economic life, and imperialist expansion and inter-imperialist wars.

In his theory of imperialism Hilferding argued that tariffs, once used only to protect infant industries, were now employed to bolster cartels, giving them permanent security against import competition and permitting them to dump their excess production overseas. High prices and correspondingly restricted markets at home were intensifying the search for export opportunities for surplus commodities, while the banks were increasingly involved in the export of surplus capital to underdeveloped countries, where the organic composition of capital was low and the rate of profit was high. In each major capitalist nation, finance capital aimed to establish the largest possible economic territory, closing that territory to foreign competition by means of protective tariffs and thereby reserving it as an exclusive area of highly profitable exploitation.

Hilferding's description of imperialism as "the policy of finance capital" has given rise to some misunderstanding. He was not suggesting that imperialism was a policy option. On the contrary, in the epoch of finance capital it was a necessity: capitalism could pursue no other policy than that of imperialism. This had enormous political consequences. First, since global cartels were more difficult to form and even less stable than purely domestic price agreements, the struggle for economic territory would lead inevitably to a sharpening of international tensions. Second, because each national finance capital needed a strong government to defend its interests against foreign interlopers, the traditional bourgeois hostility to the state had become a thing of the past. Third, the cosmopolitan capitalism of the nineteenth century had given way to an aggressive nationalism. Hilferding concluded that the increasing danger of war, and the growing tax burden of armaments expenditures, would convert both the proletariat and, eventually, the middle classes into enemies of imperialism.

The Austro-Marxist philosopher Max Adler (1915) agreed with Hilferding that imperialism resulted from the insatiable and uncontrolled drive of capital to realise itself in circumstances in which the export of capital had become even more essential than the export of commodities. Capital was now driven by a new, much more violent desire for investment opportunities that would provide new sources of surplus value. This had radically and brutally transformed the earlier, more peaceful nature of the capitalist system. But it also confirmed the correctness of the materialist interpretation of history, and offered real hope for the future. Economic development had outgrown the existing political and economic forms, and now required a new supra-national order to eliminate external conflicts at the same time as internal conflicts were overcome. Such a new international system could only be a socialist one. In this way, Adler concluded, the ideology of imperialism would give way to the idea of socialism.

Communists and their Opponents, 1914–45

These optimistic words were written soon after the outbreak of the First World War, which had already led to a deep and permanent split in the international socialist movement. The divisions became even greater with the October Revolution in Russia in 1917. Although Hilferding did not resist the war, and was no friend of Lenin or the Bolsheviks, the impact of *Finance Capital* was substantial, and sustained. Many of its principal themes were taken up by Rosa Luxemburg, in her *Accumulation of Capital* (Luxemburg 1913 [1951]) and by Nikolai Bukharin, whose *Imperialism and World Economy* (Bukharin 1915) was the major direct influence on V.I. Lenin's much better-known *Imperialism: the Highest Stage of Capitalism* (Lenin 1916 [1968]). After the Bolshevik revolution in

October 1917, Lenin's text soon became the principal authority on these matters in the Marxism of the newly established Third International (Howard and King 1989: ch. 13).

In fact the basic ideas of Hilferding, Bukharin and Lenin were broadly similar, and owed much to the work of contemporary liberal anti-imperialists, especially J.A. Hobson. They all identified a direct link between imperialism and the economic contradictions of advanced European capitalism, in Hobson's case a strong tendency to underconsumption in the metropolitan countries resulting from the maldistribution of income; Kautsky had made a similar case as early as 1884 in his analysis of the French colonisation of Indochina. Luxemburg took the argument even further, using Marx's two-sector models of accumulation to claim – wrongly – that the continued expansion of any capitalist economy was in principle impossible without constant access to new non-capitalist markets.

When the First World War overwhelmed the international socialist movement, Kautsky sought desperately to show that imperialist conflict was not inevitable, pointing to the strong possibility of an ultra-imperialism, a sort of global cartel of the leading capitalist powers that would agree to the peaceful partition of the world and to a harmonious division of the spoils of imperialist penetration. Bukharin and Lenin denied that this was possible, invoking the law of uneven and combined development. Just as cartels were weakened and eventually destroyed by differences in the cost levels and rates of technical progress in individual companies, they argued, so international agreements between imperialist powers would founder on the conflict between new and dynamic capitalist states and the less progressive, longer-established powers with a large vested interest in the status quo. The core principle of Communist political economy between the wars, derived from Lenin's *Imperialism*, was the claim that capitalism had reached a new, final and extremely dangerous stage in its history, in which the means of violence monopolised by the state were used by capitalists to suppress the working class at home and to extend their reach across the globe. In the 1930s this crystallised into the Stalinist conception of state monopoly capitalism, or *stamocap*, which was depicted by writers such as Eugen Varga as the last, most decadent and easily the most vicious stage of the capitalist mode of production.

This carried very clear implications for the economic prospects of not just the advanced capitalist nations but also the backward, dependent, colonial or semi-colonial regions. Marx himself had argued that imperialism was indispensable in spreading capitalist relations throughout the globe. He claimed that non-European societies lacked internal dynamism, so that imperialism was essential to introduce progress (Warren 1980). Luxemburg took a very similar position, which was stridently denied by Communist theorists after 1917. Capitalism was no longer a source of progress, they argued, but instead represented an insuperable barrier to successful industrialisation, using its military and economic power to retard development in backward areas. Only through adopting the Soviet model could colonial peoples hope to achieve any substantial social progress.

This Soviet model itself was largely improvised, since Marx and Engels had provided little or no guidance on the economic operations of a post-capitalist economy. In the Second International, too, the economic problems of socialism were essentially assumed away, since it was supposed that the development of capitalism itself would solve them. Hilferding's assertion that the proletariat need only seize the six largest Berlin banks was typical, and entirely unhelpful. Bourgeois writers like Enrico Barone, who claimed that rational economic calculation under communism would inevitably require the imple-mentation of capitalist economic principles, were not taken seriously until Oskar Lange's advocacy of market socialism in the late 1930s. Such arguments were in any case of very doubtful relevance to the central problem faced by Soviet Russia, which was how to introduce modern industry into a backward and overwhelmingly peasant society suffi-ciently rapidly to allow it to resist a new invasion by hostile capitalist powers. After 1917 there were genuine debates on the course that the new Communist regime should follow, and significant advances in the theory of socialist growth were made by theorists such as Evgeny Preobrazhensky and G.A. Feld'man until the early 1930s, when the Stalinist dic-tatorship made further serious intellectual activity impossible (Howard and King 1989: ch. 15; 1992: chs 2–3). After 1945, Western Communists drew on the Soviet experience to set out a development strategy for the ex-colonial nations.

Some social democrats, like Kautsky, were early and sustained critics of the Soviet model while others, like Otto Bauer, took a more favourable position. In the 1920s Hilferding identified a new stage of development, organised capitalism, in which the most objectionable features of competitive capitalism had been superseded by the growth of monopoly, increased trade union power, and government regulation of the market in the interests of the working class. In effect Hilferding had (belatedly) made his peace with the revisionists, though his expectations of a gradual and peaceful path to socialism through piecemeal reform were very soon shattered by events (Howard and King 1989: ch. 14). In 1929 the Polish socialist, Henryk Grossmann, foreshadowed the economic breakdown of capitalism with an elaborate version of the falling rate of profit model that Marx had set out in *Capital*, volume III (Howard and King 1989: ch. 16).

In the 1930s the length and severity of the Great Depression and the rise of fascism stimulated interest in Marxian crisis theory throughout the capitalist world, including (at long last) the United States (Howard and King 1992: chs 1, 5). Marx's recognition of the need for surplus value to be realised through the profitable sale of commodities, and his dismissal of Say's law as "childish babble", seemed to place him on the same side as John Maynard Keynes. One of Keynes's most prominent disciples, Joan Robinson, wrote a book-length comparison of Marx and Keynes, not always to the latter's advantage (Robinson 1942). She had come under the influence of the Polish social democrat Michał Kalecki, who had discovered the main features of Keynes's theory independently, and was an admirer of the Marxian work of Luxemburg and Mikhail Tugan-Baranovsky.

Meanwhile Bauer had produced the first mathematical model of underconsumption, which was introduced to a wider readership by Paul Sweezy, an American with Keynesian sympathies. Sweezy's *Theory of Capitalist Development* was probably the most important English-language text on Marxian political economy to appear in the twentieth century (Sweezy 1942 [1970]). Rejecting both the falling rate of profit theory and the necessity of expressing the analysis in labour value terms, Sweezy argued that underconsumption was the principal cause of realisation crises (crises of effective demand). It was offset to some extent by the growth of unproductive consumption, including the huge sales costs of monopolistic corporations, and by increasing state expenditure, above all on war and preparations for war. The broad outlines of the post-1945 theory of monopoly capital, and the closely related critique of military Keynesianism, were already evident here.

Another Austro-Marxist, Max Adler, took a rather different line. Influenced by his compatriot Emil Lederer, Adler argued that permanent mass unemployment was a necessary consequence of the continuing and rapid development of capitalist technology. In the unlikely event of a new upswing in the world economy, Adler maintained, only a part of the unemployed would be employed again. The continued operation of the capitalist system was now possible only by eliminating millions of workers from production and reducing the wages of the others. This, he concluded, was a fatal measure that would intensify the crisis rather than overcoming it. Thus the growth of technological unemployment was reinforcing the tendency towards underconsumption (Adler 1933).

Marxian Political Economy in the Cold War, 1945–91

Most of the significant developments in Marxian political economy in the first two decades after the war came from Western Europe and, to a lesser extent, the United States. Important work was also done in Japan, where Kei Shibata had made impressive contributions in the 1930s and the postwar period saw the emergence of the idiosyncratic and largely non-transferable Japanese Marxism of the Uno School. More influential was Nobuo Okishio, writing in the early 1960s, who gave his name to a theorem demonstrating that technical progress could only reduce the rate of profit if it also led to an increase in real wages. The significance of the Okishio theorem was, however, soon challenged by Western writers such as Neri Salvadori and Anwar Shaikh (Howard and King 1992: 316–17). The full history of Marxian political economy in Japan is yet to be written (or at least translated into English); it will prove to be a rich and complicated story.

Nothing of any consequence emerged in this period from the Soviet Union or from most of its eastern European satellites, although Poland, where Kalecki returned in 1954, was something of an exception to the rule. An influential study by the Frankfurt School philosopher Herbert Marcuse, now living in the United States, stressed the magical and ritual elements in Soviet Marxism (Marcuse 1961). The moribund nature of Stalinism was confirmed by the way in which even its intellectual sympathisers in the West took increasingly heretical positions on questions of political economy. Maurice Dobb, for example, attempted a marriage between Marx and Marshall; Sweezy preferred Mao's China, and later Castro's Cuba, to the Soviet Union; and, rather later, Ian Steedman sought to replace Marx's theory of value with that of Ricardo. The Communist authorities did make one valuable contribution, with the publication (at least before 1991 at greatly subsidised prices) of the collected works of Marx and Engels, first in German and then in other European languages. The final book in the 50-volume series appeared in 2005 (Marx and Engels 1975–2005); it is reported, however, that a project to publish the pair's complete works (in German) will require no less than 120 volumes.

Most important was the appearance of Marx's early writings, above all the *Economic and Philosophical Manuscripts* (1844), and other major unpublished work, including his *Grundrisse* (1857) and *Theories of Surplus Value* (1862–63). These writings were a very powerful influence on the distinctively Western variety of Marxism that emerged after 1945 (Anderson 1976). They highlighted the Hegelian influence on Marx's own thinking, both in his youth and later, as he prepared to write *Capital*, and had a profound impact on many Western Marxists. It was not always a benign influence, since it tended to encourage a dogmatically essentialist interpretation of Marxian political economy, especially with respect to crisis theory. Since the tendency for the rate of profit to fall was an essential feature of capitalism, the Hegelian Marxists maintained, it could not be overcome, and therefore capitalism itself could not be seriously reformed. This easily transmuted itself into a fatalism reminiscent of the orthodox Marxism of the Second International, no less debilitating for now being confined to revolutionary Maoists and Trotskyists. Later, once it became apparent that capitalism was here to stay, essentialist Marxism proved a popular road to conservatism and neoliberalism.

This was only one strand of Western Marxism, which was also characterised by a strong reaction against narrowly economistic thinking that minimised the role of social and political institutions, of ideology and values, in the evolution of the capitalist mode of production. Western Marxism was characterised by a pronounced shift in theoretical concerns, away from economics narrowly defined and towards philosophy (again, see Anderson 1976). The Frankfurt School was an important influence after 1945, as (rather later) were the French regulation school and proponents of the social structure of accumulation in the United States. In Italy, Lucio Colletti (1972) made an influential critique of the prevailing mechanistic conception of the economy as something distinct from conscious human action and subject to impersonal, quasi-natural laws of motion (Redhead 2010).

Earlier theories of imperialism continued to influence Marxian analysis of the problems facing the poor, backward or under-developed countries of the Third World. The most important single text was Paul Baran's *Political Economy of Growth*, which was broadly in the Leninist tradition but also contained some notably unorthodox themes, above all the new concept of economic surplus. Baran defined the actual surplus as the difference between current output and current consumption; the potential surplus was the difference between potential output and essential consumption (Baran 1957: 132–3). These concepts were derived from, but not equivalent to, the conventional Marxian notion of aggregate surplus value. Baran used them to criticise advanced capitalism for its propensity to waste a large proportion of the potential surplus, both because actual output was almost always well below its potential level and because actual consumption was invariably much larger than essential consumption.

These ideas underpinned his approach to development economics. Despite the deep and widespread poverty, Baran noted, poor colonial and ex-colonial countries always produced a very substantial (actual) economic surplus; if they did not, the peasants would be unable to pay rent to the landlords. However, this actual surplus was much smaller than the potential surplus, and it was largely wasted – on inessential consumption by landed elites, and through being siphoned off by the advanced capitalist countries by means of naked plunder, colonial taxation, super-profits from overseas investments, and unequal exchange in international trade. Formal independence, Baran argued, made little or no difference to this massive process of international exploitation, which was responsible for perpetuating economic backwardness. Thus surplus transfer from poor to rich countries played the central role in Baran's analysis of informal imperialism in the post-colonial age. His book was immensely influential, for example, on Samir Amin (1974) and Arghiri Emmanuel, the latter claiming that the most important source of surplus transfer was unequal exchange (and not super-profits from the export of capital). Wages were so very much lower in poor countries than in the metropolitan heartlands, for work of equal skill and intensity, that commodities containing very small amounts of American labour (for example) exchanged for commodities in which very much larger quantities of (for example) Lebanese labour were embodied (Emmanuel 1972).

The political implications of surplus transfer were profound. It explained both the passivity of the working class in the United States, which had been bought off by a small share in the proceeds of imperialism and constituted a sort of super-aristocracy of labour, and the revolutionary potential of the proletarian and (especially) the peasant masses in the colonial and ex-colonial territories, which really did have "nothing to lose but their chains". It also gave the world as a whole a revolutionary subject, which was palpably lacking in Sweezy's earlier work. However, it gave no cause to expect a revolutionary upsurge in the advanced capitalist countries, where all classes were benefiting, to a greater or lesser extent, at the expense of "the wretched of the earth". According to Mao Tse-tung and his supporters, by the 1960s the Soviet Union itself had become an important part of this exploitative labour aristocracy.

Marxian reactions to the remarkable and unexpected success of the advanced capitalist economies during the Golden Age (1945–1973) were mixed. Had advanced capitalism changed so fundamentally that earlier crisis theories needed to be radically revised? This again raised the question of the relationship between Marx and Keynes. If underconsumption was the fundamental contraction of capitalism, and if the social democratic reforms inspired by Keynesian macroeconomics had overcome it, then perhaps the system was no longer seriously crisis-prone. Kalecki now claimed that working-class pressure had forced capitalists reluctantly to accept a crucial reform of their own system, in which the state now guaranteed sufficient effective demand to maintain something close to full employment and, by allowing real wages to rise in line with labour productivity, had considerably improved the real incomes of the masses. This had resulted in a weakening of anti-capitalist attitudes among the Western working class, making the "crucial reform" a matter of real historical significance (King 2013).

The regulation school and social structure of accumulation theorists took a rather similar line. They claimed that, in the new "Fordist" stage of development in the advanced capitalist countries, political and social changes had overcome the earlier proneness of the system to underconsumption. The acceptance of collective wage bargaining by trade unions had kept real wages increasing at roughly the same rate as labour productivity, while the big expansion of the welfare state after 1945 had introduced built-in stabilisers that prevented effective demand from collapsing when a crisis broke out (Boyer 1990; McDonough et al. 2010). These essentially revisionist ideas had a profound influence both on European social democrats and on the reformist Eurocommunists who, by the early 1970s, controlled the Communist movement in several nations, including Italy and Spain.

Three objections were raised against them. First, underconsumption was not the only, or the most important, economic contradiction of capitalism. Second, the supposed reform of the system was itself contradictory, and therefore unstable and transient. Third, to the extent that underconsumption had been overcome, it was through quite different and much more objectionable mechanisms than those advocated by the Keynesians. The first criticism either relied on the *Capital* volume III falling rate of profit theory or drew on Marx's scattered remarks in volume I about the threat to profits posed by the sharp fall in the reserve army of the unemployed in any strong boom. This latter point reinforced the second objection: as Kalecki had recognised as early as 1943, a sustained period of full employment in peacetime would pose a serious threat to discipline in the factories. The revival of trade union militancy in the late 1960s was accompanied both by rapid wage inflation and by increasing resistance to capitalist control of the labour process that inhibited productivity growth, resulting in a severe profit squeeze. By the end of the 1970s there was clear evidence of a deep crisis of Fordism, reflected in a sharp fall in the rate of profit (Weisskopf 1979).

The third objection came from Baran and Sweezy, in their very widely read book, *Monopoly Capital*. Here they proposed a law of the rising surplus, according to which both the actual and the potential surplus tended constantly to increase as a proportion of both potential and actual output. Large oligopolistic corporations were continually reducing their costs through technical improvements to the processes of production, but since tacit collusion prevented prices from falling the result was constantly growing profit margins. The growing surplus was clear evidence of the chronic realisation problem faced by advanced capitalism, but also reflected the deeply objectionable ways in which it had been overcome. The surplus had been absorbed through rising consumption and investment expenditure by capitalists, increasing advertising and other marketing expenses, the sales effort, growth in civilian government expenditure, military expenditure and imperialism. To the extent that none of these outlets proved sufficient, they concluded, there was a constant danger of economic stagnation in monopoly capital. In practice, they claimed, militarism and imperialism could not offer a permanent cure for stagnation, but their arguments are not entirely convincing. Neither is their blunt rejection of any state capitalist, social democratic or welfare state alternatives to stagnation, even though in the mid-1960s these could be observed, and seemed to be operating quite successfully, in much of Northern and Western Europe. They were on much firmer ground in condemning the irrationality of a system that relied so heavily upon waste; in demonstrating the dependence of monopoly capital on racism, alienation and the fetishism of commodities; and in attacking "the emptiness, the degradation, and the suffering which poison human existence in this society" (Baran and Sweezy 1966: 348–9).

There was an implicit Kaleckian macroeconomic model in *Monopoly Capital*, which yet again posed the question of the analytical relationship between Marx and Keynes. One possible conclusion was that capitalist economies were precariously balanced on a knife-edge between low wages, which led to underconsumption, and high wages, which caused a profit squeeze. Reform or no reform, the system thus remained fundamentally unstable. Some post-Keynesians had strong Kaleckian sympathies and were left social democrats or Eurocommunists in politics. However, a rapprochement between Marxians and post-Keynesians faced some significant obstacles, not least the Marxians' inability to come up with a convincing theory of money and credit. Marx himself had anticipated the endogenous money approach that was being asserted, a century later, by post-Keynesians such as Nicholas Kaldor in their critique of monetarism, but he never succeeded in freeing himself from a commodity-money approach that saw the value of money (the inverse of the price level) as being determined by the labour value of gold. Non-commodity money in the form of paper money and bank deposits were merely "tokens" for gold, their value depending entirely on how many units were issued per ounce of gold. This led straight to the quantity theory of money in everything but name (Nelson 1999).

In the highly charged political atmosphere of the late 1960s and early 1970s, all these issues were very widely discussed by students and younger academics, not all of whom were willing to identify themselves as Marxists of any description. Often the less exclusive and more ambiguous label of radical economics or radical political economy was adopted, as it was by the founders of the Union for Radical Political Economics (URPE), established in the United States in 1968. This was a period in which nothing was sacred, including at least some of the fundamental principles of Marxian political economy.

One such principle was the labour theory of value. The increased interest in the Hegelian roots of Marx's thought led to a reinterpretation of the qualitative aspects of value theory (Faccarello 1997). There was also continuing discussion of the quantitative aspects. Marx had claimed that the transformation problem affected only individual values and individual surplus values. In aggregate, he insisted, the sum of values equals the sum of prices, and the sum of surplus values equals the sum of profits. But these two propositions are true only under very special circumstances: the "borderline" or numeraire commodity, with an organic composition of capital equal to the social average, must be produced by means of production which themselves have an average organic composition, and so too must their means of production, and so ad infinitum. The "new solution" proposed in the 1980s by Gérard Duménil in France and Duncan Foley in the United States reformulated the invariance conditions, so that they applied only to the net product and to variable capital, but this carried with it a different set of problems; most obviously, the rate of profit was not unaffected by the transformation process (Howard and King 1992: 276–8).

Piero Sraffa's important rehabilitation of Ricardian economics, published in 1960, was silent on these questions (as on many others), but eventually a former student of Sraffa's, Ronald Meek, discovered that it offered a solution to Marx's problem: Sraffa's standard commodity was, in fact, the borderline commodity that Marx had been looking for (Meek 1973). Unfortunately, this also pointed to the irrelevance of the entire discussion. Sraffa had provided a rigorous model of profits and prices of production in a competitive capitalist economy without making any reference to either labour value or surplus value. Thus the principle of Occam's razor could be invoked against Marx, as it soon was by Steedman (1977). A theory of value founded on the objective conditions of production rather than on the subjective preferences of individuals did not require that any reference be made to labour values, Steedman claimed, and the existence of exploitation could be established independently of the notion of surplus value. The subversive nature of Sraffa's work had already been noted by Italian theorists like Claudio Napoleoni (1975), and also by Colletti, who argued that it "implies the demolition of the entire foundations of Marx's analysis" (Colletti 1974 [2011]: 142).

Even more heretical were the Analytical Marxists who, as the name implies, made a conscious effort to apply the standards of (Anglo-Saxon) analytical philosophy to Marxism, and to eradicate Hegelian influences, or at least Hegelian modes of expression, from Marxian thought. If nothing else, this improved the clarity of the arguments and gave rise to some valuable work, especially Gerry Cohen's reformulation of the materialist conception of history (Cohen 1978). Other Analytical Marxists went too far, however, when they adopted a strong version of the principle of methodological individualism and combined it with the theory of rational choice, taken directly from neoclassical economics. Rational Choice Marxists like Jon Elster and John Roemer claimed that all propositions in Marxian political economy must be expressed in terms of (that is, reduced to) statements about the maximising behaviour of rational individuals. This required a substantial revision of the theory of exploitation, with class antagonism between capitalists and wage-labourers largely disappearing from the analysis. The legacy of Analytical Marxism remains disputed, but few have been convinced by its insistence of the need to provide microfoundations for Marxian economics (Veneziani 2012).

After the Fall: Marxian Political Economy since 1991

As a matter of strict intellectual principle, the fall of the Berlin Wall in 1989 and the disintegration of the Soviet Union two years later should have had little or no effect on Marxian political economy, since the bureaucratic gerontocracy that Mikhail Gorbachev inherited in 1985 and attempted unsuccessfully to reform had almost nothing in common with any variant of Marxism. In practice, though, the collapse of communism did undermine the influence of Marxian ideas even among radical social scientists, not least in economics. By 1995 Anthony Brewer, the author of a well-received and largely sympathetic survey of Marxian theories of imperialism, was justifying the neglect of Marxian political economy in the mainstream literature on the grounds that Marx was such a poor economist that it was entirely correct to ignore him (see Brewer 1995 and the related mini-symposium). There were also many more apostates.

The last quarter of a century has also seen a number of more or less innovative developments, which indicate that Marxian political economy has a future as well as a past. First, the temporal single system school has advocated a genuinely new approach to the transformation problem, arguing that both the Bortkiewicz and the Sraffian approaches had incorrectly applied neoclassical equilibrium theorising to a problem that must be solved without it. In a sense this had been anticipated in 1977 by Anwar Shaikh, who suggested that Marx's transformation procedure should be seen not as the conclusion to the analysis but rather as the first stage of an iterative process. However, Shaikh's proposed procedure led asymptotically to the Bortkiewicz solution, which was repudiated by advocates of the "temporal single system" approach. They in turn have been attacked, savagely so, by Ernesto Screpanti (2005), for "solving" the problem by assuming it away. Certainly any trace of Marx's "counteracting tendencies" to the falling rate of profit have disappeared; even "economy in the use of constant capital" now serves to reduce the profit rate instead of increasing it (Freeman and Carchedi 1996).

Second, an intriguing effort to marry Marxist ideas with post-modernism has been made by David Ruccio et al. (1996), who advocate a "non-deterministic" or postmodern version of Marxism that draws on American post-analytic epistemology and on French post-structuralism. They emphasise decentred, multiple, endogenous subjectivities and social processes rather than objective laws of motion, and advocate a more complex notion of causation, in which everything is seen as both cause and effect. Postmodern Marxists reject the traditional Marxian view that the base (economy) and superstructure (politics, culture and the rest of society) must be analysed hierarchically, and reinterpret the labour theory of value as a class analysis of the mutual determination of production and exchange. Thus over-determination and difference are crucial concepts. They pay great attention to questions of race, gender and exploitation within the family and other institutions. There is no single "logic of capital", they maintain, but rather open-ended, conjunctural trajectories of capitalist corporations. The relationship between the "real" economy and the monetary system is one of complex interaction, not one-directional causation. Uncertainty must be taken very seriously, which provides an alternative potential link with post-Keynesian macroeconomic theory to that supplied by Kalecki. Postmodern Marxism has something in common with the final, non-economistic, chapters of *Monopoly Capital*, and represents yet another, distinctively American, attempt to reformulate Marxian political economy.

A third innovation has seen the emergence of a Marxian variant of environmental economics, which had been anticipated by Sweezy in some of his final articles. Writers like Paul Burkett, Michael Perelman and John Bellamy Foster have argued that Marx was not an anti-ecological thinker, but rather that ecology was central to his thought. The legacy of Hegelian Marxism, Foster suggests, was to deny the possibility of applying dialectical reasoning to nature, as Engels had unconvincingly attempted to do in his *Dialectics of Nature* (1872–83). On Foster's interpretation, however, "Marx's world-view was deeply, and indeed systematically, ecological" (Foster 2000: viii). For Marx, then, the alienation of human labour was closely connected to the alienation of human beings from nature. However, Foster has little to say about the environmental destruction perpetrated in the course of Stalinist industrialisation, which was often adduced by critics of Marxism as evidence of the malign influence of the labour theory of value, a dogma which appeared to deny any role to nature in the creation of wealth.

Fourth, and with greater success, Marxian economists have taken up the challenges posed by the interpretation of globalisation. Here they are on much more natural home territory, for as Eric Hobsbawm (1998) noted in his one hundred and fiftieth anniversary edition, the *Communist Manifesto* was especially far-sighted on this question. Hobsbawm was not himself an economic theorist, but he did write the best single text on the social and economic history of twentieth-century capitalism (Hobsbawm 1994) and also co-edited a major five-volume series, in Italian, on the history of Marxism (Hobsbawm et al. 1978–82), the first volume of which was also published in English (Hobsbawm 1982). Possibly the best of a large and growing Marxian literature on globalisation is Glyn (2006). The Alter-Globalisation movement of the late 1990s, with the slogan "another world is possible", had its roots in the Marxian and other radical theories of underdevelopment that were discussed in the previous section, as did the "Occupy" movement that flourished briefly in many countries in the aftermath of the global financial crisis of 2008–09.

Fifth, and closely related, is the increasingly salient issue of imperialism. Between 1945 and 1989 a combination of the Cold War and the United States' economic and military dominance cast doubt on the relevance of the Hilferding–Lenin thesis concerning the inescapable and very dangerous rivalry between the world's leading capitalist powers. With the rapid and continuing relative decline of the United States' economy, and the rise of China, it is not only Marxians who have begun to draw historical parallels with growth of tension between Britain and German before the outbreak of global warfare in 1914. However, Marxian political economy does have something distinctive to contribute on this vitally important issue, since it emphasises competition for raw materials, markets and outlets for surplus capital as the fundamental influence on the military and diplomatic policies of capitalist nation-states (Sutcliffe 2006).

Sixth, there is the question of the rise of neoliberalism, "the return of the market", that almost no one foresaw and that falsified the most important of all Marx's long-range historical predictions. It also confounded the expectations of almost all of the theorists of the Second and Third Internationals. Howard and King (2008) claim that the rise of neoliberalism can in fact be explained in terms of the principles of historical materialism, that is, as the result of developments in both the forces of production and the social relations of production favouring the broadening and deepening of market relations and undermining resistance to them. On this account, Marx and his disciples had been asking precisely the right questions, but they gave precisely the wrong answers. Politically the rise of neoliberalism confirmed everything that the Marxists had always believed about the inherently predatory and essentially unreformable nature of the capitalist system. Capitalism, it is now clear, is indeed prone to ever-increasing inequalities in income and wealth; the capitalist state is the executive committee of the bourgeoisie, and the revisionist notion that it could be used in the interests of the working class has always been an illusion. However, this offers little consolation.

Marxian Political Economy in 2016: "What is Left?"

Marx would have been both greatly surprised and deeply disappointed to find capitalism alive and kicking 130 years after his death; the same can be said of Lenin, whose description of capitalism (in 1916) as "moribund" proved to be very wide of the mark. They would also have been saddened by the failure of all attempts to supersede the capitalist mode of production. They would not, perhaps, have been quite so surprised by the transformation of the global world economy in the course of the twentieth century, in both quantity and quality, since they regarded constant revolutionising of the means of production as part of the very essence of capitalism. Some of the challenges faced by Marxian political economists in the 2010s are thus, necessarily, very different from those faced by their predecessors in 1883 or 1917. They include pressing questions of race and gender; the prospect of imminent environmental catastrophe; and a continuing process of the financialisation of capital that was only temporarily slowed by the global financial crisis of 2008–09. Other issues are more familiar. Marx was wrong about very many things, but he was right to insist on the class nature of capitalist society, on the contradictory and unstable character of the capitalist economy, and on its essentially global reach. This gives Marxian political economy a head start over all its competitors in analysing the truly important problems of our age (Kotz 2015).

Whether Marxian ideas can inspire a viable alternative to capitalism is another question altogether. Paul Sweezy (who died in 2004) ended up as a left social democrat, regarding the abolition of capitalism as impracticable for the foreseeable future and instead arguing for a large public sector and a substantial redistribution of income and wealth within the existing social order. This would not have satisfied Herbert Marcuse, whose critique of "one-dimensional man" hinged on the way in which capitalism was whittling away individuality, freedom and the ability to dissent (Marcuse 1964 [1991]). It would certainly not have pleased Marx, whose own notion of "free individuality" (on which Marcuse drew heavily) pointed to a future society with no state (or there would be political oppression); no classes (or exploitation would continue); no markets (or alienation and fetishism would not be overcome); and no scarcity (or labour would still have to be compulsory). Marx denied that this vision was utopian, claiming instead that it was foreshadowed by developments within the capitalist mode of production itself, which would soon eliminate scarcity, greatly diminish the role of the market, and create a class-conscious proletariat that would gladly replace capitalism with a state-free, class-free, market-free, scarcity-free communist society. This was, to put it mildly, very optimistic, and there are good reasons why twenty-first century communists tend to be very suspicious of Marxism (Albert 2006).

As a political ideology Marxism is undoubtedly very much weaker than it used to be. In academia the influence of Marxian ideas remains substantial in social science departments, but among mainstream economists it is minimal – much less than it was in the early 1970s, when radical ideas could sometimes be published in the leading journals. Even among historians of economic thought there is less interest in Marx and Marxism(s) than was once the case. However, Marxian political economy is not a phenomenon of purely historical interest. It survives as one heterodox tradition among several, cooperating with and drawing upon the resources of other dissident schools in order to survive in what has again become a very cold intellectual climate. Every (roughly monthly) issue of the widely circulated *Heterodox Economics Newsletter* (www.heterodoxnews.com) advertises Marxian lectures, seminars, conferences, journal articles and books, revealing the continuing vitality of Marxism(s) in political economy.

JOHN E. KING

See also:

Ladislaus von Bortkiewicz (I); British classical political economy (II); Development economics (III); Vladimir Karpovich Dmitriev (I); Growth (III); Income distribution (III); Michał Kalecki (I); Oskar Ryszard Lange (I); Macroeconomics (III); Karl Heinrich Marx (I); Money and banking (III); Neo-Ricardian economics (II); Political philosophy and economics: freedom and labour (III); David Ricardo (I); Russian School of mathematical economics (II); Piero Sraffa (I); Mikhail Ivanovich Tugan-Baranovsky (I); Value and price (III).

References and further reading

Adler, M. (1915), 'Zur Ideologie der Weltkriege', *Der Kampf*, **8**, 123–30, translated as 'The ideology of the world war', in T. Bottomore and P. Goode (eds) (1978), *Austro-Marxism*, Oxford: Clarendon Press, pp. 125–35.
Adler, M. (1933), 'Wandlung der Arbeiterklasse', *Der Kampf*, **26**, 367–82, translated as 'The metamorphosis of the working class', in T. Bottomore and P. Goode (eds) (1978), *Austro-Marxism*, Oxford: Clarendon Press, pp. 217–48.
Albert, M. (2006), *Realizing Hope: Life Beyond Capitalism*, London: Zed Books.
Amin, S. (1974), *Accumulation on a World Scale*, New York: Monthly Review Press.
Anderson, P. (1976), *Considerations on Western Marxism*, London: New Left Books.
Baran, P.A. (1957), *The Political Economy of Growth*, New York: Monthly Review Press.
Baran, P.A. and P.M. Sweezy (1966), *Monopoly Capital: An Essay on the American Economic and Social Order*, New York: Monthly Review Press.
Boyer, R. (1990), *The Regulation School: A Critical Introduction*, New York: Columbia University Press.
Brewer, A. (1995), 'A minor post-Ricardian? Marx as an economist', *History of Political Economy*, **27** (1), 111–45.
Bukharin, N. (1915), *Imperialism and World Economy*, reprinted 1972, London: Merlin Press.
Cohen, G.A. (1978), *Karl Marx's Theory of History: A Defense*, Princeton, NJ: Princeton University Press.
Colletti, L. (1972), *From Rousseau to Lenin: Studies in Ideology and Society*, London: New Left Books, first published in 1969 as *Ideologia e Società*, Rome: Laterza.
Colletti, L. (1974), 'A political and philosophical interview', in F. Mulhern (ed.) (2011), *Lives on the Left: A Group Portrait*. London: Verso, pp. 121–49.
Dobb, M.H. (1973), *Theories of Value and Distribution since Adam Smith*, Cambridge: Cambridge University Press.
Emmanuel, A. (1972), *Unequal Exchange: a Study of the Imperialism of Trade*, New York: Monthly Review Press.
Engels, F. (1872–83), *Dialectics of Nature*, reprinted 1964, Moscow: Progress.

Faccarello, G. (1997), 'Some reflections on Marx's theory of value', in R. Bellofiore (ed.), *Marxism Revisited, Volume I*, Basingstoke: Macmillan, pp. 29–47.

Fine, B. and A. Saad-Filho (2010), *Marx's 'Capital'*, 5th edn, London: Pluto.

Foster, J.B. (2000), *Marx's Ecology: Materialism and Nature*, New York: Monthly Review Press.

Freeman, A. and G. Carchedi (eds) (1996), *Marx and Non-Equilibrium Economics*, Cheltenham, UK and Brookfield, VT, USA: Edward Elgar.

Glyn, A. (2006), *Capitalism Unleashed: Finance, Globalisation and Welfare*, Oxford: Oxford University Press.

Harvey, D. (2010), *A Companion to Marx's Capital*, London: Verso.

Hilferding, R. (1910), *Finance Capital: A Study of the Latest Phase of Capitalist Development*, reprinted 1981, London: Routledge & Kegan Paul.

Hobsbawm, E.J. (ed.) (1982), *The History of Marxism. Volume I: Marxism in Marx's Day*, Brighton: Harvester Press.

Hobsbawm, E. (1994), *Age of Extremes: The Short Twentieth Century 1914–1991*, London: Michael Joseph.

Hobsbawm, E.J. (1998), 'Introduction', in K. Marx and F. Engels, *The Communist Manifesto*, London: Verso, pp. 3–29.

Hobsbawm, E.J., G. Haupt, F. Marek, E. Ragioneri, V. Strada and C. Vivanti (eds) (1978–82), *Storia del Marxismo*, 5 vols, Turin: Einaudi.

Howard, M.C. and J.E. King (1985), *The Political Economy of Marx*, 2nd edn, Harlow: Longman.

Howard, M.C. and J.E. King (1989), *A History of Marxian Economics: Volume I, 1883–1929*, London: Macmillan, and Princeton, NJ: Princeton University Press.

Howard, M.C. and J.E. King (1992), *A History of Marxian Economics: Volume II, 1929–1990*, London: Macmillan, and Princeton, NJ: Princeton University Press.

Howard, M.C. and J.E. King (2008), *The Rise of Neoliberalism in Advanced Capitalist Economies: A Materialist Analysis*, Basingstoke: Palgrave Macmillan.

King, J.E. (2013), 'Whatever happened to the crucial reform?', in R. Bellofiore, E. Karwowski and J. Toporowski (eds), *Economic Crisis and Political Economy. Volume 2 of Essays in Honour of Tadeusz Kowalik*, Basingstoke: Palgrave Macmillan, pp. 29–41.

Kotz, D.M. (2015), *The Rise and Fall of Neoliberal Capitalism*. Cambridge, MA: Harvard University Press.

Lenin, V.I. (1916), *Imperialism, The Highest Stage of Capitalism*, reprinted 1968, Moscow: Progress.

Luxemburg, R. (1913), *The Accumulation of Capital*, reprinted 1951, London: Routledge & Kegan Paul.

Marcuse, H. (1961), *Soviet Marxism: A Critical Analysis*, New York: Vintage Books.

Marcuse, H. (1964), *One-Dimensional Man: Studies in the Ideology of Advanced Industrial Society*, reprinted 1991, London: Routledge.

Marx, K. (1844), *Economic and Philosophical Manuscripts of 1844*, reprinted 1970, London: Lawrence & Wishart.

Marx, K. (1857), *Grundrisse: Foundations of the Critique of Political Economy (Rough Draft)*, reprinted 1973, Harmondsworth: Penguin.

Marx, K. (1859), 'Preface', in K. Marx, *A Contribution to the Critique of Political Economy*, reprinted 1971, London: Lawrence & Wishart, pp. 19–23.

Marx, K. (1862–63), *Theories of Surplus Value, Volumes I, II and III*, reprinted 1971–72, London: Lawrence & Wishart.

Marx, K. (1867), *Capital: A Critical Analysis of Capitalist Production*, vol. I, reprinted 1961, Moscow: Foreign Languages Publishing House.

Marx, K. and F. Engels (1975–2005), *Collected Works, Volumes 1–50*, Moscow: Progress, London: Lawrence & Wishart, New York: International.

McDonough, T., M. Reich and D.M. Kotz (eds) (2010), *Contemporary Capitalism and Its Crises: Social Structure of Accumulation Theory for the 21st Century*, Cambridge: Cambridge University Press.

Meek, R.L. (1973), 'Introduction to the second edition', in R.L. Meek, *Studies in the Labour Theory of Value*, London: Lawrence & Wishart, pp. i–xliv.

Napoleoni, C. (1975), *Smith Ricardo Marx*, New York: Wiley, first published in 1973 as *Smith Ricardo Marx*, Turin: Editore Boringhieri.

Nelson, A. (1999), *Marx's Concept of Money: The God of Commodities*, London: Routledge.

Redhead, S. (2010), 'From Marx to Berlusconi: Lucio Colletti and the struggle for scientific Marxism', *Rethinking Marxism*, **22** (1), 148–56.

Robinson, J. (1942), *An Essay on Marxian Economics*, London: Macmillan.

Ruccio, D., J. Amariglio, A. Callari, S. Resnick and R. Wolff (1996), 'Nondeterminist Marxism: the birth of a postmodern tradition in economics', in F.E. Foldvary (ed.), *Beyond Neoclassical Economics: Heterodox Approaches to Economic Thought*, Cheltenham, UK and Brookfield, VT, USA: Edward Elgar, pp. 134–47.

Screpanti, E. (2005), 'Guglielmo Carchedi's "art of fudging" explained to the people', *Review of Political Economy*, **17** (1), 115–26.

Steedman, I. (1977), *Marx after Sraffa*, London: New Left Books.

Sutcliffe, B. (2006), 'Imperialism old and new: a comment on David Harvey's *The New Imperialism* and Ellen Meiksins Wood's *Empire of Capital*', *Historical Materialism*, **14** (4), 59–78.

Sweezy, P.M. (1942), *Theory of Capitalist Development*, reprinted 1970, New York: Monthly Review Press.

Veneziani, R. (2012), 'Analytical Marxism', *Journal of Economic Surveys*, **26** (4), 649–73.

Warren, B. (1980), *Imperialism: Pioneer of Capitalism*, London: Verso.

Weisskopf, T.E. (1979), 'Marxian crisis theory and the rate of profit in the postwar U.S. economy', *Cambridge Journal of Economics*, **3** (4), 341–78.

German and Austrian schools

Introduction

Whether there is a "German School" and an "Austrian School" of economics has been disputed not least because of the frequently heated debates amongst members of these alleged "schools". The litmus test of whether there is a school, and which author belongs to it and which not, obviously cannot be decided in terms of any *unité de doctrine* unanimously shared by all members of the school, because typically there is no such thing. A less rigid concept of school is needed. Here we use the term in the sense that the scholars we reckon to a school share a similar outlook on the economic world, subscribe to similar methods of the analysis, develop their argument around essentially the same corpus of ideas and elaborate their approach in a deliberate attempt to differentiate it from other approaches. Without too much of an effort, a German and an Austrian school can be identified along these lines and the latter can be said to have greatly benefited from certain developments of the former.

Carl Menger (2007: 39) dedicated his *Grundsätze der Volkswirthschaftslehre* (1871), commonly seen as the foundational work of Austrian economics, "with respectful esteem" to Wilhelm Roscher, the leading German economics professor at the time and a towering figure of the older Historical School. Menger wrote:

> It was a special pleasure to me that the field here treated, comprising the most general principles of our science, is in no small degree so truly the product of recent development in German political economy, and that the reform of the most important principles of our science here attempted is therefore built upon a foundation laid by previous work that was produced almost entirely by the industry of German scholars.
>
> Let this work be regarded, therefore, as a friendly greeting from a collaborator in Austria, and as a faint echo of the scientific suggestions so abundantly lavished on us Austrians by Germany through the many outstanding scholars she has sent us and through her excellent publications. (Menger 1871, 2007: 49)

Many readers of the book appear to have considered this dedication an expression of the notorious Austrian style of void courtesy. This may contribute to explaining why for a long time the view was widespread that Menger's work was largely original. However, things are a great deal more complex. First, while Menger held Roscher and other German authors in high esteem, there is reason to presume that he was also keen not to spoil the German economics market by extravagant claims to originality and by demarcating his theory too much from theirs. Close scrutiny shows that in important respects he distanced himself from the cameralist economic tradition that permeates the writings of German authors and the important role they typically attributed to the state. There is also the remarkable fact that the majority of German economists did not consider their contributions as marking a fundamental split with the received classical doctrine especially of Adam Smith, but rather a correction and elaboration of several of the ideas contained therein. Looking at German economics in the first half of the nineteenth century only from the vantage point of whether and to what extent it anticipated marginal utility theory is in danger of generating a distorted picture of the facts. It was only after marginalism had become fully established in economics that the German use value school appeared in new light. Therefore, while "the idea that Austrian economics arose armour-clad like Pallas Athena from Menger's brain" is a myth, as Streissler (1997) rightly stressed, to call the German school "proto-neoclassical", as he also did, is perhaps an exaggeration unduly emphasising one of the school's features to the detriment of important others. Streissler's (1990) rescue from oblivion of the fact that the German *Nutzwertschule* or "use value school" had anticipated marginal utility theory stimulated several other works. See Baloglou (1995), Priddat (1997) and, in particular, Chipman (2005, 2013), who scrutinised in great depth the respective German literature and related it to the Austrian and other traditions of economic thought. Yagi (2011) sees the German and especially the Austrian school as having prepared the ground for evolutionary economic thinking in the German language area.

The German Use Value School: Its Beginnings

The publication of Christian Garbe's translation of Adam Smith's *Wealth of Nations* (1776 [1976], hereafter WN) into German in 1794 paved the way to a critical discussion especially of the Scotsman's theory of value. In the course of this discussion marginal utility theory gradually took shape. The upshot of the development was the work of Karl Heinrich Rau (1826, 1828, 1832, 1833, 1837a, 1837b), who elaborated not only the concept (but not the expression *Grenznutzen*, which was coined by Wieser 1884) of marginal utility of a commodity as a function of the quantity consumed, but also, and independently of Cournot, the concept of a market as consisting of the confrontation of a demand and a supply schedule. (The concept of marginal utility had already been clearly formulated by the Swiss Daniel Bernoulli, whose work was, however, ignored for some time.)

While in early German authors we do indeed encounter anticipations of marginal utility theory, this must not distract attention away from the fact that many of them adopted large parts of the teachings of the classical economists, especially Smith, but also Ricardo. In terms of the method of analysis employed, they typically did not endorse methodological individualism, as advocates of the Austrian school would do later, but entertained a more holistic view of society and economy. The idea of "reconstructing" the latter by starting from the single needy individual was alien to them. Society shaped the individual much more than the individual shaped society. The authors under consideration stressed the existence of collective, public and cultural needs and wants alongside individual ones, which they did not consider as purely subjective, but as conditioned by the society in which people lived and the social group to which they belonged. While utility (*Nutzen*, *Nutzwerth*) became an important analytical category in their writings, it would be wrong to consider them advocates of utilitarianism or hedonism. In their writings we encounter the concept of a hierarchy of needs and wants and thus a lexicographic ordering of preferences, which defies the use of utility functions. Substitution of goods within a category of needs or wants was possible, but across categories it was not. Reflecting the cameralist tradition of German economics, the state played an important role, a great deal more important than in Smith, and was dealt with in the subject of *Finanzwissenschaft* (public finance).

The starting point of the German use value school was Smith's discussion of the "paradox of value" which revolved around his distinction between "value in use" and "value in exchange" – a distinction we encounter already in Aristotle. Smith observed: "The things which have the greatest value in use have frequently little or no value in exchange; and, on the contrary, those which have the greatest value in exchange have frequently little or no value in use" (WN I.iv.13). He exemplified this antinomy in terms of drinking water and a diamond, water being available (in Scotland) at a very low price, whereas a diamond of a given quality and size being very expensive. Smith explained what at first sight might be considered puzzling in terms of the very different costs of attaining the two kinds of commodities.

Before we turn to the early German discussions of Smith's argument, the following observations are apposite. In Smith's understanding the consumption or use of certain commodities is a social act, a form of communicating with other people. It cannot therefore be described exclusively in terms of a relationship between a single person and the commodity under consideration, as in the case of drinking water. A diamond is a case in point and it is safe to assume that Smith had chosen the example on purpose. While the demand for a diamond may be seen to express a delicacy of taste, it serves first and foremost as an ideal device to signal wealth, fortune and social position. What matters is that the diamond is seen, not by the person who wears it, but by other people. It is meant to impress them and is thus wanted, as Smith stressed, despite the fact that it "has scarce any value in use" (WN I.iv.13) for the person wearing it. It is a kind of "positional good," to use Fred Hirsch's concept. The more expensive a diamond is, the more exclusive is its possession. It seems that this aspect of Smith's argument has been widely ignored (not only) in the German literature to which we now turn. This means, of course, that Smith's critics have at least partly missed their target.

One of the first authors to express his disenchantment with Smith's analysis was Friedrich Julius Heinrich, imperial count of Soden (1754–1831), who in his book *Die Nazionalökonomie* (1805) launched an attack on Smith. Soden replaced Smith's value dichotomy by what he called "positive" and "comparative value" (*positifer* and *verglichener Werth*). While water, Soden explained, has positive value for humanity under all conditions, its comparative value depends upon its scarcity. Similarly, if diamonds were available in abundance they would lose in comparative value. Ludwig Heinrich von Jakob (1759–1827) in his *Grundsätze der National-Oeconomie* (1805) came up with a similar distinction, using different expressions. However, in a fully classical spirit he saw the prices of goods determined by costs of production, which resolved in quantities of labour needed in order to bring forth the goods. Hence, while he was convinced that the value in use of a good ought to be seen as depending on the quantity available of it, he felt no need to abandon the classical cost of production approach to exchangeable value. Gottlieb Hufeland (1761–1817) in his *Neue Grundlegung der Staatswirthschaftskunst* (1807) for the main part simply expounded Smith, but then stressed subjective aspects and put special emphasis on the role of knowledge in the estimation of value, an emphasis we later encounter also in Austrian economists. In addition he anticipated the Marshallian concepts of "supply price" and "demand price".

The idea of a hierarchy of needs and wants and thus "lexicographic preferences" is clearly expressed by Johann Friedrich Eusebius Lotz (1771–1838) in his *Revision der Grundbegriffe der Nationalwirthschaftslehre* (1811–14). Friedrich Benedict Wilhelm von Hermann in his *Staatswirthschaftliche Untersuchungen* (1832) elaborated on the idea in some depth (see also Kurz 1998).

Characteristic features of these early contributions to the German use value school are: (1) subjectivist elements in explaining exchange values gain in importance without, however, becoming all-dominant; (2) the role of the quantity available of a commodity and thus of its relative scarcity for its value as seen by the consumer is discussed, but the concept of marginal utility as a function of the quantity consumed is still missing; (3) needs and wants are typically seen to be partly shaped by society and most of them are considered to be satiable, the exception being fancied and artificial desires and the services to meet them.

The discussion moved on to a higher level with Karl Heinrich Rau (1782–1870), whose tripartite *Lehrbuch der politischen Oekonomie* (vol. I, 1826; vol. II, 1828; vol. III.1, 1832; vol. III.2, 1837) saw in total five editions up to 1867. The first three editions of volume I of the book published in 1826, 1833 and 1837 especially deserve our attention.

Karl Heinrich Rau

Rau's textbook was not only a paragon for other works, it also contained a number of ideas and concepts, often wrongly attributed to other authors, which foreshadowed and even anticipated in full later developments. In the second edition of volume I Rau put forward a distinction that paralleled Soden's: while "species value" (*Gattungswerth*) refers to a class or type of commodities and is not related to the quantity consumed, "concrete (use) value" (*konkreter Wert*) of a unit of the commodity, alternatively also called "quantitative value," is seen to depend on the quantity consumed of it and thus points in the direction of marginal utility. A first clear formulation of the principle of diminishing marginal utility is to be found in the third edition of volume I. The concept of concrete value established for the first time the idea of use value depending on quantity. By means of his two concepts of value Rau sought to solve the "paradox of value": while Smith's value in use corresponds to Rau's "species value", Smith's value in exchange corresponds to Rau's concrete value. Comparing water and diamond involves, on the one hand, comparing two incommensurables – two species values – but, on the other, it involves comparing two commensurables – two concrete values – in terms of the fact that their consumption or use generates utility for the consumer, the magnitude of which is taken to depend on the quantity consumed of each of the two goods.

In his reflections, Rau started from separable utilities derived from the consumption of different goods. He originally retained the assumption of satiability with regard to each need and want. Later he weakened this assumption, at first explicitly with regard to luxury goods "for which no limit of requirement can be specified", then also implicitly with regard to all goods, provided we are willing to follow Chipman's translation of what Rau stated into "a total utility function . . . which is strictly increasing, concave, continuous, and once-differentiable; thus satiable preferences have become insatiable." (Chipman 2013: 15) Interestingly, Rau also pointed out that commodities are typically possessed of different characteristics, or of the same characteristics in different proportions, thus foreshadowing Kevin Lancaster's (1971) view that what consumers seek to acquire are not commodities themselves, but the characteristics they contain. To the extent to which commodities have some characteristics in common (for example, caloric content in the case of food) they are substitutes and belong to the same species. While Rau does not use the term, it is clear that he has this concept in mind.

While on the one hand Rau was keen to solve the "paradox of value", he was also concerned with another Smithian problem: the estimation of the size of the wealth of a nation. He rejected Jean-Baptiste Say's proposal to measure utility by value, and he was also critical of the idea to measure it in terms of the sum total of quantities multiplied by current prices. He was on the lookout for some invariant measure of value, a search that had plagued Ricardo until the end of his life, and after some deliberation opted for using an average of prices over a period of time. Interestingly, he also advocated the idea of a diminishing marginal utility of income, which hints, of course, in the direction of finite satiation levels of goods.

In an appendix to the fourth edition of his *Lehrbuch*, published in 1841, Rau introduced intersecting demand and supply curves – only three years after and independently of the first use of demand curves in Cournot (1838). Rau's analysis was the starting point of Mangoldt's investigation (1863).

Bruno Hildebrand (1812–1878)

Hildebrand in his book *Die Nationalökonomie der Gegenwart und Zukunft* (1848) deals with the history of economic thought and via a critical scrutiny of earlier economists' ideas on value elaborates his own view. He holds Adam Smith in high esteem and actually calls him the "Immanuel Kant of economics" (1848: 285). In the same year in which the *Communist Manifesto* was published, Hildebrand puts forward an early criticism of socialist authors, especially Friedrich Engels and Pierre-Joseph Proudhon. On Hildebrand's work, see Schefold (1998).

Engels's contention that the German economists had failed to contribute anything useful to the state of the art as it had been handed down by Smith, Hildebrand rebutted by stressing that the Germans had established the view "that value is always a relationship of a thing to a person and to human society, and depends upon human estimation" (1848: 168). Proudhon, in one of his numerical examples designed to discuss the relationship between "use value" and exchange value, had insisted that an exceptionally good harvest leads to the paradoxical result that the use value exceeds the exchange value. He arrived at this conclusion by assuming that the use value is independent of the amount produced, whereas the exchange value is inversely related to the quantity produced. As regards the relationship under consideration, Proudhon made the implicit assumption of a unitary price-elasticity of demand, implying a constant share of income allocated to the good under consideration. This assumption attracted Hildebrand's attention. He stressed that "the more the quantity of a useful item is increased, the more, in a state of unchanged need, the use value [*Nutzwerth*] of each individual unit declines" (1848: 318). In this formulation we have, on the one hand, the concept of a declining marginal utility, which Rau had attempted to cover with his concept of "concrete value". On the other hand, Hildebrand speaks of "a state of unchanged need", which may be interpreted as Rau's "specie value", which now is taken to be reflected by a constant share of total income spent on a particular good. Hildebrand thus improved upon the specification of what nowadays are called preferences by not only defining the movement of marginal utility as a function of the quantity consumed, but by also specifying the demand function that corresponds to constant shares of expenditures out of national income (see Chipman 2013: 24–7).

Subsequent developments

Eberhard Friedländer (1799–1869) taught in Estonia, and in his book *Die Theorie des Werths* (1852) put forward a number of ideas that foreshadowed later developments. He insisted that "the true goal of economics is less the pursuit of wealth than that of the general welfare" (1852: 6). He rejected Jean-Baptiste Say's idea of consumer sovereignty and with explicit reference to the Chinese government's policy to curb the smoking of opium emphasised the role of the state in educating people and preventing them from consuming in ways that are detrimental to their well-being in the long run. Friedländer advocated the possibility of ranking human needs and was concerned with giving a more precise definition of "subsistence" in terms of the amounts of needs that have to be satisfied. He stressed that these needs may be met in terms of different bundles of consumption goods. The reason for this possibility is to be seen in the fact that each good typically represents a compositum mixtum of what Friedländer called *Bedürfnißeinheiten* (units of need), a concept that may be said to foreshadow Kevin Lancaster's (1971) "characteristics".

The arguments of Rau, Hildebrand and Roscher (1843) were taken a step further in a treatise by Karl Knies (1821–1898), published in 1855. (It deserves to be mentioned that the Austrian economists Böhm-Bawerk and Wieser studied with Knies in Heidelberg.) Knies distinguished sharply between use value (*Gebrauchswerth*) and usefulness (*Brauchbarkeit*) and developed the concept of species value to a hierarchy of wants, or species of wants, and took it to correspond closely to a species of goods. In each species the goods are taken to be substitutes, whereas goods belonging to different species are complements. Thus wheat and rye, for example, are subspecies that can be substituted for one another because both are carriers of calories. If only calories happen to matter, the choice will be in terms of the grain that minimises costs per unit of calorie. In case other aspects, such as taste, also matter the choice is across all aspects considered. Knies was also keen to confront his theory with historical data. Interestingly, he rejected the view that the pursuit of individual self-interest was always beneficial to society at large, a view he wrongly ascribed to Adam Smith.

The first edition of Wilhelm Roscher's (1817–1894) *Grundlagen* (1854) reflects the influence of Rau and Hildebrand, but does not go beyond their contributions. In the second edition of the treatise (1857) he approved of Knies's distinction between use value and usefulness. He applied the analyses of the aforementioned authors to the "paradox of value" (1857: 7–10), without, unfortunately, touching upon the all-important aspect of Smith's reasoning that the use or consumption of certain goods cannot be understood in terms of a simple subject–object relationship: it involves other parties the individual wishes to impress. We may conclude, however, with Chipman (2013: 42), that "Rau (1847) and the three founding members of the older historical school, Hildebrand (1848), Knies (1855), and Roscher (1857), developed ... the essential ideas of the marginal revolution later associated with the names of Gossen (1854), Menger (1871) and Jevons (1871)."

Herrmann Heinrich Gossen's book *Entwickelung der Gesetze des menschlichen Verkehrs und der daraus fließenden Regeln für menschliches Handeln* (*The Laws of Human Relations and the Rules of Human Action Derived Therefrom*) (1854) reflects Rau's overwhelming influence. Rau and other representatives of the school had not used mathematical formalisations to express their ideas. What they said with words was only later translated into the language of mathematics, especially by Chipman (2013), occasionally not without the need to interpret vague formulations. Gossen was the first author who attempted to expose the new theory directly in mathematical terms. He did so by having recourse to a number of simplifying assumptions, such as the assumption that marginal utility is a linear function of the amount consumed of each commodity. It is important to note that Gossen emphasised the fact that consumption takes time, which is the reason why he presented the decision problem of consumers as consisting first and foremost of the allocation of scarce time to alternative uses, or rather human actions, and only secondly to the purchase of goods needed to carry out those actions. He was clear that while the time constraint is always binding and has to be met, the income constraint is not necessarily so. This aspect has totally fallen into oblivion in the literature and was only retrieved by Georgescu-Roegen (1983) and then developed further by Steedman (2001). Not least because of his tedious numerical examples and cumbersome mathematics Gossen's work was entirely ignored and "discovered" more than 20 years after its publication by Léon Walras.

The limited importance attributed to the findings of the use value theorists is well expressed by Adolph Wagner's textbook (1876). Wagner was considered an important representative of classical economics. In his view marginal utility theory contributed to ascertaining the quantities produced of the various commodities, whose values however were determined by cost of production. His view in this regard resembles the views taken by authors such as Heinrich Dietzel and Karl Diehl (see Diehl 1908; see also Kurz 1995).

Several recent interpretations of the German use value school focused their attention almost exclusively on anticipations of marginal utility theory. However, in hardly any one of the German authors does this theory appear to have assumed the status of self-sufficiency: it improved our understanding of certain phenomena, but badly needed to be complemented. Several authors felt that the complement was provided by the classical labour or cost of production approach. The fact that the German authors generally did not fully embrace the outlook of marginal utility theory can also be inferred from the fact that they did not look at the economy through the lens of methodological individualism. Many of them upheld Smithian and Ricardian ideas and entertained a view of society as an object of study that exists independently of the single individual. Therefore, while the German use value school may be said to have laid the foundation of some of the ideas elaborated by the Austrians, in important respects Austrian economics involved a break with the German tradition.

The Austrian School

The name "Austrian school" was coined by one of its severest critics, Gustav von Schmoller, who in the so-called *Methodenstreit* (battle over the method) had levelled a fierce attack at Carl Menger and his followers. While Schmoller advocated a method in economics that was "historical-ethical", empirical and inductive, the Austrians were said to apply a method that was ahistorical, abstract, purely theoretical and deductive.

We may distinguish between several generations or layers of Austrian economists and economics. The first comprises Carl Menger, Eugen von Böhm-Bawerk and Friedrich von Wieser and, the second, Ludwig von Mises and Friedrich August von Hayek. Whether and to what extent other Austrian-born economists such as Joseph Alois

Schumpeter, Hans Mayer, Oskar Morgenstern, Gottfried Haberler, Fritz Machlup and Paul Rosenstein-Rodan belong to the school is an issue of much debate. John Richard Hicks cherished the temporal aspect of the Austrian and especially Böhm-Bawerk's approach, which distinguished it from the atemporal Walrasian approach, and sought to develop it in terms of his "neo-Austrian" theory (Hicks 1973). Today, Austrian-cum-libertarian doctrines are encountered especially in some universities and institutes in the United States, especially the George Mason University in Fairfax, Virginia, New York University, the Ludwig von Mises Institute and the Cato Institute. Misesians such as Israel Kirzner and Murray Rothbard developed a radically subjectivist point of view, while others, such as Peter Boettke, Roger W. Garrison, Ludwig M. Lachmann and Steven G. Horowitz followed more the tradition established by Hayek, which implied a much smaller break with mainstream economics. Austrians have founded their own journals, including the *Quarterly Journal of Austrian Economics*.

Characteristic features

While Austrian economists differ in many respects, they share certain beliefs, methodological positions and views of the world. These include the following. (1) They endorse methodological individualism, which requests the reconstruction of society starting from the needs and wants, motives and actions of single individuals. (2) Closely related to this, they endorse methodological subjectivism, tracing all economic phenomena back to the value assessments of individuals and their interaction. Many of them are opposed to macroeconomics, which argues in terms of aggregates rather than micro units. (3) The attention focuses on catallactics, which studies exchange and trade among individuals and how prices form. (4) Austrian economists emphasise the importance of time both in production and consumption and are highly critical of atemporal approaches, such as Walras's. (5) An aspect of the emphasis on time is their insistence on uncertainty and the error-proneness of human action – as Menger famously put it in the title of a section of his 1871 book: "Time – error". This leads to an analysis of the role of expectations and learning processes and an investigation of the problem of information. Without too much of an exaggeration one might say that Austrian economics is first and foremost about the generation and transmission of information and its reflection in market values. (6) The economy is considered a self-organising system that, in principle, can do without any state interference. The same applies to institutions; money is accordingly seen as an institution that emerges as a by-product of the evolution of exchange relationships. (7) Austrian economists endorse marginal utility theory, which is why their theories are typically considered variants of marginalism or what was later called "neoclassicism". (8) Major Austrian economists emphasise that explanations of economic phenomena ought to be causal-genetic (a term Hans Mayer introduced), going back to the roots of the phenomena under consideration that deserve no further examination; they reject the concept of "equilibrium" and are critical of the use of mathematics in economics. (9) Austrian economists typically mistrust governments and the state and are suspicious of the motives of its representatives: these are said to tend to present their own particular selfish interests as the interests of society at large. The baseline of Austrian economics is the advocacy of "free markets" against state interventionism and the conviction that if things go wrong in the economy it must be because of the harmful activity of the state or the central bank. (10) Politically, Austrian economists take more or less radical libertarian views, with Mises being the most radical of all. Hayek founded in 1947 together with Mises, Frank Knight, Karl Popper, George Stigler and Milton Friedman the Mont Pèlerin Society, whose declared aims were to advocate a free market economics, a "liberal order" and a "free society". Ideas of the Mont Pèlerin Society fell on fertile ground with such politicians as Margaret Thatcher and Ronald Reagan.

Austrian economists are divided on a number of issues. These concern, in particular, the following. (1) Some leading representatives like Mises are strictly opposed to the use of mathematics in economics. This use conveys the impression that economics is or ought to be very much like a natural science, preferably physics, possessed of a precision that, however, simply cannot be attained, given its subject matter. Mathematical economics is accused of treating incommensurable qualities as commensurable quantities. Hayek warned that economics must not fall victim to the "pretence of knowledge". (2) Some authors such as Böhm-Bawerk and Mises are strict adversaries of the method of simultaneous equations, which at the time began to filter into economics, whereas Wieser, Hayek and others are less adamant in this regard and see at least a heuristic role for it. (3) Most (modern) Austrian economists reject welfare economics in general and not only because it presupposes cardinal utility: welfare economics is said to involve a departure from an approach that considers individual preferences as incommensurable. (4) While the majority of Austrian economists insist on the axiom of the sovereignty of the consumer, Schumpeter points out that innovating firms mould those preferences in terms of the provision of new goods and techniques of sales promotion. (5) While the majority of Austrian economists conceive of savings as the key to individual and collective wealth, Schumpeter insists that what matters are investments by means of which new methods of production and new goods are introduced into the system, and these investments are made possible by a sophisticated monetary and credit system without preceding savings.

The writings of Austrian economists reflect numerous intellectual influences. These include, in particular, the German use value school, the School of Salamanca (and Coimbra), the Scottish Enlightenment and Austrian philosophy, especially Franz Brentano's (see Smith 1994: ch. 10). Of great importance were the writings of Richard Cantillon, Francis Hutcheson, David Hume, Adam Ferguson and partly also Adam Smith. Two closely related concepts elaborated by them assumed centre stage in Austrian eocnomics: the "invisible hand" and "spontaneous order". Eugen von Böhm-Bawerk drew attention to some of the sources mentioned in his *Kapital und Kapitalzins. Erste Abtheilung: Geschichte und Kritik der Kapitalzinstheorien* (1884). Friedrich August von Hayek variously recalled these influences in his writings and stimulated Marjorie Grice-Hutchinson (1952) to write her PhD thesis on the School of Salamanca; see also de Roover (1955). Anticipations of Austrian ideas concern in particular: a subjectivist concept of value; the conception of competition not as a state, but as a process; the importance of information and knowledge; the view of market intervention as a potential violation of natural law; the view of the particular role of banks in the economy; economic liberalism.

While Adam Smith and other authors had subdivided economic history in various phases or stages, with capitalism (or the "commercial society", as Smith called it) as only the most recent stage, Austrian economists advocated the view that the world has always seen some form of capitalism, because the latter only expresses the natural inclinations of people: crucial features of capitalism are said to be extra-historical socio-economic phenomena. For example, there has always been a positive rate of interest, which simply reflects the indubitable fact that humans are possessed of a positive rate of time preference. Attempts to fight and suppress interest are bound to fail. This explains the Austrians' positive attitude towards capitalism. Austrian economists share the conviction of Smith and others that a main difficulty economics has to cope with consists in the fact that human actions typically involve consequences that were neither intended nor could possibly have been foreseen by agents. Therefore, the Austrians are convinced, one cannot predict except patterns of development.

A main analytical concern of Austrian economists was with refuting criticisms of interest (and profit) taking. They were critical of Aristotle and the churchmen in their condemnation of interest in the doctrine of usury, of Adam Smith's view of profits and interest as a "deduction from the produce of labour", and of Karl Marx and the socialists' attack on all property incomes (profits, interest and rents of land) as originating in the "exploitation of workers". While all Austrian economists agreed that property incomes do not per se have an odious smell, but reflect the mutually advantageous exercise of individual rights and economic liberties, they differ vastly in explaining the causes and levels of profits and interest.

Carl Menger (1840–1921)

Menger (1871) insisted that economic analysis must start from the single needy individual; he took Robinson Crusoe (before the latter's encounter with "Friday") in Daniel Defoe's famous novel as the paradigmatic case in point. Via introspection and the application of procedures by means of which meaning and content may be increased and generalised to social forms of production and distribution, it is then possible to elaborate across several stages an exact theory of the economy. The method endorses the law of cause and effect: it is causal-genetic.

The realm of "goods", that is, things capable of satisfying human needs and wants, may be subdivided in the following way: goods of the first order comprise goods that are directly capable of satisfying human needs and wants, or consumption goods, whereas goods of a higher order are only capable of doing this indirectly: goods of the second order are goods used in the production of goods of the first order, goods of the third order are goods used in the production of goods of the second order, and so on. Goods of higher orders comprise not only intermediate products, or capital goods, but also different kinds of labour and the services of nature (land, mineral deposits and so on).

Since, according to Menger's point of view, the value estimation of individuals determines the prices of goods of the first order, he advocates a recursive structure of the problem of price determination. With the prices of consumption goods taken as already fixed, how are the prices of goods of higher order, including wage rates, rent rates, profits and interest, ascertained? This leads to the (in)famous imputation problem. Menger tried to solve it with reference to the "principle of loss" (which foreshadows the principle of opportunity cost): imagine a certain quantity of a good of higher order would be taken away. How much would this reduce the amount produced of the good of the first order under consideration? This amount multiplied by the pre-determined price of the good of first order gives the price of the good of higher order.

Menger's solution cannot be sustained. First, think of a bus and take away one of its wheels then it can no longer carry the tourists to the beach and the value of the wheel ought to be equal to the value of the entire transportation and nothing is left to pay the bus driver. The same argument applies also to the other three wheels and we are confronted with multiple counting. Second, what about when the number of goods of first order (*n*) is not equal to the number of all goods of higher order (*m*), $n \neq m$? In the case of $n < m$ the problem would be underdetermined, in the case of $n > m$ it would be overdetermined. Clearly, there is no presumption that $n = m$. Third, in the case of circular production, in which commodities are produced by means of commodities (corn by means of corn or steel by means of steel, and so on), which is the normal case in industrialised economies, the hierarchy of goods invoked by Menger loses much of its appeal, because in the extreme one and the same type of good may be contained in each and every order. Fourth, dealing with competitive conditions, costs of production at each and every stage must be discounted forward at the prevailing rate of interest, but how is it determined and how to deal with compound interest? Fifth, is it generally true that consumption goods (goods of the first order) are produced more capital intensively than capital goods (goods of higher order), because they obtain at a later stage of the time-phased process of production? The contention that this is indeed the case was one of the propositions that assumed almost the status of an "iron law" in marginalist or neoclassical theory and gave rise to the view that in the case of a choice of technique the higher is the interest–wage ratio (*r/w*) the lower will be the capital–labour ratio or capital intensity (*K/L*), that is:

$$\partial(K/L)/\partial(r/w) < 0 \qquad (1)$$

This is supposed to hold with regard to single firms, industries and the economy as a whole. However, as we know now this is not generally true. Demand functions for factors of production that are elastic with respect to the rates of remuneration of the factors need not be downward sloping over the entire interval of feasible levels of factor prices. See, for example, Kurz and Salvadori (1995: ch. 14) and Opocher and Steedman (2015).

As regards the determination of the rate of interest (or profit), Menger distinguished between the capital good proper, on the one hand, and its utilisation, on the other. He argued that while the price of the capital good refers only to the capital good proper, interest is a separate price paid for its utilisation.

Already during Menger's lifetime his theory was criticised harshly by other Austrians. Wieser drew attention to the fact that the proposed solution of the imputation problem was a failure and insisted that the problem cannot be tackled in the successivist manner in which Menger had attempted to solve it, starting from given prices of consumption goods which then had to be split up and divided among the various input factors collaborating in its production. In a circular framework, which is characteristic of developed economies in which products are produced by means of products, the problem rather had to be approached in terms of simultaneous equations. This ran counter to some Austrian economists' opposition to the use of mathematics. Böhm-Bawerk and, later, Schumpeter discarded Menger's explanation of interest on the ground that it amounted to double counting, because the price of the capital good includes interest and is in fact equal to the sum of the discounted stream of future net profits obtained by utilising the capital good until the end of its economic life. There was no room for a payment in addition to that.

Eugen von Böhm-Bawerk (1851–1914)

The radical subjectivists among the Austrian economists do not consider Böhm-Bawerk as belonging to the same stable. They instead see in him essentially a Ricardian, concerned with Ricardian problems and using Ricardian tools. Böhm-Bawerk saw himself firmly entrenched in the tradition established by Menger, and despite differences of opinion with his peer in important respects, such as the problem of capital and interest, he was keen to advance the latter's approach. His most important work was *Kapital und Kapitalzins*, which is in two volumes. The first (1884) provided a critical summary account of all theories of interest and profits from first pronouncements on economic matters up until Böhm-Bawerk's time, including, for example, criticisms of Marx and the socialists, John Bates Clark's marginal productivity theory and also Menger's explanation of profits. Against the background of this broad-spanned canvas, in the second volume, *Positive Theorie des Kapitales* (1889), he then elaborated his own explanation. He defended his theory against critics in debates with Clark and Schumpeter. His criticism of Marx subsequent to the publication of volume III of *Capital* edited by Friedrich Engels, "On the close of the Marxian system" (1896, see English translation 1949), had a substantial impact on the debate about Marx's theory of value and surplus value. In 1914 he published his influential essay on "Macht oder ökonomisches Gesetz?" ("Power or economic law?"), in which he attempted to refute all theories that see income distribution as reflecting economic power and defended the assumption of perfect competition as the appropriate workhorse of economics.

Here we focus attention on Böhm-Bawerk's theory of profits. He adopted essentially the long-period framework of the classical economists revolving around positions of the economic system characterised by a uniform general rate of profits, or interest, as Böhm-Bawerk preferred to call it, uniform rates of remuneration for all primary factors of production, that is, the services of labour and land, and what the classical economists called "natural" or "normal" prices. "A theorist", Böhm-Bawerk stressed in accordance with Smith and Ricardo, "may venture to abstract from the accidental and temporary fluctuations of the market prices around their normal fixed level" (Böhm-Bawerk 1949: 87). This involved assuming that the composition of the capital stock of the economy is fully adjusted to the other data of the system, the preferences of consumers and the technical alternatives available to cost-minimizing producers. He emphasised that capital is not a third original factor of production alongside with labour and land (or natural resources more generally), but is a derived factor consisting of stored up services of labour and nature. He agreed with Smith and Ricardo that interest (profit) is property income, pure and simple, and not a sort of "entrepreneurial wage" or a "risk premium". He stressed: "What forces us to think about capital interest is its labour-less flowing from a sort of conceiving mother good" (*"Was am Kapitalzins überhaupt zum Nachdenken herausfordert, ist sein arbeitsloses Hervorquellen aus einem gleichsam zeugenden Muttergut"*).

Böhm-Bawerk rejected the then existing theories of interest, which he grouped under six headings: "colourless theories" (Smith and Ricardo); "productivity theories" (from Jean-Baptiste Say via Johanna Heinrich von Thünen to J.B. Clark); "utilisation theories" (from Friedrich Benedict Wilhelm von Hermann to Carl Menger); "abstinence theories" (Nassau William Senior); "labour theories" (Jean-Baptiste Say); and "exploitation theories" (Karl Rodbertus and Karl Marx) (see Kurz 1994). The first five groups are said to be "favourable" to interest, whereas the last one is "inimical" to it. In

Böhm-Bawerk's view, Smith's *Wealth of Nations* contains the germs of almost all later theories, especially those tracing interest back to the productivity enhancing power of capital, to exploitation and to abstinence. Böhm-Bawerk was particularly keen to ward off the socialist attack on capitalism and profits, which earned him Schumpeter's label "the bourgeois Marx".

Böhm-Bawerk elaborated a particular version of the scarcity theory of income distribution, advocated by the marginalists, focusing attention on the time element in production and consumption. As regards the latter he singled out Jeremy Bentham (1748–1832), John Rae (1796–1872) and William Stanley Jevons (1835–1882) as precursors. His explanation revolved around the famous "three grounds":

1. The higher estimation of present needs and wants compared with future ones, that is, a positive rate of time preference.
2. The superiority of more roundabout processes of production, that is, the higher labour productivity of more capital-intensive processes of production.
3. The difference of provision of goods in the present and future.

Here we focus attention on the first two grounds. According to Böhm-Bawerk, interest is an intertemporal price, an "agio" on present goods relative to future goods. Only production by labour (and nature) that is unassisted by any human-made means of production Böhm-Bawerk considered to be "noncapitalist", whereas according to him the defining feature of capitalism is the use of capital goods or intermediate products. Böhm-Bawerk's definition of capitalism was meant to be innocuous and devoid of any ideological contamination. However, by construction he deliberately reduced the set of non-capitalist economies to the empty set. The production of each commodity he conceived of as a one-way avenue of finite length leading from the expenditure of certain amounts of labour (and the services of nature) across time to the maturing of the final product.

The central concept of his theory of interest is the "average period of production" designed to provide a measure of the "capitalistic" character of production of single goods, but also of an economy's output as a whole. It is the weighted average of the periods of time over which the amounts of labour remain invested until one unit of the (single or composite) commodity is obtained, with the respective amounts of labour serving as weights. By means of this device, Böhm-Bawerk thought it possible to replace in each line of production (and in the economy as a whole) a vector of physically heterogeneous capital goods with a scalar that is independent of income distribution and prices. "Capital" was thus taken to be reducible to a single dimension: time. Lengthening the production process requires a greater "subsistence fund" used to employ workers on more roundabout processes of production. It increases labour productivity, but because of diminishing returns with regard to more capital-intensive processes of production it is accompanied by a lowering of the rate of return on capital. Whether a lengthening will be effectuated depends on how the rate of return and the (average) rate of time preference compare. If the former is larger than the latter, there is an incentive to save (and invest) and thus accumulate capital, that is, increase the subsistence fund and embark on more roundabout processes, and vice versa in the opposite case.

Böhm-Bawerk was convinced that with his temporal theory of capital and interest he had spoken the "salvational word" on this hotly debated topic and had proved interest to be present in all societies that use produced means of production. Attempts at suppressing it were necessarily bound to fail. The "right to the full product of labour", called for by the socialists, cannot be denied, Böhm-Bawerk conceded, but what does it mean? "The crux of the matter", he insisted, "is the time difference between the payment of wages and the completion of the product." He added: "It is not the full merit of the labourers working today, of their industry and diligence alone, that many years later a certain larger product obtains; a part of the causation and merit belongs to a group of people having acted ahead of time and having provided for the formation and preservation of the saved-up stocks of goods [capital]" (1884 [1921]: 410).

Böhm-Bawerk's hope and expectation to have once and for all settled the issues at hand did not come true. His construction was attacked both by Austrians and non-Austrians. Menger, disenchanted with Böhm-Bawerk's criticism of his utilisation theory of interest, in private conversation is said to have told Schumpeter: "The time will come when people will realize that Böhm-Bawerk's theory is one of the greatest errors ever committed in political economy." His brother in law, Wieser, and the latter's student Schumpeter argued that the higher estimation of present over future goods is not the cause, but the consequence of a positive rate of interest. Ladislaus von Bortkiewicz (1906) insisted that a systematic undervaluation of future goods implies irrational behaviour. He also criticised the concept of the average period of production, in whose construction Böhm-Bawerk had assumed simple interest, which is incompatible with competitive conditions. As Sraffa (1960) pointed out, once compound interest is taken into account the average period is not independent of the rate of interest. This points towards a vicious circle: the average period of production, designed to measure capital intensity independently of the rate of interest and relative prices in order to determine the rate of interest, cannot be defined independently of that rate. Irving Fisher within a partial equilibrium framework dealing with the problem of the choice of technique stressed that a lower (higher) interest rate does not necessarily correspond to the adoption of a more (less) capital-intensive process of production. Schumpeter (1913) objected that there is no presumption that technical progress will always bring about a lengthening of the period of production. Finally, the concept of the average period is unable to cope with fixed capital and joint production. In the so-called Cambridge controversy in the theory of capital, the Austrian theory was scrutinised and shown to be untenable in general (see Garegnani 1960, Harcourt 1972, and Kurz and Salvadori 1995: ch. 14).

Friedrich von Wieser (1851–1926)

Wieser coined the term "*Grenznutzen*" (marginal utility) and contributed essentially two major works to economics: in 1884 his habilitation entitled *Über den Ursprung und die Hauptgesetze des wirthschaftlichen Werthes* (*On the Origin and the Main Laws of Economic Value*) and in 1889 *Der Natürliche Werth* (*The Natural Value* [1893]). He was appointed to the chair of his teacher, Menger, in 1903 and in 1926 published *Das Gesetz der Macht* (*The Law of Power*), in which he put down his concept of leadership. While much of his thinking revolved around a stationary economy and how to represent it analytically, the book may be said to reflect upon the forces that cause change. According to Wieser, all social development is determined by power. Schumpeter's concept of the "entrepreneur" was strongly influenced by Wieser, who was his teacher. Wieser's work has many facets. On the one hand, he anticipated marginalist allocation theory by combining marginal productivity theory with marginal utility theory. On the other hand, he transcended the static marginalist framework and put forward ideas with a decidedly classical flavour. Finally, he insisted on the important role of particular people, "leaders", who leave the beaten track and propel the system forward.

Wieser's starting point was the imputation problem, which Menger had left unsolved. Wieser saw quickly that it could not successfully be tackled in a purely causal-genetic way, but requested the use of mathematics (1889: 85–8). In the case of $m = n$ the problem had to be approached in terms of n simultaneous equations. However, in modern industrialised economies production is not unidirectional (as Menger and Böhm-Bawerk had assumed) but circular: "Not even the most crude tool is made without some other tool" (Wieser 1884: 115). Yet this implied that Menger's hierarchy of goods no longer applies and all values (including the values of consumption goods) are unknown and must be ascertained simultaneously. This threw doubt on the view that the values of commodities are exclusively determined by consumers' estimations.

Interestingly, Wieser also contemplated the case in which all goods are (re-)producible. He thus left the typical Austrian world of universal scarcity and entered a world of universal reproducibility. In it, he observed, a positive rate of interest presupposes a physical surplus of commodities produced above and beyond what is used up of them in the course of production. In this case, Wieser surmised, "the capital goods are to be attributed a net product, just as if they reproduced themselves with a surplus" (1889: 130). Having started from Menger's imputation problem, Wieser thus arrived at a concept of profits that bears a close resemblance to the classical surplus-based one – as Ricardo had insisted: "profits come out of the surplus produce" (Ricardo 1951–73, *Works*, II: 128). Since the physical composition of the surplus and that of the capital invested typically differ from one another, the value of social capital and the interest rate can only be determined simultaneously. Wieser also insisted, contrary to his brother-in-law, that once there is a positive rate of interest, "discounting" becomes natural (1889: 134) – time preference is the effect and not the cause of interest.

These are remarkable findings, which implied a break with crucial Austrian dogmas from which Wieser had started his analysis. In his attempt to resolve open problems of Menger's theory, Wieser gradually distanced himself from his subjectivist starting point and moved towards an increasingly more objectivist stance. It cannot therefore come as a surprise that ardent advocates of the subjectivist orientation in Austrian economics, such as Mises, saw in him "the most confused and eclectic" representative of the first generation of Austrian economists.

Ludwig von Mises (1881–1973)

Mises read Menger's *Grundsätze* in 1903 while studying law in Vienna and was deeply impressed by the book. In 1912 he published *Theorie des Geldes und der Umlaufsmittel* (*Theory of Money and the Means of Circulation*), which was followed in 1920 by his influential essay, in German, on "Economic calculation in the socialist commonwealth", and in 1926 he founded the Austrian Institute of Business Cycle Research. Then, 1940 saw the publication of his book *Nationalökonomie. Theorie des Handelns und Wirtschaftens*, an English version of which, entitled *Human Action*, appeared in 1949 and contained his concept of "praxeology".

Mises stated: "The distinguishing feature of the Austrian School and what will constitute its immortal fame is precisely that it is a doctrine of action and not a doctrine of economic equilibrium, of non-action" (1978: 21). Mises advocated a radical demarcation vis-à-vis the economic mainstream – neoclassicism in whichever form – and chastised mathematical formalism in economics. The view entertained by Jevons and his acolytes that economics should be shaped in the image of physics, Mises considered to be fundamentally misconceived and a dead end in the social sciences. He was also strictly opposed to the view that empirics and the power to forecast decide about the quality of an economic theory.

In his habilitation Mises was concerned with extending the subjectivist approach to the sphere of money. This led him to elaborate his "money-regression theorem": the demand for money is not determined by the purchasing power of money today, but by its purchasing power in the past, because every type of money is said to have had its origin in a proper good capable of satisfying the needs and wants of humans and is not rooted in an imposition made by the state or in a social contract, as received monetary theories maintained. Money is to be derived from the good that eventually assumed the role of money. In order to understand money and its role in the economic system a process analysis is required. Money ought to have only a single function – that of a means of exchange. This requires that banking policy must request a reserve coefficient with respect to deposits of 100 per cent – comparable to Peel's Bank Charter Act of 1844, according to which the Bank of England was restricted to issue new bank notes only if they were 100 per cent backed by gold. In Mises's view money ought to be neutral, that is, ought not to affect the real economic system. This, however, necessitates regulating the monetary system in the way indicated.

The implications of failing to accomplish this task Mises exemplified in terms of his explanation of business cycles. He held a monetary malinvestment theory, in which he merged ideas of the Currency School with Böhm-Bawerk's capital theory and Knut Wicksell's distinction between a "natural" (r) and a money rate of interest (i). The source of cycles is an inflationary credit expansion – a policy of "easy money": if i is reduced below r, firms are induced to embark on more roundabout processes of production, which channels productive resources from industries that produce consumption goods to industries that produce intermediate products. However, with a reduction in consumer goods output their prices will tend to increase, which improves profitability in the industries producing them. Eventually this renders the production of consumption goods more profitable than that of investment goods and reverses the process of lengthening the period of production in the economy. Investment projects will be abandoned halfway and productive resources wasted. The economic system will get stuck in a crisis. The culprit of the maldevelopment is a mistaken monetary policy. Mises's theory was the starting point of Hayek's (1931b) theory of business cycles (see below).

At the beginning of the twentieth century several authors, including Vilfredo Pareto and Enrico Barone, had raised the question whether socialism was feasible and capable of generating efficient economic outcomes. The answer given differed as between authors, but was by and large in the positive. Mises (1920) opposed these views and insisted that socialism was logically impossible, because lacking markets it was unable to calculate and therefore incapable to effectively organise a complex society. Calculation requires prices that indicate relative scarcities, which presuppose markets in which the competitive process brings them into the open. Only a market economy was capable of dealing with the calculation problem in a satisfactory way. Mises went so far as to argue that rationality was a by-product of the dealings in markets. He also advocated a kind of domino doctrine: any state intervention in the economy causes damages that will lead to a request for more state intervention in order to make good the damages, which, alas, will cause further damages, and so on, until eventually the economy ends in socialism.

In his praxeology Mises argued against logical positivism, heralded most prominently by the neoclassical school. In contradistinction to the natural sciences, especially physics, economic laws are to be obtained by logical deduction from a small set of self-evident axioms: (1) men choose aims and means to reach them; (2) the law of diminishing marginal utility applies; (3) men are possessed of a positive rate of time preference; (4) action takes time and time is scarce. While he did not argue that predictions are impossible, he insisted that they can be qualitative only.

Friedrich August von Hayek (1899–1992)

Hayek wrote his PhD thesis on the problem of imputation. He participated in Mises's so-called "private seminar" and in 1927 he was appointed to the directorship of the Austrian Institute of Business Cycle Research, founded by Mises. In 1929 he published *Geldtheorie und Konjunkturtheorie* (*Monetary Theory and Theory of Economic Fluctuations*), in which he elaborated on Mises's approach to the problems under consideration. He submitted the book as a habilitation thesis to the University of Vienna and was appointed to a lectureship (*Privatdozent*) there. In 1931 Lionel Robbins invited him to the London School of Economics to give four lectures, which were then published as *Prices and Production* (Hayek 1931b). These lectures had both a critical and a constructive part: the former was directed at Keynes's *Treatise on Money* and sought to refute the idea that the economic system was demand-constrained, whereas the latter was concerned with cross-breeding the Austrian theory of capital and interest, the Misesian theory of money and the Paretian theory of general equilibrium. Robbins also published a paper by Hayek in *Economica*, the London School of Economics (LSE) journal, which contained a frontal assault on Keynes (Hayek 1931a). This led to a famous controversy with Piero Sraffa in the *Economic Journal*, then edited by Keynes, which according to several observers Hayek lost and may have prompted him to turn to social philosophy, a field in which he made important contributions. In 1932 Hayek was appointed to the Tooke Chair at the LSE. In a final attempt to turn the defeat in the controversy with Sraffa into a victory, Hayek worked on capital theory and economic dynamics, but had to admit that the Böhm-Bawerkian approach he had endorsed could not generally be sustained. This becomes clear in his 1941 book on *The Pure Theory of Capital*, which may be considered his last major contribution to pure economic theory. In 1944 he published *The Road to Serfdom* and three years later was one of the founders of the Mont Pèlerin Society. From 1950 to 1962 he held the chair in Social and Moral Sciences at the University of Chicago. His influential book, *The Constitution of Liberty*, was published in 1960. In 1974 he was awarded, together with Gunnar Myrdal, the Sveriges Riksbank Prize in Economic Sciences in Memory of Alfred Nobel, not least, and somewhat ironically, for his "pioneering work in the theory of money and economic fluctuations".

Competition, Hayek insisted, is a procedure for discovering facts, which, without such procedure, would remain unknown and therefore could not be used. This concept of competition stands in striking contrast to the conventional concept of perfect competition in mainstream economics, in which all "data" are assumed to be known to all agents, that is, there is perfect information. In Hayek's view nothing could be further from the truth. Hayek drew the following conclusions: first, the outcomes of the process are typically unpredictable and bound to frustrate some agents by disappointing their expectations; second, conventional microeconomics does not perform all that well when confronted with the real world, because it ignores the fact just mentioned. The competitive process will result in prices that reflect the widely dispersed and fragmented information, a knowledge which no single individual can possibly ever possess, not least because some information reflected in prices is tacit.

As regards the theory of economic fluctuations and unemployment, Hayek (1931b) disputed Keynes's emphasis on the role of aggregate effective demand: the source of crises and depressions are, on the contrary, interventions by governments and central banks, which lead to a misallocation of capital and labour and trigger crises. Hayek's explanation of the world depression in the late 1920s and early 1930s can be said to revolve around his view of the problem of the choice of technique, which derives from Böhm-Bawerk's theory of capital. A money rate of interest fixed by the banking system that is lower than what he called the "equilibrium rate" prompts producers to embark on more roundabout processes of production, that is, lengthen the period of production and thus increase capital intensity. This requires a redirection of productive resources away from industries that are close to the maturing of consumption goods to industries that are far from it (invoking Menger's hierarchy of goods). This is effectuated by bidding up the prices of these resources. However, since the preferences of agents have not changed, the prices of consumption goods, whose flow of output is being diminished, will rise, which, in turn, implies "forced saving": consumers would like to consume more but are prevented from doing so because of an insufficient supply. Yet with rising prices of consumption goods profitability in the industries producing them will increase and provide an incentive to expand their production. This necessitates redirecting productive resources from spheres far away to spheres close to the maturing of consumption goods and reverses the tendency towards a lengthening of the production period. The mute witnesses of the misallocation of capital and labour are prematurely abandoned investment projects – investment "ruins" – and unemployed workers. The misguided development due to too low a money rate of interest becomes obvious and the productive capacity of the economy shrinks: the problem is not a lack of effective demand, as Keynes maintained, but a lack of effective supply. If banks in response to the inflationary pressure that has built up eventually decide to increase the money rate of interest again, the system, Hayek contended, will return to its old equilibrium position. The attempt to boost the economy by means of a policy of easy money is thus argued to be self-defeating: after a costly detour in which productive resources have been wasted the system gets back to where it started.

Keynes who had difficulty warding off Hayek's attack because he was not familiar with its building blocks (the contributions of Böhm-Bawerk, Mises and Pareto) asked Piero Sraffa to rush to his rescue. This Sraffa (1932a) did. First, he rejected Hayek's basic proposition that a divergence between the money rate and the "equilibrium rate" of interest is a characteristic feature of a monetary economy. Second, in a barter economy, he observed, loans would be made in terms of all sorts of commodities. There would be a single (uniform) rate of interest compatible with equilibrium, but there will generally be at any moment as many "natural" (or "commodity" or "own") rates of interest as there are commodities, though they would not be equilibrium rates. He explained that in equilibrium the spot and forward price coincide for all commodities, and all commodity rates are equal to one another and to the money rate. However if, for whichever reason (the weather, for example), the supply and the demand for a commodity are not in equilibrium, its spot and forward prices diverge, and the "commodity" rate of interest on that commodity diverges from the "commodity" rates on other commodities. This will trigger adjustment processes (as they have been discussed by the classical economists in terms of the process of gravitation of market prices to their natural levels) that will tend to remove the discrepancy between spot and forward prices and bring about a new equilibrium. Third, Hayek's idea that the economy will return to its old equilibrium ignores the fact that the banking policy will in the meantime have changed the distribution of wealth and income among agents and thus one of the data defining a Paretian equilibrium (the other two being the preferences of agents and the technical alternatives of production). Fourth, Hayek's idea that "voluntary saving" can be strictly discriminated from "forced saving" is naive. Sraffa concluded that Hayek had not argued correctly and was unable to explain the facts he purported to explain.

Sraffa's criticism had dealt a serious blow to Hayek's explanation of economic fluctuations and, not surprisingly, had pleased Keynes a great deal. In more recent times Hayek's theory has been invoked again in attempts to explain what has been dubbed "the great recession" in the aftermath of the bursting of the financial bubble in 2007. The theory is however difficult to reconcile with important empirical facts, in particular, the fact that in recessions and depressions we generally do not observe an increase in employment in the consumer goods industries, as Hayek contended. An overall slack demand is reflected not least in the underutilisation of productive capacity in the consumer goods sector.

Concluding Remarks

A lot more could be said and several other important German and Austrian economists, such as Christian Jakob Kraus, Heinrich Friedrich von Storch, Hans Mayer, Oskar Morgenstern, Gottfried Haberler and Fritz Machlup, would deserve to be dealt with. Space constraints do not allow this. The reader is asked to consult the works cited in this entry. Chipman (2013) contains excerpts translated into English of important contributions to the German use value school. Kirzner (1994) provides an anthology of some of the writings of Austrian economists. Boettke (1994) contains short essays on basically all themes in Austrian economics and the latter's relationship with other schools of thought.

HEINZ D. KURZ

See also:

Daniel Bernoulli (I); Eugen von Böhm-Bawerk (I); Cameralism (II); Hermann Heinrich Gossen (I); Friedrich August von Hayek (I); Bruno Hildebrand (I); Karl Heinrich Marx (I); Carl Menger (I); Ludwig Heinrich von Mises (I); Wilhelm Georg Friedrich Roscher (I); Joseph Alois Schumpeter (I); Adam Smith (I); Friedrich von Wieser (I).

References and further reading

Baloglou, C. (1995), *Die Vertreter der mathematischen Nationalökonomie in Deutschland zwischen 1838 und 1871*, Marburg: Metropolis Verlag.

Boettke, P. (1994), *The Elgar Companion to Austrian Economics*, Aldershot, UK and Brookfield, VT, USA: Edward Elgar.

Böhm-Bawerk, E. von (1884), *Kapital und Kapitalzins. Erste Abteilung: Geschichte und Kritik der Kapitalzins-Theorien*, Innsbruck: Wagner, 2nd edn 1903, 3rd edn 1914, 4th edn 1921, Jena: Gustav Fischer, English trans. of 1st edn (1890), *Capital and Interest*, London: Macmillan, English trans. of 4th edn (1959), *Capital and Interest*, vol. 1, South Holland, IL: Libertarian Press.

Böhm-Bawerk, E. von (1886–87), 'Grundzüge der Theorie des wirtschaftlichen Güterwerts', *Jahrbücher für Nationalökonomie und Statistik*, two instalments: **47** (1886), 1–82; **48** (1887), 477–541.

Böhm-Bawerk, E. von (1889), *Kapital und Kapitalzins. Zweite Abteilung: Positive Theorie des Kapitales*, Innsbruck: Wagner, 2nd edn 1902; 3rd edn in 2 vols 1909 and 1912, 4th edn in 2 vols 1921, Jena: Gustav Fischer, English trans. of 1st edn (1891), *The Positive Theory of Capital*, London: Macmillan, English trans. of 4th edn (1959), *Capital and Interest*, vols. 2 and 3, South Holland, IL: Libertarian Press.

Böhm-Bawerk, E. von (1892), 'Wert, Kosten und Grenznutzen', *Jahrbücher für Nationalökonomie und Statistik*, third series, **3**, 321–67.

Böhm-Bawerk, E. von (1914), 'Macht oder ökonomisches Gesetz?', *Zeitschrift für Volkswirtschaft, Sozialpolitik und Verwaltung*, **23**, 205–71, English trans. (2010), *Control or Economic Law*, Auburn, AL: Ludwig von Mises Institute.

Böhm-Bawerk, E. von (1949), 'Karl Marx and the close of his system', reprinted in P.M. Sweezy (ed.), *Karl Marx and the Close of His System*, New York: Augustus M. Kelley, pp. 1–118, English trans. of E. von Böhm-Bawerk (1896), 'Zum Abschluß des Marxschen Systems', in O. von Boenigk (ed.), *Staatswissenschaftliche Arbeiten. Festgaben für Karl Knies*, Berlin: Haering.

Bortkiewicz, L. von (1906), 'Der Kardinalfehler der Böhm-Bawerkschen Zinstheorie', *Schmollers Jahrbuch*, **30**, 943–72.

Chipman, J.S. (2005), 'Contributions of the older German schools to the development of utility theory', in C. Scheer (ed.), *Die Ältere Historische Schule: Wirtschaftstheoretische Beiträge und Wirtschaftspolitische Vorstellung, Studien zur Entwicklung der ökonomischen Theorie*, vol. 20, Berlin: Duncker & Humblot, pp. 157–258.

Chipman, J.S. (2013), *German Utility Theory: Analysis and Translations*, Abingdon and New York: Routledge.

Cournot, A. (1838), *Recherches sur les principe mathématiques de la théorie des richesses*, Paris: Hachette.

Diehl, K. (1908), 'Die Entwicklung der Wert- und Preistheorie im 19. Jahrhundert', in G.P. Altmann et al. (eds), *Die Entwicklung der deutschen Volkswirtschaftslehre im neunzehnten Jahrhundert. Gustav Schmoller zur siebzigsten Wiederkehr seines Geburtstages*, pt 1, Leipzig: Duncker und Humblot.

Friedländer, E. (1852), *Die Theorie des Werths*, Tartu: Druck von Heinrich Laakmann.

Garegnani, P. (1960), *Il capitale nelle teorie della distribuzione*, Milan: Giuffrè.

Georgescu-Roegen, N. (1983), 'Hermann Heinrich Gossen: his life and work in historical perspective', in H.H. Gossen (1983), *The Laws of Human Relations and the Rules of Human Action Derived Therefrom*, Cambridge, MA: MIT Press, pp. xi–cxiv.

Gossen, H.H. (1854), *Entwickelung der Gesetze des menschlichen Verkehrs und der daraus fließenden Regeln für menschliches Handeln*, Braunschweig: Vieweg and Son.

Gossen, H.H. (1983), *The Laws of Human Relations and the Rules of Human Action Derived Therefrom*, ed. and introduced by N. Georgescu-Roegen, Cambridge, MA: MIT Press.

Grice-Hutchinson, M. (1952), *The School of Salamanca: Readings in Spanish Monetary Theory, 1544–1605*, Oxford: Oxford University Press.

Harcourt, G.C. (1972), *Some Cambridge Controversies in the Theory of Capital*, Cambridge: Cambridge University Press.

Hayek, F.A. von (1929), *Geldtheorie und Konjunkturtheorie*, Vienna and Leipzig: Hölder-Pichler-Tempsk.

Hayek, F.A. von (1931a), 'Reflections on the pure theory of money of Mr. J.M. Keynes', *Economica*, **11** (33), 270–95.

Hayek, F.A. von (1931b), *Prices and Production*, London: Routledge and Kegan Paul.

Hayek, F.A. von (1932), 'Money and capital: a reply', *Economic Journal*, **42** (2), 237–49.

Hayek, F.A. von (1941), *The Pure Theory of Capital*, London: Routledge and Kegan Paul.

Hermann, F.B.W. von (1832), *Staatswirthschaftliche Untersuchungen*, Munich: Anton Weber'sche Buchhandlung.

Hicks, J.R. (1973), *Capital and Time: A Neo-Austrian Theory*, Oxford: Oxford University Press.

Hildebrand, B. (1848), *Die Nationalökonomie der Gegenwart und Zukunft*, Frankfurt: Literarische Anstalt.

Hufeland, G. (1807, 1813), *Neue Grundlegung der Staatswirthschaftskunst*, vol. 1 (1807) Biesen: Tasche and Müller, vol. 2 (1813) Biesen: Gottgetreu Müller.

Jakob, L.H. von (1805), *Grundsätze der National-Oekonomie oder National-Wirthschaftslehre*, Halle: Ruffsche Verlagshandlung.

Jevons, W.S. (1871), *The Theory of Political Economy*, London: Macmillan.

Kirzner, I. (1994), *Classics in Austrian Economics. A Sampling in the History of a Tradition*, 3 vols, London: William Pickering.

Knies, K. (1855), 'Die nationalökonomische Lehre vom Werth', *Zeitschrift für die gesamte Staatswissenschaft*, **11**, 421–75.

Knies, K. (1873), *Das Geld*, Berlin: Weidmannsche Buchhandlung.

Kurz, H.D. (1994), 'Auf der Suche nach dem "erlösenden Wort": Eugen von Böhm-Bawerk und der Kapitalzins', in B. Schefold (ed.), *Eugen von Böhm-Bawerks "Geschichte und Kritik der Kapitalzinstheorieen". Vademecum zu einem Klassiker der Theoriegeschichte*, Düsseldorf: Verlag Wirtschaft und Finanzen, pp. 45–110.

Kurz, H.D. (1995), 'Marginalism, classicism and socialism in German-speaking countries, 1871–1932', in I. Steedman (ed.), *Socialism and Marginalism in Economics, 1870–1930*, London and New York: Routledge, pp. 7–86.

Kurz, H.D. (1998), 'Friedrich Benedict Wilhelm Hermann on capital and profits', *European Journal of the History of Economic Thought*, **5** (1), 85–119.

Kurz, H.D. (ed.) (2000), *Critical Essays on Piero Sraffa's Legacy in Economics*, Cambridge and New York: Cambridge University Press.

Kurz, H.D. and N. Salvadori (1995), *Theory of Production. A Long-Period Analysis*, Cambridge: Cambridge University Press.

Kurz, H.D. and R. Sturn (1999), 'Wiesers "Ursprung" und die Entwicklung der Mikroökonomik', in B. Schefold (ed.), *Friedrich von Wiesers "Über den Ursprung und die Hauptgesetze des wirtschaftlichen Werthes". Vademecum zu einem Klassiker der Volkswirtschaftslehre*, Düsseldorf: Verlag Wirtschaft und Finanzen, pp. 59–103.

Lancaster, K.J. (1971), *Consumer Demand: A New Approach*, New York and London: Columbia University Press.

Lotz, J.F.E. (1811–14), *Revision der Grundbegriffe der Nationalwirthschaftslehre*, 4 vols, Coburg and Leipzig: Sinner'sche Buchhandlung.

Mangoldt, H. von (1863), *Grundriß der Volkswirthschaftslehre*, Stuttgart: Engelhorn.

Menger, C. (1871), *Grundsätze der Volkswirthschaftslehre*, Vienna: Wilhelm Braumüller.

Menger, C. (2007), *Principles of Economics*, trans J. Dingwall and B.F. Hoselitz, Glencoe, IL: Free Press.

Mises, L. von (1912), *Theorie des Geldes und der Umlaufsmittel*, Munich and Leipzig: Duncker and Humblot.

Mises, L. von (1920), 'Die Wirtschaftsrechnung im sozialistischen Gemeinwesen', *Archiv für Sozialwissenschaften*, **47**, English trans. "Economic calculation in the socialist commonwealth,' in F.A. Hayek (ed.) (1935), *Collectivist Economic Planning*, London: George Routledge & Sons, pp. 87–130.

Mises, L. von (1940), *Nationalökonomie. Theorie des Handelns und Wirtschaftens*, Geneva: Union.

Mises, L. von (1949), *Human Action*, Auburn, AL: Ludwig von Mises Institute, English trans. of L. von Mises (1940), *Nationalökonomie. Theorie des Handelns und Wirtschaftens*, Geneva: Union.

Mises, L. von (1978), *Erinnerungen von Ludwig v. Mises*, Stuttgart and New York: Gustav Fischer.

Opocher, A. and I. Steedman (2015), *Full Industry Equilibrium*, Cambridge: Cambridge University Press.

Priddat, B.P. (ed.) (1997), *Wert, Meinung, Bedeutung. Die Tradition der subjektiven Wertlehre in der deutschsprachigen Nationalökonomie vor Menger*, Marburg: Metropolis Verlag.

Rau, K.H. (1826), *Lehrbuch der politischen Ökonomie*, vol. 1, *Grundsätze der Volkswirthschaftslehre*, 2nd edn 1833, 3rd edn 1837, 4th edn 1841, Heidelberg: C.F. Winter.

Rau, K.H. (1828), *Lehrbuch der politischen Ökonomie*, vol. II, Heidelberg: C.F. Winter.

Rau, K.H. (1832), *Lehrbuch der politischen Ökonomie*, vol. III.1, Heidelberg: C.F. Winter.

Rau, K.H. (1837), *Lehrbuch der politischen Ökonomie*, vol. III.2, Heidelberg: C.F. Winter.

Ricardo, D. (1951–73), *The Collected Writings and Correspondence of David Ricardo*, 11 vols, ed. P. Sraffa with the collaboration of M.H. Dobb, Cambridge: Cambridge University Press.

Roover, R. de (1955), 'Scholastic economics. Survival and lasting influence from the sixteenth century to Adam Smith', *Quarterly Journal of Economics*, **69** (2), 161–90.

Roscher, W. (1843), *Grundriß zu Vorlesungen über die Staatswirthschaft. Nach geschichtlicher Methode*, Göttingen: Dieterich.

Roscher, W. (1854), *System der Volkswirthschaft*, vol. 1: *Die Grundlagen der Nationalökonomie. Ein Hand- und Lesebuch für Geschäftsmänner und Studierende*, 2nd edn 1857, Stuttgart and Tübingen: Cotta.

Schefold, B. (1998), 'Bruno Hildebrand: Die historische Perspektive eines liberalen Ökonomen', in B. Schefold (ed.), *Vademecum zu einem Klassiker der Stufenlehre*, Düsseldorf: Verlag Wirtschaft und Finanzen, pp. 5–55.

Schumpeter, J.A. (1913), 'Eine "dynamische" Theorie des Kapitalzinses. Eine Entgegnung', *Zeitschrift für Volkswirtschaft, Sozialpolitik und Verwaltung*, **22**, 411–51.

Schumpeter, J.A. (1954), *History of Economic Analysis*, New York: Oxford University Press.

Smith, A. (1776), *An Inquiry into the Nature and Causes of the Wealth of Nations*, reprinted in R.H. Campbell and A.S. Skinner (eds) (1976), *The Glasgow Edition of the Works and Correspondence of Adam Smith*, 2 vols, Oxford, Oxford University Press; in the text referred to as WN, book number, chapter number, section number, paragraph number.

Smith, B. (1994), *Austrian Philosophy. The Legacy of Franz Brentano*, Chicago and La Salle, IL: Open Court.

Soden, J.H. (1805), *Die Nazional-Oekonomie. Ein philosophischer Versuch, über die Quellen des National-Reichthums, und über die Mittel zu dessen Beförderung*, vol. 1 (of 9) Leipzig: Johann Ambrosius Barth.

Sraffa, P. (1932a), 'Dr. Hayek on money and capital', *Economic Journal*, **42** (1), 42–53.

Sraffa, P. (1932b), 'A rejoinder', *Economic Journal*, **42** (2), 249–51.

Sraffa, P. (1960), *Production of Commodities by Means of Commodities*, Cambridge: Cambridge University Press.

Steedman, I. (2001), *Consumption Takes Time. Implications for Economic Theory*, London: Routledge.

Streissler, E. (1990), 'The influence of German economics on Menger and Marshall', in B.J. Caldwell (ed.), *Carl Menger and his Legacy in Economics*, Durham: Durham University Press, pp. 31–68.

Streissler, E. (1994), 'Wilhelm Roscher als führender Wirtschaftstheoretiker', in B. Schefold (ed.), *Vademecum zu einem Klassiker der Historischen Schule*, Düsseldorf: Handelsblatt Verlag, pp. 37–121.

Streissler, E. (1997), 'Carl Menger, der deutsche Nationalökonom', in B.P. Priddat (ed.), *Wert, Meinung, Bedeutung. Die Tradition der subjektiven Wertlehre in der deutschsprachigen Nationalökonomie vor Menger*, Marburg: Metropolis Verlag, pp. 33–88.

Thünen, J.H. von (1826), *Der isolierte Staat in Beziehung auf Landwirthschaft und Nationalökonomie*, pt 1, Hamburg: Friedrich Perthes.

Wagner, A. (1876), *Allgemeine oder theoretische Volkswirthschaftslehre. Mit Benutzung von Rau's Grundsätzen der Volkswirthschaftslehre*, pt I, *Grundlegung*, Leipzig and Heidelberg: C.F. Winter.

Wieser, F. von (1884), *Über den Ursprung und die Hauptgesetze des wirthschaftlichen Werthes*, Vienna: Alfred Hölder.

Wieser, F. von (1889), *Der natürliche Werth*, Vienna: Alfred Hölder, English trans. (1893), *Natural Value*, London: Macmillan.

Wieser, F. von (1926), *Das Gesetz der Macht*, Vienna: Julius Springer.

Yagi, K. (2011), *Austrian and German Economic Thought: From Subjectivism to Social Evolution*, London: Routledge.

British marginalism

The term "English marginalism" generally refers to the work and outlook of a small group of economists working in England in roughly the last quarter of the nineteenth century. These may be thought of as pioneer neoclassical economists and include, as major figures, Jevons, Marshall, Edgeworth and Wicksteed. The latter was later a strong influence on Robbins, who provided leadership for a later generation of marginalists; see O'Brien (1988). Edgeworth was Anglo-Irish, and Jevons developed his earliest ideas in Australia, but it is obviously appropriate to group them under English marginalism. Distinctions along such national lines are of course not necessarily solid, particularly as, following the lead set by Jevons, this period can be regarded as the "high period" in the international exchange of ideas. Also, as Hutchison (1955: 9) stated, "Edgeworth, Wicksteed, Auspitz and Lieben, Wieser, Böhm-Bawerk, Wicksell, Walras, Pareto, Barone and Fisher all drew on a broad, internationally known literature". Important and original works were, "constructed essentially on the basis of a wide, eclectic, cosmopolitan reading of their contemporaries and immediate predecessors" (Hutchison 1955: 9). However, Hutchison (1955: 10) also makes the interesting point that, despite Edgeworth's international sympathies, publications by non-English economists in the *Economic Journal* were negligible. Furthermore, the journal played no part in securing translations of major works, and it seems that the only translation which Edgeworth encouraged was that of N.G. Pierson's *Principles* in 1902.

Nevertheless, it is possible to discern differences, in views and influences, between English and continental writers during this period. Walras developed his analysis of exchange, quite independently of the English writers, as an extension of Cournot's model of trade between regions involving a single good. Indeed, despite an extensive correspondence, his relationship with English authors cannot ultimately be described as congenial, particularly after Edgeworth's review of the *Elements* where he criticised, among other things, the "exuberance of algebraic foliage". It is true that there are traces of the influence of Cournot on Marshall's early unpublished work, available in Whitaker (1975), but the main influence in producing his offer curve analysis of trade was clearly J.S. Mill. Communication among the English marginalists was facilitated by closer proximity, particularly in London. There was, of course, the long-established Political Economy Club, and Herford (1931: 119) reports that between 1884 and 1888 there were regular economic discussions at the house of Henry Beeton. The circle included Wicksteed, Edgeworth, Foxwell, Sidney Webb and Bernard Shaw (Jevons had of course died in 1882). In addition, the Junior Economic Club was formed at University College in 1890. The formation of the Royal Economic Society is discussed below.

The Political Economy Club saw debates between Wicksteed, who produced his Jevonian critique of Marx in 1884, and the Fabian Socialist, Shaw. Earlier, around 1879, Edgeworth came into contact with Jevons, a near neighbour in Hampstead, through a mutual friend, James Sully, and their membership of the Savile Club. This led to Edgeworth's rapid shift of attention from moral philosophy towards economics, marked by his *Mathematical Psychics* published in 1881.

Furthermore, the English marginalists were not always in agreement. Even though Edgeworth and Wicksteed may be described as disciples of Jevons, they were by no means slavish followers. Edgeworth (1881: 109) defended Jevons's "trading body" in terms of "a sort of typical couple", but the point of departure of his work was the need to examine the role of the number of traders as an extension of Jevons's framework, where price-taking behaviour was simply assumed. Jevons and Edgeworth also had completely different attitudes towards authority, with Jevons famously rejecting any role and Edgeworth always ready to quote an authority in support of his argument, viewing authority as almost equivalent to empirical evidence. Jevons took Edgeworth to task for the lack of transparency in his writing. Furthermore, Edgeworth criticised Wicksteed's use of linear homogeneous production functions. Despite Edgeworth's admiration for Marshall, there were strong disagreements between them, for example, over indeterminacy in exchange (the "barter controversy") and Giffen goods: on contrasts between Marshall and Edgeworth, see also Creedy (1990). Furthermore, Marshall stressed the evolution of ideas and continuity with classical economics, while the others took a more revolutionary stand. Marshall saw a clear line of filiation from Smith and Ricardo through J.S. Mill, while Jevons famously explicitly rejected Mill.

The term "English marginalism" also requires discussion. This is undoubtedly the most common description used in the secondary and textbook literature. It appears to give primacy to the emphasis on the margin or the use of calculus, so that derivatives of utility and production functions became ubiquitous (though the term "marginal utility", replacing such awkward terms as "final degree of utility", owes its origin to Wicksteed). It is true that Jevons, Edgeworth and Wicksteed all produced extensive apologia or justifications for the use of mathematics in economics and that, despite relegating his analyses to appendices, many of Marshall's innovations were arrived at via the use of mathematics and diagrammatic analyses. Nevertheless, it is worth stressing that the period marks a distinct change of emphasis, rather than simply of technique, in the study of economics. Instead of the concentration by the classical economists on the great dynamic themes of growth and development, and the important and highly sophisticated monetary debates associated with the numerous banking crises of the first half of the nineteenth century, the emphasis of the neoclassical economists was on the nature of exchange.

Exchange was seen (particularly by Jevons, Edgeworth and Wicksteed) as the "central" problem in economics. For example, Hicks (1984) referred to the early neoclassicals as "catallactists", in order to emphasise their exchange focus. This neologism of Whately, used also by Edgeworth, was extensively used by Hearn (1864) in his *Plutology*, which appears to have had some influence on Jevons, who is known to have attended a lecture by Hearn while in Australia. Hicks stressed (1984: 250) that:

> while the classics looked at the economic system primarily from the production angle, the catallactists looked at it primarily from the side of exchange. It was possible, they found, to construct a "vision" of economic life out of the theory of exchange, as the classics had done out of the social product. It was quite a different vision. (1984: 250)

Edgeworth (1925, II: 288) summarised the position by suggesting that "in pure economics there is only one fundamental theorem, but that is a very difficult one: the theory of bargain in a wide sense". Edgeworth also stressed, "the fundamental principle of international trade is that general theory which Jevons called the Theory of Exchange ... which constitutes the "kernel" of most of the chief problems of economics" (1925, II: 6). He added, "distribution is the species of exchange by which produce is divided between the parties who have contributed to it" (1925, II: 13). Schumpeter (1954: 911) wrote, "they realised the central position of exchange value" which "is but a special form of a universal coefficient of transformation on the derivation of which pivots the whole logic of economic phenomena". Furthermore, in considering the central position of exchange theory, Fraser (1937: 104) stated that the view of costs in terms of foregone alternatives is "merely the extension of the exchange relationship to the whole of economic life".

The great success of the early marginalist or neoclassical economists was also associated with the fact that they provided a foundation for their exchange model in the form of a utility analysis. Utilitarianism was of course the dominant moral philosophy (despite lively debates during the period with idealists and social Darwinists) among the English marginalists, influenced particularly by J.S. Mill and Sidgwick, although none was perhaps as strong in his adherence as Edgeworth. Although it is sometimes remarked, following Hutchison (1955), that in "marginal utility", the adjective is more important than the noun, a utility approach allowed for a deeper treatment of the gains from exchange and the wider consideration of economic welfare. Furthermore, this type of welfare analysis survived the replacement of a cardinal utility concept with an ordinal concept, or the idea of a simple preference ordering. Indeed, Hicks stated that "welfare economics was captured by the catallactists and it has never got quite free" (1984: 253). Hicks was of course directly involved in developing the "new welfare economics". The issues were discussed in the famous book by another later marginalist, Robertson (1952).

The success of their agenda can thus be attributed to the fact that they did indeed manage to produce a unified theory on such foundations. In looking back on the dominance of the "marginalists", Hicks (1984: 252) argued:

> I would therefore maintain that the principal reason for the triumph of catallactics – in its day it was quite a triumph – was nothing to do with socialism or individualism; nor did it even have much to do with the changes that were then occurring in the "real world". The construction of a powerful economic theory, based on exchange, instead of production and distribution, had always been a possibility. The novelty in the work of the great catallactists is just that they achieved it.

It is only when the perceived central position of exchange analysis is recognised, along with the place of the principle of utility maximisation as the foundation, that it is possible to have some appreciation of the attitude behind Edgeworth's (1881: 12) remark, after discussing the extension of utility analysis to subjects such as production and labour supply, that:

> "Mécanique sociale" may one day take her place along with "Mécanique céleste", throned each upon the double-sided height of one maximum principle, the supreme pinnacle of moral as of physical science . . . the movements of each soul, whether selfishly isolated or linked sympathetically, may continually be realising the maximum energy of pleasure, the Divine love of the universe.

Of course, other writers were much more prosaic in their expressions than Edgeworth, but his view nicely encapsulates something of the pioneering spirit of the early neoclassical economists.

This spirit is also displayed in Jevons's letters to his sister and brother. Jevons, writing to his sister, suggested that, "in treating of Man or Society there must also be general principles and laws which underlie all the present discussions & partial arguments . . .

each individual must be a creature of cause and effect" (see Black 1977: 361). His letter to his brother stated that he had, "fortunately struck out what I have no doubt is the true theory of economy, so thorough-going and consistent, that I cannot now read other books on the subject without indignation" (see Black 1977: 410). Schumpeter argued that the utility analysis must be understood in the context of exchange as the central "pivot", and "the whole of the organism of pure economics thus finds itself unified in the light of a single principle – in a sense in which it never had before" (1954: 913). However, Marshall did not share in this enthusiasm.

The famous "equations of exchange" illustrate both a point of similarity and difference between Jevons and Walras. Using similar two-person two-good exchange models, they independently produced (in Walras's case, with help from his mathematician colleague Paul Piccard) the two simultaneous equations involved, and they both concentrated on price-taking solutions. It is recognised that some commentators would dispute this point, placing much stress on different interpretations of Walras's famous *tâtonnement* process. However, in the formal models it is hard to escape the fact that, just as in Jevons's approach, individuals are price-takers and in the equilibria considered, all exchange takes place at the corresponding prices. Jevons left the equations expressed in terms of quantities exchanged, leaving the equilibrium price ratio to be determined by the resulting ratio of quantities. Recognising the nonlinear nature of these equations for most forms of utility function, so that explicit solutions could not be obtained, Jevons therefore did not formally derive demand functions for the two goods in terms of relative prices. Edgeworth subsequently developed his indifference curve analysis of exchange within his box diagram and, given his emphasis on indeterminacy rather than price-taking, gave priority to the contract curve rather than demand curves.

Walras (1874) instead had previously extended Cournot's model of trade between two regions, involving a single good, to produce a non-utility analysis of the exchange of two goods between two traders. He produced his general equilibrium demand and supply curves in which the quantity demanded or supplied is expressed as a function of the relative price. He had explored the form these curves might take, in particular, showing that in general the supply curves would be expected to be "backward bending", essentially because suppliers also have a demand for the good of which they hold stocks. Hence, when faced with the equations of exchange, he realised that instead of trying to solve them in terms of quantities of the two goods, the concept of reciprocal supply and demand allowed him to replace one of the quantities with the product of a relative price and the other quantity, since $\frac{y}{x} = \frac{p_x}{p_y}$, where x and y are the amounts exchanged and p_x and p_y are the respective prices. This reciprocal demand relationship had of course been recognised by many earlier economists, but in order to produce an exchange model, this idea needs to be combined with the idea of demand as a function of relative price. Walras is therefore credited with showing explicitly how general equilibrium demand and supply functions can be derived from utility functions: these are not the partial equilibrium demand functions which, partly through Marshall's influence, later came to dominate economic analysis.

Formally, persons A and B hold endowments, a and b respectively, of goods X and Y. Where x and y are the amounts exchanged, utility after trade takes place can therefore be written as $U_A = U_A(a - x, y)$ for trader A, while for B it is $U_B = U_B(x, b - y)$: Jevons actually used additive utility functions. The "keystone" of the theory is the result that for utility maximisation, "*the ratio of exchange of any two commodities will be the reciprocal of the ratio of the final degrees of utility of the quantities of commodity available for consumption after the exchange is complete*" (Jevons 1871, in 1957: 95, original emphasis). This gives rise to his famous "equations of exchange", which can be expressed using modern notation as:

$$-\frac{\partial U_A/\partial x}{\partial U_A/\partial y} = \frac{dy}{dx} = -\frac{\partial U_B/\partial x}{\partial U_B/\partial y} \tag{1}$$

The term $\frac{dy}{dx}$ is the ratio of exchange of the two commodities at the margin. Jevons recognised that the integration of these differential equations presents formidable difficulties, and for this reason he restricted his attention to price-taking equilibria, using his "law of indifference" whereby there are no trades at disequilibrium ratios of exchange and "the last increments in an act of exchange must be exchanged in the same ratio as the whole quantities exchanged" (1957: 94). This means that $\frac{y}{x}$ can be substituted for $\frac{dy}{dx}$ in (1), giving two simultaneous equations in x and y. Jevons recognised that $\frac{y}{x}$ is equivalent to the ratio of prices of the two goods, $p = \frac{p_x}{p_y} = \frac{y}{x}$, but he preferred to leave p out of the equations until the equilibrium values of y and x are obtained. Recognising, as noted above, that in general the equations in (1) would be nonlinear, he did not take their formal analysis further, although he added the important but rather cryptic comment that the theory is "perfectly consistent with the laws of supply and demand; and if we had the functions of utility determined, it would be possible throw them into a form clearly expressing the equivalence of supply and demand" (Jevons 1957: 101). He showed how the equations can be used to examine some "complex cases"; see Creedy (1992).

Walras explicitly considered the step to which Jevons had merely alluded, and replaced y with px in order to suggest that the resulting equations could be solved for x and y in terms of p. He did not do this for fully specified functional forms for utility functions, and indeed the equations can be solved explicitly only for certain special cases. Launhardt (1885 [1993]) was later to be the first to do this, using quadratic utility functions. Curiously, this important step taken by Walras was not discussed by the English marginalists at all. Indeed his associated demand and supply curves seem to have been almost entirely "lost"; they do not appear in any history of economics or microeconomics texts. For further discussion see Creedy (1999).

They received their most extensive development by Launhardt (1885 [1993]), whose analysis was used heavily in a rather terse treatment by Wicksell (1895). The curves were discussed very briefly, in the comprehensive review of Walras's equilibrium economics, by van Daal and Jolink (1993: 26). They commented that, "it did not get much following", and referred to the "undeniable complexity of the figures". The only treatment in general works on the history of economic analysis seems to be the terse mention by Stigler (1965: 96), who also referred to Wicksell, but not to Launhardt.

The above discussion has focused on the essential characteristics and preoccupations of the British marginalists, and some differences from contemporary continental European writers. However, it is worth considering the special context in which these economists worked. Hicks is quoted above as describing the nature of the "victory" of the catallactists, but it is nevertheless true that any kind of victory from the point of view of the attitude of the profession as a whole had to wait many years.

British economics in the 1870s was going through a period of pessimism, reflected in Bagehot's (1880: 3) comment that it "lies rather dead in the public mind. Not only . . . it does not excite the same interest as formerly but there is not exactly the same confidence in it". A further symptom of the negative attitude was the attempt to exclude economics from the British Association (Section F, "Economic Science and Statistics"). There was also substantial tension between analytical economists and economic historians, such as Cunningham, and also the historical economists, such as Ingram, who were sympathetic to the German School.

The new technical innovations of the marginalists were greeted with the argument that economics was losing touch with reality. Jevons's *Theory of Political Economy* was greeted with more criticism than praise, particularly regarding his use of mathematics. Marshall (in Black 1981: 146) suggested that, "the book before us would be improved if the mathematics were omitted but the diagrams retained". Cairnes (in Black 1981: 152) argued that, "when mathematics are carried further . . . without constant reference to the concrete meaning of the terms for which the mathematical symbols are employed, I own I regard the practice with profound distrust". The anonymous reviewer in the *Saturday Review* concluded that, "whether anything can or cannot be done in the direction indicated – and we by no means say that it cannot – Mr. Jevons has taken us a very short way" (in Black 1981: 157). Cliff Leslie wrote, "we regret that so much of Mr. Jevons' [*sic*] own reasoning is put into a mathematical form, because it is one unintelligible or unattractive to many students of considerable intellectual power and attainments" (in Black 1981: 160).

Jevons's reputation was indeed initially based on his applied and policy analyses. Also Edgeworth did not really establish his position until after the extensive work on index numbers, in his role as secretary to the British Association Report on Index Numbers, which produced three volumes in the late 1880s. His first professorial appointment, at King's College London, was in 1890 when he was 45 years old. Edgeworth's most important publication, *Mathematical Psychics*, was privately published in 1881 and, apart from the reviews by Marshall and Jevons, it was largely ignored for many years.

The Royal Economic Society (initially the British Economic Association – BEA) was not established, along with the *Economic Journal*, until 1890 and, despite Edgeworth's editorship, the early issues contained a very broad range of studies – technical and analytical work was in a very small minority. The new journal cannot be said to have reflected a clear marginalist agenda. Indeed it was important, as Marshall stressed, to appeal to as wide a group as possible. In the same spirit no entry barriers were placed on membership of the association; for further discussion, see Coats (1968). This was not even the first economics journal in Britain: the Oxford University branch of the Christian Social Union launched its *Economic Review* before the *Economic Journal*, a move which significantly worried those who were planning to set up the BEA.

Economic debate during the period was by no means dominated by academics. Coats (1968: 370) shows that in 1891, of the 501 members of the British Economic Association who could be identified, only 86 could be described as university teachers. To this it must also be added that there were very few students of economics – even the academic economists were drawn from other disciplines. The small number of economists produced by Cambridge was a regular source of complaint by Marshall, and it took him many years to establish the economics degree (the Tripos) in Cambridge.

The introduction of a marginal utility analysis of exchange also came at a time when there was much debate in Britain regarding moral philosophy. Utilitarianism may have been dominant in Cambridge, under Sidgwick, but Oxford was dominated by Idealists such as T.H. Green and F.H. Bradley who were heavily influenced by Hegel and Kant. Other approaches, such as social Darwinism, with enthusiasts such as Herbert Spencer, were also becoming popular. Thus the welfare economics and technical analysis based on utility maximisation did not initially fall on fertile ground. While it is easy from the present perspective to write in terms of a victory for English marginalists, it is nevertheless the case that economics in England during the last quarter of the nineteenth century was carried out by a significantly heterogeneous group of writers. Furthermore, the marginalists themselves did not form a unified group with a single-minded agenda. The early death of Jevons left the marginalists without a pioneering and passionate leader, and Marshall – with his much wider sympathies and broader vision – became the undisputed leader of British economics for a generation.

JOHN CREEDY

See also:

Jeremy Bentham (I); Francis Ysidro Edgeworth (I); Formalization and mathematical modelling (III); Income distribution (III); William Stanley Jevons (I); Lausanne School (II); Alfred Marshall (I); Arthur Cecil Pigou (I); Lionel Charles Robbins (I); Utilitarianism and anti-utilitarianism (III); Value and price (III); Welfare economics (III); Philip Henry Wicksteed (I).

References and further reading

Bagehot, W. (1880), *Economic Studies*, London: Longmans Green.
Black, R.D.C. (1977), *Papers and Correspondence of William Stanley Jevons*, vol. 2. London: Macmillan.
Black, R.D.C. (1981), *Papers and Correspondence of William Stanley Jevons*, vol. 7, London: Macmillan.
Coats, A.W. (1968), 'The origins and early development of the Royal Economic Society', *Economic Journal*, **78** (310), 349–71.
Creedy, J. (1990), 'Marshall and Edgeworth', *Scottish Journal of Political Economy*, **37** (1), 18–39.
Creedy, J. (1992), 'Jevons's complex cases in the theory of exchange', *Journal of the History of Economic Thought*, **14** (Spring), 55–69.
Creedy, J. (1999), 'The rise and fall of Walras's demand and supply curves', *Manchester School*, **67** (2), 192–202.
Edgeworth, F.Y. (1881), *Mathematical Psychics*, London: Kegan Paul.
Edgeworth, F.Y. (1925), *Papers Relating to Political Economy*, 2 vols, London: Macmillan.
Fraser, L.M. (1937), *Economic Thought and Language*, London: A. and C. Black.
Hearn, W.E. (1864), *Plutology: Or the Theory of Efforts to Satisfy Human Wants*, London: Macmillan.
Herford, C.H. (1931), *Philip Wicksteed: His Life and Work*, London: J.M. Dent.
Hicks, J.R. (1984), *The Economics of John Hicks*, ed. D. Helm, Oxford: Basil Blackwell.
Hutchison, T.W. (1955), *Review of Economic Doctrines 1870–1929*, Oxford: Clarendon Press.
Jevons, W.S. (1957), *The Theory of Political Economy*, 5th edn, ed. H.S. Jevons. New York: Augustus Kelly.
Launhardt, W. (1885), *Mathematical Principles of Economics*, trans. 1993 by H. Schmidt and ed. J. Creedy, Aldershot, UK and Brookfield, VT, USA: Edward Elgar.
O'Brien, D.P. (1988), *Lionel Robbins*, London: Macmillan.
Pierson, N.G. (1902), *Principles of Economics*, London: Macmillan.
Robertson, D.H. (1952), *Utility and All That*, London: Allen and Unwin.
Schumpeter, J.A. (1954), *History of Economic Analysis*, London: Allen and Unwin.
Stigler, G.J. (1965), *Essays in the History of Economics*, Chicago, IL: University of Chicago Press.
Van Daal, J. and A. Jolink (1993), *The Equilibrium Economics of Leon Walras*, London: Routledge.
Walras, L. (1874), *Elements of Pure Economics*, trans. 1954 W. Jaffé, London: Allen and Unwin.
Whitaker, J.K. (ed.) (1975), *The Early Economic Writings of Alfred Marshall 1867–1890*, London: Macmillan.
Wicksell, K. (1895), *Value, Capital and Rent*, trans. 1954 S.H. Frowein, London: Allen and Unwin.

Lausanne School

In the current sense of the term and strictly speaking, the name École de Lausanne (Lausanne School), which dates back to the early twentieth century, refers to three economists' contributions to (pure) economics: Léon Walras, who was the founder of it and held the first chair in economics at the University of Lausanne, his successor Vilfredo Pareto and, incidentally, Pasquale Boninsegni.

In the last quarter of the nineteenth century, economists who wanted to get together a group of authors anxious to widely use mathematics in economic reasoning dubbed themselves the École mathématique (Mathematical School). A number of economists used to be called that way, namely, Antoine-Augustin Cournot, William Stanley Jevons and Irving Fisher. The name École de Lausanne first occurred in French in the subtitle to the *Petit traité d'économie politique mathématique* (*Small Treatise on Mathematical Political Economy*), written by a mathematician – Hermann Laurent – in 1902, which presented a simplified version of the general economic equilibrium. The first occurrence in English might be said to date back to 1909: Edgeworth's announcement in the *Economic Journal* of the ceremony in honor of Léon Walras, his "fifty-year Jubilee". The École de Lausanne is thus characterized by its innovative and systematic use of mathematical language in the study of economic phenomena and its consideration of the interdependencies between markets, through its formulation of the general economic equilibrium. It had first bite at the mathematical determination of equilibrium prices, that is, prices that provide equality between supply and demand simultaneously in a competitive economy composed of a large number of markets.

The influence of the École de Lausanne on twentieth-century economics is much more important than the strict development of the neo-Walrasian general equilibrium theory. It is essential in the formation of econometrics and, more broadly, has been regarded as a key paradigm since the second half of the twentieth century.

The Chair of Political Economy in Lausanne

In accordance with the new 1861 Constitution, the Canton of Vaud Parliament voted in 1869 to reform the Academy of Lausanne, and gave it the legal standing necessary to its development. Eighteen chairs were established, including in political economy, located in the Law Faculty – also a common practice in French universities. The Cantonal Minister of Education and architect of the reform, the radical Louis Ruchonnet, offered the position to Marie-Esprit-Léon Walras, at that time an employee keeping the books in a Paris bank. He had met him in Lausanne in 1860, at the Congrès international de l'impôt (International Congress on taxation), and had since kept in touch. Unlike the majority of participants to the congress who agreed on levying a single tax on income and capital, Ruchonnet had enjoyed the clear and precise communication delivered by a very young Walras, condemning the principle of proportional taxation and advocating collective land-ownership.

Owing to the Franco-Prussian war, the organization of test lessons proved impossible and the appointment of the first professor at the chair of political economy in Lausanne was made on the sole basis of his research work. Walras was unable to boast any academic title but he had a very clear scientific project, which was supported by Ruchonnet, and he was appointed as an extraordinary professor on 12 November 1870, by four votes to three. The following year, he was promoted to full professorship and on 20 October 1871 he was officially installed in the chair of political economy by Louis Ruchonnet himself. That is how the École de Lausanne got started.

The founder: Léon Walras

Upon his installation, Walras asked for his position's brief to be amended so as to make it consistent with the scientific project he had developed in the early 1860s and pursued all his life: "discovering the natural laws of value and of wealth, together with the moral laws governing the fairest distribution within the most abundant production" (Walras 1863: 159). The faculty accepted, but the structure and content of his teaching did not stabilize until the fall of 1875. Throughout his career, during the winter term, Walras delivered a four-hour weekly course in pure economics, and in the summer semester he would teach a five-hour class in applied economics and social economics, alternating them every other year.

Upon his arrival in Lausanne, besides preparing his teachings (whose trace is to be found in his *Cours*, Walras worked hard on the first volume of his triptych, the *Éléments d'économie politique pure* (*Elements of Pure Economics*), whose first issue consisted of three sections released in 1874. The second instalment of the *Éléments* was released in 1877 and contributed two extra chapters to the construction of the general economic equilibrium: next to the exchange of several commodities for one another and the circulation of money, Walras added the equations of production and those of capitalization. However, Walras was not satisfied with the resulting architecture and unconvinced by his own theory of money. Indeed, issues related to circulation and credit figure prominently in his subsequent research in pure economics, and beyond. Since the *Éléments* were completed, Walras focused his work on applied economics (where the problems of money and credit remain central) and social economics, with his studies on the "*Réalisation de l'idéal social*" (*Realization of the Social Ideal*) via land repurchase by the state and the abolition of taxation.

In 1889, the second edition of *Éléments* was released, where the general economic equilibrium was presented in a logic of increasing complexity (an exchange economy with two goods and later several ones, an economy with production, an economy with capitalization and credit, and an economy with money) and whose last volume presents a section related to "considerations on the consequences of economic progress". This structure, whose justification regarding the general economic equilibrium was educational, was never modified. Not surprisingly, in terms of content, the most important contribution of this second edition is the theory of money, revised and expanded through the addition of two chapters on bimetallism.

In 1890, the Academy eventually became the University of Lausanne. Two years later, Walras requested early retirement for health reasons and his succession was therefore open. He first proposed the chair to Ladislaus von Bortkiewicz, who turned it down as he hoped to succeed Professor Yuly Edwardovich Yanson in Saint Petersburg. Following this refusal, Walras turned to Vilfredo Pareto, whom he had met the year before through Maffeo Pantaleoni.

The reference scientist: Vilfredo Pareto

The Italian engineer (but a French native speaker), accepted willingly and in 1893 promptly delivered courses as an extraordinary professor, before he was appointed full professor the following year. His teachings were immediately greeted with great success and his research contributed decisively to the school's reputation.

A brilliant teacher, Pareto made the difference from his so illustrious predecessor, because the latter was a poor teacher. From his earliest lessons, Pareto, while paying homage to the Master, took a personal approach whose inspiration was to look more to Hermann Heinrich Gossen and the English economists. Admittedly, by appropriating the concept of '*rareté*' and dubbing the "Walras equation", Pareto demonstrated his desire for some continuity, but probably more for diplomatic than scientific reasons.

Pareto's analytical inputs to the Walrasian general equilibrium were many: a new concept of utility and of production, the notions of optimum and the modernization of mathematics. Regarding the latter, Pareto provided, throughout his contributions (marked mainly by the *Cours* and completed by the *Manuel*), a mathematicized version of the general equilibrium, which established itself as the standard for modern microeconomics. Pareto also renewed the concept of utility – which he preferred to call "ophelimity" – and rid the construction of the general equilibrium of the difficulties linked to its measurability. With his exclusive use of an ordinal ranking of different combinations of goods, modern microeconomics was born. In his production theory, Pareto reactivated the research programme on variable coefficients but in a framework of a non-circular production process (though this may not be called real progress). Finally, Pareto developed a key concept in the history of welfare theories. Based (loosely) on Walras's theorem of maximum satisfaction, Pareto developed his optimum concept, and what is now appropriately called – in the wake of Kenneth J. Arrow and Gérard Debreu – the first fundamental theorem of welfare economics: any general equilibrium is an optimum situation where increasing ophelimity in favour of some can only be achieved at the expense of the others' ophelimity.

For his part, Walras intended, though he had retired, to issue new publications and even the systematic treatise on political and social economy he had planned at the beginning of his career – the famous "triptych". However, owing to his poor health, Walras eventually had to abandon this project, deemed beyond his strength, but he did not give up on his deep conviction of the need to complement pure economics by applied and social economics. That is why, instead of the triptych, he published, along with the third edition of the *Éléments* (1896), two collections of articles: *Études d'économie sociale* (*Studies in Social Economics*, 1896) and *Études d'économie politique appliquée* (*Studies in Applied Economics*, 1898), each containing a major original text: respectively, the "Theory of property" and "An outline of an economic and social doctrine".

Meanwhile, Pareto published his *Cours d'économie politique professé à l'Université de Lausanne* (*Political Economy Course Delivered at the University of Lausanne*, 1896–97), and, on resuming the teachings in applied economics and social economics when he had to meet the faculty's new educational requirement, he replaced them with a course entitled "Socialist Systems" and another, "Principles of Sociology". Moreover, Pareto also rejected Walras's social economics because, he claimed, it is "metaphysical", which was completely incompatible with his own logico-experimental method. Not that Pareto was uninterested in applied or social considerations, but he did it differently. No doubt inspired by his experience – Pareto had long managed a forge in Italy, where he was able to actually experiment the variation in production coefficients and the effects of policies hostile to free trade – Pareto anchored his understanding of human actions in empirical facts. He therefore deemed that the theory of general equilibrium could only provide a first, rough, approximation of this understanding. In attempting to systematize this position, including for his sociology course, Pareto developed his distinction between logical and non-logical actions, a foundational one for his great second approximation. He built up his own sociological terminology, consisting of "residues" (passions, the soul of society) and "derivations" (names people give to vindicate their actions after the fact, a "varnish of logic"). On these grounds, he developed his analysis of income distribution and his theory of the circulation of elites. Pareto had some bearing on sociology at that time, but the discipline had already picked out other figureheads such as Max Weber and Emile Durkheim.

When Pareto came into some inherited money, he considered, as early as in 1898, giving up teaching to dedicate himself to research, and, after much dithering and long negotiations with the university, he obtained permission in 1900 to henceforth give only one weekly one-hour lesson. Vittorio Racca, his assistant since 1898, was appointed as "substitute" teacher. The same year, Walras published the fourth edition of *Éléments*, which includes a major innovation, *"tâtonnement sur bons"* (tâtonnement on written pledges).

Pareto did not completely retire from academic policy and played an important role in the promulgation of the 12 February 1902 Law, which established the diplomas of Bachelor of Science and Doctorate in social sciences awarded by the Faculty of Law but managed by a new institution: the École des sciences sociales et politiques (School of Social and Political Sciences), which was then established.

Twilight: Pasquale Boninsegni

In November 1903, after a rather unclear incident, Pareto requested that his new protégé, Pasquale Boninsegni, should replace Racca, which the faculty accepted. Four years later, Boninsegni was appointed as an extraordinary professor, but he had to wait almost 20 years, until 1926, to eventually access the full professorship. Boninsegni's scientific contribution to the École de Lausanne is not very original: he published three articles in the *Giornale degli Economisti* before his appointment, and a dozen in journals deemed less prestigious thereafter. Indeed, Boninsegni's academic activity focused on teaching and on the dissemination of Pareto's economic theory. In his eyes, Pareto can be credited with abandoning metaphysical research into value and its causes, to focus solely on facts, that is, how men act to procure the goods they want. Boninsegni advocated the importance of mathematization and the study of concrete social phenomena, but disagreed on Pareto's (liberal) involvement; but it did not prevent him – while President of the School of Social and Political Sciences and holder of the political economy and sociology chair – from overtly affirming his commitment to Mussolini's fascist stands. It is also at his instigation and through dubious manoeuvring that, in 1937, the university granted an honorary doctorate to Benito Mussolini.

Finally, from the perspective of a rational reconstruction of economic analysis, Pareto's work, *Manuale di economia politica con una introduzione alla scienza sociale* (*Manual of Political Economy with an Introduction to Social Science*, 1906), is the École de Lausanne's last major contribution to modern economic theory, while marking Pareto's transfer to sociology with the *Trattato di sociologia generale* (1916).

The "Nouvelle École de Lausanne": Firmin Oulès

In 1939, on Boninsegni's retirement, two successors were appointed: for teaching economics and statistics, the Law Faculty gave preference to the French Firmin Oulès over Stanislao Scalfati, an Italian; and for teaching general sociology, the School of Social and Political Sciences chose Jean Piaget, who had already been teaching general psychology there for three years. First as an Extraordinary Professor, Piaget accessed full professorship in 1945, but left Lausanne in the early 1950s and, while keeping the chair he held in Geneva, delivered lessons in genetic psychology at the Sorbonne until 1963. In 1947, Firmin Oulès was appointed full professor of political and financial economics, as well as of history of economic thought, and remained in Lausanne until his retirement in 1974. After Boninsegni's long parenthesis, Oulès sought to revive economic research in Lausanne, with the works of Walras and Pareto as springboards for further findings. On the one hand, he drastically criticized the use of mathematical language and logic, which he called "L. Walras and Pareto's evil genius"; on the other, he developed the concepts of interdependence and general economic equilibrium, which he saw as the École de Lausanne's essential and specific features. Above all, the Nouvelle École de Lausanne (New Lausanne School) highlighted the Walrasian idea of enlightening economic policy with scientific theory. Walras was then understood as "the founder of scientific economic policy" and the New School became firmly committed to economic topical issues. Yet, it was still rather confidential and it died out after Oulès retired.

However, the Chair of Political Economy in the Faculty of Law lived on, occupied since 1967 by François Schaller, who used to teach political economy and the history of economic doctrines. In 1986, Pascal Bridel succeeded him and became the latest holder of the famous chair, because the new 2004 University Act profoundly changed its organization and removed all chairs.

Well Beyond Lausanne

Despite the twilight of the École de Lausanne after Pareto, direct heirs do exist and the general equilibrium exercised considerable influence on developments in economic theory in the twentieth century, well beyond Lausanne. This undeniable influence, though modest at the beginning, is the visible tip of the École de Lausanne. Although we are unable to account for it here, it should not obscure the fascination that the concept of equilibrium has exerted in subtle ways on many disciplines.

Heirs

A few individuals have enjoyed close proximity with the École de Lausanne founders, which make them their direct heirs.

Take Léon Winiarski, for example, a Polish sociologist and disgruntled Marxist, who was fascinated by the application of the mathematical method in political economy, and especially by the general economic equilibrium. He defended a doctoral thesis on Russian finance at the University of Lausanne (1894), with Pareto as Examiner. As he shared much of the Walrasian social ideal, Winiarski attempted to disseminate the new theory, through his teaching activity at the University of Geneva, his multilingual publicist undertaking, and especially via his social mechanics (Winiarski 1967), which is a vast, unfinished attempt to extend the general economic equilibrium to a general equilibrium applied to all fields of social life.

The Russian statistician and economist of Polish descent Ladislaus Bortkiewicz could be counted in the 1890s as one of the direct heirs of this École de Lausanne, to such an extent that, as noted earlier, Walras thought he could make him his successor. However, his involvement in the construction of the general equilibrium boiled down to technical problems, which Bortkiewicz seemed to be more interested in than in the analysis of the general framework. What he would later remember about it was primarily the mathematical notion of interdependence of economic variables, which he used in other contexts without keeping the framework of the general equilibrium. Finally, Bortkiewicz's most lasting contribution to the École de Lausanne's legacy may well be his role as a knowledge broker – in Berlin, where he had settled – between Lausanne and Russia, where a whole school of mathematical economists (Vladimir Karpovich Dmitriev, Evgeny Evgenievich Slutsky, Nikolay Nikolaevich Shaposhnikov and Leonid Naumovich Yurovsky) was influenced by the Walras and Pareto theories, from the early twentieth century until the mid-1920s, while participating early on in a neo-Ricardian revival. Soviet mathematician economists (Leonid Vital'evich Kantorovich, Vasily Serge'evich Nemchinov and Viktor Valentinovich Novozhilov) became their heirs, but reference to the École de Lausanne was lost in the mean time.

Two of Vilfredo Pareto's doctoral students worked on the theory of general equilibrium. Pierre Boven, one of the master's faithful disciples, wrote an early history of the intellectual heritage of the École de Lausanne, in his thesis entitled "Les applications mathématiques à l'économie politique" ("Mathematical applications to political economy", 1912). Boven authored the French translation of Pareto's *Trattato di sociologia generale* (1917–19, translated as *The Mind and Society*), and also Roberto Murray's (1920) volume, and later became Attorney General of the Canton of Vaud, and although he was repeatedly approached to deliver courses in sociology, Pareto's sole local student departed from his master's original concerns. Much less faithful to the master, Basile Samsonoff developed the theory of rent in the spirit of the École de Lausanne, that is, as the difference between two successive general equilibriums. Little attention was paid to his thesis, "Esquisse d'une théorie générale de la rente" ("An outline of a general theory of rent", 1912). Samsonoff joined the Russian mathematician economists, but his family's staunch military tradition decided otherwise for him: he died on the battlefield during the First World War. Even if Marie Kolabinska's sociology thesis on *La circulation des élites en France* (*The Circulation of Elites in France*, 1912) is included, Pareto was not the source of intense emulation in Lausanne.

The legacy
It is essentially outside Lausanne, by way of letters, that Walras as well as Pareto maintained or even gave rise to, in the case of the founder, a network of correspondents interested in their works. However, the dissemination of the École de Lausanne's theories was achieved in different ways depending on national traditions.

Italy was the country offering the most open and benevolent reception to writings by Walras. There developed a network of correspondents interested in his work. Pareto can be included, although his interest in Walras was neither immediate – despite his friends' insistence – nor disinterested. Maffeo Pantaleoni, Enrico Barone and Gustavo Del Vecchio were authors who interacted constructively with the École de Lausanne, while others, such as Umberto Ricci, Enrico Leone, Luigi Amoroso, Guido Sensini and Stanislao Scalfati, often simply disseminated Pareto's work, without actually contributing to the development of the general equilibrium theory. In Spain, several attempts to introduce the general equilibrium were made. Among them can be included Antonio Flores de Lemus's, who learned about the Walrasian general equilibrium under Lexis and Bortkiewicz, and tried to accommodate it to the national context (Astigarraga and Zabalza 2008). In Portugal, António Horta Osório wrote a handbook entitled *A Mathematica na economia pura* (1911) based on the École de Lausanne, which was translated into French.

In France, the mathematization of political economy raised a problem: Walras was ostracized and the dissemination of the École de Lausanne in the early twentieth century was rather subdued. Some books in French about mathematical political economy were nonetheless released before the Great War: by Emile Bouvier (1901), Hermann Laurent (1902), António Horta Osório (1913), Wladimir Zawadzki (1914) and Jacques Moret in 1915. However, it is mainly through engineering schools that the general equilibrium theory ultimately prevailed subsequently, whereas the university (that is, law schools) remained indifferent – when not averse to it. Take Albert Aupetit, for example, because he failed to be appointed either in 1901 or in 1903, he gave up an academic career; and Étienne Antonelli had to wait until 1919 to get tenure. François Bompaire's (1931) book enjoyed very limited response and the lessons delivered by Gaëtan Pirou to the École pratique des hautes études in 1932–34 (Pirou 1946) long remained the only references to the École de Lausanne. Despite Georges-Henri Bousquet's efforts (he was part of Pareto's inner circle) to disseminate the master's approach, the École de Lausanne has remained on the margins of French universities and developed only through a particular tradition of French engineering schools (Maurice Allais and François Divisia, among others).

In Japan, Tokuzo Fukuda, Kinnosuke Otsuka, Ichiro Nakayama, Takuma Yasui and especially Yasuma Takata mix general equilibrium and sociology, while Michio Morishima and Takashi Negishi's combinations of general equilibrium and Marxism have proved very successful (Misaki 2006).

In Sweden, Knut Wicksell (1893, 1898) used the general equilibrium equations and the Walras *tâtonnement*, but his theoretical construction deviated from the latter when it came to thinking about the difference between real and monetary phenomena, where he mobilized Böhm-Bawerk and developed his own ideas. Gustav Cassel (1899), meanwhile, achieved the feat of presenting different versions of the Walrasian general equilibrium with much greater clarity than in the original – and in very few pages as well – but at the cost of great simplification. The general equilibrium as seen by Wicksell and Cassel left its mark through the School of Stockholm and its sequential analyses (Erik Lindahl, Gunnar Myrdal and Bertil Ohlin). However, more importantly, Wicksell and Cassel write in German, and this accounts for their predominant role in the dissemination of the general equilibrium (the same happened when their works were translated into English, but only later on).

The two Vienna schools: the Mathematisches Kolloquium and the Kreis
The École de Lausanne made its mark in Vienna in the 1920s and early 1930s. First, under the influence of Karl Menger's Mathematisches Kolloquium, a number of questions originally formulated by Walras in terms of a "number of equations and unknowns" and *"tâtonnements"* were transformed, crystallized and prioritized around the equilibrium existence, uniqueness and stability. Participants to the Mathematisches Kolloquium, mostly mathematicians such as Karl Schlesinger, Abraham Wald, Frederik Zeuthen, Hans Neisser and John von Neumann, used an axiomatic approach, and their Hilbertian formalism was applied to the Walrasian general equilibrium, which they were acquainted with thanks to Gustav Cassel's simplified version. The general economic equilibrium is thus seen as a system of interdependent economic variables where the issue of whether these variables account for the coordination of individual behaviour through the price mechanism is very abstract and actually quite removed from the group's concerns.

Yet, to follow the École de Lausanne via Vienna, it is necessary, besides this history, to focus on a second avenue with surprising ramifications. As brilliantly shown by Marchionatti (2009), another Viennese circle was interested in the general equilibrium: Moritz Schlick's Kreis. Very different from the Mathematisches Kolloquium, the Kreis was essentially the birthplace of neo-positivism. In this circle, Pareto's writings were known and read and his programme for epistemological revision of political economy had a direct echo in "The scientific conception of the world", written in 1929 by Hans Hahn, Otto Neurath and Rudolf Carnap. A critical analysis of the foundations of political economy, the abandonment of all "metaphysical" residual elements, a similar verificationist paradigm – Pareto's logico-experimental method indeed agrees well with the empirical-logical method – together with the project of a unified science, these are all points of contact between Pareto and the Kreis.

In the USA
Both the École de Lausanne's Viennese legacies ran in parallel over the twentieth century, and sometimes intersected, particularly in the United States and at the Cowles Commission especially. The Kreis's posterity expressed itself there in the early development of econometrics and its neo-positivist concerns, and the legacy of the Mathematisches Kolloquium gave rise to the neo-Walrasian programme with leanings towards Bourbaki (Debreu). In the beginning, the general equilibrium became a type of applied economics and was operationalized. Pareto's work was called upon in the emergence of the movement for econometrics and in the development of the input–output approach as well as linear programming. The influence of the Kreis's neo-positivist Vienna seems dominant in this case and, for that matter, the latter's programme is explicitly associated with the rise of econometrics. Cowles Commission members (and affiliates), such as Tjalling Koopmans, Wassily Leontief, George Dantzig and Jacob Marschak, took part in the empirical vision of the general equilibrium, while departing from *à la* National Bureau of Economic Research (NBER) empiricism, as evidenced by the controversy over "measurement without theory". However, because members of the Mathematische Kolloquium such as von Neumann and Wald, emigrated to the United States, the Cowles Commission became a meeting place between the two Viennese schools, fostering the development of the neo-Walrasian programme.

In 1954, Arrow and Debreu identified the conditions of existence of the general equilibrium. This demonstration, plus Lionel McKenzie's in 1959, as well as the one on the uniqueness of the equilibrium, raised hopes that were soon qualified by doubts about its stability (Scarf 1960) and finally challenged by Hugo Sonnenschein's (1972), Rolf Mantel's (1974) and Debreu's (1974) results. The general equilibrium as a research programme suffered a breakpoint then, which did not prevent it from keeping up its status of a preferred way to look at reality in a number of contemporary theories. Above all, the applied aspect of the general equilibrium outweighs axiomatic issues in computable general equilibrium models, whose numerical algorithms are rather indifferent to the equilibrium theoretical lack of stability.

Harvard is the other landmark of American participation in the legacy of the École de Lausanne's general equilibrium. On one hand, within the Harvard Pareto circle, members had read the *Treatise of general sociology* and discussed the concept of general equilibrium from very different perspectives. On the other hand, Harvard hosted in the 1930s a number of European economists familiar with the general equilibrium, such as Joseph Schumpeter and Wassily Leontief. It was in this context that an occasional member of the Harvard Pareto circle, Paul Anthony Samuelson, wrote a doctoral thesis whose publication in 1947, entitled *Foundations of Economic Analysis*, became the canonical form of mathematical economics.

The LSE

Besides Vienna, another European source enriched the heritage of the École de Lausanne's general equilibrium: the English response, localized at the London School of Economics and Political Science (LSE) against the domination of Cambridge, which stole the show over the École de Lausanne. Indeed, the general equilibrium was then mobilized against Alfred Marshall's hegemony, regarding the partial equilibrium approach and Arthur Cecil Pigou's as regards welfare economics. John Hicks, Roy Allen and Lionel Robbins's works, and especially the publication of *Value and Capital* (Hicks 1939), made Pareto's general equilibrium – together with his ordinalism – known to a wider English audience.

The socialist calculation debate, which conferred centre stage to the general equilibrium theory, also had its operational core at the LSE in 1930 (Friedrich Hayek and Abba Lerner). The debate, launched by the Austrian Ludwig von Mises, called for socialist economists such as Oskar Lange and Boris Brutzkus to react, so as to know whether the general equilibrium was able to capture the essence of a decentralized economy. While this debate helped unearth the Italian Enrico Barone's Paretian contribution, it is mainly the different perceptions of the general equilibrium by both Vienna schools that were then to be found mobilized, and transposed into a new conceptual framework. Let us suggest by the way that, though the controversy was won by Lange, it may well have had an influence on the concrete planning of Soviet economies.

Other histories

Beyond national traditions, the École de Lausanne's theoretical contributions raised expectations, and became the subject of refinement and debates throughout the past century.

Thus, many economists have also considered the general equilibrium as the stable foundation of a future dynamics theory. Wicksell, Moore and Schumpeter also participated in this effort to revitalize the general equilibrium theory.

In Pareto's version, with its ordinal concept of utility and its optimum notion, the general equilibrium was mobilized in debates on welfare economics, until Arrow's impossibility theorem (1951), while the abandoning of produced capital goods operated in the *Manuel* became, indirectly, the focus point of the debate on capital between the two Cambridges.

Finally, the issue of integrating money to the general equilibrium was raised upon the foundations provided by the Walras theories of money, with a genealogy leading up to Frank Horace Hahn's conjecture, through Arthur W. Marget and Don Patinkin.

Ultimately, the École de Lausanne's central legacy might well prove to be its general equilibrium, available in two great intersecting histories: a neo-Walrasian narrative that draws support from Mathematisches Kolloquium; and a Paretian background, drawing from the Kreis. However, the École de Lausanne, but also the general economic equilibrium, were initially much more than issues focusing on economic variables interdependencies and on the mathematization of economics.

A Similar Theory, but Two Irreconcilable Philosophies

Despite Oulès's attempt, the École de Lausanne's influence on economics lies in a general economic equilibrium formulation that is independent and free from institutions and politics. Thus, the initial Walrasian research programme to find a scientific solution to the social question, as well as Pareto's opening to sociology in a process of successive approximations, got lost along the way. Although both one and the other, each in their own ways, were certain that a scientific approach to the general equilibrium could not be isolated; that the economics is not self-sufficient in itself, the legacy that economics has metabolized has leaned towards an opposite direction: towards a self-sufficient disciplinary theory. In contrast, though these two authors agree neither on the use of mathematics nor on the epistemological status of the general economic equilibrium, it is a specific use of mathematics and a particular meaning of the general economic equilibrium that has been kept by the discipline as constituting the École de Lausanne's characteristic features. So, when we change our point of view, leaving the legacy aside to inquire about these two authors' works, the very definition of the school proves problematic.

Regarding the use of mathematics

Walras thought that "the theory of value in exchange is really a branch of mathematics which mathematicians have hitherto neglected and left undeveloped" (Walras 1954: 70). Since the exchange value is a mathematical fact, resorting to mathematics for pure economics purposes is indeed possible and even necessary for science to make progress. Formal language is clearer and more specific; it is indispensable on account of its heuristic value, and allows distinguishing true from false with certainty. Indeed, only formal language makes it possible to account for the complexity of the general interdependence of economic equilibrium, whereas natural language strays into apparent tautologies. Through the use of mathematics, it is possible to replace some of economists' simple dogmatic assertions with rigorous demonstrations and achieve new results. Like all those who advocate applying mathematics to economics, Pareto shared Walras's views on its formal advantages, but, unlike the latter, he did not believe it could guarantee, beyond mere reasoning consistency, the substantial truth of findings.

About the referent of equations of the general economic equilibrium

The point that probably most separates the two Lausanne economists consists in the meaning they attribute to the general economic equilibrium. For Walras, as a pure science (not an applied one), it captures the essence of the phenomenon, in the specific case of the exchange value of social wealth. Pareto thought it represented the uniformities found in choices and laws, arising from the opposition between men's tastes and obstacles to satisfy them.

From Walras's point of view, the general economic equilibrium theory hinges around the establishment of exchange values once stripped of all contingent aspects, but it is also the theory of price determination in a hypothetical system of absolute free competition. This is understandable, because that regime, which is a mechanism for price determination, not a market structure, is hypothetical from the historical contingent, but necessary to the extent that it is the only mechanism able to ensure pricing in accordance with human nature. However, political economy cannot go against human nature, just as physics against the law of gravity. Walras believed that prices, when established that way, are true (in its strong sense of their connection to facts per se), though they do not reflect actual market operations, as it is not the theory that is flawed, but reality itself.

The matter of the adequacy of theory to facts is dealt with in diametrically opposed fashion to Walras and Pareto's; but it cannot be reduced, as does the latter, to the distinction between "normative" and "positive" economics, because Walras asserted that the ideal generated by science is "positive"; it is also even the only possible scientific result. Pareto understood the Walrasian stand, but could not accept it. On the part of the "most nominalist among Nominalists", Walrasian essentialism is hopelessly metaphysical, whereas true scientific approach can only be inductive. The general economic equilibrium is one of these successive approximations any science resorts to, an imperfect picture of reality, which is always to be compared with experimental facts. Far from the method of "reasoning about words", Pareto leaves more room for empirical verification of theories, with no qualms about "modifying or even abandoning any theory that could not be reconciled with experience", whereas Walras thought science required no verification.

At the ontological level, the gap was even more radical. Pareto considered that, like any scientist, an economist need not even ask this question, while Walras devoted a number of writings to it. However, Pareto inevitably took a stand when defending the existence of a complex reality which science approaches "through theories that prove ever more consistent with it". A portion of this reality is therefore the referent of the general economic equilibrium. On the contrary, Walras declared that what is at stake with the general economic equilibrium are essences that are only partially actualized in reality, but meant to completely unfold in historical time. Placed in their respective philosophical contexts, both general equilibrium theories are reminiscent of the "false friends" found when comparing two languages. Continuity within the École de Lausanne thus lies in the transmission of the sole mathematical tool for the general economic equilibrium, taken from political and social economics in the case of Walras, while being insulated from non-logical actions in Pareto's. On the contrary, there is no continuity in the referent of proposals constructed from this tool: Pareto focused on the real world while Walras aimed for the ideal world of unrealized essences. In other words, although both authors use a common formal device, their respective contents prove different.

Which School?

Finally, the meaning commonly attributed to the École de Lausanne results from it being dazzled by mathematization, thus obscuring different incommensurable meanings of the general economic equilibrium and thereby giving exclusive priority to Pareto's version. In addition, the disciplinary rift such a definition of the School implies utterly betrays the spirit of it. The École de Lausanne is built on the scientific project of the triptych; it developed together with the joint analysis of logical and non-logical actions; and the revival in favour of "politics" that occurred at the Nouvelle École de Lausanne unsuccessfully recalled the necessary interdependence between the economic, social and political arenas. Though that school's protagonists seem to beckon us to embark in that direction, it is paradoxical for historians of economic thought to use the phrase École de Lausanne in a meaning that is rather related to doxography (Rorty 1984).

ROBERTO BARANZINI AND FRANÇOIS ALLISSON

See also:

Maurice Allais (I); Kenneth Joseph Arrow (I); Enrico Barone (I); Ladislaus von Bortkiewicz (I); Gustav Cassel (I); Competition (III); Econometrics (III); Gérard Debreu (I); Formalization and mathematical modelling (III); General equilibrium theory (III); John Richard Hicks (I); Oskar Ryszard Lange (I); Robert E. Lucas (I); Michio Morishima (I); Takashi Negishi (I); Maffeo Pantaleoni (I); Vilfredo Pareto (I); Don Patinkin (I); Paul Anthony Samuelson (I); Marie-Esprit-Léon Walras (I); Welfare economics (III); Knut Wicksell (I).

References and further reading

Akhabbar, A. and J. Lallement (2011), '"Appliquer la théorie économique de l'équilibre général": de Walras à Leontief', in R. Baranzini, A. Legris and L. Ragni (eds), *Léon Walras et l'équilibre économique général. Recherches récentes*, Paris: Economica, pp. 201–31.

Allisson, F. (2015), *Value and Prices in Russian Economic Thought: A Journey Inside the Russian Synthesis, 1890–1920*, London: Routledge.

Arrow, K.J. (1951), *Social Choice and Individual Values*, New York: Wiley, London: Chapman and Hall.

Astigarraga, J. and J. Zabalza (2008), 'Walras in Spain (1874–1936)', *History of Economic Thought*, **51** (1), 1–18.

Baranzini, R. and P. Bridel (1997), 'On Pareto's first lectures on pure economics at Lausanne', *History of Economic Ideas*, **5** (3), 65–87.

Baranzini, R. and P. Bridel (2005), 'L'"École de Lausanne", l'utilité marginale moyenne et l'idée de marché', in G. Bensimon (ed.), *Histoire des représentations du marché*, Paris: Michel Houdiard, pp. 347–65.

Bavarel, E. and P. Oulès (2001), *Firmin Oulès, sa vie, son œuvre, son actualité*, Brussels: Bruylant.

Bompaire, F. (1931), *Du principe de la liberté économique dans l'œuvre de Cournot et dans celle de l'Ecole de Lausanne (Walras et Pareto)*, Paris: Recueil Sirey.

Bouvier, E. (1901), *La méthode mathématique en économie politique*, Paris: Larose.

Boven, P. (1912), *Les applications mathématiques à l'économie politique*, Lausanne: Rouge.

Busino, G. (1989), *L'Italia di Vilfredo Pareto: economia et società in un carteggio del 1873–1923*, Milan: Banca commerciale italiana.

Busino, G. and P. Bridel (1987), *L'école de Lausanne de Léon Walras à Pasquale Boninsegni*, Lausanne: Université de Lausanne.

Cassel, G. (1899), 'Grundrisse einer elementaren Preislehre', *Zeitschrift für die gesamte Staatswissenschaft*, **55** (3), 395–458.

Cot, A. and J. Lallement (2006), '1859–1959: Walras à Debreu, un siècle d'équilibre général', *Revue économique*, **57** (3), 377–88.

Debreu, G. (1974), 'Excess demande functions', *Journal of Mathematical Economics*, **1** (1), 15–21.
Dockès, P. and J.-P. Potier (2001), *La vie et l'œuvre économique de Léon Walras*, Paris: Economica.
Edgeworth, F.Y. (1909), 'Current topics', *The Economic Journal*, **19** (74), 335–40.
Hahn, H., O. Neurath and R. Carnap (1929), *Wissenschaftliche Weltauffassung. Der Wiener Kreis*, in O. Neurath (1973), *Empiricism and Sociology*, Dordrecht: Reidel, pp. 299–318.
Hicks, J.R. (1939), *Value and Capital: An Inquiry into Some Fundamental Principles of Economic Theory*, Oxford: Clarendon Press.
Ingrao, B. and G. Israel (1987), *La mano invisibile: l'equilibrio economico nella storia della scienza*, English trans. (1990), *The Invisible Hand: Economic Equilibrium in the History of Science*, Cambridge, MA: MIT Press.
Jaffé, W. (ed.) (1965), *Correspondence of Léon Walras and Related Papers*, Amsterdam: North Holland.
Laurent, H. (1902), *Petit traité d'économie politique mathématique rédigé conformément aux préceptes de l'école de Lausanne*, Paris: Charles Schmid.
Leone, E. (1911), 'Léon Walras und die hedonistisch-mathematische "Schule von Lausanne"', *Archiv für Sozialwissenschaft und Sozialpolitik*, **32** (1), 36–71.
Mantel, R.R. (1974), 'On the characterization of aggregate excess demand', *Journal of Economic Theory*, **7** (3), 348–53.
Marchionatti, R. (2009), 'Pareto's influence on modern economics', in L. Bruni and A. Montesano (eds), *New Essays on Pareto's Economic Theory*, London and New York: Routledge, pp. 110–29.
Misaki, K. (2006), 'The general equilibrium theory in Japanese economic thought: from Walras to Morishima', in J.G. Backhaus and J.A. Hans Maks (eds), *From Walras to Pareto*, New York: Springer, pp. 11–26.
Moret, J. (1915), *L'emploi des mathématiques en économie politique*, Paris: M. Giard and E. Brière.
Mornati, F. (1999), *Pasquale Boninsegni e la Scuola di Losanna*, Turin: UTET Libreria.
Murray, R.A. (1920), *Leçons d'économie politique, suivant la doctrine de l'Ecole de Lausanne*, Paris: Payot.
Osório, A.H. (1911), *A mathematica na economia pura: a troca*, Lisbon: Centro Typographico Colonial.
Osório, A.H. (1913), *Théorie mathématique de l'échange*, Paris: M. Giard et E. Brière.
Pareto, V. (1896–97), *Cours d'économie politique professé à l'Université de Lausanne*, in V. Pareto (1964–2005), *Œuvres complètes*, G. Busino (ed.), 32 vols, Geneva: Droz.
Pareto, V. (1906), *Manuale di economia politica con una introduzione alla scienza sociale*, in V. Pareto (1964–2005), *Œuvres complètes*, G. Busino (ed.), 32 vols, Geneva: Droz.
Pareto, V. (1916), *Trattato di sociologia generale*, in V. Pareto (1964–2005), *Œuvres complètes*, G. Busino (ed.), 32 vols, Geneva: Droz.
Pareto, V. (1964–2005), *Œuvres complètes*, G. Busino (ed.), 32 vols, Geneva: Droz.
Pirou, G. (1946), *Les theories de l'équilibre économique: Walras et Pareto. Conférences faites à l'École pratique des hautes études en 1932–33 et 1933–34*, Paris: Domat Montchrestien.
Rorty, R. (1984), 'The historiography of philosophy: four genres', in R. Rorty, J.B. Schneewind and Q. Skinner (eds), *Philosophy in History: Essays on Historiography of Philosophy*, Cambridge: Cambridge University Press, pp. 49–75.
Samsonoff, B. (1912), *Esquisse d'une théorie générale de la rente; suivie d'une critique des principales opinions émises sur le même sujet*, Lausanne: Imprimerie A. Petter.
Samuelson, P.A. (1947), *Foundations of Economic Analysis*, Cambridge, MA: Harvard University Press.
Schultz, H. (1932), 'Marginal productivity and the Lausanne School', *Economica*, **12** (37), 285–300.
Sonnenschein, H. (1972), 'Market excess demand functions', *Econometrica*, **40** (3), 549–63.
Tarascio, V.J. (1978), 'The political economy of the Lausanne School: Walras and Pareto', *Atlantic Economic Journal*, **6** (4), 26–34.
Tissot, L. (1996), *Politique, société et enseignement supérieur dans le canton de Vaud: l'Université de Lausanne, 1890–1916*, Lausanne: Payot and Université de Lausanne.
Walras, A. and L. Walras (1987–2005), *Œuvres économiques complètes*, P. Dockès, P.H. Goutte, C. Hébert, C. Mouchot, J.-P. Potier and J.-M. Servet (eds), 14 vols, Paris: Economica.
Walras, L. (1863), 'Principes de la théorie des richesses, par M. Cournot', *L'indépandant de la Moselle [Metz (France)]*, **33**, 1.
Walras, L. (1874), *Éléments d'économie politique pure*, in A. Walras and L. Walras (1987–2005), *Œuvres économiques complètes*, P. Dockès, P.-H. Goutte, C. Hébert, C. Mouchot, J.-P. Potier and J.-M. Servet (eds), 14 vols, Paris: Economica.
Walras, L. (1877), *Éléments d'économie politique pure*, in A. Walras and L. Walras (1987–2005), *Œuvres économiques complètes*, P. Dockès, P.-H. Goutte, C. Hébert, C. Mouchot, J.-P. Potier and J.-M. Servet (eds), 14 vols, Paris: Economica.
Walras, L. (1889), *Éléments d'économie politique pure*, 2nd edn, in A. Walras and L. Walras (1987–2005), *Œuvres économiques complètes*, P. Dockès, P.-H. Goutte, C. Hébert, C. Mouchot, J.-P. Potier and J.-M. Servet (eds), 14 vols, Paris: Economica.
Walras, L. (1896), *Éléments d'économie politique pure*, 3rd edn, in A. Walras and L. Walras (1987–2005),

Œuvres économiques complètes, P. Dockès, P.-H. Goutte, C. Hébert, C. Mouchot, J.-P. Potier and J.-M. Servet (eds), 14 vols, Paris: Economica.

Walras, L. (1896), *Éléments d'économie sociale*, in A. Walras and L. Walras (1987–2005), *Œuvres économiques complètes*, P. Dockès, P.-H. Goutte, C. Hébert, C. Mouchot, J.-P. Potier and J.-M. Servet (eds), 14 vols, Paris: Economica.

Walras, L. (1898), *Éléments d'économie politique appliquée*, in A. Walras and L. Walras (1987–2005), *Œuvres économiques complètes*, P. Dockès, P.-H. Goutte, C. Hébert, C. Mouchot, J.-P. Potier and J.-M. Servet (eds), 14 vols, Paris: Economica.

Walras, L. (1898), *Éléments d'économie politique pure*, 4th edn, in A. Walras and L. Walras (1987–2005), *Œuvres économiques complètes*, P. Dockès, P.-H. Goutte, C. Hébert, C. Mouchot, J.-P. Potier and J.-M. Servet (eds), 14 vols, Paris: Economica.

Walras, L. (1954), *Elements of Pure Economics, or the Theory of Social Wealth*, trans. W. Jaffé, Homewood, IL: Irwin, London: Allen and Unwin.

Weintraub, E.R. (1983), 'On the existence of a competitive equilibrium: 1930–1954', *Journal of Economic Literature*, **21** (1), 1–39.

Wicksell, K. (1893), *Über Wert, Kapital und Rente nach den neueren nationalökonomischen Theorien*, Jena: Gustav Fischer.

Wicksell, K. (1898), *Geldzins und Güterpreise: Eine Studie über die den Tauschwert des Geldes bestimmenden Ursachen*, Jena: Gustav Fischer.

Winiarski, L. (1967), *Essais sur la mécanique sociale*, G. Busino (ed.), Geneva: Droz.

Zawadzki, W. (1914), *Les mathématiques appliquées à l'économie politique*, Paris: M. Rivière.

Zylberberg, A. (1990), *L'économie mathématique en France 1870–1914*, Paris: Economica.

Historical economics

During the second half of the nineteenth century, as "political economy" gave way to a new academically shaped "economics", the argument was made that the development of economic thought should have a historical basis. The argument was most consistently made in Germany, and since the German university and its scholars enjoyed international pre-eminence across many fields, the "German Historical School" became central to this idea of a "historical economics". As university systems were developed around the world, "German Historical Economics" carried a powerful resonance, but it was only in Great Britain that this reputation linked into existing historical studies. This entry examines the origins and early development of this attempt to construct a "historical economics", first outlining German developments, then English, without however exploring more recent writings which largely recycle the reputation, rather than the substance, of these arguments about history and economics.

Political economy first emerged in early nineteenth-century Britain and France as a discourse concerned less with the general progress of nations, and more with abstract doctrines concerning the relationships of wages, rents and profits, and the relationship of price to value. By mid-century, arguments had gelled into a more or less settled doctrine, notoriously represented by John Stuart Mill's declaration that there was, happily, "nothing in the laws of Value which remains for the present or any future writer to clear up; the theory of the subject is complete: the only difficulty to be overcome is that of so stating it as to solve by anticipation the chief perplexities which occur in applying it" (1848 [1965]: 456). The second half of the century saw the eclipse of this presumption: not only did a new subjectivist approach develop which shifted attention from the properties of a good to the decisions made by an economic agent, the precursor to twentieth-century developments; the older model also became increasingly criticised from the standpoint of logic, politics and history. Quite soon a new story developed around this last perspective: that political economy's abstract, universalist approach divorced it from the real history of nations, seeking explanation of the fluctuations of prices, wages, rents and interest in a causal mechanics, rather than in the diverse institutions whose particular configurations and interactions shaped these movements. Historians, it was said, eschewed theory in favour of an approach akin to that of biology, "the detailed description and historical explanation of the constitution and economic life of every nation".

So wrote Charles Rist in the first modern history of economic thought, Gide and Rist's *Histoire des doctrines économiques depuis les Physiocrates jusqu'à nos jours* (1909: 464), in which "The Historical School and the dispute on methods" is the first of four chapters in the section on "The dissidents", dissident, that is, from the economic liberalism of Bastiat and Carey, on the one hand, and John Stuart Mill, on the other. The remaining three chapters in this section are on state socialism, Marxism, and Christian doctrines. The sketch Rist gives of the "Historical School" is by now a familiar one: the "School" was inaugurated by Roscher in 1843, elaborated by Hildebrand in 1848, and reinforced by Knies in 1853, together forming what later became known as the "Older Historical School". From the 1870s a new wave developed around the figure of Gustav Schmoller, what became the "Younger Historical School", which abandoned any concern with economic laws, turned increasingly away from any connection with theoretical approaches, and for the first time produced a substantial body of economic-historical studies. "From

Germany, this impulse propagated abroad where it encountered especially favourable circumstances" (Gide and Rist 1909: 446) – although besides some passing remarks about France, where the introduction of political economy in the teaching of law faculties in 1878 provided some opening for a historical approach, the impact of these impulses is only detailed for Britain. Here in 1875 John Elliott Cairnes brought out the second edition of his *Character and Logical Method of Political Economy*, reaffirming a classical deductive approach to political economy that was criticised in 1879 by Cliffe Leslie, a criticism backed up by Arnold Toynbee in his posthumous *Lectures on the Industrial Revolution of the 18th Century in England* (1884). The positive adoption of a historical and institutional approach to economic development was then, Rist suggested, reinforced in the writings of William Cunningham, W.J. Ashley, Sidney and Beatrice Webb, and Charles Booth (Gide and Rist 1909: 448).

Rist was here attempting to sketch out a broad trend in the recent development of economic thought; and it is not so much that the narrative he created is faulty, but that it has never been subjected to any reassessment. Absent in Rist, and also today, is any consideration of contemporary historical studies, the status of a modern history detached from classical studies, and linked to conceptions of human development as reflected in the study of language and archaeology – what history meant in a nineteenth-century context. It is also widely assumed today that "historical economics" was, if briefly, a real alternative option to a more theoretical economics in the later nineteenth century, an option supposedly closed down by academic economists who engineered a diversion into economic history, which could be tidily segregated from the real business of economics. Rist was making a first pass at the role of the "Historical School"; but this story should by rights have been superseded decades ago by a serious reconsideration of his arguments. In this entry we will try to provide some elements for a reassessment of "Historical Economics", using material drawn from Germany and Britain. We deal first with German developments, not because of their alleged "influence", but because it was only in Germany that we can talk of a fully fledged and self-conscious "Historical School of Economics". It could also be said that the three members of the German "Older" School, necessarily so-called only retrospectively, never asserted themselves as pursuing some kind of common programme in the way that their "successors" did. The distinction between "Older" and "Younger" is therefore somewhat specious, being an invention of later nineteenth century German economists. Moreover, this division fails to account for the real diversity of German teaching and writing on economic matters during the mid to late nineteenth century.

Roscher, Hildebrand and Knies

Wilhelm Roscher (1817–1894) began his studies in 1835, first in Göttingen where he read history and philosophy, then in Berlin, where he studied ancient philology with Boeckh, and history with Ranke. By 1840 he had completed his habilitation, and in 1843 he was appointed to an assistant professorship in history and state science (*Staatswissenschaft*) in Göttingen, being promoted the next year to a full professor. For his first lectures on *Staatswirtschaft* in 1843 he prepared an outline which is usually taken as the foundation stone of German historical economics, the *Grundriß zu Vorlesungen über die Staatswirthschaft. Nach geschichtlicher Methode*. The fact that he had studied with

Dahlmann, Gervinus and Ranke might suggest that his "historical method" was inspired by these founding fathers of German history; but this would be only partially true. The real clue to his orientation is his contact with philology, and especially the work of Boeckh.

Karl Otfried Müller, whose lectures Roscher attended in Göttingen, had published in 1833 an edition of Aeschylus' *Eumenides* which drew on art and archaeology as well as textual sources, prompting the criticism from Gottfried Hermann that use of such sources was not appropriate for the study of texts. Müller had studied with Boeckh, whose defence of his favourite student led to a schism between the *Wortphilologie* of Hermann and what became known as *Realphilologie*, which supplemented the textual study of classical texts with ancient history, literature and art (Gerber 2010: 104–5). Boeckh had published a major work of this kind in 1817 devoted to the *Staatshaushaltung der Athener*, book 1 of volume 1 dealing with "Prices, wages and interest in Attica", the second book dealing with financial administration and expenditures – apart from being addressed to ancient Greece, the work clearly owes a great deal to the descriptions of states and their economic organisation that can be found in the writings of contemporary *Staatswissenschaften* and *Statistik*.

Roscher's initial interest lay in this projection of the *Staatswissenschaften* into ancient society; the year before the *Grundriß* appeared he had published a substantial book on Thucydides, announcing in the preface that:

> Hitherto my lectures have been limited to the history of political theories, *Staatswirthschaft*, *Politik* and *Statistik*; from now on they will extend to real history (*die eigentliche Historie*). I regard *Politik* as the doctrine of the developmental laws of the State; *Staatswirthschaft* and *Statistik* as especially important and detailed branches and aspects of *Politik*. I believe I can find these developmental laws through a comparison of those histories of peoples with which I am familiar. (Roscher 1842: vii)

Despite the fact that he went on to contrast philology and ancient history, and identify himself with the latter, it is Boeckh's version of ancient history that is the clear source for his thinking. For the "histories of peoples" to which he was here referring concern the peoples of Ancient Greece and Rome, not the ancient Germanic tribes, and even less so the peoples of medieval and early modern Europe. This is apparent both in his book on Thucydides and the programmatic statement he made the following year in the context of his lectures on *Staatswirtschaft*. This was described as a "political science":

> Our aim is to present an account of what people have, from an economic perspective, thought, wanted and felt; what they have striven for and achieved, why they have so striven, and why they have achieved what they have . . . The people is not however just the mass of those living today. Whoever wishes to study the economy cannot just stop at the observation of present-day economic relationships. The study of earlier cultural stages seems to have almost the same importance, since it is the best teacher about the more primitive peoples of the present . . . The difficulty of finding the essential, law-like regularities in the great mass of phenomena impels us to compare economically all those peoples known to us. (Roscher 1843: iv)

Roscher suggested a comparison with the work of Savigny, who had studied the early development of relations of property and possession and spawned the "Historical School of Law". However, he never developed this allusion; nor, in fact, did his comparative history ever get off the starting blocks. The nearest thing to any such comparative history is his study of Thucydides, announced as the first part of a major work that never materialised. The programmatic intent of identifying developmental laws – *Staatswirtschaft* is "the doctrine of the developmental laws of the economy", politics is "the doctrine of the developmental laws of the state" (Roscher 1843: 4) – through the pursuit of comparative history remained unfulfilled. Instead, Roscher produced a popular five-volume *System der Volkswirthschaft (1854–94)* that combined extensive description of economic organisation with a conventional German textbook exposition of the main principles of political economy, and in 1874 a history of German economics that drew on many essays that he had written in the previous 20 years. The identification of the developmental laws of the economy from a systematic comparative study of human history remained an aspiration that barely seems to have survived its first articulation. Roscher remained an important figure, publishing in 1892 his *Politik* as a "historical natural doctrine of monarchy, aristocracy and democracy", which in its closing sections examined the development of plutocracy, the proletariat and Caesarism, this last beginning in ancient Rome and culminating with Cromwell and Napoleon.

Bruno Hildebrand (1812–1878) had a more conventionally historical training at Leipzig and Breslau, but his career was from the first student semester onwards dogged by his activism. Appointed to a chair in the *Staatswissenschaften* at Marburg in 1841, during 1848 he was a deputy to the National Assembly in Frankfurt; but this political involvement brought retribution, and by 1851 he had fled to Switzerland, where he first held a chair in Zürich, and then in Bern, returning to Germany only in 1861 to an appointment at Jena. His declared membership of an "older" school is owed mainly to a programmatic statement made as a book published in 1848, *Die Nationalökonomie der Gegenwart und Zukunft*, which was intended as the first part of a work that would contribute to the elaboration of "the economic laws of development of peoples" (1848: v).

This first part, "The systems of political economy", is divided into five sections – on Smith and Ricardo, Adam Müller, Friedrich List, socialism and Proudhon – and never moves beyond a critique of existing work:

> The Smithian system represented itself as a general theory of human economy, but was only an expression of a money economy just become pre-eminent . . . Economics was treated by the entire Smithian school as a natural science of commerce, in which the individual was assumed to be a purely selfish force, active like any natural force in a constant direction and which, given similar conditions, will produce the same results. For this reason its laws and regularities were called both in Germany and in England natural economic laws, and eternal duration attributed to them, like other natural laws. (Hildebrand 1848: 29, 33–4)

Knies would later point out that Hildebrand's association of Smith with "selfishness" or "egoism" was a mistaken idea originating in a faulty German translation of *The Wealth of Nations* by Max Stirner, but Hildebrand's association of Smith's analysis with natural laws distinguishes his critique from that of Friedrich List, who had in *Das nationale System der politischen Oekonomie* (1841) argued primarily against the nationalism of Smith's account of commercial economy. List had organised his critique of Adam Smith's "cosmopolitical economics" around the idea that in the present it only served Britain's national interests, whereas Smith's principles belonged properly to a future international economy. Hildebrand maintained that List's criticisms had made him a "benefactor of the German people" despite the fact that he was otherwise "partisan, superficial, exaggerating, really only repeating one single idea in a thousand variations" (1848: 69); a stimulus to historical study, but no historian himself.

Hence List's criticism of British political economy for being "unhistorical" did not necessarily entail an explicitly historical stance. But the same argument can be made of Hildebrand's own work: he never completed his promised account of the real method of political economy; no further parts to his book were ever published. However, once back in Jena he founded the *Jahrbücher für Nationalökonomie und Statistik* in 1862, the first German periodical dedicated to political economy broadly conceived, and which remained the leading publication for German-language economists into the 1890s, given that the *Jahrbuch für Gesetzgebung, Verwaltung und Volkswirtschaft im Deutschen Reiche* that Schmoller took over in 1881 always had a more broadly legislative and historical profile. Hildebrand was also, in 1872, a founding member of the Verein für Socialpolitik (see below), a broad association whose main function was to encourage systematic research into social and economic questions and debate them at an annual conference.

Hildebrand did therefore overlap with the "Younger" generation, as did Carl Knies (1821–1898), who had a similarly rocky start to his career before settling into a 30-year tenure of the Heidelberg chair. Knies began in 1841 as a student of history and the *Staatswissenschaften* in Marburg, thus overlapping with Hildebrand, but he never described himself as a student of Hildebrand, nor indeed did any of these three academics form any kind of "school" themselves. Having completed in 1846 a dissertation on the Roman city of Palestrina, he was hampered in finding an academic post by his lack of publications, although he had already deputised as a lecturer for Hildebrand and von Sybel. He was therefore sent to a training school in Kassel to write a book, publishing in 1850 a study of *Statistik*. Returning to Marburg, there had been a ministerial changeover and no appointment materialised, and so he left once more to teach in a school, quickly writing up *Die politische Oekonomie vom Standpunkte der geschichtlichen Methode* (1853). As he later complained, the book sold very slowly, but it did lend him a high enough profile to be appointed to a chair in Freiburg in 1861. Here he became politically active, sitting as a deputy in the Baden Lower Assembly, and becoming Middle School Director for Baden. In 1865 he was appointed (by the Baden Ministry of Culture) to the chair at Heidelberg, where he lectured among others to John Bates Clark, Edwin Seligman, and Max Weber, while Eugen von Böhm-Bawerk and Friedrich Wieser joined his seminar in 1876. A new edition of his *Politische Oekonomie* was published in 1883 under a revised title: *Die politische Oekonomie vom geschichtlichen Standpuncte,* reflecting his distaste for "historical method" and preference for a "historical perspective". Knies added new passages to the volume, clarifying the object of political economy as he saw it, and in so doing marking his distance from the work of Schmoller and Lujo Brentano:

> The object of study for the sciences of the state and society consists in the actions or works of men, and the conditions of a societised and legally ordered living community (*vergesellschafteten und rechtlich geordneten Lebensgemeinschaft*) founded upon the actions and works of many individuals and entire peoples. This is not a matter of a world of thoughts and ideas within man, as with the human sciences, but rather process and circumstances that can be found in the external world of sensually perceptible phenomena. (Knies 1883: 6)

Fortunately, student lecture notes from his courses in 1880 and 1886 have also survived, and demonstrate that in his teaching of political economy Knies followed a predictable path, beginning with definitions of "wants" and "goods", just like Roscher, or any other German teacher of economics for that matter. The exposition of the leading concepts – of production, distribution, value and price – is geared primarily to a critique of socialist theory, especially the doctrines of Marx, associated by Knies with the English political economists. Rejecting the idea that price is determined by cost of production, Knies argues that if this were true then prices would not fluctuate in the manner that they do while costs of production remained stable. Instead he identifies the interaction of supply and demand as the dominant factor, in effect adopting the position Jean-Baptiste Say had taken in his criticism of Ricardo some 70 years earlier:

> The significance of production costs in price formation is determined by the extension or contraction of supply . . . Where production cannot be expanded or reduced prices will rise with higher demand, or fall with less demand. If production can be varied, then prices do not vary so greatly, despite altered demand. (Knies 1886 [2000]: 48)

There is no suggestion in these lectures that the principles expounded should be founded inductively; as with Roscher and Hildebrand, the principal historical element involved reference to the classics of economics such as the Physiocrats, Adam Smith and David Ricardo. While he retained a strong interest in systems of communication and money, publishing separate works on these topics, his exposition of the principles of political economy was not merely unremarkable, it was continuous with the understanding of many other German economists not usually assigned to either "Historical School". Turning, for example, to Lorenz von Stein's *Die Volkswirthschaftslehre* (1878), finds a "historical" or institutional account of the economy by a writer not normally associated with any Historical School. The work of Roscher, Hildebrand and Knies is only one part of an extensive, if unexplored, hinterland of writing associated with the *Staatswissenschaften*, shading off into ancient history and philology. Not only are there significant differences between the work of these three members of the "Older School", each of them can be related more directly to other contemporaries than to each other.

The "Younger" Historical School

Roscher, Hildebrand and Knies did all develop a critique of the "abstract" and "unhistorical" economics associated especially with the British economists of the early nineteenth century, while proclaiming their belief in the existence of the "laws of development" of society and economy. Their successors reversed this: they proclaimed a belief in the abstract and unhistorical nature of existing economic thought, while going some way to develop analyses of trades, commerce and administration that demonstrated the existence of determinate stages of economic development. Rather than imitate their predecessors and simply adopt, for the sake of convenience, the basic analytical armoury of classical economics, this new generation simply dismissed it, and turned to what now would be regarded as economic history. Whereas we might say of the "Older" School that they failed to develop the historical analysis they had proposed, it could be said of the "Younger" School that their work had little bearing on contemporary economic analysis, however broadly understood.

Nevertheless, the "Younger School" successfully established itself within the German universities of the later nineteenth century, and established as a common institutional support in 1872 the Verein für Socialpolitik, having its inaugural annual meeting in 1873 and which became a vehicle for the study of the "social question", the varied and contradictory forces arising from industrialisation and urbanisation. The Verein was a broadly reformist organisation, but one which conceived the German state as the embodiment of the will of the German people. Many of its members came to be known as Kathedersozialisten, "academic socialists". Gustav Schmoller (1838–1917) had argued at the 1872 meeting that it was the task of German academics to uncover a common basis for the reform of social relations, and persuade a broader public of the need for such reform (Schmoller 1872 [2000]: 595). He warned of the threat from social revolution engendered by the division between employer and worker, propertied and propertyless classes, and suggested that popular economic beliefs concerning commercial freedom and economic individualism could well create even greater disorder, rather than the rosy future they imagined. Germany had been united the previous year; but, argued Schmoller, social divisions already posed a threat to the young nation, and for the reduction of social tension one had to look to the German state, which stood above selfish class interests, "legislating, guiding administration with a just hand, protecting the weak, raising the lower classes", the culmination of two centuries of Prussian endeavour (Schmoller 1872 [2000]: 599–60).

We can better appreciate how this broad objective of social reform and the emergence of the German state was linked to historical study from Schmoller's account of Frederick the Great's "economic policy", published in 12 separate articles over 500 pages in the flagship journal of which he assumed control in 1881, the *Jahrbuch für Gesetzgebung, Verwaltung und Volkswirtschaft*. Schmoller began by remarking that Roscher's own treatment of Frederick the Great's economic policy reflected the prevailing certainties of nineteenth-century economics: he evaluated policies by reference to the economic rationality of Frederick's explicit pronouncements on economic matters (Tribe 1993). Assuming the rationality of prevailing economic principles, "successful" policies followed from rational decisions plus unimpeded execution; while "unsuccessful policies" suffered from countervailing distortions not part of the policy process itself. There was therefore no need to examine the objectives and actual performance of Prussian economic administration independently of the economic principles articulated by the Prussian monarch. In contrast to this approach, Schmoller sought to develop the rationality of policy from a study of the organisation of economic life, shifting the emphasis away from statements of economic principle towards the actual process of economic organisation. This represented a step forward in the historical understanding of economic evolution, and was to provide the model upon which the new economic history of, among others, Ashley and Cunningham was built.

However, Schmoller also here introduced a major step backwards, reviving Smith's treatment in *The Wealth of Nations* book IV of the "mercantile system" and converting it into a new term, "mercantilism", which brought together all those policies which positively contributed to the formation of the Prussian state. It was therefore not only teleological, the founding myth of German unification; ironically, much like Adam Smith's own account, it focused on "policy" and not on the writings of contemporary writers who had debated the merits of policy. "Mercantilism" entered the conceptual armoury of historians of economic thought as a general designation for the beliefs and assumptions of those engaged in economic activity who are in fact notable for their absence from Schmoller's historical perspective. Also, it was not as though this absence went unrecognised at the time: the year after Schmoller's articles began to appear, Gustav Marchet not only presented the doctrines of Seckendorff, Becher, Sonnenfels and Justi with exemplary clarity, he also reacted strongly against their alleged "mercantilist" pedigree. Marchet lays proper emphasis on the ubiquity of state activity, in which the functioning of the economy depended upon the preparedness of the state to intervene "and regulate, and provide assistance, and also protection, and create order, and impose restrictions" (Marchet 1885: 50). However, the sources that Marchet employed are those supplied by contemporary arguments, and these are not linked by Marchet to any mythology of the Prussian state and its origins.

Quite apart from the prominence which his role in the *Verein* gave him, Schmoller's own extensive writings were distinguished by their focus on the social and economic forces underlying the development of the German state. His early study of small enterprise (1870) examined the pressures on small and craft businesses in increasingly international markets, arguing for a measure of protective legislation that would enable such enterprises to adapt to new conditions. Historical and comparative investigation of financial, agrarian or industrial conditions was linked in this manner to the forces of industrialisation and the role of the state in moderating the negative effects of economic progress. This approach was shared with others, such as Lujo Brentano, whose early studies of British trade unions prompted a comparative analysis of labour organisation, establishing that British wages were higher and working hours shorter than those in Germany. His conclusion from this research, that economic progress would only result from a reduction of working hours in Germany, exemplifies the manner in which the comparative study originally envisaged by Roscher could be linked to social reform (Brentano 1877).

In time a division emerged within the *Verein* between founding members who had experienced unification and who shared Schmoller's ethical evaluation of the state – Adolph Wagner, Wilhelm Lexis, Johannes Conrad – and a younger generation, primarily of economists, more concerned with the social and political disintegration of the 1880s and 1890s – Carl Grünberg, Max Sering, Ferdinand Tönnies, and of course Max and Alfred Weber. Although some of these latter academics did conduct detailed empirical investigation, they were also more open to theoretical argument. So when Carl Menger published his methodological critique of German historicism (1883) and Schmoller unleashed what became known as the *Methodenstreit*, or "Dispute on method", the idea that this was a root and branch assault on the principles of the Historical School was always one held by the older generation within the "Younger" school, and not the younger.

If we examine dispassionately the arguments made by Menger, the "dispute on method" shrinks in significance. He made a clear distinction between the historical and statistical study of economic forms; theoretical economics; and practical fields such as economic policy and finance. Historical study of economic structures had its place, but was complementary to, not a substitute for, the development of theoretical principles (1883 [1969]: 12–13). The prime task of economic analysis was therefore the elaboration of theory and policy, not the simple accumulation of economic facts. Empirical knowledge could not be acquired through reflection, and the search for theoretical knowledge was not directly served by extensive empirical work. This was the core of Menger's argument. Schmoller's generation knew little of contemporary economic theory, and for years he had devoted his energy to detailed studies of economic organisation on the basis of administrative records. However, in response he simply reversed the point that Menger had made, and argued that economic analysis could not be derived from general principles of psychology, but must arise from the study of individual economic action. Historical study, he suggested, had no need of "theoretical" economics (1883 [1969]: 967–77). Of course, Schmoller never did study individual action, historical or otherwise, in the manner that he implied. There was no more to the *Methodenstreit* than this. Menger argued, on the one hand, that theory was not susceptible to inductive elaboration – something which Schmoller in truth never even attempted – while Schmoller asserted, on the other, that it was, but never sought to demonstrate how. Despite its insubstantial nature, this "dispute on method" came to symbolise the gulf that separated historical from theoretical economics in the later nineteenth century.

Arguments over the relationship of economics to economic history do, however, distract attention from the focus of historical economists on national economic development. An important thread in this approach was the idea of developmental stages in economic development, elaborated by Karl Bücher in lectures during the later 1880s, and first published as *Die Entstehung der Volkswirtschaft* in 1893. This was a three-step evolutionary ideal type, beginning with the household economy in which goods were produced and consumed within the same economic form; developing into an urban economy in which goods moved directly from producer to consumer; and ending with *Volkswirtschaft*, where goods were produced as commodities and circulated as such. The transition from household to urban economy was brought about by difficulties the former had in meeting all its own needs; this engendered the development of markets, but Bücher did not argue that this new feature in turn led to the commoditisation of production and consumption. Instead, it was the political centralisation brought about by the early modern territorial state that created the modern economy. The problem posed by Bücher linked therefore to Brentano: to explain how European societies had evolved from earlier, non-profit-oriented forms to a modern, commercial reality. Shiro Takebayashi has outlined in great detail exactly how Bucher's "stages" were constructed around this problem, mapping Bücher's conceptual schema on to Schmoller's much more discursive accounts. In so doing, he is able to show the degree to which Brentano, Schmoller and Bücher shared a common perspective with respect to conceptualisation of the evolutionary path taken by modern enterprise; and that, while they might increasingly have taken into account Marx's own arguments as outlined in *Capital* volume I, there is little ground for arguing that they were in dialogue with Marx, or that Marx had initiated an argument that they then took up. Takebayashi sums up the relationship with Marx's evolutionary history as follows:

> If one compares Brentano's view with Marx's "industrial morphology" it is clear that, for Brentano, the decisive turning point in industrial history lay not in the development of manufacture, but instead in the transition from manual crafts to domestic industry. He is of the opinion that it was only with domestic industry that industrial organisations emerged in association with trading relationships linked to the world market. Brentano therefore sees the

emergence of an "acquisitive impulse" (*Erwerbstrieb*) in the historical transition of the economic enterprise from manual crafts to domestic industry. (Takebayashi 2003: 78)

It was the origin of this "acquisitive impulse" that formed the object of Max Weber's essays on the "Protestant ethic" in 1904/05, conceived by him as "illuminating the manner in which 'ideas' become effective in history . . . the main thing is to discover the psychological *drives* which led people to behave in a certain way and held them firmly in this path" (Weber 1904/05 [2002]: 35, 69).

Historical Economics in England

In conventional accounts of English historical economics two distinct stages may be discerned. In the first, between roughly 1870 and 1885, various individuals raised a protest against orthodox economic theory by way of an appeal to history. Then, from around 1885 through to the early years of the twentieth century, historical economists became bound up, first in a battle over the professionalisation of economics, and then in the national political debate over tariff reform (becoming, as one historian has put it, "the house intellectuals of the Edwardian Conservative party"; Green 1996: 183). Both the political and academic battles are deemed to have ended in defeat. The victor on the academic front was Alfred Marshall, who is said to have established university economics as a neoclassical science in which economic theory retained its old deductive methodology albeit in a new marginal guise. Effectively retiring from the academic fray and resigning any claim to the economic crown, the historical economists now settled down as economic historians.

The discussion that follows demonstrates the various ways in which this conventional account is not tenable. One problem that immediately presents itself is that many of the strands that are told of the second stage bear only an accidental or contingent relationship to historical thought. Edwardian arguments over tariff reform, for example, might have divided economists into two camps, but there was nothing inherently historical in the idea of increased state intervention in the interest of national or imperial preference. The grounds for including such arguments as part of an "English *Methodenstreit*" (Koot 1988: 4) are sociological rather than intellectual, relating, that is, to a contingent distribution of opinions among academic factions as opposed to anything inherently historical about those opinions themselves.

A more unsettling problem concerns the place of Alfred Marshall in the conventional narrative. Marshall usually appears only in the second stage, a star actor in the story of professionalisation, playing the role of hero or villain according to the sympathies of the audience. So cast as the leader of the new theoretical economics, Marshall is the arch-enemy of the historians who plays what proves to be a winning strategy of "conciliation without concessions" (Maloney 1976: 440). In so representing Marshall as the founder of a modern deductive and ahistorical neoclassical economics, students of historical economics have of course but reflected what, until very recently, has been the general consensus about Marshall held by historians of economics. Nevertheless, and as demonstrated below, Marshall, no less than (say) T.E. Cliffe Leslie or Arnold Toynbee, warrants inclusion among that handful of individuals who, in the 1870s, engaged with the historicist challenge to current economic orthodoxy.

Bringing to light Marshall's place in the first stage of English historical economics undermines further the coherency of the standard account of the second stage. For once we recognise that Marshall's own contributions to theoretical economics arose at least to some degree by way of his early encounter with historical thought, and that his conciliatory statements on method were more than mere rhetoric, then the standard binary framework that structures conventional interpretations of the "English *Methodenstreit*" falls apart. This is not to deny the reality of both academic and political controversy in the three decades after 1885; but it is to raise seemingly terminal doubts as to the value of interpreting such arguments within a single framework itself reducible to some profound clash between historicist and theoretical paradigms.

In what follows our primary concern is to illuminate the first stage of English historical economics, laying particular emphasis upon the place of the younger Marshall in the key intellectual developments. The conclusion to which we are led is that the intellectual momentum behind the drive to create a genuinely historical economics was pretty much spent in England by around 1890. If this conclusion is accepted, then it follows that, whatever the sound and fury generated by historically minded economists (or economically minded historians) after this date, its significance for historical thought was very limited, and that nothing warranting identification as a *Methodenstreit* ever occurred.

Henry Maine

In the prefatory remarks to his collection of *Essays in Political and Moral Philosophy*, Cliffe Leslie famously pronounced that "the English economist of the future must study in the schools of both Mr. Stubbs and Sir Henry Maine, as well as in that of Mr. Mill" (1879: vii). While the work of Stubbs remained a closed book to most outside of Oxford, two books of Maine had, already by the end of the 1870s, exerted a profound impact upon English students of economics: *Ancient Law* (1861) and *Village Communities in the East and West* (1871). The first book outlined a history of jurisprudence from primitive times, proposing the central thesis that progress had entailed a movement in the conception – and hence legal reality – of social relations, from primitive ideas of status as determined by rules of kinship through to modern ideas of individuals freely contracting with one another. The second book proposed a model of institutional development, from the primitive social form of the village community through to the various institutions of modern commercial society. In distinctive ways, these two books stand behind much of the methodological criticism and the substantive historical thought of English students of economics in the 1870s.

Cliffe Leslie made Maine's *Ancient Law* a foundational text in his methodological revolt against orthodox deductive political economy. In his seminal essay of 1870, "The political economy of Adam Smith", he argued that Smith had originated two economic "schools one deductive the other inductive". The latter, the historical school, had hitherto been eclipsed by the former. However, the recent work of Henry Maine, Cliffe Leslie argued, had discredited the deductive methodology that the orthodox school had inherited from Smith. The orthodox deductive methodology, so Cliffe Leslie claimed, rested upon ideas of "Nature" and "Natural Law" that Maine had recently shown to be derived from the jurisprudential thinking of Roman Stoicism, resting upon a fallacious conflation of natural and moral orders (Cliffe Leslie 1870: 552). By way of the strange survival of natural law philosophy into the modern age, an ancient – and otherwise long-superseded – framing of particular social relationships and states of society as "natural" had come to be embedded at the heart of eighteenth-century political economy. For Cliffe Leslie in 1870 the lesson to be derived from *Ancient Law* was that the entire deductive tradition of political economy must be discarded: the future belonged to the historical school.

Marshall engaged with the relevant arguments of Maine, ultimately arriving at different conclusions to Cliffe Leslie. In his early manuscripts we find notes on both Cliffe Leslie's 1870s paper (Marshall 2010: M 4/19, f.6) and Maine's discussion in *Ancient Law* of the modern history of the ancient idea of the "Law of Nature" (unpublished manuscript: M 4/13, f.20). The fruit of this engagement is made clear when we turn to the *Principles of Economics*, which was first published in 1890, nearly two decades later. Here we find Marshall echoing Maine as he directed Cliffe Leslie's arguments on to the Physiocrats who, Marshall complains, placed at the heart of their thought the idea of "the Law of Nature which had been developed by the Stoic lawyers of the later Roman Empire", with the inevitable result that they confused "the laws of economic science and the ethical precepts of conformity to nature" – a confusion, Marshall adds, that Adam Smith "had not quite got rid of" (Marshall 1890 [1961] I: 756, n. 2). This theme is developed further in the introduction to the theory of distribution in (what became) book VI of the *Principles*, where Smith and Ricardo are criticised for adopting the physiocratic terminology of natural law and, thereby, suggesting that a state of society in which wages barely cover the necessaries of life is in some way natural (Marshall 1890 [1961] I: 507–8). These early notes, and later discussions in the *Principles*, reveal that Marshall was in agreement with Cliffe Leslie's view that Maine's *Ancient Law* shed light upon the problematic way in which ancient natural law philosophy had become entwined in the early history of modern economic theory. However, what the discussions in the *Principles* also illustrate is that Marshall drew from this historicist criticism the lesson that the traditional theory must be revised, or at least restated, rather than discarded.

This is not the place to enter into a general discussion of the role of historicism in Marshall's methodological and theoretical innovations (on this, see Cook 2009: chs 6–8). It can certainly be argued that Marshall developed a revised deductivism, in which theory was applied in a local rather than general manner, and in which appreciation of the particularities of local context became extremely important; and, indeed, this is very much the image of Marshall that emerges from the most recent scholarship (see, especially, Raffaelli et al. 2006) and which has begun to replace the older portrait of Marshall as the founder of a new "neoclassical" orthodoxy. However, what matters to us here is, in the first place, the evident flaw in any picture of an English *Methodenstreit* in which historical economists do battle with intransient deductivist theorists under the leadership of Marshall. At the very least, the reality was more complicated; and a case could clearly be made for characterising later disputes as taking place within some general historicist consensus. However, this is not all. It is certainly possible to quibble with the value of the particular theoretical revisions that Marshall made to orthodoxy in light of Maine's historicism. But by 1890 Cliffe Leslie's more radical alternative of completely jettisoning theory in favour of a purely inductive science had lost credibility. To see how this came about and what it meant we need to turn to the reception of Maine's *Village Communities*.

Maine's *Village Communities* built upon the work of the German Historical School of law, most notably G.L. von Maurer's *Einleitung zur Geschichte der Mark* (1854). Earlier in the century the great historical jurist, Friedrich Carl von Savigny, aided by the famous historian of ancient Rome, Barthold Niebuhr, had pioneered an account of the development of private property from the nomadic tribe to the ancient city, in which some of the land in ancient Rome (the *ager publicus*) was shown to have been publicly owned but possessed and farmed by private persons. In the mid-century von Maurer had described the early Germanic village or *mark* community as also containing mixed forms of property ownership. Maine's first innovation was to recognise von Maurer's early Germanic *mark* community in the village community of nineteenth-century India. His second innovation was to build upon the genealogical connections established by nineteenth-century comparative philology and bring Indian, ancient Roman, and Germanic (including English) social forms together within a single account of so-called Aryan social evolution. The starting-point of this account was the nomadic tribe, in which all property was held in common and individual identity entirely defined in terms of kinship relations within the tribe. The basic idea was that, when a tribe bound together by ties of kinship and holding its land in common settled down to till the soil, two changes commenced: the gradual transformation of the social bond – from ties of kinship to ties based on shared territory (from being a Frank to being a citizen of France, as it were); and the gradual transformation of common into private property.

Maine's model of social progress was developed by several students of history in the 1870s. Perhaps the most important of such studies was E.A. Freeman's *Comparative Politics* (1873), which was carefully read by Marshall. Essentially, Freeman used Maine's model in order to explain the difference between ancient and modern societies as the products of two distinct paths of development out of an original primitive Aryan village community: in the ancient city-state citizenship remained bound up with kinship and blood ties and property was not wholly liberated from its initial communal state; the Germanic village community, by contrast, had undergone a more far-reaching transformation, through feudalism, and ultimately generating (by a process of amalgamation) the modern nations of Europe. Specifically, economic adaptations of Maine's model in this period can be found in several of Cliffe Leslie's essays of the 1870s, Marshall's various historical writings of the same decade, and the first book of William Cunningham's *Growth of English Industry and Commerce*, which was first published in 1882.

Cunningham's rendering of early English history is worth reviewing, not least because just about every element of it had been rejected by 1914. Cunningham begins with the English tribes prior to their invasion of (what would become) England. Like "other Aryan tribes", the English are said to have but recently migrated out of Asia and, according to the accounts of the German tribes given by Caesar and Tacitus, to be only just emerging from a state of nomadic pastoralism. Cunningham's first book tells the story of how these English tribes settled down and gradually established private ownership of the land together with that system of inherited and forced contracts known as feudalism. To give but one example: a key early step in this organic development occurs when the extensive occasional agriculture of nomads gives way to the intensive cultivation of a village community. At this point an incentive arises to bestow care and forethought on that plot of arable land that is repeatedly cultivated, and Cunningham suggests that at this point the communal tillage of the village is parcelled out into private holdings. That his story is deduced from a general model rather than inferred from local evidence is indicated by his comment at this point in his chapter that it is "impossible to decide with certainty" whether this development had occurred before or after the English settled in England (Cunningham 1882 [1890]: 41–2).

By the time that Cunningham brought out a second edition of *The Growth of English Industry*, in 1890, this first book of his volume appeared out of date and untenable. Such, at any rate, was the opinion expressed by the economic historian W.J. Ashley (1891: 154), who in a review of Cunningham's second edition observed that when his first edition had appeared in 1882 "English historical students were still under the spell of Maurer and Nasse and Maine: they all believed devoutly in the primitive Teutonic freeman and the mark, or free village community. Since then, however, Mr. Seebohm has arisen". Ashley was referring to Frederic Seebohm's *English Village Community* (1883), which did for ploughed fields what others in the 1880s were doing for the skulls of British ploughmen. Seebohm's basic claim was that "the continuity between the Roman and English system of land management was not really broken" by the Anglo-Saxon conquest (1883 [1905]: 418). Such claims fitted into a growing conviction among archaeologists and anthropologists that the evidence of skull types suggested a general continuity of population before and after the English invasion. In place of the older story of organic English social development together with folk migration and genocidal conquest of parts of the British Isles, a new historical picture was emerging. According to the new wisdom, Anglo-Saxon warriors simply took over existing Romano-British institutions and turned the British population into serfs. From this new historiographical perspective, as Ashley tartly put it, Cunningham needed to rewrite the first part of his book (Ashley 1891: 155).

The various responses to the work of Seebohm (and others) reveal the intellectual bankruptcy of English historical economics in the 1890s. Seebohm's arguments were bound up with a model of invasion and subsequent overlordship that was fundamentally incompatible with Maine's model of folk migration and organic social development. That a village community contains within itself a seed of development that may one day generate a medieval town is quite irrelevant if that village community is invaded by a band of warriors who enslave the inhabitants and force them to work as agricultural serfs. Marshall's response was to stick to his original plan of introducing his *Principles* with a long introductory historical discussion, but to remove the account of the evolution of village community into a modern nation state that had once been its kernel. The result was the emasculation of Marshall's historical thought (Cook 2013). Cunningham, as we have seen, resolutely refused to acknowledge any crisis and stuck with his original account through his second – and subsequent – editions; thereby attracting Ashley's rebuke and appearing ever more outdated as the years went by. Ashley's response was to discard the entire pre-feudal part of the story: as he put it in his *Introduction to English Economic History and Theory* (1888: 13), an economic history of England must begin with the eleventh century, at which date England was known to be covered by feudal manors, "and we cannot begin earlier because it is by no means agreed how that condition of things came about". However, one cannot amputate the initial stages of an organic evolutionary model and continue to maintain that the later stages still follow the earlier established pattern. By the early 1890s Ashley had repudiated Cliffe Leslie's ambition to transform economics into a historical discipline and henceforth directed his energy rather to the establishment of economic history as a separate discipline (Koot 1988: 110).

It is from this perspective that we should view the various spats and skirmishes of the 1890s and beyond. Cunningham is no doubt the historical actor most responsible for generating the misleading impression that the arguments of these years amounted to an English *Methodenstreit*. What was needed in the wake of the challenge to Maine's organic model was a revised or even new model of social development. Cunningham in this period went on the offensive, but signally failed to engage with the real issues. In the 1890 edition of his *Growth of English Industry* he actually intensified his reliance upon Maine's model, arguing that the role of custom identified by Maine as a hallmark of the primitive (but not the modern) world was also fundamental in the modern world. Then, in the pages of the *Economic Journal* of 1892, he launched his infamous attack upon Marshall's historical introduction to the *Principles*, published under the title "The perversion of economic history". Thus Cunningham's response to the intellectual crisis faced by traditional English historicism was vociferous, but singularly lacking in theoretical acumen. He refused to acknowledge (other than implicitly) that Maine's historical model was a theoretical model, and his ever-louder protestations of the virtues of inductivism simply betray an inability to come to grips with the real challenges facing that model. Perhaps the most notable element of this whole story is that later historians, on encountering Cunningham's wasteland of futile gesture and empty rhetoric, declared it a *Methodenstreit*.

New Constellations

Our conclusions may be reinforced by way of a brief review of subsequent developments in English historicism. Seebohm's *English Village Community* was the first in a series of publications that would utterly revise not only the orthodox picture of Anglo-Saxon history but also the conventional borders of the disciplinary constellations. Of particular importance was F.W. Maitland's *Domesday Book and Beyond* (1897), written very much as an attempt "to answer Mr Seebohm" (Maitland 1897: v). Maitland returned historical orthodoxy to an identification of Anglo-Saxon villages as neither Celtic nor Roman but "very purely and typically German" (Maitland 1897: 222). Nevertheless, he also insisted that Anglo-Saxon society had not been divided into clans, that the English "village community was not a *gens*" (Maitland 1897: 349), and that "so far back as we can see, the German village had a solid core of individualism" (Maitland 1897: 348). In other words, there could be no story told of a transformation of kinship group into contractual society of individuals, at least not on English soil. Elsewhere, Maitland went further. The attempt to trace the origins of individualism into some distant Continental past, he declared, "should be placed for our race beyond the limit of history" (Pollock and Maitland 1895: 240). What this meant in practice, at least at Maitland's Cambridge in the early years of the twentieth century, was that study of the early history of the English henceforth passed out of the hands of historians and into those of archaeologists and anthropologists.

The year 1907 also saw the publication of H.M. Chadwick's seminal *The Origin of the English Nation*, the arguments of which were developed and generalised in his

1912 *The Heroic Age*. Significantly, both books were published within the "Cambridge Archaeological and Ethnological Series". Chadwick marks the definitive rejection of the origin story accepted by, among others, Maine, Cunningham, and the early Marshall. Chadwick's starting-point was the finding of recent archaeological research that agriculture had been practiced continuously around the North Sea and Baltic coasts since the Stone Age (1907: 343–4). The pre-conquest English were not nomadic pastoralists recently arrived from Asia, but sedentary farmers, and they had been so for time out of mind. From this it followed that the origins of English individualism were not to be sought in some organic story of settlement and cultivation of the land. Anglo-Saxon individualism, Chadwick argued, had its roots in the corruption of traditional society that began when the young men began to see a life of war and plunder as a viable alternative to following their fathers behind the plough: spurning the bonds of kin and the ties of custom, young warriors now swore loyalty to any war-leader who promised loot, pillage and newly conquered slave-worked land.

Chadwick's research fed into a bold new picture of the past emerging by way of the various lectures given under the auspices of the new Board of Anthropological Studies at Cambridge University. Another of the lecturers in these years was W.H. Rivers, just then in the process of conversion to the diffusionist theory according to which civilisation was a single package that had emerged only once and in one place – ancient Egypt. In his *Growth of Civilization* (1924), W.J. Perry, who had attended lectures in anthropology while studying mathematics in Edwardian Cambridge, brought together the ideas of Rivers and Chadwick. Perry's account of prehistory, which contains more than a hint of nineteenth-century Manchester liberalism, begins with the global dissemination of a peaceful Egyptian civilisation by traders and prospectors. A mutation then occurs on the periphery, which results in the emergence of individualistic warrior societies that conquer the civilised world and proceed to govern it over several millennia as a parasitical aristocracy, the bellicose activities of which had but recently plunged the nations of the globe into a world war.

What has all this to do with economics and historical economics? The short answer is: nothing. And this is precisely the point. It is evident that the discrediting of Maine's historicist model by no means spelled the end of historicist thought in England. Indeed, the two decades after 1890 witnessed the construction of a completely new model of the emergence of modern civilisation, but neither economists nor economic historians had anything to do with these developments. This absence can be lamented from the point of view of a paucity of economic acumen in the work of these Cambridge anthropologists (and note that when this deficiency was rectified by archaeologists it was by way of a drawing upon the Marxist tradition, and not any indigenous tradition of English historical economics). Be that as it may, our present purposes are met by the observation that after around 1890 it was not historicist thought that in England was ossified and moribund, but merely the idea of founding an alternative inductive school of economics upon it.

SIMON COOK AND KEITH TRIBE

See also:

Institutionalism (II); Alfred Marshall (I).

References and further reading

Ashley, W.J. (1888), *An Introduction to English Economic History and Theory: The Middle Ages*, London: Rivingtons.

Ashley, W.J. (1891), 'Cunningham's growth of English industry', *Political Science Quarterly* **6** (1), 152–61.

Boeckh, A. (1817), *Die Staatshaushaltung der Athener*, Berlin: Realschulbuchhandlung.

Brentano, L. (1877), *Das Arbeitsverhältniss gemäss dem heutigen Recht*, Leipzig: Duncker and Humblot.

Bücher, K. (1893), *Die Entstehung der Volkswirtschaft*, 2nd edn 1898, Tübingen: Verlag der H. Laupp'schen Buchhandlung.

Cairnes, J.E. (1875), *Character and Logical Method of Political Economy*, London: Macmillan.

Cliffe Leslie, T.E. (1870), 'The political economy of Adam Smith', *Fortnightly Review*, **8** (November), 549–63.

Cliffe Leslie, T.E. (1879), *Essays in Political and Moral Philosophy*, London: Longmans, Green.

Chadwick, H.M. (1907), *The Origin of the English Nation*, Cambridge: Cambridge University Press.

Chadwick, H.M. (1912), *The Heroic Age*, Cambridge: Cambridge University Press.

Cook, S. (2009), *The Intellectual Foundations of Alfred Marshall's Economic Science*, Cambridge: Cambridge University Press.

Cook, S. (2013), 'Race and nation in Marshall's histories', *European Journal of the History of Economic Thought*, **20** (6), 940–56.

Cunningham, W. (1882), *The Growth of English Industry and Commerce, During the Early and Middle Ages*, 2nd edn 1890, Cambridge: Cambridge University Press.

Cunningham, W. (1892), 'The perversion of economic history', *Economic Journal*, **2** (3), 491–506.

Freeman, E.A. (1873), *Comparative Politics*, New York: Macmillan.

Gerber, A. (2010), *Deissmann the Philologist*, Berlin: Walter de Gruyter.

Gide, C. and C. Rist (1909), *Histoire des doctrines économiques depuis les Physiocrates jusqu'à nos jours*, Paris: J.-B. Sirey.

Green, E.H.H. (1996), *The Crisis of Conservatism: The Politics, Economics and Ideology of the British Conservative Party, 1880–1914*, London: Routledge.

Hildebrand, B. (1848), *Die Nationalökonomie der Gegenwart und Zukunft*, Frankfurt am Main: Literarische Anstalt.

Knies, K. (1883), *Die politische Oekonomie vom geschichtlichen Standpuncte*, Neue Auflage, Brunswick: C.A. Schwetschke und Sohn (M. Bruhn).

Knies, K. (1886), 'Allgemeine (theoretische) Volkswirtschaftslehre (1886)', reprinted 2000 in *Kyoto University Economic Review*, **69** (1 & 2).

Koot, G.M. (1988), *English Historical Economics, 1870–1926: The Rise of Economic History and Neomercantilism*, Cambridge: Cambridge University Press.

List, F. (1841), *Das Nationale System der politischen Oekonomie*, Schriften/Reden/Briefe vol. 6, reprinted 1930, Berlin: Verlag von Reimar Hobbing.

Maine, H. (1861), *Ancient Law: Its Connection with the Early History Society, and its Relation to Modern Ideas*, London: John Murray.

Maine, H. (1871), *Village-Communities in the East and West*, London: John Murray.

Maitland, F.W. (1897), *Domesday Book and Beyond: Three Essays in the Early History of England*, Cambridge: Cambridge University Press.

Maloney, J. (1976), 'Marshall, Cunningham and the emerging economics profession', *Economic History Review*, **29** (3), 440–51.

Marchet, G. (1885), *Studien über die Entwickelung der Verwaltungslehre in Deutschland von der zweiten Hälfte des 17. bis zum Ende des 18. Jahrhunderts*, Munich: R. Oldenbourg.

Marshall, A. unpublished manuscript: M 4/13 (circa 1872), Marshall Archive, Marshall Library, Cambridge University.

Marshall, A. (1890), *Principles of Economics*, 2 vols, 9th (Variorum) edn 1961, London: Macmillan.

Marshall, A. (2010), 'Marshall's notes for his advanced course in political economy, ca. 1871', eds S. Cook and T. Foresti, *Marshall Studies Bulletin*, **11**.

Maurer, G.L von (1854), *Einleitung zur Geschichte der Mark-, Hof-, Dorf- und Stadt-Verfassung und der öffentlichen Gewalt*, Munich: Christian Kaiser.

Menger, C. (1883), *Untersuchungen über die Methode der Socialwissenschaften, under der Politischen Oekonomie insbesondere*, in F.A. von Hayek (ed.) (1969), *Carl Menger. Gesammelte Werke*, vol. 2, Tübingen: J.C.B. Mohr (Paul Siebeck).

Mill, J.S. ([1848] 1965), *Principles of Political Economy*, reprinted in J.M. Robson (ed.), *Collected Works of John Stuart Mill*, vol. 3, Toronto: University of Toronto Press.

Perry, W.J. (1924), *The Growth of Civilization*, London: Penguin.

Pollock, F. and F.W. Maitland (1895), *The History of English Law before the time of Edward I*, vol. 2, Cambridge: Cambridge University Press.

Raffaelli, T., M. Dardi and G. Becattini (2006), *The Elgar Companion to Alfred Marshall*, Cheltenham, UK and Northampton, MA, USA: Edward Elgar.

Roscher, W. (1842), *Leben, Werk und Zeitalter des Thukydides*, Göttingen: Vandenhoeck und Ruprecht.

Roscher, W. (1843), *Grundriß zu Vorlesungen über die Staatswirthschaft. Nach geschichtlicher Methode*, Göttingen: Dieterische Buchhandlung.

Roscher, W. (1854–94), *System der Volkswirthschaft*, 5 vols, Stuttgart: J.G. Cotta.

Roscher, W. (1892), *Politik: Geschichtliche Naturlehre der Monarchie, Aristokratie und Demokratie*, Stuttgart: J.G. Cotta.

Schmoller, G. (1870), *Zur Geschichte der deutschen Kleingewerbe im 19.Jahrhundert*, Halle: Verlag der Buchhandlung des Waisenhauses.

Schmoller, G. (1872), 'Eröffnungsrede auf der Eisenacher Versammlung zur Besprechung der sozialen Frage', reprinted in J. Burkhardt, and B.P. Priddat (eds) (2000), *Geschichte der Ökonomie*, Frankfurt am Main: Deutscher Klassiker Verlag.

Schmoller, G. (1883), 'Zur Methodologie der Staats- und Sozialwissenschaften', *Jahrbuch für Gesetzgebung, Verwaltung und Volkswirtschaft*, N. F. Jg. 7, 975–1058.

Schmoller, G. (1884–87), 'Studien über die wirtschaftliche Politik Friedrich des Großens und Preußens überhaupt von 1680–1786', *Jahrbuch für Gesetzgebung, Verwaltung und Volkswirtschaft*, **8–11**.

Seebohm, F. (1883), *The English Village Community*, reprinted 1905, London: Longmans, Green.

Stein, L. von (1878), *Die Volkswirthschaftslehre*, Vienna: Wilhelm Braumüller.

Takebayashi, S. (2003), *Die Entstehung der Kapitalismustheorie in der Gründungsphase der deutschen Soziologie*, Berlin: Duncker and Humblot.

Toynbee, A. (1884), *Lectures on the Industrial Revolution of the 18th Century in England*, London: Rivingtons.

Tribe, K. (1993), 'Mercantilism and the economics of state formation', in L. Magnusson (ed.), *Mercantilism*, Boston, MA: Kluwer, pp. 175–86.

Weber, M. (1904–05), *The Protestant Ethic and the Spirit of Capitalism and other Writings*, reprinted 2002, London: Penguin Books.

Institutionalism

The term "institutionalism" denotes a movement that was a major part of American economics during the interwar period, and is a tradition of economics that still exists today. As the name suggests, it is an approach to economics that stresses the central role of institutions in shaping economic behavior, and is usually identified with the work of Thorstein Veblen, Wesley Mitchell, Walton Hamilton, John M. Clark, John R. Commons, and Clarence Ayres, although many other individuals were, and are, involved.

The explicit identification of something called the "institutional approach" to economics, or "institutional economics," goes back to 1918 and to Walton Hamilton's American Economic Association (AEA) conference paper, "The institutional approach to economic theory" (Hamilton 1919). Hamilton's paper was deliberately a manifesto for an institutional economics. For Hamilton, this institutional approach was to be relevant to the problem of "social control" or the solution of social problems; related to institutions as the agencies through which the "changeable elements of life could be directed"; concerned with "process" in the form of an awareness of the constantly changing nature of institutions; and based on an acceptable theory of human behavior, one in harmony with the conclusions of "modern" psychology (Hamilton 1919: 312–14). Walter Stewart (Hamilton's friend and colleague) chaired the session, and argued that economics needed to be "organized around the central problem of control", should utilize the "most competent thought in the related sciences of psychology and sociology", and combine "the statistical method and the institutional approach" (Stewart 1919: 319), a reference to his own and Wesley Mitchell's quantitative work. J.M. Clark and William Ogburn also participated in the session. The organization of the session also involved Harold Moulton who discussed the idea with Veblen and Mitchell (Rutherford 2000a).

There were other early attempts to define institutional economics by J.M. Clark, Wesley Mitchell, by many of the contributor to Rexford Tugwell's 1924 volume *The Trend of Economics*, as well as by others. In all of these efforts there is a stress on the significance of institutions in shaping human behavior, the need for new psychological foundations for economics, the central importance of directing economics to the development of new forms of "social control" to supplement (or replace) the market, and the need for economics to become more "scientific" in the senses of being more investigative, more empirical, and more consistent with findings in related fields.

In terms of social control, Helen Everett, a student of Hamilton's, defined the concept as the "active intelligent guidance of social processes" or "the consciously planned guidance of economic processes", and argued that the concept formed a "central organizing principle" for the "institutionalist school of economics" (Everett 1931: 345). In terms of the need for economics to become more "scientific," Wesley Mitchell's empirical work on business cycles (Mitchell 1913) was often referred to as a paradigm. Mitchell explicitly linked quantitative and statistical work to an institutional perspective. He argued that it is institutions that standardize behavior and that create the patterns, regularities, and cycles that are to be observed in the data (Mitchell 1924 [1971]: 27). In his Presidential address Mitchell suggested that quantitative methods would transform economics by displacing traditional theory and leading to a much greater stress on institutions (Mitchell 1925: 7). Lionel Edie called this address "a genuine manifesto of quantitative and

institutional economics", that stated "the faith of a very large part of the younger generation of economists" (Edie 1927: 417). The notion of "science" in institutional economics
was, however, not limited to quantitative work. As J.M. Clark argued: "Economics must
come into closer touch with facts" and achieve this "by becoming more inductive, or by
much verification of results, or by taking over the accredited results of specialists in other
fields, notably psychology, anthropology, jurisprudence and history" (Clark 1927: 221).
This particular combination of "science" and "social control" was immensely appealing.
In Dorothy Ross's words "what fuelled the institutionalist ambition was an overflow of
realism and new liberal idealism that could not be contained by neoclassical practice"
(Ross 1991: 411).

During the interwar period institutionalism developed a significant following, with a
concentrated presence at a number of major schools and research institutes. In addition
to Veblen, Hamilton, Clark, Mitchell, and Commons, who were the most visible proponents of institutionalism, there were many others associated with the movement. The
two major centers for institutionalism over the whole interwar period were Columbia
and Wisconsin, at that time among the four leading doctoral departments of economics
in the country. Wisconsin's department included Commons (until he retired in 1933),
E.E. Witte, Harold Groves, Martin Glaeser, Selig Perlman, Don Lescohier and several
others. Columbia was an even bigger centre for institutionalism with Mitchell, Clark,
Tugwell, F.C. Mills, A.R. Burns, Joseph Dorfman, Leo Wolman, Carter Goodrich,
James Bonbright and Robert Hale all in the Economics Department or Business School
at various times, and Gardiner Means, Adolf A. Berle, John Dewey and many other
people of related views in other departments. Chicago had an institutionalist contingent
at least until Clark left for Columbia in 1926, and Walton Hamilton was at the center of
groups first at Amherst (1915–23) and later at the Robert Brookings Graduate School
(1923–28). Other institutionalist groups existed at Texas, where Clarence Ayres joined
Robert Montgomery in 1930, and in a number of other schools and colleges (Rutherford
2003, 2004, 2006).

Among research institutes, the Institute of Economics, which later became part of the
Brookings Institution, was heavily institutionalist in character. The institute was headed
by Harold Moulton and the research staff included Isador Lubin and Edwin Nourse
among others. The National Bureau of Economic Research (NBER) was founded by
Wesley Mitchell and closely associated with Mitchell's quantitative approach and his
program of business cycle research, and employed many of his Columbia colleagues and
students. The quantitative and policy orientation of the work done by these organizations attracted funding from foundations such as Carnegie and Rockefeller (Rutherford
2005a).

The Sources of Institutional Economics

The elements that went to make up the core of the institutional approach as defined
above were all present in American economics before 1918. Institutionalism as it formed
in the interwar period was an approach to economics that derived from several sources.
The single most significant source of inspiration for institutionalism was the work of
Thorstein Veblen. It would be impossible to think of institutionalism without giving
Veblen's work a central place, but at the same time he did not uniquely define the

research agenda or methodology of what became institutionalism in the interwar period. Veblen's influence, whether direct or indirect, was one of the major elements providing a commonality and a bond between the members of the institutionalist movement mentioned above. Veblen was important in a number of crucial respects. He provided a strong criticism of hedonism, including marginal utility theory, satirizing its conception of man as a "lightning calculator of pleasures and pains" (Veblen 1898 [1961]: 389), and arguing that economics should look to more modern social-psychological theories of behavior based on instinct and habit. This was a theme actively pursued by Mitchell, Clark, and numerous others.

Veblen's overall evolutionary framework was one which stressed the cumulative and path-dependent nature of institutional change, the role of new technology in bringing about institutional change (by changing the underlying, habitual ways of living and thinking), and the predominantly "pecuniary" character of the existing set of American institutions (that is, expressing the "business" values of pecuniary success and individual gain by money making, to the virtual exclusion of all other values). For Veblen, as for other institutionalists, institutions were more than merely constraints on individual action, but embodied generally accepted ways of thinking and behaving, and worked to mold the preferences and values of individuals brought up under their sway. Within this framework Veblen developed his analyses of "conspicuous consumption" and consumption norms; the effect of corporate finance on the ownership and control of firms; the role of intangible property and the ability to capitalize intangibles; business and financial strategies for profit-making; salesmanship and advertising; the emergence of a specialist managerial class; business fluctuations; and many other topics (Veblen 1899 [1924]; 1904 [1975]).

Veblen did not think of existing institutions as necessarily functioning to promote the social benefit – in fact, rather the opposite. Existing institutions, due both to the inertia inherent in any established scheme and to the defensive activities of vested interests, tended to become out of step with new technological means and with the economic issues and social problems they generated. Thus, for Veblen, the existing legal and social institutions of his America were outmoded and inadequate to the task of the social control of modern large-scale industry. Again, this became a central argument in virtually all later institutional economics.

Veblen was pointing to what he perceived as a systemic failure of "business" institutions to channel private economic activity in ways consistent with the public interest. For Veblen, the "invisible hand" notion of the market may have been applicable to conditions of small-scale manufacturing, but not to conditions of large scale production, corporate finance, and salesmanship. Veblen was particularly harsh in his attack on the manipulative, restrictive, and unproductive tactics used by business to generate income (including consolidations, control via holding companies and interlocking directorates, financial manipulation, insider dealing, sharp practices of various kinds, and unscrupulous salesmanship), and on the "waste" generated by monopoly restriction, business cycles, unemployment, and competitive advertising. Veblen held out little hope of change short of a complete rejection of "business" principles (Veblen 1904 [1975]; 1921).

Many of these aspects of Veblen's thinking had significant influence on other institutionalists, and can easily be found displayed in the work of Hamilton, Mitchell, Clark, and others. Even Commons, who took less from Veblen than most other institutionalists, gave central importance to his analysis of intangible property, and spent considerable space discussing his ideas (Commons 1934: 649–77).

Not all aspects of Veblen's work, however, were adopted by interwar institutionalists, and it is not difficult to find criticisms of Veblen's methodology and of some of his specific theories. As mentioned above, institutional economics was frequently and explicitly linked to quantitative and other forms of empirical research. Veblen's own research agenda was one of providing sweeping dissections of existing institutional arrangements, but often without the careful investigation or close consideration of factual evidence that might seem to have been implied by his own many references to the "matter of fact" approach of "modern science" (Veblen 1906). Many later institutionalists, including Hamilton, Mitchell, Clark, and Tugwell, all commented adversely on Veblen's lack of attention to what they considered proper scientific methodology (Rutherford 1999). For Hamilton, Veblen was an "emancipator," someone who inspired but who could not have done the detailed empirical work of Hoxie, Stewart, or Mitchell (Hamilton 1958: 21–2). For Clark, Veblen provided "orientation", a "conception of the problem", but neglected "scientific procedure" (Clark 1927: 248–9). For Mitchell, Veblen's conceptions of human nature were "a vast improvement" and he had "uncanny insights" (Mitchell 1928 [1936]: 412), but "like other intrepid explorers of new lands, Veblen made hasty traverses" and his "sketch maps" were "not accurate in detail" (Mitchell 1929: 68). Mitchell was highly suspicious of "speculative" approaches and he included applications of Darwinian theory to social evolution in that category. For Mitchell the path of progress in social science lay in the methods of physics and chemistry: "They had been built up not in grand systems like soap bubbles; but by the patient processes of observation and testing – always critical testing – of the relations between the working hypotheses and the processes observed" (Mitchell 1928 [1936]: 413).

In addition, Veblen's overall evolutionary scheme was found to have more specific problems. Veblen's theory of institutional evolution emphasized the role of new technology bringing about institutional change via a causal process of habituation to new "disciplines" of life. Here rational appraisal of consequences plays no significant role, the process being one whereby new ways of thinking are somehow induced by new patterns of life. In the early years of the century, both Mitchell and Robert Hoxie attempted to apply Veblen's theory, but each ran into difficulty. Mitchell's work on the development of the "money economy" found many more factors at work in institutional evolution than Veblen suggested, and Hoxie came to reject Veblen's hypothesis, expressed in *The Theory of Business Enterprise* (Veblen 1904 [1975]: 306–60), that the discipline of machine industry would tend to turn the habits of thought of unionized workers in a socialistic direction (Rutherford 1998).

Institutionalists in the interwar period obviously did share Veblen's conception of the institutional scheme as evolving over time, of institutions establishing the context within which economic activity takes place and is to be explained, and of the "pecuniary" nature of existing economic institutions, but they did not pursue the development of Veblen's specific theory of institutional evolution. Indeed, for most institutionalists the issues of the current performance of economic institutions and matters of immediate social concern took center stage, while issues of longer term institutional change were largely left aside. The major exception to this is the later work of J.R. Commons, but Commons explicitly rejected Veblen's basic dichotomization of industry and business (or technology and institutions), and his own theory of institutional evolution stressed processes of legal evolution through courts, legislatures, and processes of conflict resolution. Commons was not closely involved with the initial founding of the institutionalist movement, but became included as an institutionalist after the publication of his *The Legal Foundations of Capitalism* in 1924.

Outside of Veblen, institutionalists were influenced by the earlier generation of American progressive economists and social theorists such as Richard T. Ely, and H.C. Adams. Writers such as these were also concerned with institutions and institutional change, but they did not share Veblen's radicalism and imparted a much more reformist position to their students. Although Veblen is often included as a part of American progressivism, along with people such as Ely, H.C. Adams, and pragmatist philosophers such as John Dewey, Veblen's evolutionary theory gives little room for deliberative social guidance and legislative reform (Ross 1991: 213), and his work did not focus on issues such as labor law or business regulation that held a central place in the progressive literature more generally.

In the hands of institutionalists such as Hamilton, Clark, Mitchell, and Commons the problem became one of supplementing (rather than replacing) the market with other forms of "social control," or one of "how to make production for profit turn out a larger supply of useful goods under conditions more conducive to welfare" (Mitchell 1923 [1950]: 148). While Veblen's influence made institutionalists somewhat more critical of existing institutions than many of the previous generation of progressives, it does have to be understood that it was not Veblen alone who was the fountainhead for interwar institutionalism, but Veblen moderated by pragmatic and progressive views of science and social reform.

On the other side, this is not to say that institutionalism was simply a continuation of the work of the generation of German trained economists who had brought historicist ideas and a progressive reform agenda to American economics in the 1880s. Institutionalists certainly claimed H.C. Adams and R.T. Ely as predecessors, and it is also noteworthy that the combination of quantitative and statistical research with progressive reformism which formed such a significant part of institutionalism had its roots in the work of German economists such as Ernest Engel and others (Grimmer-Solem 2003: 127–68). However, institutionalists saw themselves not merely as continuing that tradition, but as significantly updating, modernizing, and revitalizing it in a number of ways.

Institutionalists, following Veblen's opinion of Schmoller (Veblen 1901), tended to be critical of German historicism for its tendency to descriptivism, and it is very noticeable that institutionalists did not usually refer to German historicists as predecessors. Veblen thought of himself as providing a more theoretical approach to institutions, and the Veblenian influence on institutionalism is an important element that separates institutionalists from the previous generation of American progressive economists. Another important difference is to be found in the Social Christianity of Ely, Adams, J.B. Clark, and the younger Commons. The institutionalist literature is thoroughly secular with no important reference to the church or to Christian morality as important agents of reform (Bateman 1998). The references instead are to science, pragmatic philosophy, and to the actions of the state. Another difference is that many of the German trained economists had subsequently made an accommodation with marginalism (Yonay 1998:

39–46). This can be seen especially in the later editions of Ely's introductory text book (Ely et al. 1908), in J.B. Clark's work on marginal productivity theory, and also in the work done by E.R.A. Seligman and many others. Institutionalists largely rejected this accommodation. Finally, some of the progressives of the previous generation had become increasingly conservative; Ely certainly had become so. The Veblenian critique of business institutions and marginalist economics, placed together with the ideas of empirical science and Dewey's pragmatic reformism, worked to refocus and re-energize the progressive impulse.

One final source of inspiration that needs to be mentioned is the part played by many of those involved in the formation of institutionalism in the economic planning developed as a part of World War I. The war brought economists into government agencies in an unprecedented fashion. Mitchell headed the Prices Section of the War Industries Board (WIB) and worked on a large study of prices during the war, work that also involved Isador Lubin, Leo Wolman and Walter Stewart. The WIB was chaired by Robert Brookings and Brookings' endowment of research agencies in public administration and economics was inspired by his wartime experience. Mitchell's concern with statistical and factual knowledge, and the need for improved research in the social sciences was also given special urgency by his experience of wartime administration. In 1918 Mitchell became President of the American Statistical Association. His Presidential Address, "Statistics and government" (Mitchell 1919) specifically related his war experience to the need for more work on "social statistics," and gave impetus to the founding of the NBER. Hamilton and Moulton worked with the War Labor Policies Board as economic experts dealing mainly with reconstruction issues and were keen to see some of the wartime planning apparatus retained to manage the period of reconstruction. That economists both could and should share in fixing the "foundations of a new economic organization" was the theme of Irving Fisher's 1918 Presidential Address to the AEA (Fisher 1919: 21). Economics had established itself as an important tool for government policy formation, and the possibilities for the discipline seemed immense. This provided a critical background to the ideals of scientific investigation and social control that are so apparent in Hamilton's manifesto and the conference session of which it was a part.

The Contributions of Interwar Institutionalism

Mark Blaug has stated that institutionalism "was never more than a tenuous inclination to dissent from orthodox economics" (Blaug 1978: 712), and this view still finds wide currency. In fact, institutionalism in the interwar period was a major part of a pluralistic mainstream economics (Morgan and Rutherford, 1998). That institutionalists did have a positive program of research in mind should be clear from the above. Not all elements of this program were pursued successfully, but there can be no doubt that institutionalists did make important positive contributions to economics, and this is particularly true of the period when institutionalism was at its peak. Just a few of these contributions will be highlighted.

Institutionalists took the task of improving economic measurement seriously. The NBER not only produced many empirical studies relating to business cycles, labor, and price movements, but also played a vital role in the development of national income accounting, through the work of Mitchell's student, Simon Kuznets. In conjunction with the Federal Reserve, the NBER also did much to develop monetary and financial data and Morris Copeland developed flow of funds accounts. During the New Deal institutionalists were heavily involved in the effort to improve the statistical work of government agencies (Rutherford 2002).

As noted above, one of the claims of institutionalists was that a scientific economics would have to be consistent with "modern psychology". A typical argument was that economics "is a science of human behavior" and any conception of human behavior that the economist may adopt "is a matter of psychology" (Clark 1918: 4). Mitchell made important early contributions in his discussions of the limitations of rational choice theory (Mitchell 1910a; 1910b), but Clark made perhaps the most interesting effort to develop the psychological basis of institutional economics (Clark 1918). Building on the work of William James and C.H. Cooley, he argued that the "effort of decision" is an important cost, and one that prevents utility maximization. Clark was considering both the costs of information gathering and of calculation, and his argument is a clear precursor of more recent conceptions of bounded rationality leading to the use of habits or routines.

Interesting work on the economics of consumption and the household was pursued by Hazel Kyrk and Theresa McMahon. McMahon made use of Veblen's conception of emulation in consumption, while Kyrk was critical of marginal utility theory as a basis for a theory of consumption and emphasized the social nature of the formation of consumption values. Consumption patterns relate to habitual "standards of living", and Kyrk undertook to measure and critically analyze existing standards of living, and to create policy to help achieve higher standards of living. In her later work she discussed the household in both its producing and consuming roles, the division of labor between the sexes, employment and earnings of women, adequacy of family incomes, and issues of risks of disability, unemployment, provision for the future and social security, and the protection and education of the consumer (Kyrk 1923, 1933; McMahon 1925).

There was much work dealing with the inadequacy of the standard models of perfect competition and pure monopoly. The soft coal industry received particular attention. In that industry, investigators such as Hamilton found little that corresponded to the ideal of a competitive industry. Competition within the industry had resulted not in efficient low-cost production but in persistent excess capacity, inefficiency, irregular operation, poor working conditions and low earnings (Hamilton and Wright 1925). This represented a common institutionalist theme – that, particularly under conditions of high overheads and rapid technological advance, competition could lead to "disorder" and inefficiency rather than to order and efficiency. Institutionalists also studied such things as common pool problems in the oil industry, production cycles in agriculture, including the cobweb model and its implications for the orthodox view of self–regulating markets, and the vast array of restrictive practices to be found in many industries (Hamilton and Associates 1938).

A related theme was that technological change had altered the structure of costs faced by firms and had altered their behavior. This argument derived from Clark's *Studies in the Economics of Overhead Costs* (1923). For Clark, the growth of overhead costs as a result of capital-intensive methods of production had resulted in price discrimination, an extension of monopoly and an increase in price inflexibility over the cycle. A little later

Gardiner Means (1935) developed his theory of administered pricing, which sparked a vast literature on relative price inflexibility.

On issues of corporate finance and ownership, Bonbright and Means co-authored *The Holding Company*, and Berle and Means *The Modern Corporation and Private Property*, both in 1932. These works much extended Veblen's earlier discussions of corporate consolidation and the separation of ownership and control. Berle and Means's work raised important issues of agency, and whether managers would maximize profits.

On labor market issues, institutionalists concerned themselves with studying unions and the history of the labor movement, developing in the process both classifications of unions and explanations for the particular pattern of trade union development in America (Perlman 1928). Wage determination was also a problem that attracted the attention of institutionalists. Walton Hamilton's (with Stacy May) 1923 book *The Control of Wages* was praised by Clark for providing not an "abstract formulation of the characteristic outcome" but a "directory of the forces to be studied" in any particular case (Clark 1927: 276–7). Discussions of trade unions and wage bargaining were provided by many other institutional labor economists such as Commons (1924) and Sumner Slichter (1931). In this work much attention was given to issues of collective bargaining and systems of conciliation and mediation.

Public utilities, including issues relating to the valuation of utility property and the proper basis for rate regulation, were major areas of institutionalist research. Both Clark and Commons devoted considerable attention to the concept of intangible property, goodwill, and valuation issues (Commons 1924; Clark 1926). Bonbright dealt with the difference between commercial and social valuation in connection with public utilities. Bonbright, Hale, and Martin Glaeser all wrote extensively on issues of public utility regulation, with Hale probably having the greatest impact with his campaign of criticism of the "fair value" concept as a basis for rate regulation (Hale 1921; Bonbright 1961: 164).

In his *Social Control of Business* (1926) Clark argued that business cannot be regarded as a purely private affair. This idea of private business being broadly "affected with a public interest" was absolutely central to the institutionalist argument for regulation of business. Clark expresses the idea in his claim that "every business is 'affected with a public interest' of one sort or another" (Clark 1926: 185), and the argument also appears as a central theme in Tugwell's early work on regulation (Tugwell 1921, 1922), and in Walton Hamilton's and Robert Hale's extensive writings on law and economics (Rutherford 2005b; Fried 1998).

More general interconnections between law and economics and the operation of markets were addressed by Hale, Commons, and Hamilton. Commons's approach was the most developed and was built on his notions of the pervasiveness of distributional conflicts, of legislatures and courts as attempting to resolve conflicts (at least between those interest groups with representation), and of the evolution of the law as the outcome of these ongoing processes of conflict resolution. He developed his concept of the "transaction" as the basic unit of analysis (later adopted by Oliver Williamson). In turn, the terms of transactions were determined by legal rights and by economic (bargaining) power. Market transactions always involved some degree of coercion, in the sense of some degree of restriction upon alternatives (Commons 1924, 1932; Hale 1923). He also provided a theory of the behavior of legislatures based on log-rolling, and a theory of judicial decision-making based on the concept of reasonableness (Commons 1932, 1934).

The institutionalist program dealing with business cycles, in the period before the depression, was centered on Wesley Mitchell's work and that he promoted through the NBER. As noted above, Mitchell explicitly placed his work on business cycles within an institutional context by associating cycles with the functioning of the system of pecuniary institutions. Mitchell's 1913 volume *Business Cycles*, with its discussion of the four-phase cycle driven by an interaction of factors such as the behavior of profit-seeking firms, the behavior of banks, and the leads and lags in the adjustment of prices and wages, became the standard institutionalist reference. At the NBER, Mitchell focused heavily on promoting work that would add to the understanding of business cycles, generating a stream of research studies far too long to list here, but contributing to the development of national income measures, business cycle indicators, and much more. In addition, Clark developed his concept of the accelerator out of his study of Mitchell's 1913 work, and the accelerator mechanism soon became a standard part of cycle theory (Clark 1917). Mitchell's work was not the only approach to business cycles to be found within institutionalism. Many institutionalists, including Hamilton, had an interest in the work of J.A. Hobson, and Hobson's underconsumptionism became popular among institutionalists in the 1930s (Rutherford and DesRoches 2008).

On issues of market failure, broadly conceived, Clark (1926) discussed a large number of types of market failure in his *Social Control of Business*. These included monopoly, maintaining the ethical level of competition, protecting individuals where they are unable to properly judge alternatives, problems of agency, relief for people displaced by rapid economic and technological change, relief of poverty (including social security and minimum wages), regulation of advertising and the provision of information and standards, increasing equality of opportunity, externalities (unpaid costs of industry), public goods (inappropriable services), the wastes of arms race types of competition (such as competitive advertising), unemployment, the interests of posterity or future generations, and any other discrepancy between private and social accounting. Slichter (1924) provided a list of problems almost as long, including the pro-cyclical behavior of banks, overexploitation of natural resources, discrimination in employment, advertising and salesmanship, lack of market information, pollution and other external effects, uncertainty and unemployment, economic waste and inefficiency, and economic conflict. All these problems were seen as justifying some additional social control of business activity.

Finally, and intimately related to the above, institutionalists made important contributions to policy in their roles in the development of unemployment insurance, workmen's compensation, social security, labor legislation, public utility regulation, agricultural price support programs, and in the promotion of government planning to create high and stable levels of output. Commons had pioneered public utility regulation, unemployment insurance, and workmen's compensation in Wisconsin, and the Wisconsin model was widely influential. Many institutionalists were active members of the American Association of Labor Legislation (AALL), and the AALL promoted many reforms to labor legislation. Medical insurance programs were also pursued by the AALL, and also by the Committee on the Costs of Medical Care, which involved both Hamilton and Mitchell.

Institutionalists had significant influence within the New Deal. Many of Commons's students played leading roles in the development of the federal social security program. Berle and Tugwell were two of Roosevelt's original Brains Trust, and Tugwell, Means, and Mordecai Ezekiel were the leading advocates of the structuralist or planning approach that had influence in the early part of the New Deal (Barber 1996). Hamilton, Lubin, and several others were deeply involved in the labor legislation and consumer protection aspects of the New Deal. Hamilton later worked with Thurman Arnold in developing their case by case approach to anti-trust (Rutherford 2005b).

The Decline of Institutional Economics

Institutionalism attained a significant position in American economics in the interwar period, both in academia and in government, but then declined in position and prestige after the Second World War. At this point institutionalism fell out of the mainstream of American economics to become a heterodox tradition on the margins of the discipline. There are quite a number of overlapping reasons for this, some of which reach back into the 1920s and 1930s, but the focus here will be limited to just a few of the more important issues.

Institutionalism clearly did not live up to its own early promise, particularly in its failure to pin down exactly what foundations in modern psychology it was supposed to have. After the mid-1920s, psychologists abandoned the instinct/habit approach in favor of a behaviorism that became increasingly narrow and difficult to see as an adequate foundation for institutional economics. In this climate, the enthusiasm for new psychological approaches that had played such a role in the institutionalist movement's beginnings could not be sustained. Institutionalism probably played a part in ridding economics of explicitly hedonistic language, but it did not develop the alternative basis to convince the profession as a whole to abandon its traditional views of rationality (Lewin 1996).

It must also be said that institutionalists failed to develop their theories of social norms, technological change, legislative and judicial decision-making, transactions, and forms of business enterprise (apart from issues of ownership and control) much beyond the stage reached by Veblen and Commons. The reasons for this lack of development relate partly to the focus of interwar institutionalists on immediate and pressing policy problems, like business cycles, labor law, and social security. In addition, from the late 1920s on, sociology separated itself from economics and became established in separate departments, taking much of the subject matter of social norms and institutions with it.

It is also the case that, from the 1930s onwards, many new developments in theory and methods occurred within economics, developments that tended to displace institutionalist ideas and methods. Hicks's revision of demand theory seemed to free economics from the shifting basis of psychology, while the work of Joan Robinson and Edward Chamberlin provided treatments of imperfect competition more amenable to neoclassical approaches. The discussion of externalities in terms of market failure was also much clarified. Neoclassicism developed a language capable of encompassing at least some of the issues of concern to institutionalists; issues that had formerly fallen outside the neoclassical theoretical compass.

Moreover, institutionalist approaches to business cycles were replaced by Keynesian ideas. In many respects, Keynesian economics took over the role of the exciting new economics that institutionalism had played in the early 1920s (Rutherford and DesRoches

2008). In addition, neoclassical and Keynesian economics gained an empirical component with the rise of econometrics. Institutionalists could no longer claim greater "scientific" standing because of their empiricism.

In these ways more orthodox economic theory took over those aspects of institutionalism amenable to "model analysis" (Copeland 1951) while other aspects were absorbed into what became applied field areas, such as industrial organization, labor economics, and industrial relations. At least until the 1960s these field areas had only loose ties to the theoretical core of the discipline, and maintained a substantial institutional component.

All of this was combined with a shift in the view of proper scientific method as applied to economics. Interwar institutionalists had frequently claimed the mantle of science on the basis of an empirical and instrumental view of science taken largely from John Dewey. Over the same period orthodox economists had been much more cautious in their claims to science, but this was to change. Orthodox economists came to adopt either the logical empiricism of Rudolf Carnap, Carl Hempel and Ernest Nagel, or Friedman's version of positive economics. Logical empiricism emphasizes the "hypothetico-deductive" nature of theories. Theories contain axioms and statements derived from them. The axioms "may refer to either observables or theoretical entities," and the "system is given empirical meaningfulness only when the system is given some empirical interpretation" via the translation of some of the theoretical statements into observational language (Caldwell 1982: 25). It is usually the "lower level" deduced consequences of a theory that will describe observables and that are subject to empirical verification. Friedman's version of instrumentalism is much less formal and simply focuses attention on the testing of a theory's predictions with no attention being given to the realism of assumptions. Both positions, however, provided a view of science that could counter institutionalist demands for realism. Both gave wide range to deductive theorizing with the emphasis only on the empirical testing (by verification or falsification) of some specific implications of the theoretical model. This gradually displaced the broader institutionalist concern with realism. Logical empiricism, in addition, claimed to be a general description of scientific procedure, applicable to both the natural and physical sciences, and it largely displaced pragmatism as the ruling philosophy of science in the United States. Increasingly, institutionalism was criticized for lacking theory. As one example, Mitchell was accused by Koopmans (1947) of "measurement without theory;" an exaggerated view, but one often repeated and widely accepted.

Finally, a significant part of the institutionalist agenda of social reform had come to pass, both removing some of the original causes of the institutionalist movement, and prompting a reaction in the form of critiques of the expanded role for government that institutionalists had done so much to put forward.

Under these circumstances, it is not difficult to see why institutionalism slipped from being a central part of American economics to a more marginalized position. This change did not happen overnight, but was hastened by the significant amount of new hiring on the part of American universities immediately after the Second World War. These new faculties were predominantly Keynesians or neoclassicals equipped with the latest in mathematical and econometric tools. The retirement of the last of the older generation of institutionalists in the 1950s completed the process (Rutherford 2011).

Institutional Economics after 1945

American institutionalism did not disappear, but it certainly changed. As the other centers of institutionalism declined, the group at the University of Texas and Clarence Ayres gained in importance. When Ayres arrived at the University of Texas in 1930 he found himself in a department that was already heavily institutionalist. A.B. Wolfe taught at Texas between 1914 and 1923, Max Handman between 1917 and 1930, Robert Montgomery began teaching at Texas in 1922, even before going to Brookings for his PhD, E.E. Hale joined the faculty in 1923, George Stocking was there between 1925 and 1946, and Ruth Allen joined in 1933. Until this time Ayres had taught philosophy but he transitioned into economics, although always retaining a philosophical orientation. A number of writers on institutionalism have commented on this "Texas School" (see Phillips 1995).

Ayres's first major work in economics was a book *The Problem of Economic Order* (1938). Ayres sent copies of this book to all and sundry with a covering note emphasizing the use of the definite article. The problem of the economic order, according to Ayres, lay in the unequal distribution of income that was responsible for the economic problem of depressions and more besides. Greater equality would be an instrumently effective change. This remained a theme in Ayres's work, but he was to very much broaden his scope in his next major book *The Theory of Economic Progress* (1944).

Ayres was to argue that one of his concerns in writing this book was to respond to the criticism of institutionalism as lacking in theory. In the book itself he seems to agree that institutionalism had been largely descriptive (Ayres 1944: 11–12). In order to develop his theory of progress Ayres turned back to Veblen: on the one hand, to Veblen's emphasis on technology as the engine of economic growth and progress, and, on the other hand, to Veblen's view of the existing institutional system as often blocking further progress through the power of established ways of thinking and doing. Ayres took these ideas and gave them a particular interpretation, identifying technology with instrumental ways of thinking and institutions with "ceremonialism" (Ayres 1944). This "dichotomy" between the instrumental and the ceremonial is at the heart of Ayres's system. For Ayres the institutions of the market and of orthodox economics were ceremonial in nature. Neither is seen as being instrumental in the service of human progress, which in turn is defined very broadly as a life process consisting at base of the growth of instrumental capacities.

Ayres's effort to define institutionalism in terms of his instrumental/ceremonial dichotomy was, at the time, not particularly well received by other institutionalists, and completely failed to make any headway among other economists. Even those who knew Ayres well, such as Dorfman and Clark, were decidedly cool. Other old friends, such as Alexander Meiklejohn and Morris Copeland, exchanged long and critical correspondences with Ayres concerning his dichotomy, neither becoming convinced by Ayres's arguments (Rutherford 2000b).

There are key differences between Ayres and the institutionalist program as expressed by most of the interwar members of the movement. Hamilton, Mitchell, Clark, Commons, and Copeland always gave the market an important instrumental role, even while suggesting the need for new forms of social control, and none of them would have found Ayres's tendency to see institutions as almost entirely ceremonial as a useful approach. Ayres's attitude towards markets and the price system is much closer to Veblen's than anyone else's. Nevertheless, and despite the criticisms that can be made of Ayres, his work represents in an important way the primary institutionalist reaction to the new situation facing them. This reaction was to turn attention back to the ideas of Thorstein Veblen, as representing a source of more theoretical ideas and a more thorough rejection of orthodox economics. Ayres was able to produce a number of students (such as Fagg Foster, David Hamilton, and many others) who spread his ideas throughout many of the universities of the Southwest, and this Veblen/Ayres version of institutionalism became a major part of the post 1945 institutionalist movement. Of course, not everyone in the movement adopted the Ayresian system. J.K. Galbraith developed a different analysis of American capitalism, although also derived from Veblen. Galbraith's main arguments concerned the coexistence of private affluence and public squalor, and the emergence of a "new industrial state" controlled by managers and technocrats (Galbraith 1958, 1967). Allan Gruchy also maintained a greater emphasis on the structure of industry and on economic policy issues (Gruchy 1974, 1987), while Warren Samuels (1971), Allan Schmid (1978) and Dan Bromley (1989) have carried on very much in the Commons tradition. Overall, the movement became less coherent and more subject to internal disagreement than had previously been the case.

Texas itself remained a center for institutionalism for many years with people such as Wendell Gordon, Walter Neal, and H.H. Liebhafsky. Outside Texas and the Southwest small institutionalist groups came to exist at Maryland (Allan Gruchy), the University of Massachusetts at Amherst (Ben Seligman), Cornell (Douglas Dowd), Michigan State (Samuels, Schmid, and Trebing) (Schmid 2004), and at a few other places, but nothing on the earlier scale. J.K. Galbraith was by far the highest profile institutionalist of the post-1945 period, but he was a lone figure at Harvard and did not produce academic followers. Interestingly, Gruchy, Dowd, and Galbraith all appear to have been introduced to institutionalism at Berkeley. Many economists continued to have concerns with neoclassical economics but became unwilling to associate themselves with "institutional economics".

In 1959 a small group of ten people met at the Windsor Hotel (formerly the Wardman Hotel) during an AEA conference to discuss the future of institutional economics. The meeting had been called by Allan Gruchy. As a clear indication of the disrepute into which the term "institutional economics" had fallen, one of the major items of business was the name that the group should adopt. As an interim measure and in the face of nothing better, the group called itself the Wardman Group. Joseph Gambs undertook to survey American economists with respect to their interest in institutional economics and produced a brief description of his talks with 45 economists described as "dissenters". The largest group were those in the Veblen/Ayres tradition, but Gambs also noted another group who did not see themselves as in the tradition of Veblen or as institutionalists, but who were interested in the "reconstruction" of economics.

The Wardman Group continued to meet at AEA conferences, growing to about 150 people on the mailing list by 1963. Two years later the Association for Evolutionary Economics was formed with a broad statement of purpose designed to attract both groups identified by Gambs, and a paid membership for 1966 of 110. Those involved at this point included Clarence Ayres, John Blair, Joseph Dorfman, Douglas Dowd, Fagg Foster, John Gambs, J.K. Galbraith, Carter Goodrich, Wendell Gordon, Allan Gruchy, Forest Hill, Louis Junker, William Kapp, Gardiner Means, Walter Neale,

Warren Samuels, Ben Seligman, Marc Tool, and Harry Trebing. With some delay and difficulty the association's *Journal of Economic Issues* appeared in 1966. The institutionalist tradition in America continues to exist, but it remains a relatively small heterodox movement existing, for the most part, outside the mainstream of American economics.

Perhaps the most important recent development within the institutionalist tradition has been the growing interest in the work of Veblen and Commons among a new generation of European economists attracted to institutional and evolutionary ideas. One outstanding example of this is to be found in the work of Geoffrey Hodgson, who has argued forcefully for the development of an institutional economics along lines he sees as having been originally pioneered by Veblen in his evolutionary and Darwinian approach to institutions and institutional change (Hodgson 1988, 2004).

MALCOLM RUTHERFORD

See also:

John Bates Clark (I); Historical economics (II); Institutional economics (III); Wesley Clair Mitchell (I); Gustav Friedrich von Schmoller (I); Thorstein Bunde Veblen (I).

References and further reading

Ayres, C.E. (1938), *The Problem of Economic Order*, New York: Farrar and Rinehart.
Ayres, C.E. (1944), *The Theory of Economic Progress*, Chapel Hill, NC: University of North Carolina.
Barber, W.J. (1996), *Designs within Disorder: Franklin D. Roosevelt, the Economists, and the Shaping of Economic Policy, 1933–1945*, New York: Cambridge University Press.
Bateman, B.W. (1998), 'Clearing the ground: the demise of the social gospel movement and the rise of neo-classicism in American economics', in M.S. Morgan and M. Rutherford (eds), *From Interwar Pluralism to Postwar Neoclassicism*, Annual Supplement to Volume 30 of *History of Political Economy*, Durham, NC: Duke University Press.
Berle, A.A. and G.C. Means (1932), *The Modern Corporation and Private Property*, New York: Macmillan.
Blaug, M. (1978), *Economic Theory in Retrospect*, 3rd edn, London: Cambridge University Press.
Bonbright, J.C. (1961), *Principles of Public Utility Rates*, New York: Columbia University Press.
Bonbright, J.C. and G.C. Means (1932), *The Holding Company*, New York: McGraw Hill.
Bromley, D.W. (1989), *Economic Interests and Institutions: The Conceptual Foundations of Public Policy*, Oxford: Basil Blackwell.
Caldwell, B.J. (1982), *Beyond Positivism: Economic Methodology in the Twentieth Century*, London: George Allen and Unwin.
Clark, J.M. (1917), 'Business acceleration and the law of demand: a technical factor in business cycles', *Journal of Political Economy*, **25** (March), 217–35.
Clark, J.M. (1918), 'Economics and modern psychology', parts I and II, *Journal of Political Economy*, **26** (January–February), 1–30, 136–66.
Clark, J.M. (1923), *Studies in the Economics of Overhead Costs*, Chicago, IL: University of Chicago Press.
Clark, J.M. (1926), *Social Control of Business*, Chicago, IL: University of Chicago Press.
Clark, J.M. (1927), 'Recent developments in economics', in E.C. Hayes (ed.), *Recent Developments in the Social Sciences*, Philadelphia, PA: Lippencott.
Commons, J.R. (1924), *The Legal Foundations of Capitalism*, New York: Macmillan.
Commons, J.R. (1932), 'The problem of correlating law, economics and ethics', *Wisconsin Law Review*, **8** (December), 3–26.
Commons, J.R. (1934), *Institutional Economics: Its Place in Political Economy*, New York: Macmillan.
Copeland, M.A. (1951), 'Institutional economics and model analysis', *American Economic Review*, **41** (May), 56–65.
Edie, L.D. (1927), 'Some positive contributions of the institutional concept', *Quarterly Journal of Economics*, **41** (May), 405–40.
Ely, R.T., T.S. Adams, M.O. Lorenz, and A.A. Young (1908), *Outlines of Economics*, revised edn, New York: Macmillan.
Everett, H. (1931), 'Social control', *Encyclopaedia of the Social Sciences*, vol. 4, New York: Macmillan, pp. 344–9.

Fisher, I. (1919), 'Economists and the public service', *American Economic Review*, **9** (March), 5–21.

Fried, B.H. (1998), *The Progressive Assault on Laissez Faire: Robert Hale and the First Law and Economics Movement*, Cambridge, MA: Harvard University Press.

Galbraith, J.K. (1958), *The Affluent Society*, Boston, MA: Houghton Mifflin.

Galbraith, J.K. (1967), *The New Industrial State*, Boston, MA: Houghton Mifflin.

Grimmer-Solem, E. (2003), *The Rise of Historical Economics and Social Reform in Germany 1864–1894*, Oxford: Oxford University Press.

Gruchy, A.G. (1974), 'Government intervention and the social control of business: the neoinstitutionalist position', *Journal of Economic Issues*, **8** (June), 235–49.

Gruchy, A.G. (1987), *The Reconstruction of Economics*, Westport, CT: Greenwood Press.

Hale, R.L. (1921), 'The "physical value" fallacy in rate cases', *Yale Law Journal*, **30** (May), 710–31.

Hale, R.L. (1923), 'Coercion and distribution in a supposedly non-coercive state', *Political Science Quarterly*, **38** (September), 470–94.

Hamilton, W.H. (1919), 'The institutional approach to economic theory', *American Economic Review*, **9** (March), 309–18.

Hamilton, W.H. (1958), 'Veblen – then and now', in D. Dowd (ed.), *Thorstein Veblen: A Critical Reappraisal*, Ithaca, NY: Cornell University Press.

Hamilton, W.H. and Associates (1938), *Price and Price Policies*, New York: McGraw Hill.

Hamilton, W.H. and S. May (1923), *The Control of Wages*, reprinted 1968, New York: Augustus M. Kelley.

Hamilton, W. H. and H.R. Wright (1925), *The Case of Bituminous Coal*, New York: Macmillan.

Hodgson, G.M. (1988), *Institutions and Economics: A Manifesto for a Modern Institutional Economics*, Cambridge: Polity Press.

Hodgson, G.M. (2004), *The Evolution of Institutional Economics: Agency, Structure and Darwinism in American Institutionalism*, London: Routledge.

Koopmans, T.C. (1947), 'Measurement without theory', *Review of Economic Statistics*, **29** (August), 161–72.

Kyrk, H. (1923), *A Theory of Consumption*, Boston, MA: Houghton Mifflin.

Kyrk, H. (1933), *Economic Problems of the Family*, New York: Harper.

Lewin, S. (1996), 'Economics and psychology: lessons for our own day from the early twentieth century', *Journal of Economic Literature*, **35** (September), 1293–323.

McMahon, T. (1925), *Social and Economic Standards of Living*, Boston, MA: D.C. Heath.

Means, G.C. (1935), *Industrial Prices and their Relative Inflexibility*, Senate Document 13, 74th Congress, 1st Session, Washington, DC: US Government Printing Office.

Mitchell, W.C. (1910a), 'The rationality of economic activity', pt I, *Journal of Political Economy*, **18** (February), 97–113.

Mitchell, W.C. (1910b), 'The rationality of economic activity', pt II, *Journal of Political Economy*, **18** (March), 197–216.

Mitchell, W.C. (1913), *Business Cycles*, Berkeley, CA: University of California Press.

Mitchell, W.C. (1919), 'Statistics and government', reprinted in W.C. Mitchell (1950), *The Backward Art of Spending Money*. New York: Augustus M. Kelley, pp. 42–57.

Mitchell, W.C. (1923), 'Making goods and making money', reprinted in W.C. Mitchell (1950), *The Backward Art of Spending Money*, New York: Augustus M. Kelly, pp. 137–48.

Mitchell, W.C. (1924), 'The prospects of economics', in R.G. Tugwell (ed.) (1971), *The Trend of Economics*, Port Washington, NY: Kennikat Press.

Mitchell, W.C. (1925), 'Quantitative analysis in economic theory', *American Economic Review*, **15** (March), 1–12.

Mitchell, W.C. (1927), *Business Cycles: The Problem and its Setting*, New York: NBER.

Mitchell, W.C. (1928), 'Letter from Wesley C. Mitchell to John M. Clark', in J.M. Clark (1936), *Preface to Social Economics*, New York: Farrar and Rinehart, pp. 410–16.

Mitchell, W.C. (1929), 'Thorstein Veblen, 1857–1929', *New Republic*, **60** (4 September), 66–8.

Morgan, M.S. and M. Rutherford (1998), *From Interwar Pluralism to Postwar Neoclassicism*, annual supplement to vol. 30 of *History of Political Economy*, Durham, NC: Duke University Press.

Perlman, S. (1928), *A Theory of the Labor Movement*, New York: Macmillan.

Phillips, R.J. (ed.) (1995), *Economic Mavericks: The Texas Institutionalists*, Greenwich, CN: JAI Press.

Ross, D. (1991), *The Origins of American Social Science*, Cambridge: Cambridge University Press.

Rutherford, M. (1998), 'Thorstein Veblen's evolutionary programme: a promise unfulfilled', *Cambridge Journal of Economics*, **22** (July), 463–77.

Rutherford, M. (1999), 'Institutionalism as "scientific" economics', in R. Backhouse and J. Creedy (eds), *From Classical Economics to the Theory of the Firm: Essays in Honour of D.P. O'Brien*, Aldershot, UK and Brookfield, VT, USA: Edward Elgar.

Rutherford, M. (2000a), 'Understanding institutional economics: 1918–1929', *Journal of the History of Economic Thought*, **22** (June), 277–308.

Rutherford, M. (2000b), 'Institutionalism between the wars', *Journal of Economic Issues*, **34** (September), 291–303.

Rutherford, M. (2002), 'Morris A. Copeland: a case study in the history of institutional economics', *Journal of the History of Economic Thought*, **24** (September), 261–90.

Rutherford, M. (2003), 'Walton Hamilton, Amherst, and the Brookings graduate school: institutional economics and education', *History of Political Economy*, **35** (Winter), 611–53.

Rutherford, M. (2004), 'Institutional economics at Columbia University', *History of Political Economy*, **36** (Spring), 31–78.

Rutherford, M. (2005a), 'Who's afraid of Arthur Burns? The NBER and the foundations', *Journal of the History of Economic Thought*, **27** (June), 109–39.

Rutherford, M. (2005b), 'Walton H. Hamilton and the public control of business', in S. Medema and P. Boettke (eds), *The Role of Government in the History of Political Economy*, supplement to vol. 37 of *History of Political Economy*, Durham, NC: Duke University Press.

Rutherford, M. (2006), 'Wisconsin institutionalism: John R. Commons and his students', *Labor History*, **47** (May), 161–88.

Rutherford, M. (2010), 'Chicago economics and institutionalism', in R. Emmett (ed.), *Elgar Companion to the Chicago School of Economics*, Cheltenham, UK and Northampton, MA, USA: Edward Elgar, pp. 25–39.

Rutherford, M. (2011), *The Institutionalist Movement in American Economics, 1918–1947: Science and Social Control*, Cambridge: Cambridge University Press.

Rutherford, M. and T. DesRoches (2008), 'The institutionalist reaction to Keynesian economics', *Journal of the History of Economic Thought*, **30** (March), 29–48.

Samuels, W.J. (1971), 'The interrelations between legal and economic processes', *Journal of Law and Economics*, **14** (October), 435–50.

Schmid, A.A. (1978), *Property, Power, and Public Choice*, New York: Praeger.

Schmid, A.A. (2004), 'The Spartan School of political economy at Michigan State University', *Research in the History of Economic Thought and Methodology*, **22-C**, 207–43.

Slichter, S.H. (1924), 'The organization and control of economic activity', in R.G. Tugwell (ed.) (1971), *The Trend of Economics*, Port Washington, NY: Kennikat Press.

Slichter, S.H. (1931), *Modern Economic Society*, New York: H. Holt.

Stewart, W.W. (1919), 'Economic theory: discussion', *American Economic Review*, **9** (March), 319–20.

Tugwell, R.G. (1921), The economic basis for business regulation, *American Economic Review*, **11** (March), 643–58.

Tugwell, R.G. (1922), *The Economic Basis of Public Interest*, reprinted 1938, New York: Augustus M. Kelley.

Tugwell, R.G. (ed.) (1924), *The Trend of Economics*, reprinted 1971, Port Washington, NY: Kennikat Press.

Veblen, T. (1898), 'Why is economics not an evolutionary science?', reprinted 1961 in *The Place of Science in Modern Civilisation*, New York: Russell and Russell.

Veblen, T. (1899), *The Theory of the Leisure Class*, reprinted 1924, London: George Allen and Unwin.

Veblen, T. (1904), *The Theory of Business Enterprise*, reprinted 1975, Clifton, NJ: Augustus M. Kelley.

Veblen, T. (1906), 'The place of science in modern civilization', *American Journal of Sociology*, **11** (March), 585–609.

Veblen, T. (1921), *The Engineers and the Price System*, New York: B.W. Huebsch.

Yonay, Y.P. (1998), *The Struggle over the Soul of Economics: Institutionalist and Neoclassical Economists in America between the Wars*, Princeton, NJ: Princeton University Press.

Russian School of mathematical economics

In the twentieth century Russian scholars who applied mathematical methods in economics made a major contribution to the development of the discipline. In this period the discipline of economics in Russia was to a considerable extent influenced by political and economic processes and the history of mathematical economics can, accordingly, be divided into six periods: (1) from the end of the nineteenth century to the revolution of 1917; (2) the period of the New Economic Policy when significant progress was made; (3) from the 1930s to the mid-1950s (notable for the work of L.V. Kantorovich and V.V. Novozhilov); (4) from the mid-1950s to the mid-1960s (when the Russian School of mathematical economics was created); (5) from the mid-1960s to the mid-1980s (during which period there was little progress before "perestroika"); (6) and from the mid-1980s to the present day (when Russia joined the mainstream of world economic thought). However, the most significant results had been achieved by the early 1960s. (For more details, see Belykh 2007).

The Early Twentieth Century

By comparison with the rest of the world the Russian School of economics in the nineteenth century was rather backward. In 1890, when Alfred Marshall's *Principles of Economics* were published, a publication appeared in Russia, in which an attempt was made to create a so-called "neo-classical approach", that is, to combine classical value theory with marginal utility and marginal productivity theories. It was an article by M.I. Tugan-Baranovsky (1890), which did not display originality, but did mark the beginning of a closer exchange with Western economics. Similar approaches were adopted in the works of V.K. Dmitriev, W.S. Woitinsky, A.D. Bilimovich, N.N. Shaposhnikov and E.E. Slutsky. All of these scholars worked independently of each other and their works were of varying quality. The works of Dmitriev (1904 [1974]) and Slutsky (1915 [1952]) became known worldwide, but much later. (For assessments of the contribution of Dmitriev and Slutsky, see the entries devoted to them in Volume I of this *Handbook*. A separate entry is also devoted to Ladislaus von Bortkiewich, who was born in Russia and graduated from St Petersburg University and who can, to a certain extent, also be considered a Russian mathematical economist.)

Essays on the Theory of Labour Household (1912) by A.V. Chayanov has been undeservedly forgotten for a long time. In this work Chayanov attempted to produce a mathematical model of the labouring household. As an example he took the separate peasant family that exploited only the labour of its own members. Chayanov put forward two functions as determining the balance of the labouring household. Let x be the total income of the working family in roubles. Then the first function $f(x)$, being a monotonously increasing function, indicates the drudgery entailed in the acquisition of a marginal rouble, while the second monotonously decreasing function $\varphi(x)$ describes the value of marginal utility of these roubles (see Figure 2).

Chayanov's idea was that as the amount of work increases, the subjective value of a marginal rouble will always decrease and the difficulty of its acquisition will always increase. Therefore, the plots of these functions will intersect at a single point x_1, reflecting

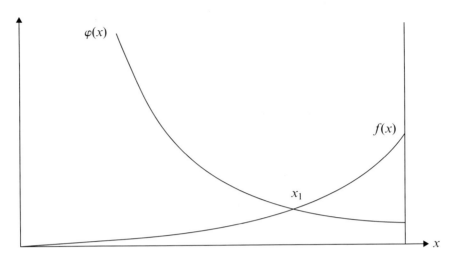

Figure 2   Equilibrium of the working household

the equality $f(x_1) = \varphi(x_1)$. This led him to an important conclusion that any labour household has the natural limit of its production determined by a balance between the yearly labour effort and the level of demand satisfaction of a given working family (Chayanov 1966). His analysis of the labouring household brought Chayanov to another important conclusion, namely, that a peasant household is a specific type of household without motive to gain profit or to maximize income. Using this model, Chayanov managed to carry out a thorough investigation of the contribution of labour productivity to the establishment of economic equilibrium. He suggested that the higher labour productivity is, the less difficult is the acquisition of a marginal unit of the sum x, which means that a new balance will be established at a higher level of needs satisfaction. He tried to prove his hypotheses using data on peasants' household budgets in Switzerland in 1909 and 1910 collected by Ernst Laur, as well as data on the Volokolamsk region of Moscow province collected by himself.

Chayanov was not a pioneer in the development of marginal utility theory. Being fluent in German and French he probably knew Western works in this field. The importance of his approach consisted in efforts to construct utility functions based on actual statistical data on consumers' budgets in different countries (Belguim, Germany, Russia and Switzerland). This enabled Chayanov to produce a corrected model containing new conclusions on functions describing the condition of equilibrium. Later his approach received due attention and was consequently developed by Western scholars (see Durrenberger 1984).

During this period, the basis was laid for further developments in the field of mathematical economics. Mathematical methods gained general acceptance and some experience was acquired in the mathematical modelling of economic phenomena. Russian economists obtained their first serious scientific results. However, this progress was interrupted by the Revolution and the Civil War.

The 1920s

During the 1920s, mathematical methods made rapid progress in Soviet economics for a variety of reasons. Difficult economic conditions meant that solutions to many economic problems had to be found rapidly, especially in the fields of organization of planning and in finance. Under the New Economic Policy (NEP), many non-communist economists worked for the government. Some of them were quite competent in mathematics. The relative freedom of discussion and publication at this time was also important. As L. Smolinski noted:

> [T]he rise of mathematical economics during the NEP period can be interpreted as a response to the challenge posed by the emergence of the Soviet economy during the years of War Communism. When their Western colleagues were still largely preoccupied with the finer points of marginal utility theory . . . Soviet mathematical economists were opening up new frontiers in economic research. (Smolinski 1971: 140)

These new frontiers included: planning of the national economy, the theory of inflation and problems of economic growth. Some pioneering works on optimization models were produced.

Most attention was given to problems of planning – first, to economic balances and then, later, to problems of economic growth. Discussions on the methodology of planning began in 1920. It was only natural that the system of War Communism, with its administrative allocation of resources and high inflation, led to approaches in planning that utilized physical indicators. Accordingly, major contributions were made in the field of input–output analysis.

In January 1921, A.A. Bogdanov delivered a report to a conference on the Scientific Organization of Labour and Production, in which he advocated a particular system of planning (Bogdanov 1921). Central to his approach was the idea of chain links between branches of the economy. The existence of such links, including feedback links, determines certain proportions in the economy. Any possible increase in the output of a particular good would be dependent upon the input factor in scarcest supply. Bogdanov named this rule "the law of the minimum".

The starting point of Bogdanov's planning methodology was a calculation of the ultimate needs of the population. To cater for these needs, consumer goods had to be produced which entailed the utilization of producer goods. The production of producer goods entailed, in turn, the production of other producer goods. The elaboration of the plan was conceived as an iterative process. Bogdanov does not use the terms "technological" or "input–output" coefficients, but he does make it clear that for the output of any given product, inputs of other specific products have to be calculated. This was an important contribution to what later became input–output analysis.

L.M. Kritsman adopted the same approach. He published several articles on the methodology of planning. Kritsman further developed Bogdanov's iterative process, adapting it to the real economy and dividing products into three groups: those produced in the state sector, those purchased in the private sector and those purchased from abroad. Kritsman formulated the task of planning as follows: "to determine the sizes of branches of the economy in such a way that they will be able to develop without disturbance, producing the maximum possible by utilizing existing resources" (Kritsman 1921: 44).

Kritsman already used the term "input coefficients" and emphasized that the reliability of planning rests upon the reliability of these coefficients. Later, in 1922, he proposed the use in planning of a kind of chess-board table (Kritsman 1922: 24–5).

Another important contribution to the development of planning theory was made by S.G. Strumilin. In January 1921, Strumilin put forward a solution to the optimization problem. The utility function (a kind of social welfare function) was to be maximized. The quantities of labour devoted to the production of different goods were variables and the single constraint was the total labour fund for the year. This approach, from a formal point of view, did not in fact differ greatly from Western models of consumer behaviour. What is important, however, is that Strumilin tried to elaborate the notion of objective social utility and to apply the concept of optimization to planning of the national economy (Strumilin 1921).

V.A. Bazarov, a prominent economist, also made a contribution to the theory of optimization during this period. For Bazarov, there were three requirements for any optimal economic plan:

> Firstly, the progress of the national economy from its present state to the target indicated in the General Plan must be smooth . . . Secondly, the economy must be conceived of as a harmonious, organic whole – a system of mobile equilibrium that is as stable as possible . . . The third precondition of optimality is that the path chosen as leading towards the goal projected in the General Plan should be the shortest possible path. (Bazarov 1926 [1964]: 366–7)

However, during the 1920s neither Bazarov, nor any other Russian economist, was able to develop a formal optimization model for such an approach.

Better practical results were achieved in the construction of economic balances. In 1926 the Central Statistical Board published the Balance of the National Economy of the USSR (the first versions of this balance were published in 1925). This work was positively reviewed by W. Leontiev:

> What is essentially new in this balance when it is compared with the usual economic investigations such as the American and English censuses, is the attempt to embrace in figures not only the output but also the distribution of the national product, so as to obtain in this way a comprehensive picture of the whole process of reproduction in the form of a kind of "Tableau Economique". (Leontiev 1925 [1964]: 88)

A further step was taken by M. Barengolts, who in 1928 created a chess-board table for 12 branches of the economy of the USSR. He also discussed the idea of technological coefficients and argued that in the absence of technical and price changes these coefficients can be considered as stable. In his opinion, such coefficients would help to explain the links between branches of the economy (Barengolts 1928 [1964]: 329). The history of input–output analysis has been analysed by several authors (Treml 1967; Clark 1984; Belykh 1989, 2007). We do not know currently to what extent Leontiev was familiar with the works mentioned above and how far they influenced his own theory. It is well known that he denied any such influence. What can be said, without in any way diminishing the significance of Leontiev's theory, is that the abovementioned works made an important contribution to the development of mathematical economics.

The creation of the planning system in the USSR and the introduction of Five Year Plans raised questions of long-term planning and rates of further economic growth. In

1928, G.A. Feld'man put forward his own model of economic growth, which can be considered as a further contribution to mathematical economics. Feld'man's model was used for the calculation of the general plan of the national economy for the period of 15 years. Feld'man was convinced that "it is impossible to imagine that a phenomenon as complicated as the national economy could be planned by a simple method" and that "the perfect planning can be implemented only on the basis of mathematical theory" (Feld'man 1928 [1964]: 177–8). Feld'man modified the Marxian theory of reproduction and divided the economy into two parts: one in which "simple reproduction" (replacement investment) took place and another, which provided the means for "expanded reproduction" (net investment). E. Domar, who was the first in the West to draw attention to Feld'man, interpreted Feld'man's binary distinction along Marxian lines as referring to, on the one hand, the production of the means of production and, on the other, to the production of consumer goods. Domar considered Feld'man's model to be similar to the later developed Western models of economic growth (Domar 1957).

During the 1920s mathematical economics as a branch of Soviet economic science developed rapidly. Its impact on the concept of planning was significant. Achievements in other areas were also important: Chayanov applied optimization ideas to agriculture (Chayanov 1917, 1922, 1928); mathematical models of money issue were developed (Bazarov 1923; Schmidt 1923; Slutsky 1923); major works were published by scholars of the famous Conjuncture Institute (Institute of Business Cycles) where the director, N.D. Kondratiev, put forward the theory of long waves in economics. Modelling was quite widely practiced by Soviet economists during the 1920s and the first "Control figures for the economy for the year 1925/26" were prepared under the guidance of three economists: V.G. Groman, V.A. Bazarov and S.G. Strumilin.

This promising development of mathematical economics in the Soviet Union was interrupted at the end of the 1920s. Radical changes in economic policy that revived the methods of War Communism, the political defeat within the Communist Party of the so-called "right wing" headed by Bukharin, the end of the NEP – all these events had important consequences for Soviet economics. In his speech to a conference of Agrarian Marxists in 1929, Stalin denounced equilibrium theory as anti-Marxist. Instead he called for "the development of reproduction theory and the balance of national economy", because "what the Central Statistical Board published in 1926 as the balance sheet of the national economy is not a balance sheet, but juggling with figures. Nor is the manner in which Bazarov and Groman treat the problem of the balance sheet of the national economy suitable" (Stalin 1929: 178). Soon afterwards, both Groman and Bazarov as well as many other gifted mathematical economists (Chayanov, Kondratiev, Litoshenko, Yurovskii) were arrested. Bogdanov died in 1928. Strumilin was severely criticized and lost the important position of the Deputy Head of GOSPLAN (the State Planning Committee). Feld'man was arrested in 1937 and was released only in 1953.

1930–53

In the early 1930s, the dictatorship of the proletariat was proclaimed to be the basic economic law of socialism. Prices were deemed to be a political, rather than an economic matter. Theories of the optimal sizes of industrial and agriculture enterprises were denounced as "bourgeois". An obsessive search for "wreckers and saboteurs" greatly damaged the institutions responsible for planning. Increasingly, mathematical methods in economics were condemned as "juggling with figures", "formalism", later "idealism" and, finally, "bourgeois" and "anti-Marxist". From 1930 until Stalin's death in 1953 the use of mathematics was to all intents and purposes banned in Soviet economics.

Even so, it was during this very period that the foundations of the theory of optimal planning were laid. In 1937, L.V. Kantorovich, then a young mathematician at Leningrad University, was approached by representatives of industrial enterprise – Plywood Trust. The problem was formulated as follows. The trust had eight different peeling machines and five different types of wood to be peeled. How could one determine a use of machines that would maximize wood production in specific fixed proportions? Resolving this problem Kantorovich created the method of optimal planning. This provided an important mathematical tool for the description of the national economy. In 1975 he was awarded the Sveriges Riksbank Prize in Economic Sciences in memory of Alfred Nobel for his work on optimum allocation of resources (the co-recipient of the prize was T. Koopmans).

Kantorovich discovered that the problem of Plywood Trust was an example of a whole group of mathematical problems, namely, that of arriving at an optimum of a linear function with linear constraints. The plywood problem was formalized in a general way as follows: there are n machines, which can produce m different products. Let α_{ik} be the amount of the k product k which machine i can produce during a working day. The output is fixed in the proportion of products $- p_1 : p_2 : \ldots : p_m$. (In fact this limitation can be avoided by introducing new coefficients $- \overline{\alpha}_{ik} = \alpha_{ik}/p_k$). Let h_{ik} be the time of machine i allocated to product k. Then the problem is to determine amounts of h_{ik}, which maximize z with several constraints:

$$h_{ik} \geq 0, i \in 1{:}n, k \in 1{:}m \tag{1}$$

$$\sum_{k=1}^{m} h_{ik} = 1, i \in 1{:}n \tag{2}$$

$$\frac{\sum_{i=1}^{n} h_{i1}\alpha_{i1}}{p_1} = \cdots = \frac{\sum_{i=1}^{n} h_{im}\alpha_{im}}{p_m} = z \tag{3}$$

It is clear that in such a problem the optimal solution is on the boundary of the possibility set. Therefore the classical approach of Lagrangian multipliers was not applicable. Kantorovich invented his own method. Each constraint has a corresponding variable which he called a resolving multiplier. This idea can be explained in terms of the following example with two products. Then the problem is to determine h_{i1} and h_{i2} which maximize z with constraints:

$$1)\ h_{i1} \geq 0, h_{i2} \geq 0 \tag{4}$$

$$2)\ h_{i1} + h_{i2} = 1 \tag{5}$$

$$3) \ \sum_{i=1}^{n}\alpha_{i1}h_{i1} = \sum_{i=1}^{n}\alpha_{i2}h_{i2} = z \tag{6}$$

The main idea was to introduce $k_i = \alpha_{i2}/\alpha_{i1}$. It is possible to consider the case $k_1 \leq k_2 \leq k_3$ and so on, which means that machines are ranged and numbered by productivity of the first product. In such a case it is efficient to use machines with Smaller numbers to produce the first product and to use machines with bigger numbers to produce second product. Then a number s should be determined such that $\sum_{i=1}^{s-1}\alpha_{i1} < \sum_{i=s}^{n}\alpha_{i2}$ and $\sum_{i=1}^{s}\alpha_{i1} \geq \sum_{i=s+1}^{n}\alpha_{i2}$. This means that to produce the first product with $(s - 1)$ machines will not be enough, and to produce it with s machines will be more then enough. Then the solution is: $h_{i2} = 0$, $h_{i1} = 1$, for $i \in (1; s - 1)$ and $h_{i1} = 0$, $h_{i2} = 1$ for $i \in (s + 1; n)$. Amounts h_{s1} and h_{s2} are determined by the following equations:

$$h_{s1} + h_{s2} = 1 \tag{7}$$

and

$$\sum_{i=1}^{s-1}\alpha_{i1} + h_{s1}\alpha_{s1} = \sum_{i=s}^{n}\alpha_{i2} + h_{s2}\alpha_{s2}. \tag{8}$$

Kantorovich noted that the solution of the initial problem is equivalent to the determination of the following quantities: $k_s = \frac{\alpha_{s2}}{\alpha_{s1}} = \frac{\lambda_2}{\lambda_1}$, which determine the optimal plan. He called quantities λ_1 and λ_2 resolving multipliers. Obviously such an approach was valid for any number of products.

Kantorovich published these results in 1939 in a brochure at Leningrad University (Kantorovich 1939 [1960], reprinted in Nemchinov 1959 [1964]). In addition to the Plywood Trust problem, he analysed numerous other economic problems. In a supplement, he provided analytical and geometrical proofs of the resolving multipliers method. In the geometrical proof it was shown that resolving multipliers characterize a hyperplane separating two convex sets determined by the conditions of the optimization problem. In fact, even at that time Kantorovich understood that an optimal plan is inseparable from prices. "It is somewhat ironic that at practically the same time that the great debate over the feasibility of socialism was taking place between Lange and Hayek in England, a Russian unknown to them had proved the mathematical existence of planned socialist prices" (Gardner 1990: 644).

At this time, however, Kantorovich was unable to apply his approach to national economic planning. Even the use of mathematics for the solution of local economic problems was politically dangerous since the mathematical school in economics was considered to be consorting with capitalism. During one discussion a professor of statistics, B.S. Yastremskii, even accused Kantorovich of "speaking about the optimum, whilst the fascist Pareto also spoke of the optimum" (Kantorovich 1986: 60). In his memoirs, Kantorovich writes that in view of such attitudes he tried in his brochure (1939) to avoid using the term "economic" referring instead to the "organization of production". Also, he could not openly discuss the implications of resolving multipliers (Kantorovich 1986: 55).

What he could do, however, was to publish a mathematical version of his results. In his article of 1940 Kantorovich proved that for the problem of minimization of convex objective function with a compact feasibility set the criteria for the optimal solution is the existence of a linear function passing through the optimal solution and having the same value as the objective function. It is clear that in modern terms this linear function determines the optimal plan of the dual problem.

The general mathematical solution of the optimization problem made feasible the solution of a number of practical economic problems. The first was the transportation problem. In 1940 Kantorovich and M.K. Gavurin drafted an article on this problem, but owing to the negative attitude to mathematical economics that prevailed at the time, it was not published. The mathematical version was published later (Kantorovich 1942 [1958]).

After the beginning of the war with Germany in 1941, Kantorovich was involved in military research and served in the Naval Engineering College. In January 1942, the college was transferred to Yaroslavl, where Kantorovich had started and in November completed the first version of his book on the efficient use of economic resources. He delivered lectures on this work in a number of institutions, but economists by and large did not support him. This activity became dangerous for him and he abandoned economic research. After the war, however, he became involved in mathematical work related to the atomic programme. For this work, in 1949, he was awarded the Stalin prize and this enabled him to return to economics.

In 1949 it became possible to publish Kantorovich and Gavurin's article on transport problems. In this particular case, resolving multipliers are named potentials, which were interpreted as regional prices of transported cargos. In the same year Kantorovich in collaboration with V.A. Zalgaller solved the problem of the optimal cutting of materials (Kantorovich 1949; Kantorovich and Zalgaller 1951). Their work proved that the application of optimal cutting methods produced economies of up to 5 per cent of materials. Zalgaller was the first in the world to apply optimal methods in practice – at the Leningrad Railway Carriage-Building Plant.

Kantorovich's ideas influenced V.V. Novozhilov, who had begun his work on the efficiency of investments during the late 1930s. In 1943, Novozhilov wrote an important article (published in 1946) in which he outlined the procedure for planning (English translation Novozhilov 1956). The elaboration of the plan was considered to be the solution of an optimization problem in which the total sum of labour inputs was to be minimized, given constraints on the availability of capital goods, which were to be allocated to different investment projects. In his procedure, the so-called norms of "inversely related expenditures of labour" play a crucial role. Using what was, in fact, Kantorovich's method of resolving multipliers, Novozhilov showed that the optimal solution of his problem is attained if, for each final product, that investment project is adopted which has the lowest sum of actual labour costs plus other input values at their norms of inversely related expenditures. As G. Grossman has pointed out, "these norms are, of course, actually the interest rate on capital and the scarcity rents of physical resources" and Novozhilov's concept resembled the concept of opportunity costs (Grossman 1953: 330).

Although Novozhilov's theory is well known, some points are worth mentioning. First, Novozhilov's problem of plan construction was actually a mixed-integer linear problem, but he did not present it in its fully explicit form. Thus, his recourse to a method of solution by linear programming and his use of shadow prices were not entirely justified. Secondly, and more importantly, his new approach to planning implied radical changes in the entire economic system. Opportunity costs ought to be included in prices, cost accounting ought to be introduced on this basis and the procedures for planning would have to be changed. Moreover, the theory of value would have to be further developed.

Grossman thought that Novozhilov's solution was close to the general equilibrium systems of Walras and Barone. However, this was officially denied by Novozhilov. Being a competent economist and a graduate of the Kiev University before the Revolution, Novozhilov should have been familiar with Walras's theory. It seems, however, that his knowledge of Soviet planning, with its iterative calculation of the balances of physical products and of distribution of limited resources, had a much greater influence upon his thought.

Another important development during this period was V.S. Nemchinov's appeal in 1946 for the creation of Soviet econometrics, which he interpreted as a theory of mathematical calculations in planning (Nemchinov 1967: 182). This proposal was rejected at that time as being "bourgeois", econometrics being considered to be a Western invention.

The approaches of mathematical economists were totally unacceptable in Stalin's time. Kantorovich enjoyed some protection, because he worked in the military sphere. Novozhilov, on the other hand, was severely criticized and eventually dismissed from the Leningrad Polytechnical Institute. Nemchinov, who was the President of the Academy of Agricultural Sciences, was dismissed from this position in 1948. He was accused of "idealism", which was thought to be the application of the formalist bourgeois methodology of mathematics to the fields of biology and economics.

From the Mid-1950s to the Mid-1960s

It was only after Stalin's death that changes became possible. It was now understood that if there was to be economic development, new approaches in economics were needed. 1957 saw the first experiments in the calculation of input–output tables and in that year Kantorovich was able to publish his article on an optimization model for the planning of the national economy (Kantorovich 1957). In 1958, Nemchinov organized the Laboratory of Mathematical Methods in Economics in the Academy of Sciences of the USSR and became its Director. The Laboratory was the centre of input–output studies and in 1958–59 it produced several regional input–output balances. On the basis of this work, the Central Statistical Administration began preparing an input–output balance of the national economy.

There were several crucial developments during the years 1959 and 1960. In 1959, Kantorovich was able to publish his main book *Ekonomicheskii raschet nailuchshego ispol'zonvaniia resursov* (English translation *Optimal Use of Economic Resources* published in 1965). Nemchinov edited the first volume of *Primenenie matematiki v ekonomicheskikh issledovaniniakh* (English translation *The Application of Mathematics in EconomicResearch* published on 1964). In this collection, Kantorovich's work of 1939 was republished and Novozhilov's major article "Evaluation of costs and results in a socialist economy" was included. In April 1960, an All-Union Conference on the Application of Mathematical Methods in Economics was organized by Nemchinov and the materials of the conference were published in six volumes. This conference laid the organizational foundations and completed the official recognition of a new branch of Soviet economic science: the so-called "mathematical revolution" in Soviet economic science was launched. In 1963 the Central Institute of Mathematical Economics (TsEMI) of the Academy of Sciences was created, and in 1965 a new journal, *Ekonomika i matematicheskie metody*, was published.

At the core of this "revolution" was the concept of optimal planning, developed (albeit conceived somewhat differently) by Kantorovich (1959 [1965]) and Novozhilov (1967 [1970]). Kantorovich aptly renamed resolving multipliers as "objectively determined valuations" (ODV). Kantorovich's ODV and Novozhilov's "differential costs" were connected as a result of the calculation of an optimal plan to every scarce resource and basically coincided with the optimal solution of the dual problem. Their idea was that they should play a major role in the transformation of planning and pricing. The main features of optimal planning were summarized by Kantorovich as follows: it will consist in the simultaneous drawing up of the outlines of a plan and of economic indicators (ODV); it will be calculated for implementation at various levels; it will proceed by consecutive stages, by gradual implementation and by coordination of short-term with long-term planning; it will furnish planning solutions of a flexible rather than a final character. These should be adjusted in the process of plan fulfilment and be supported by economic accounting and a system of incentives (Kantorovich 1959 [1965]: 146–7). After explaining the mechanism of planning and the process of gradual increase in the accuracy of the ODV, Kantorovich emphasizes that whilst his approach is "outwardly reminiscent of the process of competition in the capitalist world", in reality his scheme is a "competition among plans and methods in the process of planning calculations" (ibid.: 150). Thus, there was no real market and there were no real prices; rather there were valuations used in the process of elaboration of the plan. It seems that at this time Kantorovich was not acquainted with the famous "Socialist Calculation Debate", but in fact his work had much in common with the arguments used by Lange against von Mises. Later, Kantorovich explicitly expressed his belief that the ODV concept undermined the arguments of Hayek and von Mises as to the ineffectiveness of the socialist economy (Gaetano 1984: 79). Novozhilov's concept of indirect centralization, his proposals for the regulation of prices and cost accounting contributed to the elaboration of the economic reform of 1965. On the other hand, his model of the determination of an optimal plan presupposed a fully centralized system.

Up to the mid-1960s, mathematical economists made significant contributions to the theory of planning. Input–output studies flourished, and a variety of optimal models were created. Planning processes remained, however, basically unaffected. Even input–output models were not wholly integrated into the planning process because of various informational, organizational and institutional impediments (Hardt et al. 1967). The optimization approach made even less of an impact. The 1965 economic reform, which incorporated some of the ideas of the mathematical economists, held out some prospect of improvement. Among the basic ideas of the reform were an increase in enterprise autonomy and a greater role of the market. However, the reform was not based upon a mathematical model of the new economic system or of the planning process. In a sense, the situation was similar to that of the mid-1920s: the planning system did not directly make use of plans based upon mathematical models, but was influenced indirectly through the implementation of procedures elaborated by economists who were familiar with quantitative analysis.

From the Mid-1960s to 1985

In the second half of the 1960s, the development of mathematical economics resulted in the system of optimal functioning of the economy (SOFE) concept created by the scholars of the TsEMI, headed by N.P. Fedorenko. The SOFE concept views the economy as a hierarchical system with an inherent objective function. Planning was seen as the problem of optimization of the objective function, under the constraints of scarce resources. Given the complexity of the economy, total centralized planning was deemed to be impossible. The regulation of local economic entities was to be based on prices, calculated as ODVs. From this general approach, several major proposals for the reform of the planning system were derived. Planning was to be an iterative process, integrating plans with different horizons. An all-union system of collecting, processing and transmitting of information was needed to provide the technical basis for planning. At the top level, decisions were to be made in aggregate terms; at the lower levels, there would be disaggregation for all scarce resources, ODVs (or shadow prices) would be calculated and economic accountability would be widely used.

Some of these ideas were implemented during the economic reform of 1965. This reform, however, was not comprehensive in character, nor was it accompanied by any political reform. Implementation proceeded very slowly. There was a gradual return to centralization.

During the 1970s the performance of the Soviet economy deteriorated, as a diminution in the rates of growth of basic economic indicators made clear. The authorities attempted to solve the problem by reinforcing the centralization of the economy and by modest changes in the system of management. Proposals for improvement of the economic mechanism, made by mathematical economists, became less and less radical.

Theoretical discussion was accompanied by some integration of mathematical methods into planning practice but on a piece-meal basis only and at a snail's pace. Even simple optimization problems were very rarely solved in the planning process. As problems in the real economy increased, theories of optimal functioning of the economy were increasingly looked upon as being unrealistic. The impact of mathematical methods on planning remained marginal and this, in turn, exposed mathematical economics to criticism. It became increasingly evident that any successful application of mathematical methods in planning and of scientific methods of management in general were incompatible with the command economy.

After 1985

"Perestroika" and the transition to the market economy that followed had important implications for the discipline of economics. For mathematical economists there were several important consequences. The object of research changed dramatically, ideological obstacles were removed and some traditional spheres of study simply became obsolete. The new priorities were to catch up with contemporary Western economics and to analyse and resolve new economic problems.

To sum up, we have seen that there was a great flourishing of mathematical economics in the Soviet Union during the 1920s. During the Stalinist years, despite restrictions, there were important further theoretical innovations. In the post-Stalin period, mathematical economics gained a reputable place in Soviet economics, but the discipline was not incorporated into the Soviet planning process. At the present time, Russian mathematical economists have joined the mainstream of world economics. It will be for future historians to evaluate their achievements.

ANDREI A. BELYKH

See also:

Ladislaus von Bortkiewicz (I); Vladimir Karpovich Dmitriev (I); Wassily W. Leontief (I); Evgeni Evgenievich Slutsky (I).

References and further reading

Barengolts, M. (1928), 'E'mkosts promyshlennogo rynka v SSSR', *Planovoe khoziastvo*, **7**, 325–98, English trans. M. Barengolts (1964) 'Capacity of the industrial market in the USSR', in N. Spulber (ed.) *Foundations of Soviet Strategy for Economic Growth, Selected Short Soviet Essays 1924–1930*, Bloomington, IN: Indiana University Press, pp. 99–123.

Bazarov, V.A. (1923), 'K metodologii izucheniia denezhnoi emissii', *Vestnik Kommunisticheskoi akademii*, **3**, 28–100.

Bazarov, V.A. (1926), 'O metodologii postroeniia perspectivnykh planov', *Planovoe khoziastvo*, Moscow, **7**, 7–21, English trans. V.A. Bazarov (1964) 'On the methodology for drafting perspective plans', in N. Spulber (ed.) *Foundations of Soviet Strategy for Economic Growth, Selected Short Soviet Essays 1924–1930*, Bloomington, IN: Indiana University Press, pp. 365–78.

Belykh, A.A. (1989), 'A note on the origins of input–output analysis and the contribution of the early Soviet economists: Chayanov, Bogdanov and Kritsman', *Soviet Studies*, **3** (41), 426–9.

Belykh, A.A. (2007), *Istoriia rossiiskikh ekonomiko-matematicheskikh issledovanii. Pervye sto let*, Moscow: Editorial URSS.

Bogdanov, A.A. (1921), 'Organizatsionnaya nauka i khozyaistvennaya planomernosts', *Trudy Pervoi Vserossiiskoi Initsiativnoi Konferentsii po nauchnoi organizatsii truda i proizvodstva*, Moscow, reprinted in abridged form in *Ekonomika i matematicheskie metody*, **24** (5), 798–801.

Chayanov, A.V. (1912), *Ocherki po teorii trudovogo khoziaistva*, Moscow: Pechatnoe delo.

Chayanov, A.V. (1917), 'Ocherki po teorii vodnogo khoziaistva', *Vestnik selskogo khoziaistva*, **49–50**, 5–8; **51–2**, 8–12.

Chayanov, A.V. (1922), 'Optimalnye razmery zemledelcheskikh khoziaistv', in A.V. Chayanov, *Optimalnye razmery selskokhoziaistvennykh predpriiatii (problemy zemleustroistva)*, Moscow: Novaia derevnia, pp. 5–82.

Chayanov, A.V. (1928), *Optimalnye razmery selskokhoziaistvennykh predpriiatii*, 3rd edn, Moscow: Novaia derevnia, German trans. A.W. Tschajanow (1930) *Die optimalen Betriebsgrossen In der Landwirtschaft*. Berlin: Parey, Japanese trans. 1957, *Nogyo kelel tekisel kiboron: sono riron to kelsoku*. Tokyo.

Chayanov, A.V. (1966), *On the Theory of Peasant Economy*, B. Kerblay, D. Thorner and R.E.F. Smith (eds), Homewood, IL: American Economic Association.

Clark, D.L. (1984), 'Planning and the real origins of input–output analysis', *Journal of Contemporary Asia*, **4** (14), 408–15.

Dmitriev, V.K. (1904), *Ekonomicheskie ocherki. Opyt organicheskogo sinteza teorii tsennosti I teorii predelnoi poleznosti*, Moscow: Tipografiia V. Rikhktera, French trans. 1968, *Essais Economiques – Esquisse de synthse organique de la théorie de la valeur travail et de la théorie de l'utilité marginale*, Paris: Éditions du Centre national de la recherche scientifique, English trans. 1974, ed. with an introduction by D. Nuti, *Economic Essays on Value, Competition and Utility*, Cambridge: Cambridge University Press.

Domar, E.D. (1957), 'A Soviet model of growth', in E.D. Domar, *Essays in the Theory of Economic Growth*, New York: Oxford University Press, pp. 223–61.

Durrenberger, E.P. (1984), 'Operationalizing Chayanov', in E.P. Durrenberger (ed.), *Chayanov, Peasants and Economic Anthropology*, Orlando, FL: Academic Press, pp. 27–38.

Feld'man, G.A. (1928), 'K teorii tempov rosta narodnogo dokhoda', *Planovoe khoziaistvo*, **11**, 146–70, **12**, 151–78, English trans. 'On the theory of growth rates of national income', in N. Spulber (ed.) (1964) *Foundations of Soviet Strategy for Economic Growth: Selected Soviet Essays, 1924–1930*, Bloomington: IN University Press, pp. 174–99, 304–41.

Gaetano, D. (1984), *L'economia sovietica: Uno sguardo dall'interno*, Milan: Franco Angeli.

Gardner, R. (1990), 'L.V. Kantorovich: the price implications of optimal planning', *Journal of Economic Literature*, **28** (June), 638–48.

Grossman, G. (1953), 'Scarce capital and Soviet doctrine', *Quarterly Journal of Economics*, **67** (3), 311–43.

Hardt, J.P., M. Hoffenberg, N. Kaplan and H.S. Levine (eds) (1967), *Mathematics and Computers in Soviet Economic Planning*, New Haven, CT, and London: Yale University Press.

Kantorovich, L.V. (1939), *Matematicheskie metody organizatsii i planirovaniia proizvodstva*, Leningrad: Leningrad State University, English trans. 1960, 'Mathematical methods of organizing and planning production', *Management Science*, **4** (6), 366–422.

Kantorovich, L.V. (1940), 'Ob odnom effectivnom metode resheniia nekotorykh klassov ekstremalnykh problem', *Doklady Akademii nauk SSSR*, new series, **28** (3), 212–15.

Kantorovich, L.V. (1942), 'O peremeshchenii mass', *Doklady Akademii nauk SSSR*, **37** (7–8), 227–30, French trans. 1942, 'Sur la translocation des masses ', *Comptes Rendus (Doklady) de l'Académie des Sciences de l'URSS*, **37** (7–8), 199–201, English trans. 1958, 'On the translocation of masses', *Management Science*, **5** (1), 1–4.

Kantorovich, L.V. (1949), 'Podbor postavov obespechivaiushchikh maksimalnyi vykhod produktsii v zadannom assortimente', *Lesnaia promyshlennost*, **7**, 15–17, **8**, 17–18.

Kantorovich, L.V. (1957), 'O metodakh analiza nekotorykh ekstremalnykh planovo-proizvodstvennykh zadach', *Doklady Academii Nauk*, **115** (3), 441–4.

Kantorovich, L.V. (1959), *Ekonomicheskii raschet nailychshego ispolzovaniia resursov.* Moscow: AN SSSR, English trans. 1965, *The Best Uses of Economic Resource*, Oxford: Pergamon Press.

Kantorovich, L.V. (1986), 'Moi put v nauke', in V.L. Kantorovich, S.S. Kutateladze and I.I. Fet (eds) (2002), *Leonid Vitalevich Kantorovich: chelovek i uchenyi*, vol. 1, Novosibirsk: SO RAN, pp. 22–75.

Kantorovich, L.V. and M.K. Gavurin (1949), 'Primenenie matematichesikgh metodov v voprosakh analiza gruzopotokov', in V.V. Zvonkov (ed.), *Problemy povysheniia effectivnosti raboty transporta*, Moscow: Transzheldorizdat, pp. 110–38.

Kantorovich, L.V. and V.A. Zalgaller (1951), *Raschet ratsionalnogo raskroia promyshlennykh materialov*, Leningrad: Lenizdat.

Kritsman, L.N. (1921), *O edinom khoziastvennom plane*, Moscow: Gosizdat.

Kritsman, L.N. (1922), *Novaya ekonomicheskaya politika i planovoe raspredelenie*, Moscow: Gosizdat.

Leontiev, V.V. (1925), 'Balans narodnogo khoziastava SSSR – metodicheskii razbor raboty TsSU', *Planovoe Khoziaistvo*, **12**, 254–58, English trans. 'The balance of the economy of the USSR', in N. Spulber (ed.) (1964), *Foundations of Soviet Strategy for Economic Growth, Selected Short Soviet Essays 1924–1930*, Bloomington, IN: Indiana University Press, pp. 88–94.

Marshall, A. (1890), *Principles of Economics*, 8th edn 1920, London: Macmillan.

Nemchinov, V.S. (ed.) (1959), *Primenenie matematiki v ekonomicheskikh issledovaniiakh*, vol. 1, Moscow: Sotsekgiz, English trans. 1964, *The Use of Mathematics in Economics*, Cambridge, MA: MIT Press.

Nemchinov, V.S. (1967), *Izbrannye proizvedeniia*, vol. 1, Moscow: Nauka.

Novozhilov, V.V. (1946), 'Metody nakhozhdeniia minimuma zatrat v sotsialisticheskom khoziastve', *Trudy Leningradskogo politekhnicheskogo instituta im. M.I. Kalinina*, **1**, 322–37.

Novozhilov, V.V. (1956), 'On choosing between investment projects', *International Economic Papers*, vol. 6, London: International Economic Association.

Novozhilov, V.V. (1967), *Problemy izmereniia zatrat i resultatov pri optimalnom planirovanii*, Moscow: Ekonomika, English trans. 1970, *Problems of Cost–Benefit Analysis in Optimal Planning*, White Plains, NY: International Arts and Sciences Press.

Schmidt, O.I. (1923), *Matematicheskie zakony denezhnot emissii*, Moscow: Gosizdat.

Slutsky, E.E. (1915), 'Sulla teoria del bilancio del consumatore', *Giornale degli economisti e rivista di statistica*, **51** (July), 1–26, English trans., E.E. Slutsky (1952), 'On the theory of the budget of the consumer', in G.J. Stigler and K.E. Boulding (eds), *Readings in Price Theory*, Homewood, IL: Richard D. Irwin, 1952, pp. 27–56.

Slutsky, E.E. (1923), 'Matematicheskie zametki k teorii kony emissii', *Ekonomicheskii biulleten Kon'iunkturnogo instituta*, **2**, 53–60.

Smolinski, L. (1971), 'The origins of Soviet mathematical economics', *Jahrbuch der Wirtschaft Osteuropas (Yearbook of East-European Economics)*, B.2, Munich: Veroffentlichung des Osteuropa Institute, pp. 137–53.

Spulber, N. (ed.) (1964), *Foundations of Soviet Strategy for Economic Growth: Selected Soviet Essays, 1924–1930*, Bloomington, IN: Indiana University Press.

Stalin, I.V. (1929), 'Concerning questions of agrarian policy in the USSR', in I.V. Stalin, *Collected Works*, vol. 12, Moscow: Foreign Languages Publishing House.

Strumilin, S.G. (1921), 'Formula khozaistvennogo plana', *Ekonomicheskaia zhizn*, **22** (14 November), pp. 1–2.

Treml, V.G. (1967), 'Input–output analysis and Soviet panning', in J. Hardt, *Mathematics and Computers in Soviet Economic Planning*, New Haven, CT: Yale University Press, pp. 68–146.

Tugan-Baranovsky, M.I. (1890), 'Uchenie o predelnoi poleznosti khoziaistvennykh blag kak prichine ikh tsennosti', *Iuridicheskoi vestnik*, Moscow, **6** (2), (VI), 192–230.

Cambridge School of economics

Even though references to the "Cambridge School" are frequent in history of economic thought literature, what this term designates is far from being univocal, being used sometimes in relation to Marshall and his disciples, sometimes to Keynes and his followers, sometimes to the approach to economics prevailing in Cambridge throughout the period spanning from the early days of the twentieth century to the 1970s, when Cambridge enjoyed international prestige as one of the leading centres of scientific investigation in economics. As in any other science, there is more than one definition of what it takes to constitute a school in economics. If we accept as the definition of school "an alliance of persons, a community of ideas, an acknowledged authority, and a combination in purpose, which banded them into a society apart" (Higgs 1897 [2001]: 7), then this would hold only for the first decades of the Cambridge School, when Marshall introduced the new degree in economics in 1903 and created a community of disciples that kept his teachings alive well after his death. They spread the ideas of the master as presented in his *Principles of Economics* (Marshall 1920), acknowledged his authority, shared the mission he set for economics and were perceived and perceived themselves as a group of scholars with a well-defined identity. Keynes himself, in his introduction to the Cambridge Handbooks in 1922, could speak of the authors contributing to this output as "orthodox members of the Cambridge School of economics" whose "ideas about the subject, and even [whose] prejudices, are traceable to the contact they have enjoyed with the writings and lectures of the two economists who have chiefly influenced Cambridge thought for the past fifty years, Dr. Marshall and Prof. Pigou" (Keynes 1971–89, hereafter CWK, XII: 857). The School included almost all the members of the Faculty of Economics and Politics, Claude William Guillebaud (1890–1971), Hubert Douglas Henderson (1890–1952), Frederick Lavington (1881–1927), Gerald Frank Shove (1887–1947), Dennis Holme Robertson (1890–1963), Maurice Herbert Dobb (1900–76), and Edward Austin Grossage Robinson (1897–1993).

When the term "school" is applied to the Keynes era and more so to the post-Keynes period, the above definition is more problematic. First there is the issue of whom should be included. Until Keynes's death in 1946 the list would certainly have included Roy Forbes Harrod (1900–78), Richard Ferdinand Kahn (1905–89), Nicholas Kaldor (1908–86), Michal Kalecki (1899–1970), James Edward Meade (1907–95), Joan Violet Robinson (1903–83), Piero Sraffa (1898–1983) and Richard Nicholas Stone (1913–91), while for the post-war period the names of Wynne Godley (1926–2010), Richard Murphey Goodwin (1913–96), Geoffrey Colin Harcourt, Robin Marris (1924–2012), Luigi Pasinetti and Ajit Singh (1940–2015) are to be added. Secondly there is the issue of what exactly they shared and whether it is sufficiently broad to consider them a school.

Most of these economists shared common times and places, but this is neither a necessary nor a sufficient condition to constitute a school. A school is, after all, marked out by shared approach and doctrinal content, and we can speak of schools of thought also in the absence of unity of time and place. Conversely, a shared place and time do not lead to the formation of a school if there is no common pursuit or recognized leader. While the role of "master" might, in the first period after Marshall, have been performed by Keynes, who was the pivotal figure in the inter-war Cambridge, after his death it is hard to identify a "master" around whom the school regrouped.

However, in the literature the term "Cambridge School" is generally applied without qualification to Keynes's immediate circle in the inter-war years, and to his followers in the later period.

Schumpeter (1954: 223) argues that Keynes and the "orthodox Keynesians . . . were a school by virtue of doctrinal and personal bonds, and always acted as a group, praising one another, fighting one another's fights, each member taking his share in group propaganda".

Pasinetti (2007: 61) maintains that Joan Robinson, Richard Kahn, Nicholas Kaldor and Piero Sraffa formed "a powerful school on the track of Keynes's economic theory". He recognizes that this "school" was in reality a motley, argumentative group united and divided by strong emotional bonds, although he discerned "something . . . much deeper, that shaped their intellectual affinities or attractiveness and at the same time gave rise to their strong and stormy personal relationship" (ibid.). That "deep something", Pasinetti argues, derived from adopting a common approach to economics.

On the other hand, Bliss (2010: 632–3) wrote: "Keynes created a circle of true believers and a corresponding group of heretical others. . . . The characters listed in Pasinetti's book [2007] were each different, and where their paths crossed they were frequently in ill-tempered opposition . . . The exception would be the twin stars Richard Kahn and Joan Robinson".

For our part, we have characterized the Cambridge economists in the inter-war years as a group rather than as a school (Marcuzzo and Rosselli 2005; Marcuzzo et al. 2008). We maintained that:

> Unlike a "school", a "group" does not subscribe to a common body of doctrine, although there may be internal cohesion and shared contents; . . . this group identity stemmed from motivations, values, life-styles and work-styles, leaving room for reciprocal respect, overriding many contrasts, and keeping the sense of belonging alive; . . . the points of theoretical division, precisely because they generated discussion, did not break the group up but served to form a connective tissue; . . . precisely because there was no common *corpus* of accepted ideas to defend, the characteristic feature seems rather to have been elitism – a system of co-optation based on characteristics that were neither ideology nor exactly academic performance or success, but rather the features of a moral and intellectual aristocracy. (Marcuzzo et al. 2008: 582–3)

As to the period after World War II, there is certainly a recognizable group of economists in Cambridge that shared an opposition to neoclassical economics and drew mainly on Keynes's heritage, but they can hardly be considered a school given the nature of their research agenda, which was highly diversified and, in the case of Sraffa, radically so.

Whether in the form of opposition or endorsement, the Cambridge group or school is a landmark in the history of twentieth century economic thought, because of its outstanding characteristic of being associated with the most powerful attempt at building an approach to economics alternative to the mainstream. For this reason it is still capable of arousing strong reactions in friends and foes alike. In the following pages we reconstruct the main elements of this tradition, the stages of its developments and the nature of its heritage. For the purpose of reconstructing the main features of the "Cambridge School" it is useful to identify four stages of its history: (1) the Marshall era, up to the mid-1920s; (2) the Keynes era, up to the mid-1940s; (3) the Golden Age, up to the early 1970s; and (4) the "fall from grace", up to the early 1980s.

The Marshall Era

Marshall was the first to believe in the possibility of making economics an independent discipline, and indeed a major one in the academic system of Cambridge, hitherto dominated by classical and mathematical studies (see Coats 1993: 106–13; Groenewegen 1995: ch. 15). It was Marshall who set the process moving by instituting the Economics Tripos, supporting the birth of a faculty of economics, selecting the teaching staff and courses, and guiding and coordinating the academic life and assignments of the various members. A few years later it was his pupil, Pigou, who took over this role, making a decisive contribution to the consolidation of the academic status of Cambridge economics. The operation proved an unqualified success, seeing that just a few years later – from the 1920s – Cambridge drew the attention of the rest of the world as a paragon for the study of economics, while those engaged there in research and teaching had a distinct sense of belonging to a concentrated microcosm with a clear identity of its own.

Much of this imprinting was forged by Marshall's vision of where the ultimate purpose of economics lay and consequently how economists should be trained. Both "visions" can be traced back to his inaugural lecture in Cambridge (Marshall 1885 [1925]). There we find sketched out his conception of modern economics as an *organon*, as a means of reasoning; it was the approach with which "Cambridge economists up to and beyond the 1930s positively associated themselves" (Tribe 2000: 223). He also made eloquently clear his vision of what the purpose of training economists in Cambridge was:

> It will be my most cherished ambition, my highest endeavour, to do what with my poor ability and my limited strength I may, to increase the numbers of those, whom Cambridge, the great mother of strong men, sends out into the world with cool heads but warm hearts, willing to give some at least of their best powers to grappling with the social suffering around them; resolved not to rest content till they have done what in them lies to discover how far it is possible to open up to all the material means of a refined and noble life. (Marshall 1885 [1925]: 177)

The type of economics Marshall favoured was application of the tools of economic analysis to reality, be it districts, trades or markets, "always with acute awareness of its embeddedness in historically determined totalities" (Becattini 2006: 614).

In the curriculum of students great weight was given to modern economic and political history and applied economics, which were to provide the framework for an economic interpretation of social reality. Recourse to mathematical formalism was discouraged because "excessive reliance on this instrument . . . might distort our sense of proportion by causing us to neglect factors that could not easily be worked up in the mathematical machine" (Pigou 1925: 84). Equally distrusted was the appeal of the raw statistical material, pre-eminence being attributed to theoretical analysis over simple data collection or manipulation. Moreover, biological metaphors served the purpose of stressing the evolutionary nature of most economic institutions, which should be studied like living organisms, of which they follow similar life-cycle patterns.

While Keynes, the most outstanding of Marshall's pupils, went on to pursue a research path of his own, which eventually led his economics to differ in many and fundamental respects from that of Marshall, there remained in Cambridge well after Marshall's death a Marshallian "old guard" of faithful pupils – Pigou, Robertson and Shove – who resisted the "Keynesian revolution" and, as far as language and substance of the theory were concerned, stuck to unadulterated Marshall. A small group of Marshall's pupils, Sydney Chapman, David Macgregor, Walter Layton, Frederick Lavington and Philip Sargant Florence, constituting what has been labelled the Marshallian school of industrial economics (see Raffaelli 2004), should also be considered as a distinctive thread in the warp of the Cambridge School in its early stage.

Developments in economics along the lines identified by Marshall did not end with his death. Important new fields were explored and approaches were created that dominated economic thinking well into the 1960s. This was the case of Pigou's welfare economics, built on Marshall's marginal benefit–marginal cost framework and based on identification and analysis of the divergences between marginal private net product and marginal social net product. The market failures that arise when pursuit of self-interest does not lead to the best results for the society as a whole was for decades the justification for the corrective action of the state.

Other efforts were less successful. The book that Shove had meant to write on the theory of costs, which should have taken into account the heterogeneity of factors of production and all the different types of relation between firm and industry, never came to light. Shove had assumed, like Marshall, that each firm had a private market, but his idea of "imperfect competition" was too vague and intractable in formal representation, and eventually it was Joan Robinson's geometrical approach that prevailed.

The Keynes Era

The arrival of Sraffa in Cambridge in 1927 marked the onset of upheaval with new and subversive ideas. He had criticized Marshall in the famous 1925 and 1926 articles which had driven Keynes to invite him to Cambridge, showing that Marshall's supply curve of an industry in perfect competition was built on assumptions both unrealistic and inconsistent with the partial equilibrium approach. Inconsistent because decreasing costs must be explained by "external" economies, since in perfect competition "internal" economies would turn the most efficient firm into a monopoly. Yet external economies also usually affect the other sectors, so the clause *ceteris paribus* does not hold. Similarly, Sraffa argued, it is hard to conceive of the price of a factor that increases in one sector only and generates increasing costs exclusively in that sector.

Keynes thought Sraffa's criticism disruptive and indeed it deeply impacted on the Marshallian hegemony, marking a new phase. The old guard of Marshall's disciples (Robertson and Shove) tried to defend Marshall's theory of value and his supply curve. In their defence an important role was played by marketing expenses and by the idea that the firm is subject to a life cycle and natural decline (Robertson 1930; Shove 1930). Their arguments, however, failed to convince the younger generation, who enthusiastically pursued the way out of Marshall's inconsistencies suggested by Sraffa's 1926 article: the idea was to drop the assumption of perfect competition and to focus on markets where each firm faces its own negative sloping demand curve.

The original idea of developing a theory of imperfect competition has always been credited to Sraffa. However, it is still doubtful how convinced he himself was of its fruitfulness, apart from its role in exposing Marshall's weaknesses. Sraffa did not follow this line of research for long, and during the preparation of his course on advanced theory of value, which he taught in Cambridge from 1928 to 1931, he took a completely different route. This was based on two elements. The first was a reappraisal of the theory of value of classical political economy as antagonist to the Marshallian "fundamental symmetry" of supply and demand and based on a definition of cost as "physical" cost, which does not include any subjective factors, such as "sacrifice" and "waiting". The second element was investigation into the exchange ratios between commodities that enable the exchanges between productive sectors which warrant reproduction of the economic system. However, very little of what Sraffa was working on was known to his Cambridge colleagues, and the prolonged work on the book, which was to appear 33 years later, has only recently been reconstructed on the basis of his unpublished papers.

In the period under consideration two major works, *The Treatise on Probability* (1921) and *The General Theory of Employment, Interest and Money* (1936), signpost Keynes's contribution to Cambridge economics. During the same period Keynes produced another landmark work, the *Treatise on Money* (1930), besides *A Tract of Monetary Reform* (1923). Philosophically and methodologically he remained faithful to the approach to human behaviour resting on the two pillars of conventions and expectations, supported by a notion of probability, to be evaluated with evidence and judgement, as guide to action. Understanding how opinions are formed is instrumental to transforming them through the joint effects of persuasion and artfully designed institutions, with the ultimate aim of attaining the common good.

The premise of Keynesian economics, as we find it in the *General Theory*, is that the economic system is not ruled by "natural forces" that economists can discover and order in a neat pattern of causes and effects, but that their task, rather, is to control and manage the key variables for attainment of a social goal. Against the "classical" conclusion that market forces are at work to bring the economic system to the full employment of resources, Keynes counter-posed the argument that aggregate economic behaviour does not have the same outcome as the pursuit of individual self-interest, so that what is good for the individual may not be good for the whole. It was not against the market, but rather against unfettered laissez-faire that his economics stood, for, as he wrote in the last chapter of the *General Theory*, it is "wise and prudent statesmanship to allow the game to be played, *subject to rules and limitations*" (CWK VII: 374, emphasis added).

Keynes's first tenet against traditional thinking is based on reverting the causality relation between budget deficit, income and expenditure; the means to reduce unemployment is through an increase in effective demand (having public expenditure to supplement private investment when necessary) rather than adjusting supply to the existing level of demand. The "digging holes in the ground" argument – it does not matter how public money is spent, as long as it is spent – is meant to illustrate the principle that expenditure will generate income and through the multiplier the savings necessary to finance it.

Keynes's other fundamental contribution to macroeconomics, besides effective demand, is the notion of liquidity preference. He argued against the "classical tradition" whereby thrift and capital productivity are the "real forces" at work in determining the rate of interest, considering it a highly conventional phenomenon, determined by the strength of the desire of individuals to hold money (as protection against an uncertain future) and the quantity of money provided by the banking system.

At the international level he struggled to make the logic of cooperation and coordination prevail over the working of blind market forces, which would not be able to correct imbalances and asymmetries between creditor and debtor countries. He fought for the creation of international institutions to oversee the system of payments and the alloca-tion of international capital.

These pillars are the foundations of the Keynesian full employment policies and reforms of the international monetary order, which informed the so-called Keynesian consensus in the post-war years.

In all his activities, Keynes could rely on his "favourite pupil" Richard Kahn, who stood for the preservation of Keynes's heritage. At the beginning of his career, follow-ing a path opened up by Marshall, Kahn stressed the importance of the short period because of the nature of the particular decisions involved, characterized by the time horizon to which they apply. The "Economics of the short period" was the title of the dissertation which in 1930 earned him a Fellowship at King's College and was much later (it remained unpublished for nearly 50 years) to be recognized as a landmark in the "imperfect competition revolution". However, Kahn's association with Cambridge economics in the period under consideration is certainly to be identified with the Keynesian revolution, to which he contributed more significantly than anyone else in the circle around Keynes. First, there is the forging of a formidable analytical tool – the multiplier – which allowed Keynes to reverse the causality relationship between saving and investment: it is investment which generates savings. Secondly, again expanding on Marshall's apparatus, Kahn introduced the aggregate supply function as a means, together with the aggregate demand function, to determine the price level. Many years later he prided himself on "finally disposing of the idea that the price level is determined by the quantity of money" (Patinkin and Leith 1977: 147). Unlike Keynes, adept in the use of rhetoric as a technique for persuasion, Kahn invariably favoured the use of deductive reasoning. His "great repugnance to the thought that there might be an error attached to his name", according to Joan Robinson (JVR papers i/8/7, King's College, Cambridge) did not make him a prolific writer, but his extraordinary influence is to be seen in the two most important books of the Cambridge economics of the 1930s, the *Economics of Imperfect Competition* (Robinson 1969) and the *General Theory* (Keynes 1936).

Joan Robinson, "after Keynes. . . . the most prominent name associated with the Cambridge School of Economics" according to Kaldor's obituary written for the King's College 1984 Annual Report (p. 34), was a latecomer and potentially an outcast in the all-male club of Cambridge economists. Early on she gained Kahn's enthusiastic support and Keynes's consideration, which sustained her in the production of many articles and books in the 1930s and 1940s. Her contributions span from imperfect competition to extension of the *General Theory* to an open economy and the long period, and they include the attempt to legitimate some Marxian concepts within the accepted box of tools drawn upon by the economist. Her encounter with Kalecki (who was in Cambridge during 1937–39) and constant engagement with Sraffa made her more willing than Kahn to enlarge her approach beyond the boundaries of Keynesian economics. "For me" – she wrote much later – "the main message of Marx was the need to think in terms of history, not of equilibrium" (Robinson 1973: x). Pursuit in this direction became her main endeavour in the last part of her life, when she strongly argued that Kalecki, who "brought imperfect competition into touch with the theory of employment" (Robinson 1969: viii), had a system of analysis in some respects superior to Keynes's (Robinson 1979: 186).

The very idea of a Keynesian "revolution" was resisted and, to some extent, opposed by the old Marshallian guard. Robertson, on the basis of his own approach to the problems of economic fluctuations and cycles in terms of a succession of periods, objected to Keynes's short-period approach whereby the current level of saving is a function of current income, without any reference to the past level of savings. Moreover, he challenged Keynes's theory of liquidity preference, adhering to the theory that the rate of interest is the price that brings the demand and supply of loanable funds into equilibrium. In the case of Pigou, the main point of disagreement was whether a cut in money wages would cure unemployment. In October 1937 Pigou presented his argument, based on the quantity theory of money, that "if a cut in wages leaves employment unchanged, money income has no ground for change" (CWK XIV: 256–7); Keynes's position was, instead, "that, if there is a cut in wages, unemployment being unchanged, there is a ground for a change in money income" (CWK XIV: 257). At the time there was no room for conciliation, and notwithstanding Pigou's later admission that he did not grant Keynes due recognition (Pigou 1950), the ground was paved for presenting the main result of the *General Theory* – equilibrium with unemployment – as dependent on wage rigidity only, as Marshall and subsequent neoclassical economics would have it.

The Golden Age

In the first decades after War World II the reputation enjoyed by the most famous Cambridge economists attracted students from all over the world to their courses. Taking the academic year 1961–62 as an example, they went to Cambridge to study "Economic dynamics" with Kaldor, "Employment, prices and growth" with J. Robinson, "Wages policy" with Kahn, "Planned economies" and "Welfare economics" with Dobb, and "Price and production in an expanding economy" with Goodwin and Pasinetti (*Cambridge University Reporter*, 1962). The number of students sitting part II of the Economics Tripos nearly trebled in less than 20 years, from 72 students in 1952 to 212 in 1968, with a growing non-British percentage. However, not many changes were made to the composition of the faculty, nor to its size. For a long time there were only two professors in economics, Kahn and Austin Robinson, who had been appointed a few years after the end of the war. Robertson, who had returned to Cambridge after the war as professor of political economy, retired in 1957. When A. Robinson retired in 1965, his place was taken by his wife J. Robinson, joined, one year later, by Kaldor. They left the small group of readers to which they had belonged since the early 1950s, and to which Dobb and David Champernowne had been admitted in 1959 and Goodwin only in 1966. Until the end of the 1960s, then, it was the generation who had personally been under the influence of Keynes who ruled the faculty and taught the main courses in economics, with the support of no more than a dozen younger lecturers, some of whom, like Harcourt and Pasinetti, kept the tradition of their mentors alive, while others, like Frank Horace Hahn, Christopher Bliss or Amartya Sen, took different routes. The size of the Faculty of Economics and Politics was matched by that of the Department of Applied Economics, established in 1939 to manage the research projects funded by external institutions, and put under the direction first of Stone, and later of Brian Reddaway.

In the post-war period Cambridge economics developed along two routes which converged for a few years subsequent to publication of Sraffa's *Production of Commodities by Means of Commodities* (1960), as the capital controversy raged throughout the 1960s and 1970s, only to diverge again in its aftermath.

The first route has been labelled (Harcourt 2006) the Post-Keynesian theory of growth and distribution: it originated as a joint effort, first by J. Robinson, Kahn and Kaldor, and later by Goodwin and Pasinetti. The aim was to go beyond the static approach of the *General Theory* and model the working of an economic system which moves through time. One of the protagonists of these efforts, Kaldor, was not a born and bred Cambridge economist, but a Hungarian émigré who soon became identified with the Cambridge School. Although he was already in Cambridge when the London School of Economics was evacuated there in wartime, he joined the economics faculty only in 1949, when he also became a fellow of King's College. He was a prolific writer both in his academic output and in his contributions to the political debates on economic issues, advising governments and the general public alike.

Kaldor's main contributions in the field of pure economic theory are his economic growth models and his theory of income distribution, which followed up the thread of a Keynesian idea, namely, that profit earners have a higher propensity to save than wage earners (Kaldor 1956). So he became "the joint architect with Joan Robinson and Richard Kahn of the Post Keynesian School of Economics which extended Keynesian modes of thinking to the long run" (Thirlwall 2003: 221).

Joan Robinson, in her *Accumulation of Capital* (1956), pursued a different method, seeking to determine what the consequences are for an economy when it moves off its golden path, that is, when the rate of accumulation and the rates of growth of population and technical change are not such as to guarantee a steady growth in equilibrium with full employment.

Goodwin, an American Marxist who arrived in Cambridge in 1951, contributed to this literature in 1967 with a model of growth cycle, exhibiting the dynamic interaction between the distribution of income and the accumulation of capital, which formalized Marx's general law of accumulation:

> Labour market conditions drive profit rates, profit rates drive the rate of accumulation, and the rate of accumulation feeds back to affect labour market conditions. When placed in a multiplier-accelerator framework, this generates cyclical growth, with a full-employment profit rate squeeze sending the economy into a phase of slower growth with rising unemployment that lasts until the profit rate has recovered. (Palley 2003: 185; see also Desai and Ormerod 1998)

Pasinetti arrived from Italy to Cambridge in 1956 as a student, having both Kaldor and Goodwin as mentors; he later became a member of the faculty and a recognized leader of post-Keynesian economics. In his 1962 article he presented the famous theorem associated with his name that "in steady growth the rate of profit is equal to the ratio between the rate of growth and the capitalists' propensity to save and does not depend on technology or on the workers' propensity to save" (Panico 2003: 171).

The second route developed in Cambridge after the war – the alternative to the Marshallian determination of prices (both of goods and factors) – surfaced with the publication of Sraffa's introduction to Ricardo's *Principles* (Sraffa 1951) and was fully laid down in his 1960 book, where reappraisal of classical political economy led the way towards the construction of a theory in which the principle of equating marginal costs and benefits found no room. The monumental editorial work on Ricardo's *Works and*

Correspondence, for which he was universally praised, led Sraffa to challenge the interpretation of Ricardo which had prevailed in the British tradition.

Sraffa showed that in Ricardo the "laws which regulate the distribution" of the surplus between profits and rent constituted the main problem in political economy. To this end, the labour theory of value, despite its limitations, of which Ricardo was well aware, and which he sought to overcome with his search for an invariant measure of value, played the essential role of determining the rate of profit as a ratio between surplus and wages. The same role had been played in his "early theory of profits" by corn, which appeared both as input and output in the agricultural sector (known as Ricardo's corn-ratio theory of profits).

Sraffa's interpretation was translated into a geometrical model by Kaldor (1956) in a famous article which pointed out the differences between alternative theories of distribution (Ricardian, Marxian, neoclassical and Keynesian), and, by Pasinetti (1960), into a mathematical model. The introduction to the *Principles* was the first step toward a revival of that surplus approach, "submerged and forgotten", which Sraffa promoted in his 1960 book.

Production of Commodities by Means of Commodities (Sraffa 1960) had a great impact on Cambridge economics and seemed to satisfy two different needs. On the one hand, it presented an alternative theory of prices and distribution. Given the quantities produced and the technical conditions of production for each commodity, the prices are determined by a system of simultaneous equations, under the assumption that in a capitalist society the rate of profit must be equal in all sectors. The distribution of the surplus was not made dependent exclusively on the technical conditions of production and the relative scarcity of productive factors, since one of the distributive variables was determined outside the system of prices and could be influenced by other economic, or even political and social, causes. Moreover, it was a theory that underscored the antithetical interests of labourers and capitalists by drawing an inverse relationship between rate of profit and wage. On the other hand, Sraffa brought compelling elements to the critique of the concept of capital outside the short period that Joan Robinson had begun in her 1954 article, where she drew attention to the "profound methodological error" (Robinson 1954 [1964]: 120) connected with the concept of quantity of capital outside the short period. She pointed up the neoclassical failure to distinguish between changes in the conditions of producing a given output, when the quantity of physical capital is altered, from changes in the value of that capital, due to variations in wages and profits. The implication is that "different factor ratios cannot be used to analyse changes in the factor ratio taking place through time", because over time the value of the quantity of capital may change as a consequence of a change in distribution, and we will not be comparing the same quantities. She concluded that "it is impossible to discuss changes (as opposed to differences) in neo-classical terms" (Robinson 1954 [1964]: 129).

The substitution of labour for capital when the rate of profit rises relatively to the wage lost any meaning after Sraffa showed that the same technique could be adopted as the most profitable at different rates of wages (the so-called "reswitching"). Therefore Sraffa's critique had implications not only for the theory of distribution based on the aggregate production function, but also for the contention that market forces always bring the system to the full employment equilibrium via changes in the wage rate. It was the same battle the Keynesians were fighting.

The "Fall from Grace"

By the late 1970s the generation which had given Cambridge its fame and prestige had amply passed retirement age. While still active, opinioned and vociferous on the public and academic scene, they had lost power in the faculty. It has been said that there was a failure, "an unwise behaviour" (Pasinetti 2007: 199–204), on their part in selecting and promoting suitable candidates to become their successors. "The trouble is that the post-Keynesian school has not proved to be at all good at replicating itself" (Bliss 2010: 650).

As a result Cambridge was conquered by a very able new generation of economists who, however, set themselves up as opponents rather than followers. With the appointment of Frank Hahn as professor in 1972, the shift towards mathematical models of general equilibrium and formalism was accomplished. This opened a rift between the "old" Keynesians, who saw these developments as betrayal of the ideas they had fought for, and those who believed that they were a necessary step to break away from Cambridge insularity and engage in competition with the academic world at large.

Since the 1960s, the top US universities had established themselves as the leading centres of postgraduate education in economics. The prominence of their graduate schools in training and supplying cohorts of professional economists to cater for the growing demand coming from institutions and academia worldwide overshadowed the dominant position hitherto enjoyed by Cambridge, which was holding on to its old-fashioned system of teaching mainly to undergraduates and through supervisions, giving little weight to postgraduate lectures and courses (see Tribe 2000: 245).

If we look at the internal development of economics as an academic subject, we find other reasons which may account for the decline of the Cambridge School. As we have seen, the research strategy embraced by Cambridge economists in the post-war years followed two routes: extension and generalization to the long period of the Keynesian theory, and critique of neoclassical theory with a return to classical political economy. Both enterprises turned out to be at odds with what was being pursued on the research frontier in the major universities, mainly in the US, but also elsewhere (Desai 1983).

As far back as the early 1950s, Milton Friedman had launched his attack on Keynesian policies. Not only in Chicago but also elsewhere, increasing dissatisfaction with the neo-classical synthesis had given way to a kind of macroeconomics which discarded many Keynesian features to find more congenial ground in general equilibrium analysis. Monetarism and the "rational expectations" revolution were conquering the discipline within and outside the academic world.

The heated response, by Joan Robinson against "bastard Keynesism" and by Kahn and Kaldor against the "scourge of monetarism", raised the contraposition between Cambridge and the outside world to an extreme degree. It deepened the gulf between "us and them", enforcing the perception of isolation and sectarianism of the Cambridge School.

Similarly, Sraffa's critique of neoclassical theory was rejected by the establishment in the academic world, and the Cambridge economists became increasingly isolated and dismissed. The controversy over the theory of capital between Cambridge, UK, and Cambridge, USA, had raged for two decades. It reached its peak in the late 1960s, when Paul Samuelson tried to defend the theory of capital under attack, first, by constructing a special case of production function and, secondly, by denying the possibility of reswitching. In both cases he ended by honestly admitting that he had been wrong. At this point, Sraffa's critique, which could not be proven wrong, was accused of being irrelevant: either reswitching was an "exception" that could be ignored or the critique of the concept of capital held only for obsolete versions of the neoclassical theory, the intertemporal general equilibrium models being free from any notion of capital as a single magnitude. In the mid-1970s the approach to the controversy went through a further development. It was argued by its opponents (see, for instance, Hahn 1982) not only that Sraffian theory was ineffective as a critique of the up-to-date versions of mainstream economics, but also that it was just an application of the general equilibrium theory under special assumptions. This is the interpretation of Sraffa's book that still prevails in the literature.

To the list of factors which may account for the "fall from grace" of the Cambridge School, it must be added the change in the political climate whereby the ideological pendulum swung from government intervention to free market and liberalism, from the endorsement of the Welfare State and participation in mass movements of the late 1960s, to the encouragement of individualism and the philosophy of "homo faber fortunae suae" ("every man is the artisan of his own fortune") which characterized the age of President Reagan and Mrs Thatcher.

The sea-change may have been prompted by the economic facts of high inflation and high unemployment of the 1970s, which contradicted the trade-off between unemployment and inflation predicted by the Phillips curve and made Keynesian policy appear totally ineffective, but it had much deeper reasons which are beyond the scope of this paper (for an overview see Bateman et al. 2010).

In this critical impasse, its internal divisions did not help the cause of the Cambridge School, with the neo-Ricardians accusing the post-Keynesians of not having sufficiently shaken off certain neoclassical traits (for instance, acceptance of the inverse relationship – based on the marginal productivity of factors – between investment and the rate of interest, or between real wage and employment) and the post-Keynesians retorting that in Sraffa's system there is no room for money and uncertainty, which are the distinct features of a capitalist economy.

The Cambridge Tradition is Alive and Well

In spite of the loss of centrality in the academic world and the oblivion of the victories in the theoretical battle against neoclassical economics, it is not to be inferred that the Cambridge tradition is dead and buried. On the contrary, it is alive and kicking, as witnessed by the number of scientific societies which have Cambridge authors as their source of inspiration, by the great number of articles coming out that relate to the Cambridge School, either in choice of topic or approach, and by a sense of belonging, strongly felt by those who are committed to hold on to that heritage. Nowadays we can single out at least three research environments which purportedly draw and build upon what we have identified as the main threads of the Cambridge tradition, that is, the Marshallian, post-Keynesian and Sraffian approaches.

The tradition stemming from Marshall is enjoying a revival thanks to the work of a group of scholars bringing to light a conceptual tool of his analysis which has proved of great utility in interpreting the peculiarity of a contemporary economic phenomenon. Marshall's concept of "industrial district", discussed in book IV of the *Principles*, describing "the concentration of specialised industries in particular localities", pointed to a form of organization governed by trust and co-operation, which characterizes clusters of firms within well-defined regional boundaries in various parts of the world.

Becattini (1979), who was the first to apply this concept to explain the success stories of several industrial regions in Central Italy (mainly in the textile sector), provided the key idea that in order for an industrial district to rise and grow a congruence must be there between the organization of the production process and the social and cultural characteristics of the people involved in it. It is "the active presence of both a community of people and a population of firms in one naturally and historically bounded area" (Becattini 1990: 38) which provides the necessary ingredients. The district can be seen, then, as a relatively stable community which has evolved out of a strong local cultural identity and shared industrial expertise. (A recent assessment of the theoretical aspects of this literature can be found in Raffaelli et al. 2010.)

This attention to the social and historical embeddedness of the economic process within which firms operate is a far cry from the approach to industrial economics which has become fashionable nowadays (industrial organization and its focus on strategic interaction and incentives). Marshall's concern with the costs of coordination and the knowledge, skills and experience of the firm is a source of inspiration for those who are dissatisfied with formal production theory focusing on optimization. This is one of the areas in which the Cambridge School heritage has proved to be more fruitful.

Another and equally successful endorsement of the Marshallian apparatus draws on his evolutionary vision of the organic development of firms and society at large. Economic progress is seen as the cumulative result of increasing division of labour, of the development of specialized skills, knowledge and machinery and, at the same time, of the ability to coordinate them. Economic change is represented by concepts such as adaptive behaviour, variation and selection through industrial competition. The object of study is a population of firms, each different from the other and continuously evolving through interaction among themselves and with their social environment. Although this evolutionary approach is not unique to Marshall, having its recognized forefather in Schumpeter, several interesting research trends in cognitive and industrial economics have exploited the richness of this Marshallian tradition.

The idea that mental models matter in explaining economic processes, and the role of personal learning in the problem-solving process, together with the importance attached to the development of mental faculties – all of Marshallian ancestry (Egidi and Rizzello 2004) – are the basis of the cognitive approach to economics, which has grown into a specialized and successful discipline in recent years.

However, nowadays the best-known and most widespread approach in economics associated with the Cambridge School is post-Keynesianism, which emerged in the 1960s as a reaction against the "perversions of Keynes's original vision" (King 2003: xiv). In recent years the insights of Hyman Minsky into the causes of the financial meltdown have given more visibility and credibility to an approach which had always stressed the role of uncertainty, as well as the importance of money and income distribution in capitalist economies. The role of effective demand in generating employment, rejection of the idea that public investment crowds out private investment, the monetary nature of the interest rate, mistrust in the flexibility of prices as a way to redress fundamental market imbalances, and the importance of cost in generating inflation and of incomes policy in controlling it and fostering growth are the main ingredients of the post-Keynesian approach.

There is indeed variety within the group of post-Keynesians, in terms of emphasis and research agenda, while the (smaller) Sraffian group appears more cohesive and focused. It is for expository purposes that the division is made here between the two approaches, since many heterodox economists would see no contradiction in endorsing both.

Sraffa's research programme has been carried forward along three different lines. The first is investigation into the properties of the so-called "core", that is, the set of equations that determine long-period relative prices and the wage rate or rate of profit, under the assumption that outputs and the alternative techniques that produce them are given. The analytical complexities of the system when joint production is involved and/or the inputs include at least one natural resource have been explored. Another issue that drew the attention of Sraffian scholars is the convergence (or the non-explosive oscillations) of market prices to their long-run positions characterized by the uniformity of the profit rate. Important results have been reached in this field and the related literature is quite large (Kurz and Salvadori 1995; Chiodi and Ditta 2008).

The second line of research lies in the "closure of the system" or determination of the distributive variable which is assumed as given. The classical tradition of assuming constant real wage is rejected and attention is focused on the rate of profit. Two routes have been pursued here. One, following Pasinetti and his Cambridge growth equation, is to consider the rate of profit determined by the rate of growth of the system, which, in turn, depends on the investment decisions of capitalists. The other route, following Sraffa's suggestion, is to assume the rate of interest to be equal to the rate of profit (allowing for differences in liquidity and risks). In this way the possibility for monetary policy to impact on income distribution – a clear case of non-neutrality of money – is posited.

Note that the two lines of research described above well represent what Pasinetti has labelled the "separation theorem", that is, the division between "those investigations that concern the foundational bases of economic relations – to be detected at a strictly essential level of basic economic analysis – from those investigations that must be carried out at the level of the actual economic institutions" (Pasinetti 2007: 275). The separation concerns not only the objects, but the level of abstraction and generality that the analysis must and can achieve (Garegnani 2002).

The third line of research lies in a critique of general equilibrium theory in its more recent versions of temporal and intertemporal equilibrium, in order to show that even this version, with disaggregated capital endowments, is based on the notion of capital as a single magnitude and therefore falls under Sraffa's critique. The debate is still going on (Garegnani 2003; Schefold 2008).

We may conclude by saying that the Cambridge tradition has handed down to us a heritage resting on two pillars. The first is rejection of the "classical" conclusion that market forces are always at work to bring the economic system to full employment of resources, implicated by the belief that there is no discontinuity between individual and aggregate behaviour, so that what is good for a single player in the market is good for the whole. The second is the Sraffian theme that the market, taken as synonymous with supply and demand, is a misleading arena for representation of the rules of production and distribution. To accept being part of this tradition implies not only a commitment against the "free market" ideology but also the need to work strenuously towards an alternative theory, and indeed a better society.

MARIA CRISTINA MARCUZZO AND ANNALISA ROSSELLI

See also:

Business cycles and growth (III); Richard Ferdinand Kahn (I); Nicholas Kaldor (I); John Maynard Keynes (I); Keynesianism (II); Labour and employment (III); Macroeconomics (III); James Edward Meade (I); Money and banking (III); Post-Keynesianism (II); Joan Violet Robinson (I); Piero Sraffa (I); Uncertainty and information (III).

References and further reading

Bateman, B., T. Hirai and M.C. Marcuzzo (eds) (2010), 'Introduction', *The Return to Keynes*, Cambridge, MA: Harvard University Press.
Becattini, G. (1979), 'Dal "settore" industriale al "distretto" industriale: alcune considerazioni sull'unità d'indagine dell'economia industriale', *Rivista di economia e politica industriale*, **5** (1), 7–21.
Becattini, G. (1990), 'The Marshallian industrial district as a socio-economic notion', in F. Pike, G. Becattini and W. Sengenberger (eds), *Industrial Districts and Interfirm Cooperation in Italy*, Geneva: International Institute for Labor Studies, pp. 37–51.
Becattini, G. (2006), 'The Marshallian school of economics', in T. Raffaelli, G. Becattini and M. Dardi (eds), *The Elgar Companion to Alfred Marshall*, Cheltenham, UK and Northampton, MA, USA: Edward Elgar, pp. 664–71.
Bliss, C. (2010), 'The Cambridge post-Keynesians: an outsider's insider view', *History of Political Economy*, **42** (4), 631–52.
Chiodi, G. and L. Ditta (2008), *Sraffa or an Alternative Economics*, Basingstoke: Palgrave Macmillan.
Coats, A.W. (ed.) (1993), *The Sociology and Professionalization of Economics*, London: Routledge.
Desai, M. (1983), 'Fall from grace', *Times Literary Supplement*, 6 June.
Desai, M. and P. Ormerod (1998), 'Richard Goodwin: a short appreciation', *Economic Journal*, **108** (450), 1431–5.
Egidi, M. and S. Rizzello (2004), 'Cognitive economics: foundations and historical roots', in M. Egidi and S. Rizzello (eds), *Cognitive Economics*, Cheltenham, UK and Northampton, MA, USA: Edward Elgar, pp. 1–22.
Garegnani, P. (2002), 'Misunderstanding classical economics? A reply to Blaug', *History of Political Economy*, **34** (1), 241–54.
Garegnani, P. (2003), 'Savings, investment and capital in a system of general intertemporal equilibrium', with two appendices and a mathematical note by M. Tucci, in F. Petri and F. Hahn (eds), *General Equilibrium. Problems and Prospects*, London: Routledge, pp. 117–75.
Goodwin, R.M. (1967), 'A growth cycle', in C.H. Feinstein (ed.), *Socialism, Capitalism and Economic Growth*, Cambridge: Cambridge University Press, pp. 54–8.
Groenewegen, P. (1995), *A Soaring Eagle: Alfred Marshall 1842–1924*, Aldershot, UK and Brookfield, VT, USA: Edward Elgar.
Hahn, F.H. (1982), 'The neo-Ricardians', *Cambridge Journal of Economics*, **6** (4), 353–74.
Harcourt, G (2006), *The Structure of Post-Keynesian Economics*, Cambridge: Cambridge University Press.
Higgs, H. (1897), *The Physiocrats*, reprinted 2001, Kitchener, Ontario: Batoche Books.
Kahn, R.F. (1989), *The Economics of the Short Period*, London, Macmillan.
Kaldor, N. (1956), 'Alternative theories of distribution', *Review of Economic Studies*, **23** (2), 83–100.
Keynes, J.M. (1971–89), *The Collected Writings of John Maynard Keynes*, edited by E. Johnson and D.E. Moggridge, London: Macmillan:
    Vol. IV: *A Tract on Monetary Reform* [1923], 1973.
    Vol. V: *A Treatise on Money: I. The Pure Theory of Money* [1930], 1971.
    Vol. VI: *A Treatise on Money: II. The Applied Theory of Money* [1930], 1971.
    Vol. VII: *The General Theory of Employment, Interest and Money* [1936], 1973.
    Vol. VIII: *A Treatise on Probability* [1921], 1973.
    Vol. XII: *Economic Articles and Correspondence: Investment and Editorial*, 1983.
    Vol. XIV: *The General Theory and After. Part II: Defence and Development*, 1973.
King, J. (2003), 'Introduction' to J.E. King (ed.), *The Elgar Companion to Post Keynesian Economics*, Cheltenham, UK and Northampton, MA, USA: Edward Elgar.
Kurz, H. and N. Salvadori (1995), *Theory of Production. A Long-Period Analysis*, Cambridge: Cambridge University Press.

Marcuzzo, M.C. and A. Rosselli (eds) (2005), *Economists in Cambridge: A Study through the Correspondence, 1907–46*, Abingdon: Routledge.

Marcuzzo, M.C., N. Naldi, A. Rosselli and E. Sanfilippo (2008), 'Cambridge as a place in economics', *History of Political Economy*, **40** (4), 569–94.

Marshall, A. (1885), 'The present position of economics', in A.C. Pigou (ed.) (1925), *Memorials of Alfred Marshall*, London: Macmillan.

Marshall, A. (1920), *Principles of Economics*, 8th edn, London: Macmillan.

Palley, T. (2003), 'Income distribution' in J.E. King (ed.), *The Elgar Companion to Post Keynesian Economics*, Cheltenham, UK and Northampton, MA, USA: Edward Elgar, pp. 283–7.

Panico, C. (2003), 'Growth and income distribution', in J.E. King (ed), *The Elgar Companion to Post Keynesian Economics*, Cheltenham, UK and Northampton, MA, USA: Edward Elgar, pp. 264–71.

Pasinetti, L. (1960), 'A mathematical formulation of the Ricardian system', *Review of Economic Studies*, **27** (2), 78–98.

Pasinetti, L. (2007), *Keynes and the Cambridge Keynesians. A 'Revolution in Economics' to be Accomplished*, Cambridge: Cambridge University.

Patinkin, D. and J.C. Leith (eds) (1977), *Keynes, Cambridge and the General Theory*, London: Macmillan.

Pigou, A.C. (ed.) (1925), *Memorials of Alfred Marshall*, London: Macmillan.

Pigou, A.C. (1950), *Keynes's General Theory. A Retrospective View*, London: Macmillan.

Raffaelli, T. (2004), 'Whatever happened to Marshall's industrial economics?', *European Journal of the History of Economic Thought*, **11** (2), 209–29.

Raffaelli, T., T. Nishizawa and S. Cook (eds) (2010), *Marshall, Marshallians and Industrial Economics*, Abingdon: Routledge.

Robertson, D.H. (1930), 'The trees of the forest', *Economic Journal*, **40** (157), 80–89.

Robinson, J. (1954), 'The production function and the theory of capital', reprinted 1964 in *Collected Economic Papers*, vol. 2, Oxford: Blackwell, pp. 114–31.

Robinson, J. (1956), *The Accumulation of Capital*, London: Macmillan.

Robinson, J. (1969), *The Economics of Imperfect Competition*, 2nd edn, London: Macmillan.

Robinson, J. (1973), 'Preface', in J.A. Kregel, *The Reconstruction of Political Economy: An Introduction to Post-Keynesian Economics*, London: Macmillan, pp. ix–xiii.

Robinson, J. (1979), 'Michal Kalecki', in J. Robinson, *Collected Economic Papers*, vol. 5, Oxford: Blackwell, pp. 184–96.

Schefold, B. (2008), 'Savings, investment and capital in a system of general intertemporal equilibrium – an extended comment on Garegnani with a note on Parinello', in G. Chiodi and L. Ditta (eds), *Sraffa or an Alternative Economics*, Basingstoke: Macmillan, pp. 127–84.

Schumpeter, J. (1954), *The History of Economic Analysis*, Oxford: Oxford University Press.

Shove, G.F. (1930), 'The representative firm and increasing returns', *Economic Journal*, **40** (157), 94–116.

Sraffa, P. (1925), 'Sulle relazioni fra costo and quantità prodotta', *Annali di Economia*, **2**, 277–328.

Sraffa, P. (1926), 'The laws of returns under competitive conditions', *Economic Journal*, **36** (144), 535–50.

Sraffa, P. (1951), 'Introduction', in D. Ricardo, *Principles of Political Economy and Taxation*, ed. P. Sraffa with the collaboration of M.H. Dobb, *Works and Correspondence of David Ricardo*, vol. 1, Cambridge: Cambridge University Press, pp. xiii–lxii.

Sraffa, P. (1960), *Production of Commodities by Means of Commodities*, Cambridge: Cambridge University Press.

Thirlwall, A.P. (2003), 'Kaldorian economics', in J.E. King (ed.), *The Elgar Companion to Post Keynesian Economics*, Cheltenham, UK and Northampton, MA, USA: Edward Elgar, pp. 338–43.

Tribe, K. (2000), 'The Cambridge Economics Tripos 1903–55 and the training of economists', *Manchester School*, **68** (2), 222–48.

Stockholm (Swedish) School

The label Stockholm School refers to a group of Swedish economists who, between 1927 and 1939, developed dynamic methods for macroeconomic analysis. The most prominent members of the school were Erik Lindahl (1891–1960), Gunnar Myrdal (1898–1987), Bertil Ohlin (1899–1979) and Erik Lundberg (1907–1987). Important contributions were also made by Alf Johansson (1901–1981), Dag Hammarskjöld (1905–1961) and Ingvar Svennilson (1908–1972). The trademarks of the Stockholm School are the use of sequence analysis and the twin concept of *ex ante/ex post* to explore the formation of expectations and coordination of incongruent plans through adjustments of prices and quantities in interdependent markets.

The school label came into international circulation through Ohlin's "Some notes on the Stockholm theory of savings and investment" (1937), a critical review of Keynes's *General Theory* (1936) from the vantage point of contemporaneous Swedish macro-economics. The article, published in the *Economic Journal*, was a reaction to the lecture "My grounds for departure from orthodox economic traditions" that Keynes had given at Stockholm in October 1936, on invitation from the local Political Economy Club (Henriksson 1991: 41). Half a century later, the club secretary remembered that:

> [i]t was certainly a remarkable event when the great prophet came to Stockholm pretending that he had seen a new light, only to be taken down by the Swedish youngsters – Myrdal and Ohlin were around thirty-five, Hammarskjöld thirty, Lundberg and Svennilson under thirty – who told him that he was rather old-fashioned, that the Swedish economists had gone much further, and that his, Keynes's, very method, the equilibrium method, was unsuitable for the treatment of dynamic problems. (Cederwall 1991: 76)

In his article, Ohlin presented this critique as a coherent body of research that he named the "Stockholm school of thought" (1937: 57).

Most of Ohlin's colleagues were quick to point out that they did not consider themselves to be members of any school – "in the case of Gunnar Myrdal not of the same school as Bertil Ohlin at least" (Jonung 1991: 7) – and that Lindahl, the senior of the circle, was not based in Stockholm. Lundberg (1994: 491, original emphasis) observed that "[t]he view that the Stockholm School was and is a *myth* is, surely, generally accepted". Yet, he also pointed out that "[e]ven a myth has its real base: the myth may become at least as real as reality itself" (ibid.). The following account of the Stockholm School's development will demonstrate that, in spite of large differences between the approaches and positions of its members, there was enough common substance to warrant the school label. The chronological order of the main contributions coincides largely with the logical sequences in the development of dynamic methods and proposals for macroeconomic stabilization policies (see Ohlin 1937; Hansson 1982; Lundberg 1996: 19–37).

On the Shoulders of Wicksell and Cassel

The formation of the Stockholm School was strongly influenced by works of Knut Wicksell and Gustav Cassel, the key figures in the prior generation of Swedish economists. Wicksell's *Interest and Prices* (1898 [1936]), with its theory of cumulative changes in the price level, opened an avenue for thinking about macroeconomic dynamics, while Cassel's *Theory of Social Economy* (1918 [1923]) provided the starting point. In 1927 Cassel's student Myrdal published his doctoral dissertation on *The Problem of Price Formation and the Factor of Change* – a work frequently cited, but never translated. In its first part, Myrdal (1927: 25–7) criticized Cassel's general equilibrium analysis for neglecting the influence of "anticipations of future events" on the formation of prices, capital values and investment plans. He acknowledged that Marshall (1916: bk V) had taken expectations into account, when he attempted to construct a dynamic theory of long-run equilibrium. Yet he rejected Marshall's postulate of the fulfillment of "the expectations in the long run", as it ignored the problem of demonstrating how markets coordinate plans that are based on subjective risk valuations. In a similar vein, Myrdal criticized Irving Fisher for reducing risk considerations in the capitalization of income to objective probabilities, and Frank Knight for failing to integrate his subtler distinctions between risk and uncertainty into a theory of price formation (1927: 104–9). In the second part of his dissertation, Myrdal provided a sophisticated classification of risks in order to describe how subjective valuations of objective probabilities influence the profit expectations and investment plans of entrepreneurs. In the last part, Myrdal emphasized that general equilibrium cannot be determined on the base of given consumer preferences, production technology and factor endowments alone. Expectations of future changes need to be included into the data-set, as they affect the equilibrium position of the system before the changes actually take place.

Myrdal's approach met with a fundamental critique from young Lundberg, who was a student of both Cassel and Myrdal at the University of Stockholm. In an article "On the concept of economic equilibrium", which was based on his licentiate thesis, Lundberg (1930 [1994]: 35) pointed out that expectations of price changes are not independent of the given price structure, "except when changes are wholly exogenous to the economic context". He argued that Myrdal, moreover, had failed to show how a general equilibrium would develop from a market constellation with incongruent expectations. If, on the other hand, "individuals' expectations are 'rational', in the sense that they are realized", the analysis would not supersede Cassel's static theory. "By assuming that the time distance does not have any effect, the time element . . . is eliminated" (Lundberg 1930 [1994]: 34).

Lundberg's early use of the notion of "rational expectations" is noteworthy. Yet it was Lindahl who gave it a precise meaning by examining the conditions under which "the individual anticipations of coming price developments are to a certain extent the causes of the actual developments themselves" (1939: 147). In his "Place of capital in the theory of price" (1929a), translated in his *Studies in the Theory of Money and Capital* (1939: pt III), Lindahl addressed "the problem of price formation" by taking "into account some of the complications due to the existence of a time factor in production, i.e. to the complex of problems where the theory of capital and interest and the general theory of price meet" (1939: 271). The valuation of capital goods was clearly a Wicksellian theme, but Lindahl was critical of the Böhm-Bawerkian approach used by Wicksell. He started, like Myrdal (1927), from the static Walras–Cassel system, but used a different track for its extension to dynamics. He subdivided the "dynamic process" of price changes into a sequence of moving equilibrium states, defined by equality of supply and demand in the final goods markets during the corresponding periods:

In order to analyse such a dynamic process, we imagine it to be subdivided into periods of time so short that the factors directly affecting prices, and therefore also the prices themselves, can be regarded as unchanged in each period. All such changes are therefore assumed to take place at the transition points between periods. (Lindahl 1939: 158)

The first exposition of Stockholm-style sequence analysis is thus found in Lindahl (1929a), where the examination of the "pricing problem" proceeded step by step from perfect foresight and stationary conditions to imperfect foresight and dynamic conditions. In this context, Lindahl (1929a) made essential contributions to the concepts of intertemporal equilibrium and temporary equilibrium, independently of Hayek (1928) and prior to Hicks (1939), even though he did not use these terms at the time (see Kurz and Salvadori 1995: 456–58). Intertemporal equilibrium is characterized by the correct anticipation of all changes at transition points, such that the prices, quantities and interest rates of all periods are simultaneously determined. This construction was just an intermittent step from static to dynamic analysis in "approximation to reality", so Lindahl (1929a: s. 4) relaxed the assumption of perfect foresight and discussed changes in intertemporal price relations that are connected with unforeseen gains and losses and subsequent shifts of budget constraints. Assuming that the unforeseen changes occur at the transition points between the periods, Lindahl (1929a) described the latter as temporary equilibria.

In his classic essay on "The means of monetary policy", included as "The rate of interest and the price level" in the *Studies* (1939: pt 2), Lindahl took the temporary-equilibrium method to its limits by applying it to a generalization of Wicksell's (1898 [1936]) theory of cumulative inflation and deflation. The essay was the sequel to a (hitherto untranslated) monograph on *The Ends of Monetary Policy* (1929b), in which Lindahl argued that "rational monetary policy" should follow two principles: the authorities ought to publicize and follow a clear norm for monetary policy, so as to inspire trust in credit and other economic relations that take time; and the norm should be chosen so as to minimize the deviations between intended and actual outcomes of all monetary transactions. A credible strategy along these lines would facilitate the formation of rational expectations in the markets (see Boianovsky and Trautwein 2006: 886–8). As an example, Lindahl (1929b) presented Wicksell's norm of price-level stabilization, by which monetary authorities ought to vary interest rates so as to control inflation.

In *The Means of Monetary Policy*, Lindahl (1930 [1939]) reversed the procedure. Like Wicksell (1898 [1936]), he chose the setting of a completely centralized pure credit economy, in which the central bank sets the level of interest rates autonomously. Lindahl explored "the cumulative process caused by lowering or raising the level of interest rates" (1939: ch. 2) in different scenarios, varying the assumptions about the states of information (perfect, imperfect foresight) and expectations (static, adaptive, forward-looking), the degrees of unemployment, capacity utilization and investment irreversibility in different sectors, and the structure of interest rates. Each scenario was analysed "as a series of temporary equilibria, between which there occur unforeseen events with consequent gains and losses" (Lindahl 1939: 11). The immediate result of an unexpected lowering of the interest rate is an increase in all capital values, greater for long-term investments and smaller for short-term investments. In the following periods markets would clear, but not always at the expected prices. The size and distribution of gains and losses is determined by the constellation of assumptions that defines the scenarios. In cases of unemployed resources in the capital goods industries the gains from a lowering of the level of interest rates would be greatest, as it tends to generate a rise in total real income through a sustainable expansion of credit and production. Wicksell (1898 [1936]), on the other hand, had based his scenario of an upward cumulative process on the assumptions of full employment and "non-rigid investment periods". In this setting, a credit expansion triggers inflation and a redistribution of purchasing power from earners of fixed incomes towards entrepreneurs. Adhering to the neutrality postulates of the quantity theory, Wicksell (1898 [1936]) had asserted that total real income would not change. This is not necessarily the case in Lindahl's theory, where the windfall profits from inflation are described as "unplanned saving" of entrepreneurs. As the latters' propensity to save and invest is normally higher than average, they tend to plough back windfall profits into further investment, thus enlarging the capital stock and increasing total real income until a final equilibrium is reached in which planned saving equals investment.

Lindahl (1930 [1939]) was nevertheless critical of policy strategies that attempt to exploit this redistributive income mechanism. He was convinced that people would learn from their inflation experience, such that the state of expectations would turn from static to adaptive and even forward-looking. In the end, inflation might accelerate to the extent that it would become "necessary to arrest the movement before the amount of capital appropriate to the lower rate of interest has been accumulated" (1939: 182–3). In contrast with much of modern mainstream macroeconomics, Lindahl considered rational expectations to be endogenous, both to inflation and to credible anti-inflation policies. He was also critical of Wicksell's concept of a "natural or real rate of interest" and demonstrated that, outside a one-good economy, "the real rate of interest does not depend only on technical conditions, but also on the price situation, and cannot be regarded as existing independently of the loan rate of interest" (1939: 248). Based on his concept of capital as present value of expected, risk-adjusted income flows, Lindahl concluded that the "real rate of interest on capital", defined as the prospective profit rate, "has a tendency to adjust itself to the actual loan rate of interest in every period" (1939: 249). This raised the question, however, which level of interest rates the central bank should target. Lindahl (1930 [1939]: 252) finally arrived at the definition of a "normal" or "neutral rate of interest" that brings investment in line with planned saving. It "does not necessarily imply an unchanged price level, but rather such a development of prices that is in accordance with the expectations of the public".

In an additional note to the 1939 translation of the 1930 essay, Lindahl qualified his views on the cumulative process and the neutral rate of interest. In closer connection with Wicksell's original approach, he now argued that, compared to his earlier temporary-equilibrium approach, a sequence analysis, "by which economic processes are regarded as series of successive *disequilibria*, must undoubtedly be held to be more generally applicable" (1939: 260–61, emphasis added). Lindahl also acknowledged that prospective profit rates could systematically differ from the actual loan rates of interest, and that the normal rate of interest (capital market equilibrium) is not necessarily neutral with regard to the expectations of the public, the distribution of income or the volume of production. In all this, Lindahl explicitly reacted to Myrdal's critique of his 1930 essay.

In the 1931 volume of *Ekonomisk Tidskrift* (now the *Scandinavian Journal of Economics*), Myrdal published a long article "On the theoretical concept of monetary equilibrium", advertised by its subtitle as "a study of the 'normal rate of interest' in Wicksell's monetary theory". A more widely read German version appeared in 1933 in an anthology edited by Friedrich A. Hayek; it was translated into English and published as a monograph in 1939. Together with Lindahl's *Studies* (1939), Myrdal's *Monetary Equilibrium* (1939) has come to be regarded as a landmark contribution to the macroeconomics of the Stockholm School. The Swedish version contains a critique of Lindahl (1930 [1939]), through which Myrdal attempted to reconstruct Wicksell's concepts of monetary equilibrium and cumulative processes by way of immanent criticism. The German and English versions were largely cleared of critical comments on Lindahl and presented as an extension of the dissertation project, intended "to include anticipations in the monetary system" (Myrdal 1939: 32; cf. Hansson 1982: ch. 6).

Myrdal (1931) examined the three conditions by which Wicksell (1898 [1936]) had defined monetary equilibrium: "The 'normal rate of interest' must . . . (1) equal the marginal technical productivity of real capital (i.e. the 'real' or 'natural' rate of interest); (2) equate the supply of and demand for savings; and, finally, (3) guarantee a stable price level" (Myrdal 1939: 37–8). Myrdal went even further than Lindahl in demonstrating that Wicksell's conditions were either imprecise (2) or false (1 and 3). He showed that Wicksell's notion of a natural rate of interest was incompatible with his assumptions of a credit economy and of innovations as causes of the shifts in the "yield of real capital" that generate cumulative inflation. In a non-stationary monetary economy, the yield of real capital includes expectations about money prices and loan rates of interest. Hence, changes in the levels of prices and interest rates feed back to the yield of real capital in terms of prospective profitability. Myrdal (1931 [1939]: 84–97) accordingly redefined the equilibrium rate of interest as the rate at which the "cost of production of new investment" equals "free capital disposal" in terms of "savings proper" and "value change defined as anticipated depreciation minus appreciation" of the investment in question. The equality of the value of real capital and its costs of reproduction implies the equality of investment and saving. In this way, Myrdal's definition of monetary equilibrium essentially anticipated the formulation of Tobin's q.

Another innovation of Myrdal's study helped to make the analysis of cumulative processes more operational by describing them in terms of balanced bookkeeping. This innovation, which was more clearly developed in the German version (1931 [1933]), was the distinction between *ex ante* and *ex post*, i.e. between expected and realized values, or between plans and outcomes (1939: 45–7, 116–25). If the *ex post* values correspond to the *ex ante* values, the economy is in a state of monetary equilibrium; if they do not, unplanned adjustments of prices, quantities and the capital stock take place, eventually amounting to a cumulative process. Myrdal (1931 [1939]) criticized Lindahl (1930 [1994]) for being unable to analyse such out-of-equilibrium adjustments. Myrdal's own treatment of cumulative processes was largely limited to verbal conjectures about the "inner mechanics of the depressive process", induced by a tightening of the credit conditions (1931 [1939]: 164–9). Yet his *ex ante/ex post* terminology stimulated formal exercises in disequilibrium analysis, carried out by Hammarskjöld (1933), Lundberg (1937) and Svennilson (1938) in their doctoral dissertations, and by Lindahl in preparation of his *Studies* (1939). Despite the differences in publication dates, these works were essentially composed and discussed between 1932 and 1935.

Further Explorations in Sequence Analysis

Hammarskjöld made two important contributions to sequence analysis. The first was his "Outline of an algebraic method for dynamic price analysis" (1932), the second his doctoral dissertation on "The transmission of economic fluctuations" (1933); none of them was ever translated into English. Hammarskjöld (1932: 171–6) was very critical of Myrdal's (1931 [1939]) definition of monetary equilibrium and based his "algebraic method" on Lindahl's (1929a [1939]) temporary-equilibrium approach. Yet he translated Myrdal's critique of Lindahl into a "continuation analysis", by which consecutive periods of the dynamic process are explicitly linked through the reactions of economic agents to changes in their respective "strategic factor". The strategic factor for the firms is their net profit, and – in the perspective of Hammarskjöld in particular, and the Stockholm School in general – the entrepreneurs as leaders of the firms are the key agents in the system. Hence, (unexpected) windfall profits are the strategic factor in the system, which in Myrdalian terms could now be described as the discrepancy between the *ex ante* and *ex post* values of the same variable. The changes in plans and uses of windfall profits, which Hammarskjöld captured through reaction functions, provide the links between the periods, within which the plans are coordinated through market processes (see Lindahl 1939: 152; Hansson 1982: 157–66).

At the microeconomic level, and closer to Myrdal (1927, 1931 [1939]), Svennilson (1938) used sequence analysis to discuss the typical firm's intertemporal planning under risk. His focus was set on developing a toolkit of formal concepts of probability and constrained optimization in the short term and the long, rather than on providing a theory of coordination (see Siven 1991). Svennilson's dissertation, too, remained untranslated.

Lundberg's dissertation was directly published in English. His *Studies in the Theory of Economic Expansion* (1937) are generally regarded as the peak in Stockholm-style sequence analysis. The core part of the book is chapter 9, "The construction of model sequences", where Lundberg (1937: 183) declared:

> The subject of our analysis is an economic system during a period of expansion . . . Production, consumption, income, savings, and investments are all increasing at certain rates, and we ask whether this growth can continue in some sort of dynamic equilibrium, or whether discrepancies must automatically come into being within the system itself, which have the tendency to interrupt the process. The conditions for continued growth may not be reconcilable to the cumulative effects of the expansion during previous periods. . . Cassel's simple assumption of a [uniformly progressive economy] is hence viewed as a problem to be investigated.

Lundberg (1937: 185, 240) formalized Cassel's conditions for steady-state growth, clearly anticipating the core of the Harrod and Domar growth models by several years (see Berg 1991). He employed these conditions as benchmarks for the construction of numerical model sequences, in which he first used multiplier analysis with exogenous investment and the famous Lundberg-lag, then sequences in which the multiplier interacts with accelerators related to variations of inventories and investments in fixed capital, and finally sequences in which investment is endogenous to a variable rate of interest. Lundberg reconstructed Wicksell's cumulative process as a general framework of disequilibrium sequence analysis, in which he nested Keynesian "oversaving" as well as Hayekian "undersaving" sequences. Even though he was well versed in mathematics and used systems of difference equations for his dynamic analysis, he did not attempt a formal generalization of his approach. This was done in a reduced fashion in 1939, when "Harvard professor Alvin Hansen gave a talented young student with mathematical skills the assignment to formalize Lundberg's argument. The student, 23 years of age, was Paul Samuelson, and the result was the famous article about the interaction between the multiplier and the accelerator that led to Samuelson's international breakthrough" (Lindbeck and Persson 1990: 276, author's translation).

Lindahl (1939: pt 1) had the final word about sequence analysis in the era of the Stockholm School, at least in terms of the publication date. It has already been mentioned that his methodological focus had turned from temporary equilibria to disequilibria after 1930. While he had earlier assumed that markets clear within all periods, though not always at the expected prices, he now favoured an approach in which "no price movements occur during the periods themselves" (Lindahl 1939: 61), while quantities adjust to unforeseen events. Excess demands and supplies manifest themselves in unplanned orders and inventories of producers and traders, who will then change prices between the periods. While Lundberg (1937) had taken sequence analysis to a general framework for casuistic modelling, Lindahl (1939: pt 1) offered the nucleus of a general theory of out-of-equilibrium dynamics, based on a systematic comparison of the different approaches to dynamic theory developed in the Stockholm School, to which he appended an "algebraic discussion of the relations between some fundamental concepts", both at micro- and macroeconomic levels. The ground for this formalization was laid by a "Note on the dynamic pricing problem", which he had circulated in 1934 (see Steiger 1971: 204–11). Upon a visit at the London School of Economics in the same year, Lindahl and his note had made an impression on John Hicks, inspiring him to develop his concept of temporary equilibrium in *Value and Capital* (1939). Hicks and his wife Ursula also cooperated with Lindahl in the publication of the latter's *Studies*, which were published simultaneously (see Hicks 1991).

Impact on Concepts of Economic Policy

The members of the Stockholm School were not only involved in the development of dynamic theory; they were also engaged in designing policy strategies for macroeconomic stabilization. With the exception of Lundberg (who studied in the USA at the time), all of them worked for the governmental Committee on Unemployment in the years between 1927 until 1935 (see Wadensjö 1991). The committee and its publication series provided a forum for their theoretical and political discourse. All members of the Stockholm School wrote, moreover, memoranda and reports for the central bank, the ministry of finance, the League of Nations and many other political institutions at domestic and international levels. This forced them to form expert opinions on how to solve the macroeconomic problems connected with the Great Depression in the early 1930s. Among the many contributions made by Stockholm School members in this context, four are especially noteworthy.

The first contribution is Lindahl's persistent struggle for price-level stabilization as adviser to the central bank (see Boianovsky and Trautwein 2006). Even though he personally favoured nominal GDP targeting (Lindahl 1929b, 1939: 223–44), he supported the shift from exchange-rate targeting to price-level targeting when Sweden went off the gold standard in 1931. He did this mainly for pragmatic reasons, as national accounting was not yet developed. In Lindahl's view, setting the focus on the general price index, which he helped to develop and maintain, was more operational for anchoring the inflation expectations of the public. The Riksbank was the first central bank in history to control inflation by such a strategy. At the same time, Lindahl's work on concepts of estimating national income, which was closely related to his work on monetary economics and dynamic analysis, laid some grounds for social accounting theory (Lindahl 1937).

The second contribution is the concept of countercyclical fiscal policy, which Lindahl and Myrdal developed between 1930 and 1935. They argued that monetary policy would not always be sufficient for stabilizing the economy, when interest rates failed to coordinate saving and investment. In a section later omitted from the English translation, Lindahl (1930: 63–8) discussed strategies of stabilization by variations of public revenues and expenditures. In a memorandum on *The Economic Effects of Fiscal Policy*, Myrdal (1934) outlined a strategy of countercyclical fiscal policy that would balance the public budget over the business cycle instead of each and every fiscal year. Lindahl (1935 [1939]: 351–82) showed how macroeconomic stabilization and fiscal soundness could be made compatible and operational as principles for balancing the budget.

The third contribution is Ohlin's work on aggregate income mechanisms and an employment norm for economic policy. Among his publications on these issues, his report on *Monetary Policy, Public Works, Subsidies and Tariff Policy as Remedies for Unemployment* (1934) stands out, together with an article "On the formulation of monetary theory" (1933, translated 1978). Ohlin rejected the approaches of Lindahl and Myrdal, who interpreted Wicksell's cumulative process as a failure of the interest-rate mechanism to coordinate intertemporal plans. In his view, Wicksell's achievement was to describe imbalances of aggregate demand and supply. These need not be caused by interest-rate gaps; they could also be generated by autonomous changes in consumption, both private and public. Ohlin (1933 [1978]: 368–80) argued that such impulses induce changes in investment demand which generate the levels of output and income that *ex post* bring saving in line with investment. Contrary to the clichés of political geography, Ohlin, a liberal by conviction and affiliation (later to become opposition leader in the Swedish parliament), favoured the minimization of unemployment as a norm for monetary policy (see Wadensjö 1991), whereas this norm was criticized by Myrdal, the social democrat, because it would lead to unintended "cumulative price movements . . . or else require quite extensive public regulations of markets" (Myrdal 1939: 195–6). Ohlin and Myrdal agreed nevertheless on the uses of fiscal policies for counteracting contractions of aggregate demand. "Myrdal and Ohlin were quite effective in showing that no 'crowding out' need follow an increase in the government budget deficit, provided an accommodating monetary policy was adopted" (Lundberg 1996: 32).

Finally, these positions were supported by Alf Johansson's *Wage Changes and Unemployment* (1934), which showed – with reference to the depression in the early 1920s – that wage cuts are not a safe remedy for curing depressions. They tend to reduce aggregate demand and to make depressions even worse by their negative effects on expected profits and investment. Both Johansson and Ohlin combined elements of multiplier and accelerator analysis, but did not contribute to the debates about dynamic method.

Looking back on the achievements of the Swedish economists between 1930 and 1935, it should not be surprising that Keynes failed to make much of an impression on them in October 1936. They found his *General Theory* less general than their own work and his conclusions nested in their own approaches. Since then, there have been debates again and again, to which extent the Stockholm School anticipated the core ideas of Keynes's *General Theory* (see Lundberg 1996: 19–37). There are similarities in the rejection of the "classical" concepts of a natural rate of interest, the stability of full-employment equilibrium and strictly balanced public budgets. However, as Lundberg (1996: 36) summarized it:

> [T]he Swedish economists focused on the dynamics of expansion and contraction, whilst Keynes concentrated mainly on those factors that determined an under-employment equilibrium. Furthermore, the economists of the Stockholm School also dealt with the analysis of booms, with supply constraints during periods of expansion and with period-to-period dynamics of contraction.

Many of the Swedish insights were complementary to Keynesian theory and became standard fare in macroeconomics. The label of the Stockholm School faded away, because it was never a school in the sense of a unifying "core model" or body of doctrines. Its members had a common research agenda in terms of dynamic theory and stabilization policy. But they had a tendency of agreeing to disagree in order to expand the scope of their analysis. Furthermore, their discourse ended in the second half of the 1930s, when all of them, except Lindahl, left academia, and in some cases even the country. They went into applied research, administration and politics. Some of them made impressive careers, such as Dag Hammarskjöld, who became UN General Secretary. Others, such as Ohlin and Myrdal, received Nobel Prizes – although not essentially for their contributions to the economics of the Stockholm School.

Hans-Michael Trautwein

See also:

Gustav Cassel (I); Erik Lindahl (I); Keynesianism (II); Macroeconomics (III); Gunnar Myrdal (I); Knut Wicksell (I).

References and further reading

Berg, C. (1991), 'Lundberg, Keynes, and the riddles of a general theory', in L. Jonung (ed.), *The Stockholm School Revisited*, Cambridge: Cambridge University Press, pp. 205–28.
Boianovsky, M. and H.-M. Trautwein (2006), 'Price expectations, capital accumulation and employment: Lindahl's macroeconomics from the 1920s to the 1950s', *Cambridge Journal of Economics*, **30**, 881–900.
Cassel, G. (1918), *Theoretische Sozialökonomie*, Leipzig: C.F. Winter, English trans. 1923, *The Theory of Social Economy*, London: Ernest Benn.
Cederwall, G. (1991), 'Comment on Henriksson', in L. Jonung (ed.), *The Stockholm School Revisited*, Cambridge: Cambridge University Press, pp. 74–77.
Hammarskjöld, D. (1932), 'Utkast till en algebraisk metod för dynamisk prisanalys', *Ekonomisk tidskrift*, **34**, 157–76.
Hammarskjöld, D. (1933), *Konjunkturspridningen: en teoretisk och historisk undersökning*, Arbetslöshetsutredningens Betänkande I, bilagor, vol. 1; Statens Offentliga Utredningar 1933: 29, Stockholm: P.A. Norstedt.
Hansson, B. (1982), *The Stockholm School and the Development of Dynamic Method*, London: Croom Helm.
Hayek, F.A. (1928), 'Das intertemporale Gleichgewichtssystem der Preise und die Bewegungen des "Geldwertes"', *Weltwirtschaftliches Archiv*, **28** (2), 33–76, English trans. 'Intertemporal price equilibrium and movement in the value of money', in R. McCloughry (ed.) (1928), *Money, Capital and Fluctuations. Early Essays*, London: Routledge & Kegan Paul, pp. 71–117.

Henriksson, R. (1991), 'The Political Economy Club and the Stockholm School, 1917–51', in L. Jonung (ed.), *The Stockholm School Revisited*, Cambridge: Cambridge University Press, pp. 41–74.

Hicks, J. (1939), *Value and Capital*, Oxford: Clarendon Press.

Hicks, J. (1991), 'The Swedish influence on *Value and Capital*', in L. Jonung (ed.), *The Stockholm School Revisited*, Cambridge: Cambridge University Press, pp. 369–76.

Johansson, A. (1934), *Löneutveckling och arbetslösheten*, Arbetslöshetsutredningens betänkande II, bilagor, vol. 3 Statens Offentliga Utredningar 1934:2, Stockholm: P.A. Norstedt.

Jonung, L. (ed.) (1991), *The Stockholm School Revisited*, Cambridge: Cambridge University Press.

Keynes, J.M. (1936), *The General Theory of Employment, Interest and Money*, London: Macmillan.

Kurz, H.D. and N. Salvadori (1995), *Theory of Production. A Long-Period Analysis*, Cambridge: Cambridge University Press.

Lindahl, E. (1929a), 'Prisbildningsproblemets uppläggning från kapitalteoretisk synpunkt', *Ekonomisk Tidskrift*, **31**, 31–81, English trans., 'The place of capital in the theory of price', in E. Lindahl (1939), *Studies in the Theory of Money and Capital*, London: Allen & Unwin, pt 3.

Lindahl, E. (1929b), *Penningpolitikens Mål*, Malmö: Förlagsaktiebolaget.

Lindahl, E. (1930), *Penningpolitikens Medel*, Malmö: Förlagsaktiebolaget; English trans. 'The rate of interest and the price level', in E. Lindahl (1939), *Studies in the Theory of Money and Capital*, London: Allen & Unwin, pt II.

Lindahl, E. (1934), 'A note on the dynamic pricing problem', in O. Steiger (1971), *Studien zur Entstehung der Neuen Wirtschaftslehre in Schweden. Eine Anti-Kritik*, Berlin: Duncker & Humblot, pp. 204–11.

Lindahl, E. (1935), 'The problem of balancing the budget', in E. Lindahl (1939), *Studies in the Theory of Money and Capital*, London: Allen & Unwin, pp. 351–84.

Lindahl, E. (1937), 'National income. The concept and methods of estimation', in E. Lindahl, E. Dahlgren and K. Kock, *National Income of Sweden, 1861–1930*, London: P.S. King, pp. 1–25.

Lindahl, E. (1939), *Studies in the Theory of Money and Capital*. London: Allen & Unwin.

Lindbeck, A. and M. Persson (1990), 'Erik Lundberg', in C. Jonung and A.-C. Ståhlberg (eds), *Ekonomporträtt*, Stockholm: SNS förlag, pp. 273–85.

Lundberg, E. (1930), 'Om begreppet ekonomisk jämvikt och dess tillämpning', *Ekonomisk Tidskrift*, **32**, 133–60, English trans. 'On the concept of economic equilibrium', in E. Lundberg (1994), *Studies in Economic Instability and Change*, Stockholm: SNS förlag, pp. 13–47.

Lundberg, E. (1937), *Studies in the Theory of Economic Expansion*, London: P.S. King.

Lundberg, E. (1994), 'Memories of the Stockholm School', in E. Lundberg, *Studies in Economic Instability and Change*, Stockholm: SNS förlag, pp. 491–9.

Lundberg, E. (1996), *The Development of Swedish and Keynesian Macroeconomic Theory and its Impact on Economic Policy*, Cambridge: Cambridge University Press.

Marshall, A. (1916), *Principles of Economics*, 7th edn, London: Macmillan.

Myrdal, G. (1927), *Prisbildningsproblemet och föränderligheten*, Uppsala: Almqvist & Wiksell.

Myrdal, G. (1931), 'Om penningteoretisk jämvikt. En studie över den "normala räntan" i Wicksells penninglära', *Ekonomisk Tidskrift*, **33**, 191–302; German trans., 'Der Gleichgewichtsbegriff als Instrument der geldtheoretischen Analyse', in F.A. Hayek (ed.) (1933), *Beiträge zur Geldtheorie*, Vienna: Julius Springer, pp. 361–487; English trans. in G. Myrdal (1939), *Monetary Equilibrium*, London: William Hodge.

Myrdal, G. (1939), *Monetary Equilibrium*, London: William Hodge.

Ohlin, B. (1933), 'Till frågan om penningteoriens uppläggning', *Ekonomisk Tidskrift*, **35**, 45–87, English trans. 1978: 'On the *Formulation of Monetary Theory*', *History of Political Economy*, **10**, 353–88.

Ohlin, B. (1934), *Penningpolitik, offentliga arbeten, subventioner och tullar som medel mot arbetslöshet*, Statens offentliga utredningar 1934: 12, Stockholm: P.A. Norstedt.

Ohlin, B. (1937), 'Some notes on the Stockholm theory of savings and investment', *Economic Journal*, **47**, pt 1: 53–69, pt 2: 221–40.

Siven, C.-H. (1991), 'The microeconomics of the Stockholm School', in L. Jonung (ed.), *The Stockholm School Revisited*, Cambridge: Cambridge University Press, pp. 141–66.

Steiger, O. (1971), *Studien zur Entstehung der Neuen Wirtschaftslehre in Schweden. Eine Anti-Kritik*, Berlin: Duncker & Humblot.

Svennilson, I. (1938), *Ekonomisk planering: Teoretiska studier*, Uppsala: Almqvist & Wiksell.

Wadensjö, E. (1991), 'The Committee on Unemployment and the Stockholm School', in L. Jonung (ed.), *The Stockholm School Revisited*, Cambridge: Cambridge University Press, pp. 103–24.

Wicksell, K. (1898), *Geldzins und Güterpreise. Eine Studie über die den Tauschwert des Geldes bestimmenden Ursachen*, Jena: Gustav Fischer, English trans. 1936: *Interest and Prices. A Study of the Causes Regulating the Value of Money*, London: Macmillan.

Chicago School

The Chicago School was a group of postwar economists, primarily located at the University of Chicago, who shared a common theoretical and methodological approach to economics as an applied policy science. The school's commitment to economics as an applied policy science, and their common scientific approach, distinguished them from the mainstream of the economics discipline in the postwar era. The success of their approach, both within the economics discipline and in economic policy around the world, led Andrei Shleifer (2009) to name the last quarter of the twentieth century after the school's most famous member: "The age of Milton Friedman."

At the core of the Chicago approach were two themes which guided their work: (1) the relevance of Marshallian price theory to policy analysis; and (2) the necessity of empirically testing that relevance against the outcomes of policy initiatives. So armed, the Chicago School not only launched assaults on Keynesian macroeconomics and traditional structure–conduct–performance theories of industrial organization, but also led in the development of modern financial economics, labor economics, economic history, public finance, applied econometrics, and social economics. Members of the School advised governments around the world, and University of Chicago graduates have been policy leaders in government ministries, central banks, the International Monetary Fund, and other national and international organizations. The School's influence in the Reagan and Thatcher administrations, as well as the role of the Chicago Boys in Chile, brought global attention to the School's policy framework. Their leadership, both in the economics discipline and in economic policy, has been recognized by the awarding of the Sveriges Riksbank Prize in Economic Sciences in Memory of Alfred Nobel to ten economists directly associated with the Chicago School: Milton Friedman, T.W. Schultz, George Stigler, Merton Miller, Ronald Coase, Gary Becker, Robert Fogel, Robert Lucas, Myron Scholes, and James Heckman. Numerous other laureates spent time in Chicago as either graduate students or post-doctoral researchers associated with the School or the Cowles Commission.

Pre-War Chicago Economics and the Chicago School

The analytical connection between the postwar Chicago School and various aspects of the work of earlier Chicago economists has often led to the effort to collapse them into one, divided into "early" and "late," "old" and "new," or "first" and "second" versions (Bronfenbrenner 1962; Miller 1962; Reder 1982; van Overtveldt 2007). It is more appropriate, however, to identify the School as a uniquely postwar phenomenon, without denying its reliance on Jacob Viner's emphasis on Marshallian price theory, the policy impetus of members of the pre-war circle that gathered around Frank H. Knight, or even the empirical emphases of Henry Schultz and Paul Douglas.

Until the early 1950s, Chicago's economists were largely concentrated in the department, and used a diverse set of approaches with little coordination among them. Knight can hardly be conceived of as the founder of the School (Reder 1982: 6; Emmett 2009), and Viner departed Chicago for Princeton in 1945, at about the same time as T.W. Schultz arrived. Schultz was a superb program builder, and under his oversight Friedman, Stigler, Fogel, D. Gale Johnson, H. Gregg Lewis, Lester Telser, D.N. McCloskey, and others forged not only a common economic approach but the institutional framework of teaching and research that supported it (van Horn et al. 2011). By the mid-1950s a coordinated departmental effort had appeared, and the Chicago School grew as those identified with it spread into the university's business and law schools.

The Analytical Relevance of Price Theory

Viner, the Knight circle and other members of Chicago's prewar department did provide members of the Chicago School with an appreciation for the socially efficacious regulation of human behavior in free markets through the price mechanism (Reder 1982: 13). In the 1930s and 1940s, Knight's clear explanation of the operation of the price system in a free market introduced many Chicago students to an argument that was uncommon among American economists at the time (Knight 1951, originally published for classroom use in 1933), and Viner's price theory course reinforced the message. Yet the Marshallian perspective was actually strengthened when Milton Friedman took over teaching the course in the late 1940s (Hammond 2010). Remarkably, from the 1930s to the 1980s, Chicago's core price theory course, required of all graduate students in their first year, was primarily taught by a sequence of Viner or Knight (until the late 1940s), Friedman (until the 1970s), Arnold Harberger (until the early 1980s), and Gary Becker (1970s and 1980s; he continued teaching a section of the course into the twenty-first century). Consistency in content and quality across five decades in the core price theory course helped establish the school.

However, teaching price theory was one thing, making it an analytical policy tool was another. While the rest of the economics discipline sought greater "descriptive accuracy" in the underlying assumptions of their models, members of the Chicago School continued, and in fact extended, the earlier Chicago emphasis on the "analytical relevance" of basic economic principles to policy analysis (Friedman 1953). Henry C. Simons, who had joined his former teacher Knight at Chicago in the late 1920s and moved to the university's law school in the 1930s, had advocated a "positive program" for economic reform (Simons 1934) that many point to as the first formulation of a Chicago School policy agenda. Knight (1944) himself directly defended analytical relevance over realism in his criticism of Hicksian demand theory, although he refused to acknowledge the predictive power of economics as an applied policy science in the same manner that Friedman and company did shortly thereafter. Friedman's (1953) essay called for the "analytical relevance" of Marshallian price theory to be tested against the empirical evidence provided by existing policies. It quickly became the *locus classicus* of the Chicago School's methodology.

A good example of the difference that the Chicago approach made can be found in the early postwar debate between Stigler and Richard Lester over the effect of minimum wage legislation. Lester argued, as had many American institutionalist labor economists, that price theory was irrelevant to the evaluation of minimum wage legislation because (1) labor markets were not competitive; and (2) neither employers nor workers were profit maximizers in labor market transactions (Lester 1946). Stigler's (1946) response re-affirmed the analytical relevance of Marshallian price theory to considerations of applied policy, even in labor markets. Despite the standoff between Stigler and Lester in the late 1940s, the increasing acceptance of the Chicago approach meant that, by the

1970s, Stigler's conclusions had become the disciplinary standard. Similar controversies over other applied price theory topics solidified the Chicago approach. Stigler's role was crucial in debates over imperfect or monopolistic competition (Stigler 1949) and kinked demand curves in oligopolistic industries (Stigler 1947), both of which started as challenges to the descriptive accuracy of competitive models. But other Chicago economists were also involved. Aaron Director led the battle in re-evaluating monopoly as the basis for trust busting; Eugene Fama extended price theory to financial market activity in the efficient market hypothesis; and Lester Telser led the critical appraisal of anticompetitive measures such as re-sale price maintenance agreements.

The predictive power of the Chicago approach, however, required the specification of a second methodological assumption to accompany Friedman's principle. The necessary assumption, which came to be known by the name Stigler and Becker used as the title of the article in which they articulated it – "De gustibus non est disputandum" (Stigler and Becker 1977) – was implicit in Friedman's essay when he "ventured the judgment" that disagreements about policies depend on different predictions of the policies' outcomes rather than "fundamental differences in basic values" and, hence, that the progress of positive economic science could solve policy disagreements (Friedman 1953: 5). Essentially, price theory taught Friedman, Stigler and the rest of the Chicago School to focus on changes in the measurable cost structures surrounding market participants for scientific explanation, rather than changes in tastes, preferences and values. It was this lesson that Stigler and Becker codified for methodological purposes: assume that tastes and values are stable over time and among people. *De gustibus non est disputandum* joined Friedman's "analytical relevance" as the methodological principles upon which the Chicago School was built, and became particularly important as the School broadened its reach across the entire breadth of human behavior (Becker 1976).

An Empirically Based Applied Policy Science, Chicago Style

So much attention has been paid to the Chicago School's price theoretic approach that, until recently, the school's development of empirical tools to facilitate the application of that approach to policy questions has often been overlooked. Here, too, members of the Chicago School followed in the footsteps of earlier Chicago economists, especially Wesley Mitchell and Henry Schultz. Both Friedman and Lewis served as research assistants for Schultz; and Lewis, who had also studied with Chicago statistician Theodore O. Yntema, was appointed to the faculty following Schultz's death in 1938. However, it was Mitchell, one of the Chicago economics department's first doctoral students, who perhaps had the greatest early impact on the empirical method of Chicago economists, albeit indirectly. Mitchell entered in the first class of students at Chicago in 1892 and remained as a student and then instructor until 1903. He eventually ended up at Columbia University in New York, where he founded the National Bureau of Economic Research (NBER) in the 1920s. Many Chicago economists have had connections to the NBER; none more important than Friedman, who finished his doctorate at Columbia with Arthur F. Burns, who had succeeded Mitchell as the NBER director. Friedman subsequently collaborated with Simon Kuznets on a NBER study of professional incomes (Friedman and Kuznets 1945) that introduced the notion of permanent income, which became the basis for Friedman's own theory of consumption (Friedman

1957). Friedman then teamed up with NBER researcher Anna Jacobson Schwartz on a long-term study of Anglo-American monetary history, often viewed as the foundational empirical support for Friedman's monetarist policy framework (Friedman and Schwartz 1963).

Lewis served as a bridge between the emerging Chicago School and the older Chicago empirical tradition. He had studied with both Schultz and Simons, became the graduate student advisor through most of the postwar period, and served on many dissertation committees. After 1950, he focused his research on unionism, a topic which had occupied earlier Chicago economists like Douglas and the departing Albert Rees. Lewis's approach combined the Chicago price theoretic approach with careful empirical investigation into union power. His first publication on unions echoed the title of Simons positive policy program (Lewis 1951), and his most important work characterized the applied scientific work that the Chicago School's labor economics made the standard for the sub-field (Lewis 1963).

By 1950 Lewis was not alone. Friedman had joined the department in 1946, and equally importantly, the mid-1940s also saw the arrival of agricultural economist T.W. Schultz from Iowa State University. Schultz chaired the department from 1945 until the 1970s, and managed to reunite several of his Iowa State colleagues at Chicago, including Margaret Reid and his former student D. Gale Johnson. While Friedman was the star and taught the central courses that all students took in price theory and money, behind the scenes, Schultz was building a coordinated program of education and research that was unrivaled (van Horn et al. 2011). His connections with foundations, government agencies and the university administration provided resources for both graduate education and research by both faculty and students. He, Lewis, D. Gale Johnson and Friedman were responsible for the creation of the Chicago workshops, which became central to the School's success (Emmett 2011). Schultz, Lewis and Harberger also built the program's connections with the Catholic University of Chile in the 1950s. Latin American students entering the Chicago graduate program joined others from Israel; after the postwar period, the focus of international recruitment shifted to eastern Europe.

Schultz's leadership, Friedman's dynamic teaching, the applied policy focus of its studies in agricultural economics, public finance, monetary economics, Latin American economic development, and labor economics, and the presence of D. Gale Johnson, Zvi Griliches, Lewis, Al Harberger, and the group of economic historians led by Fogel and D.N. McCloskey, provided the context within which the Chicago School found empirical methods that complemented its price theoretic approach. More recently, Chicago econometric policy analysis has been carried further by Nobel laureate James Heckman, whose work has transformed labor, education and social policy evaluation.

Key Chicago School Analytical Developments

The Chicago School is best known, of course, for monetarism: a macroeconomic policy regime of stable long-term economic growth with minimal inflation guided by a stable rule for growth of the monetary base. Monetarism was designed to counter the Keynesian manipulation of fiscal policy levers to achieve the same goals, thus wedding a monetary theory which enabled market prices to function efficiently with a critique of interventionist policies in the macroeconomic realm that paralleled the Chicago School's other economic policy arguments. The controversy between Keynesians and monetarists raged over the late 1960s and 1970s (Johnson 1972) and spilled over into international economics as Harry Johnson and Robert Mundell created the monetary approach to the balance of payments (Frenkel and Johnson 1976).

The formal basis for the monetary rule was a restatement of the quantity theory of money (Friedman 1956). The restatement was rooted, however, in an implication of Friedman's consumption theory (1957): a stable relation between consumption and permanent income implied that savings would not be a stable function of current income, which had been the operative assumption in earlier macroeconomic theories. Friedman's permanent income hypothesis, then, enabled monetarists to focus attention on the policy implications of a stable demand for money in a quantity theory of money setting.

But monetarism is only one of several key Chicago School contributions to modern economic analysis. In microeconomic and industrial organization theory, Stigler led a group of scholars who challenged assumptions about the analytical relevance of price theory to a wide range of industrial policy. Stigler's interest in how knowledge acquisition affects an economic agent's market behavior led him through the application of statistical decision theory within a competitive price model to information search theory (Stigler 1961), a theme which Chicago economists, following Stigler's lead, made central to labor economics and industrial organization, among other applications. Stigler also turned his attention to regulation. With his long-time research assistant Claire Friedland, he examined systematically the empirical evidence on the effects of public utility regulation, showing that regulation had little or no impact on utility pricing (Stigler and Friedland 1962). He also argued that the existence of demanders of regulation as well as suppliers created a market-like environment for government regulation of economic affairs. However, in a political context without competitive pressures, demanders would capture the suppliers, rendering regulation socially inefficient (Stigler 1971). Stigler's empirical work on regulation also led him to join Director in becoming more sanguine about the benefits of antitrust action.

Two related developments emerged from the work of Ronald H. Coase, who arrived at the University of Chicago's law school in 1964, and took over editorship of the *Journal of Law & Economics*. Coase's two major articles, on the firm (Coase 1937) and on private versus social costs (Coase 1960), both continue the Chicago notion of using the basic insights of price theory to examine the operation of real markets. The first article introduced the costs of creating and sustaining markets, initiating the modern theory of the firm and the development of transaction cost economics, which reaches beyond industrial organization to law and economics, economic history, and the emergence of new institutional economics. Indeed, the field of law and economics is commonly said to have been created by the Chicago School; certainly, several of its most famous members – Coase, Becker, Richard Posner, Henry Manne, and Robert Bork – were faculty or students in the university's law school. Coase's second article also played an important part in the development of law and economics, as well as informing almost every area of economic policy analysis. Within the Chicago School, the use of Coase (1960) was largely shaped by Stigler's interpretation, labeled the "Coase theorem": in perfect competition, private and social costs would be equal (Stigler 1966: 113). Harold Demsetz, who was a faculty member in the university's graduate business school from 1963 to 1971, drew upon Coase and Stigler in developing a theory of property rights which contributed not only to law and economics, but also to the emergence of the new institutionalist economics (Demsetz 1967).

A third theme of modern economic analysis that owes much to its development in the Chicago School is human capital. Schultz had long stressed the relationship between economic development and investment in human capabilities, and sought in the late 1950s to measure the impact of education on capital formation (Schultz 1960). At the same time, Becker and his Columbia University colleague Jacob Mincer were also examining the monetary return to post-secondary education. Becker's *Human Capital* (1964) provided a formulation of the concept that enabled several generations of Chicago School students – among them Kevin M. Murphy, Finis Welch, and Richard Freeman – to apply price theory to lifelong individual decisions and public investment questions.

The Chicago School that emerged in the postwar period created an approach to the economic analysis of policy issues that tested the basic insights of price theory against empirical evidence provided by policy outcomes. While the Chicago approach initially differed substantively both in method and findings from the disciplinary mainstream, it eventually became the vanguard of developments across the discipline, as well as a leader in pushing the discipline into areas of social analysis into which it previously had not ventured.

Ross B. Emmett

See also:

Ronald Harry Coase (I); Milton Friedman (I); Frank H. Knight (I); Robert E. Lucas (I); Monetarism (II).

References and further reading
Becker, G.S. (1964), *Human Capital: A Theoretical and Empirical Analysis, with Special Reference to Education*, New York: Columbia University Press.
Becker, G.S. (1976), *The Economic Approach to Human Behavior*, Chicago, IL: University of Chicago Press.
Bronfenbrenner, M. (1962), 'Observation on the "Chicago school(s)"', *Journal of Political Economy*, **70** (1), 72–5.
Coase, R.H. (1937), 'The nature of the firm', *Economica*, new series, **4** (16), 386–405.
Coase, R.H. (1960), 'The problem of social cost', *Journal of Law & Economics*, **3** (October), 1–44.
Demsetz, H. (1967), 'Toward a theory of property rights', *American Economic Review*, **57** (2), Papers and Proceedings, 347–59.
Emmett, R.B. (2009), 'Did the Chicago School reject Frank Knight?', in R.B. Emmett, *Frank Knight and the Chicago School in American Economics*, New York: Routledge, pp. 145–55.
Emmett, R.B. (2011), 'Sharpening tools in the workshop: the workshop system and the Chicago School's success', in R. Van Horn, P. Mirowski and T. Stapleford (eds), *Building Chicago Economics: New Perspectives on the History of America's Most Powerful Economics Program*, Cambridge: Cambridge University Press, pp. 93–115.
Frenkel, J.A. and H.G. Johnson (eds) (1976), *The Monetary Approach to the Balance of Payments*, Toronto: University of Toronto Press.
Friedman, M. (1953), 'The methodology of positive economics', in M. Friedman, *Essays in Positive Economics*, Chicago, IL: University of Chicago Press, pp. 3–43.
Friedman, M. (1956), 'The quantity theory of money – a restatement', in M. Friedman (ed.), *Studies in the Quantity Theory of Money*, Chicago, IL: University of Chicago Press, pp. 3–21.
Friedman, M. (1957), *Theory of the Consumption Function*, Princeton, NJ: Princeton University Press.
Friedman, M. and A. Jacobson Schwartz (1963), *A Monetary History of the United States, 1867–1960*, Princeton, NJ: Princeton University Press.
Friedman, M. and S. Kuznets (1945), *Income from Independent Professional Practice*, New York: National Bureau of Economic Research.
Hammond, J.D. (2010), 'The development of post-war Chicago price theory', in R.B. Emmett (ed.), *The Elgar Companion to the Chicago School of Economics*, Cheltenham, UK and Northampton, MA, USA: Edward Elgar, pp. 7–24.

Johnson, H.G. (1972), *Inflation and the Monetarist Controversy*, Amsterdam: North-Holland.
Knight, F.H. (1944), 'Realism and relevance in the theory of demand', *Journal of Political Economy*, **52** (4), 289–318.
Knight, F.H. (1951), *The Economic Organization, with an Article 'Notes on Cost and Utility'*, New York: Augustus M. Kelley.
Lester, R.A. (1946), 'Shortcoming of marginal analysis for wage-employment problems', *American Economic Review*, **36** (1), 62–82.
Lewis, H.G. (1951), 'The labor-monopoly problem: a positive program', *Journal of Political Economy* **59** (4), 277–87.
Lewis, H.G. (1963), *Unionism and Relatives Wages in the United States: An Empirical Inquiry*, Chicago, IL: University of Chicago Press.
Miller, H.L. Jr (1962), '"On the Chicago school of economics"', *Journal of Political Economy*, **70** (1), 64–9.
Reder, M.W. (1982), 'Chicago economics: permanence and change', *Journal of Economic Literature*, **20** (1), 1–38.
Schultz, T.W. (1960), 'Capital formation by education', *Journal of Political Economy*, **68** (6), 571–83.
Shleifer, A. (2009), 'The age of Milton Friedman', *Journal of Economic Literature*, **47** (1), 123–35.
Simons, H.C. (1934), *A Positive Program for Laissez Faire: Some Proposals for a Liberal Economic Policy*, Public Policy Pamphlet No. 15, Chicago, IL: University of Chicago Press.
Stigler, G.J. (1946), 'The economics of minimum wage legislation', *American Economic Review*, **36** (3), 358–65.
Stigler, G.J. (1947), 'The kinky oligopoly demand curve and rigid prices', *Journal of Political Economy*, **55** (5), 432–49.
Stigler, G.J. (1949), 'Monopolistic competition in retrospect', in G.J. Stigler, *Five Lectures on Economic Problems*, London: Longmans, Green, pp. 12–34.
Stigler, G.J. (1961), 'The economics of information', *Journal of Political Economy*, **69** (3), 213–25.
Stigler, G.J. (1966), *The Theory of Price*, 3rd edn, New York: Macmillan.
Stigler, G.J. (1971), 'The theory of economic regulation', *Bell Journal of Economics and Management Science*, **2** (1), 3–21.
Stigler, G.J. and G.S. Becker (1977), 'De gustibus non est disputandum', *American Economic Review*, **67** (March), 76–90.
Stigler, G.J. and C. Friedland (1962), 'What can regulators regulate? The case of electricity', *Journal of Law & Economics*, **5** (October), 1–16.
Van Horn, R., P. Mirowski and T. Stapleford (eds) (2011), *Building Chicago Economics: New Perspectives on the History of America's Most Powerful Economics Program*, Cambridge: Cambridge University Press.
Van Overtveldt, J. (2007), *The Chicago School: How the University of Chicago Assembled the Thinkers Who Revolutionized Economics and Business*, Chicago, IL: Agate.

Monetarism

Monetarism in a Nutshell

The term "monetarism" was coined by Karl Brunner to label a specific set of analytical and empirical propositions brought forward to contest the conventional wisdom of post-World War II macroeconomics (Brunner 1968). The first contributions to what came to be known as monetarism were published during the 1950s. Within the economics profession, it had its heydays in the 1970s due to its ability to predict the US stagflation by means of the expectations-augmented Phillips curve. Monetarist policy views spread quickly and rose to dominance in the 1980s (with the rise of "Ronald Thatcher", see Laidler 2012: 24, fn 27). Whereas the success of monetarism within the economics profession was largely due to the expectations-augmented Phillips curve, its sway over public opinion was fostered by the monetarist short-run and policy-orientated quantity theory of money.

The towering figure of the monetarist school was Milton Friedman, who set the tone in an, at times, heated controversy with the proponents of the neoclassical synthesis. Other prominent members are Karl Brunner, Bennett McCallum, David Laidler, Allan Meltzer, Anna Schwartz, and Carl Warburton (who is the "pioneer monetarist"; see Bordo and Schwartz 1979). It is, however, the work of Friedman that is generally acknowledged to define "monetarist orthodoxy", that is, the beliefs and methods that characterize the monetarist school. He did no less than to invert the prevailing view of why the Great Depression had happened, and of what had proven to be an effective remedy.

Before the rise of monetarism, the dominant view was Keynesian in that it held responsible for the Great Depression the inherent instability of the private sector. According to this view, investment choice reflects consensual market expectations that are prone to fads and collective passions ("animal spirits"). Fickle market sentiments translate into volatile investment spending and expose the economy to self-fulfilling prophecies. If the private sector is left on its own, there exists a multiplicity of demand-constrained equilibria so that full-employment becomes a matter of chance. Government intervention is beneficial as it is able to select for the right equilibrium: whenever private spending collapses, the government is able to offset the impact on aggregate demand and, thus, to defend the output level consistent with full-employment.

In their seminal monograph *A Monetary History of the United States*, Friedman and Schwartz argued the opposite (1963: ch. 7). According to their "monetarist view", a small shock that would otherwise have caused a minor recession was turned into a deep slump by a series of blunt policy mistakes. In particular, monetary policy stood by as the money multiplier collapsed in consequence of a bank run. Monetarists believe that, in general, the monetary authority always and completely controls the level of nominal income. In the short run, when nominal rigidities prevail, monetary policy is fully accountable for the level of real income. Accordingly, significant inflationary booms, like the post-World War I inflation, and significant deflationary busts, like the Great Depression, cannot be blamed on the private sector, which they believed to be inherently stable (Mayer 1978: 2, 14–15). Instability is rather inflicted upon the private sector by monetary policy: "The contraction is in fact a tragic testimonial to the importance of monetary forces" (Friedman and Schwartz 1963: 300).

Further, because nominal income in monetarist analysis is always and everywhere controlled by monetary policy, deficit spending has no impact on aggregate demand, output, and employment. If not accommodated by a monetary authority, fiscal policy just induces a reallocation of resources, crowding out private investment to finance unproductive government consumption instead (on the "fiscalist–monetarist debate", see Brunner 1989: 259–80). In the longer run, which in monetarist analysis is not necessarily a steady state, it is in vain to target real variables like output and the rate of unemployment. Because the private sector is not exposed to money illusion and, thus, cannot be fooled permanently, there is no exploitable long-run trade-off between inflation (a nominal target) and unemployment (a real target).

Monetarism and the Quantity-Theory Tradition

From Hume to Keynes: "internal stability" as a goal of monetary policy

Most of the major propositions of monetarism follow from Friedman's restatement of the quantity theory of money (Friedman 1956). The quantity theory, which in one form or another dominated monetary orthodoxy until the rise of Keynesian economics, has been subject to many different interpretations throughout the history of economic thought (see Laidler 1991). Common to all variants of the quantity theory is the view that there exists a tight relationship between the stock of nominal money balances, the flow of nominal income and, in the long run, the purchasing power of money. It was further argued that the causal chain runs from stocks to flows and prices, and not otherwise. To appreciate Friedman's variation on the theme, it is important to go beyond the similarities, and to highlight some differences between the classical, neoclassical, and monetarist tradition (see Patinkin 1969, 1974). All versions of the quantity theory state a "quantity equation".

A basic variant is given by:

$$Mv = PY, \tag{1}$$

where M denotes the nominal supply of money (usually, the monetary base), Y the level of aggregate real income, and P the corresponding price level. The "velocity of money", denoted by v, measures money's average rate of turnover (the number of transactions enabled by a unit of money per period), reflecting the fact that the quantity equation relates the stock of money to the flow of nominal income (PY). The Cambridge-reciprocal, $k \equiv 1/v$, measures the average period over which money balances are held (as a fraction of the elementary period). If k is determined by economic behaviour, it is a measure of the real *transaction* demand for money.

The use of the equality sign is pure convention. In fact, the "quantity equation" is a flow identity and, as such, tautological. Its left-hand side simply specifies nominal spending as "money in circulation". It states the trivial fact that nominal spending in the aggregate is always and by necessity equal to nominal income; that what is spent (decumulation of cash balances) is by definition received (accumulation of cash balances). So far, the analysis is empirically empty and, in some form or another, common to all variants of the quantity theory of money. To arrive at predictions, assumptions were made, and it is in the details of these assumptions that the variations differ:

(A1)   The "relevant" definition of nominal money supply is exogenous: $M = \bar{M}$.

(A2)   There exists no systematic relationship between the nominal stock of money and its velocity (or the real demand for money). Equivalently, v (or k) is independent of M. In studying the impact of money supply on income and prices, it is therefore feasible to fix the velocity of money: $v = \bar{v}$.

(A3)   Classical dichotomy: monetary factors exert no persistent influence on the level of real output. The output level in stationary equilibrium (the classical centre of gravitation) is fully determined by "real" factors. Thus, in the long-run: $Y = \bar{Y}$.

Given the quantity equation, (A1)–(A2) already yield a simple theory of nominal income. Changes in the stock of money supply suggest equi-proportional changes in nominal spending and, thus, income. The theory of nominal income suggests no particular equilibrium specification. It may hold in static (neoclassical) and stationary (classical and neoclassical) equilibria; it also holds in disequilibrium. All assumptions together then yield the prediction of "quantity of money theory of the price level" (Tobin 1974: 86):

> (*Quantity Theorem*) Given equation (1), if (A1)–(A3) hold for whatever reason, then the following statements are true and equivalent in a closed economy in long-run (steady-state) equilibrium: the purchasing power of the aggregate money supply (M/P) is independent of the level of nominal balances; money-supply variations are reflected in equi-proportional changes in the price level; monetary policy fully controls nominal variables; monetary policy has zero grip on quantities (real variables); *money is neutral.*

Or, in the words of Hume, whom Friedman (2008) celebrated as the best early advocate of the quantity theory: "*If we consider any one kingdom by itself*, it is evident, that the greater or less plenty of money is of no consequence; since the prices of commodities are always proportioned to the plenty of money" (Hume 1752 [1955]: 33; emphasis added).

Hume's quantity theory must be seen as a vital contribution to a general attack on mercantilistic principles. It ridicules the goal of increasing a nation's "riches" by maximizing the domestic stock of gold. Mercantilism is irrational, so the message, in the sense that it is founded on a money illusion, the confusion of nominal and real economic magnitudes. In the aggregate, it is impossible to accumulate wealth by hoarding gold, since money's purchasing power adjusts until any nominal supply purchases the equilibrium level of output. Friedman, at least, always expressed greatest sympathy for this interpretation of Hume's quantity theory (Friedman 1956: 10–11, 1966 [1969]: 145, 1974: 1–3, 2008).

In the quotation above, Hume explicitly refers to a closed economy (see italics). In general, however, he was concerned with open economies, considering international trade between pre-industrial commercial clusters that share gold and silver as common media of exchange. His quantity theorem is a statement of pure logic, directed against the profound irrationality of mercantilist thought and policy. According to his famous price-specie flow mechanism, money supply is endogenous (A1 does not apply): any national increase in the nominal money supply would disturb the international balance-of-payment equilibrium. According to the quantity theory, such an expansionary impulse leads to an increase in the domestic price level and, thus, deteriorates the terms of trade. In response, the trade balance turns into deficit, financed by an outflow of money (or monies). Falling prices, as again predicted by the quantity theory, then restore the initial terms of trade and rebalance the current account. In new and old equilibrium, the global stock of gold and silver is distributed across nations in proportion to their real transaction demand for money (Dimand 2013: 293–7). Given free financial markets, a monetary authority committed to maintaining the convertibility of national currency into gold and silver cannot persistently influence nominal variables.

By contrast, the monetarist orthodoxy champions flexible exchange rates (Friedman 1953a). It argues that nominal exchange rate adjustments serve as a buffer against external shocks. Most importantly, flexible exchange rates restore monetary sovereignty and, thus, the exogeneity of money. Even though the monetarists celebrated Hume and the classical quantity-theory tradition, they advocated a completely different monetary regime and, therewith, a different interpretation of the quantity theory. In case of inconvertible currency and flexible exchange rates, the quantity theory suggests the monetary authority's long-run responsibility for price stability (and the responsibility for stable money income in the short run). In fact, monetarists are Keynesian in that they are willing to sacrifice "external stability" for the sake of such "internal stability ".

Thus, it comes as no surprise that Friedman admired Keynes's early work as a Marshallian quantity theorist, especially his advocacy of monetary sovereignty and price stability as the primary long-run goal of monetary policy (see Keynes 1923 [1971]; Friedman 1974: 171, 1997: 2). Irrespective of vital differences (discussed below), Friedman's restatement of the quantity theory is best understood as an attempt to improve upon Keynes's early monetary analysis. This view is not in conflict with Friedman's firm belief that his restatement was consistent with the *General Theory* (1936 [1973]), for he also believed that Keynes's theory of output in a monetary economy was meant to be a refinement of his earlier work in the Cambridge tradition:

> Keynes was a quantity theorist long before he was a Keynesian, and he continued to be one after he became a Keynesian. . . . I maintain that Keynes's discussion of the demand curve for money in the *General Theory* is for the most part a continuation of earlier quantity theory approaches, improved and refined but not basically modified. As evidence, I shall cite Keynes's own writings in the *Tract on Monetary Reform*. (Friedman 1974: 159, 168)

The quantity theory as a theory of money demand
In general, Friedman expressed highest esteem for the neoclassical "Cambridge cash-balance approach" (Friedman 1974: 8–10). Whereas classical analysis assumed velocity to be an institutional datum, determined by the properties of the payment system and the length of the income period, Alfred Marshall and the Cambridge tradition invoked the real demand for money as a stable behavioural relationship (Pigou 1917 is the epitome of the Cambridge tradition). Like classical monetary economics, early neoclassical analysis was primarily concerned with the transaction motive (money is held to be spent). The real transaction demand for money was then specified as a linear function of real income:

$$L = kY, \tag{2}$$

where L denotes the aggregate demand for real balances. Linearity isolates the impact of income on money demand.

Further, neoclassical analysis would be incomplete without market-clearing conditions, supplementing the individual conditions of optimality. As a result, the quantity theory came to rely on an equilibrium condition. The money-market equilibrium condition is given by:

$$\frac{M}{P} = L(Y), \tag{3}$$

where M/P measures the purchasing power of all money (real balances in the aggregate). Substituting (2) into (3) yields relationship (1) after simple rearrangements; this time, however, as a genuine equation. Given (A2)–(A3), the real demand for money in the stationary state is independent of the nominal supply of money. In the hands of Pigou, the quantity theorem became identified with the "unitary elasticity" of an aggregate cash-balance demand function (a "rectangular hyperbola", Pigou 1917: 42), which was primarily employed in comparative-static analysis. The absence of money illusion was translated to mean that individual excess demand functions are homogeneous of degree zero. The real-balance effect then described the convergence process at the vicinity of the stationary state (for the inconsistency of this approach; see Patinkin 1949, 1965).

The focus of the Cambridge School on the behavioural foundations of money demand was a game-changing event in the history of the quantity theory. The involvement of the money market equilibrium condition changed the way the quantity theorem was presented. This impact may explain Friedman's famous exaggeration that "the quantity theory is in the first instance a theory of the demand for money. It is not a theory of output, or of money income, or of the price level" (Friedman 1956: 4; see also Friedman 1974: 3). Taken seriously, this statement would suggest a quantity theory without its prediction, the quantity theorem. Right because Pigou's quantity theory is centred on a market-clearing condition, it should be clear that no meaningful restatement can ignore the supply side of the money market. In fact, the money-supply theory of nominal income figures prominently in the monetarist restatement of the quantity theory. After all, monetarism owes its name to the fact that its advocates persistently stressed the predominance of money supply as a determinant of money income.

What is true, however, is that the long-run neutrality of money is of secondary importance in monetarist analysis. Otherwise, monetarism would be far less controversial. Friedman was rather interested in "a more subtle and relevant version, one in which the quantity theory" becomes "a flexible and sensitive tool for interpreting movements in aggregate economic activity and for developing relevant policy prescriptions" (Friedman 1956: 3; see also Friedman 1974: 158–9). Pigou's real-balance effect was regarded as analytically valid, but of minor empirical relevance (Friedman 1974: 159–60, 1997: 16). Instead of this sterile convergence process, monetarist monetary analysis is concerned with how a monetary impulse is transmitted through financial markets (the portfolio-balance effect), and how it impacts "real" variables on the evidence of nominal rigidities. In the best tradition of non-Pigovian studies on the quantity theory – from Hume to Fisher and the young Keynes (see Dimand 1988, 2013) – Friedman and the monetarists were primarily interested in the short-run non-neutrality of money. In short, monetarism resurrects the one-equation approach to business cycle analysis.

In his restatement, Friedman (1956: 3–4) traced his short-run, policy-orientated version of the quantity theory back to an "oral tradition" at the University of Chicago "throughout the 1930s and 1940s", in the teachings of Henry Simons, Lloyd Mints and, "at one remove", Frank Knight and Jacob Viner (for a critical discussion, see Patinkin

1974: 112–18, then Friedman 1974: 162–8, and then Steindl 1990). This oral tradition, in turn, Friedman traced back to Keynes's *Tract* (Friedman 1974: 168–9). There, Keynes dismissed the relevance of the long-run neutrality of money on the ground that "this long run is a misleading guide to current affairs". In fact, "[e]conomists set themselves too easy, too useless a task if in tempestuous seasons they can only tell us that when the storm is long past the ocean will be flat again" (Keynes 1923 [1971]: 80). Keynes's often misunderstood dictum – "*In the long run* we are all dead" (ibid.: original emphasis) – is just a trenchant summary of this view.

The Monetarist Transmission Mechanism

Monetarists of all types emphasized the heterogeneity of wealth. But they did so for different reasons. Brunner and Meltzer (1976) focused on the specifics of the portfolio-balance effect by which a monetary impulse is transmitted to aggregate spending and production. They were also concerned with asset market conditions that could stifle fiscal impulses and contain the multiplier. They believed that the IS–LM model is generically unable to accommodate the heterogeneity of assets, and drafted eclectic macro-models instead. Brunner, in particular, was hostile to the IS–LM apparatus, which dominated the macro-economic discourse during that period. He considered the implicit assumption that equity and other "real assets are frozen into portfolios by forbidding transaction costs" to be backward and even "schizophrenic" (Brunner 1978: 56). He liked to call the IS–LM model the "islamic framework", and to talk of the "contamination" of post-World War II theory and policy advice (ibid.: 56, 60–62). He rather emphasized that there exists for each asset, including monetary assets, "a *general* and *imperfect* range of substitution in all directions over the whole spectrum of assets" (Brunner 1978: 61; original emphasis). Friedman, by contrast, was not interested in the details of the portfolio-balance effect (Friedman 1974: 134–7). For him, the variety of yields affected by the portfolio-balance effect allowed for a complete specification of the money demand function, accounting for a stable functional relationship (Friedman 1956: 15–16).

Common to both approaches is the asset space, introduced as a continuum of close substitutes. That is, for each out of an infinite number of assets there exists a neighbourhood of "similar" assets. Assets outside of this local neighbourhood are rather "dissimilar". In particular, the two polar assets have nothing in common. Yet, they are connected via infinitely many overlapping neighbourhoods. Although the polar assets, say equity and currency, are highly "dissimilar", their respective yields are interrelated. They are gross substitutes. The topology (the "neighbourhood-system") of the asset space is generated by risk characteristics: assets are "similar", if they expose the asset-holder to similar types of risk. In the example, with equity and money as polar assets, money is characterized by real risk, yet it is nominally riskless, whereas equity is immune to inflation risk, yet it is exposed to all other types of risk associated with a capitalistic society. Nevertheless, the monetarist risk topology suggests that money market conditions co-determine the equity yield in equilibrium.

Accordingly, the transmission of a monetary impulse is wave-like, crossing an entire ocean of assets until it hits the facing coast. To simplify things, monetarist analysis reduces this ocean to a few asset classes: equities, bonds, and money. The goal of the monetarist transmission mechanism is to show that a monetary impulse affects the yields of a large variety of assets such that, even if some specific transmission channels are broken (in a Keynesian manner), the impulse is transmitted to the "real" sector. Money, so the argument, is never "trapped". Further, monetarism is founded on the (false) belief that "proper" micro-foundations for the money demand function could resurrect the predominance of the money supply as determinant of nominal income. In fact, Friedman's restatement of the quantity theory as a theory of money demand has at its core a risk-averse representative "wealth-owning unit", introduced as a problem of portfolio optimization (Friedman 1956: 4, 8–9, 14, 1974: 13–14).

In modern parlance, Friedman's representative portfolio holder maximizes a utility function characterized by constant relative risk aversion subject to a wealth constraint such that the warranted composition of wealth is invariant to its level. Due to the homothetic property of preferences, the optimal wealth composition is independent of the wealth level (including the discounted perpetual payoff of human capital; Friedman 1956: 10, 1974: 13–14). The representative agent is just concerned with the composition of his portfolio, which includes real as well as nominal assets (real claims to real/human capital payoff versus dollar-denominated government liabilities). Nominal assets, in turn, are composed of monetary and non-monetary assets. The former contains central bank liabilities and other information-insensitive and, thus, liquid assets, while the latter contains those assets exposed to nominal risks. In studying the demand for money as portfolio choice, monetarism accepts Keynes's liquidity preference theory and, thus, money as a store of value.

Given the monetarist insistence of the importance of real assets for the transmission mechanism, providing a direct link between money supply and investment spending, the Fisher equation plays a significant role (Friedman 1956: 6–7, 9–10, 1974: 13, 36; Brunner and Meltzer 1976: 72, 179). It provides the one-period no-arbitrage condition between real and nominal assets. For sufficiently small values, the Fisher relation is approximated by:

$$i = r + \pi^e, \tag{4}$$

where i denotes the nominal rate of interest, r denotes the ex-ante real rate of interest (in monetarist analysis equal to the rate of return on equity), and π^e gives the expected inflation rate. Irving Fisher (1896 [1997]) introduced the no-arbitrage condition to "move up one derivative beyond" the long-run neutrality prediction of Hume's static quantity theory (Dimand 2013: 287; see also Dimand 2012). The real rate of interest is unaffected by expected changes in the value of money, which reformulates "the divorce between monetary and real factors" in the context of a perfect-foresight equilibrium.

Real yields are equally governed by a no-arbitrage condition, invoking the fundamental theorem of finance – equilibrium returns linearly increase in risk:

$$r = r_f + e, \tag{5}$$

with $e \geq 0$, where r_f gives the risk-free, inflation-adjusted rate of return on bonds with certain nominal payoffs, e denotes the equity premium, that is, the excess returns necessary to compensate for undiversifiable risk. Friedman assumed that diversification eliminates all risk so that the interrelation of aggregate variables fits a deterministic model: "The society, though stationary, is not static. Aggregates are constant, but individuals are subject to uncertainty and change" (Friedman 1969: 2). In this case, equity is a perfect substitute of an asset that is not exposed to market risk, that is, $e = 0$. This is also Keynes's specification in the *General Theory*. Brunner and Meltzer, however, insisted on imperfect substitutability: the risk topology is such that diversification does not eliminate all risk. Some "systematic risk" remains, differentiating equity from bonds and money. In equilibrium, equity trades at a discount, That is, $e > 0$.

What matters for the monetarist transmission mechanism is that risky and riskless returns co-vary. This they do irrespective of the equity premium level, which is a "deep parameter ". In contrast to what Brunner and Meltzer believed, their eclectic models are no substantial improvement upon Friedman's early exposition of the transmission mechanism. Nor is there any substantial difference between the monetarist transmission mechanism and the Keynesian portfolio-balance effect as developed by Tobin (1958 [1987], 1969 [1987]) and Blinder and Solow (1973). To conclude with Benjamin Friedman (1978: 109–10; see also Dornbusch 1976: 123–4):

> What is one to make of all this? Perhaps Brunner and Meltzer are not monetarists. Or perhaps Tobin is not a Keynesian. Perhaps. A more likely conclusion, however, is that, once monetarists and Keynesians specify clearly a "transmission mechanism" by which monetary policy has its effect in their respective theoretical models, these alternative mechanisms are by and large identical. On this key issue, which is the essence of the theoretical dimension of the monetarist debate, it is hard to find significant disagreement.

The Monetarist Restatement of the Quantity Theory

The portfolio optimization exemplified above yields Friedman's restatement of the quantity theory as a theory of money demand. Given the no-arbitrage conditions (4) and (5), the real money demand of the representative agent is:

$$L(r_f, e, \pi^e, \Omega, Y), \tag{6}$$

with

$$\Omega = \frac{Y_\infty}{\tilde{r}}, \tag{7}$$

where Ω is the aggregate wealth constraint (a real value) which – in equilibrium – equals the present value of real "permanent income", denoted by Y_∞ (Friedman 1956: 4–5, 10–11, 1974: 11–12). Permanent income is defined as the mean or mathematical expectation of a stationary real income process (more prominently formulated in Friedman 1957: 21). Finally, $\tilde{r}$ is the portfolio-weighted average over the net returns of the different asset classes.

Because preferences are assumed to be homothetic, the demand for any asset class, including money, is linearly increasing in wealth or permanent income. Linking short-run money demand to a steady-state variable renders it more stable: by specifying CRRA utility, the portfolio weight of liquid assets is unaffected by random income shocks, or by "transitory" deviations of "actual income" from steady state. The first three arguments of the money demand altogether represent the Keynesian liquidity preference theory.

The real demand for money decreases in the nominal interest rate, $i = r_f + e + \pi^e$, the relevant opportunity cost of liquidity. It follows that the money demand function decreases in its first three arguments (enabling the portfolio-balance effect).

Finally, actual or current income Y accounts for the transaction motive (demand is increasing in actual income). In contrast to Tobin (1958 [1987]), Friedman did not provide micro-foundations for transaction demand. He rejected the hypothetical distinction between "active" and "idle" balances. To him, Keynes's liquidity preference theory in the *General Theory* is a refinement of the *Tract*, which is a refinement of Marshall's *Principles of Economics*, the latter's exposition being "*precisely* the liquidity preference theory of the *General Theory*: $M = M_1 + M_2 = L_1(Y) + L_2(r)$, except that Marshall expressed the part M_2 as a fraction of wealth, whereas Keynes expressed it as a function of the interest rate" (Friedman 1974: 170; emphasis added).

Friedman systematically de-emphasized the general-equilibrium implications of Keynes's liquidity preference theory in a short-run model of output and employment, which is also his setting. He, like other monetarists, regarded Keynes's "momentous deviation" from the neoclassical Cambridge tradition "in reversing the roles assigned to price and quantity" in Marshall's market period, thereby "[merging] the market period and the short-run period." "At least for changes in aggregate demand, quantity was the variable that adjusted rapidly, while price was the variable that adjusted slowly" (Friedman 1974: 18). By introducing short-run income as an endogenous variable, monetarism accepts the possibility of demand-constrained equilibrium income (the principle of effective demand). "Friedman, like Keynes, offers a theory of the level of income." (Meltzer 1983: 7). Then, however, there are two unknowns – the real risk-free rate of interest (r_f) and actual income (Y) – which require two market-clearing conditions for a short-run equilibrium to exist. Yet, monetarism insists on one equation, which is the gist of Friedman's restatement:

> I regard the description of our position [Friedman and Schwartz (1963)] as "money is all that matters for changes in *nominal* income and for *short-run* changes in real income" as an exaggeration, but one that gives the right flavor of our conclusions. I regard the statement that "money is all that matters," period, as a basic misrepresentation of our conclusions. (Friedman 1974: 27; original emphasis)

To demonstrate the compatibility between the quantity theory as a theory of income and Keynes's liquidity preference theory, Friedman formulates a "simply common" IS–LM model (1974: 29–30). For a closed economy with a public sector (that borrows to consume), the monetarist money market equilibrium condition is:

$$\frac{M}{P} = L(r_f, e, \pi^e, Y_\infty, Y), \tag{8}$$

and a plausible monetarist IS condition is given by:

$$I(r_f, e) + G = S(r_f, e, Y, Y_\infty), \tag{9}$$

where G denotes government consumption, I is the investment function, and S the saving function. The investment function is standard, decreasing in required rate of equity return. In this short-run model, the exogenous variables are M, P, Y_∞, G, π^e and e.

The saving function is specified according to Friedman's permanent income hypothesis (PIH), which was an essential leverage point of the monetarist counterrevolution (Friedman 1957). The hypothesis dissolves the tight link between consumption and actual income, defined to include unpredictable and transitory deviations from the mean. Assuming risk aversion, optimization dampens the impact of transitory income fluctuations on consumption (precautionary savings). Current saving is increasing in actual income, because current consumption is not. It is increasing in interest rates. Friedman's restatement suggests that the use of the money market condition (8) to determine real income is a first step. Then, in a separate step, the real interest rate is determined via (9), given the value of income derived in the first step (or vice versa). This procedure is only feasible, if and only if the marginal propensity to consume out of transitory income and the interest-elasticity of money demand are both zero. The first condition is substantiated by the PIH, which suspends the Keynesian multiplier.

The zero interest-elasticity of money demand, however, involves the major analytical contradiction of monetarism. It is a necessary assumption for any variant of the quantity theory, as in fact acknowledged by Friedman (1966 [1969]: 146). A positive interest-elasticity, however small, suggests that some increase in the money supply is absorbed by higher money demand, which would violate the equi-proportionality between money and nominal income. This, however, means that Keynes's liquidity theory does not apply (Johnson 1965: 396), an implication Friedman denied (Friedman 1966 [1969]: 142). He did not see this contradiction. Since money demand is a stable functional relationship (derived from deep parameters), the stability of its arguments would translate into a stable functional value and, therewith, guarantee the independence of the demand for real balances from money supply (A2). Most importantly, *"if interest rates are stable*, knowledge of interest rates is not necessary to predict changes in nominal income or in prices, so exclusion of interest rates is not even a necessary condition for a divorce" of money and commodity markets (Friedman 1966 [1969]: 146; emphasis added). His reliance on a stable interest rate, however, involves a presumption about the commodity market clearing condition. According to the IS condition, a stable short-run interest rate suggests a stable level of actual income. Friedman's argument for stable income, in turn, is a stable money supply, which however involves (A2). Friedman argued in a circle.

This analytical contradiction had far-reaching consequences for the empirical controversies that ensued after Friedman's restatement (excellently summarized by Laidler 1993). His Keynesian opponents brought forward overwhelming evidence of positive interest-rate elasticity, yet Friedman remained unimpressed and thought he had been misunderstood. Unaware of the circularity of his theoretical reasoning, he denied that a positive interest elasticity of money demand could falsify his theory. The resurrection of the quantity theory tradition, so he believed, would rather depend on a positive but "low" semi-elasticity of money demand with respect to short-run interest rates, that is, an interest rate elasticity smaller one (Friedman 1966 [1969]: 142–4). The same empirical evidence that led his opponents to reject the monetarist quantity theory convinced Friedman that he was right.

Monetarist Transitional Dynamics

Monetarist orthodoxy is not conclusively defined without reference to important works on the dynamics of the modified quantity theory. Friedman is again pivotal (see Friedman

1968, 1974, 1977). The horizon of his short-run, policy-oriented quantity theory also includes the transitional dynamics towards a unique steady-state equilibrium. Monetary orthodoxy introduces transitional dynamics as a disequilibrium process (monetary non-neutrality). At the core of the theory is the assumption of *adaptive expectations*, that is, expected inflation is a weighted average of all current and past realized inflation rates. Even though the representative agent is not irrational (not subject to money illusion), he must "learn" to improve his forecast. Expectations are sluggish, because learning takes time. Accordingly, the speed of convergence depends on the persistence of past experience. In case only last period's experience matters, inflation expectations are given by:

$$\pi_t^e = \pi_{t-1}^e + \lambda(\pi_{t-1} - \pi_{t-1}^e), \tag{10}$$

where π_t^e denotes next period inflation rate currently expected, and λ gives the elasticity of expectations. Changes in the stance of monetary policy always come by surprise and are, therefore, non-neutral.

During the convergence process, the demand for money is predominantly determined by permanent income and inflation expectations. As a proxy for the steady-state wealth level, permanent income is thought to stabilize the money demand function. Of equal importance is the role of inflation expectations. Nothing in the *Tract* impressed Friedman more than Keynes's "excellent and explicit discussion of inflation as a tax and of the [negative] effect of the tax on the quantity of real balances demanded" (Friedman 1974: 171). He was well aware that Keynes anticipated the Cagan model, which is a foundational contribution to monetarist orthodoxy (Cagan 1956). Here, inflation expectations may account for bubbles (dynamic instability). Monetary policy is advised to rule out such explosive paths (hyperinflations) by committing to non-accelerating money-supply rules.

Permanent income is of minor importance in the neighbourhood of a steady-state equilibrium of a stable real economy. It does no harm to set the steady-state real growth rate equal to zero. Then, for $v_t = 1/L(\pi_t^e, Y_\infty)$, the dynamic version of the quantity equation is taken to yield the growth rate of nominal income:

$$\dot{Y}_t = \dot{m}_t + \dot{v}(\pi_t^e - \pi_{t-1}^e), \tag{11}$$

where dotted lower case letter variables denote the percentage growth rates of the upper case letter variables, respectively. Note that growth of nominal income, given by $\dot{Y}$, is a separate variable. Furthermore, given that money supply is supposed to have an immediate impact on nominal income (as shown above), all variables are indexed with respect to the same time period. This is the monetarist theory of nominal income beyond the very short run.

To distinguish between the impact of money supply on transitional real-income growth and on inflation, Friedman introduced his variant of the Phillips curve relationship. Prior to Friedman (1968) and Phelps (1967), the Phillips curve implied a relationship between wage-driven inflation and an excess demand on the labour market. It was understood to explain inflation as disequilibrium phenomena: an excess demand (supply) for commodities translates into an excess demand for labour (involuntary unemployment), driving up (down) the nominal wage rate and – via mark-up pricing – the price level (for example,

Lipsey 1960). Friedman rejected this early Phillips curve on the ground that it involves money illusion. Wage setters remain on their short-run labour supply curves, meaning that firms have to pay higher real wages to buy additional labour force. This results in the monetarist or expectations-augmented Phillips curve:

$$\dot{w} - \pi_t^e = \ell(u_t - u^*), \tag{12}$$

where ℓ denotes the elasticity of labour supply, $\dot{w}$ is wage inflation, u the actual unemployment rate, and u^* the potentially inefficient steady-state rate of unemployment (due to labour market frictions of any type). Friedman's controversial notion of the "natural rate of unemployment" is basically "the equilibrium reached by labor markets unaided and undistorted by governmental fine tuning" (Tobin 1972: 2).

Nominal wages were assumed to be more sluggish than commodity prices, such that rational wage setters must involve inflation expectations to protect their real claims. Given marginal productivity pricing in a competitive economy, there exists – for any given level of actual income – a close relationship between nominal wage growth and realized inflation. Let us assume that $\dot{w}_t = \pi_t$. Substitution and rearrangement yield the Lucas–Rapping "surprise" function (Lucas and Rapping 1969), a cornerstone of monetarism:

$$u_t = u^* - (\pi_t - \pi_t^e)/\ell, \tag{13}$$

summarizing one of the most important propositions of monetarism: deviations of unemployment from its natural level occur only in case of unanticipated inflation rates. To "stimulate the economy", inflation must rise by surprise. Solving for realized inflation then gives:

$$\pi_t = \pi_t^e + \ell(u_t - u^*), \tag{14}$$

introducing inflation expectations as a shift variable. Finally, transitional real-income growth is trivially given by:

$$\dot{y}_t = \dot{Y}_t - \pi_t, \tag{15}$$

which just completes the quantity equation. The variables $\pi_{-1} = \pi_0^e, \dot{m}, u^*$ are exogenous. Given initial values, the seven equations solve for the disequilibrium dynamics of $\pi, \pi^e, \dot{w}, v, \dot{y}, \dot{Y}$. Given proper parameter values, the dynamic system converges to a perfect-foresight equilibrium, characterized by $\dot{w} = \pi = \pi^e = \dot{Y} = \dot{m}$, and $u = u^*, \dot{y} = \dot{v} = 0$. In the steady state, nominal variables grow at the same constant rate determined by monetary policy. Furthermore, the classical dichotomy prevails in long-run equilibrium (the quantity prediction). Augmenting the Phillips curve with expectations suggests that there exists no long-run trade-off between inflation and unemployment, since the curve shifts as soon as wage setters start to learn the money growth rate.

Assume that a monetary authority decides to realize higher money supply growth. According to equation (11), the growth rate of nominal income *immediately* adjusts (the money-supply theory of nominal income). Given the actual inflation rate, equations (13) and (15) suggest that the monetary impulse immediately induces output growth, thereby pushing the unemployment rate below its natural level. The monetarist disequilibrium dynamics display monetary non-neutrality. Realized inflation rises from the onset, due to an increasingly overheating labour market (equation 14). According to (10), they subsequently learn the stance of monetary policy; expectations catch up successively.

The velocity of money increases due to the eroding base of the expected inflation tax on real balances. This amplifies the monetary impulse: during the "early" stages of the transition, nominal and real incomes grow at a faster rate than money supply. The non-accelerating money supply path rules out the explosive solutions. Note that the real wage rate is pro-cyclical in Friedman's analysis, which is not confirmed by the facts.

The fame of the dynamic monetarist model is based on its ability to predict "stagflation", a period of high inflation and low growth. Old variants of the Phillips curve (pure cost-push/demand-pull inflation explanations) suggested a persistent and exploitable trade-off between inflation and unemployment. The US stagflation during the 1970s could not be predicted by the "Keynesian" workhorse models. This was the momentum for the monetarist school, because stagflation is the predicted response to a monetary impulse during the late stages of the transition process. Because the early phase of the monetarist transition is one of "bamboozlement" (Tobin 1972), its late phase, when expected and realized inflation are already close, is a hangover. Given equation (15), a convergent inflation process suggests decreasing real growth (stagflation). The role of the monetarist Phillips curve is decisive: the convergence is driven by its successive shifts during the learning process. In turn, the assumption underlying the expectations-augmented Phillips curve is the absence of money illusion.

Rationality of the private sector is the key to Friedman's dynamic analysis. Irrational behaviour, according to Friedman, cannot survive in a competitive market (Friedman 1953b: 22–3). As animal spirits and other irrationality are driven out by the impersonal market selection process, the observed amplitude of the business cycle must be largely due to policy failures. Friedman and the monetarists, of course, admitted that real and nominal variables are prone to demand and supply shocks. Yet, monetarism is founded on the presumption of a stochastically stable economy (like much of contemporary macroeconomics). This leaves little room for governmental fine-tuning.

Even worse, because fine-tuning works only with "long and variable lags", discretionary monetary policy is highly pro-cyclical, even if well intended. Because money-supply management is highly effective, so much that there is nothing left for fiscal policy, central banks represent a permanent source of danger. A socially efficient solution, according to Friedman's *A Program for Monetary Stability* (1960), would be to fire the money managers, and to replace them by a computer, programmed to increase the monetary base each month at a steady percentage rate (see also Simons 1936). Of course, the so-called "k-percent rule" is an extreme example. Monetarism usually prescribes nominal-income rules, that is, rules that counteract velocity shocks (see McCallum 1981). Friedman's rule is illuminating, because it carries to extremes the spirit of monetarist orthodoxy.

Concluding Remarks

Monetary orthodoxy is anti-Keynesian in its preference for rules over discretion. It shares the classical school's sympathy for credible commitments to well established, openly communicated, and non-contingent rules. Monetarism advocates monetary policy by law, not by genius. Yet, whereas classical monetary orthodoxy proposes the commitment to "external stability", monetarism favours "internal stability ". In this, it is Keynesian. Monetarist money-supply rules are best understood as an attempt to combine the best of two worlds: the rationality of the Gold Standard with the advantages of flexible exchange rates.

One of the reasons why monetarism became so popular, until governments actually tried (some of) it out, was its simplicity. Like progressive policy circles, which upheld simplistic versions of Keynes's *General Theory*, conservative policy circles felt comfortable with the monetarist hyperbole that markets never fail, while governments always do. Even prime ministers and presidents could grasp the gist of Friedman's one-equation macroeconomics. Monetarism, however, did not stand the test of time. The money demand function was found to be unstable. Accordingly, money supply targeting proved to increase interest rate volatility and, therefore, to destabilize the real economy. David Laidler, himself a leading monetarist, closed the book on monetarism in 1989: "The simple fact remains that a further 30 years of monetarist analysis has not been able to demonstrate the empirical existence of a structurally stable transmission mechanism between money and inflation to the satisfaction of its own practitioners, let alone its critics" (Laidler 1989: 1157; see also Laidler 1993).

This is not to say that monetarism was without any merit. Friedman's permanent-income hypothesis and the expectations-augmented Phillips curve remain the most influential monetarist contributions. The lasting impact of monetarism is evident in undergraduate textbooks. Further, monetarism is to be responsible for an intellectual climate that made possible the Volcker disinflation and the subsequent great moderation. In 2002, as a freshly appointed member of the Federal Reserve Board of Governors, Ben Bernanke canonized Friedman's and Schwartz's *Monetary History*: "I would like to say to Milton and Anna: Regarding the Great Depression. You're right, we did it. We're very sorry. But thanks to you, we won't do it again" (Bernanke 2002). A few years later, not long after he was promoted to become chairman, Bernanke found himself and the Federal Reserve caught in a liquidity trap, and witnessed the return of the "fiscal stimulus". Even unconventional policy measures that have more than tripled the Federal Reserve's balance sheet could not prevent a collapse of output and inflation.

ARASH MOLAVI VASSÉI

See also:

Bullionist and anti-bullionist schools (II); Banking and currency schools (II); Chicago School (II); Milton Friedman (I); David Hume (I); Macroeconomics (III); Money and banking (III); New classical macroeconomics (II).

References and further reading

Bernanke, B. (2002), Remarks at the conference to honor Milton Friedman, University of Chicago, accessed at http://www.federalreserve.gov/BOARDDOCS/SPEECHES/2002/20021108/.
Blinder, A.S. and R.M. Solow (1973), 'Does fiscal policy matter?', *Journal of Public Economics*, **2** (4), 319–37.
Bordo, M.D. and A.J. Schwartz (1979), 'Clark Warburton: pioneer monetarist', *Journal of Monetary Economics*, **5** (1), 43–65.
Brunner, K. (1968), 'The role of money and monetary policy', *Federal Reserve Bank of St. Louis Review*, **50**, 8–24.

Brunner, K. (1978), 'Issues of post-Keynesian monetary analysis', in T. Mayer (ed.), *The Structure of Monetarism*, New York: W.W. Norton, pp. 56–84.

Brunner, K. (1989), 'Fiscal policy in macro theory: a survey and evaluation', in K. Brunner and A.H. Meltzer (eds), *Monetary Economics*, New York: Basil Blackwell, pp. 259–338.

Brunner, K. and A. Meltzer (1976), 'An aggregate theory for a closed economy (and reply – monetarism)', in J.L. Stein (ed.), *Monetarism*, New York: North Holland, pp. 69–103, 150–82.

Cagan, P. (1956), 'The monetary dynamics of hyperinflation', in M. Friedman (ed.), *Studies in the Quantity Theory of Money*, Chicago, IL: University of Chicago Press, pp. 25–115.

Dimand, R.W. (1988), *The Origins of the Keynesian Revolution: The Development of Keynes' Theory of Employment and Output*, Aldershot, UK and Brookfield, VT, USA: Edward Elgar.

Dimand, R.W. (2013), 'David Hume and Irving Fisher on the quantity theory of money in the long run and the short run', *European Journal of the History of Economic Thought*, **20** (2), 284–304.

Dimand, R.W. and R.G. Betancourt (2012), 'Irving Fisher's Appreciation and Interest (1896) and the Fisher relation', *Journal of Economic Perspectives*, **26** (4), 185–96.

Dornbusch, R. (1976), 'Comments on an aggregative theory for a closed economy', in J.L. Stein (ed.), *Monetarism*, New York: North Holland, pp. 104–25.

Fisher, I. (1896), *Appreciation and Interest*, reprinted in W. Barber (ed.) (1997), *The Works of Irving Fisher*, vol. 1, London: Pickering & Chatto.

Friedman, B. (1978), 'The theoretical non-debate about monetarism', in T. Mayer (ed.), *The Structure of Monetarism*, New York: W.W. Norton, pp. 94–112.

Friedman, M. (1953a), 'The case for flexible exchange rates', in M. Friedman (ed.), *Essays in Positive Economics*, Chicago, IL: University of Chicago Press, pp. 157–203.

Friedman, M. (1953b), 'The methodology of positive economics', in M. Friedman (ed.), *Essays in Positive Economics*, Chicago, IL: University of Chicago Press, pp. 3–46.

Friedman, M. (1956), 'The quantity theory of money – a restatement', in M. Friedman (ed.), *Studies in the Quantity Theory of Money*, Chicago, IL: University of Chicago Press.

Friedman, M. (1957), *A Theory of the Consumption Function*, Princeton, NJ: Princeton University Press.

Friedman, M. (1960), *A Program for Monetary Stability*, New York: Fordham University Press.

Friedman, M. (1966), 'Interest rates and the demand for money', reprinted in M. Friedman (ed.) (1969), *The Optimum Quantity of Money and Other Essays*, Chicago, IL: Aldine, pp. 141–56.

Friedman, M. (1968), 'The role of monetary policy', *American Economic Review*, **58** (1), 1–17.

Friedman, M. (1969), 'The optimum quantity of money', in M. Friedman (ed.), *The Optimum Quantity of Money and Other Essays*, Chicago, IL: Aldine, pp. 1–50.

Friedman, M. (1974), 'A theoretical framework for monetary analysis. Comments on the critics', in R.J. Gordon (ed.), *Milton Friedman's Monetary Framework – A Debate with His Critics*, Chicago, IL: University of Chicago Press, pp. 1–62, 132–77.

Friedman, M. (1977), 'Nobel lecture: inflation and unemployment', *Journal of Political Economy*, **85** (3), 451–72.

Friedman, M. (1997), 'John Maynard Keynes', *Federal Reserve Bank of Richmond Economic Quarterly*, **82** (2), 1–23.

Friedman, M. (2008), 'Quantity theory of money', in S.N. Durlauf and L.E. Blume (eds), *The New Palgrave Dictionary of Economics*, Basingstoke: Palgrave Macmillan.

Friedman, M. and A.J. Schwartz (1963), *A Monetary History of the United States, 1867–1960*, Princeton, NJ: Princeton University Press.

Hume, D. (1752), *Political Discourses*, reprinted 1955, E. Rotwein (ed.), Madison, WI: University of Wisconsin Press.

Johnson, H.G. (1965), 'A quantity theorist's monetary history of the United States', *The Economic Journal*, **75** (298), 388–96.

Keynes, J.M. (1923), *A Tract on Monetary Reform*, reprinted 1971 in *The Collected Writings of John Maynard Keynes*, vol. IV, London: Macmillan and Cambridge University Press.

Keynes, J.M. (1936), *The General Theory of Employment, Interest, and Money*, reprinted 1973 in *The Collected Writings of John Maynard Keynes*, vol. VII, London: Macmillan and Cambridge University Press.

Laidler, D.E.W. (1989), 'Dow and Saville's critique of monetary policy – a review essay', *Journal of Economic Literature*, **27** (3), 1147–59.

Laidler, D.E.W. (1991), *The Golden Age of the Quantity Theory*, Princeton, NJ: Princeton University Press.

Laidler, D.E.W. (1993), *The Demand for Money: Theories, Evidence and Problems*, 4th edn, New York: HarperCollins.

Laidler, D.E.W. (2012), 'Milton Friedman's contributions to macroeconomics and their influence', EPRI Working Paper Series, 2012(2).

Lipsey, R.G. (1960), 'The relation between unemployment and the rate of change of money wage rates in the United Kingdom 1862–1957', *Economica*, **27** (1), 1–31.

Lucas, E.L. Jr and L.A. Rapping (1969), 'Price expectations and the Phillips curve', *American Economic Review*, **59** (3), 342–50.

Mayer, T. (1978), 'The structure of monetarism', part I, in T. Mayer (ed.), *The Structure of Monetarism*, New York: W.W. Norton, pp. 1–25.

McCallum, B.T. (1981), 'Monetarist principles and the money stock growth rule', *American Economic Review*, **71** (2), 134–8.

Meltzer, A.H. (1983), 'On Keynes and monetarism', in D. Worswick and J. Trevithick (eds), *Keynes and the Modern World: Proceedings of the Keynes Centenary Conference*, Cambridge: Cambridge University Press, pp. 1–26.

Patinkin, D. (1949), 'The indeterminacy of absolute prices in classical economics', *Econometrica*, **17**(1), 1–27.

Patinkin, D. (1965), *Money, Interest, and Prices*, New York: Harper & Row.

Patinkin, D. (1969), 'The Chicago tradition, the quantity theory and Friedman', *Journal of Money, Credit and Banking*, **1** (2), 46–70.

Patinkin, D. (1974), 'Friedman on the quantity theory and Keynesian economics', in R.J. Gordon (ed.), *Milton Friedman's Monetary Framework – A Debate with His Critics*, Chicago, IL: University of Chicago Press, pp. 111–31.

Phelps, E.S. (1967), 'Phillips curves, expectations of inflation and optimal unemployment over time', *Economica*, new series, **34** (135), 254–81.

Pigou, A.C. (1917), 'The value of money', *Quarterly Journal of Economics*, **32** (1), 38–65.

Simons, H.C. (1936), 'Rule versus authorities in monetary policy', *Journal of Political Economy*, **44** (1), 1–30.

Steindl, F.G. (1990), 'The "Oral Tradition" at Chicago in the 1930s', *Journal of Political Economy*, **98** (2), 430–32.

Tobin, J. (1958), 'Liquidity preference as the behavior towards risk', reprinted in J. Tobin (ed.) (1987), *Essays in Economics: Macroeconomics*, Cambridge, MA: MIT Press, pp. 242–71.

Tobin, J. (1969), 'A general equilibrium approach to monetary theory', reprinted in J. Tobin (ed.) (1987), *Essays in Economics: Macroeconomics*, Cambridge, MA: MIT Press, pp. 322–38.

Tobin, J. (1972), 'Inflation and unemployment', *American Economic Review*, **62** (1), 1–18.

Tobin, J. (1974), 'Friedman's theoretical framework', in R.J. Gordon (ed.), *Milton Friedman's Monetary Framework – A Debate with His Critics*, Chicago, IL: University of Chicago Press, pp. 77–89.

New classical macroeconomics

New Classical Macroeconomics as Monetarism Mark II

At its heyday in the 1980s, new classical macroeconomics (NCM) was widely considered to have accomplished the monetarist campaign against Keynesianism. This campaign had been driven most forcefully by Friedman (1968) in his well-known presidential address to the American Economic Association: monetary policy cannot establish and maintain any inflation–unemployment combination on a given Phillips curve at will, because adaptive inflation expectations let the curve shift upwards (in case of an expansionary monetary impulse). Thus there is no Phillips curve trade-off in the long run; there is only the choice between high or low inflation at the given level of the non-accelerating inflation rate of unemployment (NAIRU), that is, the level of the unemployment rate that represents a macroeconomic equilibrium of the labour market, ruling out excess demand or excess supply pressure on wage inflation.

As Friedman left no doubt that he discussed a scenario where policy aimed to keep unemployment below the natural rate, it remains a mystery why Keynesians felt the need to object to this monetarist attack. The "discovery" that money growth beyond the point of full employment will necessarily lead to inflation without increasing output can already be found in the *General Theory* (Keynes 1936 [1973]: 303). There is hardly any deviation from Friedman's acceleration principle, although it has to be conceded that a systematic treatment of inflation expectation is missing in Keynes (but note that trend inflation is a post-World War II phenomenon).

A reasonable understanding of Friedman's scenario would build on a realistic assumption of data uncertainty: when suffering from an imprecise estimation of the natural rate, policymakers, as in Wicksell's (1898: 189) early recommendation for interest rate policy, learn only by a rise or fall in the price level about deviations from equilibrium. However, the problem of scant information on the economy's resource constraints was not prominent in the 1960s and 1970s discussion on the Phillips curve; it was ranked higher only in retrospect (Orphanides 2002).

The same is true with regard to hysteresis: there is an incentive to increase employment beyond the current natural rate if that level is endogenous, but this argument was missing in Friedman's attack on Keynesian demand policy. Friedman provides no detailed explanation of how the natural rate is determined, he simply contends that it results from the Walrasian system of general equilibrium equations. According to Lucas (1980: 709), owing to a lack of analytical capabilities Friedman is "not able to put such a system down on paper", and, according to McCallum (1989), the natural rate hypothesis is not incompatible with hysteresis as it is not monetary policy as such that changes the NAIRU, but endogenous mechanisms of human capital building triggered by a monetary policy impulse.

Taking Friedman's scenario as the stage, Lucas and the NCM, named Monetarism Mark II by Tobin (1980), offered a more radical play where agents immediately jump to their new equilibrium positions whenever they expect rationally that the policymaker is about to increase the money growth rate. As a consequence, there are not even temporary employment gains during a monetary expansion. There is no Phillips Curve that can be exploited on the part of an employment-oriented policymaker. What comes as a surprise, however, is that Hahn (1982: 74–5) seemed to be the only person who understood that, so far, the Keynesian camp should not be bothered by the messages of both Friedman and Lucas:

> It is puzzling to find it put forward as a discovery that a higher inflation rate will not increase the full-employment level of employment: Keynes and Keynesians would not have claimed otherwise ... The Lucasians, by denying the possibility of involuntary unemployment – indeed, they profess not to know what it means – have given no reason why anyone should be interested in their trade-off even if it existed. In fact, the world that they describe quite plainly needs no macro-policy. Keynesians were concerned with the problem of pushing the economy to its natural rate, not beyond it. If the economy is already there, we can all go home.

Shocks and Missing Responses: The Variety of Macroeconomic Disequilibria

The confusion in the debate between the Keynesian and the monetarist and new classical schools has its roots first and foremost in the fact that also Keynesians seemed to believe that a key problem in macroeconomics is nominal wage rigidity. In contrast, Keynes in his famous chapter 19 of the *General Theory* had shown that flexible nominal wages in no way guaranteed the dynamic stability of a full-employment equilibrium in case of demand shocks that mainly emanate from the volatility of the marginal efficiency of capital. Prospects of lower rates of return represent a real shock that, according to Keynes, is not absorbed by adjustments of the (real) rate of interest because the latter (with constant inflation) is governed by liquidity preference and/or rigid yield aspirations.

Following the taxonomy suggested by Leijonhufvud (1983), the *General Theory* addressed an R/R type of macro disequilibrium where a real shock is not properly offset by an adjustment of a real market variable: a change of the marginal efficiency of capital (*d mec*) coming up against a constant real interest rate ($\bar{r}$), basically an intertemporal coordination failure between investment and saving (Table 1). However, during the era of the neoclassical synthesis, debates were located in the R/N cell where a real *mec* shock was said to cause unemployment due to a rigid nominal wage ($\bar{w}$). This, however, is a misguided diagnosis as the cause of the trouble is not rooted in the labour market. Keynes already had shown that nominal wage flexibility cannot help to stabilise the macro effects of expected-profitability shocks.

Table 1   The "Swedish flag"

		Adjustment failures	
		Nominal	Real
Shocks	Nominal	N/N $dM \sim \bar{w}$	N/R $dM \sim E(r)$
	Real	R/N $d\,mec \sim \bar{w}$	R/R $d\,mec \sim \bar{r}$

Source: Leijonhufvud (1983: 187).

Monetarism then activated the N/N issue on money neutrality: wage stickiness may cause employment to vary temporarily with money supply changes (dM). This is less of an important discovery in Friedman's story of expansive monetary policy, but more so when assessing the economic costs of disinflation. In any case, Keynes's message somehow seemed to have been forgotten. The new classicals turned their attention to the N/R constellation: a nominal monetary policy impulse induces an increase of output as producers take a general price increase as a sign of a profitable move of firm-specific prices; the expected rate of profit $E(r)$ moves although it should not.

> The positive association of price changes and output arises because suppliers misinterpret general price movements for relative price changes. (Lucas 1973: 333)

> Monetary changes have real consequences only because agents cannot discriminate perfectly between real and monetary demand shifts. Since their ability to discriminate should not be altered by a proportional change in the *scale* of monetary policy, intuition suggests that such scale changes should have no real consequences. (Lucas 1972: 116, original emphasis)

In the monetarist case, workers suffer from incomplete information on consumer prices (or from money illusion), hence they interpret higher nominal as higher real wages, which allows a period of temporary over-employment. New classical macroeconomics shifts the information problem onto producers. They bear the profit risk of ill-founded supply decisions whereas workers no longer are fooled: flexible nominal and real wages let them reach positions on the labour supply curve at any time (the possibility of parallel movements of wages and prices, and the involuntary persistence of a disequilibrium real wage, are ignored). The NCM story can best be understood as a description of self-employed market agents searching profitable sales contracts. Apart from misinterpreted price movements, we have market clearing throughout.

The argument of disappointed expectations on relative prices p_j/P (where p_j is the supply price of firm j and P the price level) is important for a possible explanation of disinflation costs: firms may hesitate to lower the rate of increase of their supply prices (and workers likewise their wage growth aspirations) in a period of monetary restraint because there may be signs that the firm's market position is upheld in the ongoing process of competition and structural change; thus it appears rational to wait until firm-specific demand starts to weaken. If many firms suffer from a too optimistic assessment of their market position, downward price rigidity may ensue.

However, the aforementioned line of argument rests on a misjudgement of the expected market forces affecting p_j, not on a wrong estimation of P. The NCM story has it the other way round, which is much harder to swallow. It can be justified only by specific assumptions on information dissemination in a segmented market structure; this sounds convincing in Lucas's (1972, 1975) island model where producers visit separated market places in a sequential order, but in general the information on the path of money and inflation is readily available without any costs. This may not hold if policy follows an erratic activist strategy, hence Lucas (1975: 1139) finds that his analysis "provides a rationalization for rules which smooth monetary policy" – surely a trivial recommendation drawn from a model where all market disturbances result from the field of macro policy.

Time Inconsistency: The Temptation to Organise Surprise Inflation

Starting from this latter insight, the stage was prepared for an analysis of the misuse of the policymaker's discretion. Following Kydland and Prescott (1977), Barro and Gordon (1983) see the policymaker minimise a loss function of the form:

$$L = \pi^2 + b[y - (y^* + k)]^2 \tag{1}$$

where π is inflation, y is log output and k some positive desired deviation from market equilibrium y^*. According to the Lucas supply function, output depends on surprise inflation, i.e. the difference between actual and expected inflation:

$$y = y^* + \alpha(\pi - \pi^e) \tag{2}$$

The form of this supply function, with quantities following price signals, reveals the Walrasian roots of NCM; this is a further difference compared to the Marshallian tradition of Friedman's monetarism (Hoover 1984).

It is assumed "for the sake of simplification" that the policymaker can control inflation directly. Then, taking expected inflation π^e as given, an optimal rate of inflation can be derived, increasing in k, which allows output to approach $y^* + k$. If market agents however respond by adjusting $\pi^e = \pi$, inflation settles at $\pi = \alpha bk$, and $y = y^*$. This constellation is the stable rational-expectations equilibrium as private agents keep $\pi^e = \alpha bk$, bearing in mind the $k > 0$ term in the policymaker's loss function. His promise to stick to $\pi = 0$ is not credible; it is not time consistent because, after the public's change of belief to $\pi^e = 0$, it is optimal to organise a surprise inflation.

This simple game-theoretic exercise nicely demonstrates NCM's simplistic attitude towards the relationship between politics and markets: policymakers appear as inclined to fool private agents, in order to aim for a policy target that does not conform to a direct aggregation of individual preferences. This justifies the recommendation to abolish the policymaker's discretionary powers (that is, let him optimise a per-period loss function) and to impose an obligation to obey predictable rules of decision making.

The list of critical points that can be raised against the surprise-inflation theory is long (Forder 2001). The arguments given for the $k > 0$ target are hardly convincing: if income taxes produce a distortion in individual labour supply so that private and social benefits of work do not conform, one might consider a tax reform, but not expansive monetary policy. Blinder (1997) claims never to have met central bankers who succumb to the temptation of initiating a surprise inflation because they can easily anticipate the inevitable damage in their *intertemporal* loss function. Finally, we should not regard the rate of inflation as a policy instrument. However, it took 15 years before the simple argument of Goodhart and Huang (1998: 393, 378–9) appeared in the literature that organising a surprise inflation is impossible owing to the well-known lags in monetary policy-making:

> Game theoretic models of time inconsistency have been so popular, because we have wanted to believe them, despite these models being unrealistic in several respects . . . [They] have ignored the fact that there are long lags between monetary policy adjustments and their effect on the real economy, and that both inflation and output have persistence. But so long as wages and

prices are fully flexible, such monetary policy lags would imply that the policy would be transparently observed before it affects the economy; consequently the Central Bank could not fool anybody . . . If monetary instruments operate with a lag, then a rational public would observe them and adjust their expectations accordingly if they have not bound themselves into a contract longer than that lag. Hence the public would not be fooled, and the time inconsistency problem would vanish.

Policy Ineffectiveness, the Lucas Critique and Money Neutrality

The view that macro policy is often used in order to fool agents is an extreme variant of NCM's more essential message that macro policy is useless. The basic model consists of the Lucas supply function (now expressed in log price-level terms with $y^* = 0$):

$$y = \alpha(p - p^e) + \varepsilon^s \tag{3}$$

and a demand function where, in a monetarist fashion, the log of nominal money m is the central bank's policy instrument and g represents the log of autonomous (fiscal) spending:

$$y = \theta g + \beta(m - p) + \varepsilon^d \tag{4}$$

The solution reveals that only non-anticipated expansionary policy moves exert an impact on output. Given rational expectations, only random shocks ε^d and ε^s let output and prices deviate from their equilibrium values $y^* = 0$ and $p^* = m + \theta g/\beta$, respectively. Thus any policy that follows a predictable rule fails to affect real variables, and it is often further assumed that the policymaker cannot perceive and respond to shocks more timely and efficiently than market agents. Policy inefficiency is to be understood in a dynamic sense: we should not assume that market behaviour remains unaffected from changes of economic policy strategies. This finding, the Lucas critique, is appreciated also on the part of NCM critics like Hahn (1980: 3): "Monetary policy, or indeed any government policy, is part of the economic environment of agents who can learn or deduce what this policy is. But then, in evaluating the policy we must not model the actions of agents as if they were independent of the government's policy."

In order to elaborate this argument, Sargent and Wallace (1976) first show that in general there are "activist" policy strategies, which dominate Friedman's fixed-rule recommendation if market expectations remain unchanged. Let the "true" one-equation model be:

$$y_t = \theta g + \beta (m_t - m_t^e) + \varphi y_{t-1} + \varepsilon_t \tag{5}$$

With constant expectations this will be estimated as:

$$y_t = c + \beta m_t + \varphi y_{t-1} + \varepsilon_t \tag{6}$$

The central bank now seeks an optimal policy rule of the form $m_t = \mu_0 + \mu_1 y_{t-1}$ in order to minimise the variance of y_t around a desired mean y^*. Application of that rule yields:

$$y_t = (\beta\mu_0 + c) + (\beta\mu_1 + \varphi)y_{t-1} + \varepsilon_t \tag{7}$$

The variance of the process (7) is:

$$var(y_t) = \frac{var(\varepsilon_t)}{1 - (\beta\mu_1 + \varphi)^2} \tag{8}$$

which is minimised by choosing $\mu_1 = -\varphi/\beta$. Equating the mean of process (7) with the policy target:

$$y^* = \frac{\beta\mu_0 + c}{1 - (\beta\mu_1 + \varphi)} \tag{9}$$

leads to the selection of $\mu_0 = (y^* - c)/\beta$. Thus running the activist policy rule with optimised coefficients yields the best available result:

$$y_t = y^* + \varepsilon_t \tag{10}$$

This outcome obviously outperforms any fixed-m rule. However, this depends crucially on a no-learning behaviour of market agents who stick to their former fixed-m^e belief. If, on the other hand, people understand and recalculate the motives and mechanisms of activist policy strategies, the central bank loses its influence on the process (5) due to $m_t = m_t^e$.

The extent to which market agents are able to grasp the macroeconomic logic of policy strategies is much under dispute. Sargent and Wallace (1976: 181) believe that rational individuals should anticipate reforms that can be expected to happen, from an analysis of the society's list of urgent problems:

If rational agents live in a world in which rules can be and are changed, their behavior should take into account such possibilities and should depend on the process generating the rule changes. But invoking this kind of complete rationality seems to rule out normative economics completely by, in effect, ruling out freedom for the policymaker. For in a model with completely rational expectations, including a rich enough description of policy, it seems impossible to define a sense in which there is any scope for discussing the optimal design of policy rules. That is because the equilibrium values of the endogenous variables already reflect, in the proper way, the parameters describing the authorities' prospective subsequent behavior, including the probability that this or that proposal for reforming policy will be adopted.

The whole argument appears rather hypothetical and normative. It is obvious that NCM aims to establish the money neutrality postulate in an even stronger version compared to simple monetarism. In his Nobel Lecture, Lucas (1996) opposes David Hume on account of the latter's view that a recession is unavoidable following a monetary contraction. This is illogical, according to Lucas, because a gradual change of the money supply should be regarded as basically equivalent to an administrative change in the standard of the money of account, for example, redefining 1000 old francs as 10 new francs. This finding, however, was said to be too complicated for an economist like Hume, "equipped with only verbal methods". Lucas restricts the asserted equivalence of a money-of-account recalibration and a change of money growth to a state of perfect markets. So, how could a perceptive observer of the world like David Hume ever be convinced to believe that market societies tend to be organised in a series of Walras auctions?

After some years of debate within the scientific community, the view gained momentum that the NCM project was running into diminishing returns. On the one hand, the rational-expectation campaign appeared as a somewhat sterile exercise of pure logic; it did not prove the convergence of individual learning processes in a dynamic scenario of different beliefs:

> Individuals, just as they have their own subjective preferences, have their own subjective ways of learning from experience and thus will develop their own forecasts. Though each of these forecasts may be perfectly rational in the light of the individual's experience, they may well look irrational in the light of the particular model of an economic observer and they will generally differ from each other. (Niehans 1987: 412; cf. also DeCanio 1979)

On the other hand, the distinction between anticipated and "surprising" actions of monetary policy did not help to understand the pattern of the macro process since the mid-1970s. NCM was stuck in a dead-end.

> The original Lucas model of the business cycle proved to be *too* successful at explaining why business fluctuations should not be much of a problem; under plausible assumptions about the speed with which information circulates in a modern economy, the model could not explain why monetary disturbances should have any significant effects (and above all, any *persistent* effects) at all. (Woodford 1999: 23, original emphasis)

Business Cycles in a Robinson Crusoe Economy

The empirical observation that macro activity was linked to broad, but less so to narrow money, finally prompted NCM to depart from its monetarist tradition. Monetary policy and banking behaviour now were considered as responses to market dynamics, which according to the new view of the Real Business Cycle (RBC) theory is driven by real shocks (Barro 1989). They emanate mainly from the sphere of technology as productivity shocks, but this approach can be generalised to comprise also shifts of the marginal efficiency of investment resulting from demand shocks (Stadler 1994). Thus, after a long detour in the history of macroeconomic thought, the neoclassicals seemed to have found their way back to Keynes's world (see cell R/R in Table 1).

However, this would be a misleading conclusion. Keynesian economics are criticised for lacking a proper choice-theoretic framework and their assertion of market failures, which may be compared to unexplained and unexploited gains from trade. On the contrary, the core of the RBC approach consists of the optimisation calculus of a representative agent who decides on his path of work, leisure, consumption, saving and investment over time, thus responding to random choices of his opponent player: Mother Nature. These exogenous impulses drive a productivity growth process; shocks and (in the case of specific utility functions) responses may show a pattern of serial correlation so that the stylised image of a macroeconomic cycle can be formally reproduced. It is supposed to be an equilibrium business cycle that does not call for economic policy interventions.

"Microfoundation of macroeconomics", NCM's methodological principle, aims to derive the path of all macro variables directly from the optimisation calculus of a single agent. This ideal of collapsing macroeconomics into a series of microeconomic choices comes into its own in the world of Robinson Crusoe. It is, by definition, a full-employment scenario where coordination failures between saving and investment, liquidity shortages and distributional conflicts have no role to play.

Some proponents of RBC frankly admit that "this model is clearly simple and unrealistic" (Plosser 1989: 54). They claim, but do not prove that results from studying Robinson Crusoe economics continue to hold in a competitive setting with many agents and incomplete markets. Nevertheless, Lucas (1987: 67–9) does not hesitate to conclude that all unemployment in the real word must be of the voluntary type, and – if people spend too much time on being unemployed – that welfare can be improved by imposing a tax on this "activity". The representative agent who dominates the RBC model exhibits conspicuously close ties to a social planner, but is hardly able to aggregate individual preferences of heterogeneous agents in a free market society (Kirman 1992).

On a more technical level, it proved to be difficult to explain slumps and crises by simultaneous negative productivity shocks in most of a country's industries. Moreover, RBC was not able to account for the power of monetary policy in a world of partly rigid wages and prices. This paved the way for the next step in macro theory: new Keynesian macroeconomics, which however is a misnomer as seen from the development of the history of economic thought (Spahn 2009).

Techniques of Model Building and Scientific Progress

Lucas as one of the "founding fathers" of NCM sees progress in economics as an entirely technical matter: mathematical and statistical methods improve over time; and he often pities previous economists for not being equipped with modern computational capabilities. At the same time, he rightly emphasises that economics does not evolve by mere empirical observation:

> A "theory" is not a collection of assertions about the behavior of the actual economy but rather an explicit set of instructions for building a parallel or analogue system–a mechanical, imitation economy. A "good" model, from this point of view, will not be exactly more "real" than a poor one, but will provide better imitations. Of course, what one means by a "better imitation" will depend on the particular questions to which one wishes answers. (Lucas 1980: 697)

Thus scientific progress depends on the growth of technical abilities to construct models, but also on the changes of questions posed. This is very similar to Keynes's (1938 [1987]: 296–7, original emphasis) view:

> Economics is a branch of logic, a way of thinking . . . One cannot get very far except by devising new and improved models . . . *Progress* in economics consists almost entirely in a progressive improvement in the choice of models. . . . Economics is a science of thinking in terms of models joined with the art of choosing models which are relevant to the contemporary world. It is compelled to be this, because, unlike the typical natural science, the material to which it is applied is, in too many respects, not homogeneous through time . . . Economics is essentially a moral science and not a natural science. That is to say, it employs introspection and judgement of value.

Thus it is all the more astonishing that both authors do not at agree on issues such as macroeconomic market failures and the need for stabilisation policies. The conclusion is that progress in model-building techniques hardly suffices to understand paradigm shifts in economics. Here, views on the conception of the world do not seem to converge. However, this is hard to concede among rational-expectation believers.

PETER SPAHN

See also:
Milton Friedman (I); Robert E. Lucas (I); Macroeconomics (III); Monetarism (II).

References and further reading

Barro, R.J. (1989), 'New classicals and Keynesians, or the good guys and the bad guys', *Schweizerische Zeitschrift für Volkswirtschaft und Statistik*, **125** (3), 263–73.
Barro, R.J. and D.B. Gordon (1983), 'Rules, discretion and reputation in a model of monetary policy', *Journal of Monetary Economics*, **12** (1), 101–21.
Blinder, A.S. (1997), 'What central bankers could learn from academics – and vice versa', *Journal of Economic Perspectives*, **11** (2), 3–19.
DeCanio, S.J. (1979), 'Rational expectations and learning from experience', *Quarterly Journal of Economics*, **94** (1), 47–57.
Forder, J. (2001), 'The theory of credibility and the reputation-bias of policy', *Review of Political Economy*, **13** (1), 5–25.
Friedman, M. (1968), 'The role of monetary policy', *American Economic Review*, **58** (1), 1–17.
Goodhart, C.A.E. and H. Huang (1998), 'Time inconsistency in a model with lags, persistence, and overlapping wage contracts', *Oxford Economic Papers*, **50** (3), 378–96.
Hahn, F.H. (1980), 'Monetarism and economic theory', *Economica*, **47** (February), 1–17.
Hahn, F.H. (1982), *Money and Inflation*, Oxford: Blackwell.
Hoover, K.D. (1984), 'Two types of monetarism', *Journal of Economic Literature*, **22** (1), 58–76.
Keynes, J.M. (1936), *The General Theory of Employment, Interest, and Money*, reprinted 1973, London: Macmillan.
Keynes, J.M. (1938), 'Letter to R.F. Harrod', in D. Moggridge (ed.), *The Collected Writings of John Maynard Keynes*, vol. 14, *The General Theory and After*, pt II, *Defence and Development*, reprinted 1987, London: Macmillan, 295–7.
Kirman, A. (1992), 'Whom or what does the representative individual represent?', *Journal of Economic Perspectives*, **6** (2), 117–36.
Klamer, A. (1984), *The New Classical Macroeconomics – Conversations with New Classical Economists and Their Opponents*, Brighton: Wheatsheaf Books.
Kydland, F.E. and E.C. Prescott (1977), 'Rules rather than discretion – the inconsistency of optimal plans', *Journal of Political Economy*, **85** (3), 473–91.
Leijonhufvud, A. (1983), 'What would Keynes have thought of rational expectations?', in D. Worswick and J. Trevithick (eds), *Keynes and the Modern World*, Cambridge: Cambridge University Press, pp. 179–205.
Lucas, R.E. (1972), 'Expectations and the neutrality of money', *Journal of Economic Theory*, **4** (2), 103–24.
Lucas, R.E. (1973), 'Some international evidence on output-inflation tradeoffs', *American Economic Review*, **63** (3), 326–34.
Lucas, R.E. (1975), 'An equilibrium model of the business cycle', *Journal of Political Economy*, **83** (6), 1113–44.
Lucas, R.E. (1980), 'Methods and problems in business cycle theory', *Journal of Money, Credit, and Banking*, **12** (4), 696–715.
Lucas, R.E. (1987), *Models of Business Cycles*, Oxford and New York: Blackwell.
Lucas, R.E. (1996), 'Nobel Lecture – monetary neutrality', *Journal of Political Economy*, **104** (4), 661–82.
McCallum, B.T. (1989), 'New classical macroeconomics – a sympathetic account', *Scandinavian Journal of Economics*, **91** (2), 223–52.
Niehans, J. (1987), 'Classical monetary theory, new and old', *Journal of Money, Credit, and Banking*, **19** (4), 409–24.
Orphanides, A. (2002), 'Monetary-policy rules and the great inflation', *American Economic Review, Papers and Proceedings*, **92** (2), 115–20.
Plosser, C.I. (1989), 'Understanding real business cycles', *Journal of Economic Perspectives*, **3** (3), 51–77.
Sargent, T.J. and N. Wallace (1976), 'Rational expectations and the theory of economic policy', *Journal of Monetary Economics*, **2** (2), 169–83.

Spahn, P. (2009), 'The new Keynesian microfoundation of macroeconomics', *Jahrbuch für Wirtschaftswissenschaften*, **60** (3), 181–203.

Stadler, G.W. (1994), 'Real business cycles', *Journal of Economic Literature*, **32** (4), 1750–83.

Tobin, J. (1980), *Asset Accumulation and Economic Activity – Reflections on Contemporary Macroeconomic Theory*, Chicago, IL: University of Chicago Press.

Wicksell, K. (1898), *Interest and Prices – A Study of the Causes Regulating the Value of Money*, reprinted 1936, London and New York: Macmillan.

Woodford, M. (1999), *Revolution and Evolution in Twentieth-Century Macroeconomics*, Princeton, NJ: Princeton University.

Public choice

The Sources of Public Choice

In the *Wealth of Nations* published in 1776, Adam Smith convincingly explains the fundamental importance of freedom for the prosperity of a nation. Incidentally, the year of the publication of the *Wealth of Nations* coincides with the year of the Declaration of Independence of the United States of America. Not incidentally, however, Smith's book has enormously inspired the US Constitution framers in writing the *Federalist Papers* in the years 1787–88. In Britain, Smith's home country, the echo of the *Wealth* was more mixed. Smith has been praised as an anti-mercantilist. However, his commitment to liberty has become less acknowledged. Smith had to convince his compatriot readers against the theories of competing writers. In 1780, only a few years after the publication of the *Wealth*, Jeremy Bentham published his *Introduction to the Principles of Morals and Legislation* in which he proposed utilitarianism as a leading doctrine for the British public. Bentham fought for a moral society against phenomena such as usury and prodigality. His follower John Stuart Mill saw utilitarianism as a principle to obtain a better society. He has adopted the ideas of an equal sacrifice of taxation first proposed by Horace and Jean-Baptiste Say (Faccarello 2006). Mill, too, thought that the rich and poor citizens should both contribute to the state, but as utility of income and wealth was assumed to decline with higher income, Mill's equal sacrifice principle implied a higher taxation of the rich compared with the taxation of the poor. The amount of the total sacrifice, in fact the amount of money to be raised has not been questioned. The expenditure side of the budget was not explicitly considered. Therefore public choice has remained outside economic analysis. Bentham and Mill both had a large influence in Britain. It is due to their publications that utilitarianism became a leading philosophy in nineteenth- up to twentieth-century Britain. As utility was regarded as cardinally measurable, welfare maximization became a policy goal for governments. Welfare maximization had its own justification. It was imposed and hence independent of individuals' choices. So the spirit of liberty of Adam Smith has been crowded out of public policy.

The utilitarian view was contested by three neoclassical economists: Carl Menger of Vienna, Stanley Jevons of London and Léon Walras of Lausanne who succeeded in explaining prices in a market economy as a result of consistent individual market evaluations of private goods around 1870. However, individual market evaluations were alien to the British utilitarians who neglected to notice that the great neoclassical triad has opened a new research programme from private to public goods. The study of the economics of public goods has been exiled to the Continent to Germany, Italy and Sweden.

In Germany Adolph Wagner of Berlin was an important trailblazer. Wagner did not believe much in the relevance of individual choices in the public sector, but he understood the relevance of public goods, which were unknown to the then leading British public finance economists Bentham and Mill (see Blaug 1978). On the one hand, Wagner gave an important signal to the economists of the Italian School of public finance to study public goods on the basis of the marginal utility principle, which they appreciated from reading the publications of Menger, Jevons and Walras. On the other hand, the Italians have already become familiar in terms of *quid pro quo* for public goods, inherited from

French economists A.-R.-J. Turgot and M.-J.-A.-N. Caritat de Condorcet (Faccarello and Sturn 2010) and from Francesco Ferrara.

Antonio De Viti de Marco (1888) and Ugo Mazzola (1890) concluded that the principle of choice had to be extended from private goods to public goods: this was a new world, quite different from the utilitarian world of Bentham and Mill. But how should choice be organized as public goods were consumed collectively? All individuals had to contribute according to their joint evaluation, said De Viti de Marco, and each individual according to his or her own evaluation in terms of his or her "godimento" (pleasure) as Mazzola has suggested. How could this bridge be built? De Viti de Marco thought that the actual state should become something like a cooperative. Mazzola thought that coercion was necessary (Fausto 2006: 77). However, coercion would disregard the idea of individual evaluation: in fact the heart of the whole Italian scientific venture. No doubt; marginal evaluation had to be voluntary. At this critical point the Swedish economist Knut Wicksell made the decisive contribution. He linked the idea of quid pro quo inherited from Turgot, Concorcet, Ferrara and Sax and combined it with the institutions of the parliamentary decision process:

> The principle is as such nothing, but the interest principle, the well known principle of reciprocity between contribution and return whose range of application and usefulness I try to extend in two directions: On the one hand, following the example of Sax and his followers, towards applying the modern view of marginal utility and of subjective evaluation consistently to public services and private individuals' response payments . . . and – herein I could not indeed quote a forerunner – by linking the principle . . . with the form which tax power has adopted nowadays . . . namely the parliamentary principle of tax approval and by trying to establish the conditions under which the principle of quid pro quo. . . can be brought into effect automatically. (Wicksell 1896: vi–vii, author's translation)

To Wicksell it was necessary that individuals' consent was voluntary. So the link to neoclassical economics was established, and the result was indeed a choice. Wicksell effectively closed the gap from private to public goods; the problem which was left open by Menger, Jevons and Walras, who only considered private goods. The importance of linking choice from private to public goods has never been fully grasped by the established Anglo-Saxon School of public finance until today. James Mirrlees, for example, admittedly acknowledges the existence of public goods in Diamond and Mirrlees (1971a, 1971b). He spared an amount of resources for public goods in his theory of optimal taxation. However, he leaves the question unanswered how public goods should be evaluated and how many public goods are desired (Blankart 2014).

The light disseminated by the Swedish and Italian economists remained unnoticed until Richard Musgrave popularized their views in his 1939 paper "Voluntary exchange theory of public economy". However, the fundamental attack on the welfare approach of the Anglo-Saxon School was due to the publication of Lionel Robbins's book *An Essay on the Nature and Significance of Economic Science* (London 1932 [1935]). Robbins argued that the economists should stop studying normative issues about the welfare of a society, but rather analyse positively how individuals use scarce means to achieve alternative ends. So Robbins has repatriated choice in the centre of economics.

Robbins gave confidence to economists studying positive economics in the new world of public choice. Duncan Black (1948) and Kenneth Arrow (1951 [1963]) were the first who tested the new trail. They extended the study of free markets to the study of free democracies. Their first results were a great surprise. Black found that separate individual orderings, when compared pairwise, might end in a cycle. He popularized earlier but forgotten results by the French scientist Marie-Jean-Antoine-Nicolas Caritat de Condorcet (1785) and the English logician Charles Dodgson (1876).

Arrow (1951 [1963]) has proven that, when voters have to choose between three or more distinct alternatives, individual rankings cannot be converted in a consistent set of collectively ranked preferences if individuals' domain of alternatives is unrestricted, if dictatorship is to be absent, if Pareto efficiency and independence of irrelevant alternatives have to hold.

If one or more of the four conditions are relaxed, a consistent ordering may not be obtained. The most famous invention is due to Black (1948). He found that if it is possible to array the alternatives in such a way that each voter's preferences exhibit single-peakedness, then cycles could be avoided and in fact the median voter decides for the whole community (median voter theorem). Is Black's condition realistic? Single-peakedness seems plausible if the community has to decide on whether to have one, two or three football fields. The football fans, on the one hand, are confronted with the football grumpies, on the other. But single-peakedness is much less plausible when the community has to decide how to use the last plot of land in a local community. Should the plot be used for a football field, an ecological park or a building site? There is no reason whatsoever that the voters have single peaked preferences (Mueller 2003).

Gerald Kramer (1973) asked the question: how much homogeneity of preferences is necessary to avoid a cycle. He found that only when individuals have non-crossing personal indifference curves can a cycle be avoided. This is a very strong condition. For non-crossing can be expected for one individual, but not among several individuals. Non-crossing between several individuals in fact implies unanimity between these individuals. However, with unanimity, preferences are simply juxtaposed and not really aggregated. An aggregation of preferences leading us to a social welfare function as aimed at by Abram Bergson (1938) or Paul A. Samuelson (1947), indicating what is good and what is bad for the society, is not possible. This again shows the importance of Arrow's impossibility theorem. An implication of these results is that we should not rely too much on political and the rationality of collective choice. In fact, we should rather avoid voting processes.

Black has shown what single majority rule cannot produce. But what can single majority rule do? Kenneth O. May (1952) found that, under two alternatives, the sum of yes (+1) and no (−1) will generate a group decision function which is a simple majority rule if and only if it satisfies the following four conditions:

1. Decisiveness (that is, no ambiguity);
2. positive responsiveness (of the outcome when either the pros or the cons increase);
3. anonymity (among ballots of voters); and
4. neutrality (on particular issues) (Mueller 2003: 133–6).

If we add transitivity as an additional condition it follows from May's theorem that no voting rule will satisfy all five conditions, not even the simple majority rule.

Neutrality means that all issues are of the same importance, anonymity that all individuals are equally affected. Dropping these two conditions opens a multidimensional issue space and hence opportunities for trading votes (logrolling) between issues of unequal importance and between individuals with different intensities of preferences. Decisiveness will break down and majority rule will lead to cycles. A further consequence of this analysis is that logrolling opens no escape from Arrow's impossibility theorem (Bernholz 1978).

Under these new conditions another set of very strict conditions has to be met to restore a stable outcome of majority rule. Charles Plott (1967) has shown that a majority rule equilibrium exists if it is a maximum for one and only one voter while the other voters are evenly paired off so that any change improving the position for one individual is balanced by another individual being made worse off (see Mueller 2003).

Political Entrepreneurs

What will individuals do? Inconsistencies of voting open new perspectives for political entrepreneurship. Anthony Downs (1957) has suggested that party leaders who maximize votes may contribute to general welfare in the same way as competitive private entrepreneurs who maximize profits under competition in private markets. The analogy holds, however, only if the political process fulfils a number of restrictive conditions. Political issues can be arranged in a single left–right policy space consistent with Duncan Black's condition of single-peakedness. Moreover, perfect information and permanent voting are required. Eventually two competing parties will meet in equilibrium at the programme which is most preferred by the median voter.

Chance decides which party will come to government. If individuals, however, believe that parties' positions are far off the median, the probability that an individual's vote is decisive for the election outcome is very small and not worth the personal costs of voting. Nevertheless, people vote. This is the "paradox of voting" first pointed out by Downs (1957). The paradox of voting is an unexplained anomaly in economics.

The Downsian conditions of a voting equilibrium are, however, very restrictive. Peter Coughlin and Shmuel Nitzan (1981) asked the question: is it possible to find a voting equilibrium between two competing parties if preferences are more than one dimensional? They found that under deterministic preferences even small changes in a platform will motivate voters to reallocate their votes so that cycles again occur as soon as a party transgresses the yes/no threshold of a voter's preferences. Cycles can, however, be avoided when voters and parties are both incompletely informed about each others' reactions so that only the probability of a yes or no increases or decreases when a party modifies its programme, and voters therefore adjust their voting decisions probabilistically in every direction. Under these conditions again a stable median voter outcome may emerge.

In the more general case in which the equilibrium conditions are not fulfilled, vote competition generates an endless cycle. One majority beats the other without an improvement in sight. The danger increases that individuals get frustrated and find their hope in the autocracy of a powerful dictator.

The Economic Theory of Constitutions

What can economists propose in the bleak world of endless cycles? James Buchanan and Gordon Tullock (1962) propose the idea of a constitutional contract. A constitutional contract contains the basic rules on which the potential participants of a polity can agree. Agreement is the basis of legitimacy and stability of the polity. Those who do not agree do not take part. They may "go West" and establish a community elsewhere.

Buchanan was very much inspired by Knut Wicksell (1896) when he wrote chapters on the Constitution in Buchanan and Tullock's (1962) *Calculus of Consent*. Wicksell thought that a tax which is imposed by the franchised rich on the dis-enfranchised poor cannot be just. "Just taxation" (the subtitle of Wicksell's 1896 book) had to be unanimous. Buchanan does not go so far; he does not insist on justice, only on legitimacy. He writes: "the legitimacy of social-organizational structures is to be judged against the voluntary agreement of those who are to live or are living under the arrangements that are judged" (Buchanan 1999: 288). The legitimate constitutional contract is the basis from which all further arrangements have to start. It opens a perspective for further agreements. "The central premise of individuals as sovereigns does allow for delegation of decision-making authority to agents, so long as it remains understood that individuals remain as principals" (Buchanan 1999: 288). Delegation implies the power to make less than unanimous decisions. Individuals are aware of all the intricacies of less than unanimity decisions as found by Arrow, Black, May, Kramer and others, but they come to the conclusion that less than unanimity can be advantageous within the previously agreed contract. Their yes to less than unanimity decisions is encouraged by the veil of ignorance. They may correctly predict the consequences of a collective decision rule, but they are behind the veil of uncertainty and cannot predict whether they will be on the winning or on the losing side of a coalition. Therefore they can separate the characteristics of the rule from their personal interests, which are disguised.

Open exit ("to go West") is an important precondition of the legitimacy of a constitution. However, what should be done if exit is blocked and the problem of the distribution of rights comes up. Musgrave proposes that the constitution framers should solve the distribution issue before they proceed to the allocation issue (Buchanan and Musgrave 2000). Once the problem of a just distribution is solved, the Wicksellian unanimity test may be applied and efficiency may be reached, but not before. However, Musgrave remains silent on how the distribution problem should be solved. To re-introduce welfare economic judgements through the back door would certainly not be a satisfactory way. It would push economic analysis back behind Robbins's 1932 plea for an economics of choice. The problem is therefore not how to allocate resources, but how to define decision rules for allocating rights in a situation of conflict.

Rae (1969) and Taylor (1969) assume that an individual seeks to avoid having issues imposed on him, which he opposes, but that he favours the imposition of issues he prefers on others so that, on average, preferences can be assumed to be of equal intensity on both sides. Rae and Taylor ask, what rule minimizes the probability of supporting an issue that loses or opposing an issue that wins? The authors show that simple majority is the only rule that satisfies both criteria (Mueller 2003: 136–7).

Brian Barry (1965) illustrates this case in a lucid example: five people occupy a (once closed) railroad car. No sign either allows or prohibits smoking. Under the assumption of equal intensity of preferences and of uncertainty whether one is a smoker or a non-smoker, majority rule is the best decision rule. It maximizes the expected utility of a constitutional decision maker (Mueller 2003).

The Rae–Taylor rule shows that a constitutional contract is also feasible when individuals are locked-in. But simple majority rule becomes more attractive.

Federalism, Competition and Public Choice

A simple way to solve the public good problem is to privatize public goods. Charles E. Tiebout (1956) has shown that local public goods can be privatized if localities are separated from each other. The problem of non-exclusion within a locality is avoided by exclusion between localities. It is thought that an individual pays a fixed access price to the community and consumes the good internally as a free public good. Competition among local communities guarantees an efficient supply at least costs. In the literature this form of pricing is known under the name two-part or Disneyland pricing (Oi 1971).

Tiebout competition generates important adjustment processes. First, local communities will specialize in particular services and hence induce citizens with similar preferences to cluster in specialized local communities. Second, as far as the market is a discovery process (Hayek 1968 [2002]), local jurisdictions under competition will search for new products and processes, hence dynamically improve the quality of local public services. Third, competitive federalism is a laboratory for new ideas (see Oates's concept of "laboratory federalism" in Oates 1999). Fourth, federalism may crowd out inefficient bureaucratic and Leviathan solutions (Weingast 1995); and fifth, federalism may bring a local community on to a steeper growth path (Feld and Schnellenbach 2011).

The pure Tiebout model does not provide for public choice. Local governments work in the same way as markets work. They find the efficient solution themselves. Public choice is not only not necessary, it would even interfere with the market and destroy Tiebout's efficiency. Public choice can, however, help to support federalism where the latter is not strong enough to bring about an efficient spatial specialization.

Suppose that the 100000 inhabitants of jurisdiction J, which consists of two local communities A and B with 55000 and 45000 inhabitants respectively, are debating the introduction of a progressive school system X or a conservative school system Y, see Table 2. If individuals are not motivated enough to segregate in specialized jurisdictions democracy can help to reveal citizens' preferences.

If jurisdictions A and B vote in their entirety between the two school systems, the progressive school system X will be chosen. The preferences of 55000 voters will be fulfilled, while 45000 inhabitants are outvoted. If the inhabitants of A and B vote separately,

Table 2　Collective choice of school system X and Y

	Options	
	School system X	School system Y
Inhabitants of A	20000	30000
Inhabitants of B	35000	15000
All inhabitants	55000	45000

Sources:　Wagner (1983); Blankart (2011).

however, the *A* inhabitants would choose the conservative school system *Y*, while the *B* inhabitants would opt for the progressive school system *X*. As can be seen, only 35 000 inhabitants are outvoted: this is a clear advantage of decentralized voting (under the assumption that the inhabitants in *A* are equally concerned about school systems as those in *B*). Decentralized vote reveals that voters have different preferences.

Note that with the same overall, but another inter-local, distribution of votes, both communities might vote for the progressive school system so that decentralized decision making does not seem necessary. The equality of the two outcomes is, however, not an argument against decentralized voting, for how could one know that an aggregated vote is enough if not proved by decentralized voting? Therefore it is more reliable to start with decentralized government before centralized solutions are considered. This insight has been anchored in Oates's decentralization theorem:

> For a public good – the consumption of which is defined over geographical subsets of the total population, and for which the costs of providing each level of output of the good in each jurisdiction are the same for the central or the respective local government – it will always be more efficient (or at least as efficient) for local governments to provide the Pareto-efficient levels of output for their respective jurisdictions than for the central government to provide any specified and uniform level of output across all jurisdictions. (Oates 1972: 35)

The conclusion is that a democracy can support federalism where its own forces are not strong enough to bring about an efficient outcome, but that democracy cannot replace federalism; for how could the vote districts be formed without the prior evidence provided by federalism?

Oates's decentralization theorem requires calculating the relative costs of alternative levels of government in each case. This, too, is often not possible. A more practical alternative is provided by the subsidiarity principle. The principle says that if a problem can be tackled individually or within an individual's family it should not be delegated to the local or a higher-level government. The burden of the proof of centralization is always with the next higher entity. If the subsidiarity test is negative the issue remains with the lower level. The subsidiarity principle has been accepted as a general principle in politics. It is also embedded in article 5 of the Treaty of Lisbon of the European Union: "The use of Union competences is governed by the principles of subsidiarity and proportionality." The subsidiarity principle is related to the principle of institutional congruency. Only when the citizens of a jurisdiction bear the full costs of a public service can they calculate rationally whether it is worthwhile to increase taxes for its extension or vice versa to decrease taxes. However, if ambitious politicians believe that they can obtain power by redistributing costs they will not hesitate to do so. Therefore, the subsidiarity principle is weak in politics. It is often violated in order to attract more votes.

Multi-Level Constitutions

Many constituencies try to restrict uncontrolled centralization by constitutional rules. These rules are often not as consensual as in the model of Buchanan and Tullock, but exempt from day-to-day politics so that they can only be changed by consent of a qualified majority. Theory and practice of public choice have developed several models to restrict or at least to channel centralization, three of which are of importance: the model of an association of states, the model of a federal state and the model of a unitary state (Blankart 2011).

In an association of states a motion to centralize an issue from a lower to a higher level of government is only adopted if it obtains a "gross majority", that is, if it is adopted by a majority of each member state according to its constitution. In a unitary state a "net majority" of all citizens, independent of their place of residence, is sufficient to centralize an issue. A federal state usually requires a qualified majority somewhere between a gross and net majority. The European Union (EU) is an association of states, the United States and Germany are federal states, and France is a unitary state. Therefore a centralization of government is more likely in the unitary state of France than in an association of states as the EU. On the other hand, it may be more difficult to control the decisions of governments of an association of states than the government of a unitary state, so that an association of states is not exempt from the danger of over-centralization.

Which Form of Democracy?

Citizens of an association of states, of a federal state and of a unitary state, may practice different forms of democracies. Some have direct democracies, some representative democracies and some two party systems, but which form of democracy should be chosen? In a direct democracy the voters vote on issues, in a representative democracy the voters elect representatives who vote on issues. These two cases, however, need to be defined more closely. A direct democracy usually means that a representative democracy is supplemented by direct voting if required by a referendum or an initiative, and a representative democracy means that the parliament exclusively and definitely decides. In some representative democracies, the government is elected by the parliament, in others the government or the president is elected directly by the citizens. Though both democracies are representative, the latter are often called "presidential".

Direct and representative democracies differ in the way in which government and parliament are controlled. In a representative democracy members of parliament are confronted only at election time with voters' preferences. During the mandate they are shielded from strict adherence to voters' will. In a direct democracy, in contrast, government and parliament have less leeway. They are checked by referenda and popular initiatives during the mandate and in the elections. Therefore more compliance with voter preferences has to be expected in direct democracies than in representative democracies.

An important question is therefore who does benefit from the leeway, which is generated by voters' incomplete control in representative democracies? Economists say that the leeway establishes a common pool for which interest groups compete. In equilibrium the total costs of competition for rents are equal to the total benefits and nothing is left over for interest groups (theorem of the dissipation of rents, Tullock 1980). In so far as competition for rents is restricted, rents do not fully dissipate and result in benefits for staff and bureaucrats within the government (Lüchinger et al. 2010). For these reasons interest groups have an important influence in representative democracies. However, what about rents in a direct democracy? In general it is said that the political influence of interest groups and bureaucrats is smaller in a direct democracy than in a representative democracy for it is more expensive to convince millions of voters than a handful of representatives (Kirchgässner et al. 1999: 31–2).

Rent-seeking is not without social costs to voters: what interest groups gain is lost by voters. Especially vaguely defined and blurred voter interests such as disguised taxes, general expenditures and public debt are likely to be neglected by politicians in parliamentary democracies in favour of interest groups' goals. Amilcare Puviani (1903) has observed this phenomenon more than 100 years ago. In empirical studies it has been corroborated later that taxes, expenditures and public debt are significantly lower in direct than in parliamentary democracies (Kirchgässner et al. 1999).

Rent-seeking occurs mostly in public production which cannot be easily controlled by voters. Quite a number of nineteenth-century French economists therefore advocated an outright privatization of state enterprises, the transformation of the state into a new organization designed on the model of a private company. The state should disappear into a new private company (see Faccarello 2010 for a survey). A well-organized private economy is always better than a corrupt public economy. In reality, however, a state which is run as a private company usually needs regulation.

Blankart and Mueller (2014) ask: what could be done to increase citizens' influence in politics? In public choice, two models of democracies can be distinguished:

1. A pure representative democracy is established in two stages. At the outset each citizen is by definition a member of the parliament. However, he or she does not have to take office. He or she may delegate his or her vote to a person he or she trusts. Under utility maximization, citizens choose the members of parliament who come closest to their personal preferences. Should the resulting parliament be too big to be operational a second vote is held in which only (say) the 100 candidates who have received most votes remain in the parliament. Traditional political parties may act as intermediators. The resulting parliament is truly representative because the nomination of representatives is free and unrestricted. No political party pre-selects the candidates. Preference formation, discussion and vote take place in the parliament.
2. In a pure two-party democracy, the parties try to identify and to amalgamate voters' preferences in their premises. Party leaders then submit the chosen programme to the voters. After a run-off election among different party programmes, it is revealed which of the two remaining programmes attracts more votes. The government is formed by the leader who has won the election and hence the absolute majority of the votes.

There is a role for referenda in a pure representative democracy. Representatives may have missed the exact voter preferences in their debate that can be corrected in a referendum, but there is barely a scope for referenda in a pure two-party system. The election is about issues and not about the preferences generating the issues. Therefore it is logical not to allow direct democracy through referenda and initiatives during the election period, as they would blur government's responsibility. It is preferable to have shorter election periods in order to keep the government under control.

It is often said that the so-called Westminster system inherited from the British democratic tradition is equivalent to the pure two-party system, but this is not the case. In the Westminster system candidates are elected in local districts by relative majority according to the first-past-the-post system. The overall majority of the votes is not necessarily reflected in the majority of the seats in parliament. If the voters shift from left to the right or vice versa, politics are not constrained to follow. The gap may be filled by preferences of interest groups (Blankart and Mueller 2014).

Parliamentary Democracy and the Political Business Cycle

The temporary monopoly provided to governments in an election not only promotes a policy in favour of interest groups, it may also have a dynamic impact on promoting political business cycles.

This basic hypothesis was first proposed by William D. Nordhaus (1975). In the elections, voters evaluate the government's past ability to steer the economy between unemployment and inflation under the assumption of a Phillips curve. They weigh unemployment more negatively than inflation. The government can gain votes if it steers the economy in a way that unemployment is low at election time (even if inflation is somewhat higher). If, after the election, inflation has to be reduced again and unemployment increases, the government's popularity decreases. However, before the next elections, voters will have forgotten these hardships and will vote again for the government if unemployment is low, even if inflation is high.

These considerations are diametrically opposed to the traditional economic policy paradigm: whereas in traditional public finance it is assumed that a government controls its expenditures and revenues in a way that the economic fluctuations are dampened, Nordhaus concludes from his model that the government can use incentives to generate these fluctuations. In other words, if the private sector of the economy does not generate fluctuations on its own, then the government of a representative democracy, which has to be re-elected periodically, would cause them. Therefore, the attention of public choice economists should focus more on endogenous cycles than on exogenous cycles.

The Nordhaus hypothesis has triggered an intensive discussion. Three alternative models have been proposed: the partisan theory by Douglas A. Hibbs (1977), the theory of rational expectations by Alberto Alesina (1987) and an intermediary theory by Bruno S. Frey and Friedrich Schneider (1978).

1. Hibbs argues that parties have their partisans and they will support the interests of their partisans if they come to power. Hibbs, therefore, does not follow the Nordhaus (and Downs) hypothesis according to which parties make their programmes according to vote maximization. In Hibbs's model, parties follow a political science attitude in that they try to win an election with the ideology of their partisans. Left-wing parties pursue an expansive and inflationary labour market policy favouring inflation rather than unemployment for their lower middle-class clientele. Right-wing parties pursue an opposite policy for their upper middle-class clientele. As a consequence, Hibbs predicts a political business cycle when the governing party changes.
2. Alesina and other proponents of the political economics school are critical of the theory of the political business cycle of Nordhaus whom they include in the public choice school. Their approach is "anti-public choice" (Blankart and Koester 2006). They argue that the Nordhaus public choice theories contradict the theory of rational expectations. A government acting according to the Nordhaus model systematically and permanently deceives the voters. If, for example, the government pursues an

inflationary policy to lower unemployment, it is allegedly assumed that workers do not understand that this policy is accompanied by a decrease in the real wage. Only under this illusion will they be willing to work more, and only in this case is a drift along the Phillips curve possible for the government. If, however, rational expectations are assumed, individuals do not evaluate the government on the performance in the expired legislative period, but rather on the impact that governmental actions will have in the future. The individuals see through the intentions of the government, they do their appropriate disposals and attempt to block their impacts: for example, unions will anticipate the inflation effects of an expansive tax and spending policy; they will not accept the decrease in real wages and therefore will demand higher wages, and similar, with the consequence that a positive employment effect will not be initiated and there will be no political business cycle.

Indeed it makes no sense why a government should try to create political business cycles. A political influence on the economic cycle – if any – has to be justified in another way. Alesina takes Hibbs's partisan theory as a starting point and introduces the assumption of an uncertain election outcome. Before the election, voters do not exactly know if a left-wing party with a preference for an expansive national budget or a right-wing party favouring a contractionary budget will come to power. Therefore the citizens will behave cautiously in their function as workers and union agents. They will assume an average budgetary policy for their wage claim if the labour agreement will hold beyond the election date. If one party comes to power, there will be surprises and real (expansive or contractionary) effects. From this perspective, politics will keep its influence on the economy. However, it remains an open question why workers with rational expectations do not adjust their labour agreements to the election dates. Then there would be no political business cycles. Thus the question remains: why do really rational unions and employers not adjust their negotiations to the election dates? In this way they could avoid surprises. In as much as Alesina leaves this question open, his unions do not seem to have fully rational expectations.

Mueller (2003: ch.19) puts the different models to the test and analyses which one better explains the US business cycles between 1949 and 2000. Hibbs's partisan theory performs best. If the president is a democrat, unemployment decreases whereas it increases if the president is a republican. The theories of political business cycles of Nordhaus perform slightly less satisfactorily and the theoretically ambitious models of Alesina (in Alesina and Rosenthal 1995) perform definitely worse.

While Hibbs's partisan theory seemed to work well for the United States it was less successful for other countries. For Germany, Gerrit B. Koester (2009) shows that, contrary to the partisan theory, governments led by social democrats between 1994 and 2004 lowered the progressive income tax and increased the more regressive value added tax, while governments dominated by Christian democrats behaved conversely.

3. An intermediate approach between Nordhaus and Alesina has been developed by Frey and Schneider (1978). In their theory, incentives of the government to become budgetary politically active depend on the electoral-political need. This is given if elections are about to be held and the economic situation is bad. With a bad economic situation, for example, high unemployment or high inflation, the regularly measured

Table 3   Government budgetary policy dependent on election dates and economic situation

	Upcoming elections	No upcoming elections
Economic situation bad, popularity low	*Active anticyclical budgetary policy*	Ideological budgetary policy
Economic situation good, popularity high	Ideological budgetary policy	Ideological budgetary policy

Source: Frey and Schneider (1978).

popularity of the government is low. With upcoming elections, the government sees itself forced to take immediate budgetary counteractions. In the case of high unemployment, it will raise the expenditures (especially transfers) and lower taxes. In case of high inflation, it will lower the expenditures for goods and services and, possibly, raise taxes. In doing so, it hopes to win back lost popularity and to avoid an election loss. This case is illustrated in the upper left field in Table 3. In all other cases where either the economic situation is good and the popularity is high or no elections are coming up, the government does not need to become politically active. The government can plan its incomes and expenditures in the long run dependent on its ideology and does not have to directly consider the interests of the voters. The approach of Frey and Schneider has been successfully tested for different countries.

Conclusion

The purpose of public choice is to discover what a society of individuals prefers. Nineteenth-century utilitarians thought that individual utilities could be measured and aggregated. This view has been refuted by Lionel Robbins (1932), who argues that only individual choices between ends and scarce means can uncover individual preferences. This new approach has opened the door to public choice.

The first and still most significant scholar of public choice is Kenneth Arrow with his treatise on *Social Choice and Individual Values* (1951 [1963]). Arrow shows that consistent social preferences cannot be derived from individual wants if they are to be compatible with four fundamental axioms: (1) the domain of individual preferences is unrestricted; (2) dictatorship is absent; (3) Pareto efficiency obtains; and (4) the social preferences are independent of irrelevant alternatives. No society can fulfil all four axioms together. All societies of all times have to compromise.

The history of mankind can be regarded as a mirror of how people have coped with Arrow's axioms. Primitive societies of primeval times were mostly dictatorships. They disregarded the axiom of non-dictatorship as well as most of the other axioms. Later in history, individuals became more mobile increasing their domain of individual preferences. However, with different beliefs, they developed different ideologies, which generated wars and other cruelties inflicting the Pareto axiom. This was an endless tragedy. Arrow's fourth axiom, the independence of irrelevant alternatives, however, seems immune against the above intricacies of human conflicts. Arrow has introduced the independence axiom because he wanted to avoid comparisons between more than two alternatives and hence cardinal (strategic) evaluations (Arrow 1951 [1963]: 110). But the restriction to pairwise comparisons has its price. It leads directly into cyclical decisions if the independence axiom does not hold, in particular if issues are linked by externalities.

This can be illustrated by the actual euro crisis. If a bank is systemically interconnected with other banks, a single drop out may generate a large and endless crisis. Suppose banker of country X declares: "I fail", then this is enough for the rest of the euro bankers to ask: how can we survive? They approach the European Central Bank (ECB) to bail them out. The ECB bailout may encourage moral hazard of the first banker who starts a new round of failure and bailout and so on. These sorts of externalities show that once the independence axiom is violated, an endless chain of crises may follows. The example illustrates the dismal message of Kenneth Arrow: a crisis is not an exception. It is the ordinary stem of the tide.

CHARLES B. BLANKART

See also:

Kenneth Joseph Arrow (I); Jeremy Bentham (I); Abram Bergson [Abram Burk] (I); James M. Buchanan (I); Marie-Jean-Antoine-Nicolas Caritat de Condorcet (I); Antonio De Viti de Marco (I); Friedrich August von Hayek (I); Social choice (III); Knut Wicksell (I).

References and further reading

Alesina, A. (1987), 'Macroeconomic policy in a two-party system as a repeated game', *Quarterly Journal of Economics*, **102** (3), 651–78.
Alesina, A. and H. Rosental (1995), *Partisan Politics, Divided Government and the Economy,* Cambridge: Cambridge University Press.
Arrow, K.J. (1951), *Social Choice and Individual Values*, 2nd edn 1963, New York: John Wiley.
Barry, B. (1965), *Political Argument*, London: Routledge and Kegan Paul and New York: Humanities Press.
Bentham, J. (1789), *Introduction to the Principles of Morals and Legislation*, in J.H. Burns and H.L.A. Hart (eds) (1996), *The Collected Works of Jeremy Bentham*, Oxford: Clarendon.
Bergson, A. (1938), 'A reformulation of certain aspects of welfare economics', *Quarterly Journal of Economics*, **52** (7), 314–44.
Bernholz, P. (1978), 'On the stability of logrolling outcomes in stochastic games', *Public Choice*, **33** (3), 65–82.
Black, D. (1948), 'On the rationale of group decision making', *Journal of Political Economy*, **56** (February), 23–34.
Blankart, C.B. (2011), *Öffentliche Finanzen in der Demokratie (Public Finance in a Democracy)*, 8th edn, Munich: Vahlen.
Blankart, C.B. (2013), 'Oil and vinegar. A fiscal theory of the euro crisis', *Kyklos*, **66** (4), 497–528.
Blankart, C.B. (2014), 'From friends to foes? The euro as a cause of new nationalism', in A. Varsori and M. Poettinger (eds) (2014), *Economic Crisis and New Nationalisms, German Political Economy as Perceived by European Partners*, Brussels: P.I.E. Peter Lang SA, pp. 99–114.
Blankart, C.B. and E.R. Fasten (2011), 'Knut Wicksell's principle of just taxation revisited', in V. Caspari (ed.), *The Evolution of Economic Theory: Essays in Honour of Bertram Schefold*, London: Routledge, pp. 132–41.
Blankart, C.B. and G. Koester (2006), 'Political economics versus public choice', *Kyklos*, **59** (2), 171–200.
Blankart, C.B. and D.C. Mueller (2004), 'The advantages of pure forms of parliamentary democracy over mixed forms', *Public Choice*, **122** (3–4), 431–53.
Blankart, C.B. and D.C. Mueller (2014), 'Who is to represent the citizens in the state?', *Ifo Schnelldienst*, **67** (15), 31–4.
Blaug, M. (1978), *Economic Theory in Retrospect*, Cambridge: Cambridge University Press.
Buchanan, J. (1999), 'The foundations for normative individualism', in *The Logical Foundations of Constitutional Liberty*, Indianapolis, IN: Liberty Fund.
Buchanan, J.M. and R.A. Musgrave (2000), *Public Finance and Public Choice: Two Contrasting Visions of the State*, Cambridge, MA: MIT Press.
Buchanan, J.M. and G. Tullock (1962), *The Calculus of Consent*, Ann Arbor, MI: University of Michigan Press.

Condorcet, M.-J.-A.-N. Caritat de (1785), *Essai sur l'application de l'analyse à la probabilité des décisions rendues à la pluralité des voix*, Paris: Imprimerie Royale.

Coughlin, P. and S. Nitzan (1981), 'Electoral outcomes with probabilistic voting and Nash social welfare maxima', *Journal of Public Economics*, **15** (1), 113–22.

De Viti de Marco, A. (1888), *Il carattere teorico dell'economia finanziaria*, Rome: Pasqualucci.

Diamond, P.A. and J.A. Mirrlees (1971a), 'Optimal taxation and public production I: production efficiency', *American Economic Review*, **61** (1), 8–27.

Diamond, P.A. and J.A. Mirrlees (1971b), 'Optimal taxation and public production II: tax rules', *American Economic Review*, **61** (2), 261–78.

Dogson, C.L. (1876), 'Suggestions as to the best method of taking votes, where more than two issues are to be voted on', in D. Black (1958), *The Theory of Committees and Elections*, Cambridge: Cambridge University Press, pp. 222–34.

Downs, A. (1957), *An Economic Theory of Democracy*, New York: Harper & Row.

Faccarello, G. (2006), 'An "exception culturelle"? French Sensationist political economy and the shaping of public economics', *European Journal of the History of Economic Thought*, **13** (1), 1–38.

Faccarello, G. (2010), 'Bold ideas. French liberal economists and public economics in 19th century France', *European Journal of the History of Economic Thought*, **17** (4), 719–58.

Faccarello, G. and R. Sturn (2010), 'The challenge of the history of public economics', *European Journal of the History of Economic Thought*, **17** (4), 537–42.

Fausto, D. (2006), 'The Italian approach to the theory of public goods', *European Journal of the History of Economic Thought*, **13** (1), 69–98.

Feld, L.P. and J. Schnellenbach (2011), 'Fiscal federalism and long-run macroeconomic performance: a survey of recent research (with Lars P. Feld)', *EPC: Government and Policy*, **29** (2), 224–43.

Frey, B.S. and F. Schneider (1978), 'An empirical study of a politico-economic interaction in the U.S.', *Review of Economics and Statistics*, **60** (May), 174–83.

Hayek, F.A. (1968), 'The market as a discovery procedure', trans. and reprinted 2002 in *Quarterly Journal of Austrian Economics*, **5** (3), 9–23.

Hibbs, D.A. (1977), 'Political parties and macroeconomic policy', *American Political Science Review*, **71** (December), 1467–87.

Jevons, W.S. (1871), *The Theory of Political Economy*, London: Macmillan.

Kirchgässner, G., L. Feld and M.R. Savioz (1999), *Direkte Demokratie. Modern, erfolgreich, entwicklungs- und exportfähig*, Basle and Munich: Helbing und Lichtenhahn, Vahlen.

Koester, G.B. (2009), *The Political Economy of Tax Reforms*, Berlin: Humboldt-Universität zu Berlin, Baden-Baden: Nomos.

Kramer, G.H. (1973), 'On a class of equilibrium conditions for majority rule', *Econometrica*, **41** (2), 285–97.

Lüchinger, S., A. Stutzer and S. Meier (2008), 'Bureaucratic rents and life satisfaction', *Journal of Law, Economics & Organization*, **24** (2), 476–88.

Lüchinger, S., S. Meier and A. Stutzer (2010), 'Why does unemployment hurt the employed? Evidence from the life satisfaction gap between the public and the private sector', *Journal of Human Resources*, **45** (4), 998–1045.

May, K.O. (1952), 'A set of independent, necessary and sufficient conditions for simple majority decisions', *Econometrica*, **20** (4), 680–84.

Mazzola, U. (1890), 'The formation of prices of public goods', in A.T. Peacock and R.A. Musgrave (1958), *Classics in the Theory of Public Finance*, Houndsmill: Macmillan, pp. 37–47.

Menger, C. (1871), *Grundsätze der Volkswirtschaftslehre*, Vienne: W. Braumüller.

Mueller, D.C. (2003), *Public Choice III*, Cambridge: Cambridge University Press.

Musgrave, R.A. (1939), 'The voluntary exchange theory of public economy', *Quarterly Journal of Economics*, **53** (2), 213–37.

Nordhaus, W.D. (1975), 'The political business cycle', *Review of Economic Studies*, **42** (2), 169–90.

Oates, W.E. (1972), *Fiscal Federalism*, London: Harcourt Brace.

Oates, W.E. (1999), 'An essay on fiscal federalism', *Journal of Economic Literature*, **37** (3), 1120–49.

Oi, W.Y. (1971), 'A Disneyland dilemma: two-part tariffs', *Quarterly Journal of Economics*, **85** (1), 77–96.

Peacock, A. (1992), *Pubic Choice in Historical Perspective* (Raffaele Mattioli Lectures 1989), Milan: Banca Commerciale Italiana, Cambridge: Cambridge University Press.

Puviani, A. (1903), *Teoria della illusione finanziaria*, Palermo: Sandron.

Rae, D.W. (1969), 'Decision-rules and individual values in constitutional choice', *American Political Science Review*, **63** (1), 40–56.

Robbins, L. (1932), *An Essay on the Nature and Significance of Economic Science*, 2nd edn 1935, London: Macmillan.

Samuelson, P. (1947), *Foundations of Economic Analysis*, Cambridge, MA: Harvard University Press.
Smith, A. (1776), *An Inquiry into the Nature and Causes of the Wealth of Nations*, 2 vols, London, Strahan and Cadell, reprinted in R.H. Campbell, A.S. Skinner and W.B. Todd (eds) (1976) *Adam Smith. An Inquiry into the Nature and Causes of the Wealth of Nations* (Glasgow Edition of the Works and Correspondence of Adam Smith, vol. 2), 2 vols, Oxford: Clarendon Press.
Taylor, M.D. (1969), 'Proof of a theorem on majority rule', *Behavioral Science*, **24** (May), 228–31.
Tiebout, C.M. (1956), 'A pure theory of local expenditures', *Journal of Political Economy*, **64** (5), 416–24.
Tullock, G. (1967a), 'The welfare costs of tariffs, monopoly and theft', *Western Economic Journal*, **5** (3), 224–32.
Tullock, G. (1967b), *Toward Mathematics of Politics*, Ann Arbor, MI: University of Michigan Press.
Tullock, G. (1971), 'The paradox of revolutions', *Public Choice*, **11** (Fall), 89–100.
Tullock, G. (1980), 'Efficient rent-seeking', in J.M. Buchanan, R. Tollison and G. Tullock (eds), *Toward a Theory of the Rent-Seeking Society*, College Station, TX: Texas A&M University Press, pp. 97–112.
Wagner, R.E. (1983), *Public Finance, Revenues and Expenditures in a Democratic Society*, Boston, MA and Toronto: Little, Brown.
Walras, L. (1874), *Eléments d'économie politique pure ou théorie de la richesse sociale*, final edn 1926, Paris: Pichon and Duriaz-Anzias.
Weingast, B.R. (1995), 'The economic role of political institutions: market-preserving federalism and economic development', *Journal of Law, Economics and Organization*, **11** (1), 1–31.
Wicksell, K. (1896), *Finanztheoretische Untersuchen nebst Darstellung und Kritik des Steuerwesens Schwedens*, Jena: Gustav Fischer.

Neo-Ricardian economics

The term "neo-Ricardian" became prominent in the aftermath of the publication of *The Works and Correspondence of David Ricardo* (hereafter *Works*), edited by Piero Sraffa with the collaboration of Maurice H. Dobb (Ricardo 1951–73), and the publication of Sraffa's *Production of Commodities by Means of Commodities* (Sraffa 1960). Rowthorn (1974) used it to distinguish Sraffa's approach to the theory of value and distribution in strictly material terms (that is, quantities of commodities and labour) from Marx's labour-value based reasoning. Rowthorn considered Sraffa's analysis as a variant of "vulgar economics", dealing with "appearances" only, whereas Marx's theory was credited with investigating "the real relations in bourgeois society" (Marx 1954a: 84 n.). A second meaning simply refers to the fact that Sraffa saw his reconstructive work as a return to the "standpoint of the old classical economists from Adam Smith to Ricardo, [which] has been submerged and forgotten since the advent of the 'marginal' method" (Sraffa 1960: v). Finally, some neoclassical or marginalist economists (for example, Hahn 1982) used the term to describe the analysis of the critics of marginalism in the so-called Cambridge controversies in the theory of capital. For a summary account of the criticism put forward, see Kurz and Salvadori (1995: ch. 14). Variously also the label "Sraffian economics" is used.

What Sraffa in fact provides in the Ricardo edition and in his book is a reformulation of the classical approach to the problem of value and distribution that sheds the weaknesses and builds upon the strengths of its earlier formulations. Hence it would be more appropriate to speak of a revival and development of "classical economics". It is a characteristic feature of classical economics that profits and all property incomes (such as the rents of land and interest) are seen to be based on the social surplus left over after the necessary means of production and the wages in the support of workers have been deducted from the gross outputs produced during a year. In Ricardo's words: "Profits come out of the surplus produce" (*Works* II: 130–31; similarly I: 95). A characteristic feature of the classical approach is that wages and profits are treated asymmetrically: while one of the distributive variables is assumed to be a known magnitude (its level being determined in another part of the theory, that is, the theory of capital accumulation and technical progress), the other is regarded as a residual. In the classical economists the theory of value and distribution was designed to lay the foundation of all other economic analysis, including the investigation of economic development and growth; of social transformation and structural change; and of taxation and public debt. The pivotal role of the theory of value and distribution in the classical authors can be inferred from the fact that it typically occupies a place right at the beginning of major classical works: in Smith it is dealt with in book I of *The Wealth of Nations* (1776 [1976]) and in Ricardo in chapter 1 of the *Principles* (*Works* I). Sraffa is to be credited with having elaborated a logically coherent and general analysis of the problem under consideration. He was thus able to show that it had been prematurely abandoned, because its defects had wrongly been considered to be irremediable. In addition to this constructive task Sraffa also pursued a critical task: the propositions of his book were explicitly "designed to serve as the basis for a critique of [the marginal theory of value and distribution]" (Sraffa 1960: vi).

The Analytical Method of the Classical Economists

The classical economists were keen to unravel the economic laws governing the emerging capitalist economy, characterized by the stratification of society into three classes: workers, land owners, and the rising class of capitalists; wage labour as the dominant form of the appropriation of other people's capacity to work; an increasingly sophisticated division of labour within and between firms; the co-ordination of economic activity via a system of interdependent markets in which transactions are mediated through money; and ongoing technical, organizational and institutional change. That is, they were concerned with an economic system incessantly in motion. The classical authors tried to understand the complexities of the modern economy by distinguishing between the "actual" values of the relevant variables – the distributive rates and prices – and their "normal" values. The former were taken to reflect all kinds of influences, many of an accidental or temporary nature, about which no general propositions are possible, whereas the latter were seen to express the persistent, non-accidental and non-temporary factors governing the economic system. Only the latter could be systematically studied.

The method of the analysis adopted by the classical economists is known as the method of long-period positions of the economy. Any such position is the situation towards which the system is taken to gravitate as the result of the self-seeking actions of agents, especially capitalists, thereby putting into sharp relief the fundamental forces at work. In conditions of free competition, characterized by the absence of marked barriers to entry into and exit from the various markets, the resulting long-period position is characterized by a uniform rate of profits (subject perhaps to persistent inter-industry differentials reflecting different levels of risk and of agreeableness of the business; see Kurz and Salvadori 1995: ch. 11) and uniform rates of remuneration for each particular kind of primary input, that is, each kind of labour and each kind of land. Competitive conditions were taken to enforce cost-minimizing behaviour of profit-seeking producers.

Alfred Marshall (1890) had interpreted the classical economists as essentially early advocates of demand and supply theory, with an undeveloped demand side. Sraffa challenged this interpretation and the underlying continuity thesis in economics, which was later dubbed "Whig history" of economics by Paul A. Samuelson (1987). As Sraffa showed, the classical economists' approach to the theory of value and distribution was fundamentally different from the later marginalist approach. It explained profits in terms of two data: (1) the system of production in use and (2) a given real wage rate (or, alternatively, a given share of wages). Profits (and rents) were thus conceived of as a residual income. Whereas in marginalist theory wages and profits are treated symmetrically, in classical theory they are treated asymmetrically. Also, whereas in marginalist theory prices are scarcity indexes of goods (and of factor services), in classical theory they support the given distribution of income and only some of them reflect the scarcity of the thing under consideration. That is, while the rent of a particular kind of land typically expresses the scarcity of that kind, profits do not express the scarcity of "capital" in general or of particular capital goods. In contrast to land, capital goods are reproducible and therefore it makes no sense in a long-period framework, which was also adopted by major marginalist theorists, to apply the principle of scarcity to them. On a still deeper methodological level, the divide between the classical and the marginalist authors could hardly be more pronounced: while the classical authors took the economic system to exist prior to and independently of the single agent and actually exert a considerable influence upon the latter as worker, capitalist or proprietor of land, the marginalist authors advocated "methodological individualism", which takes a set of optimizing agents to exist independently of the system as a whole and where the agents shape the system rather than being shaped by it.

Tools versus Concepts

The classical economists proceeded essentially in the following two steps. (1) They isolated the kinds of factors that were seen to determine income distribution and the prices supporting that distribution in well specified situations, that is, in a given place and time. The task of the theory of value and distribution was to identify *in abstracto* the dominant and persistent forces at work and to investigate their interaction. (2) They then turned to an investigation of the causes, which over time affected these forces from within the economic system, and, as a consequence, the system itself. The second step concerned the analysis of the working of these forces over time in the theory of capital accumulation, technical and organizational improvements (technical progress), economic growth and socio-economic development.

It is another characteristic feature of the classical approach to profits, rents and relative prices that these are explained essentially in terms of magnitudes that can, in principle, be observed, measured or calculated. The objectivist orientation of classical economics has received its perhaps strongest expression in a famous proclamation by William Petty, who was arguably its founding father. Keen to assume what he called the "'physician's' outlook", Petty in his *Political Arithmetick*, published in 1690, stressed that he was to express himself exclusively "in Terms of *Number, Weight* or *Measure*" (Petty 1899 [1986]: 244), citing the Bible. James Mill noted significantly that "*The agents of production are the commodities themselves* . . . They are the food of the labourer, the tools and the machinery with which he works, and the raw materials which he works upon" (Mill 1826 [1844]: 165, emphasis added). Sraffa thus interpreted the classical authors as advocating a concept of physical real cost. Man cannot create matter, but can only change its form and move it. Production involves destruction, and the real cost of a commodity consists of the commodities that of necessity have to be destroyed in order to get it. This concept differs markedly from the marginalist concepts, with their emphasis on "psychic cost", reflected in such notions as "utility" and "disutility".

The classical authors saw modern production as a circular flow. This concept can be traced back to William Petty and Richard Cantillon, and was most effectively advocated by François Quesnay (1759 [1972]) in the *Tableau économique*. Accordingly, commodities are produced by means of commodities. This is in stark contrast with the view of production as a one-way avenue leading from the services of original factors of production, typically the services of labour and land, via some intermediate products to consumption goods, as it is entertained not only by "Austrian" economists. However, the classical economists failed to elaborate a consistent theory of value and distribution on the basis of the twin concepts of (1) physical real costs and (2) a circular flow of production. According to Sraffa (see Kurz and Salvadori 2005; Kurz 2012), a main, if not the main, reason for this consisted in a discrepancy between highly sophisticated analytical concepts, on the one hand, and inadequate tools available to the classical authors to deal with them, on the other. More specifically, the tool needed in order to bring to fruition one with another conceptual elements (1) and (2) were simultaneous equations and the knowledge how to solve them and what their properties are. Unfortunately, this tool was not at the disposal of the classical authors. They therefore tried to solve the problems they encountered in a roundabout way, typically by first identifying an "ultimate stand-ard of value" by means of which heterogeneous commodities were meant to be rendered homogeneous and thus commensurate. Several authors, especially Ricardo, Robert Torrens and Marx, had then reached the conclusion that "labour" was the sought stand-ard and had therefore arrived in one way or another at some version of the labour theory of value. This theory allowed them to preserve the objectivist character of their analyses by taking as data, or known quantities, only measurable things, such as the amounts of commodities actually produced and the amounts of them actually used up in production, including the means of subsistence in the support of workers. This was understandable in view of the unresolved tension between concepts and tools. However, with production as a circular flow, even labour values of commodities cannot be known independently of solving a system of simultaneous equations. Hence the route via labour values was not really a way out of the impasse in which the classical authors found themselves: it rather landed them right in that impasse again. Commodities were produced by means of com-modities and there was no way to circumnavigate the simultaneous equations approach.

Equations of Production

What prevented the classical authors from seeing that the theory of value and distribu-tion could be firmly grounded in the concept of physical real cost? Given their primitive tools of analysis, they did not see that the information about (1) the system of production actually in use and (2) the quantities of the means of subsistence in support of workers was all that was needed in order to determine directly (without any need to go through labour values) the system of necessary prices and the general rate of profits. This Sraffa understood as early as November 1927, as we can see from his hitherto unpublished papers kept at Trinity College Library, Cambridge (UK), with respect to what he called his "first" (without a surplus) and "second equations" (with a surplus); see Kurz (2012).

We may illustrate his argument by starting from James Mill's above case with three types of commodities – tools (t), raw materials (m), and the food of the labourer (f). Production in the three industries may then be tabulated in the following way:

$$T_t \oplus M_t \oplus F_t \to T$$

$$T_m \oplus M_m \oplus F_m \to M \tag{1}$$

$$T_f \oplus M_f \oplus F_f \to F$$

Here T_i, M_i and F_i designate the inputs of the three commodities (employed as means of production and means of subsistence) in industry i ($i = t, m, f$), and T, M and F total outputs in the three industries; the symbol "$\oplus$" indicates that all inputs on the left-hand side (LHS) of "$\to$", representing production, are required to generate the output on its right-hand side (RHS). Adopting the terminology of the classical authors, Sraffa calls these relations "the methods of production and productive consumption" (Sraffa 1960: 3). In the hypothetical case in which the economy is just viable, that is, able to reproduce itself without any surplus (or deficiency), we have $T = \Sigma_i T_i$, $M = \Sigma_i M_i$, and $F = \Sigma_i F_i$.

From this schema of reproduction and reproductive consumption we may directly derive the corresponding system of "absolute" or "natural" values, which expresses the concept of physical real cost-based values in an unadulterated way. Denoting the value of one unit of commodity i by p_i ($i = t, m, f$), we have:

$$T_t p_t + M_t p_m + F_t p_f = T p_t$$

$$T_m p_t + M_m p_m + F_m p_f = M p_m$$

$$T_f p_t + M_f p_m + F_f p_f = F p_f$$

Since only two of the three equations are independent of one another, fixing a standard of value, whose price is *ex definitione* equal to unity, provides an additional equation without adding a further unknown and allows one to solve for the remaining dependent variables.

The reasoning up until now shows that there is no need whatsoever to invoke labour values. In fact, it would not be clear what could be meant by them vis-à-vis the undeniable heterogeneity of labour performed in the different lines of production. Also, with regard to the next stage, which refers to a system with a surplus and given commodity (or real) wages advanced at the beginning of the production period, the same applies: information about the system of production in use and real wages is all that is needed in order to ascertain relative prices and the additional variable that reflects the distribution of the surplus product in conditions of free competition: the general rate of profits. This rate applies to the values of the "capitals" advanced in the different industries by capitalists.

We start once more from the system of quantities consumed productively and produced (1), but now we assume that $T \geq \Sigma_i T_i$, $M \geq \Sigma_i M_i$, and $F \geq \Sigma_i F_i$, where at least with regard to one commodity the strict inequality sign applies. In the extremely special case of a uniform rate of physical surplus across all commodities, as it was contemplated by such diverse authors as Ricardo, Torrens, and John von Neumann (1945), we have:

$$\frac{T - \Sigma_i T_i}{\Sigma_i T_i} = \frac{M - \Sigma_i M_i}{\Sigma_i M_i} = \frac{F - \Sigma_i F_i}{\Sigma_i F_i} = r$$

In it the general rate of profits, r, equals the uniform material rate of produce. As Sraffa emphasized, here we see the rate of profits in the commodities themselves as having nothing to do with their values. However, in general the rates of physical surplus will differ as between different commodities (and some of these rates might even be negative).

Yet, unequal rates of commodity surplus do not, by themselves, necessarily imply unequal rates of profit across industries. In conditions of free competition the concept of "normal" prices (Smith, Ricardo), or "prices of production" (Torrens and Ricardo), implies that the social surplus is divided in such a way between the different employments of capital that a uniform rate of profits obtains. This condition is met by the following system of production equations:

$$(T_t p_t + M_t p_m + F_t p_f)(1 + r) = Tp_t$$

$$(T_m p_t + M_m p_m + F_m p_f)(1 + r) = Mp_m$$

$$(T_f p_t + M_f p_m + F_f p_f)(1 + r) = Fp_f$$

These three equations are independent of one another. Fixing a standard of value provides a fourth equation and no extra unknown, so that the system of equations can be solved for the dependent variables: the general rate of profits and prices.

This result is startling and implicitly puts in sharp relief the shortcomings of some received economic doctrines. To see its far-reaching implications we turn to the way in which Sraffa introduces it right at the beginning of his 1960 book. With the real wage rate given and paid at the beginning of the periodical production cycle, the problem of the determination of the rate of profits consists in distributing the surplus product in proportion to the capital advanced in each industry. Clearly, Sraffa observes,

> such a proportion between two aggregates of heterogeneous goods (in other words, the rate of profits) cannot be determined before we know the prices of the goods. On the other hand, we cannot defer the allotment of the surplus till after the prices are known, for . . . the prices cannot be determined before knowing the rate of profits. *The result is that the distribution of the surplus must be determined through the same mechanism and at the same time as are the prices of commodities.* (Sraffa 1960: 6, emphasis added)

This passage shows that the concept of "capital" as a magnitude that can be known prior to and independently of the prices of commodities and the rate of profits (the rate of interest) cannot generally be sustained. We encounter a variant of this concept in Marx's labour value-based reasoning, another in the marginalist concept of a given "quantity of capital". Marx attempted to determine the general rate of profits and prices of production in two steps, which Ladislaus von Bortkiewicz (1906–07, essay II: 38) aptly dubbed "successivist" (as opposed to "simultaneous"). In a first step Marx assumed that the general rate of profits is determined independently of, and prior to, the determination of prices as the ratio between the labour value of the social surplus and that of the social capital, consisting of a "constant capital" (means of production) and a "variable capital" (wages or means of subsistence). In a second step he then used the rate of profits ascertained in this way to calculate prices. Underlying his approach is the hypothesis that while the "transformation" of values into prices is relevant with regard to each single commodity, it is irrelevant with regard to commodity aggregates, such as the surplus product or the social capital, and the ratio of such aggregates. Yet this is not generally the case: the value of the sum total of heterogeneous capital goods (as well as the value of the sum total of the commodities forming the surplus product) cannot be taken as given and independent of the rate of profits, but has to be determined simultaneously with the rate of profits.

The Wage Curve

Up until now the argument was based on the assumption that real wages are given in kind at some level of subsistence. The classical economists however saw clearly that the share of wages in the product may rise above mere sustenance of labourers. As early as in the *Essay on Profits* of 1815, Ricardo had stressed that "it is no longer questioned" that improved machinery "has a decided tendency to raise the real wage of labour" (*Works* IV: 35). In this case a new wage concept was needed. This case had already been studied by Ricardo and had made him establish the inverse relationship between wages, conceived as a share in the product, and the rate of profits: "The greater the *portion of the result of labour* that is given to the labourer, the smaller must be the *rate* of profits, and vice versa" (*Works* VIII: 194; emphasis added). Sraffa also adopted the concept of "proportional wages", as he was to call it, albeit with two important changes. First, when workers partake in the sharing out of the surplus product, the original classical idea of wages being an integral part of social capital, that is, advanced at the beginning of the period of production, is difficult to sustain. Sraffa after some deliberation therefore decided to treat wages as a whole as paid out of the product, that is, paid *post factum*. Secondly, he expressed the share of wages as the ratio of total wages to the net product assessed in terms of normal prices, w. These changes necessitated reformulating the price equations by taking explicitly into account the amounts of labour expended in the different industries, L_i ($i = t, m, f$), because wages are taken to be paid in proportion to those amounts, and by defining these amounts as fractions of the total annual labour of society, that is, $L_t + L_m + L_f = 1$. In addition it is assumed, following the classical economists, that differences in the quality of labour have been previously reduced to equivalent differences in quantity so that each unit of labour receives the same wage rate (see Kurz and Salvadori 1995: ch. 11).

We may now formulate the corresponding system of production equations for the case of the three kinds of commodities mentioned by Mill, where now the quantities represented by T_i, M_i and F_i refer exclusively to the inputs of the three commodities employed as means of production. We get:

$$(T_t p_t + M_t p_m + F_t p_f)(1 + r) + L_t w = T p_t$$

$$(T_m p_t + M_m p_m + F_m p_f)(1 + r) + L_m w = M p_m \qquad (2)$$

$$(T_f p_t + M_f p_m + F_f p_f)(1 + r) + L_f w = F p_f$$

Taking the net product as standard of value, we have the following additional equation:

$$(T - \Sigma_i T_i)p_t + (M - \Sigma_i M_i)p_m + (F - \Sigma_i F_i)p_f = 1.$$

Taking one of the distributive variables, the share of wages w (or the rate of profits r) as given, one can determine the remaining variables: r (or w) and the prices of commodities. In the case of single production contemplated in equations (2), Sraffa corroborates Ricardo's finding of an inverse relationship between the share of wages and the rate of profits, also known as the *w-r* relationship or wage frontier:

$$r = \phi(w)$$

where $\phi'(w) < 0$.

He also establishes the fact, which was already known to Marx, that in the case in which commodities are produced by means of commodities, the maximum rate of profits, R, which obtains when wages are hypothetically equal to zero, is finite. Sraffa constructs a particular standard of value, the Standard commodity, which has the property that, if applied, renders the wage frontier linear:

$$r = R(1 - w).$$

We may replace in the equation of a commodity the different means of production used with a series of quantities of labour, each with its appropriate "date", and thus arrive at what is known as "reduction to dated quantities of labour" (see Sraffa 1960: ch. 6).

Sraffa shows that, whereas the wage rate as a function of the rate of profits is necessarily decreasing (but does not need to be so in the case of joint production), any relative price as a function of the rate of profits typically does not follow a simple rule: the function can alternately be increasing or decreasing, and can pass through a specific real number several times (which is constrained by the overall number of commodities involved).

Finally, we owe Sraffa the distinction between "basic" and "non-basic commodities". Basic commodities enter directly or indirectly the production of all commodities, whereas non-basics do not. (Mill's above scheme with three industries knows only basic commodities.) Only basic commodities play a role in the construction of the Standard commodity and the determination of the maximum rate of profits.

Choice of Technique

The fact mentioned above concerning relative prices as a function of the rate of profits is important also because the problem of the choice of technique from among several alternatives can be studied by making use of it. Suppose, for instance, that commodity t can be produced also with method:

$$T_t' \oplus M_t' \oplus F_t' \rightarrow T'$$

Then the following equation can be added to system (2)

$$(T_t'p_t + M_t'p_m + F_t'p_f)(1 + r) + L_t'w = T'p_t' \tag{3}$$

with the additional unknown p_t'. The study of the ratio p_t'/p_t allows one to say when it is profitable to use the old method and when the new one: if p_t'/p_t is smaller than unity, cost-minimizing producers will choose the new method, whereas if it is larger than unity they will stick to the old method; in case the ratio happens to be equal to unity, the two methods can co-exist, because they are equi-profitable.

If the new method is cost minimizing and has replaced the old one and on the further assumption that the rate of profits is unchanged, then equations (2) are replaced by the following equations, which represent the new system of production:

$$(T'_t p'_t + M'_t p'_m + F'_t p'_f)(1 + r) + L'_t w' = T' p'_t$$

$$(T_m p'_t + M_m p'_m + F_m p'_f)(1 + r) + L_m w' = M p'_m \qquad (4)$$

$$(T_f p'_t + M_f p'_m + F_f p'_f)(1 + r) + L_f w' = F p'_f$$

In this new system prices and the wage are different ($p'_j \neq p_j$ and $w' \neq w$) except in the case in which the two methods happen to be both cost-minimizing and thus can coexist (that is when $p'_t/p_t = 1$ in system (2)–(3)); in this latter case prices and the wage rate are the same in both systems.

Assessing the old method in terms of the prices and the wage corresponding to the new system requires combining system (4) and the equation:

$$(T_t p'_t + M_t p'_m + F_t p'_f)(1 + r) + L_t w' = T p'_t \qquad (5)$$

Then calculate again the ratio p'_t/p_t. The property that prices and the wage in the two systems coincide when $p'_t/p_t = 1$ suffices to prove that p'_t/p_t is larger (lower) than unity for a given r in system (4)–(5), if and only if it is so in system (2)–(3). Hence the new and the old method can be compared both at the prices of the new and the old system with the result being the same.

A technique is called a system involving a number of methods of production equal to the number of commodities involved, each method producing a different commodity. A technique that is chosen at a given income distribution (a given w or a given r) is called a cost-minimizing technique at that income distribution. The fact that a relative price can pass through a given value at several (feasible) income distributions implies that a technique can be cost-minimizing at different values of the rate of profits, with other techniques being cost-minimizing in the interval in between. This possibility is known as reswitching; it played an important role in the criticism of neoclassical theory during the so-called Cambridge controversies in the theory of capital (see Harcourt 1972).

The argument above presupposes the special case of single production or circulating capital only. The circulating items of capital advanced in production contribute entirely and exclusively to the output generated in the period under consideration, that is, they "disappear" from the scene during the period. Things are different with regard to the fixed items that contribute to a sequence of outputs over several periods, that is, after a single round of production its items are still there – older but still useful. The appropriate framework for analysing durable instruments of production would therefore be a system with multiple-product industries or joint production. For a discussion of joint production proper, like the familiar cases of mutton and wool or coal and coke gas, a discussion of fixed capital and of scarce natural resources, such as land, see Sraffa (1960), Pasinetti (1977), Schefold (1989), Kurz and Salvadori (1995) and Bidard (2004).

The Recent Controversy in the Theory of Capital

Sraffa's statement cited above (1960: 6) contains the key not only to a critique of Marx's labour-value based reasoning, but also of the long-period marginalist concept of capital. This concept rests on the possibility of defining the "quantity of capital", whose relative scarcity and thus marginal productivity is supposed to determine the rate of profits, independently of that rate. Following the logic of Sraffa's argument, this is not possible other than in highly special and in fact uninteresting cases: with heterogeneous capital goods the quantity of capital can only be conceived of as a value magnitude ($\Sigma_i T_i p_i + \Sigma_i M_i p_m + \Sigma_i F_i p_f$) that has to be ascertained simultaneously with the rate of profits. Neither Marx's nor the marginalist variant of successivism can be sustained.

The difficulties besetting the marginalist concept of capital may be clarified with reference to the concepts of "Wicksell effects". Joan Robinson (1953: 95) introduced the term during the Cambridge debate in the theory of capital (see Kurz and Salvadori 1995: ch. 14) and distinguished between price Wicksell and real Wicksell effects (hereafter PWE and RWE, respectively). A PWE refers to a change in relative prices corresponding to a change in income distribution, given the system of production in use, as we already discussed it in the above. An RWE refers instead to a change in technique in response to a change in income distribution. Recall that when two techniques are cost minimizing at a given income distribution (a given w or, alternatively, a given r), they exhibit the same prices (and the same r and w). (Clearly, one of them will be cost minimizing at a higher and the other one at a lower rate of profits.) Speaking of "change" in this context refers, of course, to the comparison of long-period positions of the economic system.

A positive PWE means that with a rise (fall) in the rate of profits (rate of interest) prices of consumption goods will tend to rise (fall) relative to those of capital goods. (Wicksell had adopted a variant of the Austrian concept of production as a one-way avenue of finite length that leads from original factor services of labour – and land – via a sequence of intermediate products or capital goods to the final product.) In this perspective consumption goods are taken to be produced more capital intensively than capital goods: consumption goods emerge at the end of the production process, whereas capital goods are intermediate products that gradually "mature" towards the final product. The higher (lower) is the rate of profits, the argument goes, the less (more) expensive are the intermediate products in terms of a standard consisting of a (basket of) consumption good(s). Considering a stationary economy (in which the net product contains only consumption goods) as a whole, this implies that with a rise in the rate of profits the value of the net social product rises relatively to the value of the aggregate of intermediate or capital goods employed. Seen from a marginalist perspective, a positive PWE with regard to the relative price of the two aggregates of commodities under consideration – the net product and the capital employed – involves a negative relationship between the aggregate capital-output ratio, on the one hand, and the profit rate, on the other.

Let $K/Y = \mathbf{x}\mathbf{p}(r)/\mathbf{y}\mathbf{p}(r)$ – $\mathbf{x}$ is the row vector of capital goods, $\mathbf{y}$ the row vector of net outputs, and $\mathbf{p}(r)$ the column vector of prices (in terms of the bundle of consumption goods), which depends on r – designate the capital-output ratio, then marginalist theory claims that:

$$\frac{\partial (K/Y)}{\partial r} \leq 0$$

Since for a given system of production the amount of labour is constant irrespective of the level of the rate of profits, also the ratio of the value of the capital goods and the amount of labour employed, or capital-labour ratio, K/L, would tend to fall (rise) with a rise (fall) in the rate of profits:

$$\frac{\partial (K/L)}{\partial r} \leq 0 \qquad (6)$$

This is the first claim of marginalist theory. The second claim is that RWEs are also positive. A positive RWE means that with a rise (fall) in the rate of profits – and the corresponding fall (rise) in the wage rate – cost-minimizing producers switch to methods of production that generally exhibit higher (lower) labour intensities, thereby "substituting" for the "factor of production" that has become more expensive – "capital" (labour) – the one that has become less expensive – labour ("capital"). Hence (6) is taken to apply also in the case with a choice of technique. The assumed positivity of the RWE involves the marginalist concept of a demand function for labour (capital) that is inversely related to the real wage rate (the rate of profits).

Careful scrutiny of the marginalist reasoning shows that it cannot generally be sustained: there is no presumption that PWEs and RWEs are invariably positive. In fact there is no presumption that techniques can be ordered monotonically with the rate of profits (Sraffa 1960). Reswitching implies that, even if PWEs happen to be positive, RWEs cannot always be positive. As Mas-Colell (1989) stressed, the relationship between K/L and r can have almost any shape whatsoever. The intervals in which K/L is an increasing function of r are spoken of as capital reversal. This implies that, if the neoclassical approach to value and distribution is followed, the "demand for capital" is not decreasing, and therefore the resulting equilibrium, provided there is one, is not stable. Hence the finding that PWEs and RWEs need not be positive challenges the received doctrine of the working of the economic system, as it is portrayed by conventional economic theory (see Pasinetti 1966; Garegnani 1970; see also Harcourt 1972; Kurz and Salvadori 1995: ch. 14; 1998c).

Recent Work in the Classical Tradition

More recently, the focus of attention of authors working in the classical tradition was especially, but not exclusively, on the following problems. First, there has been a lively interest in generalizing the results provided by Sraffa on joint production, fixed capital, and land. Then the approach was extended to cover the cases of international trade, taxation, renewable and exhaustible resources and to allow for the more realistic case of costly disposal, which leads to the concept of negative prices of products that have to be disposed of. There is also a renewed interest in the problem of economic growth and development. Freed from the straitjacket of Say's law, which can be said to be an implication of the finding that conventional equilibrium analysis cannot be sustained, there is no presumption that the economy will consistently follow a full-employment–full-capacity path of economic expansion. Hence the problem of different degrees and modes of utilization of productive capacity and the role of effectual demand (Adam Smith) has been analysed. This avenue has opened up avenues for cross-fertilization between classical economics, on the one hand, and Keynesian economics, based on the principle of effective demand, and evolutionary economics, concerned with complex dynamics, on the other. This fact is also highlighted in comparisons with the so-called new growth theory, and allows one to better understand the latter's merits and demerits (see Kurz and Salvadori 1998a: ch. 4, 1999).

In the 1960s and 1970s the long-period versions of marginalist theory revolving around the concept of a uniform rate of return on capital were called into question on logical grounds. While many marginalist authors accepted this criticism, some of them contended that intertemporal equilibrium theory, the "highbrow version" of neoclassicism, was not affected by it (see especially Bliss 1975; Hahn 1982). This claim has been subjected to closer scrutiny (see Garegnani 2000, Schefold 2000, and the special issue of *Metroeconomica*, **56** (2), in 2006).

The significance of "reswitching" of entire systems of production or economy-level techniques has sometimes been denied on the grounds of its purportedly low probability. More recently Arrigo Opocher and Ian Steedman (2015) have drawn the attention to the question whether the employment of one or several or all inputs may return in different full long-period equilibria at the industry level. They argue that such "recurrence" is generically far more probable than the return of entire systems of production. Interestingly, these recurrences can be associated not only with changes in income distribution (changes in the rate of profits), but also with changes in the relative prices of primary inputs. Opocher and Steedman insist that recurrence alone, without reswitching, undermines standard marginalist theory. Therefore, a low "probability of reswitching" must not be taken to weaken the case of the critics of marginalist theory.

While the criticism of the long-period versions of marginalist theory is irrefutable, as authors from Paul Samuelson to Andreu Mas-Colell have admitted, this has not prevented the economics profession at large from still using this theory. This is perhaps so because in more recent years the way of theorizing in large parts of mainstream economics has fundamentally changed. Whether this change is a response to the criticism need not concern us here. It suffices to draw the reader's attention to a statement by Paul Romer in one of his papers on endogenous growth in which he self-critically pointed out a slip in his earlier argument. The error he had committed, he wrote, "may seem a trifling matter in an area of theory that depends on so many other short cuts. After all, if one is going to do violence to the complexity of economic activity by assuming that there is an aggregate production function, how much more harm can it do to be sloppy about the difference between rival and non-rival goods?" (Romer 1994: 15–16). We can only wonder where this ends. Once economic theory has taken the road indicated, criticism becomes a barren instrument. Indeed, why should someone who seeks to provide "microfoundations" in terms of a representative agent with an infinite time horizon find fault with the counter-factual but attractive assumption that there is only a single (capital) good?

HEINZ D. KURZ AND NERI SALVADORI

See also:

Ladislaus von Bortkiewicz (I); British classical political economy (II); Cambridge School of economics (II); Capital theory (III); Competition (III); Keynesianism (II); Vladimir Karpovich Dmitriev (I); Growth (III); Income distribution (III); Input–output analysis (III); Karl Heinrich Marx (I); Methods in the history of economic thought (III); Resource and environmental economics (III); David Ricardo (I); Scottish Enlightenment (II); Adam Smith (I); Piero Sraffa (I); Technical change and innovation (III); Value and price (III).

References and further reading

Aspromourgos, T. (1996), *On the Origins of Classical Economics. Distribution and Value from William Petty to Adam Smith*, London and New York: Routledge.
Bidard, C. (2004), *Prices, Reproduction, Scarcity*, Cambridge, New York and Melbourne: Cambridge University Press.
Bliss, C. (1975), *Capital Theory and the Distribution of Income*, Amsterdam: North Holland.
Bortkiewicz, L. von (1906–07), 'Wertrechnung und Preisrechnung im Marxschen System', *Archiv für Sozialwissenschaft und Sozialpolitik*, **23** (1906), 1–50 (essay I), **25** (1907), 10–51 (essay II) and 445–88 (essay III).
Garegnani, P. (1970), 'Heterogeneous capital, the production function and the theory of distribution'. *Review of Economic Studies*, **37** (3), 407–36.
Garegnani, P. (1984), 'Value and distribution in the classical economists and Marx', *Oxford Economic Papers*, **36** (2), 291–325.
Garegnani, P. (1987), 'Surplus approach to value and distribution', in J. Eatwell, M. Milgate, and P. Newman (eds), *The New Palgrave. A Dictionary of Economics*, vol. 4, London: Macmillan, pp. 560–74.
Garegnani, P. (2000), 'Savings, investment and capital in a system of general intertemporal equilibrium', in H.D. Kurz (ed.), *Critical Essays on Piero Sraffa's Legacy in Economics*. Cambridge: Cambridge University Press, pp. 392–445.
Hahn, F. (1982), 'The neo-Ricardians', *Cambridge Journal of Economics*, **6** (4), 353–74.
Harcourt, G.C. (1972), *Some Cambridge Controversies in the Theory of Capital*, Cambridge: Cambridge University Press.
Kurz, H.D. (2012), 'Don't treat too ill my Piero! Interpreting Sraffa's papers', *Cambridge Journal of Economics*, **36** (6), 1535–69.
Kurz, H.D. and N. Salvadori (1993), 'The "Standard commodity" and Ricardo's search for an "invariable measure of value"', in M. Baranzini and G.C. Harcourt (eds), *The Dynamics of the Wealth of Nations. Growth, Distribution and Structural Change. Essays in Honour of Luigi Pasinetti*, New York: St. Martin's Press, pp. 95–123.
Kurz, H.D. and N. Salvadori (1995), *Theory of Production. A Long-Period Analysis*, Cambridge, New York and Melbourne: Cambridge University Press.
Kurz, H.D. and N. Salvadori (1998a), *Understanding 'Classical' Economics: Studies in Long-Period Theory*, London: Routledge.
Kurz, H.D. and N. Salvadori (eds) (1998b), *The Elgar Companion to Classical Economics*, 2 vols, Cheltenham, UK and Northampton, MA, USA: Edward Elgar.
Kurz, H.D. and N. Salvadori (1998c), 'Reverse capital deepening and the numeraire: a note', *Review of Political Economy*, **10** (4), 415–26.
Kurz, H.D. and N. Salvadori (1999), 'Theories of "endogenous" growth in historical perspective', in M.R. Sertel (ed.), *Contemporary Economic Issues. Proceedings of the Eleventh World Congress of the International Economic Association, Tunis, Volume 4 Economic Behaviour and Design*, London: Macmillan, and New York: St Martin's Press.
Kurz, H.D. and N. Salvadori (2000), '"Classical" roots of input-output analysis: a short account of its long prehistory', *Economic Systems Research*, **12** (2), 153–79.
Kurz, H.D. and N. Salvadori (2002), 'The surplus interpretation of the classical economists: a reply to Mark Blaug', *History of Political Economy*, **34** (1), 227–38.
Kurz, H.D. and N. Salvadori (2005), 'Representing the production and circulation of commodities in material terms: on Sraffa's objectivism', *Review of Political Economy*, **17** (3), 413–41.
Kurz, H.D. and N. Salvadori (2008), 'Neo-Ricardian economics', in S.N. Durlauf and L.E. Blume (eds), *The New Palgrave Dictionary of Economics*, 2nd edn, vol. 5, London: Palgrave Macmillan, pp. 899–906.
Marshall, A. (1890), *Principles of Economics*, London: Macmillan.
Marx, K. (1954a), *Theories of Surplus Value*, Moscow: Progress, English trans. of *Theorien über den Mehrwert*.
Marx, K. (1954b), *Capital*, vol. 1, Moscow: Progress, English trans. of *Das Kapital*, vol. 1 (1867), Hamburg: Meissner.

Marx, K. (1959), *Capital*, vol. 3, Moscow: Progress, English trans. of *Das Kapital*, vol. 3, ed. F. Engels (1894), Hamburg: Meissner.

Mas-Colell, A. (1989), 'Capital theory paradoxes: anything goes', in R. Feiwel (ed.), *Joan Robinson and Modern Economic Theory*, London: Macmillan, pp. 505–20.

Mill, J. (1826), *Elements of Political Economy*, 3rd edn, reprinted 1844, London: Henry G. Bohn.

Neumann, J. von (1945), 'A model of general economic equilibrium', *Review of Economic Studies*, **13** (1), 1–9.

Pasinetti, L.L. (1966), 'Changes in the rate of profit and switches of techniques', *Quarterly Journal of Economics*, **80** (4), 503–17.

Pasinetti, L.L. (1977), *Lectures on the Theory of Production*, London: Macmillan.

Petty, W. (1899), *The Economic Writings of Sir William Petty*, 2 vols, Cambridge: Cambridge University Press, reprinted 1986 as 1 vol., C.H. Hull (ed.), New York: Kelley.

Quesnay, F. (1759), *Quesnay's Tableau Economique*, reprinted 1972, eds M. Kuczynski and R.L. Meek, London: Macmillan.

Opocher, A. and I. Steedman (2015), *Full Industry Equilibrium*, Cambridge: Cambridge University Press.

Ricardo, D. (1951–73), *The Works and Correspondence of David Ricardo*, 11 vols, ed. by P. Sraffa with the collaboration of M.H. Dobb, Cambridge: Cambridge University Press.

Robinson, J.V. (1953), 'The production function and the theory of capital', *Review of Economic Studies*, **21** (2), 81–106.

Romer, P. (1994), 'The origins of endogenous growth', *Journal of Economic Perspectives*, **8** (1), 3–22.

Rowthorn, B. (1974), 'Neo-classicism, neo-Ricardianism and Marxism', *New Left Review*, **86** (July–August), 63–87.

Samuelson, P.A. (1987), 'Out of the closet: a program for the Whig history of economic science: keynote address at History of Economics Society Boston Meeting, June 20', *History of Economics Society Bulletin*, **9** (1), 51–60.

Schefold, B. (1989), *Mr Sraffa on Joint Production and Other Essays*, London: Unwin Hyman.

Schefold, B. (2000), 'Paradoxes of capital and counterintuitive changes of distribution in an intertemporal equilibrium model', in H.D. Kurz (ed.), *Critical Essays on Piero Sraffa's Legacy in Economics*, Cambridge: Cambridge University Press, pp. 363–91.

Smith, A. (1776), *An Inquiry into the Nature and Causes of the Wealth of Nations*, reprinted 1976 in *The Glasgow Edition of the Works and Correspondence of Adam Smith*, 2 vols, Oxford: Oxford University Press.

Sraffa, P. (1951), 'Introduction', in D. Ricardo, *The Works and Correspondence of David Ricardo*, ed. P. Sraffa with the collaboration of M.H. Dobb, vol. I, Cambridge: Cambridge University Press, pp. xiii–lxii.

Sraffa, P. (1960), *Production of Commodities by Means of Commodities. Prelude to a Critique of Economic Theory*, Cambridge: Cambridge University Press.

Steedman, I. (1977), *Marx after Sraffa*, London: New Left Books.

Torrens, R. (2000), *Collected Works of Robert Torrens*, 8 vols, ed. and introduced by G. de Vivo, Bristol: Thoemmes Press.

Keynesianism

A.K. Dasgupta published *Epochs of Economic Theory* in 1985. It quickly became a classic. Its major theme was that the development of dominant theories in economics reflected the historical events of the epochs with which they were associated. Dasgupta identified three epochs: classical including Marx, marginalist (he objected to the use of neoclassical to describe the second epoch) and Keynesian. He took a long – and correct – perspective, for the death of Keynes, over 80 years on from the publication of *The General Theory*, now resembles the greatly exaggerated notice of the death of Mark Twain. Why? To answer, it is useful, first, to examine the elements of the major approach that Keynes inherited from his teachers, especially Marshall and Pigou, and also from Malthus and Ricardo, and to show how he modified or scrapped them in order to build his own new system. Secondly, we point out that though in essence what Joan Robinson (1964) dubbed pre-Keynesian theory after Keynes, has dominated the past 40 years and more of economic theory and sometimes policy, yet it is now being proved wrong-headed and inapplicable, just as it appeared to Keynes, and was, as he moved from *A Tract* (1923) to *A Treatise on Money* (1930) (which had feet in both worlds) to *The General Theory* (1936) and after.

It may be argued that Keynes had to rationally reconstruct the system which he (inappropriately) named classical until Pigou's 1933 book on the theory of unemployment provided him with a detailed and comprehensive example of what he had in mind. (Ambrosi (2003) makes the definitive case for this reading.) Finally, it is argued that because of the particular ways in which Keynes's thought developed, his system, though still relevant and applicable (the "tract for our times" most convincingly arguing this is Taylor (2010)) nevertheless may be set out even more appropriately and relevantly within the approach of Michal Kalecki.

Kalecki's own development drew on the classical political economists and Marx's schemes of reproduction. He set the new proposition within the theory of the trade cycle, which itself ultimately became a theory of cyclical growth. His final views are similar in essence to the independent development of the same approach by Richard Goodwin. The major influences on Goodwin coincided with those on Kalecki, together with Wicksell, Schumpeter, Leontif and Joan Robinson.

So the emphasis in this entry is on, first, Keynes's contributions and approach and, secondly, on the most appropriate and promising ways forward. The alternative approaches under the rubric of Keynesianism which ruled the roost from Hicks 1937 on are only mentioned in passing.

Keynes came to economics with a background in mathematics and philosophy. He always regarded economics as a moral science. The development of his own philosophical ideas constituted an integral and essential part of the way he thought economics should be done and of his own revolutionary contributions to economic theory. Three aspects stand out. First, he argued that in a subject like economics, a whole spectrum of languages applies, running all the way from intuition and poetry through lawyer-like arguments (weight) to formal logic and mathematics. All have roles to play, depending upon what issues, or what aspects of issues, are being analysed.

Secondly, there is his emphasis that the whole may be more than the sum of the parts, a vital ingredient of his leading insight in the analysis in *The General Theory* and other of his writings of the processes at work in the economy as a whole. Much modern macro-economics is done in terms of one representative agent models which by their nature preclude Keynes's insight and especially the implications of the fallacy of composition.

Thirdly, there is his stress, also to be found in Marshall, that sensible, and sometimes not so sensible, people have to make important decisions in environments of inescapable fundamental uncertainty and so must develop behaviour and act in ways which are not implied by the assumption of *homo economicus* at work in all situations. This implies that much economic theory which has been developed either by assuming away the presence of uncertainty or by treating it as the equivalent of risk, is inapplicable – or, if applied, seriously misleading.

So what was the system that Keynes was brought up on? Marshall only produced one fully finished volume of the, at least three, volumes he thought should make up a comprehensive principles of economics: volume 1, theories of the formation of relative equilibrium prices and quantities in market, short and long periods in mainly competi-tive situations; volume 2, theories of the determination of the general price level and the roles of monetary and financial variables and institutions; and volume 3, economic history based around the theme of economic progress. (Keynes himself said he would spend his eighth decade on economic history.) Marshall did leave in various places his views on money, finance and related matters, international trade and capital flows, as well as his unsatisfactory volume, *Money, Credit and Commerce* (1923) published in his old age. From these sources, Keynes constituted what he was to call the classical system.

In the simplest outline, there was, first, a strict dichotomy between the real and the monetary so that the formation of relative prices and quantities in firms, industries and the economy as a whole could be analysed without there being any analytical role for money (other than as a ticket) and finance. Especially was this so for the analysis of long-period competitive prices and quantities, what Richard Kahn was later to call "the real business" of Marshall's *Principles*, Kahn (1929 [1989], xxviii). Money was essentially a veil, that is, had no impact on real economic activity. A corollary of this view was that in a competitive environment there was a tendency for prices and quantities to become such that all markets cleared, including those for the services of all classes of labour and capital goods. This implied in turn at least the long-period existence of Say's law. General gluts were impossible (as Malthus failed to persuade Ricardo) and so the theory of output and employment as a whole was no more than an adding up exercise.

Accumulation was seen as the transformation of delayed consumption today into more consumption tomorrow through saving, a psychological choice at the margin, by what we now call agents but were then regarded as people, and investment (accumula-tion) by business people who transformed flows of consumption foregone today through investment in capital goods into higher flows of consumption in the future. The flows of each were equalized when their respective rates of swapping at the margin, one sub-jective, the other technical, matched each other and the nominal rate of interest. Irving Fisher became the principal expositor of this view which is still the dominant account of the accumulation process of the mainstream today. It lies behind the commonly held view that saving determines investment, especially at the level of the world economy, rather than the Keynesian view that investment leads and saving follows. The classic ref-erence is Feldstein and Horioka (1980), but see also for a critique which contains James Meade's counterattack, Dalziel and Harcourt (1997) and Harcourt (2001).

The establishment of the Say's law position of the economy as a whole was the vital link to the analysis of the general price level by the quantity theory of money. If we state it in its Fisherian form, $MV \equiv PT$, where M is the quantity of money, V is the velocity of circulation, P is the general price level and T is the total number of transactions in the period concerned, we see immediately how its principal long-period proposition is obtained. With M determined by the monetary authorities, V by historical, social and institutional factors, and T corresponding to the Say's law level of transactions, the value of P is the only unknown to be endogenously determined. The identity becomes an equation and P is proportional to M via $P = \frac{MV}{T}$. This was the base on which could be erected theories of how the economy tended to settle at this level and, if the fundamental determinants of tastes and techniques changed, how the economy could move most smoothly to the new long-period equilibrium situation. Keynes, who was clearly working within this framework, told us in the preface to *A Treatise on Money* (1930) that he was proposing "a novel means of approach to the fundamental problems of monetary theory [, that his] object [was] to find a method which is useful in describing not merely the characteristics of static equilibrium, but also those of disequilibrium, and to discover the dynamical laws governing the passage of a monetary system from one position of equilibrium to another" (1930 [*CW* 1971 V]: xvii).

Short-term fluctuations around such levels were part of the various theories of the trade and credit cycle and role of monetary policy and the nominal rate of interest in them. Basically, though, the natural rate of interest ruled the roost and the nominal rate had to be consistent with it in order to avoid cumulative processes of inflation and deflation. (Wicksell was the pioneer here.)

This was Keynes's basic structure in both the *Tract* (1923) and *A Treatise on Money* (1930). He made modifications and extensions – in the *Tract* putting emphasis on the role of monetary policy in the short run in order to attack inflation and deflation, leaving the long run to the dead; in *A Treatise on Money*, he developed within a quantity theory framework theories of sectorial as well as the overall price level – his "fundamental equations". He also analysed the banana plantation parable which cried out for the concept of the multiplier to rid the analysis of ad hocery and provide a reason for why the cumulative downturns in prices, quantities and employment would come to an end endogenously (1930 [*CW* 1973 V]: 158–60). However, Keynes was still betwixt and between, providing, as Joan Robinson later pointed out, "a new theory of the *long-period* analysis of output" without realizing it (Robinson 1933 [1951], I: 56, original emphasis).

When Keynes published *The General Theory* in February 1936, and his major responses to his critics in 1937 (see *CW* 1973 XIV: 109–23), together with the essential addition to his new system of the finance motive (see *CW* 1973 XIV: 215–23), the key components of his revolution were brought together.

First, he rejected the dichotomy between the real and the monetary, insisting that monetary matters be integrated in the analysis right from the start. In particular, he argued that the nominal rate of interest ruled the roost in both the short and the long period, and that his version of the natural rate – the marginal efficiency of capital or, as it should have been, the marginal efficiency of investment – had to measure up to it rather than the other way around as in the old system. The rate of interest in turn was the outcome of the interaction between the demand for and the supply of money.

Secondly, investment led and saving had to follow, even at full employment. The components of aggregate demand resulting from the decisions of business people concerning production, accumulation and employment in the light of their expected sales for their products drove the system along. In the absence of government intervention, and given the state of long-term expectations, the ultimate constraint on investment became the cost and availability of finance. Meade and Keynes have left us succinct statements that bring all this altogether. "Keynes's intellectual revolution was to shift economists from thinking normally in terms of a model of reality in which a dog called *savings* wagged his tail labeled *investment* to thinking in terms of a model in which a dog called *investment* wagged his tail labeled *savings*" (Meade 1975: 82, original emphases). "The investment market can become congested through shortage of cash. It can never become congested through shortage of saving ... the most fundamental of my conclusions" (*CW* 1973 XIV: 222).

Thirdly, the emphasis on the short period as worthy of study in its own right began with the *Tract*, was given credence by Richard Kahn for the firm and the industry in his 1929 dissertation for King's, "The economics of the short period", and came into its own for the economy as a whole in *The General Theory* itself. (This is not an uncontroversial view, of course, for it is not accepted by Eatwell, Garegnani and Milgate, for example, nor, I suspect, by the joint editor of this *Handbook*, Heinz Kurz.) Disposable income becomes a dominant determinant of both consumption expenditure and saving. The multiplier, first worked out in Cambridge by Kahn and Meade using the apparatus of *A Treatise on Money*, is the means by which a change in desired investment is equalized with desired saving, and aggregate demand and aggregate supply are equalized at the point of effective demand (Kahn 1931). The periodic flow of saving is regarded as a residual though the forms in which present saving and past savings are held result from conscious economic decision making.

The major determinants of investment and consumption spending are such that there is no presumption that even on average they will be at levels which ensure the full employment of labour and normal capacity working of the existing stock of capital goods. That is, sustained levels of involuntary unemployment become probable possibilities as does over full employment, especially in war time.

Finally, because Say's law was refuted by Keynes's arguments, the quantity theory no longer provided a theory of the general price level even in the long period. Keynes himself replaced it in *The General Theory* by adapting Marshall's theory of short-period competitive pricing at the firm and industry level to the economy as a whole. The general price level now reflects the short-period aggregate marginal cost of producing overall national output. While Keynes put in provisos about the modifications that would be needed if imperfect competition prevailed in goods and factor markets, in order to get his main point across, he did not stress this. For his particular purposes, market structures, and their impact on price formation, were of secondary importance in that they did not affect his main qualitative conclusions.

Keynes was happy in 1939 to accept Dunlop's, Tarshis's and Kalecki's overthrow of the expected regularities that would be found if his theory of the general price level was dominant. He did not think it changed the essence of his argument and it made it easier politically to advocate expansion by government expenditure and tax cuts in periods of recession, because the impetus to inflation associated with higher marginal costs and therefore prices would not necessarily occur (see Keynes 1939 [*CW* 1973 VII]: 394–412).

However, when, at the beginning of World War II, he explicitly extended his analysis to analyse full and overfull employment in "How to pay for the war" (1940 [*CW* 1972 IX]: 367–439), his concept of an inflationary gap drew on his theory of overall pricing in *The General Theory*. Whether market structures are or are not crucial is still being debated (see, for example, Marris 1997; Shapiro 1997). It is significant that Kalecki in his review article of *The General Theory* (Kalecki 1936; Targetti and Kinda-Hass 1982) did not believe that they were, and illustrated why.

The post-war arguments that Keynes's system had a fixed price system are certainly not supported by Keynes's own contributions, nor is the argument that Keynes-type results depend upon assuming a given money wage. Moreover, Keynes did not accept that stable, dependable long-run relationships were a feature of economies which could be relied on when making policy decisions so that the argument that the Phillips curve could be regarded as an integral part of his system, that it provided a missing link, is foreign to his methodology (see Harcourt 2000; 2001).

In *The General Theory* Keynes put little emphasis on the open economy aspects of his new theory and the role of international capital movements. However, in his wartime writings and papers prepared for the creation of the post-war international institutions, Keynes set out the conceptual bases of the open economy macroeconomics which has been developed in the post-war period (see Vines 2003 and below).

In Keynes's discussion of the determinants of investment expenditure, the impact of the demand for money and finance, the workings of stock exchanges, and the dominant importance of analysing decision making under uncertainty are brought together. This provides a sounder base on which to erect explanations of the recent financial crisis and its impact on the real economy than any of the approaches developed by mainstream economists in the past 40 years and more. As we noted, the most incisive statement of this view point is Lance Taylor's "tract for our times", appropriately entitled *Maynard's Revenge* (2010), see also Joe Stiglitz's *Freefall* (2010).

Keynes never insisted on the adoption of the particular detailed ways he put these strands all together, only that they all be considered and that his theory not be regarded as an alternative way of stating the loanable funds theory of the rate of interest. This was primarily because the loanable funds theory was dominated by the interplay of flows and largely ignored the role of stocks in the determination of the role of interest. It is, moreover, linked excessively to the forces of productivity and thrift which dominated Keynes's definition of classical theory and was what he objected to in it.

Keynes's analysis of and criticisms of the workings of the stock exchange are as fresh today as when he wrote chapter 12 of *The General Theory*, probably his own favourite chapter. There, he identified first the stock exchange's role in "enterprise" – the bringing together and gathering up of new saving, a flow, and the rearrangement of old savings (a stock), in directing funds towards the holding of financial assets, the prices of which were meant to reflect the expected profitability of newly established and long established physical assets of firms, the shares and debentures of which were quoted on the stock exchange. Keynes pointed out that if "speculation" was only a bubble on the pool of "enterprise", the stock exchange would be a socially valuable institution, doing the tasks described above tolerably well. But if the roles were reversed, so that "speculation" was dominant, the stock exchange then more resembled a casino and did a very poor job in trying to fulfil its tradition and proper role.

Speculators may do no harm as bubbles on a steady stream of enterprise. But the position is serious when enterprise becomes the bubble on a whirlpool of speculation. When the capital development of the country becomes a by-product of the activities of a casino, the job is likely to be ill-done. The measure of success attained by Wall Street, regarded as an institution of which the proper social purpose is to direct new investment into the most profitable channels in terms of future yield, cannot be claimed as one of the outstanding triumphs of *laissez-faire* capitalism . . . not surprising, if the best brains of Wall Street have been . . . directed towards a different object. (Keynes 1936 [*CW* 1973 VII]: 159)

These considerations also apply to business people making decisions concerning accumulation in an uncertain environment. Keynes in *The General Theory* had an unsatisfactory, in details, theory of aggregate investment flows in Chapter 11, in which the marginal efficiency of capital (investment) and the rate of interest match off against each other, with the rate of interest dominating. However, he clearly thought that what he called the "animal spirits" of business people and the cost and availability of finance and credit were dominant for most periods in determining the desired level of accumulation. He argued that conventions – regarding the future as akin to the present and past unless there were very good reasons for expecting otherwise, for example – dominated decision making and allowed actions to occur, usually at levels which would not match full employment voluntary saving. In so arguing, he was anticipating the themes of Nicholas Kaldor's greatest theoretical article, "Speculation and economic stability" (1939). Kaldor analysed markets where stocks dominated flows and expectations about future events and other people's behaviour dominated the usual fundamentals in markets in determining prices. With this was associated a most important Kaldorian and Keynesian insight, the importance of established norms set by expert market makers for the attainment of stability in individual markets and economic systems as a whole. In their absence, speculative activity feeds on itself in a cumulative process of destabilization.

Keynes always remained a Marshallian in method, even in his most radical theory of shifting equilibrium (Keynes 1936 [*CW* 1973 VII]: 293–4), on which the basis of the post-Keynesian theory of distribution and growth in the post-war period (for example, Joan Robinson's 1956 *The Accumulation of Capital*), was erected. Keynes's approach was recursive and he recognized mutual determination; but because of his keen sense of the different lengths of actual time that components of interrelated processes needed to work themselves out, he was wary of suggesting simultaneous determination. Keynes also never developed (nor would he probably have accepted) the theory of cumulative causation which comes from Adam Smith through Allyn Young (1928) and then Kaldor and Myrdal in the post-war period. The theory rejects the traditional neoclassical approach to economic theory whereby the factors responsible for uniqueness or otherwise of equilibrium are independent of those responsible for local and global stability. In turn, this implies that the factors responsible for the trend are independent of those responsible for the cycle. As this too is rejected, it is one reason why cumulative causation and cyclical growth theory are closely related to each other. The most succinct statement of all this is by Kalecki: "The long-run trend [is] but a slowly changing component of a chain of short-period situations . . . [not an] independent entity" (Kalecki 1968 [1971]: 165).

Whether Keynes would have accepted IS–LM as a representation of his views, a proposition consistently and vehemently denied by those closest to him, Joan Robinson and Richard Kahn, is a moot point. An IS–LM interpretation may be read into page

173 of *The General Theory* "We have now introduced money into our causal nexus for the first time, and we are able to catch a first glimpse of the way in which changes in the quantity of money work their way into the economic system" (*CW* 1973 VII: 173). Then, fortified by *ceteris paribus* which in the event may not actually hold, he sets out monetary and real relationships which may be captured in IS–LM terms and were in fact done so by, for example, Reddaway, Champernowne, Meade, Harrod and Hicks when *The General Theory* was first published. However, the limitations of this representation are also clearly implied – it requires that the IS and LM relationships be independent of each other – as Donald Moggridge set out succinctly and persuasively in the appendix to his *Modern Masters* volume on Keynes (1976).

Another major area that comes under the rubric of Keynesianism is the hotly debated question of whether money and finance are exogenous or endogenous variables. For Keynes, over his lifetime, the evidence is that he thought of them as endogenous. This must be coupled with his methodological view that whether variables are regarded as endogenous, to be determined, or exogenous, to determine, was a relative not an absolute judgement. It depended on the issue being analysed and how far processes had gone before analysis of a particular situation started.

As Sheila Dow (1997) has argued, this explains why many interpreters (including Kaldor) have criticized Keynes for taking the money supply as exogenous in *The General Theory* (even if not in the rest of his writings). Dow argues that it should be regarded as a given for Keynes's then major purpose. This allows Dow to develop an analysis in which the significance of Keynes's theory of liquidity preference in an explanation of the demand for money and other financial assets, and of banks extending credit guided by their own states of liquidity preference, so that not all demand is accommodated, are brought together in her arguments. Therefore, Dow distinguishes the demand for and supply of money from the corresponding demands for and supplies of credit. This interpretation places Keynes himself sensibly in between the extreme horizontalists (for example, Basil Moore) and the extreme verticalists (for example, Milton Friedman) (see Harcourt 2006: ch. 5). As we have noted above, Keynes's view is encrusted in "the most fundamental of [his] conclusions", coupled with Meade's Keynesian investment dog, saving tail, turn around.

The General Theory has been interpreted as way off Keynes's usual regression line. This is especially so with regard to the quantity of money, as we noted above but rejected, but also with regard to the principal setting of *The General Theory* being a closed economy, in which reading there is more substance. However, if the whole span of Keynes's interests and contributions over his life are taken into account, it is clear that he analysed open economy interactions and proposed international institutions and policies with which to tackle the problems they threw up. Vines (2003) points out that much of *A Treatise on Money* is concerned with these issues of international macroeconomics, that Keynes had already recognized the major problems but had not yet made a completely satisfactory analysis of why they arose and what to do about them, mainly because the analytical system of *A Treatise on Money* was a halfway house between the old and the new.

A more satisfactory analysis was to come in the years following *The General Theory* when Keynes worked on wartime finance in open economies, especially in the United Kingdom, the workings of the world economy with emphasis on the source of contractionary biases in it, and the interrelationships of internal and external balance in individual economies and the world as a whole.

Keynes was concerned to show why creditor nations could be bad world citizens and to design carrot and stick measures, and the institutions to implement them, to redeem this. He also emphasized the prior need for economies to reach internal balance before tackling the issues of external balance. The role of international institutions was partly to devise measures which allowed interrelated processes of vastly different lengths of historical time to operate in systemically acceptable manners. Keynes was much more favourable to freer trade than to unregulated international capital movements even when internal balance had been obtained. He wanted international institutions to create adequate liquidity so as to tide over economies that had to make structural adjustments without being forced to ally them with contractionary measures.

Keynes also analysed the problems of post-war reconstruction, especially the United Kingdom's plight owing to inescapable changes associated with fighting World War II, and the United States' dominant role in the post-war period. All these issues lay behind setting up the International Monetary Fund and the World Bank, and negotiating the post-war loan from the USA to the UK.

As we know, the Americans dominated the forms and conditions all these took, bringing in a modified form of the Gold Standard. They failed to create adequate provisions of liquidity and appropriate checks and balances within institutions to encourage good behaviour by creditor nations. Thus Bretton Woods built into its foundations its ultimate break down. Keynes was aware of all this but lost the battle. He did though leave the conceptual bases for overcoming these problems if only economists and politicians had had the goodwill to do so.

G.C. HARCOURT

See also:

Business cycles and growth (III); Cambridge School of economics (II); John Richard Hicks (I); Richard Ferdinand Kahn (I); Nicholas Kaldor (I); John Maynard Keynes (I); Labour and employment (III); Macroeconomics (III); James Edward Meade (I); Money and banking (III); Post-Keynesianism (II); Joan Violet Robinson (I); Piero Sraffa (I); Uncertainty and information (III).

References and further reading

Ambrosi, G.M. (2003), *Keynes, Pigou and Cambridge Keynesians. Authenticity and Analytical Perspective in the Keynes-Classics Debate*, Basingstoke: Palgrave Macmillan.
Dalziel, P. and G.C. Harcourt (1997), 'A note on "Mr Meade's relation" and international capital movements', *Cambridge Journal of Economics*, **21** (5), 621–31, reprinted in G.C. Harcourt (2001), *50 Years a Keynesian and Other Essays*, Basingstoke: Palgrave, pp. 72–87.
Dasgupta, A.K. (1985), *Epochs in Economic Theory*, Oxford: Basil Blackwell.
Dow, S.C. (1997), 'Endogenous money', in G.C. Harcourt and P.A. Riach (eds), *A 'Second Edition' of The General Theory*, vol. 2, London: Routledge, pp. 61–78.
Feldstein, M. and C. Horioka (1980), 'Domestic saving and international capital flows', *Economic Journal*, **90** (358), 314–29.
Harcourt, G.C. (2000), 'A left Keynesian view of the Phillips curve trade-off', in R. Leeson (ed.), *A.W.H. Phillips. Collected Works in Contemporary Perspective*, Cambridge: Cambridge University Press, pp. 304–7, reprinted in G.C. Harcourt (2001), *50 Years a Keynesian and Other Essays*, Basingstoke: Palgrave, pp. 183–7.
Harcourt, G.C. (2001), *50 Years a Keynesian and Other Essays*, Basingstoke: Palgrave.
Harcourt, G.C. (2006), *The Structure of Post-Keynesian Economics. The Core Contributions of the Pioneers*, Cambridge: Cambridge University Press.
Harcourt, G.C. and P.A. Riach (eds) (1997), *A 'Second Edition' of The General Theory*, vol. 2, London: Routledge.

Hicks, J.R. (1937), 'Mr Keynes and the classics: a suggested interpretation', *Econometrica*, **5** (2), 147–59.
Kahn, R.F. (1929), *The Economics of the Short Period*, reprinted 1989, Basingstoke: Macmillan.
Kahn, R.F. (1931), 'The relation of home investment to unemployment', *Economic Journal*, **41** (June), 173–98.
Kalecki, M. (1936), 'Pare uwag o teorii Keynesa' ('Some remarks on Keynes's theory'), *Ekonomista*, **3** (3), 18–26, reprinted in J. Osiatynski (ed.) (1990), *Collected Works of Michał Kalecki*, vol. 1, Oxford: Clarendon Press, pp. 223–32.
Kalecki, M. (1968), 'Trend and business cycles reconsidered', *Economic Journal*, **78** (310), 263–76, reprinted in M. Kalecki (1971), *Selected Essays on the Dynamics of the Capitalist Economy, 1933–1970*, Cambridge: Cambridge University Press, pp. 165–83.
Kalecki, M. (1971), *Selected Essays on the Dynamics of the Capitalist Economy, 1933–1970*, Cambridge: Cambridge University Press.
Kaldor, N. (1939), 'Speculation and economic stability', *Review of Economic Studies*, **7** (1), 1–27.
Keynes, J.M. (1923), *A Tract on Monetary Reform*, reprinted in E. Johnson and D. Moggridge (eds) (1971), *The Collected Writings of John Maynard Keynes*, vol. IV, London: Macmillan and Cambridge University Press.
Keynes, J.M. (1930), *A Treatise on Money*, reprinted in E. Johnson and D. Moggridge (eds) (1971), *The Collected Writings of John Maynard Keynes*, vols V and VI, London: Macmillan and Cambridge University Press.
Keynes, J.M. (1936), *The General Theory of Employment, Interest and Money*, reprinted in E. Johnson and D. Moggridge (eds) (1973), *The Collected Writings of John Maynard Keynes*, vol. VII, London: Macmillan and Cambridge University Press.
Keynes, J.M. (1939), 'Relative movement of real wages and output', *The Economic Journal*, **49** (193), pp. 34–51, reprinted in E. Johnson and D. Moggridge (eds) (1973), *The Collected Writings of John Maynard Keynes*, vol. VII, London: Macmillan and Cambridge University Press, app. 3, pp. 394–412.
Keynes, J.M. (1940), *How to Pay for the War*, reprinted in E. Johnson and D. Moggridge (eds) (1972), *The Collected Writings of John Maynard Keynes*, vol. IX, London: Macmillan and Cambridge University Press.
Keynes, J.M. (1972), *Essays in Persuasion*, in E. Johnson and D. Moggridge (eds), *The Collected Writings of John Maynard Keynes*, vol. IX, London: Macmillan and Cambridge University Press.
Keynes, J.M. (1973), *The General Theory and After, Part II: Defence and Development*, reprinted in E. Johnson and D. Moggridge (eds), *The Collected Writings of John Maynard Keynes*, vol. XIV, London: Macmillan and Cambridge University Press.
Keynes, M. (ed.) (1975), *Essays on John Maynard Keynes*, Cambridge: Cambridge University Press.
Leeson, R. (ed.) (2000), *A. W. H. Phillips. Collected Works in Contemporary Perspective*, Cambridge: Cambridge University Press.
Marris, R. (1997), 'Yes Mrs Robinson! *The General Theory* and imperfect competition', in G.C. Harcourt and P.A. Riach (eds), *A 'Second Edition' of The General Theory*, vol. 1, London: Routledge, pp. 52–82.
Marshall, A. (1923), *Money, Credit and Commerce*, London: Macmillan.
Meade, J.E. (1975), 'The Keynesian revolution', in M. Keynes (ed.), *Essays on John Maynard Keynes*, Cambridge: Cambridge University Press, pp. 82–8.
Moggridge, D.E. (1976), *Keynes*, London: Macmillan.
Pigou, A.C. (1933), *Theory of Unemployment*, London: Macmillan.
Robinson, J. (1933), 'The theory of money and the analysis of output', *Review of Economic Studies*, **1** (1), 22–8, reprinted in J. Robinson (1951), *Collected Economic Papers*, vol. 1, London: Macmillan, pp. 52–8.
Robinson, J. (1951), *Collected Economic Papers*, vol. 1, London: Macmillan.
Robinson, J. (1956), *The Accumulation of Capital*, 2nd edn 1965, 3rd edn 1969, London: Macmillan.
Robinson, J. (1964), 'Pre-Keynesian theory after Keynes', *Australian Economic Papers*, **3** (1–2), 25–35.
Shapiro, N. (1997), 'Imperfect competition and Keynes', in G.C. Harcourt and P.A. Riach (eds), *A 'Second Edition' of The General Theory*, vol. 1, London: Routledge, pp. 83–92.
Stiglitz, J.E. (2010), *Freefall. Free Markets and the Sinking of the Global Economy*, London: Allen Lane, Penguin.
Targetti, F. and B. Kinda-Hass (1982), 'Kalecki's review of Keynes' *General Theory*', *Australian Economic Papers*, **21** (December), 244–60.
Taylor, L. (2010), *Maynard's Revenge, The Collapse of Free Market Economics*, Cambridge, MA: Harvard University Press.
Vines, D. (2003), 'John Maynard Keynes 1937–1946: the creation of international macroeconomics', *Economic Journal*, **113** (488), F338–F361.
Young, A. (1928), 'Increasing returns and economic progress', *Economic Journal*, **38** (152), 527–42.

Post-Keynesianism

Post-Keynesian economics is a body of economic thought that developed since the mid-1950s, but of course its origins can be traced back to Keynes's *General Theory*, and to the group of young economists, called the Circus, who discussed and criticized Keynes's earlier *Treatise on Money*. Among the economists to be found in the first volume of this *Handbook*, post-Keynesian economics is primarily associated with the names of Keynes, Sraffa, Kalecki, Joan Robinson, Kahn, Kaldor and Minsky, but other influential figures, for very diverse reasons, could include Veblen, Fisher, Schumpeter, Lowe, Harrod, Lerner, Shackle, Hicks, Leontief and Simon.

Up until the beginning of the 1970s, this dissident school of thought was mainly known as the neo-Keynesian school, but also as the Anglo-Italian school or the Cambridge school (of Keynesian economics). It became mostly known for its models of growth and distribution, the so-called Kaldor–Pasinetti models (Baranzini and Mirante 2013), which were an alternative to the neoclassical theory of income distribution based on marginal productivity theory. The main initial purpose of the school was to bring Keynes's analysis into the realm of capital accumulation and the long period, as exemplified by Joan Robinson's (1956) remarkable achievement. Then in the early 1970s, following letter exchanges between Alfred Eichner and Joan Robinson, the term post-Keynesian was put forward, a name that had been used occasionally before by both Nicholas Kaldor and Robinson. The name post-Keynesian stuck when Jan Kregel (1973) used it in the subtitle of his book summarizing the main views of Cambridge Keynesians, and when Eichner and Kregel (1975) used it in the title of their survey article for the *Journal of Economic Literature*. Finally, Paul Davidson and Sidney Weintraub created the *Journal of Post Keynesian Economics* in 1978, purposefully omitting the hyphen in an effort to go beyond the growth and distribution issues that had been at the heart of the Cambridge Keynesian work. Both spellings are still in use.

An overall history of post-Keynesian economics can be found in King (2002). Pasinetti (2007) has done the same for the Cambridge branch, and Lee (2000) provides an account, with the relevant correspondence, of the amalgamation of the early Cambridge and American members of the school. Arestis and Sawyer (2006) and Setterfield (2010) offer recent surveys of what are essentially post-Keynesian monetary and growth theories, while Lavoie (2014) provides a synthesis of the various post-Keynesian theories. A fair outside assessment of post-Keynesianism can be found in Screpanti and Zamagni (2005).

Many observers have complained that it is difficult to identify a simple running thread among self-assessed post-Keynesian writers, something that would be comparable to the neoclassical framework of constrained optimization informed by relative prices and scarcity. The issue of a lack of coherence, in theory and in methodology, within post-Keynesian economics, has often been brought up. Post-Keynesians themselves seem to have diverse opinions as to what is really essential or special about post-Keynesian economics. To some extent, these differences of opinion are related to the different strands that coexist within post-Keynesian economics. After having defined these strands, it will be shown that there exist some key characteristics that are common to all these strands and that there is more agreement among post-Keynesians than is often perceived.

The Five Strands

The best-known classification of post-Keynesian economists is that of Hamouda and Harcourt (1988). They identify three strands. The first strand is composed of the American post-Keynesians, also called Marshallian post-Keynesians, fundamental post-Keynesians, financial Keynesians, or simply Post Keynesians or even Keynes's school. The second strand consists of the Kaleckians, which Hamouda and Harcourt (1988) associate with Michał Kalecki, his student Joseph Steindl, and Joan Robinson, who had a great admiration for Kalecki and thought that Kalecki's theory provided a better foundation than Keynes's for an alternative theory. Indeed, Philip Arestis (1996) calls this group the Robinsonians. Finally, the third strand is that of Sraffians, those who follow Sraffa. For a long time they were better known as the neo-Ricardians, and are occasionally called neo-Ricardian Keynesians.

The Sraffian school is discussed elsewhere in this *Handbook*, therefore little more will be said about it, but it should be noted that several methodologists argue that removing the Sraffians would bring more coherence to post-Keynesianism. This may be so, but there is little doubt that Sraffians are intimately linked with post-Keynesian analysis by tradition and by history. Indeed, as argued by Mata (2004), the post-Keynesian identity and the realization that Cambridge Keynesianism was different from the neoclassical Keynesian synthesis arose in large part as a consequence of the Cambridge capital controversies that occurred in the 1960s and early 1970s as a consequence of Sraffa's work and his critique of neoclassical economics. Secondly, many Sraffians are in close agreement with other post-Keynesians on key defining characteristics of post-Keynesianism, such as the causality between investment and saving, the role of effective demand both in the short and the long run, the endogeneity of the money supply, and the need to start from production rather than exchange relationships. Finally, Sraffians provide a much needed explanation of prices in an interdependent setting, something that is lacking in the other strands, and they provide a link with multi-sectoral production systems, which are, for example, of particular interest to ecological economists who wish to track the overall impact of production on the use of energy, natural resources and pollution.

The classification provided above should however be extended by the addition of two strands. Hamouda and Harcourt (1988) wonder where, within their three-way classification, they should put authors such as Kaldor and Wynne Godley. It seems that adding a fourth strand – the Kaldorians – would greatly simplify the exercise of assigning various well-known post-Keynesian authors to their respective boxes. Finally, in accordance with Arestis (1996), the institutionalist Keynesians constitute a fifth strand inside the post-Keynesian school.

This classification can be epitomized in the determination of a distribution variable – the normal profit rate: fundamentalists would deny its relevance; Kaleckians would argue that it is determined by class struggle or the ability of firms to prevent the entry of rivals; most Sraffians would claim that the interest rate set by the central bank, with some risk premium, determines the normal profit rate; Kaldorians would argue instead that the rate of accumulation is the main determinant of the normal profit rate, along the lines of the Cambridge equation, $r = g/s_p$, where s_p is the propensity to save out of profits; finally, Institutionalists would argue that financial norms on rates of return on equity, along with acceptable leverage ratios, imply a normal profit rate in the real sector. Naturally, there is nothing to prevent us from believing that all these factors have an impact on the normal profit rate.

The main concerns of the fundamental post-Keynesians – the first strand – are the description of a monetized production economy with their contracts in money terms, the fragility and instability of the financial system, questions tied to the liquidity preference and the liquidity needs of investors and financial institutions, and the all-crucial notion of radical uncertainty where, as described by George Shackle, any decision modifies the economic environment so that the future is always uncertain. Their work is focused on short-run issues, as it is believed that little useful can be said about the long run. An important concern of several of these authors is to amplify the true and fundamental meaning of Keynes's writings. This branch is sometimes named American because its initial proponents – Weintraub, Davidson, Hyman Minsky, Victoria Chick, Basil Moore – came from the United States, although members of this branch can now be found all over the world. Most work on post-Keynesian methodology would be associated with this branch, since much of this work was devoted to Keynes's writings on probability theory, with many misgivings about econometrics.

The Kaleckians – the second strand – besides the three names already mentioned, have as important members authors such as Tom Asimakopulos, Amit Bhaduri, Malcolm Sawyer, Amitava Dutt, Robert Blecker, Steve Fazzari, and Eckhard Hein, to which one could add Robert Rowthorn and Richard Goodwin. Similar to fundamental Keynesians, Kaleckians are concerned with short-run output and employment, but also with business cycles, long-run growth theory, as well as pricing issues, in particular the link between mark-ups and growth, and hence income distribution. The potential conflicts regarding income distribution are an important object of analysis. Another major concern is that of the realization of profit, using here the Marxist expression. An important topic over the past years has been empirical studies devoted to finding out whether economies are wage-led or profit-led, that is, whether a redistribution towards wages and away from profits generates higher output and faster growth. Arestis (1996) associates Kaleckians with the monetary circuit school that has developed in France and Italy, with Alain Parguez and Augusto Graziani at the vanguard, thus supplementing the Kaleckian strand with a more obvious monetary element. The Kaleckian strand may also be associated with the Structuralist school, which used to be mainly concerned with economic development, as exemplified by the works of Lance Taylor and Valpy Fitzgerald.

Skipping the Sraffians, we move on to the fourth strand, that of the Kaldorians. This strand is mostly concerned with monetary issues, cumulative causation, and productivity growth. A lot of attention has been devoted to the constraints arising from open economy considerations, such as the balance of payment constraints, or the fundamental identity that links financial private saving, public deficits, and the current account balance – an identity that has been used in work carried out by Wynne Godley and his colleagues, first at the Department of Applied Economics at Cambridge with Francis Cripps and Ken Coutts, and then at the Levy Institute in the USA. Besides Kaldor and Godley, to which one could add John Cornwall and his student Mark Setterfield, the names of John McCombie and Anthony Thirlwall (1994) stand out, as the empirical work of the latter has inspired a large following, especially from Latin America. Also it could be claimed that the modern work being pursued on path dependence, persistence and hysteresis can be traced back to Kaldor's (1934) remarkable article on unstable equilibria, multiple equilibria and path dependence. Like most Kaleckians, Kaldorians do not hesitate to engage in empirical work, and this has led to an extension of the Cambridge capital controversies, through the provision of *reductio ad absurdum* proofs showing that empirical estimates of neoclassical production function elasticities and of neoclassical labour demand curves are meaningless artefacts. These studies have given support to Kaldor's earlier claim that neoclassical theorists could only decorate their theories but could not corroborate them.

The fifth and final strand is that of the institutionalist Keynesians. When identifying this strand, Arestis (1996: 114) mentions wage and debt contracts, administered prices, conventions, routines, and habits. Sources of inspiration have been Thorstein Veblen, but also John Kenneth Galbraith, who was a founding patron of the *Journal of Post Keynesian Economics*. While institutionalists do not really have a macroeconomic theory of their own, post-Keynesian macroeconomics is the macroeconomic theory of institutionalism. On the other hand, besides Kalecki's mark-up pricing, there is not much of post-Keynesian microeconomics, so that, besides Sraffian prices, institutionalists provide post-Keynesians with microeconomic tools. The administered pricing literature, with full cost pricing, normal cost pricing, target return pricing and limit entry pricing, associated with Means, Andrews and Brunner, Kaplan and Lanzillotti, Sylos Labini, Godley and Nordhaus, Wood and Eichner, is closely tied to post-Keynesian microeconomics as understood by Frederic Lee (1998). Similarly, institutionalists provide post-Keynesianism with its foundations of labour economics, with authors such as Eileen Appelbaum, Jill Rubery, Frank Wilkinson and Michael Piore.

On routines, heuristics, conventions and habits, there is a substantial body of work within behavioural economics or psychological economics which is akin to the concerns and methods of post-Keynesians, getting away from the standard search for small deviations from constrained optimization and adopting instead Herbert Simon's notion of satisficing, with frugal rationality and non-compensatory choice criteria (Earl 1986; Berg and Gigerenzer 2010), something that can also be found in the description of consumer theory of ecological economists (Holt et al. 2009). Within the fifth strand, one would thus also include some works of the French convention school, which has formalized the role of conventions in Keynes's view of speculation (Orléan 1998). There is also a substantial amount of work, linked to industrial organization, which examines the evolution of corporations as part of a financialization process. This work, which is at the juncture of the Marxist, institutionalist and French Regulation school traditions, has certainly informed post-Keynesian thinking. Indeed, there is clear evidence that at least some members of the Regulation school, such as Robert Boyer, Pascal Petit and Jacques Mazier, were heavily influenced by Cambridge post-Keynesians, so that one could argue that some streams of the Regulation School are part of the institutionalist strand of post-Keynesianism. Finally, the neo-chartalist school, as found in Wray (2012) and now known as modern monetary theory (MMT) on the web, can be considered as part of institutionalist post-Keynesianism, since the neo-chartalists base their policy recommendations on a detailed analysis of monetary institutions and implementation procedures, in particular the functioning of the central bank and of the clearing and settlement system.

The identification of these various strands is only indicative. Several eclectic authors – such as Geoffrey Harcourt and Edward Nell – go across all, or at least several, of the identified strands.

Post-Keynesianism versus Orthodox Economics

As pointed out in the introduction, it is not so easy to define post-Keynesian economics. Luigi Pasinetti (2007: 37, 200, 219) believes that this difficulty arose from the beginning, as the founding members of post-Keynesianism did not bother to discuss the fundamentals of the new paradigm. Some outsiders have claimed that it is easier to say what post-Keynesians do not stand for. Here are some constructs which are most certainly rejected by post-Keynesians: (1) marginal productivity theory; (2) the natural rate of unemployment or the NAIRU; (3) a unique natural rate of interest; (4) the loanable funds theory; (5) crowding-out effects (except through possible psychological effects); (6) the efficient market hypothesis in its various incarnations; (7) bank reserves as a cause of bank loans and bank deposits; (8) the excess supply of money as the cause of inflation; (9) Say's law that supply creates its own demand; (10) aggregate employment as determined in the labour market; (11) sticky wages as the cause of unemployment; (12) the government financial and debt constraints as being analogous to those of households; and (13) unit costs with a U-shape.

Several authors have attempted to identify the key constructive characteristics of post-Keynesian economics, starting with Eichner and Kregel (1975). Although there is a substantial degree of overlap in the identified characteristics, about 15 different features could be listed (Lavoie 2014: 34). One problem arises from the fact that some lists contain methodological precepts while others entertain theoretical constructs and policy consequences. The problem is compounded by the fact that post-Keynesian economics is part of a larger group of heterodox schools of thought – dissidents who share common methodological principles that can be contrasted to those that are implicitly followed by neoclassical authors. It may be simpler to start by identifying these methodological principles that are shared by heterodox authors and by post-Keynesian authors in particular.

Some have argued that there are five key methodological beliefs, or presuppositions, which separate heterodox from orthodox economics. These presuppositions are very widely found in the writings of various well-known post-Keynesians who have attempted to define the field. For instance, one finds four of these five presuppositions in the list of Pasinetti (2007: 219–37). The heterodox presuppositions are realism, organicism, reasonable rationality, a concern with production and growth, and a belief in the need for tamed markets.

Tony Lawson (1994) has long been arguing that critical realism is the key methodological distinguishing feature, claiming that any other distinctive factor derives from taking a critical realist position. While others would tend to favour a more naive form of realism – *empirical* realism, as did Eichner and Kregel (1975) – there is an agreement that the analysis must start with first approximations of the real world, with Kaldor's stylized facts or some empirical regularities, and not with a fictional abstraction that does not even attempt to represent reality. By contrast orthodox economists strive under instrumentalism, that is, the belief that an assumption need not be realistic provided it is conductive to predictions, preferably numerical ones, even if these predictions turn out to be mistaken and even misleading, as is the case with the measured elasticities of the aggregate neoclassical production function. Post-Keynesians prefer to develop accurate simplified versions of the real world instead of polished irrelevant models.

Perhaps related to realism is the kind of rationality which is assumed in our economic models. Following the rational expectations revolution, the only type of rationality admissible to mainstream economists is model-consistent hyper-rationality. Not only are economic agents assumed to know all contingencies, from now to infinity, they are assumed to know how the world operates. As pointed out by Berg and Gigerenzer (2010: 141), the effort "to add behavioral elements as extensions of neoclassical models, paradoxically leads to optimization problems that are more complex to solve", and hence involves even more hyper-rationality. By contrast, heterodox authors rely on "reasonable rationality" – bounded rationality as Simon used to call it. Agents follow decisions processes that match their economic environment and the time and resources they can devote to their decision making, reacting to disequilibria from established norms, making informed guesses, attempting to satisfice some target, and following non-compensatory decision procedures. This justifies the rules of thumb and sensible expectations used by post-Keynesians in their models. These are much less ad hoc than the mainstream assumption of rational expectations.

The third presupposition of heterodox economics is organicism, by opposition to the orthodox use of methodological individualism, or holism versus atomicism. It is well known that heterodox schools of thought such as Marxism rely on class analysis, without starting from the optimizing individual. In post-Keynesian economics, this is often reflected by the concern for functional income distribution and the slogan that microeconomics needs macroeconomic foundations. What is really meant is that fallacies of composition are ever present in economics, that the whole is more than the sum of its parts, and that attention must be paid to the possibility of macroeconomic paradoxes that contradict the pure aggregation of a representative agent. The most famous paradox is Keynes's paradox of thrift, according to which higher saving rates lead to reduced output. However, there are many others, many of which were highly relevant during the subprime financial crisis. There is the paradox of public deficits, according to which higher government deficits raise private profits (Kalecki); the paradox of debt, where efforts to deleverage might lead to higher leverage ratios (Steindl); the paradox of liquidity, where new ways to create liquidity end up reducing it; or the paradox of risk, where the availability of individual risk cover leads to more risk overall.

About the fourth pair of presuppositions, it need only be pointed out that the most common definition of economics in orthodox textbooks is the study of the efficient allocation of scarce resources. Exchange of endowments and substitution effects here play a key role. By contrast, heterodox economists are mostly concerned with production, the (less than 100 per cent) degree of utilization of existing resources, the causes and the consequences of growth, and the ability of the economic system to create a surplus. They do not assume that resources are fully utilized and hence focus on income effects.

This leads us to the fifth and last of our key presuppositions, that of the role of markets relative to the role of the state. Mainstream economists exhibit great confidence in the ability of free markets to deliver stability and full employment. By contrast heterodox economists are very much distrustful of unfettered markets. They suspect their unfairness, their inability to self-regulate, their tendency for destabilizing paths, their squandering of resources. Post-Keynesians believe that markets must be tamed, as is especially obvious from Minsky's financial fragility hypothesis, that is, the thesis that there are endogenous destabilizing forces at work. This fifth presupposition can be clearly brought back to Keynes, who argued that the main cleavage in economics was between those who believed in a self-adjusting system and those that did not.

Post-Keynesianism versus Heterodox Economics

We now need to tackle the characteristics that truly distinguish post-Keynesian economics from the other heterodox schools. We shall identify two sets of characteristics. The most important feature is the principle of effective demand, as recognized by all recent accounts of post-Keynesianism. The principle of effective demand says that aggregate demand is the main force that determines output and employment (except for some temporary situations where productive capacity is the barrier to expansion). However, while most economists would agree or concede that the economy is demand led in the short run, few would agree with the claim that the economy is demand-led even in the long run, and thus the assertion that the economy is demand-led both in the short and the long run is most likely the most crucial feature of post-Keynesian economists, one upon which all strands agree. More concretely, this means that post-Keynesians believe that the actual demand-led path taken by the economy has an impact on the supply-side determinants of long-run growth, a point made by Kaldor, Robinson, and Cornwall. Another way to state the principle of effective demand is to claim the autonomy of investment from the intertemporal saving decisions of households, and hence to underline the causality running from investment to saving.

Giuseppe Fontana (2009: 2) sums this up by saying that post-Keynesian economists believe in three concrete propositions, which, in contrast to some other heterodox schools and neoclassical Keynesians, are assumed to be valid both in the short and the long run: the principle of effective demand, the possibility of involuntary unemployment, and the principle of policy effectiveness, according to which judicious fiscal and monetary policies are effective in improving employment and growth.

The second key characteristic of post-Keynesianism is the importance accorded to the notion of historical time. Post-Keynesians emphasize its irreversibility, as the long run is essentially the result of a sequence of short-run positions. Indeed, in their debates with their critiques, post-Keynesians have been adamant in forcing them to consider and describe the transition from one position to another, recognizing that the conditions under which this transition occurs may affect the final position of equilibrium. Thus post-Keynesians consider path-dependence and hysteresis as being typical of their vision of economic phenomena set in historical time, rather than being exceptions.

Some authors prefer to say that fundamental uncertainty *à la* Shackle is the second most important characteristic of post-Keynesianism, often linking it to the notion of non-ergodicity put forth by Davidson (1982–83), meaning that time and space averages may not coincide, implying that we cannot rely on current or past information to discover what ought to happen in the future. There is some link also with the previously mentioned notion of reasonable rationality, although many post-Keynesians would argue that reasonable rationality only implies some kind of epistemological uncertainty whereas true uncertainty refers to ontological uncertainty – the world and its future are themselves uncertain, being subjected to the free will of economic agents.

Some other post-Keynesians say the concern with a monetized production economy is the second key feature of post-Keynesianism. It is not easy to disentangle the notions of historical time, fundamental uncertainty, non-ergodicity, and monetized production economy. This latter concept could also be associated with the principle of effective demand since it is difficult to imagine an investment function independent from saving without a monetized economy. In orthodox state-of-the-art macro models, such as the dynamic general equilibrium approach, there are no nominal magnitudes nor is there any need for money. Some commodity acts as a numeraire or unit of account. As in neo-Walrasian models, everything is known until the end of time, with some probabilistic degree. Time in such models is an artificial construct, since all decisions are taken on day zero and money plays no useful role. In post-Keynesian models fundamental uncertainty is assumed from the start, by considering that contracts, debts, and assets are denominated in money terms, and by rejecting the possibility of proceeding to the maximization of intertemporal utility. Indeed, it could be claimed that any model that rejects these state-of-the-art constructs integrates in some manner the concepts of fundamental uncertainty in a monetized economy. Minsky (1996: 73) is particularly keen in emphasizing the relevance of a monetized economy, arguing that "the salient contention that makes a thesis Keynesian is that the behaviour and structure of financial (and money) markets and of product (and labor) markets are integral to the determination of the path of the economy through time".

It would be proper to finish this assessment by recalling that the Holy Grail of post-Keynesian economics has been, for a long time, the search for a way to integrate real and monetary analyses – tangible and financial capital – as well as to proceed to the coherent integration of stocks and flows. While a number of post-Keynesian authors – Davidson, Minsky, Eichner, Arestis, Skott, Dalziel – have tackled these or similar issues, the most persistent attempts have arisen from Godley over the past 30 years. His efforts have given rise to the stock-flow consistent (SFC) approach, described in Godley and Lavoie (2007). The book exemplifies the views of Minsky (1996: 77), according to whom one ought to look "at a capitalist economy as a set of interrelated balance sheets and income statements, recognizing that items in balance sheets set up cash flows through time".

MARC LAVOIE

See also:

Cambridge School of economics (II); Institutionalism (II); Richard Ferdinand Kahn (I); Nicholas Kaldor (I); Michał Kalecki (I); John Maynard Keynes (I); Keynesianism (II); Hyman Philip Minsky (I); Neo-Ricardian economics (II); Joan Violet Robinson (I); Piero Sraffa (I).

References and further reading

Arestis, P. (1996), 'Post-Keynesian economics: towards coherence', *Cambridge Journal of Economics*, **20** (1), 111–35.
Arestis, P. and M. Sawyer (eds) (2006), *A Handbook of Alternative Monetary Economics*, Cheltenham, UK and Northampton, MA, USA: Edward Elgar.
Baranzini, A. and A. Mirante (2013), 'The Cambridge post-Keynesian school of income and wealth distribution', in G.C. Harcourt and P. Kriesler (eds), *Oxford Handbook of Post-Keynesian Economics*, vol. 1, Oxford: Oxford University Press, pp. 288–361.

Berg, N. and G. Gigerenzer (2010), 'As-if behavioral economics: neoclassical economics in disguise', *History of Economics Ideas*, **18** (1), 133–66.

Davidson, P. (1982–83), 'Rational expectations: a fallacious foundation for studying crucial decision-making processes', *Journal of Post Keynesian Economics*, **5** (2), 182–98.

Earl, P. (1986), *Lifestyle Economics: Consumer Behaviour in a Turbulent World*, Brighton: Wheatsheaf Books.

Eichner, A.S. and J.A. Kregel (1975), 'An essay on post-Keynesian theory: a new paradigm in economics', *Journal of Economic Literature*, **13** (4), 1293–311.

Fontana, G. (2009), *Money, Uncertainty and Time*, London: Routledge.

Godley, W. and M. Lavoie (2007), *Monetary Economics: An Integrated Approach to Credit, Money, Income, Production and Wealth*, Basingstoke: Palgrave/Macmillan.

Hamouda, O.F. and G.C. Harcourt (1988), 'Post Keynesianism: from criticism to coherence?', *Bulletin of Economic Research*, **40** (1), 1–33.

Holt, R.P.F., S. Pressman and C.L. Spash (eds) (2009), *Post Keynesian and Ecological Economics: Confronting Environmental Issues*, Cheltenham, UK and Northampton, MA, USA: Edward Elgar.

Kaldor, N. (1934), 'A classificatory note on the determinateness of equilibrium', *Review of Economic Studies*, **1** (2), 122–36.

King, J.E. (2002), *A History of Post Keynesian Economics Since 1936*, Cheltenham, UK and Northampton, MA, USA: Edward Elgar.

Kregel, J.A. (1973), *The Reconstruction of Political Economy: An Introduction to Post-Keynesian Economics*, London: Macmillan.

Lavoie, M. (2014), *Post-Keynesian Economics: New Foundations*, Cheltenham, UK and Northampton, MA, USA: Edward Elgar.

Lawson, T. (1994), 'The nature of Post Keynesianism and its links to other traditions: a realist perspective', *Journal of Post Keynesian Economics*, **16** (4), 503–38.

Lee, F.S. (1998), *Post Keynesian Price Theory*, Cambridge: Cambridge University Press.

Lee, F.S. (2000), 'Alfred S. Eichner, Joan Robinson and the founding of post Keynesian economics', in W.J. Samuels (ed.), *Research in the History of Economic Thought and Methodology: Twentieth-Century Economics*, vol. 18-C, New York: Elsevier, pp. 9–40.

Mata, T. (2004), 'Constructing identity: the post Keynesians and the capital controversies', *Journal of the History of Economic Thought*, **26** (2), 241–59.

McCombie, J.S.L. and A.P. Thirlwall (1994), *Economic Growth and the Balance-of-Payments Constraint*, London: Macmillan.

Minsky, H.P. (1996), 'The essential characteristics of Post Keynesian economics', in G. Deleplace and E.J. Nell (eds), *Money in Motion: The Post Keynesian and the Circulation Approaches*, London: Macmillan, pp. 70–88.

Orléan, A. (1998), *Le pouvoir de la finance*, Paris: Odile Jacob.

Pasinetti, L.L. (2007), *Keynes and the Cambridge Keynesians: A Revolution in Economics to be Accomplished*, Cambridge: Cambridge University Press.

Robinson, J. (1956), *The Accumulation of Capital*, London: Macmillan.

Screpanti, E. and S. Zamagni (2005), *An Outline of the History of Economic Thought*, Oxford: Oxford University Press.

Setterfield, M. (ed.) (2010), *Handbook of Alternative Theories of Economic Growth*, Cheltenham, UK and Northampton, MA, USA: Edward Elgar.

Wray, L.R. (2012), *Modern Money Theory: A Primer on Macroeconomics for Sovereign Monetary Systems*, Basingstoke: Palgrave Macmillan.

New Keynesianism

It is well known that John Maynard Keynes meant his *General Theory* as a piece of work "chiefly addressed to [his] fellow economists" (Keynes 1936: ii), and he was not to be disappointed: over the following 20 years the economic profession wondered about the relationship between "Keynes and the classics" – starting in 1937 with Hicks on, indeed, "Mr Keynes and the 'classics'", and plausibly ending, or so Axel Leijohuvfud (1981: 44) argues, in 1956 with Patinkin on *Money Interest and Prices*. While after the Second World War, Keynesian perspectives on policy were quickly gaining ground in the public discourse, by the early 1960s Keynesianism as a theoretical framework came to be identified with the "neoclassical synthesis" (NeoS), within which, however, the question as to whether Keynes contributed any major theoretical innovation was implicitly being answered in the negative: in most textbook versions, the "Keynesian case" came down to (nominal) wage rigidity – arguably an empirical general feature, but hardly consistent with Keynes's own claim to theoretical generality.

To this short sketch should be added that in Keynes's work another channel could be found through which Say's law would fail: the theory of liquidity preference, and the idea that investment is mainly expectation driven, provided a second "Keynesian case" drawn from the *General Theory*, which, however, was often thought to matter only in very extreme (and hence allegedly rare) situations, such as the Great Depression – a view which the NeoS interpretation of Keynes did nothing to dispel. Disagreement on this very point was arguably what set the so-called post-Keynesians apart from mainstream Keynesians. If the *General Theory* was to be read as the first instalment of the "Monetary theory of production" Keynes had considered in his Cambridge lectures, surely the money/output nexus should be seen as crucial: and though the interpretations of this nexus were many, all shared the idea that Keynes did contribute a novel theory of the working of market economies – a theory where aggregate demand was largely independent of the general price level, and active fiscal policy was required to steer the economy toward full employment.

This historical premise on "old" Keynesianism is in order for two reasons. First, it shows that since its inception, the discussion on Keynes's views focused on the issue of price (notably wage) rigidity: this emphasis did not go unchallenged, but left a permanent mark on subsequent developments leading to "new" brands of Keynesianism. Secondly, it also shows that the old brand provided however no proper theory of price rigidity: the idea that one such was the missing bit of a consistent Keynesian model was in many ways the starting point of much of the new Keynesian (NK) economics developed in the 1980s and 1990s.

Historically, the passage from old to new Keynesianism is to be seen against the background of the debates of the 1970s and the rise of new classical (NC) economics, which led to challenging mainstream Keynesianism on the twin charges of poor empirical performance and theoretical weakness. Since the NeoS relied on the one basic empirical argument of nominal stickiness, with the benefit of hindsight it is not surprising that by the end of the 1960s it came increasingly under scrutiny: "stagflation" (significant inflation rates coupled with significant unemployment rates) cast many doubts on the idea that the trade-off between unemployment and inflation, if any, was stable enough to offer a recipe policy makers could rely on. At the same time (nay, somehow presciently), the theoretical underpinnings of the basic model were themselves called into question, most remarkably by Milton Friedman's celebrated address to the American Economic Association (AEA) in 1968: if firms and workers are rational, any increase in the nominal wage rate will embody expected inflation – the latter is accordingly a major determinant of observed inflation, and any observed correlation between inflation and employment is conditional upon unobservable expectations.

This new "expectation-augmented" framework was to change even the language of macroeconomics. Keynesians could account for the imperfect nominal wage adjustment to inflation borne out by the evidence in terms of "money illusion"; but with no proper theory forthcoming of why such an illusion should persist, Friedman's argument proved final, with dramatic consequences on the theory of economic policy: not only no permanent trade-off between inflation and unemployment should be expected, but discretionary monetary policy as such, far from being a way to control aggregate demand, is likely to have a positively destabilizing effect for being inevitably inflation prone. This was the first step towards making expectations crucial to macroeconomics, the final step coming to the fore with the so-called NC economics, with a disruptive effect in the Keynesian camp: when expectations are modelled in the spirit of the "rational expectation revolution" most Keynesian models would be exposed as based on "free parameters" – parameters about which (micro) theory places no restriction, and which accordingly should not be regarded as independent of the economic environment. Accordingly, key Keynesian concepts such as the marginal propensity to consume or the multiplier were to be jettisoned as theoretically empty; and, as to the Phillips curve, if the correlation between inflation and unemployment is considered within a properly detailed model, it will be seen that forward-looking expectations about the future stance of monetary policy play a key role – recorded values of the Phillips coefficient are no guide for policy simulations – and, one might add, the methodological ground was elegantly cut from under the Keynesian feet.

Or was it? The charge against the NeoS model amounted in many ways to a methodological indictment of shaky foundations: the "classical" label of the NC school did not just refer to its scepticism about monetary policy (in the 1970s the main substantive part of the "rational expectation revolution"); it was also an explicit call for a "classical" methodology, such that, when this is properly adhered to, a Walrasian picture is bound to emerge: after all, Keynes never really challenged the framework of perfect competition. Though this conclusion seemed inescapable to many, however, the new theoretical ground being trod was itself slippery, as the NC framework rested on premises, which soon began to be questioned. Prominent among these, the Walrasian picture itself: even granting that the Keynesian model was suffering from a micro-foundations problem, that in itself should not imply that the Walrasian framework provides the apt microstructure upon which macroeconomics should be built. In this sense, what came to be called the NK economics can be looked at as taking up the challenge launched by the NC economists, to argue that Keynesian perspectives could be gained by playing by the same (micro-foundations) rules using a different stack of cards.

This entry gathers some general perspectives on the way this game was actually played out in the 1980s and 1990s. Before laying down the main NK cards, however, one prior warning is in order: "NK economics" is a somewhat vague term, to which many approaches have come to be associated. As a consequence this entry cannot help setting some boundaries, and committing itself to some taxonomy: we shall consider only static models bearing out the Keynesian message that unemployment is an equilibrium feature of the economy; and we shall rely on the time-honoured distinction between partial and general equilibrium approach. Thus in the sequel we shall consider the main NK contributions looking first at partial equilibrium models, and then at the general equilibrium approach. For general assessments on the new Keynesianism, the reader is referred to, among others, Anderson (1994), Benassi et al. (1994), Dixon and Rankin (1995), Greenwald and Stiglitz (1988; 1993), Mankiw and Romer (1991) and Mankiw (1992).

Labour, Credit and Commodity Markets: The Partial Equilibrium Approach

Arguably, one of Keynes's most successful methodological innovations was "macro-markets": macroeconomics' distinctive way of theorizing makes sense of the economy as a whole by aggregating all markets in the three "representative" markets for labour, capital and goods. Thus equilibria with Keynesian features may be thought of as resulting from some specific failure in the working of these markets. The underlying idea is that both theory and empirics militate against the traditional strategy of using the perfect competition, auction-like models as a first approximation to reality. Two observations are called for in this respect. First, this change of focus was made possible by the many novel results on asymmetric information, contract theory, and so on, which were increasingly available by the end of the 1970s. These made it clear that there existed key assumptions (most notably perfect information), which could not be maintained as sensible approximations justified by practical considerations: for example, markets where information is imperfect work in their own way, and one had better take this into account. This in turn allowed an explicit analysis of many features, which had long been recognized as relevant, but the theory for which had not been available before: thus, for example, adverse selection on the credit market is clearly mentioned by Adam Smith but, according to Stiglitz and Weiss (1981: 394), it was their own paper which offered "the first theoretical justification of true credit rationing".

Secondly, in most instances this approach led to models where endogenous rationing is an equilibrium, thus providing theoretical support for prices not adjusting in the face of excess demand or supply in key markets: equilibrium is inconsistent with full employment. However, precisely because rationing is grounded on rational behaviour, the price rigidity one is concerned with is real (as opposed to nominal) – it is about relative prices. This, in spite of its currently uncontroversial label, left some authors in doubt as to the Keynesian ancestry of this brand of new Keynesianism.

As is well known, the basic neoclassical account of the labour market is based on perfect competition: under standard assumptions, an equilibrium (real) wage rate exists, such that the allocation of labour is "optimal", and no involuntary unemployment occurs: no worker is unable, when willing, to work at the equilibrium wage rate. In this setup, involuntary unemployment can be observed only if the wage rate is above market clearing, and for some reason no tendency arises for it to fall. Add in that in practice this is also somewhat of an empirical statement, as in general the real wage rate does seem to be pretty slow to react to unemployment (if at all), and the case is set for asking, what theoretical reasons can be given for this downward rigidity? No straightforward answer presents itself, as a standard answer is available which is deep-rooted in

elementary economics: if workers are rationed, they are off their supply curve of labour
they should be willing to accept a lower wage rate, which would benefit the firm. That is, there are obvious gains from trade to be reaped, and it is not clear why they should not materialize.

One way to introduce the NK approach is by noticing that the picture outlined above rests on an underbidding argument: gains from trade are realized by arbitrage across workers leading to full employment. Put in a nutshell, the NK argument is that the arbitrage picture of the labour market is not warranted at all: it is not obvious that gains from trade are correctly perceived, neither is it obvious that, when perceived, they are seized upon. More precisely, that the unemployed be able to exert a downward pressure on the wage rate, and that firms find it convenient to pay a lower one, are both necessary conditions which on closer scrutiny turn out to be far from trivial. Notice that they are not independent of each other: if for some reason firms are unwilling to cut down on wages, this prevents outside workers from competing with the insiders – which the latter can turn to their own advantage, whenever they have it in their power to affect the firm's wage policy. The NK objections to the underbidding argument are meant to be consistent with the agents' rationality, which means that utility or profit maximization should take into account some additional constraint: usually known as the "wage setting schedule" (WSS), this prevents the real wage from clearing the market – the WSS includes the key information assumed away in the NC picture, thus giving a formal account of why the labour market is not an auction market. The two main classes of NK models, which convey these ideas, go under the name of efficiency wage (Akerlof and Yellen 1986), and insider–outsider (Linbeck and Snower 1988) models. Both deliver a WSS: in the former case, to the effect that firms may be loath to accept lower wages as this may affect productivity; in the latter, to account for the turnover costs borne by the firm, which make inside workers imperfectly substitutable with outsiders.

Suppose that labour productivity increases with the real wage. Then to any employment level there corresponds a cost minimizing wage w^e, say, which will not be zero, as the cost-raising effect of higher wages for given productivity will be reduced by its cost-reducing effect via higher productivity: this is the efficiency wage. Clearly, if w^e is higher than the wage required by workers on their supply curve, involuntary unemployment will ensue: the potential increase in the firm's profits given by a lower wage would be more than compensated by the higher costs due to low productivity. This is in a nutshell the logic of the efficiency wage theory, whose linchpin rests with the relationship between productivity and the real wage rate, which much of the NK literature grounded on asymmetric information: if the quality of the worker's labour input is not observable by the firm, higher wages may be required to elicit unobservable effort on the worker's part. In the work by Shapiro and Stiglitz (1984), perhaps the best known along these lines, equilibrium unemployment acts as a "workers' discipline device": for unobservable effort to be forthcoming a "high" wage is called for, while the implied unemployment deters unobservable shirking.

Suppose instead that substituting inside workers with outsiders implies some specific cost: hiring may require the firm to put up resources for training new workers; firing may entail a severance pay. This in itself will drive a wedge between the firm's opportunity cost and the workers' – if insiders are paid w, outsiders will be able to compete with them only by accepting $(w - c)$. Moreover, c (the turnover cost) may be endogenous: a typical distinction is between hiring costs (in the main technology driven) and firing costs (over which insiders will have a say, more obviously so when unionised). If wage setting is somehow affected by the insiders' own objective, turnover costs and actual wage may be so set as to price outsiders out of the market: it is enough that the resulting $(w - c)$ is lower than their reservation wage.

Models of this kind make a case for equilibrium rationing on the labour market: they provide an equilibrium theory of involuntary unemployment, and no doubt this is why they are regarded as part of the NK research programme. However, they predict that the real wage rate will fail to clear the market: in both cases the WSS embodies constraints to utility or profit maximization, and no rational agent would care about purely nominal constraints. As a result, macro models built on these premises will deliver a *vertical* aggregate supply curve.

As Joseph Stiglitz (1992: 269) put it, "capital is at the heart of capitalism: it is, accordingly, not surprising that we should look to failures in the capital markets to account for ... fluctuations in output and employment". The significance of this remark lies in the underlying account of these failures, which the NK approach firmly grounds on informational considerations. Two points stand out in this respect: the idea that capital market imperfections should be seen as the rule, as they can be traced back to pervasive informational problems; and the claim that such imperfections make a case for unemployment as an equilibrium.

Credit rationing is perhaps the best-known instance. That "a fringe of unsatisfied borrowers" was a possibility is clearly envisaged by Keynes himself in the *Treatise* (1930: 327), and the NK approach gave a new foundation to the idea. The starting point is again asymmetric information. Suppose there is an excess demand for credit at the going interest rate: the profitable move for the lender (a bank, say) might apparently be to raise its rate at the market clearing level; however, if investment projects are distinguished by their "riskiness", and the latter cannot be observed by the bank (though it is known to the borrower), the positive effect on profits from such a choice can be offset by a higher probability of the borrower defaulting – in which case the profit maximizing rate will be kept below market clearing, and credit will be rationed. This may happen, as higher lending rates lead to worsening the average quality of the pool of credit applicant – as Adam Smith put it, "sober people ... would not venture into the competition" (1776 [1976], hereafter WN, II.iv.15) for highly priced credit. That is, risky projects are more likely to be drawn into the market, because of limited liability: a high risk investment can bear a high interest cost, since high risk means high expected profit for the borrower, his liability being indeed limited (that is, expected losses bounded); on the other hand, asymmetric information means the lender is unable to discriminate borrowers ex ante, and so adjust its rate to riskiness. Among models based on this intuition, Stiglitz and Weiss (1981) had perhaps the greatest impact; this literature grew enormously in the 1980s (for a general assessment, see Jaffee and Stiglitz 1990).

One immediate implication of this kind of result concerns policy: if credit markets are rationed, interest rate variations are a poor explanation for aggregate demand fluctuations – which does seem to be empirically the case, as the interest-elasticity of aggregate spending is typically low. Hence, monetary policy should work best when centred on managing the quantity of credit rather than the quantity of money. This, however, is a statement about the working of monetary policy, not its effectiveness: for a theory of unemployment, a theory of aggregate supply is needed – do imperfections on the capital markets have any bearing on equilibrium output?

The answer to such a question is best seen by looking at credit rationing as an instance of a more general principle: under asymmetric information the Modigliani–Miller (MM) theorem does not hold. The theorem works out a key consequence of perfect capital markets: the financial structure (for example, debt/equity ratio) of the firm is immaterial to its choices, as the cost of capital is independent of the legal form under which capital is forthcoming – investors will require the same rate of return, whatever the asset they hold. Clearly, if credit is rationed this is not the case: equity cannot be substituted with debt at no additional cost, if the latter option is constrained; but, more generally, contract forms should be seen as solutions to informational (and hence incentive) problems: thus, for instance, whether capital is raised by issuing equity or debt is not immaterial – for example, the latter entails the possibility of default, that is, a switch in the control of the firm's assets.

One important implication of these premises is that information costs are a key component of the cost of raising capital, as different contract forms embody different solutions to different information asymmetries – internal capital will be cheapest as no contract with external investors is required, consistently with firms apparently having a strong preference for own financing. Moreover, while these diverse costs affect the firm's choices as to its financial structure, the latter will influence its input and output choices: if (say) a negative shock hits its business, the firm's reaction will depend on the way capital has been raised – contrary to the MM theorem, the debt- and the equity-funded companies behave differently. In short, incentive compatibility constraints are both a real cost in the allocation of capital, and a key explanatory variable to the firms' behaviour.

All of which brings about at least two noteworthy macroeconomic consequences. First, the firm's employment and output choices are constrained by its asset structure. Though this point is developed differently in different models, as a general principle a high value of the firm's assets will lower its cost of raising external finance, while high (perceived) bankruptcy risk will lower output, as the firm will tend to shun risk; given that the linchpin of these models is the real cost of capital, this means that they deliver a vertical supply curve, the position of which will typically be below full employment. Secondly, as this position depends on variables like the asset composition of the economy and the value of such assets, the relevant dynamic issue of financial fragility is brought to bear on the matter (Bernanke and Gertler, 1990): for example, an unexpected drop in money supply, via its effect on prices, will typically lower the firm's equity value, hence raise bankruptcy risk and the cost of external capital, with negative effect on output and employment – it may also trigger multiplier effects through the consumers' permanent income, which feeds back via demand on to the firms' asset value. It should be noticed that, though this framework does in general provide a scope for policy, the latter is different from traditional Keynesian demand management – two otherwise identical economies will react differently to external shocks depending on their asset structures, which accordingly provide a key dimension along which policy should be assessed (for example, Gertler 1988).

We conclude this section with two general remarks. First, the NK research programme is sometimes held to include also models where imperfect competition on the goods market delivers a counter-cyclical behaviour of the firms' mark-up – the idea being that markets tend to be more competitive in the boom phases (for example, growing demand may make collusion more costly: Rotenberg and Saloner 1986), a higher elasticity of the demand for goods feeding an increase in the demand for labour. In a way, this takes up a point about old Keynesianism famously raised by Dunlop: any interpretation of the Keynesian model having firms on their demand for labour schedule should predict that output expansion requires a fall in real wages, which is not easily detected in the data. Empirically, whether on average the mark-up is anti-cyclical is, overall, controversial.

Secondly, generally speaking this brand of New Keynesianism accounts for unemployment in a framework where the aggregate supply curve is vertical – the nominal price level is immaterial. Unemployment is traced back to turnover costs or incentive compatibility constraints driving a wedge between individual optimality and maximum social welfare: while endogenous rationing entails an equilibrium real wage (or real interest rate) inconsistent with full employment, there is no room for nominal sluggishness, and hence for policies centred on managing nominal aggregates. Since real constraints are imposed on an otherwise neoclassical setup, the NK label attached to this approach did not go unchallenged: commenting on one model along these lines, Hall (1988: 263) observes that:

> [the authors] write as if there were a huge gulf between their own model and the real business-cycle model, a gulf as great as the one between Keynes and the Classics. They could equally well have portrayed themselves as members of the real business-cycle school . . . A much more significant watershed in macroeconomics . . . is between the real school . . . and the nominal school.

This "nominal school", which relies on a general equilibrium approach to address the issue of nominal rigidity and stresses coordination problems as the foundations of Keynesian economics, does so within a novel framework: that of general equilibrium with imperfect competition.

General Equilibrium: From Fixed Prices to Imperfect Competition

In 1977 the International Economic Association (IEA) published a well-known collection of essays devoted to the *Microeconomic Foundations of Macroeconomics*. In his contribution, Frank Hahn (1977: 25) summed up nicely the gist of the problem: after forty years, Keynesian economics was still "plainly in need of proper theoretical foundations". Indeed, the so-called micro-foundations debate had taken centre-stage at that time, following up the stark diagnosis made by Robert Clower (1965: 110): "either Walras' Law is incompatible with Keynesian economics, or Keynes had nothing fundamentally new to add to orthodox economic theory". Clower's very language points to the twofold problem being raised: how to give *a general equilibrium* account of an economy *with price rigidities* – indeed, Walras's law is the general-equilibrium aggregate constraint which, under price flexibility, rules out generalized unemployment. Hence, the need for a proper understanding of rationing in a multi-market setting, where rationing in one market "spills over" to other markets, so that, for example, labour rationing links up with the low aggregate demand yielding unemployment itself.

Models of such a kind were provided in the 1970s under the label of "disequilib-rium" analysis (an extensive appraisal is provided by Galc 1983), most remarkably by Jacques Drèze and Jean-Pascal Bénassy. Though different in their formalization of rationing, they share one basic feature: assuming prices as given, the focus is on the general equilibrium consistency of exchange and production choices under rationing. While this fixed-price methodology left one key question unanswered, it did provide a clear microeconomic account of spillover effects – the most popular instance of which is the well-known Keynesian multiplier. That key question, of course, concerns prices. Different "régimes" and policy options could be studied, as the given price constellation allocates rationing across markets: indeed, a Keynesian situation could be characterized as one where the workers' rationing on the labour market links up with the firms' on the commodity markets; but price determination, and hence what pushes the economy in a Keynesian régime, was left as an unsolved problem.

The NK literature offers a solution to that problem by dropping the commonly made assumption that agents are perfect competitors (see Hart 1982: 109): an approach, pio-neered by Hahn's work on conjectural equilibria, which came to the forefront in the early 1980s and was rich in important implications. It can be looked at as providing an answer to two related, though different, general questions: whether price making behaviour can shed any light on nominal rigidities; and whether the interaction among price making agents can account for equilibrium unemployment, beyond the microeconomic ineffi-ciency we standardly associate with imperfect competition. While historically both per-spectives can be questioned as being somehow beyond Keynes's own theoretical outlook, many results do have a Keynesian ring to them: notably, the emphasis on equilibrium unemployment as the upshot of "low" aggregate demand.

In principle, imperfect competition with price-making agents cannot in itself lead to nominal price rigidity: agents are no less rational for being price makers, and their con-trolling their own price should not in itself prevent them from adjusting it to its optimal (utility or profit maximizing) level – a change in (say) money supply should lead to a rea-lignment of nominal variables, leaving relative prices unchanged irrespective of competi-tion being perfect or imperfect. This being so, the NK approach focuses on price making to ask how indeed prices are made: it is the process whereby a price is set, which becomes the issue – in fact, a long-standing issue in Keynesian economics, from mark-up pricing seen as the upshot of rule-of-thumb behaviour, to the analysis of monopoly pricing when the demand curve is kinked.

In general, NK models differ from this tradition by emphasizing the distinction between the individual cost of non-optimal choices, and the resulting aggregate effect. Any theory having agents not reacting optimally to an exogenous shock, has to confront itself with the problem that suboptimal behaviour involves by definition some loss – why then should it persist? The two main approaches to nominal sluggishness in this vein go under the names of near rationality (for example, Akerlof and Yellen 1985) and menu cost (for example, Blanchard and Kiyotaki 1987): both answer that question by arguing that the cost of maladjustment may be "negligible", the former using first order approxi-mations, and the latter "small" adjustment cost, to define precisely what "negligible" means. Also, both make the important point that inertial behaviour involving such negligible individual losses may nevertheless result in significant aggregate effects – an amplifying mechanism relying on macroeconomic externalities.

The standard framework to convey these ideas is that of monopolistic competition – a suitable setup for macro analysis, for each agent's market power is by assumption consistent with his perceiving no aggregate effect of his own choices. In a general equilibrium model so conceived, an increase in money supply would result in each firm facing an outward shift in its own demand, and increasing its own price to the new profit maximizing level – therefore, money would be "neutral", as output and employment would settle at their initial values. However, menu costs or near rationality may lead firms to refrain from price changes, as by doing so they perceive just a negligible loss – a perception owing to the single producer not taking into account how his own choice affects his own demand, via its indirect effect on aggregate demand. In this case the macroeconomic externality would work through the aggregate price level: in fact, the latter will not adjust to the new money stock, real money balances will be higher, and monetary policy effective on output and employment.

This aggregate demand externality thus provides an important argument for nominal rigidity, as real, first-order aggregate effects of nominal shocks are supported by second-order (negligible) losses at the individual level. However, it also points to a more general interpretation of the working of the economy, which is broadly consistent with traditional Keynesian concerns and, in fact, independent of the role of money.

Whenever firms are endowed with market power, equilibrium price will be above marginal cost – firms would like to expand production at given prices, but are constrained from doing so by the quantity the market is willing to take at that price. In a sense, they are rationed; and, if *ceteris paribus* those prices were exogenously given to competitive firms, one would recover the Keynesian régime modelled by the fixed-price literature considered above (Grandmont 1989). If, now, prices were arbitrarily lowered to equal marginal cost, a better allocation would result: *ceteris paribus*, real demand, output and profits would be higher – a full employment situation. What prevents this from being an equilibrium is precisely the aggregate demand externality: when price is above marginal cost, no single firm has an incentive to lower its price and expand production, since it cannot internalize the positive effect of such a move on aggregate demand; and conversely, if prices were set at marginal cost, the single firm would have an incentive to raise its price and free ride on the other firms which, by keeping low prices, support a high real demand. By a slight *abuse de language*, the features discussed above can be seen as a standard inefficiency result associated with a Nash situation. Why would such a framework be relevant in a Keynesian perspective? The answer lies in the characterization of such an equilibrium as a situation where output is below full employment, due to a binding demand constraint endogenously generated by the working of the economy, namely, by the lack of coordination underlying the wedge between individual optimality and aggregate welfare. This supports the aggregate demand externality whenever agents enjoy some market power – an assumption all the more reasonable, considering that this is consistent with the single agent having a negligible weight on aggregates, and that in practice perfect competition is best looked at as a limit situation.

This being so, two points are worth stressing. First, equilibrium unemployment in this framework is not simply due to the standard (partial equilibrium) effect of imperfect competition: the macroeconomic externality is grounded in the coordination failure among agents, and cannot be reduced to the market power of the single agent vis-à-vis his own market. Secondly, under appropriate conditions (notably, increasing returns) models of this kind can yield multiple equilibria, typically a "low activity" and a welfare-superior "high activity" equilibrium (for example, Manning 1990; see also Silvestre 1993). This is consistent with the Keynesian idea that an economy can be stuck in a "bad" situation while a better alternative is available – though the policy leading from the former to the latter should play upon "coordination", presumably by emphasizing the regulatory role of policy makers, which is not an obvious Keynesian prescription.

As a final remark, it should be borne in mind that some might deny this approach to the Keynesian label: equilibrium "underemployment", rather than "unemployment", should be used to emphasize the inefficiency associated with imperfect competition. To this one can retort that in a general equilibrium of this sort firms and workers are rationed, in what is arguably a "Keynesian" situation where both would like to supply more at the going prices – the traditional definition of rationing makes sense only under perfect competition, and switching to imperfect competition does involve a different reference framework.

Concluding Remarks

The new Keynesianism developed in the 1980s and 1990s is clearly very different from the "old" brand and, some would argue, from Keynes's own perspective as well. The one Keynesian feature shared by all the (otherwise very different) models of new Keynesianism is providing new arguments for the traditional claim that capitalist economies have an in-built tendency to settle at equilibria with unemployment. However, the adjective "new" applies to both methodology and policy prescriptions. As to the former, emphasis on the macro relevance of market imperfections meant to a large extent drifting away from the perfect competition framework Keynes himself perhaps had in mind – though the general equilibrium models considered last do provide a consistent theory of unemployment as owing to low aggregate demand. As to the latter, that very emphasis implies that policy makers should go beyond their traditional concerns about monetary and fiscal mechanisms to control aggregate spending, and be careful about their regulatory powers. This is a lesson which definitely left its mark on the policy debates of the 2000s.

CORRADO BENASSI

See also:

Keynesianism (II); Macroeconomics (III); Monetarism (II); New classical macroeconomics (II); Post-Keynesianism (II).

References and further reading

Akerlof, G.A. and J. Yellen (1985), 'A near-rational model of the business cycle with wage and price inertia', *Quarterly Journal of Economics*, **100** (supplement), 823–38.
Akerlof, G.A. and J. Yellen (eds) (1986), *Efficiency Wage Models of the Labor Market*, Cambridge: Cambridge University Press.
Andersen, T.M. (1994), *Price Rigidities. Causes and Macroeconomic Implications*, Oxford: Clarendon Press.
Benassi, C., A. Chirco and C. Colombo (1994), *The New Keynesian Economics*, Oxford: Blackwell.
Bernanke, B. and M. Gertler (1990), 'Financial fragility and economic performance', *Quarterly Journal of Economics*, **105** (1), 87–114.
Blanchard, O.J. and N. Kiyotaki (1987), 'Monopolistic competition and the effects of aggregate demand', *American Economic Review*, **77** (4), 647–66.

Clower, R. (1965), 'The Keynesian counterrevolution: a theoretical appraisal', in F. Brechling and F.H. Hahn (eds), *The Theory of Interest Rates*, London: Macmillan, pp. 103–25.

Dixon, H.D. and N. Rankin (eds) (1995), *The New Macroeconomics*, Cambridge: Cambridge University Press.

Friedman, M. (1968), 'The role of monetary policy', *American Economic Review*, **58** (1), 1–17.

Gale, D. (1983), *Money: in Disequilibrium*, Cambridge: Cambridge University Press.

Gertler, M (1988), 'Financial structure and aggregate economic activity', *Journal of Money, Credit and Banking*, **20** (3), pt 2, 559–88.

Grandmont, J.M. (1989), 'Keynesian issues and economic theory', *Scandinavian Journal of Economics*, **91** (2), 265–93.

Greenwald, B.C. and J.E. Stiglitz (1988), 'Examining alternative macroeconomic theories', *Brookings Papers on Economic Activity*, no. 1, 207–70.

Greenwald, B.C. and J.E. Stiglitz (1993), 'New and old Keynesians', *Journal of Economic Perspectives*, **7** (1), 23–44.

Hahn, F.H. (1977), 'Keynesian economics and general equilibrium theory: reflections on some current debates', in G. Harcourt (ed.), *The Microeconomic Foundations of Macroeconomics*, London: Macmillan, pp. 25–40.

Hall, R. (1988), 'Comments and discussion on Greenwald and Stiglitz', *Brookings Papers on Economic Activity*, no. 1, 261–4.

Hart, O.D. (1982), 'A model of imperfect competition with Keynesian features', *Quarterly Journal of Economics*, **97** (1), 109–38.

Hicks, J.R. (1937), 'Mr Keynes and the "classics": a suggested interpretation', *Econometrica*, **5** (2), 147–59, reprinted in J.R. Hicks (1967), *Critical Essays in Monetary Theory*, Oxford: Oxford University Press, pp. 126–42.

Jaffee, D. and J.E. Stiglitz (1990), 'Credit rationing', in B.M. Friedman and F.H. Hahn (eds), *Handbook of Monetary Economics*, vol. 2, Amsterdam: North Holland, pp. 837–88.

Keynes, J.M. (1930), *A Treatise on Money*, vol. II: 'The Applied Theory of Money', reprinted 1971 in *The Collected Writings of J.M. Keynes*, vol. VI, London: Macmillan.

Keynes, J.M. (1936), *The General Theory of Employment, Interest and Money*, reprinted 1973 in *The Collected writings of J.M. Keynes*, vol. VIII, London: Macmillan.

Leijonhufvud, A (1981), 'Keynes and the classics: first lecture', in A. Leijonhufvud, *Information and Coordination. Essays in Macroeconomic Theory*, New York: Oxford University Press, pp. 39–54.

Linbeck, A. and D. Snower (1988), *The Insider–Outsider Theory of Unemployment*, Cambridge, MA: MIT Press.

Mankiw, G. (1992), 'The reincarnation of Keynesian economics', *European Economic Review*, **36** (2–3), 559–65.

Mankiw, N.G. and D. Romer (eds) (1991), *New Keynesian Economics*, Cambridge, MA: MIT Press.

Manning, A. (1990), 'Imperfect competition, multiple equilibria and unemployment policy', *Economic Journal*, **100** (400), 151–62.

Patinkin, D. (1956), *Money, Interest and Prices*, New York: Row, Peterson.

Rotenberg, J.J. and G. Saloner (1986), 'A supergame-theoretic model of price wars during booms', *American Economic Review*, **76** (3), 390–407.

Shapiro, C. and J.E. Stiglitz (1984), 'Equilibrium unemployment as a worker discipline device', *American Economic Review*, **74** (3), 433–44.

Silvestre, J. (1993), 'The market power foundations of macroeconomic policy', *Journal of Economic Literature*, **31** (1), 105–41.

Smith, A. (1776), *An Inquiry into the Nature and Causes of the Wealth of Nations*, reprinted 1976, eds A.H. Campbell, A.S. Skinner and W.B. Todd, Oxford: Clarendon Press.

Stiglitz, J.E. (1992), 'Capital markets and economic fluctuations in capitalist economies', *European Economic Review*, **36** (2–3), 269–306.

Stiglitz, J.E. and A. Weiss (1981), 'Credit rationing in markets with imperfect information', *American Economic Review*, **71** (3), 393–410.

Index